British Columbia & the Yukon

Ryan Ver Berkmoes

John Lee

LEGEND

Tollway
Freeway
Primary Road
Secondary Road
Tertiary Road
Unsealed Road

0 ____ 200 km
0 ____ 120 miles

TOMBSTONE TERRITORIAL PARK (p416)
See what the wild in wilderness means at this accessible park

DAWSON CITY (p407)
A legendary Klondike town as intoxicating as the quest for gold

Nunavut

Victoria Island

Banks Island

Amundsen Gulf

Beaufort Sea

Tuktoyaktuk
Inuvik

Northwest Territories

Franklin Mountains

Great Bear Lake

Mackenzie River

Anderson R

Great Slave Lake

YELLOWKNIFE

Lac la Martre

Wood Buffalo National Park

Lake Athabasca

Saskatchewan

Nahanni National Park Reserve

Mackenzie Mountains

Watson Lake

Yukon Territory

Arctic Circle

USA
CANADA

Alaska

Fairbanks

Dawson City

Yukon River

WHITEHORSE

Alaska Hwy

Kluane National Park & Reserve

Skagway
Haines

Atlin Provincial Park

Gulf of Alaska

150°W
140°W
130°W
120°W
110°W

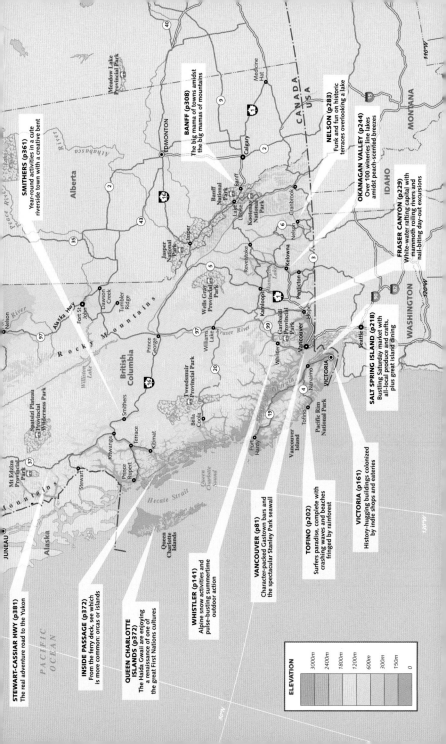

STEWART-CASSIAR HWY (p381)
The real adventure road to the Yukon

SMITHERS (p361)
Year-round activities in a cute riverside town with a creative bent

BANFF (p308)
The big mama of towns amidst the big mamas of mountains

NELSON (p283)
Funk and fun on historic terraces overlooking a lake

INSIDE PASSAGE (p372)
From the ferry deck, see which is more common: orcas or islands

QUEEN CHARLOTTE ISLANDS (p372)
The Haida Gwaii are enjoying a renaissance of one of the great First Nations cultures

OKANAGAN VALLEY (p244)
Over 100 wineries line lakes amidst peach-scented breezes

FRASER CANYON (p229)
White-water rafting capital with mammoth rolling rivers and nail-biting day-out excursions

SALT SPRING ISLAND (p218)
Bustling Saturday market with all-local produce and crafts, plus great island dining

WHISTLER (p141)
Alpine snow activities and pulse-busting summertime outdoor action

VANCOUVER (p81)
Character-packed Gastown bars and the spectacular Stanley Park seawall

TOFINO (p202)
Surfers paradise, complete with crashing waves and beaches fringed by rainforest

VICTORIA (p161)
History-hugging buildings colonized by indie shops and eateries

ELEVATION

3000m
2400m
1800m
1200m
600m
300m
150m
0

On the Road

RYAN VER BERKMOES COORDINATING AUTHOR

I've always felt the pull of the open road, and the end of the road is like the magnetic center. I just have to see what's there. On the Queen Charlotte Islands, Tow Hill Rd on the north coast of Graham Island (p379) is the perfect road to nowhere. For 26km it runs along the pounding Pacific Ocean, often under a cathedral of cedar trees dripping with moss. At its end is a deserted beach that seems to stretch to infinity. It's misty with mystery. Strange things wash ashore, adrift since Japan or Russia or who knows?

JOHN LEE I hadn't been to the Richmond Night Market for more than a year, but I remembered how important it was not to eat all day before arriving. It didn't take long to wander the stalls of trashy trinkets and odd miracle gadgets that no one needs, but heading to the steamy food area is what this place is all about. I circled the rows of hawker stalls twice before deciding what to have – these are prawn dumplings on a skewer – and then I circled again for some fried noodles and a hearty serving of fish balls. Three meals for the price of one.

For full author biographies see p441

British Columbia & the Yukon Highlights

Like a bear caught in a berry patch next to a stream full of salmon who gets popped on the head by a falling hive full of honey, you may not know which way to turn in British Columbia and the Yukon. The pleasures are myriad. To help you avoid being stung, we've herded together Lonely Planet authors, staff and travelers. Old hands at having fun, they've offered their ideas on what's essential to see and do amid all the temptations. Yes, it's random. Yes, it's biased. But that's what makes it better than hibernation. Enjoy foraging through the following pages.

RANDY LINCKS/PHOTOLIBRARY

 SKIING WHISTLER MOUNTAIN

Surrounded by breathtaking mountains and fresh powder as far as the eye can see, Whistler (p141) is a cute village that leaves you wanting more. You can feel the crisp snow crunch under foot as you cruise along the glacier, through the terrain park and then down to the village for a hot chocolate in front of an open fire. So strap on those boots and get ready for the ski trip of a lifetime, because Whistler has it all.

Charity Mackinnon, Lonely Planet staff, Australia

SAILING THE INSIDE PASSAGE

It's one of the world's most beautiful journeys and the way to do it is aboard one of the big ships operated by BC Ferries (p432). There are no such diversions as endless buffets or floor shows or casinos that you'd find on cruise ships. Rather there's simply the beautiful BC and Alaska coast. Pull up a deck chair and see orcas swim past, eagles hover overhead and moose staring at you from one of hundreds of deserted islands.

Ryan Ver Berkmoes, Lonely Planet author, USA

RALPH HOPKINS

2

MARK NEW

3 ### BEARS

Everything you saw on *Yogi Bear* was true, well, almost. Although seemingly calm here, a grizzly can erupt into the most extreme violence with little provocation. Long time residents have nothing but respect for these huge beasts, which vary in color from beige to brown to black.

Ryan Ver Berkmoes, Lonely Planet author, USA

RICHARD CUMM

4 ### THE HEART OF VANCOUVER

Whenever I take anyone to visit Stanley Park (p97) they immediately fall in love with Vancouver (if they hadn't already!). Right on the edge of the city and cozied up to sandy Kitsilano (p100), it's an oasis of lush forest. The walkway around the perimeter dishes up incredible views of the city, the Gulf Islands and the distant mountains. You'd never guess that you're just minutes away from cocktails and trendy eateries.

Korina Miller, traveler, Canada

JASPER & BANFF NATIONAL PARKS

We instantaneously fell in love with Jasper (p324) and the feel of a 'small' resort town in the Canadian Rockies. After long days of killer snowboarding at Marmot Basin we quenched our thirst at Jasper Brewing Company with some of the best beer we've ever had. On our drive to Banff (p308) we encountered a wolf trotting along the side of the road and numerous big horn sheep. Lake Louise (p320) was frozen over and we took advantage of nighttime ice skating with impressive ice sculptures for company.

Marc Visnick, Lonely Planet staff, USA

MARC VISNICK

ICEFIELDS PARKWAY

Everybody drives the Icefields Parkway (p322) in the summer. You see bits of glaciers, a mountain goat or two and some looming peaks frosted with ice. You also see a lot of other people enjoying the same scenes. But in winter, the road truly lives up to its name. It wends a lonely path through a wonderland of forest hushed by deep drifts, with the only noise the echo of a distant avalanche down the snow-packed hillsides.

Ryan Ver Berkmoes, Lonely Planet author, USA

PHILIP & KAREN SMITH

5

6

SOARING OVER PEMBERTON VALLEY

You're sitting in the front of a slender, two-person glider capsule, but you don't have to do anything but keep your eyes open. The pilot behind you will do all the work as you're towed into the sky by a light aircraft then released onto the wind like a feather. The silence is deep and enveloping as you weave close to the glacial crags and peer down at the toy town tapestry unfurling below. After a roll or two (or even a loop-the-loop), your time is up and you bump gently along the runway to a stop. Your first instinct? Let's go again (p151).

John Lee, Lonely Planet author, Canada

FRANK CAF

THE YUKON

Winter comes early and lasts a long time in the Yukon (p386). By early September the birch trees are turning golden in waves and you can sense snow forming over the horizon. A stiff wind blows you south, past the hardy locals getting ready to chop wood, batten down the storm windows and curl up for many months of solitude.

Ryan Ver Berkmoes, Lonely Planet author, USA

RYAN VER BERK

BC FRUIT MARKET

Just imagine the smell. In fall more than 60 varieties of the best apples grown in the Okanagan Valley are sold at this cooperative in Kelowna (p265). It's run by small growers, whose often rare and otherwise unattainable fruit creates a carnival of color.

Ryan Ver Berkmoes, Lonely Planet author, USA

KRAIG LIEB

9 WATCHING WILDLIFE

On an otherwise mundane stretch of the Alaska Hwy (p355) in Northern BC, we rounded a bend to find a stone sheep licking salt by the road. It quickly sped away but just another few hundred meters and we encountered a mother bear and cub and then a herd of deer and then…

Ryan Ver Berkmoes, Lonely Planet author, USA

RYAN VER BERKMOES

MARK NEWMAN

11 KLUANE NATIONAL PARK & RESERVE

From the Alaska Hwy you get just a glimpse of the awesome beauty within the vast 22,015 sq km Kluane National Park (p400). Hike for a day to the interior – or hop on a helicopter – and you'll witness an other-worldly beauty that has garnered Unesco recognition. Huge icebergs break off glaciers and the water at the shoreline freezes.

Ryan Ver Berkmoes, Lonely Planet author, USA

SALMON GLACIER

Giving meaning to 'a river of ice,' the Salmon Glacier (p383) wends through huge granite peaks near Stewart in the far north of BC. Looking down from a dirt road above it, you feel an icy breath even on a hot day. It's like you've opened the door of a refrigerator. The ice stretches for many kilometers and you realize that the mountains are mere sideshows, ready to be breached at nature's whim.

Ryan Ver Berkmoes, Lonely Planet author, USA

12

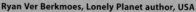

MIDNIGHT SUN

It's sometime near midnight on a summer 'night' in the Yukon. Look north and you might wonder if the first gold-seekers were inspired by the rich hues on the horizon. It was in that direction they went prospecting in the 1890s. Or were they like people today: driven by the eternal light to do things they'd never contemplate in the darkness of night?

Ryan Ver Berkmoes, Lonely Planet author, USA

13

14

STEWART-CASSIAR HIGHWAY

People talk about the Alaska Highway but this is the way to drive north through some of the last great wilderness in BC. From Northern BC not far from Prince Rupert, the Stewart-Cassiar Hwy (p381) runs for 727km straight to the Yukon. Maybe you'll see another car but more likely you'll see a moose.

Ryan Ver Berkmoes, Lonely Planet author, USA

15 SUN PEAKS ICEWINE FESTIVAL

While many wine festivals come with a side dish of snobbery, this winter event in the gabled, Christmas card resort village of Sun Peaks (p241) is dramatically different. The usual workshops and gala dinners are offered, but the Saturday night Progressive Tasting is more like a pub crawl. You'll be slipping among the lodges looking for stations that will happily fill your glass with icewine, that velvety, ultra-sweet tonic that easily chases away alpine chills. The next day is all about some hangover-busting skiing and snowboarding.

John Lee, Lonely Planet author, Canada

NORMAN POGSON/DREAMSTIME

STEPHEN SAKS

16 VANCOUVER ISLAND TRAIN TRIP

Few Victoria visitors know about the little VIA Rail *Malahat* train that departs daily from its tiny downtown station and trundles up-island though the forests and communities of Chemainus, Duncan, Parksville, Nanaimo and Courtenay. An idyllic and highly relaxing way to see the island, you'll encounter rusting trestle bridges, dense forest and the backs of homes and gardens rarely seen by those driving through. Fellow passengers are usually up for a chat and the gregarious guard often has a joke or two to impart along the way.

John Lee, Lonely Planet author, Canada

17 THE BRITISH COLUMBIA COAST

The weather changes by the hour – the minute really – along the long, craggy coast of BC. Sitting on an overnight ferry sailing the Inside Passage, the play of light on the ever-changing sky is a continuous magnificent light show. It's as if the clouds in the sky need to compete with the amazing scenery down at water's edge.

Ryan Ver Berkmoes, Lonely Planet author, USA

18 SEA KAYAKING BARKLEY SOUND

We loaded up two sea kayaks with plentiful supplies for three days and paddled off into the Broken Group Islands on the west coast of Vancouver Island. During three idyllic days we explored parts of Barkley Sound (p200), picking our way between small islands dotted with pine trees and rocky outcrops. One bay was full of sea lions, which warned us off with sharp dog-like barks. In other bays we saw huge birds hunting for fish, and porpoises. At night we surfed on the waves back to our island camp, tired out but satisfied with the day's exploring.

Lucy Monie, Lonely Planet staff, UK

FRESH WILD SALMON

The color is bright, and the meat rich and oily. Grilled to perfection, with just some lemon, garlic and butter, there is nothing more satisfying than a fresh fillet of king salmon.

Catherine Bodry, Lonely Planet author, USA

19

20

VANCOUVER'S INDIE SHOPS

Vancouver's Main St is the spend-triggering capital of great indie shopping (p122). Quirky little clothing shops dress the city's pale and interesting set, while eclectic gift and accessory stores make shopping for presents suddenly seem like an easy proposition.

Chris Olsen, traveler, Canada

21 DAWSON CITY

You're bouncing around for hours on some rickety old bus on the Klondike Hwy in the height of summer, not knowing whether it's three o'clock in the morning or afternoon, and suddenly you arrive in Dawson City (p407). Frilly-skirted ladies, straight out of the gambling hall, chat on wooden sidewalks, and a buzz of stories about gold can be heard everywhere – it's like stumbling into another world. True adventurers will try the infamous Sourtoe cocktail, and all who encounter Dawson City will brag about their experience.

Heather Dickson, Lonely Planet staff, USA

MANFRED GOTTS

22 TOTEM POLES

Ravens and killer whales, thunderbirds and sea serpents are among the figures magnificently carved out of cedar to create towering totem poles, which can be found throughout BC. The most visited display of totem poles is at Brockton Point in Stanley Park (p97), but more – representing not only family and kinship but also First Nations artistry and heritage – can be seen at Thunderbird Park (p165) and Alert Bay (p213), and in Northern BC (p365).

Heather Dickson, Lonely Planet staff, US

IGLOO CAMPING NEAR SQUAMISH

Anyone can stay in a hotel but not everyone is willing to make their own igloo and then be trusting enough to sleep in it overnight (p140). Strapping on the snowshoes and tramping several hours into an icicle-covered provincial park is followed by several hours of block cutting and placing – making sure to arrange the blocks on top of each other in an inward-spiraling curve. The reward? A night of toasting architectural success under the stars – complete with a much-needed hip flask.

John Lee, Lonely Planet author, Canada

TYLER OLSON/DREAMSTIME

VICTORIA

These days, Victoria (p161) is not the clichéd incarnation of olde-worlde England that it used to be. Yes, there are still copious tearooms and great fish and chips, but there are also swanky boutique hotels, surprisingly innovative restaurants and a hipster shopping scene on Lower Johnson that rivals much bigger and supposedly cooler cities. So if you've come here with your monocle and pith helmet, wear them ironically and you'll fit right in.

John Lee, Lonely Planet author, Canada

JOHN ELK III

BARD ON THE BEACH

Such a West Coast concept: staging Shakespeare's finest in open-backed tents on the waterfront. Vancouver's Vanier Park (p100) is the venue and the sunset-luring North Shore mountains are the backdrop for spirited productions that sell out to capacity almost every night of the summer-long run. Expect to be lulled by the poetry, then head to the gift shop in the intermission to buy that essential Shakespeare action figure, complete with its posable quill pen.

John Lee, Lonely Planet author, Canada

CAPE SCOTT PROVINCIAL PARK

The northern tip of Vancouver Island is remote enough that casual holidaymakers rarely make the trip, which only adds to the reward for those that do. Pushing though the dense, ferny undergrowth of Cape Scott (p215), you suddenly emerge blinking in the sunlight on an empty, white-sand beach studded with tide pools and rocky outcrops. The waves lap gently at the shore, while marine birds swoop around as if they own the place. It's the kind of place where falling in love with nature happens automatically.

John Lee, Lonely Planet author, Canada

Contents

Regional Map Contents

Yukon Territory
p387

Northern BC
pp348–9

Cariboo-Chilcotin & Coast
p334

Whistler & the
Sunshine Coast
p137

Fraser-Thompson
Region pp230–1

The Rockies
p302

The Kootenays
p272

Vancouver
Island
pp162–3

Vancouver
& Around
pp84–5

Okanagan Valley
p246

Southern Gulf
Islands
p217

Destination British Columbia & the Yukon

Like a nervous teen in the hours before prom night, British Columbia spent the better part of the nascent 21st century preparing for its date with the world: the 2010 Olympic & Paralympic Winter Games in Vancouver. The joy of winning the games in 2003 spawned a euphoria that lasted for several years, at least until the global economy tanked late in the decade. Then tough economic times conspired with a bad case of nerves to spawn Olympic-sized worries that weren't that much different from those of the teen contemplating her big night: Was too much spent? What would everybody else think? What would happen after?

It was an uncharacteristic bit of doubt for a province that has been on a roll for years. Vancouver goes from one strength to the next, a beautiful city of glass reflecting the surrounding mountains and water. A destination for hopeful immigrants who want to join a progressive population that takes good food, good living and good times for granted.

Reality Bites

But just like the complexion of our prom date, all is never perfect. Seemingly intractable poverty in downtrodden neighborhoods like downtown's Eastside and outbreaks of gang violence more typical of South Central LA are proof that the dream hasn't been shared by all.

After being teased by gold rushes in the 19th century, British Columbia found its real wealth all around it. The millions of spruce, cedar, fir and other trees growing in profusion from the stormy Pacific edge of Vancouver Island right across to the flanks of the Rocky Mountains found ready buyers around the world. Later, BC's underground riches of lead, zinc and more brought further wealth. Even the wild rivers that cleave the province were dammed, creating vast inland oceans of water for generating hydropower.

During the last half of the 20th century, BC could bring the modern age to almost every corner and citizen because it could feed upon itself. But in a worldwide depression there's not much need for raw materials and BC has had to deal with the collapse of its previously core industries of logging, mining and water. Towns in rural enclaves from the Kootenays right through the north have struggled.

Natural Wealth

If British Columbia was built by exploiting itself to exhaustion, its future may just come from cherishing itself. Instead of realizing wealth through destruction, it is realizing wealth through *tasteful* construction. The Powder Hwy is the marketing name coined recently for a series of roads already winding up and around the mountain ranges of the Kootenays. The name's genesis is easy: 12m of the most perfect skiing and boarding snow falls on average each year on the ranges of saw-toothed peaks across the region. Enthusiasts unblushingly call it 'champagne powder.'

Still in the Kootenays and near the American border, Rossland has found its natural wealth during the summer when the world's best mountain-bikers crash along its steep, granite slopes on trails that can best be described as sick. Just up the hill from Trail, a town living with the legacy

FAST FACTS

BC population: 4.51 million

BC area: 944,735 sq km

BC sq km per person: 0.21

Cost of 1976 Montréal Olympics: $1.5 billion

Final estimated cost of 2010 Olympics: $6 billion

Yukon population: 30,600

Yukon area: 483,450 sq km

Yukon sq km per person: 15.8

Yukon sq km per moose: 8.1

of years of destructive mining, Rossland is merrily moving forward by getting folks to go downhill.

Elsewhere in BC, the Okanagan Valley has literally uncorked a fortune by shifting some of its fertile, sun-drenched hillsides from orchards to vineyards, supplying more than 100 wineries – many world-class.

In the north, even Prince George is shaking off its image as the pulp mill of the west by discovering the natural beauty long ignored in the surrounding hills. Out in the Pacific, the Queen Charlotte Islands are perfect symbols of the renaissance of BC's rich First Nations cultures. Official prejudices and discrimination are fading as the native Haida people flex their artistic muscles and again show the world what you can carve from a huge cedar log.

Finding Balance

Of course finding a future based on environmental stewardship is as complex as BC's very environment. Competing budget pressures on the provincial government (above and beyond Olympics budget blowouts) for critical needs like health care and education mean that niceties such as the parks system remain critically underfunded.

And it's hard to tell communities that made their living off the land to wait patiently through hardship for a new future based on green pursuits. Pipeline and exploration schemes tied to the insatiable demand for energy offer the promise of billions despite their potential to muck up whole swaths of the north.

The very charms that make BC such a good date also make it potentially too hot a date, with growing crowds and traffic jams. Still, in an era when the magnificent and pristine coastal Great Bear Rainforest can at least receive partial protection, there's cause for hope that BC will find a way to become a dream date while preserving a modicum of virtue.

Meanwhile in the Yukon

Although British Columbia and the Yukon Territory share a long border, they really share little else. The history of the Yukon has always been more closely linked to that of neighboring Alaska than to its sibling to the south. Until the Alaska Hwy was built, you had to travel through the Alaskan ports of Haines and Skagway to reach the Yukon. Even today those are the preferred routes for travelers who want to combine a trip north with the exquisite joy of sailing the stunning Inside Passage.

The Yukon remains in many ways as it was 200 years ago: a forbidding wilderness that bursts into life during a brief summer that offers unparalleled opportunities for the adventurous. Most people today live in Whitehorse, the agreeable and low-key capital. Their politics lean towards the conservative, an outgrowth of the popular image of self-reliance promoted in both bluster and reality. But you can't escape the irony of trying to square a philosophy of small government with a territory that receives far more from Ottawa than it gives. The arts budget alone would be the envy of cities with many more zeros after the citizen count.

Few doubt that enormous energy and mineral riches lie under the Yukon – despite the best efforts of the Klondike gold miners and their successors. The territory's remoteness – for now – limits efforts to explore further. A worrisome glimpse of future challenges can be found in the far north where even the ancient and magnificent herds of caribou don't tread. Herschel Island, just off the coast, is threatened by the warming waters of the Arctic Ocean. In the meantime, however, this storied territory returns exponential rewards for every effort you invest in enjoying it.

Getting Started

Spend your time dreaming and planning a fabulous trip; don't spend it sweating the question of how you're going to get there or other nitty gritty details. BC and the Yukon are easy. Spur of the moment trips are a breeze, it's easy to get around and there are offerings for every budget. Visitor Centers (VCs), which can help with details big and small, abound.

See Climate Charts (p421) for more information.

WHEN TO GO

There's never really a bad time to visit BC. Vancouver is definitely a year-round destination – you can partake of its urban pleasures at any time. Other major areas in the south, such as Victoria and the Okanagan Valley, are good for most of the year when the weather is temperate. And all that rain you've heard about? Just assume it can rain at any time and get on with it.

Lots of the most beautiful parts of BC are year-round destinations in that you hike, bike and explore in the summer and ski in the winter. Whistler and the ski resorts of the Okanagan, the Kootenays and the parks of the Rockies have split personalities – both appealing. The fabulous BC coast is really most enjoyable when the harsh winter storms are not pounding though, and the Yukon is best enjoyed during the short summer from mid-June until early September. During the summer especially, you'll find festivals and events across the region (p26).

COSTS & MONEY

You can enjoy BC and the Yukon on any budget. With the freedom of your own vehicle, count on $225 to $300 per day, which will allow for comfortable rooms, activities, good meals and fuel. Traveling on a budget, you can do it for $100 a day or a bit less staying in hostels or camping and riding the bus. A group can pool their resources to enjoy the freedom of a cheap rental car.

In Vancouver, Victoria and the resorts of Whistler and the Rockies, prices for activities include skiing (average lift ticket $65) and white-water rafting ($100 or more). Families can save as there are often group prices and deals letting kids stay for free in their parents' rooms are common.

The Yukon is generally a bit more expensive, say 20%.

HOW MUCH?

A pint of a Vancouver microbrew $5

One-day lift ticket for Whistler $90

Day ferry on BC's Inside Passage (driver and car) $500

Spotting wildlife on land and sea $0

Yukon Territorial Parks admission $0

TRAVELING RESPONSIBLY

BC and the Yukon already have a pretty good vibe when it comes to green issues. A few points to consider:

- Travel in a high-mileage car; SUVs *might* only be needed for the most ambitious backcountry travel.

DON'T LEAVE HOME WITHOUT...

- Fully broken-in hiking shoes
- A corkscrew for your Okanagan Valley (p244) explorations
- Bug repellent for backcountry and Yukon summer nights
- Something for staying dry on rainy days
- Extra memory for the camera

TOP PICKS

BRITISH COLUMBIA

Part of the fun of traveling the region is making your own 'Best of...' lists of the extraordinary things you've seen and done. Here are some of ours.

WATCHING WILDLIFE

You'll see whales, moose, spawning salmon, bears, orcas, mountain goats and dozens more species on land and in the water of BC and the Yukon.

- The Inside Passage of the BC coast teems with every kind of iconic sea creature. The best way to see the spectacle is by boat (see p431)
- The Icefields Parkway isn't just about glaciers, it's about the myriad of protected species blithely ignoring you by the side of the road (p322)

- Kluane National Park & Reserve has it all, including Dall sheep performing amazing cliffside feats (p400)
- Saturna Island is the place to see passing whales (p224)
- The Bella Coola Valley has untouched rivers you can float down while viewing bears on shore (p343)

SMALL TOWNS

Scores of idiosyncratic small towns in BC and the Yukon are the cure for a homogenous age.

- Nelson, where marching to the beat of a different drummer is reality (p283)
- Fernie, with ski bums still awed by the ring of peaks (p292)
- Dawson City, a classic end-of-the-road town that avoids cliché through creativity (p407)

- Cowichan Bay, with polychromatic buildings on stilts over the water and plenty of funky characters (p184)
- Armstrong, the gloss-free northern outpost of the Okanagan Valley (p270)

SCENIC ROUTES

BC and the Yukon are a scenic route. But some roads are more equal than others.

- The sublime Sea to Sky Hwy from Vancouver to Whistler (p137)
- It doesn't get any more dramatic than the glacial canyons of the monumental Fraser Canyon (p231)
- On the road to Rossland, Hwy 3B surmounts Strawberry Pass amidst gorgeous alpine scenery (p291)

- Glaciers that will stop you in your tracks line the road to Stewart and Hyder (p382)
- More bald eagles than you can count plus scenery that changes from high alpine to lush forest in a just a few kilometers are among the highlights of the Haines Hwy (p402)

- Offset your carbon emissions with groups such as Vancouver-based Offsetters Carbon Neutral Society (www.offsetters.ca).
- Bus links between major towns are good. Biking is popular from Vancouver year-round to Dawson City in the summer. Environmentally friendly slow ferries link destinations up and down the coast.
- If you see a hotel with a 'green key' rating, it's a property that has gone through the Hotel Association of Canada's voluntary audit to assess

sustainability practices. But bear in mind it is based on self-reporting by the hotels. See www.hacgreenhotels.com for listings.

■ BC is home of the *100 Mile Diet* craze (a book that details a Vancouver couple's attempt to eat only local ingredients for one year); restaurants serving locally grown, organic, in-season food are common, as are farmers markets (detailed throughout this book).

■ Seafood is a popular menu item, but make sure the species you're ordering is one that's sustainably harvested; check Seafood Watch (www.mbayaq.org/cr/seafoodwatch.asp) for details.

■ Check out the GreenDex (p462), which indexes listings in this book that can be a part of traveling sustainability.

For more on protecting the environment in BC and the Yukon, see p80.

TRAVEL LITERATURE

Reading books about your destination can be a great way to get a feel for a place before you go. BC and the Yukon have inspired many books (including some classics) so you can delve right in.

Souvenir of Canada and the sequel, *Souvenir of Canada 2*, are books of essays by renowned Vancouver author Douglas Coupland. Canadian topics and icons such as the Yukon, moose and hockey are explored.

The Golden Spruce by John Vaillant is an award-winning page-turner that chronicles the bizarre, true tale of a logger who cuts down a sacred tree in the Queen Charlotte Islands to protest against logging.

Robert Service: Under the Spell of the Yukon by Enid Mallory is the definitive book on one of the region's greatest writers. Once a shy bank clerk, Service gained fame in his life and continues to wow with works such as *The Spell of the Yukon*.

A Land Gone Lonesome, An Inland Voyage Along the Yukon River by Dan O'Neil is an excellent work by the noted Alaskan author. Characters who cling to strangeness along the deserted banks of the vast Yukon River are featured.

Writing the West Coast is a collection of essays – serious and humorous – by a variety of writers about life on BC's coast.

The Klondike Fever by Pierre Berton is the most readable account of the enormous yet futile efforts of thousands to rush to Dawson City and get rich during the gold rush.

Following the Curve of Time by Cathy Converse traces the life and voyages of skipper and mother M Wylie Blanchet. Her 1925 *The Curve of Time* remains a classic.

INTERNET RESOURCES

You'll find many good special-interest websites listed in the front chapters of this book. Here are some general-purpose ones:

BC Parks (www.env.gov.bc.ca/bcparks/explore/explore.html) The official site to BC's 830 provincial parks (!) is loaded with info on every one.

Go BC (www.gobc.ca) Travel planner for the province with an emphasis on culture and history.

Lonely Planet (www.lonelyplanet.com) Book travel, exchange information with other travelers and much more.

Parks Canada (www.parkscanada.ca) The official site for national parks has information on all facets of the parks in BC and the Yukon.

Tourism British Columbia (www.hellobc.com) The official site for Tourism BC; has lots of good trip-planning ideas.

The Yukon (http://travelyukon.com) The official site for Yukon tourism is a Kluane-sized resource. The maps section is comprehensive.

Events Calendar

Summer may be the time of plenty but events worth your while can be found year-round in BC and the Yukon.

JANUARY-FEBRUARY

BANFF/LAKE LOUISE WINTER FESTIVAL
late Jan-early Feb
Annual town-wide party held in late January and early February since 1919, offering much mirth and merriment.

YUKON QUEST
Feb
This legendary 1600km dog sled race goes from Whitehorse to Fairbanks, Alaska through darkness and −50°C temperatures.

APRIL

TELUS WORLD SKI & SNOWBOARD FESTIVAL
mid-Apr
Whistler's giant nine-day showcase of pro ski and snowboard competitions, plus live music concerts.

MAY

VANCOUVER INTERNATIONAL CHILDREN'S FESTIVAL
mid-May
Storytelling, performances and activities in a delightful multi-tented, family-friendly site in Vanier Park.

JUNE

BARD ON THE BEACH
Jun–Sep
Up to four Shakespeare productions performed per season in tented pavilions in Vancouver's Vanier Park.

VANCOUVER INTERNATIONAL JAZZ FESTIVAL
mid-Jun
Mammoth music celebration, staged in Gastown, Yaletown and around Vancouver over 10 days. Superstar performers plus free outdoor shows.

ELVIS FESTIVAL
late Jun
Dozens of impersonators of The King invade Penticton. It could be your idea of heaven or hound dog hell, especially the ersatz Elvises at the pub-based karaoke.

MIDSUMMER MUSIC FESTIVAL
late Jun
More than 75 bands, including 45 from the Smithers area, enliven the river town with folk music and more.

WILLIAMS LAKE STAMPEDE
late Jun-early Jul
Annual four-day hoedown at the venerable Williams Lake Stampede Grounds: rodeo stunts, country crooners and various pageants.

JULY

VICTORIA SKA FEST
mid-Jul
Canada's largest nothing-but-ska festival brings the BC capital to life every summer.

KELOWNA MUSIC & ARTS FESTIVAL
late Jul
Performers of all types, artists and general entertainers and spectacle-makers take to Kelowna's streets and venues.

CELEBRATION OF LIGHT
late Jul & early Aug
Four-day international fireworks showcase crowd-pleaser, staged on barges in Vancouver's English Bay.

AUGUST

PEACH FESTIVAL
early Aug
Penticton's premier event is basically a week-long party in early August that has taken place since 1947, loosely centered on crowning a Peach Queen. The Saturday parade is a local fave.

PRIDE WEEK
early Aug
Vancouver's multi-day fiesta of gay-, lesbian- and bisexual-friendly fashion shows, gala parties, concerts and the city's largest street parade.

UDDERFEST
early Aug
Prince Rupert enjoys five days of captivating fringe theater performed by local groups and national performers.

KOKANEE CRANKWORX
mid-Aug
Whistler's nine-day mud-splattered showcase of bike stunts, speed events and world-leading two-wheel legends.

PACIFIC NATIONAL EXHIBITION   mid-Aug
BC's biggest country fair is staged in Vancouver
and includes two weeks of live shows, music
concerts, farm animals and a fairground with great
rollercoaster.

DISCOVERY DAYS   mid-Aug
The Yukon celebrates the discovery of gold in
1896. Dawson City is party central with a week-
long event.

SEPTEMBER

**VANCOUVER INTERNATIONAL FRINGE
FESTIVAL**   mid-Sep
Eleven days of eclectic performances at theaters
and unconventional venues dotted around Granville
Island.

OCTOBER

OKANAGAN FALL WINE FESTIVAL   early Oct
The valley's largest wine festival. For details on
others, see p252.

**VANCOUVER INTERNATIONAL FILM
FESTIVAL**   early Oct
Sixteen days of screenings, workshops and galas
celebrating Canadian and international movie-
making.

NOVEMBER

CORNUCOPIA   mid-Nov
An indulgent Whistler showcase of fine wining
and dining, with seminars, gala parties and tasting opportunities.

Itineraries

CLASSIC ROUTES

NORTH TO THE YUKON & BACK   One Month / Vancouver to Vancouver

From **Vancouver** (p81), take the **Sea to Ski Hwy** (p137) to the natural beauty of **Squamish** (p137). Then go for the gold in **Whistler** (p141) and head up through cowboy country in the **Chilcotin** (p341) to **Williams Lake** (p335). Then it's up to **Prince George** (p350). Yellowhead it on Hwy 16 west through **Smithers** (p361) and on to **Prince Rupert** (p367). Catch a ferry to the **Queen Charlotte Islands** (p372) and plunge into **Gwaii Haanas National Park Reserve and Haida Heritage Site** (p380). Catch the ferry back to Prince Rupert and get an **Alaska Marine Highway ferry** (p431) to **Haines, AK** (p403). From here enjoy **Kluane National Park** (p400) in the Yukon before crossing into Alaska briefly for the **Top of the World Highway** (p415) to **Dawson City** (p407) in the Yukon. Now you head south, passing through **Whitehorse** (p390) before joining the **Alaska Highway** (p397) all the way to **Dawson Creek** (p355). Jog through Prince George and east on Hwy 16 to **Jasper** (p324) and the Canadian Rockies. Head south on the **Icefields Parkway** (p322) to **Banff** (p308) and then out via **Yoho National Park** (p303) and south via Hwys 23 and 6 to funky **Nelson** (p283). Then go straight west on Hwy 3 for an **Okanagan Valley** (p244) romp and you're back in Vancouver.

This 7900km route has everything you could hope for: the best of the Olympics sites, the storied Yukon, long and beautiful ferry rides and drives, and the Rockies. What makes BC, the Rockies and the Yukon such a jaw-dropping destination can be found along this route.

A LONG WEEKEND
Three to Four Days / Vancouver to Vancouver

Head north from **Vancouver** (p81) on Hwy 99 through **Stanley Park** (p97) and make for West Van's Horseshoe Bay ferry terminal. Take the **Sunshine Coast** (p153) vessel to Langdale and hit Hwy 101, the region's main artery. After a few minutes, you'll be in **Gibsons** (p153), an ideal stop for lunch and a stroll. Rejoining Hwy 101, continue past **Sechelt** (p155), take the short ferry hop from Saltery Bay to Earls Cove and drive on to historic **Powell River** (p157). Wander around the old part of town and find a quaint spot for dinner, then consider a guided sunset kayaking trip.

Up early the next day, take the 15-minute ferry trip to **Comox** (p207) on **Vancouver Island** (p160), then weave south on Hwy 19. Be sure to drop by little **Cumberland** (p207), where the pioneer buildings now house cool eateries and colorful hangouts, then continue on to **Qualicum Beach** (p193). It's not hard to find great fish and chips here, as well as a smattering of quirky attractions. Continue southwards to **Nanaimo** (p186), the island's second city. Wander around the Old City Quarter, lined with enticing shops and restaurants.

Back on the road the next day, continue southwards on Hwy 1 and stop off at **Chemainus** (p186), an old logging town that's now covered with a kaleidoscope of painted murals. Heading towards the southern tip of the island, allow yourself plenty of time to enjoy **Victoria** (p161), the provincial capital. Check in to your hotel then wander the Inner Harbour and maybe hit a brewpub or two.

Weave northwards from the city on Hwy 17 the next morning and take the Swartz Bay ferry back to the mainland. It's a one-hour drive from where the ferry lands at Tsawwassen to Vancouver.

Vancouver, Victoria and Vancouver Island are your palette on this 500km trip that's perfect for a long weekend. The Sunshine Coast is an added pleasure in an itinerary that gives you time to explore local charms and natural beauty.

CIRCLE OF DISCOVERY   Two Weeks / Vancouver to Vancouver

Start your journey of discovery in **Vancouver** (p81). Catch the ferry for the short ride to **Nanaimo** (p186), where you can start to enjoy the Vancouver Island culture, which is distinctly more independent and small-town than the Lower Mainland. After spending the night, meander up Hwy 19 to **Port Hardy** (p213), stopping at villages that catch your fancy. Time your journey so that you make one of the daytime sailings (in summer only) of a BC Ferries **Discovery Coast Ferry** (p345). Spend a full 12 hours spotting whales and more from the deck. Arriving in tiny **Bella Coola** (p344), which sits at the end of a long fjord, find rustic retreat for a few nights in the **Bella Coola Valley** (p343). Spend your days exploring trails past huge old cedars and make the hike to pounding **Odegaard Falls** (p344). Go for a river float and lose count of the grizzlies wandering the shores. When you leave, tackle the thrill-ride for cars called **The Hill** (p342) and head east through the lonely **Chilcotin** (p341). Stop at the alpine waters of **Nimpo Lake** (p342) or just take any little tributary road and lose civilization – what little there is – altogether. At **Williams Lake** (p335) say yee-ha! to cowboy country. Turn south on the **Cariboo Hwy** (Hwy 97; p335). Otherwise known as the Gold Rush Trail, the road follows the route of the first pioneers and gold-seekers who settled in the hardy conditions of BC's unforgiving interior. At **Lytton** (p236) go white-water rafting on the Fraser and Thompson Rivers. After these chilly waters, warm up with a soak in **Harrison Hot Springs** (p231). From here it is a short drive back to Vancouver on the Trans-Canada Hwy.

Over 2400km, you'll enjoy BC's isolated coast while you sail the vaunted Inside Passage. The Bella Coola Valley combines First Nations culture, fearsome natural beauty and oodles of bears. Go cowboy in BC's interior and get wet and silly in waters hot and cold.

TAILORED TRIPS

FOODIE BC

With a full menu of lip-smacking treats, it's hard to go hungry on the road in BC. And you don't even have to drive far for your first meal: **Vancouver** (p81) is one of Canada's top dining cities and is lined with restaurants specializing in authentic ethnic cuisine as well as regional, seasonal nosh. You can follow this food to the source with a taste trip around the friendly, family-owned farms of nearby **Abbotsford** (p134) or the small farmsteads and inviting wineries of Vancouver Island's verdant **Cowichan Valley** (p184). And even among the undeniable surfeit of **Okanagan Valley** (p244) wineries, you'll find plenty of foodie farm stops – think artisan cheese and fruit stands piled high with cherries and peaches. Of course, seafood is also one of the province's favorite culinary lures: check out the local fish and shellfish (salmon, halibut or scallops are never a mistake) at chatty, homestyle restaurants on the coastline and beyond, including the rustic **Queen Charlotte Islands** (p372). And if you're finally stuffed, consider a restorative cuppa in **Victoria** (p161), where afternoon tea experiences range from the traditional to fusion international. Alternatively, just continue scoffing in **Richmond** (p132), where some of BC's best contemporary Asian dining awaits.

MORE WINE!

The **Okanagan Valley** (p244) has dozens of world-class wineries, with new ones opening every year. **Osoyoos** (p245) is a good place to start and there are farm stands on the way to **Oliver** (p248), which is surrounded by a veritable moat of wineries. **Penticton** (p249) honors both its peaches and its excellent vintages. **Naramata** (p256) is at the end of a scenic lakeside drive and is protected from the valley's bustle. **Kelowna** (p258) is the fun-filled center of the action, with a great culture, excellent local organic foods and literally intoxicating nightlife. **Vernon** (p266) has more outstanding farms you can visit. Crossing out of the valley, **Revelstoke** (p273) is the heart of BC's best ski country and a cozy place for après-ski. **New Denver** (p281) is a base for wilderness camping (and campfire wine-drinking) at nearby Valhalla Provincial Park. **Kaslo** (p283) has wine-sipping overlooking Kootenay Lake. Finally, you can bring it all together in fun and funky **Nelson** (p283), where you can drink up the atmosphere – and wine – in a bevy of cute bistros and bars.

UNESCO WORLD HERITAGE SITES

BC, the Rockies and the Yukon contain three of Canada's 13 World Heritage Sites. **Canadian Rocky Mountain Parks** (p301) is the Unesco-recognized place where Canadian tourism began. Covering 23,000 sq km it consists of **Banff** (p308), **Jasper** (p324), **Kootenay** (p306) and **Yoho** (p303) National Parks, **Mt Robson** (p331) and **Mt Assiniboine** (p307) Provincial Parks in BC and Hamber Provincial Park in Alberta. Kluane/Wrangell-St Elias/Glacier Bay/Tatshenshini-Alsek is the mouthful of a designated name for a region teeming with glaciers and raw landscape spanning two countries. **Kluane National Park** (p400) is solidly in the Yukon, abutting **Tatshenshini-Alsek Provincial Wilderness Park** (p385) in BC, while **Glacier Bay** (p385) and Wrangell-St Elias National Parks are found in adjoining Alaska. **SGaang Gwaii** (p380) is the

island home to the abandoned Haida village of Ninstints in Gwaii Haanas National Park Reserve in the Queen Charlotte Islands. In addition to these, Canada is working towards Unesco designation for the following places: the **Klondike** (p404), which covers the gold-rush area from the **Chilkoot Trail** (p405) area near **Skagway** (p404) to **Dawson City** (p407); remote – and melting – **Herschel Island** (p418) and its companion Arctic National Parks, **Ivvavik** (p417) and **Vuntut** (p417). World Heritage Site status is also being sought for all of **Gwaii Haanas National Park Reserve and Haida Heritage Site** (p380) beyond the already listed SGaang Gwaii.

GET LOST

Stewart, BC and **Hyder, AK** (p383) sit at the end of a long fjord and are within earshot of vast glaciers slowly grinding along. With no ferry service in, you enter via long, glacier-lined Hwy 37A. This road is a branch of the **Stewart-Cassiar Highway** (Hwy 37; p381), the 727km-long road linking BC and the Yukon. Most people think of the **Alaska Highway** (p397) when they think of driving north, but Hwy 37 in many ways bests the more famous route. Along its mostly paved route, you pass through some of the north's most unspoiled lands. Take a detour to ghostly **Telegraph Creek** (p384). Another excellent drive is the **Klondike Highway** (p404) from **Skagway** (p404) through **Carcross** (p406) and on to **Dawson City** (p407). Follow the

route of the gold-mad prospectors in 1897–98, many of whom simply ended up mad. For real adventure, take the all-gravel **Dempster Highway** (p416) to **Inuvik** (p416) in the Northwest Territories and arrange a trip to one of the Yukon's **Arctic parks** (p417).

History

BRITISH COLUMBIA

BC's growth and development since European arrival centers first on Vancouver Island's Fort Victoria and later on Vancouver. The history of the Yukon is a separate story (p38).

Living Off the Land

The ancestors of BC's First Nations peoples showed up in North America at least 15,000 to 20,000 years ago. It's likely that, after the last Ice Age, they crossed to Alaska on a land bridge over what is now the Bering Strait. Some settled along the Pacific Coast, while others found their way to the interior and the Yukon.

The Pacific Coast First Nations included the Nuxalk (Bella Coola, p344), Cowichan (Cowichan Valley, p184), Gitksan, Haida (Queen Charlotte Islands, p374), Kwakwaka'wakw, Nisga'a, Nuu-chah-nulth, Salish, Sechelt and Tsimshian groups. The relative abundance of food (salmon flopping into canoes, and so on) meant that there was time to develop artistic pursuits, among the most prominent being totem poles. See p37 and p43 for more on these.

These First Nations people were also able to evolve a sophisticated, structured culture and an intricate trade network. Coastal peoples dwelled as extended families in large, single-roofed cedar lodges. Living off the land and the sea, they staked out hunting and fishing grounds and good places to collect berries, bark and roots.

Inland, where climate extremes are greater than on the coast, the people led nomadic lives, where mere subsistence was something of a victory. In the north they followed the migratory herds of animals such as the caribou and the moose; in the south they pursued the bison. Most of these people were Athapaskans (now called Dene, pronounced 'de-nay'), which included such groups as Chilcotin, Sekani and Tahltan. Other important groups were the Interior Salish and the Kootenay.

Europeans Wash Ashore

During the mid-18th century, European explorers in search of new sources of wealth appeared off the West Coast. Alexsey Chirikov is thought to have been first (at least, that's what noted Russophile Ensign Chekov on *Star Trek* would have said), exploring for Russia in 1741, though his travels were mainly along what is now the Alaskan coast. Spaniards were next: Juan Pérez Hernández sailed from Mexico to the Queen Charlotte Islands and Nootka Sound in 1774, followed by Juan

In *Greetings from British Columbia*, Fred Thirkell and Bob Scullion present a collection of old postcard views of BC communities. Many have changed beyond recognition: the cannery town of Port Essington is long gone while Kelowna today is unrecognizable.

For a website almost as large as BC's history, check out the wide-ranging bchistoryportal.tc.ca.

TIMELINE

800	1778	1793
An ash-spewing eruption of the volcano today known as Mt Churchill in the Yukon destroys the environment and causes many to flee to southwest USA, where they may have evolved into the Navajo and Apaches.	Captain James Cook spreads word of BC's riches to Great Britain. He had been looking for a water route across North America from the Pacific to the Atlantic – the legendary Northwest Passage.	Having crossed the continent, Alexander Mackenzie almost reaches the Pacific Ocean near Bella Coola. Blocked by the Nuxalk in war canoes, he wrote his name on a rock then headed back east for good.

Francisco de la Bodega y Quadra in 1775. (And just to further complicate matters, there's a whole school of thought – mostly pirate fans – that contends that Sir Francis Drake turned up in the 1570s.)

But just as many came to North America from Europe before Columbus got the credit for 'discovering America', it is Captain James Cook who gets the credit for putting the future BC on the map. The outrageous sums his crew made selling sea-otter pelts bought (stolen?) on Vancouver Island brought traders eager to cash in. It would not be the last time that word of riches brought people running to the region.

Ultimately, too many people tried to profit from the fur trade and the English and Spanish came into near conflict. Only a treaty signed at Nootka in 1794 prevented war, and then only because the Spaniards caved and said in effect 'you keep the marbles, we're going home.'

In the 1800s more than 30 native languages were spoken in BC.

Huntin' Beaver

The most famous of trappers were Alexander Mackenzie, Simon Fraser and David Thompson, who explored overland routes from the east and generously lent their names to mapmakers and region-namers. Fort St John (p356), on the Peace River, became the first European settlement in 1794; in its wake came many more trading posts which, by the 1820s, went under the control of the Hudson's Bay Company (HBC). For a good idea of how HBC settlements worked (and to get an idea of the relative value of a beaver pelt), visit the restored Fort St James (p360), which is a national historic site in a now quiet corner of the north.

Of the early explorers, Alexander Mackenzie is probably the most interesting. Often compared to the Lewis and Clark expedition in the US, he crossed Canada in 1793, more than 10 years before the Americans crossed their country to the south. And he did so with almost no funding and mostly because he was always restless. (Lewis and Clark, on the other hand, set off at the behest of the US government on a journey that by contemporary standards was well funded and with a platoon of men.)

Mackenzie crossed the Rockies, the continental divide and the Fraser River to name just a few achievements. Mackenzie later wrote a book of his adventures titled *Voyages…to the Frozen and Pacific Oceans*; it was all the rage in 1801. And although his exploits in many ways topped Lewis and Clark, the Americans had the last laugh. When David Thompson followed the Columbia River to its mouth on the Pacific Ocean, he found that Lewis and Clark had already claimed everything in sight.

In the meantime, initially to counter the Spanish presence, Captain George Vancouver had circumnavigated and claimed Vancouver Island for Britain from 1792 to 1794. 'The serenity of the climate, the innumerable pleasing landscapes and the abundant fertility that unassisted nature puts forth requires only to be enriched by man to render it the most lovely country that can be imagined,' Vancouver verbosely observed in

For a treasure trove of photos including ones showing Vancouver through the decades, hardy pioneers and First Nations sites before they were plundered, see www.historicphotos.ca.

1805	1846	1866
The Northwest Trading Company establishes a fur-trading post at Hudson's Hope in northeast BC. It was later taken over by Hudson's Bay Company (HBC).	After years of debate, the US and Britain agree to the Oregon Treaty, which is meant to settle the border between the US and BC. However, the devil is in the details, and more years of debate ensue.	Mainland BC and Vancouver Island unite, not out of any love but rather because mainland BC had nowhere to turn after it overspent on infrastructure (a foreshadowing of Olympic spending habits).

THE PIG WAR

Just because BC and the US agreed to the Oregon Treaty didn't mean that the matter of the border was settled. The numerous islands around Vancouver Island were still subject to negotiation: were they part of Vancouver Island or were they separate and part of the US? In 1859 a hungry pig on San Juan Island brought matters to a head and almost started a war.

The island had been claimed both by the US and BC and, in the 13 years since the treaty, efforts at solving the imbroglio were fruitless. People went hog wild after the porker in question ate some potatoes growing on an American's plot. In a move that wouldn't surprise even today, the American shot the pig, which belonged to an Irishman working for the all-powerful HBC. Within weeks the US and Britain were rushing troops and ships to the island in preparation for war. However, the looming Civil War diverted US attention and it was agreed to continue the joint governance. (The matter was finally settled in 1872 when the US won sole possession of the islands.)

1792. Not surprisingly, the comment has long been a source of ire to First Nations people, who resent Vancouver's implication that there was no one around when he arrived. Evidence shows that the local population was about 80,000 at the time.

Vancouver also explored far up BC's north coast. By the 1840s the HBC was warily watching the USA make an increasingly indisputable claim to the Oregon country anchored by HBC's Fort Vancouver on the Columbia River near present-day Portland. In 1843, the HBC dispatched James Douglas to Vancouver Island, where he established Fort Victoria. Vancouver Island became a crown colony in 1849. You can see a lot about these early days and the nascent development of modern BC at the Royal British Columbia Museum (p165) in Victoria. Eventually the territorial claims between the British and the Americans were settled under the Oregon Treaty, which ran the border across the 49th parallel. It included the proviso that all of Vancouver Island would remain with BC, thus ensuring that tourists to Victoria would enjoy high tea as opposed to the mocha-decaf-soy-milk-half-shot lattes found south across the border.

An anti-immigration law in 1908 required Sikhs arriving from India to pay $200. Few could.

Gold I

The discovery of gold along the Fraser River in 1858 brought a flood of people seeking their fortunes, and led to mainland BC also being declared a crown colony, with New Westminster its capital. A second wave of fortune hunters arrived when gold was discovered further north in the Cariboo region. Although the gold rush only lasted a few years, many of those who came remained behind to form more permanent settlements. Experience a sanitized version of a gold-rush town at restored Barkerville (p338), which spares you streets of goop and poop comingling in a yucky soup.

1887	1896	1914
The Canadian Pacific Railway arrives in Vancouver, linking Canada's west with the east and conquering range after range of mountains arrayed across BC like swells at sea. It was an engineering marvel.	Gold found on Bonanza Creek near today's Dawson City sets off the legendary Klondike Gold Rush. Within three years the madness subsides.	The opening of the Panama Canal considerably shortens ocean journeys between BC and Europe. This is particularly good for Vancouver and contributes to the port's growth in grain exports.

After Mainland BC and Vancouver Island were united, Victoria was named capital in 1868. Meanwhile, in 1867, the British government passed the British North American Act, creating the Dominion of Canada, a confederation that maintained British ties (beyond even the Queen's mug on money) but conferred many powers to a central Canadian government and individual provinces. The eastern provinces of Canada united under the confederation, and BC decided to join in 1871 on the rather substantial condition that a transcontinental railroad be extended to the West Coast. Fledgling BC timber barons needed transport to meet the demands of settlers in the prairies who wanted to replace their sod-and-dung huts with houses made with timber.

The late 19th century proved a tough time for BC's First Nations people. The gold-rush era got them booted from their traditional lands, leading to violence among both the First Nations and the Whites. Moreover, the Canadian government, heeding complaints from missionaries and other philistines about 'pagan' native practices, outlawed potlatches in the 1880s with legislation that was not repealed until 1951.

Protests, Prejudice & Prohibition

The building of the Panama Canal, which was completed in 1914, made it easier for BC to peddle its lumber to the US East Coast and Europe. The province's interior profited too, with the completion of the Grand Trunk Railway from Edmonton, Alberta, to Prince Rupert (p369). As big business grew, so did big unions. Workers in great numbers organized into labor unions in the 1910s, protesting about working conditions and pay rates. A number of strikes targeted key industries like lumber mills and shipping; in several instances the government sided with its business-owning patrons and sent armed thugs after workers. However, the unions, the government and businesses found common ground in racial prejudice – all felt that the growing Chinese and Japanese population should be harassed, banned and beaten. During WWII, Japanese Canadians were removed from their land and their fishing boats, and were interned inland in places like New Denver, which has a good museum (p281) recalling this outrage.

When not abusing foreigners, BC's elite showed a remarkable ability to get rich. Canada very controversially tried prohibiting alcohol from 1917 to 1921. Besides enraging hockey fans, it had predictable results in that a vast black market for the stuff sprang up and dealers earned huge amounts. When the Americans ignored Canada's lesson (as always!) and instituted their own prohibition later in the 1920s, the old bootleg network was able to spring back to life and vast wealth flowed to places like Vancouver. Many see parallels in BC's thriving, albeit slightly underground, pot-exporting business now.

BC had prohibition from 1917 to 1921, when the law was ended allowing locals to get rich as rum-runners supplying the still-dry US to the south.

1915	1920	1921
The Vancouver Millionaires win hockey's Stanley Cup. They are the last local team to strike it rich on the ice. Today's Vancouver Canucks date back to 1945 and have lost both times they've made the finals.	Having dropped significantly since the turn of the century, the population of the Yukon falls below 5,000. It won't increase greatly until after the Alaska Hwy is built in 1942-43.	Kwakwaka'wakw chief Dan Cranmer defies the ban on potlatches by staging what may have been the largest gathering ever to celebrate and exchange gifts. Scores are arrested at the Alert Bay event.

HISTORY OF TOTEMS

The artistry of northwest coast native groups – Tsimshian, Haida, Tlingit, Kwakwaka'wakw and Nuxalk – is as intricate as it is simple. One of the most spectacular examples of this is the totem pole, which has become such a symbolic icon that it's part of popular culture, not least because of the entire concept of the low man.

The carving of totem poles was largely squashed after the Canadian government outlawed the potlatch ceremony in 1884. Most totems only last 60 to 80 years, though some on the Queen Charlotte Islands are more than 100 years old. When a totem falls, tradition says that it should be left there until another is erected in its place.

Today, totem carving is again widespread, though the poles are often constructed for non-traditional uses, such as public art. Modern totems commissioned for college campuses, museums and public buildings no longer recount the lineage of any one household but instead stand to honor the First Nations, their outstanding artistry and their beliefs.

Totem poles abound in Northern BC. See p364 for details. Elsewhere, you can see a clutch of exceptional poles in Thunderbird Park at the Royal British Columbia Museum in Victoria (p165). There are a lot of other amazing First Nations works there as well. You can see a huge totem at the museum in Alert Bay (p213) and there are many more examples across BC. For a guide to their symbology, see p43.

First Nations people also received their share of prejudice. The notorious 1884 ban on potlatches reached its peak with the huge one held by chief Dan Cranmer. The arrests became a focal point of outrage, even as the gifts and other artifacts wound up enshrined at the National Museum of Canada in Ottawa, which finally agreed to return them in the 1980s. Some can be seen in the museum at Alert Bay (p213). The ban was not fully lifted until 1951.

The effects of discrimination of First Nations people can be fully seen in and around Prince Rupert. As documented at the Museum of Northern British Columbia (p368), the coastal region of BC while wet was also literally swimming with food. Prior to the arrival of Europeans in 1834, the area was one of the most densely populated in all of North America. At various times more than 20 distinct native cultures lived near the rich waters. Most were (and still are) Tsimshian (poetically pronounced sim-she-an), as evidenced by the remains of 55 villages dotted around the harbor.

After the Europeans arrived, they built a fort and an HBC trading post that lured the Tsimshians into regular contact. The usual slew of diseases weakened the First Nations populations, while the repressive laws aimed at eradicating their way of life meant bleak times not just for the Tsimshians but also other coastal First Nations with rich cultures, such as the Haida across the channel on the Queen Charlotte Islands (p374).

Madness, Betrayal and the Lash is the cheery and accurate title of a book by Stephen Bown that documents the Pacific voyages of George Vancouver from 1792 to 1795.

1941	1953	1960
The December 7 attack on Pearl Harbor spurs the US to work closely with Canada to open up the north for their common defense. The effects are many, but the real enduring legacy is the Alaska Hwy.	Whitehorse becomes the Yukon's capital, replacing Dawson City. It is a transport hub (mostly American-funded), having the Alaska Hwy, a good airport and the railway to Skagway.	First Nations people finally get the right to vote in BC. This is one of the more important changes that are part of a decades-long effort to first restore the rights of BC's original residents and agree to compensation.

Making Amends & Making Money

After WWII, BC couldn't mine its minerals and chop its trees down fast enough to keep up with the demand and a lot of money flowed into the province. Road and rail links were pushed into all manner of formerly remote places, such as those along the Stewart-Cassiar Hwy (p381). The 1961 Columbia River Treaty with the US resulted in massive dam-building projects that flooded pristine valleys and displaced people. The Americans paid BC to hold back huge amounts of water that could be released to hydroelectric plants south of the border whenever power use demanded.

Scores of family-run logging mills have all been replaced by vast paper, pulp and plywood operations run by a just a few huge conglomerates. The world can thank BC for a market-flooding supply of cheap particle board, the bowed backbone of budget bookcases everywhere.

In another switch from the recent past, Vancouver hung out the welcome sign to Asians in a big way starting in the 1980s. The property boom in the years since has transformed the city, made elevator repairmen happy and changed the racial makeup of a place that had looked a lot like Glasgow.

Meanwhile, the process of negotiating treaties with First Nations people proceeds in fits and starts. James Douglas actually signed a treaty for part of Vancouver Island back in the 1800s, otherwise settlers just took what they wanted. A process to change this (and to negotiate treaties that were nothing like the 'treaties' signed in the US during westward expansion) has been proceeding irregularly for almost 20 years. A federal Supreme Court decision against BC in 1997 established aboriginal claim.

The first treaty signed – with the Nisga'a Nation – provided about $200 million and allowed some self-governance. Given the money involved, it's easy to see why the treaty process is one big vat of contention in BC (eg much of the land under downtown Vancouver is subject to First Nations claims). Only 20% of First Nation groups have even begun negotiations.

While the metaphor might be hackneyed to the point of cliché, BC spent much of the new century readying itself for a gold rush in the form of the 2010 Winter Olympics, although weary taxpayers may be forgiven if they think the rush has been for the gold in their wallets as budgets have soared. It was a narrow win for Vancouver, beating out Salzburg, Austria and PyeongChang, South Korea.

THE YUKON

Until the 1940s you traveled to the Yukon primarily through Alaskan ports because of the region's isolation, giving the Yukon a history quite different from BC, where events were closely tied to the rest of Canada.

The first people to arrive in the region were part of the groups that crossed the land bridge linking Asia and the Americas. Forswearing

Soapy Smith by Stan Sauerwein is a page-turner about one of history's great scammers. Smith employed teams of fake ministers, fake police and fake friends to fleece hapless gold seekers before they could even set out for Dawson.

1964	1971	1998
Implementation of the Columbia River Treaty starts the construction of huge dams that forever change the Kootenays. One creates the Arrow Lakes, causing Nakusp to be moved while obliterating many other towns.	Greenpeace is founded in Vancouver. A small group of activists set sail in a fishing boat to 'bear witness' to US underground nuclear tests on an island off the west coast of Alaska.	BC, the federal government and the Nisga'a Nation reach the first modern-day treaty. It is an enormous settlement for an otherwise impoverished group of people living at Nass Camp near the Nisga'a Lava Bed.

guidebooks, they followed the woolly mammoths, mastodons and steppe bison. Archaeologists date their arrival in the Porcupine River area near Old Crow from between 15,000 and 20,000 years ago. Volcanic activity coupled with weather that would make even a polar bear pause, caused hardship and the area was thinly populated.

In the 1840s Robert Campbell, an HBC door-to-door salesman and/or explorer, was the first European to travel extensively in the district. Fur traders, prospectors, whalers and – as always – missionaries followed him. In addition to an upswing in inner guilt by sinners who hadn't previously known they were sinners, diseases decimated the First Nations population even as they were being saved. Campbell established Fort Selkirk on the Yukon River as a trading post. It survived in various forms until bypassed by roads in the 20th century and today is a well-preserved artifact you can visit (p407).

Gold II

In 1870 the region became part of the Northwest Territories. During the next two decades, the few people in the region regularly found bits of gold in its streams but never enough to amount to much. The 1896 discovery on a tributary of the Klondike River near what became Dawson City changed everything. The ensuing gold rush attracted hopefuls from around the world, over 99% of whom found no fortune while losing their own (see p407).

Wealth from gold and revenue from people looking for it helped the Yukon become a separate territory in 1898, with Dawson City the capital. But the party was shortlived and, by 1920, the population was under 5000. The entire territory began a long and slow economic descent in the first decades of the 20th century as gold discoveries dwindled. WWII and the construction of the Alaska Hwy in 1942 (p398) opened up the territory to development and provided it with its first tangible link to BC.

There are 14 First Nations groups in the Yukon, speaking eight languages. Isolation has spared them some of the ravages enjoyed by First Nations in BC, and remote pockets of people still maintain traditional lives in places like Old Crow (p417).

Martha Black by Flo Whyard is a tremendous biography of a woman who fought her way to Dawson City with the prospectors and then owned her own business, became the hostess of the territory and eventually was elected to the Canadian parliament.

2003	2003	2009
Vancouver is named the site of the 2010 Winter Olympics, capping a bidding process that had gone on for almost a decade. It bested Quebec City and Calgary to be the Canadian candidate.	BC and Ontario lead the way in North America by making same-sex marriage legal. Many gay and lesbian couples travel to Vancouver to be married.	In the general elections the Liberal Party's Gordon Campbell makes it a hat trick, by winning a rare third term in office as Premier of BC.

The Culture

Culture in BC is as varied as the land. Although for decades the only acceptable culture could be linked back to Britain, today it is multifaceted. Influences are drawn from the resurgent First Nations, immigrants from around the world, especially Asia, and yes, the traditional Dominion culture of Canada. More importantly, a distinctive character has emerged that manages to be both edgy and irreverent without being aggressive or rude. The Yukon continues as a place that celebrates the hardy individual.

REGIONAL IDENTITY

BC and the Yukon cover such a huge area and have such a diverse population that it is hard to sum up any one characteristic of the people. You can't call the people green as many make their living through resources such as logging and mining. And you can't pigeonhole a majority with any political beliefs as both left and right governments have been in power for long periods.

Perhaps the one unifying characteristic is a love of where they live. People play hard all year round as you can see on pp61-72. People are rarely at a loss for words when asked what they like most about their region. Visitors find that they are not really considered strangers. Your reason for coming will never be questioned; it's obvious why you come – to enjoy what those lucky enough to live here never take for granted.

It is easier to define the many subregional identities. Vancouver blends an Asian vibe that at times makes it feel like a small version of Hong Kong with solidly affluent suburbs and a more rugged heart that is happy to hit the ski slopes visible from downtown or invent a new and edgier form of mountain biking.

Vancouver Islanders are a bit happily smug on their surprisingly large coastal island. Elsewhere in the province there is a very strong streak of independence that comes from living in small towns that are often dwarfed by the grandeur of the land around them. Individualism is celebrated in towns like Nelson or in remote places like the Queen Charlotte Islands.

The Yukon is like a boiled-down version of rural BC. Both the independence and the characters in this cold and remote territory are stronger. Reflecting on her definition of a good man, a single woman in Dawson City said: 'He's willing to get up before me and chop wood in the snow for the stove.'

LIFESTYLE

Community plays a big role in life in BC and the Yukon. Curling clubs, community fund-raisers, family gatherings, idiosyncratic festivals and more give locals an excuse to gather. Maybe it is because during the formative century here people often lived isolated lives and valued contact with others highly.

Just as the regional identity varies, so do lifestyles. The Lower Mainland comprising the greater Vancouver area is solidly first world and mostly suburban in lifestyle. The average household income is $80,000 for two-income households where both partners work (75% of women do). However, not every household in BC or the Yukon is composed of a man and a woman. Gays and lesbians enjoy a tolerant culture and same-sex marriage has been legal in Canada since 2005.

Reflect on this while stuck in the Saturday morning mob having an impromptu community event at a Tim Hortons: Canadians eat three times as many doughnuts as people in the US.

Adbusters is a magazine published in Vancouver that promotes an anti-corporate, anti-consumerism lifestyle even as it uses a slick design to do so.

In rural areas the suburban lifestyle fades and the emphasis on living is much more on getting by. Incomes are more variable with many subject to the whims of the markets. In small communities across BC, the price of lumber and/or minerals decide if people have money for a new pick-up or for new clothes for kids to go to school.

Social problems such as poverty and drug use are thorny issues in some parts of the Lower Mainland. Although polls consistently show a majority support legalizing marijuana, governments continue to push for tougher laws for marijuana and other narcotic use. Much of this is due to problems with rival gangs supplying the huge US market. Still, don't be surprised if you see a local here and there openly puffing away.

POPULATION

It's well documented that 90% of the Canadian population live within 160km of the US border, but a lesser-known statistic is that 75% of BC's four million people live within 60km of the coast. These results are obviously skewed by the fact that the Lower Mainland's two million people satisfy both requirements and 650,000-resident Vancouver Island is only 100km wide; but they also show just how much BC's people identify with the province's ocean setting.

Moving away from the Lower Mainland into the interior of the region, you'll find oodles of small towns with their own unique flavor. The few larger cities with populations over 50,000 are usually tied into an area with dominant industries like Kelowna (agriculture), Prince George (forestry) or Victoria (government and tourism).

Canwest, publisher of most of the newspapers in the Lower Mainland and Vancouver Island, has a website with content from across BC and the rest of Canada: www.canada.com.

MULTICULTURALISM & RELIGION

Canada west of the Rocky Mountains is the quintessential melting pot of cultures, ideals, rituals, creeds and ethnicities, making the region as varied culturally as it is ecologically. Canada aims to promote cultural diversity and the west coast in particular has been a portal for immigrants from Asia, India and Eastern Europe. Vancouver is a cultural hodgepodge and you'll find a long history of Asian populations across the province. Japanese and Chinese laborers helped build the railroads even as the greater society was yanking out the welcome mat.

Still, as multicultural as parts of Vancouver may seem, you won't travel far before the stark whiteness of the population is apparent: over 60% of people say their heritage is English, Scottish or Irish. In contrast 10% say Chinese and 5% East Indian.

First Nations groups and their rights to cultural heritage and lands claimed by white people are a constant topic in BC. The exception are the Inuit in the north, who don't face the problems on such a large scale. They've inhabited northern BC and the Yukon for centuries and their traditions are still practiced today. Reservations are found throughout the region. These communities vary – some are downtrodden villages but many others have cultural museums, big houses, totem-pole carvers and other traditional aspects of their culture. About 10% of the population has First Nations roots. For more, see p42.

BC and the Yukon are predominantly Christian, with the major denominations being Catholic and Protestant, and no real territorial claim by either. Most Jewish people arriving in BC move to the Vancouver region, which is now the third-largest Jewish community in Canada. With the influx of various cultures over the years, so too their beliefs – Buddhist, Sikh and Hindu temples are found all over the Lower Mainland.

Avoid the Canwest monopoly on print journalism in Vancouver by going online to read from a choice of alternative media at http://thetyee.ca.

FIRST NATIONS

The lush coast of BC supported a rich variety of cultures over thousands of years. Because food such as salmon was relatively plentiful, people like the Haida, Nuxalk and Tsimshian had time to develop complex and sophisticated art like totem poles. Canoes were carved from enormous spruce and cedar trees.

Inland BC didn't feature the same bounty literally swimming past and the First Nations Salish people in places like the Okanagan Valley had to devote much more of their time to subsistence living and surviving the long winters. In the far north, the Tagish, Gwich'in and others depended on migrating moose and caribou.

Disease brought by early visitors such as Captain Cook started the long slide for these peoples. Outright racism was rampant as well as official discrimination. In 1859 the governor of BC, James Douglas, declared that all the land and any wealth underneath belonged to the crown.

Laws enacted during much of the 20th century brutalized First Nations culture. A notorious one banned the potlatch, a vital ceremony held over many days by communities to mark special occasions, and establish ranks and privileges. Dancing, feasting and elaborate gift-giving from the chief to his people are features. Today, one of the ceremonies can cost a clan well over $30,000 to stage.

The last 40 years have seen both an effort by governments to reverse the grim course of previous decades and a resurgence of First Nations culture. A long and difficult process has begun to settle claims from the 1859 proclamation through negotiations with the various bands. So far, the one treaty signed – with the Nisga'a Nation – provides about $200 million and allows some self-governance. Given the money involved, it's easy to see why the treaty process is one big vat of contention in BC (eg much of the land under downtown Vancouver is subject to First Nations claims). Only 20% of First Nation groups have even begun negotiations.

The Recognition and Reconciliation Act is BC's effort to literally rewrite all of its laws regarding the First Nations. It includes schemes to organize the province's 203 bands into 30 indigenous governments. That, plus provisions that would carve out a big piece of the mineral wealth pie for aboriginal people, sparked enormous debate through 2009.

Relations in the Yukon have been less contentious as the size of the land has overwhelmed the conflicts among the tiny population.

Art & Culture

First Nations art goes beyond totem poles, although these icons are the perfect medium as they require both an abundance of huge trees and extraordinary carving skills, elements common on the coast. Artworks such as masks, drums and paintings feature the distinctive black and red sweeping brush strokes depicting wolves, ravens and other animals from

---

TOP FIVE PLACES TO SEE FIRST NATIONS ART

- Museum of Anthropology (p101) in Vancouver
- Royal British Columbia Museum (p165) in Victoria
- Museum of Northern British Columbia (p368) in Prince Rupert
- Haida Heritage Centre at Qay'llnagaay (p377) on the Queen Charlotte Islands
- $20 bill, which features Bill Reid's *Raven and the First Man* and *Spirit of Haida Gwaii*

READING TOTEMS

It's easy to admire the statuesque beauty and abstract artistry of totem poles, but that's the equivalent of just enjoying a book for its cover. Discerning the meaning of these creations is another matter. Each tells a story both complex and cultural, a record of a people and their beliefs.

Carved from a single cedar trunk, totems identify a household's lineage in the same way that a family crest might identify a group or clan in Britain, although the totem pole is more of a historical pictograph depicting the entire ancestry. Like a family crest, totem poles carry a sense of prestige and prosperity.

Despite the expression 'low man on the totem pole', the most important figures are usually at eye level; figures at the bottom usually serve an integral, grounding function that supports the rest of the pole. Totem figures can represent individuals, spirits, births, deaths, catastrophes or legends.

Unless you're an expert it isn't easy to decipher a totem, but you can start with some simple paradigms. Birds are identified by their beaks: ravens have a straight, midsize beak; eagles feature a short, sharp, down-turned beak; while hawks have a short, down-turned beak that curls inward. Bears usually show large, square teeth, while beavers feature sharp incisors and a cross-stitched tail. A few animals appear as if viewed from overhead. For example, the killer whale's fin protrudes outward from the pole as if its head faces downward. The long-snouted wolf also faces downward, as does the frog. The pointy-headed shark (or dogfish), with a grimacing mouth full of sharp teeth, faces upward, as does the humpback whale.

Once you've got your bears sorted from your beavers, you can move on to figuring out the interconnected and complex relationships between the creatures, which always have certain characteristics:

- black bear – serves as a protector, guardian and spiritual link between humans and animals
- beaver – symbolizes industriousness, wisdom and determined independence
- eagle – signifies intelligence and power
- frog – represents adaptability, the ability to live in both natural and supernatural worlds
- hummingbird – embodies love, beauty and unity with nature
- killer whale – symbolizes dignity and strength (often depicted as a reincarnated spirit of a great chief)
- raven – signifies mischievousness and cunning
- salmon – typifies dependable sustenance, longevity and perseverance
- shark – exemplifies an ominous and fierce solitude
- thunderbird – represents the wisdom of proud ancestors

For more background on totem poles see p37; for some places to view them today, see p364.

the spirit world. Bill Reid (p374) is one of the best-known First Nations artists and his works in the latter half of the 20th century did much to spark a renaissance of art among his Haida people and other groups.

Though most First Nations groups lack formal written history as we know it, centuries of traditions live on through creations such as totem poles. Art has long been a method of expression, intimately linked with historical and cultural preservation, religion and social ceremony.

Today, Lawrence Paul Yuxweluptun explores politics, the environment and First Nations issues with his paintings that take inspiration from Coast Salish mythology. Shuswap actor and writer Darrell Dennis takes First Nations stereotypes head on in his thrilling one-man show *Tales of an Urban Indian*. Among the memorable lines: 'I can't even make it rain for God sakes.'

Blade Runner's bleak rainy setting may have been inspired by a stint Philip K Dick spent in a Vancouver heroin rehab home.

The Bear's Embrace by the late Patricia Van Tighem is the story of her survival from a vicious grizzly attack, her struggle with depression, electroshock treatment, and parenting in Nelson.

Sage Birchwater's book *Chiwid* tells the fantastic and true story of a Chilcotin (Tsilhqot'in) woman who suffered abuse and chose to live as a hermit in the wilderness. *Wisdom of the Elders: Sacred Native Stories of Nature*, by legendary David Suzuki and Peter Knudtson, provides a thought-provoking and insightful view of the relationship First Nations groups have with nature, and the Western world's need to learn the same.

SPORTS

The 2010 Olympics are a validation of BC's winter sports culture. Potential medalists train at resorts across the province. Hockey is the spectator sport of choice, whereas the curling hall is often the community social center in rural areas.

Year-round however, what's notable about both BC and the Yukon is that people are truly players and not just fans. Most sports and outdoor activities (pp61-72) are enjoyed by the participants, as opposed to being spectator events.

Hockey

In wintertime, frozen lakes, ponds and sloughs present the opportunity for countless hours of Canada's favorite pastime. Hockey is a religion in Canada, and BC and the Yukon are no exception. *Hockey Night in Canada* commands huge TV ratings on Saturday nights for the CBC and many bars have walls lined with TVs showing matches.

Pick any random BC town and the majority of boys and girls will be on an organized team, or play for fun on a regular basis on both indoor rinks and iced-over lakes. Bear league hockey – the name for amateur adult leagues all over the BC – claims husbands and boyfriends many nights a year. It claims a few teeth as well.

Mount Pleasant, directed by Ross Weber, relates the intense and disturbing tale of three couples who find their lives entangled after a child discovers a discarded syringe in her garden. Not a comedy.

The Vancouver Canucks (p121) represent all of BC in the National Hockey League (NHL). Team success has fluctuated since its 1970 inception and a Stanley Cup has proved elusive.

The Kamloops Blazers, Chilliwack Bruins, Prince George Cougars, Kelowna Rockets (p266) and Vancouver Giants (p121), in the 20-and-under Western Hockey League (WHL), have served as the training grounds for players moving on to the NHL.

Football

The BC Lions (p122) play in Vancouver for the Canadian Football League (CFL), which has long been considered a minor league for America's National Football League (NFL). It's partly true, since the CFL has seen players like Warren Moon, Doug Flutie and Jeff Garcia do well and then sign for big bucks south of the border. However, the CFL play a different game from the American game: there's more passing, a longer and wider field, only three chances to move the ball 10 yards and ritual doughnut

---

CURLING

Few sports allow the champion to hold a trophy in one hand, a beer in the other and have a cigarette dangling from their lips, but curling, one of Canada's cultural phenomena, is one of them. Loosely defined as shuffleboard on ice with 44lb stones, a 146-ft-long playing surface and brooms, it's a game of precision and every town in the region will have a curling rink; check www.curlbc.ca if you want to watch. And look for community-wide events centered on the curling hall – if nothing else, there will be beer.

eating after every quarter. The Lions have won the Grey Cup Championship six times, most recently in 2006.

ARTS

Thanks to creative people and generous cultural funding, the art scene thrives in BC and the Yukon. Much art uses the natural beauty as its stage or protagonist but there are also many artists doing work that reflects modern times. Almost every community will have some kind of arts or fringe festival during the year celebrating local and international talent.

The Vancouver Stories is an evocative volume of short pieces on the city by a who's-who of BC literati, including Douglas Coupland, Malcolm Lowry, William Gibson and Timothy Taylor.

Literature

Canadians are known for witty observations that make you think, then make you laugh. The dry humor of Vancouver author Douglas Coupland has earned him the slightly ponderous reputation as a chronicler of our age. His illustrated *City of Glass* was an incisive look at modern Vancouver. Also recommended is his novel *Everything's Gone Green*, about a slacker named Ryan; it was made into a movie in 2006.

Born in Chiba Prefecture, Japan, Hiromi Goto's family emigrated to BC in 1969. Her works, such as *Hopeful Monsters*, challenge readers to ponder their preconceptions about others, including such seemingly easily defined characters as the tyrannical boss, or the hostile neighbor.

William Gibson is the creator of 'cyberpunk': tough-edged science fiction. His *Neuromancer* is the archetypal work of the genre.

WP Kinsella wrote *Shoeless Joe* (which the film *Field of Dreams* is based on) and is another Vancouver stalwart. Among the many BC publishing houses, is Theytus Books, which is a highly regarded First

TOP READS

- *Red Dog, Red Dog* by Patrick Lane follows two brothers trying to navigate tough times in the 1950s Okanagan Valley. It's a gripping look at heartbreak, corruption and the tough lives of those who settled Canada.

- *The Butcher of Penetang* by Betsy Trumpener is a collection of intensely felt short stories including one about moose hunters chasing snowflakes and another about hot sex in the snow.

- *Kilter: 55 Fictions* by John Gould is an award-winning series of short stories that probe modern BC life.

- *Ana Historic* by Daphne Marlatt is the evocative tale of a modern woman who becomes obsessed researching the life of Mrs Richards, a woman who appears briefly in 1873 in the civic archives of Vancouver.

- *Stanley Park* by Timothy Taylor stirs together a haute-cuisine chef with a park's dark secrets. The result is a story capturing Vancouver's quirky modern ambience.

- *Sisters of Grass* by noted poet and essayist Theresa Kishkan is a historical novel about a young woman surviving torment internal and external in BC's interior a century ago.

- *The Cremation of Sam McGee*, by Robert W Service, the renowned Bard of the Yukon. This classic of regional prose about two gold miners, the cold and what men will sometimes do, is Service at his peak. You can tour his Dawson City cabin (p410).

- *Klondike Tales* by Jack London draws on his first-hand experiences for these 23 stories showing the hardships, triumphs and betrayals of the Yukon gold rush. *Call of the Wild* wins new fans every year. Learn more about London and his books at the Jack London Interpretive Centre in Dawson City (p411).

Nations-owned publisher based in Penticton. Its *Kou-Skelowh/We Are the People: A Trilogy of Okanagan Legends* is a classic retelling of First Nations lore and culture.

The BC Film Commission website (www.bcfilmcommission .com) includes a weekly round-up of current productions filming across the province – with contact information for those seeking extras.

The Yukon has fewer authors and many fewer people, but it does have a strong program to encourage writing, including the chance for prospective authors to spend their summers writing while living at a lovely house in Dawson City. You can never go wrong reading anything by the legendary Robert W Service.

Cinema & Television

The BC Film Commission was established in 1978 and has turned the region's filmscape from a $12-million afterthought to a multibillion-dollar industry. It has set up tax breaks and reduced costs for filming and production while creating thousands of jobs for local residents. Relatively low costs and the fact that Vancouver and BC make an endlessly flexible backdrop have lured countless producers. That and a cadre of local talents, such as Oscar-nominated set decorator Peter Lando, have lured legions of productions. Sadly, the region is consistently portrayed as some other place, or obscurely left as the backdrop to no place in particular. But Vancouver does get a few star turns. *Da Vinci's Inquest*, a show about a Mountie turned crusading coroner, won plaudits over its seven-year run and seems destined to live on forever in reruns.

Music

Vancouver is the heart of BC music. The region has given the world some big names: Bryan Adams, 54*40, Sarah McLachlan, Bif Naked, kd lang, Diana Krall, popster Nelly Furtado, Victoria punksters NoMeansNo and Celtic-tinged folk rockers Spirit of the West. Some of them call Vancouver home, but many simply used the city as a launching pad for larger careers on the world stage.

The National Film Board of Canada's website (www.nfb.ca) is a treasure trove of films it has funded over several decades. Look for *Kluane*, a stark 1981 documentary about the Yukon national park, and *Carts of Darkness*, a 2008 look at shopping cart races in North Vancouver.

The New Pornographers have been *the* indie group for a decade. Their first album, *Mass Romantic*, is considered by some to be among the best ever. Their music has been compared to Cheap Trick.

Another BC band of the moment is psychedelic Black Mountain, which scored a commercial hit with *Stay Free*. Many mourned the breakup of the Buttless Chaps in 2009.

Most towns or regions have music festivals through the year. Smithers has a big one featuring folk music (p362). Jazz festivals are also popular, especially in the Okanagan Valley, where the cool strains of jazz are a natural pairing with wine. There's a large one in Penticton (p251).

First Nations music and dances are not only a delight to the visual and aural senses, they are a fundamental part of each tribe's heritage. Check with VCs and cultural centers for information.

THE YUKON'S STAR

Only one Yukoner has a star on the Hollywood Walk of Fame and that's Victor Jory. Like any good northerner, his story is better then the plots of most of the 200 movies and TV shows that have his name in the credits. He was born in 1902 to a single mother who ran a rooming house near Dawson City. Hanging around Hollywood got him his first role in 1930 and over the next 50 years he had parts in big pictures (quarrelsome field boss in *Gone with the Wind*) and small ones (the lead in *Cat-Women of the Moon*). Reflecting the ethos of the Yukon, he never said no to anything that might put food on his plate.

Visual Arts

What with all that natural beauty, how do you elevate art depicting BC and the Yukon above the cliché? One artist who succeeds is Jeff Wall, a photorealist whose huge backlit works have the quality of a cinematic production. His iconic work is *Milk*. Brian Jungen is also based in Vancouver. His series of First Nations masks created from parts of Nike shoes brilliantly shows how traditional art forms are easily corrupted by modern consumerism.

BC's most famous painter remains Emily Carr. Born in Victoria in 1871, she was inspired by the First Nations villages and the landscape of Vancouver Island, but it wasn't until she met the acclaimed eastern-Canadian Group of Seven that she took off as an artist and found her inspiration. The Emily Carr House (p168), in Victoria, is open to the public, and her paintings are displayed at the Vancouver Art Gallery (p96) and the Art Gallery of Greater Victoria (p167).

Growing Pains is Emily Carr's autobiography. From her prim BC upbringing, she travels the world learning art but then finds despair and barely makes ends meet running a boarding house. But hers is a happy ending, with recognition as Canada's finest female artist.

Architecture

When his icon-busting book about Vancouver, *City of Glass*, came out Douglas Coupland coined another moniker almost as apt as his earlier triumph *Generation X*. Built up at a frenetic pace since the 1980s as the population has soared, Vancouver is truly a city of glass. High-rise buildings sprout like a modern-day forest of spruce or cedars across the ever-growing downtown. Inside one of these, whether hotel room, office or condo, you often literally have your head in your clouds as the famous weather closes in and mists of grey swirl outside one room to the next.

The fast pace of development means that old Victorian piles like you'd find in, say, Quebec City are all but lost. Still the past is not forgotten and Vancouver has won awards for its sensitive treatment of the streetscape. On places like Granville Island and Yaletown, old buildings have found new life in pedestrian-friendly uses as cafés, pubs, shops and more. Local architect James Cheng is currently the star of Vancouver's New Urbanism movement. His 62-story 2008 Shangri-La Hotel (p109) is the tallest building in town and shows his obsession with humanizing its interface with the street. See p106 for tours you can take of Vancouver architecture.

Elsewhere in BC, architecture tends to be functional first and possibly inspired second (ignoring the odd gem). Old late-1800s towns such as Nelson and Fernie have evocative and historic centers of stolid buildings, many restored to their original glory.

The Yukon has a surprising local firm in Kobayashi + Zedda Architects, which has won international awards for low-key buildings that use local materials while respecting the culture and making the most of the climate. Their works are already making a mark across otherwise grimly utilitarian Whitehorse.

The 160-page *Van Dop Arts and Cultural Guide to BC* lists galleries, studios and festivals across the province. It's freely viewable online at www.art-bc.com.

Theater

Vancouver has over 30 professional theater groups. The Green Thumb Theater troupe (www.greenthumb.bc.ca) raised the profile of local drama when it took the searing drama *Cranked* to Broadway.

Local theaters are found throughout the region, providing entertaining performances with local talent. Chemainus Theatre (p186), a big theater in a little town, draws people from all over the southwest, while remote towns like Barkerville have theaters putting on crowd-pleasing productions, and surprising Whitehorse (p396) often has more than one show running at once. Fringe festivals are also popular; Prince Rupert has a great one (p370).

MEDIA

The *Vancouver Sun* and the *Province* are available throughout BC each morning. They are the largest of 20 BC newspapers owned by Canwest, a right-leaning media conglomerate that dominates the newspaper business in the province. Other small local papers in BC are best at recording what's got local tongues wagging, like supersized homegrown vegetables, as opposed to providing an alternate voice to the Canwest monolith. There are scads of free newspapers out in the hinterlands posing as regular dailies – skimpy products that are far from comprehensive and, due to their price, are undercutting support for regular papers that at least tried to cover their communities.

British Columbia is a magazine about Cuba. Er, no, it provides lavish features about the province. If there's a better small regional publication than *Up Here*, we haven't seen it. Each issue has loads of fascinating and well-reported stories on the Yukon and the north.

If you're driving in the afternoon, tune in CBC Radio One to BC Almanac, a great couple of hours of BC-centric radio hosted by Mark Forsythe. Topics can start with vexing political issues and transition to the pleasures of Okanagan wines. Commercial radio stations tend to play middle-of-the-road music, inoffensive to most and interesting to few.

ECONOMY

BC's economy is driven by factors outside its control. When the world economy gets sick, as it did starting in 2008, BC feels ill as well. Although spending in the province has in recent years been conservative, that can't insulate an economy based on trade and tourism.

During the years right after 2000, BC's economy was strong, with an unemployment rate that hovered around 4%, soaring home prices and budget surpluses. World demand for lumber and other raw resources even provided steady prosperity to the notoriously fickle areas of the interior that are dependent on commodity prices for what can be dug out or grown on the ground.

But global recession slashed demand for BC's lumber and wood products like plywood and cheap pressboard. In 2009 half the forestry workers in Prince George, the BC hub of that industry, were without work. Worldwide demand for lead, coal and other products skidded away. On the coasts, the fishing fleets stayed in port, hit by a lose-lose situation of falling stocks of cash fish such as salmon and halibut plus a drop in demand as global consumers switch to cheaper alternatives to BC's top-quality seafood.

Tourism also has taken a hit as people worldwide simply have less cash to visit BC. The collapse of mortgage markets, especially for people from the US, caused condos to sit unsold at ski resorts that had counted on property sales to fuel expansion.

Longer term, few doubt that BC's recently dominant industries such as tourism and services will not return to their pre-crash zoom-zoom growth. The wild card remains the 2010 Olympics. As the cost zipped past an unthinkable $6 billion (estimates just a couple years before were half that) people debated whether the games would be the mother of all economic stimulus plans, a noose of debt that would last a generation, or some combination of both.

In the Yukon most of the 30,000 residents of working age are employed by the government in some way – either as teachers, administrators, bureaucrats or in jobs dependent on government funding. Many count on the short tourist season for their livelihoods – with some wise characters working in southern winter retreats in Mexico or the Caribbean

Prince Rupert's Museum of Northern BC (www
.museumofnorthernbc
.com; p368) has a gift shop with an enormous collection of BC and Yukon books. You can browse the hundreds of titles and order online.

Geist magazine (www
.geist.com) is BC's top literary journal. Read short works of fiction plus prose and poetry online or look for a copy in bookshops.

before enjoying profitable summers in the north. Placer mining is also an economic factor, as worthwhile quantities of gold and silver continue to be extracted from the land, particularly around Dawson City. For more, see the boxed text, p412.

GOVERNMENT & POLITICS

British Columbia has a parliamentary government, with a 79-member unicameral legislature that meets in the capital, Victoria. The lieutenant governor is the formal head of state, but real power goes to the premier, who is usually the head of the majority party. The premier is Gordon Campbell of the Liberal Party, who was elected by a wide margin in 2001 then re-elected by a slimmer one in 2005. In 2009 Campbell won a rare third term, being able to campaign on being the smart choice in tough economic times and as the leader best able to launch the 2010 Olympics. The split in the legislature remained roughly the same, with the Liberals having a modest majority.

BC also sends representatives to the national House of Commons and Senate in Ottawa. But, since Canadian power is concentrated on the provincial level, most people in BC pay little heed to what's happening in the national capital. The Social Credit Party (Socreds), ostensibly the party of small business, came to power in BC in the 1950s and governed into the 1970s. During the 1960s the New Democratic Party (NDP) emerged, advocating a form of limited socialism. Beset by scandals, the Socreds fell out of favor by 1990. The NDP was in charge during much of the 1990s, but also fell to scandal. The successor to the besmirched Socreds, the Liberals, belie their name and any association with Canada's national Liberal Party (which has an eponymous name) by taking moderate to conservative stands on most issues.

The ongoing effort to resolve aboriginal land claims is a major issue in BC politics. In 1993 the provincial government established the BC Treaty Commission, intended to set up a framework by which land claims can be worked out. See p38 for details on the first treaty successfully negotiated. The BC Liberals have proven to be lightning rods on many issues. For instance, Campbell campaigned by saying provincial assets like railroads and ferries wouldn't be sold off. They were. The party's stands on global warming are derided by the left, especially the Green Party. Although they enjoy support in the low double digits, the Greens have not managed to win a seat in the legislature.

In the Yukon, the federal government appoints a commissioner who represents Ottawa; the actual governing of the territory is accomplished by the Executive Council, who are drawn from the elected Yukon Council. Major political challenges tend to center on how much money the feds are going to send north (with its tiny population and myriad needs for things like better roads, the Yukon takes in far more federal money than it pays out in taxes). Political power rests with the Yukon Party, which is conservative. First Nations claims in the Yukon have proved easier to negotiate than in BC, as so much of the land is not part of competing claims.

For obvious reasons, hard numbers are very difficult to come by but there are suggestions that BC's underground marijuana economy may be worth more than the billion-dollar forestry industry. Much of this comes from smuggling to the US.

The politics of BC's resources have impacted hard on everyone from the First Nations to pioneers trying to scratch out a living on the land. *12 Mile Remembered: Our Lives Before They Burned Our Homesteads* by Ada Domke Jarvis tells the heartbreaking story of 15 families forced off their land near Revelstoke for a dam project in the 1960s.

Food & Drink

While BC and Yukon cuisine used to involve little more than a visit to Tim Hortons, the region – like the rest of Canada – has rediscovered its distinctive indigenous larder in recent years. Restaurants that used to brag about their top-notch imported ingredients now loudly proclaim the unique West Coast bounty they've uncovered as if they were pioneers of local produce all along.

For visitors, this means a visit to BC can be a lip-smacking taste trip. Seafood fans will soon be stuffed to the gills with wild salmon, Queen Charlotte Islands halibut, Fanny Bay oysters and the kind of sweet, velvet-soft scallops that you could happily eat until you explode (don't try this, since it creates quite a mess). Carnivores can also tuck into treats like Salt Spring Island lamb and Fraser Valley duck, while they might even be persuaded (and quickly converted) by local heirloom tomatoes, earthy foraged mushrooms and the cornucopia of lush fruit and berries found throughout the region.

Whatever you decide to sink your teeth into, you don't have to go the fine dining route. The West Coast has plenty of midrange, homestyle eateries where the menus are sometimes just as impressive as top city dine-out spots. And if you're eating on the run, slow down and hit some of the farmers markets that have sprung up everywhere here like tasty morels after a warm rainstorm. Just remember: there's a huge list of increasingly excellent BC-produced wine and beer to add to the fun. Now, un-notch that belt and get feasting.

Elizabeth Levinson's *An Edible Journey: Exploring the Islands' Fine Food, Farms and Vineyards* is a lip-smacking taste trip around the foodie destinations of Vancouver Island and the Southern Gulf Islands.

STAPLES & SPECIALTIES

Breakfast in BC and the Yukon depends on where you live. While urbanites are likely to dip into some organic yoghurt as they stretch for a run, those with proper appetites tuck into much heartier fare. Brunch is the favorite weekend meal here, and dishes often have a seafood twist: expect salmon eggs benedict or seafood frittatas on many menus.

Lunch is often the least important meal in the region, but if you're in Vancouver head down the sushi route. Often regarded as hosting the best sushi and sashimi joints outside Japan, the city is teeming with midrange (and even budget) spots to indulge your nori-wrapped cravings. Outside the metropolis, seasonal soups and salads are recommended.

Local authors James MacKinnon and Alisa Smith attempted to source all their food locally for one year. Their book, *The 100-Mile Diet: A Year of Local Eating*, became a bestseller. See www.100milediet.org.

Dinner can be an event throughout the region and the seasonal option is always recommended. This can range from fresh-caught local seafood to sweet veggies and fruit: if you spot regional tomatoes, morels, cherries, peaches or blueberries on a menu, pick those immediately. And if you're traveling through rural areas, expect to have the opportunity to sample venison or caribou that's been locally caught – you'll be pleasantly surprised by the taste.

DRINKS

Mirroring the surging interest in regional food across BC and the Yukon, indulging in local wines and microbrewed beer has become a major pastime here for many people. Wherever your travels take you, it's always worth dropping in on a neighborhood bar or two and asking for the local brew.

Coffee

While Seattle is North America's self-proclaimed coffee capital, north-of-the-border java addicts find it just as easy to satisfy their leg-twitching cravings. Vancouver's Commercial Drive and South Main (SoMa) areas are lined with independent coffeeshops, while across the region you'll find that even the smallest communities spend most of their time hanging out in neighborhood cafés.

Wine

BC's lakeside Okanagan wine region will never be mistaken for Napa, but with around 100 wineries it's a must-see destination for wine fans. Winding around the area (with designated driver) delivers a tasty selection of producers in an idyllic, laid-back setting. A combination of cool winters and long summers makes whites a staple of the valley's northern region, while further south reds rise to prominence. Icewine, a dessert quaff made from grapes frozen on the vine, is also a favorite here.

The Okanagan doesn't have a lockhold on wineries, though, and you'll find producers across the region, many specializing in fruit-based tipples. Expect to stumble on a few in the Fraser Valley, Southern Gulf Islands and on southern Vancouver Island, especially in the Cowichan Valley.

> The website of the BC Wine Institute (www.winebc.com) is an invaluable resource for planning a vintage trawl around the region. It has route maps for several wine tours around the area.

Beer

BC is packed like a Saturday-night pub with fantastic microbreweries, many of them only established in the past 10 years. You'll find Nelson Brewing (Nelson), Tree Brewing (Kelowna), Phillips Brewing (Victoria), Howe Sound Brewing (Squamish), Storm Brewing (Vancouver) and the celebrated Crannóg Ales (Sorrento) among many others. The smaller the brewery, the more likely they are to produce tipples that make generic factory brews taste like something you wouldn't drink to save your life. Look out for distinctive ales, bitters, lagers, pilsners, bocks, porters, stouts and even hemp beers. If you want to see how it's all done **Granville Island Brewing** (p99) and **Vancouver Island Brewery** (p167) are among those offering short tours and leisurely tastings.

If time is tight but you'd still like to down a few regional beverages, head to Vancouver's **Alibi Room** (p119). It's the city's best spot for BC-region microbrews and it serves up to 19 local beers on tap at any given time, which means you can go on a West Coast beer crawl without even leaving town. Alternatively, try the three recommended brewpubs in Victoria (p175).

A SIX-PACK OF BEERS

On your travels around the region, sample a drink or two from some of these renowned craft brewers. Among the best producers (and their recommended tipples) are:

- **Dead Frog Brewery** (www.deadfrogbrewery.com) for copper-colored Nut Brown Ale.
- **Granville Island Brewing** (www.gib.ca) for smooth Kitsilano Maple Cream Ale.
- **Phillips Brewing** (www.phillipsbeer.com) for refreshing Phoenix Gold Lager.
- **Russell Brewing** (www.russellbeer.com) for golden Russell Pale Ale.
- **Storm Brewing** (www.stormbrewing.org) for Irish-style Black Plague Stout.
- **Vancouver Island Brewery** (www.vanislandbrewery.com) for malty Hermann's Dark Lager.

CELEBRATIONS

Food and drink is the foundation of having a good time in BC. Languid summer barbecues, fall's feast-like Thanksgiving Day and winter family get-togethers at Christmastime traditionally center on tables groaning with meat and seafood dishes, diet-ignoring fruit desserts and plenty of wine and beer.

Several BC and Yukon regions showcase their cuisines with annual festivals. Recommended events include Whistler's **Cornucopia** (www .whistlercornucopia.com) and Vancouver Island's **Cowichan Wine & Culinary Festival** (http://wines.cowichan.net). Vancouver's Feast of Fields (www .feastoffields.com) event, where local producers and top chefs combine to present an alfresco day of exemplary taste temptations, has branched out with Okanagan and Vancouver Island events in recent years.

Wine lovers are also well served when it comes to festivals, especially in the Okanagan, where there's an event for each of the four seasons. The biggest one is the 11-day **Fall Wine Festival** (www.owfs.com), while January's **Sun Peaks Icewine Festival** (www.owfs.com) is also dripping with fun. If you're in Vancouver in March, connect with the **Vancouver Playhouse International Wine Festival** (www.playhousewinefest.com), the city's largest and oldest wine-based celebration.

Under Canadian rules, icewine can only be made from grapes that have been frozen on the vine below −8°C.

WHERE TO EAT & DRINK

While Vancouver now rivals Montréal and Toronto as a fine-dining capital, it wins over both those cities with its surfeit of excellent ethnic dining options. You'll be hard-pressed to find a bad Chinese, Japanese or Vietnamese restaurant here, while its Pacific Northwest dining choices (usually fused with international influences) bring the best of the region to tables across the city. Outside Vancouver, the urban areas of Vancouver Island and the Okanagan Valley offer additional top-notch eateries.

But eating well is not just about fine dining here and you'll find places to nosh in more rustic areas of BC and the Yukon that deliver some tastebud-popping surprises. Follow the locals to waterfront seafood diners in coastal communities like Gibsons, Salt Spring Island and Prince Rupert for the kind of freshly caught aquatic treats that would often cost several times as much as in the big city.

Even the smallest towns can usually rustle up a decent meal – including those ubiquitous 'Chinese and Canadian' eateries where the menu usually combines deep-fried cheeseburgers with gelatinous sweet-and-sour pork dishes. There are also many family-oriented, mid-priced eateries for those traveling with kids. Unlike pubs in the UK and other countries, bars here are usually just as interested in serving food as they are beer.

Whichever part of BC and the Yukon you find yourself in, always ask if there's a farmers market coming up. Most of these take place once a week in the summer months and they offer a quick-hit opportunity to

---

ALCOHOL LEGALITIES

The legal drinking age in BC and the Yukon is 19, and the legal blood-alcohol limit is 0.08%, or the equivalent of two drinks for an 'average-sized' person. BC is very serious about curbing drunk driving, and you may encounter a mandatory roadside checkpoint, especially on summer evenings or around winter holidays. The provincial government operates BC Liquor Stores, where you can buy beer, wine and spirits. There are also privately-owned outlets and 'cold beer and wine stores.' These are usually more expensive than the government-run outlets. In the Yukon, alcohol is sold through government-run liquor stores as well as officially licensed private outlets.

sample local produce and bakery treats. Markets are listed throughout this book. In addition, many farms are open to culinary-minded travelers who want to drop by and sample their wares. These are especially concentrated in the Abbotsford region of the Lower Mainland, the verdant Okanagan Valley area and in the Provence-like Cowichan Valley on Vancouver Island.

VEGETARIANS & VEGANS

In urban BC there are many vegetarian and vegan options, and places that celebrate organic produce are all the rage. Vegans will salivate at Vancouver restaurants such as the **Naam** (p117) and **Foundation** (p115). Elsewhere in BC and the Yukon, vegetarian options can be limited to salads, sandwiches or mushroom burgers, with the occasional veggie-only joint standing out like a beacon in the carnivorous darkness.

EATING WITH KIDS

Children are welcome everywhere in the region; see p421 for more information. While some restaurants have kids menus, others will prepare a half-order of a regular dish if you ask nicely. White Spot, BC's very own restaurant chain, is a great place to dine with kids. Its main menu ranges from burgers (with secret 'Triple-O' sauce) to seafood pastas and Asian stir-frys, while its kids meals are served in cardboard pirate ships that are often eyed enviously by adults at other tables.

HABITS & CUSTOMS

You can easily get anything you want at almost any time in Vancouver, but outside the metropolis restaurants may shut early, even in seemingly hip places like Victoria and Whistler. Be at the restaurant by 8pm outside peak summer weekends.

Breakfast is usually eaten between 6am and 10am. Many accommodations offer a continental breakfast (a hot drink, juice, toast, muffins and maybe cereal) during these hours. Most BC residents eat breakfast at home on weekdays or grab a quick bite on the run with their morning coffee. But on weekends, a much more leisurely breakfast or brunch at a café or restaurant is a favorite pastime.

The midday meal is typically taken between 11am and 1pm. It can be as simple as a snack bought from a farmers market or hot dog stand, or a picnic taken on your hike. Dinner is served anytime from about 5pm to 8pm, often later on weekends and in large cities and resort areas such as Whistler.

Dress is casual almost everywhere. In most restaurants, you'll be fine no matter what you're wearing. For more formal places, the clichéd 'smart casual' is the norm.

Geoduck (pronounced 'gooey duck') is BC's most unusual aquatic dish. A giant saltwater clam, it's a delicacy in Chinese restaurants and is shipped to chefs around the world.

BC farmers markets are exploding across the region, bringing home-grown produce to the tables of locals and epicurious visitors. For details, see www .bcfarmersmarket.org.

Environment

The often stunning natural environment of BC and the Yukon is the number one reason why people visit. Yet it is also a prime source of profit for industry in the region. Balancing conservation and exploitation is a constant drama. Fortunately there are many protected places and parks where you can enjoy what nature offers, see p73 for details. To minimize your effects on the region's environment, see p23 and p80.

THE LAND

From the marshy, tidal southwest along the US border through to the soaring border shared with Alberta in the Rockies, BC is a land of dramatic landscapes. The troika of BC, Alaska and the Yukon meet in the northeast in a truly wild landscape of glaciers, peaks and sharp river canyons. The Yukon is washed in the north by the Arctic Ocean and separated from the flatlands of the Northwest Territories by the perilous Mackenzie Range.

BC's official symbol is the white flower of the Pacific dogwood, a tree known for springtime blossoms and autumnal red berries.

With its many inlets, BC's awe-inspiring West Coast is more than 7000km long; alongside it are hundreds of islands ranging from large (Vancouver Island) to tiny (Saturna Island).

The bulk of BC lies within the Canadian Cordillera, a system of mountain ranges running roughly northwest to southeast. Within the cordillera are several major ranges – the Rocky Mountains to the east; the Cassiar Mountains in the north; and the Columbia Mountains in the south. The glaciated Coast Mountains loom over the Pacific almost to the water's edge from Vancouver north to the Alaska panhandle.

The province has scores of freshwater lakes and fast-flowing rivers. The Fraser River is BC's longest, stretching from the Rocky Mountains to the Pacific Ocean near Vancouver. Roughly 60% of BC is covered by forest, mainly coniferous trees. About half of the forest is old-growth trees, of which only 15% are fully protected. The Peace River region in northeast BC is the only really flat area. More than 90% of BC's landmass is 'Crown Land,' and is therefore owned by the provincial government.

Vancouver's City Farm Boy Ward Teulon (www .cityfarmboy.com) grows fruit and vegetables in the gardens of many locals who are paid in produce for the privilege.

This high percentage of government-controlled land is even more the case in the Yukon, where the federal government holds more than 95% of the territory. The Rocky Mountain range eventually peters out at the Yukon border and much of the territory's interior is characterized by the broad Yukon Plateau, which is drained through the width of Alaska by the mighty Yukon River.

Geology

An Ice Age starting about a million years ago was the primary force shaping the geology of BC and the Yukon. Huge ice sheets repeatedly scraped over the lofty mountain ranges, wearing them down to bedrock and creating great valleys between the peaks. This continued until about 7000 years ago, when the last ice melted, giving rise to the province's lakes and rivers (which remain fed by annual snowmelt today). Since then, glacial, wind and water erosion have continued to alter the landscape in more subtle ways, a process being accelerated by global warming.

Mineral wealth spurred Europeans to settle in BC from the mid-19th century. The Yukon's one major boom stemmed from the fabled Klondike gold rush of 1897–98 (it's been downhill in terms of population size ever since).

Minerals remain important today. Major mineral deposits include coal on the coastal islands and the eastern slopes of the Rocky Mountains; gold in the Coast Mountains and the Yukon River and its tributaries; copper, lead, silver and zinc in the Kootenays; and natural gas – containing sandstone and shale in the Peace River region. Jade is the official mineral of BC and is widely used in jewelry and sculptures.

WILDLIFE

With all its geographical and climatic diversity, it's no surprise that BC has a wide range of plants and animals. There are 14 distinct ecological zones; nature flourishes everywhere, from the large urban parks of Vancouver and Victoria, to the tops of the Rockies, to tiny coastal tide pools. The Yukon shares many of these features and adds its vast expanse of Arctic territory.

The wildlife you see anywhere in the region is likely to be among the highlights of your trip (keep that camera ready; critters rarely pose!).

See a whale? Report it to the BC Cetacean Sightings Network (☎ 866-I-SAW-ONE, 866-472-9663; http://wildwhales.org), which tracks the huge mammals and monitors threats against them.

Animals

As a big train station is to a train spotter, BC and the Yukon are to wildlife spotters. The statistics are a checklist-obsessive's dream.

The region is habitat for more than 160 mammal species, 500 bird species, 500 fish species, 20 reptile species and 20 types of amphibians. About 100 species (including most of the whales, the burrowing owl and Vancouver Island marmot) are on the province's endangered species list; another 100 or so are considered at risk. Ecosystems are at their most diverse in southern BC, but that's also where threats from human pressures are at their strongest.

LAND MAMMALS

BC has more mountain goats than anywhere else in North America; in fact, 60% of all the world's mountain goats live here. The bear is another prominent mammal, with an estimated 160,000 black bears in BC and the Yukon, and an unknown but much smaller number of grizzlies. Kermode bears, sometimes called spirit bears, are whitish in color. Unique to BC, they're found from Bella Coola north through the Great Bear Rainforest (see p346 for details on the bears, forest and efforts to protect it) to Stewart, mostly along the lower Skeena River Valley near Prince Rupert and Terrace.

The truly white polar bear is found in the Arctic reaches of the Yukon. There has been much debate of late about the status of the bears. Anecdotal evidence told by elders in the far north says that many are washing ashore drowned as they lose track of land on vanishing ice floes.

ARE THEY KIDDING? I

In 2007, the BC government – which has an environmental record that sparks debate on all sides – implemented a plan to save BC's vanishing herds of mountain caribou. Of the province's 11 herds, it found that two groups near Golden and Nelson were so decimated that the few survivors should be caught and moved to give critical mass to other herds. Additionally, the plan said that the caribou – which have been suffering habitat loss from logging and which are especially sensitive to snowmobiles – could be saved if open season were declared on cougars and wolves. Yes, the government said that two species should be killed to save another. Meanwhile, skeptics of the plan noted that in its first two years there had been little enforcement of restrictions on snowmobiles or even logging.

WOLVES ON LAND & AT SEA

Nothing says 'outdoors' like the midnight howl of a wolf and BC has many wolves spread over the province. Although hunted by many ranchers and threatened by logging and development, you may well spot one stealthily darting across a lonely road in the early morning. Even more interesting, however, are the coastal wolves that have only received attention in recent years. Swimming and hopping between remote islands, the wolves have a diet of 75% seafood, which may or may not be the cause of the reddish tint to their hair.

Certainly it is known that, for the first time in memory, the Arctic sea ice receded completely in 2007, allowing open-water navigation right across the north.

The Biodiversity Centre for Wildlife Studies (http://wildlifebc.org) has the world's largest wildlife database, with seven million records for BC dating back 120 years. Sources include trappers, bird-watchers, government agencies and loggers.

Another unusual species, the Columbia black-tailed deer, is a small subspecies native to Vancouver Island and BC's West Coast. Other large mammals include bighorn sheep, mountain lions (also called cougars), Roosevelt elk, Dall and stone sheep, mule deer, white-tailed deer, coyote and wolves. Moose are icons of the north and the sight of one raising its moss-covered antlers out of a swamp in the morning is not soon forgotten. In the far north, the enormous herds of caribou travel ceaselessly about the tundra grazing. In winter the showshoe hare leaves its distinctive tracks everywhere as it bounds across the snow.

MARINE MAMMALS & FISH

Whales are among the best known and most sought after of BC's mammal species. About 20,000 Pacific gray whales migrate along BC's coast twice each year: southbound to Mexico from October through December and northbound to the Bering and Chukchi Seas in February through May. Less numerous and even more striking are the black-and-white orca (killer whales). Some groups (called pods) of orca live permanently off the coast of southern Vancouver Island; others range more widely in waters to the north. Other commonly sighted sea mammals include porpoises, dolphins, seals and otters. The Steller sea lion lives up to its name simply for its recovery. Since it received protection in 1970, its population has more than doubled to a modern historic high of about 24,000. One of the very best ways to see this richness of life is on one of the Inside Passage ferries (p431).

Underwater, divers can encounter a startling and often bizarre range of life. The swimming scallop looks like the fake teeth your Uncle Ed leaves in a glass by the side of the bed. In fact it is a symbiotic creature able to move under its own power, nabbing floating nutrients while a sponge attached to its shell provides protection. Like something out of Jules Verne, giant Pacific octopuses with tentacles of up to 2m or more in length are found slithering across shallow rocky ocean bottoms. The record weight to date of one of these creatures is 272kg. Finally, Wolf eels are known for their antics around divers, darting out of crevices to inspect wetsuit-clad visitors and often snuggling in the crooks of their arms.

Author, photographer and naturalist Wayne Sawchuk is one of Northern BC's foremost experts on wildlife. He's a renowned expert in identifying and following animal tracks and offers tours (www.muskwakechika.com).

Salmon rank among the most important fish in BC. Sacred to many First Nations bands, and a mainstay of the province's fishing industry, salmon come in five species: Chinook (also called king), Coho, chum, sockeye and pink. Salmon life cycles are among the most storied in the animal world. At adulthood, they leave the ocean to swim upriver to the same spawning grounds where they were born. Once there, they take their turns at reproducing, and then they die. See p59 for threats to salmon.

BIRDS

Of the 500-plus bird species, the black-and-blue Steller's jay is among the most famous; it was named the province's official bird after a government-sponsored contest. Prominent raptors include bald eagles, golden eagles, great horned owls and peregrine falcons. Look for ravens everywhere, coolly calculating their next scheme to get a meal.

Climate change means that which species you encounter is changing. Thirty years ago, seeing a nighthawk around Fort Nelson in the northeast corner of BC was nearly impossible, now the birds are common as conditions have become just balmy enough for their tastes. Over in the Chilcotin, the languorous loon has extended its summer holiday on the region's lakes by almost a month.

Plants

A succession of tree-covered hills – each one a lighter shade of blue than the last – may be both one of the most common sights in BC and the most beautiful. Yet another thing that makes the place extraordinary.

BC has always been lush, with species varying widely depending on location, climate and human impact. Its summertime wildflower displays are among the best in North America, with showy blooms of every hue scattered along trails and roadways. But BC is probably best known for its trees, which rank among the world's tallest and most majestic.

Western red cedar, Sitka spruce, hemlock and Douglas fir are prevalent trees in the moist coastal regions. Red cedar, the official provincial tree, was of special importance to indigenous coastal peoples, who used it to make everything from canoes and clothing to totem poles and medicines. The tallest tree in Canada, a Sitka spruce known as the Carmanah Giant, stands at 95m in the Carmanah Valley of western Vancouver Island (p186). As evidence of the verdant growing conditions, this tree is less than 400 years old.

Two good places to see huge old-growth trees are on the Ancient Rain Forest Trail near Prince George (p353) and near Yakoun Lake on the Queen Charlotte Islands (p377).

Coastal BC is well known for the arbutus tree, a distinctive species with twisted branches, reddish peeling bark and dark green leaves. Southern Vancouver Island and the Gulf Islands are home to Garry oak, though many of these once-prolific trees have been wiped out by human development.

Ponderosa pine, Englemann and white spruce, Douglas fir, sub-alpine fir, birch, aspen, cottonwood and larch trees are among the species

Victoria's Island Chef's Collaborative is a band of eco-concerned restaurant cooks dedicated to sourcing and supporting local farms and producers.

In 2008 geologists discovered a vast swath of permafrost near Dawson City in the Yukon that is over 740,000 years old.

AN EXPLOSION OF COLORS

Fall comes to the Yukon in August, a mere two or three months after the arrival of spring. The growing season for plants is incredibly short and they have to pack as much life as possible into a short period of sun and warmth. Maybe it's this intensity that's responsible for their going out in a blaze of glory every year. For whatever reason, every fall trees, shrubs, plants, weeds and even lichen turn a brilliant array of colors that put places like New England to shame. Birch trees turn an iridescent yellow that's akin to what you'd get if American mustard glowed in the dark. Other trees turn various angry oranges and blood reds. Underneath, purples and pinks appear. And it goes on, not for just a few kilometers but for hundreds. It's a polychromatic festival and yours to savor.

The best time for Yukon colors is mid-September; after that winter winds blow fall and travelers south. Many parts of northern BC – such as along both the Stewart-Cassiar and Alaska Hwys – reach their peak in late September. The lower Rockies and Kootenays are good in early October.

growing along the river valleys and rolling hills of the interior from Dawson City in the Yukon south. Northern landscapes are characterized by such scrappy trees as white and black spruce, tamarack and the sub-alpine fir. Hidden amongst the glacial rocks are four rare plants that biologists suspect are survivors from pre-Pleistocene times (more than 1.8 million years ago): the delicate white Walpole's poppy; the spiky, alien-looking Bering Sea dock; the beautiful yellow Northern mock goldenweed and the stubborn and hardy Baikal sedge.

The delicate tundra of the north largely consists of shrubs, grasses and lichens that eke out life during a growing season measured in weeks. Berry and mushroom pickers will be in heaven throughout the region.

ENVIRONMENTAL ISSUES

BC is a deeply conflicted place when it comes to the environment. Many see the province's vast, wild lands and coastal environments as places to protect and enjoy, while others see the many pristine and resource-rich areas as their meal ticket. Then there are areas like Tofino on Vancouver Island's West Coast, where a sometimes uneasy truce holds between people employed by extractive industries and those sworn to defend the planet from plunder.

Environmental debate is an ongoing and major part of the province's political focus. Besides the inevitable battle between those who wish to profit from natural resources and those that wish to save them, BC also

A helicopter pilot said to us: 'Politically I'm to the right of Attila the Hun, but what I've seen up here makes me believe in global warming.' He's been flying over shrinking glaciers in remote reaches of Kluane National Park & Reserve for more than 20 years.

TOP ENVIRONMENTAL GROUPS

BC has a long history of environmental activism, and even casual visitors are likely to encounter debates and perhaps protests over issues such as forestry practices and large-scale fish farming. Key groups include the following:

- David Suzuki Foundation (www.davidsuzuki.org) researches the scientific causes of environmental degradation, and studies and advocates sustainable solutions. It's Vancouver-based.

- Dogwood Initiative (www.dogwoodinitiative.org) made headlines when it distributed stickers for Loonie coins that put the duck in a pool of oil. It was protesting against proposals to allow oil tankers into the Inside Passage (p366).

- ForestEthics (www.forestethics.org) works to protect BC's constantly threatened forests and to stop the use of old-growth forest for products like toilet paper.

- Greenpeace (www.greenpeace.org) was founded in a Vancouver living room in 1969. It has achieved worldwide notoriety for its often headline-grabbing exploits to highlight environmental problems.

- Raincoast Conservation Society (www.raincoast.org) spearheaded recognition of the Great Bear Rainforest on BC's central coast as the largest contiguous tract of coastal temperate rainforest left on Earth.

- Sierra Club BC (www.sierraclub.bc.ca) is taking the lead in opposing the construction of coal-fired power plants in BC. It is also working to turn the threatened Flathead River Valley into a park (p296).

- Western Canada Wilderness Committee (www.wildernesscommittee.org) is an omnibus group with lots of ongoing coverage of environmental issues.

- Wildsight (www.wildsight.ca) is active in protecting the East Kootenays.

- Yukon Conservation Society (www.yukonconservation.org) in Whitehorse (p394) addresses a broad range of issues, including mining pollution and climate change.

ARE THEY KIDDING? II

Three of northern BC's greatest salmon rivers all spring from the ground in the same stunning sub-alpine region known as the Sacred Headwaters. It's about 120km east of the Stewart-Cassiar Hwy (p384). Bears, caribou and more roam the vast roadless plain where the Stikine, Nass and Skeena Rivers begin.

Royal Dutch Shell has obtained the rights to extract coal bed methane gas across an area of one million acres, using thousands of wells and an invasive mining procedure that produces toxic run-off and greatly changes the temperature and flow of groundwater. A coalition of groups, including the Iskut and Tahltan First Nations, Skeena Watershed Conservation Coalition, Sierra Club and Greenpeace have been fighting the plans (for environmentalist Maude Barlow's take, see p60) and in 2008 won a temporary moratorium from the BC government.

---

has urgent environmental threats from forest fires brought on by climate change and infestations of mountain pine beetles (see below) that are killing forests.

In the Yukon, concerns are often linked to climate change, such as the threats faced by Herschel Island (p418).

SALMON

Fish farming – which has been growing fast as a source of salmon – has become controversial. A major study has shown that up to 95% of young wild salmon that swim near their caged cousins catch fish lice (endemic in farm salmon) and die. The cooped up fish can't swim widely to lose the lice. Like pickpockets in a crowded mall, the lice have perfect conditions. The main way to control sea lice in farmed salmon – other than getting rid of the cages – is to give them medicated feed, which is far from organic.

Of course every cause has its effect and consumers have responded to news about lice and other concerns with farmed salmon by switching to more expensive wild-caught fish. But here too there is a problem: even as people feel they are doing the right thing, they are contributing to the monumental decline in species of salmon all along the Pacific Coast. Rivers in decline and warming ocean waters that carry less vital plankton have contributed to a near collapse of BC species like the sockeye. Chinook salmon from the mighty Yukon River are also in fast decline. In many places where record catches were the norm even a decade ago, there are now total bans on salmon fishing.

BEETLES

The mountain pine beetle is the size of a grain of rice. Its favorite meal is mature lodgepole pines, the most common trees across a swath of Canada from the Yukon, northern BC east to Alberta and beyond. Beetles attack the trees, killing them by eating the insides and leaving a fungus that chokes off the water supply. Trees try to protect themselves by emitting a white sap to entomb the beetle. But in this arms race the beetles have another weapon: when they make headway on a tree, they emit pheromones that signal to other beetles that they have found dinner. Massing beetles then overwhelm the tree's defenses.

Historically nature has held the beetles in check through long cold winters that killed the beetles. But now with global warming, the beetles are thriving to such an extent that they have killed millions of trees across BC's north, extending south through the Cariboo-Chilcotin and the Fraser-Thompson regions.

Eco-savvy locals in communities across BC meet monthly for Green Drinks (www.greendrinks.org), a social event for the environmentally interested. Guests are always welcome.

BC's carbon tax on gas at the pumps began in 2008. It will rise from 2.4 cents per liter to 7.2 cents in 2012. Deeply unpopular, it is offset by a cut in corporate taxes.

TAKE YOUR MONEY AND...

Maude Barlow is a legend among progressive Canadians. A founder of the Council of Canadians, a group dedicated to environmental issues, fair trade and more, she has always been known for speaking her mind. In 2008, Barlow was cited for Lifetime Achievement at the Canadian Environment Awards. Among the co-sponsors is Shell, and while executives sat uncomfortably in their chairs, she let loose with a speech that included the following:

'For three years, the Council of Canadians has joined [...] in the campaign to save the sacred headwaters of the Nass, Skeena and Stikene Rivers in Northern BC from a coal bed methane mining operation by Royal Dutch Shell.

'Commercial coal bed methane gas production has never before been attempted in salmon-bearing watersheds and local First Nations communities, local residents and local salmon fishermen strongly oppose the project.

'So do we at the Council of Canadians. And so I am proud to announce tonight that I will be giving my award money to the Sacred Headwaters Coalition and the First Nations in the area to support their fight to protect these pristine ancient fishing grounds in northern British Columbia. Your struggle is our struggle.'

As promised, she then turned over the $5000 award. For more on the controversy, see p59.

The award-winning *Stupid to the Last Drop* by William Marsden is a searing look at the systematic destruction of Northern Alberta to get at the oil-bearing tar sands (p366), oil that could travel to tankers on the BC coast through a pipeline.

For the bugs, their world has become a holiday in Florida. In addition, longer, drier summers are weakening trees and efforts at fire control mean that the average age of the forest is older and more infirm, a condition that allows the beetles to move right in.

The results are the swatches of brilliant red pine trees that look like an autumn dream which line the hills. But, of course, the trees should be green and efforts to stop the beetle have proven futile. This is environmental destruction on a vast scale. The one major consequence is that logging of the forests has more than doubled and the wood products industry has invoked this circular logic: if you'd let us log the forests in the first place, the beetle wouldn't have killed them. See the text, p401, for details of what the spruce beetle has done to the Yukon's forests.

One additional startling consequence, as reported by researchers in *Nature* magazine, is that so many trees are now decomposing across BC's infected 130,000 sq km that this forest is no longer reducing carbon in the atmosphere but adding to it. Parks Canada has begun some controlled burning in Yoho National Park to reduce the number of elderly trees but this also adds to carbon emissions.

British Columbia & the Yukon Outdoors

British Columbia and the Yukon are superb places for doing pretty much anything outdoors. World-class sites for hiking and kayaking are as common as bears at a salmon run. Showcased for the 21st Winter Olympics in 2010, winter sports are the real deal here.

This book is filled with activities on land and water. Some of our favorites follow.

ON LAND

Mountains, mountains everywhere. That's BC, the Rockies and the Yukon and whether you're hiking, biking, skiing or climbing, you have no shortage of options, many world-class.

CYCLING & MOUNTAIN BIKING

Mountain biking is as huge as the mountains in BC. The province is the birthplace of 'freeride' which combines downhill and dirt-jumping.

Home to some of BC's best technical trails, Rossland (p289) is the mountain biking capital of BC (and possibly Canada). You can get a ride to the top of a different trail each day and be picked up (in one piece!) at the bottom.

Whistler Mountain Bike Park (p145) has the province's best organized bike park with jumps, beams and bridges winding through 200km of maintained trails. In summer, the resort hosts the hugely popular annual Kokanee Crankworx. Nearby, you'll find 100 or so forested off-road trails twisting around the Squamish region (p139). These are freeriding dreams with narrow boards and logs spanning lush, wet ferns.

Most ski resorts ride the summer for a little cash by running some lifts that give access to trails down the now-green slopes. Most rent bikes. Fernie (p293), in a deep eastern valley, has peaks and runs that keep a year-round population of bikers waiting to hit the trails.

Cyclists can pretty much ride anywhere and hard-pumping riders are common sights all summer long on roads across BC and the Yukon. Graham Island on the Queen Charlotte Islands (p372) combines relatively quiet roads and beautiful scenery. To spice things up, you can kick up mud on old logging roads through thick surviving forests.

Winding through steep canyons, with views of vineyards, the Okanagan Valley's Kettle Valley Rail (KVR) Trail (p263) has no more than a 2% grade.

HIKING & BACKPACKING

Hitting the trails in BC, the Rockies and the Yukon ranges from simply taking in the maritime magic of Vancouver's Stanley Park (p97) to getting up close and personal with glaciers on a multi-day expedition in remote Bugaboo Provincial Park in the Kootenays (p298).

Between Squamish and Whistler, Garibaldi Provincial Park (p140) has 67km of trails and is a good place for backcountry camping close to Vancouver.

Canadian Cyclist and *Pedal* are cycling magazines available at many newsagents.

Vancouver-based *Momentum Magazine* is the publication of choice for the region's bike enthusiasts. Issues are archived and available for free download at www.momentumplanet.com.

Freeride mountain biking was invented on Vancouver's North Shore by rogue trailbuilders looking for a steeper, more technical ride.

With more than twice the number of bike commuters than any other city, Victoria claims to be the cycling capital of Canada.

On Vancouver Island, Pacific Rim National Reserve (p198) has ancient-cedar-studded rainforest and wave-pounded ocean beaches near the fun town of Tofino. The eight-day West Coast Trail (p200) was originally constructed as an escape route for shipwreck survivors. Its 75km route features rock-face ladders, stream crossings and other challenges that make it a rite of passage for serious hikers.

A little-known extension of the West Coast Trail, the Juan de Fuca Marine Trail (p183) is another good coastal hike that usually takes about four days. You can do day trips, as there are several access points.

Vancouver Island's new North Coast Trail (p214) is a demanding, waterfront hike that everyone who's done the West Coast Trail will want to try next.

Cycling BC (☎ 604-737-3034; www.cyclingbc .net), BC's governing body for mountain-bike racing, road racing and track racing, has an info-filled website. Canada Trails (www .canadatrails.ca) has ratings and links to major BC mountain biking areas.

To hear the echoes of the rich Haida First Nations culture, head out to the Queen Charlotte Islands (p372), where you will have long storm-tossed beaches and vast stands of virgin cedars and spruce to yourself.

The Okanagan Valley's Kettle Valley Rail (KVR) Trail (p263) meanders over towering wooden trestle bridges in Myra Canyon. It offers hikers the perfect chance to explore this beautiful valley without having to worry about traffic – or steep hills.

With camping spots booked months in advance, the impossibly turquoise Lake O'Hara (p305) in Yoho National Park lures hikers to a beautiful and exclusive alpine area. All the national parks in the Rockies have hikes and walks from one hour to several days. Just over the BC border, Mount Robson Provincial Park features a 22km hike to the glacier-fed Berg Lake (p332).

BEARS, OH MY

Bears are one of the top tourist draws to the north. However, you don't want it to be a fatal attraction, so here is some advice from Parks Canada for staying safe in bear country.

- On foot, travel in groups
- Keep pets on a leash
- Avoid dead animals
- Never approach a bear(!)
- Keep food and its smells away from bears; use bear-resistant food containers

If the above fails and a bear attacks, do the following:

- Don't drop your pack – it can provide protection
- Try to walk backward slowly
- Don't run – a bear will always outrun you
- Try to get somewhere safe, like a car
- If the attack is imminent, use bear spray and/or play dead, but note that bear spray is not always effective (nor is playing dead)
- If the attack occurs after a bear has stalked you or happens in your tent, fight back

Finally, two points:

- Seek out advice on bears and bear sightings from local park staff
- Be wary of 'bear whistles' as a way to make noise; some may sound like a marmot – a tasty bear snack. 'Bear bells' are a better choice.

The Bella Coola Valley (p343) is a perfect DIY hiking destination, as deserted trails abound and locals will cheerfully tell you about their favorites.

Head north so as to not miss the infamous, tortuous and steep Chilkoot Trail (p405), which is still lined with the detritus of those who desperately tried to seek their fortune in the Yukon goldfields. Reserve a spot well in advance. Elsewhere in the territory, Kluane National Park & Reserve (p400), Tombstone Territorial Park (p416) and the even more remote arctic national parks Vuntut and Ivvavik (p407) offer world-class challenges and spectacles such as thousands of caribou migrating.

HORSEBACK RIDING

Surveying BC's beautiful scenery from the back of a trusty steed is historically blessed, ecologically sound and just plain fun. Plus you get to release your inner Mountie.

The Cariboo and Chilcotin regions have dude ranches (see boxed text, p342) offering activities as diverse as trail rides and cattle drives. You can sit high in the saddle while you amble past serene lakes and atmospheric peaks. In the midst of the Great Bear Rainforest, there are plenty of trails to explore in the Bella Coola Valley (p344). You can also saddle up in Banff (p308) and Jasper (p324) National Parks; at Pemberton (p151) on the Sea to Sky Hwy and at Mt Washington (p207), near Comox and Courtenay on Vancouver Island.

ROCK CLIMBING & MOUNTAINEERING

Its numerous rocky peaks and sheer cliffs make BC a very good place for powdering up your paws and climbing up a rock.

Squamish (p137) is home to the Stawamus Chief, a world-class granite monolith within an eponymous provincial park that boasts around 200 climbing routes. Climbers also swear by the better weather at the compact gneiss rock of Skaha Bluffs near Penticton (p249), which has a long climbing season, more than 400 bolted routes and new, improved access. There's world-class climbing around Banff in the Rockies (p313). To tackle rocks both outside and inside a mountain, try Horne Lake Caves Provincial Park (p194).

SKIING & SNOWBOARDING

Powder in BC is often called 'champagne,' and with good reason: it's light and almost effervescent. But unlike the expensive bubbly from France, the amounts are limitless and affordable to all. Dry mountain air combines with an ample precipitation to produce ideal snow conditions.

Good hiking advice can be found at VCs and the national parks. Also, try these: Alpine Club of Canada (www.alpine clubofcanada.ca), Outdoor Recreation Council of British Columbia (www. orcbc.ca) and Trail Database (www .traildatabase.org /countries/canada.html).

The Grouse Grind in North Vancouver is the city's favorite outdoor workout. It's an ultra-steep 2.9km trek up the side of Grouse Mountain and usually takes about two hours.

SKI SAFETY

Because BC is so vast, backcountry skiing and boarding are popular. But understand that such adventures should not be undertaken lightly. Avalanches are a major cause of death every year, see p275 for important considerations. It's also vital to let people know if you'll be going off marked trails. In a well-publicized incident in 2009, a couple left the perimeter of the ski resort at Revelstoke and got lost. Despite having SOS signals spotted, no search and rescue effort was made because they hadn't left word of their plans with anyone. One of the pair died of exposure before help arrived nine days too late.

Finally, be sure to think about safety equipment such as helmets. This has particularly come to attention since actress Natasha Richardson died following a fall during a ski lesson in Quebec.

Vancouver and Whistler are obviously the big news given the 2010 Winter Olympics, but many would argue that the very best skiing in BC is found in the east of the province. Vast swaths of mountains, especially in the Kootenays, are covered by the 10 or more meters of snow

BC SKIING

Some of the best-known ski resorts covered in this book include the following:

Apex Mountain Resort Apex (p258) is known for its plethora of double-black-diamond and technical runs (the drop is over 600m), as well as gladed chutes and vast powdery bowls. Primarily catering to locals, the resort is rarely crowded. Close to the village you'll find 56km of accessible cross-country trails. There are 68 runs overall. Nearest town: Penticton (p249).

Banff National Park Ski Resorts Three excellent mountain resorts (p315): Ski Banff@Norquay, Sunshine Village and Lake Louise Ski Area are the triple crown of Rocky Mountain skiing. This trio is beautifully positioned and offers 250 runs of every description. All are located close to Banff, which offers the most big-time resort amenities east of Whistler. Sunshine Village is easily the most popular of the three. Nearest town: Banff (p308).

Big White Ski Resort Known for its incredible powder, Big White (p267) is one of BC's best ski resorts. The highest ski resort in the province features 118 runs, which are covered in the aforementioned deep dry snow for excellent downhill and backcountry skiing, and deep gullies that make for excellent snowboarding. The drop is 777m and you can night ski. Nearest town: Kelowna (p258).

Cypress Mountain (p129) Close to Vancouver, the wide, snow-filled Cypress Bowl sits in the heart of Cypress Provincial Park between Mt Strachan and Black Mountain. Popular with intermediate downhill skiers, the resort features 52 runs and 19km of groomed cross-country runs, as well as a snowboard park. In the evening, the lights come on for great night skiing and excellent views of Howe Sound. The Olympic venue for snowboarding and freestyle skiing, it's had a major upgrade in facilities. Nearest town: West Vancouver (p129).

Fernie Alpine Resort One of the faster growing resorts in the Kootenays, Fernie (p293) has 114 runs across five large bowls. One runs for a knee-popping 3km. Tree-skiers like going off piste here and there's plenty of virgin powder where you can leave your mark. Fully 30% of the runs are rated expert. Nearby Fernie is one of BC's best small towns. Nearest town: Fernie (p292).

Grouse Mountain Resort A mere 15-minute drive or bus ride from Vancouver, Grouse Mountain (p127) is a favorite for its night skiing and snowmaking capabilities, which ensure excellent conditions. An aerial tram whisks you to the mountaintop, offering incredible views along the way. Mogul dancers head to the Peak, or explore the mountain's backside on Blueberry or Purgatory. The drop is 384m and there are 26 daytime runs. Nearest town: North Vancouver (p126).

Kicking Horse Mountain Resort (p299) Another of the fast-growing East Kootenays resorts, a challenging 60% of the 106 runs here in the Purcell Mountains are rated advanced or expert. A gondola gives you a great vantage over the 1260 vertical meters of this relatively snow-heavy, wind-free location near the Rockies. It's best mid-week when the crowds thin. Nearest town: Golden (p299).

Kimberley Alpine Resort (p297) Boasting over 7 sq km of skiable terrain, mild weather and 80 runs, this is a good all-round resort – if you like smaller ones with minimal nightlife. There are 5 lifts and 45% of the runs are intermediate. A high-speed quad lift serves the 8200m Main Run, which has a 609m drop and is fully lighted for night skiing. A snowboard park features an exciting half-pipe. Nearest town: Kimberley (p296).

that falls annually. In fact this region now boasts the 'Powder Hwy,' a marketing moniker for a series of roads linking the major ski resorts. Major players are investing billions in resorts here, so the area will only grow in stature.

Mount Seymour (p127) Some 1000m up, this North Shore provincial park is transformed in winter, when snowboarders come to rip it up on Seymour's 23 runs, including Brockton, Mystery Peak and Mushroom Junior Park. Beginner skiers and boarders find Seymour a good place to learn, and the excellent ski/board school offers good deals on lessons. Families are catered for with cross-country trails, tobogganing and inner tube runs. Nearest town: North Vancouver (p126).

Mount Washington Alpine Resort (p207) Vancouver Island's main ski resort; there are 60 runs, a snowshoe park and 55km of cross-country trails. It has tubing runs for kids of all ages, including a floodlit one for nighttime frolics. The resort is at its best away from weekends, when it is crowded with Vancouverites. Check snow conditions in advance. Nearest town: Comox (p207).

Red Mountain Ski Resort (p290) A breeding ground for Olympic skiers, low-key 'Red' comprises two mountains – Red and Granite – and offers some of the province's best black-diamond runs. The resort is known for its steep, tree-lined runs (87 at last count). There are six lifts and a drop of 890m. The nearby cross-country area is also a favorite of medal-winners and hopefuls. Nearest town: Rossland (p289).

Revelstoke Mountain Resort BC's newest major resort, Revelstoke Mountain (p275) is close to its namesake town, which is a perfect hangout for skiers and boarders of all stripes. It currently has 40 runs with the goal of 100 by 2015. Much of the terrain was previously only accessible for backcountry skiing, and the focus remains on intermediate and advanced runs. Heli-skiing operators in town and at the resort can take you out to track-free bowls across the ranges. Nearest town: Revelstoke (p273).

Silver Star Mountain Resort With a gold rush boomtown motif and a careful design for ski-on, ski-off convenience, Silver Star (p269) attracts every level of skier and snowboarder to its 115 runs. The mountain's sunny south face, Vance Creek, features predominantly novice and intermediate runs, while the north face has black-diamond runs boasting moguls, trees and powder. The vertical drop is 760m and there are 12 lifts. A special machine carves wicked half-pipes for snowboarders; cross-country skiers enjoy 37km of groomed trails. Nearest town: Vernon (p266).

Sun Peaks Resort (p241) Legendary Olympian Nancy Greene is director of skiing here and she lends some real ski-cred to this family-friendly resort that is favored by many who'd rather avoid the Whistler madness. It's BC's second-largest resort; the three mountains boast 122 runs, 11 lifts, a snowboard park and a 881m drop. Almost 70% of the runs at Sun Peaks are novice or intermediate. Snow-shoeing, dog sledding and Nordic skiing are also popular. Nearest town: Kamloops (p239).

Whistler-Blackcomb (p144) Seen by billions during the downhill skiing events of the 2010 Winter Olympics, this world-famous, dual-mountain paradise can accommodate over 60,000 skiers and snowboarders an hour on its 38 lifts, which include a new 4.4km-long gondola linking Mts Whistler and Blackcomb. More than 200 runs and 29 sq km of bowls, glades and slopes keep the international crowd on the powder for days on end. Nearest town: Whistler (p141).

Whitewater Winter Resort (p286) Almost as charming as the nearby town of Nelson (and that's saying a lot), this small mountain (two chairs and a tow rope) tends to attract skiers and boarders venturing into the backcountry. There are local Snowcat operators and the steep terrain boasts a 400m vertical drop. It's known for its heavy powdery snowfall, which averages 10.5m per year. Nearest town: Nelson (p283).

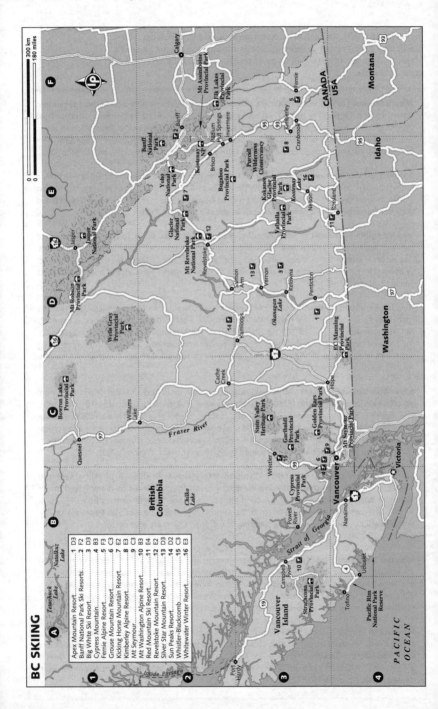

BC SKIING

Elsewhere in BC, the Okanagan Valley has some good resorts as does Vancouver Island. And, of course, the Rocky Mountain ski slopes are legendary. For detailed coverage of ski resorts across BC and the Rockies, see p64.

Slopes of any size will have a range of trails to accommodate everyone from beginners to Olympic-class experts. Skiers and boarders will find their needs equally catered for and you'll always find many kilometers of trails for cross-country skiing, snow-shoeing and snowmobiling. Lessons and rentals are widely available. Towns with resorts are also good places to organize backcountry adventures, possibly by helicopter and with or without guides. (In fact, so too are some of the almost unknown mountains in the far north off the Stewart-Cassiar Hwy; see p384.) For safety advice, see p63.

If you want something more intimate and casual than a major ski resort, BC also abounds in small and often idiosyncratic places to hit the slopes. These range from EC Manning Provincial Park (p235) near Hope to Hudson Bay Mountain near Terrace (p365). Popular with outdoorsy locals, you'll find a lift or maybe just a towrope or two. With its long winter, the entire Yukon is perfect for giving your inner-Arctic explorer its freedom.

WINTER SPORTS

Besides legendary skiing and snowboarding (p64), BC's amazing powder coupled with endlessly varied terrain mean that you don't just have to be hurtling downhill to enjoy the white stuff (although most ski areas have toboggan and tube runs). Whistler (p145) has an excellent tubing park, where you can munch a hot dog next to an open fire after bouncing down the hill.

Cross-country (Nordic) skiing is enjoyed province-wide as well as in the Yukon. In remote areas, it is still a means of transport. Also popular both for their practical and fun aspects are snow-shoeing and even dog sledding. You can find places to rent gear for the former and get tours via the latter in many places in BC as well as in Whitehorse (p390) and Dawson City (p407) in the Yukon. Both towns have famous dog sled races that attract big crowds. Ski touring is simply backpacking adapted for winter. Revelstoke (p273) and Glacier National Park (p278) are good places to organize trips. Contact the VCs for info.

Ripping across the countryside and leaving your mark with a snowmobile is an avocation for many (despite the avalanche dangers in hilly areas). Rentals are common in towns big and small. Finally, if you'd like to work up a thirst for beer while wielding a broom, curling clubs are at the center of the social scene in rural areas.

ZIPLINING

Hop into a harness and go flying down a steel cable while treetops whoosh past and perilous rocks threaten from below. That's the basic premise of ziplining, a fast-growing thrill-ride-cum-nature-experience that often starts 70m or more above the ground and gets you up to speeds of 60km/h or more. Lines are going up across BC, especially in heavily visited natural areas.

Whistler has a large, multi-line zipline park (p146) in the valley between Whistler and Blackcomb mountains. Vancouver Island has lines aplenty, including those at Strathcona Provincial Park (p211), Sooke (p182) and Nanaimo (p186).

Given the popularity of this chance to whiz along at high speeds while doing mid-air acrobatics (and taking a minute to spot that tree-top nest of baby chicks, of course), expect the craze to zip across the province.

The Kettle Valley Rail Trail (p263) is part of the 525km-long old railroad that is being converted into hiking and biking trails across the Kootenays and the Okanagan Valley.

The Cypress Mountain ski cams (www.skireport .com/bc/cypressmountain /cams) give a daily visual update on ski conditions at the 2010 Olympic venue.

Major ski resorts in the Kootenays are connected by a series of roads comprising the Powder Hwy (www.powder highway.com).

WATCHING WILDLIFE

For many, the chance to see some of BC's incredible diversity of wildlife is reason enough for a trip. For most, seeing one of these incredible critters is a lasting memory. Though wildlife viewing is good at any time of the year, there are certain high seasons along the BC coast when you're likely to see more of a particular animal (For whale-watching, see the boxed text 'There She Blows' p70).

- bald eagles – year-round but especially mid-March to mid-April
- grizzly and black bears – mid-April to June
- Kermode bears – September to mid-October
- porpoises – year-round
- seals and sea lions – year-round

Three places where you can see the full drama of nature, including bears cavorting, are:

- Bella Coola Valley – boat tours along rivers thick with grizzly bears wandering the banks (p343)
- Hyder, AK – the isolated town over the border from Stewart, BC, has a wooden walkway that takes you out over suitably named Fish Creek where bears feed on spawning salmon below (p382)
- Khutzeymateen Grizzly Bear Sanctuary – over 50 grizzlies live on this 450-sq-km refuge; eco-tour operators have permits for viewing (p372)

Away from the coast, BC and the Yukon have innumerable places to see wildlife as outlined in this book. You can see bear, caribou, deer, mountain goats, and many more animals through the year. For a guide to watching wildlife in the Rockies, see the boxed text, p332.

ON WATER

BC's *Wavelength Magazine* offers tons of great tips for serious kayakers across the region. Issues can be downloaded free at www.wavelength magazine.com.

Just looking at the map, you'll see plenty of water! From the Inside Passage and islands to pristine mountain lakes, challenging white-water rivers and more, there's just no limit to the places you can paddle, raft, swim, surf and more.

DIVING

Justly famous for its superb, albeit chilly diving conditions, BC features two of the top-ranked ocean dive spots in the world: Vancouver Island and the Gulf Islands. It's best to go in winter, when the plankton has decreased and visibility often exceeds 20m. The water temperature drops to about 7°C to 10°C in winter; in summer, it may reach 15°C. At depths of more than 15m visibility remains good throughout the year and temperatures rarely rise above 10°C. Expect to see a full range of marine life, including oodles of crabs, from tiny hermits to intimidating kings. If you're lucky you may also encounter mammals such as seals and sea lions or bizarre creatures such as the giant octopuses that thrive in the cold water (p56).

The Haida people of the Queen Charlotte Islands are great canoeists. Historically, their canoes were carved from a single cedar log and were over 20m long.

The prime diving spots lie in Georgia Strait between Vancouver Island's east coast and the mainland. Dive shops abound in this region, and they are your best sources for scuba gear as well as lessons, charters and tours. Nanaimo's Ocean Explorer's Diving (p188) will take you out to snorkel with the harbor seals or you can go deeper with a full dive at the sunken HMCS *Saskatchewan* and HMCS *Cape Breton*, two of BC's most popular dive sites.

Other popular areas include Bamfield (p198), Comox (p207), Campbell River (p209) and Quadra Island (p210).

Egmont's Porpoise Bay Charters (p156) is great for both first timers and experienced divers. They'll take you out to swim with the wolf eels and blue sharks (and maybe an octopus or two).

The crystalline waters of BC's inland lakes attract their fair share of divers. Vernon (p266) is a good base for diving 135km-long Okanagan Lake.

FISHING

Fishing, both saltwater and freshwater, draws anglers from around the world to BC. Saltwater anglers particularly like to cast their lines in the waters around Vancouver Island, where several places (Campbell River, p209, chief among them) claim the title 'salmon capital of the world,' as well as at Prince Rupert (p367), known for its halibut, and in the Queen Charlotte Islands (p372). You'll find good river and lake fishing in every region.

PADDLING

BC and the Yukon are heaven for paddlers. Lakes and rivers abound, just waiting for the dip of an oar. Some legendary spots are found inland and there are equally revered places on the coast.

Major paddling spots usually have stations where you can rent canoes, kayaks and gear. See the listings in this book for more details.

Inland

The 116km Bowron Lake canoe circuit in Bowron Lake Provincial Park (p338) is one of the world's great canoe trips, covering 10 lakes with easy portages between each. Slightly less fabled – and crowded – is a 116km-long circuit in Wells Gray Provincial Park (p340) taking in 10 alpine lakes.

Another remote canoe journey is possible on Eutsuk and neighboring lakes in the northern portion of Tweedsmuir Provincial Park (p361). For a real adventure, try Chilko Lake (see boxed text, p341) in Ts'yl-os Provincial Park, which can involve access via a floatplane.

Other good inland spots to paddle include Wells Gray Provincial Park (p340); Slocan Lake, just west of New Denver (p281); and Okanagan Lake, easily accessed from Kelowna (p258). Also accessible: Lightning Lake at EC Manning Provincial Park (p235), east of Hope; Kootenay Lake, east of Nelson (p283); and Babine Lake, north of Burns Lake (p360).

During the short Yukon summer, scores of paddlers from around the world paddle the famed Yukon River and its tributaries, the route of the Klondike gold rush. You can still experience the stunning raw wilderness that the prospectors encountered, but from a modern canoe or kayak rather than a raft of lashed-together logs. Whitehorse (p393) is the center for guides and gear.

For the ultimate in adrenaline rushes while paddling (except when you spot an orca on your tail), try creekboating some of BC's white-water rivers, such as the Kicking Horse near Golden (p299). For more on running the rapids, see p72.

The Islands & Coast

Although some people swear by their ocean-going canoes, the BC coast is truly the domain of kayaks (p71). Since humans first stretched skin over a frame and deployed a double paddle some 4000 years ago, the little craft have been an excellent marriage of man and mode.

Earthwatch Institute (☎ 800-776-0188; www.earthwatch.org) takes paying volunteers on research missions along the BC coast and the Yukon. A seven-day trip identifying whales costs $2300.

Pacific Northwest Expeditions (☎ 866-529-2522; www .seakayakbc.com) specializes in wildlife-spotting kayak trips. All-inclusive trips cost about $400 per day.

You might want to time your BC visit to coincide with the annual Vancouver Island Paddlefest (www .paddlefest.bc.ca), a major kayaking event held each May at Ladysmith.

Options are as numerous as salmon in season along BC's endlessly varied coast and islands. The greatest concentration of outfitters are on Vancouver Island, which is one big paddling playground. The Broken Group Islands (p200) offer BC's best kayaking; revered for remoteness, rugged natural beauty and the opportunity to kayak to the little islands and camp overnight.

If you don't have much time, you can always rent a kayak for a few hours or take an introductory lesson in pretty much any of the island's coastal towns. For more information, check them out in the Vancouver Island chapter: Victoria (p161), Sooke (p182), Sidney (p179), Oceanside (p194), Port Alberni (p196), Tofino (p202), Bamfield (p197), Telegraph Cove (p212), Port Hardy (p213) and Denman (p206), Hornby (p206) and Quadra Islands (p210).

In the Gulf Islands, you'll find outfitters and rental shops on each major island: Salt Spring (p218), Galiano (p226), Mayne (p225) and North Pender (p222). Pootling around the coastline of Galiano Island (p226) in a kayak is by far the best way to experience this idyllic natural paradise.

Near Vancouver, try Bowen Island (p130). The environs of Powell River (p157) also boast a wealth of options.

Further north, Prince Rupert (p367) is a hub. Many kayakers consider exploring the legendary Gwaii Haanas National Park Reserve (p380) in the Queen Charlotte Islands, an experience often propounded as the 'trip of a lifetime.'

Get BC diving info at *Diver Magazine* (www .divermag.com) and the Professional Association of Diving Instructors (www.padi.com).

SAILING & BOATING

The sheltered waters of the Inside Passage attract boaters year-round, although obviously summer is the prime time. Coastal marine parks provide safe, all-weather anchorage and offer boats for hire (powerboats as well as sailboats). Top places to sail include the Strait of Georgia and the Gulf Islands. Inland, Harrison Lake (p231) and Okanagan Lake are popular with sailors, with boats available to rent in Penticton (p249) and Kelowna (p258).

THERE SHE BLOWS

A bear foraging on land, a whale swimming at sea: two of nature's best spectacles and both easy to spot in BC (for bears, see p68).

The Inside Passage is a favorite cruising spot for gray, humpback and killer whales (among others) during migration. They regularly surprise ferries full of delighted travelers who witness the huge and magnificent creatures flipping their tails, clearing their blowholes and sometimes even breaching (p431).

Whale-watching tours are popular and are timed to catch whales during their respective seasons, which include:

- gray whales – mid-August to October
- humpback whales – August to October
- orcas (killer whales) – May to mid-July

Victoria is the top spot for joining a tour (p168) as is Sydney (p179) on the Saanich Peninsula. Elsewhere on Vancouver Island, Bamfield (p198) is good for grays and humpbacks; Pacific Rim National Park Reserve (p198) has spotting sites on land and water; Ucluelet (p201) is good for spotting from a kayak; Tofino has open-ocean tours (p202); and Telegraph Cove (p212) has a whale museum and excellent nature cruises.

In the Southern Gulf, you can spot whales from land at Saturna Island (p224). Prince Rupert (p367) is a hub for whale-watching, with several operators plying the rich waters.

SEA KAYAKING

Unlike larger boats, kayaks can hug the shoreline, offering the perfect perch for watching shore birds and other marine life (including, possibly, whales). Sea kayaks are easy to paddle, quite stable and lots of fun. Nearly every coastal and island town has at least one outfitter ready to take you on a guided trek lasting from a few hours (for about $50) to a week. These trips are a fine way to get into the sport; once you know the ropes, you can rent or buy gear and go paddling on your own.

It's always best, for safety, to kayak with other people. Someone in the group should know how to plot a course by navigational chart and compass, pilot in fog, read weather patterns, assess water hazards, interpret tide tables, handle boats in adverse conditions and perform group- and self-rescues. Always check weather forecasts before setting out and don't expect your cell phone/mobile to work.

Campsites are common on BC's many islands, but more and more people are choosing 'mothership' sea kayaking over camping. The mothership, a larger boat (often sail-powered), takes kayakers and their gear out to sea; the kayakers then spend their days paddling, with nights passed in comfort on the big boat. This is a popular way of touring the otherwise inaccessible parts of Gwaii Haanas National Park Reserve in the Queen Charlottes (p380).

Houseboating is a leisurely way to explore inland waters, including Shuswap Lake (p242) north of the Okanagan. It costs from $2000 a week, depending on location and time of year, to rent a self-contained boat that sleeps about 10 people.

SURFING

Tofino (p202) is BC's surfing mecca with surf camps and rental operators dotted around the town. Weather conditions may well be far from ideal – imagine buckets of rain and chilly temperatures – but the waves are truly awesome, rolling directly off the North Pacific. Nearby Long Beach (p198), fittingly named given its 20km length, is always popular.

SWIMMING

There's really nowhere you can't swim in BC. The water quality of the ocean, lakes and rivers is usually excellent and beaches – albeit narrow ones – abound. There's just one caveat: you might exit the water missing a few parts that have frozen off. A summer temperature of 10°C is considered pretty warm.

The beaches of Vancouver (p82) offer plenty of opportunity for a bracing dip in the Pacific with Third Beach, Kitsilano Beach and Jericho Beach among the most popular. Nelson (p283), which finds ways to have fun all year round, has a popular lakeside beach where people swim from one side to the other (possibly to stay warm). Vancouver has some good public swimming pools but the best and most family-friendly is at Second Beach in Stanley Park (p97). For other city locations, see p103. Indoor public pools are found in larger towns, including Revelstoke (p274) and Whitehorse in the Yukon (p393).

WHITE-WATER RAFTING

Rugged canyons and seasonal gushes of melting snow make BC's rivers great for white-water action. You don't need to be experienced to have a go, as licensed commercial rafting operators are government-vetted and noted for their expertise. Trips can last from three hours (average cost $100) up to a couple of weeks.

Ask at VCs and sporting goods stores for information on the profusion of fishing licenses. The BC Ministry of Environment (www .env.gov.bc.ca/fw/) controls freshwater licenses. The federal Department of Fisheries & Oceans (www.pac .dfo-mpo.gc.ca/) issues licenses for saltwater /tidal fishing.

Check out www.surfing vancouverisland.com for lots of information on surfing and some gnarly videos.

CLASSIFYING WHITE WATER

Never take to the river until you know what conditions to expect and what you can handle.

- **Class I – easy** Mostly flat water with occasional series of mild rapids.

- **Class II – medium** Frequent stretches of rapids with waves up to 3ft high and easy chutes, ledges and falls. The best route is easy to identify, and the entire river can be run in open canoes.

- **Class III – difficult** Features numerous rapids with high, irregular waves and difficult chutes and falls that often require scouting.

- **Class IV – very difficult** Long stretches of irregular waves, powerful eddies and even constricted canyons. Scouting is mandatory, and rescues can be difficult in many places.

- **Class V – extremely difficult** Continuous violent rapids, powerful rollers and high, unavoidable waves and haystacks.

- **Class VI – highest level of difficulty** Rarely run except by very experienced kayakers under ideal conditions

---

Mountain Equipment Co-op, the famed outdoor store with outlets in Vancouver and Victoria, started with 6 members in 1971 and now has 2.9 million.

The official Tourism Vancouver Island outdoor activity site (www .vancouverisland.travel /outdoor) is a one-stop portal for options across the region, including caving, hiking, surfing, kayaking and storm watching

Wherever you are in BC, you're probably close to a good whitewater river. Consider the Thompson River (p236) near Lytton for excellent white water not especially far from Vancouver. Adams River near Shuswap Lake (p242) is another fine choice.

The Kootenays are probably the best area; many consider the Kicking Horse River near Golden (p299) to offer one of the province's best raft trips. Other prime spots include the Clearwater River near Wells Gray Provincial Park (p340) and the Bulkley and Babine Rivers near Smithers (p361). For wilderness adventures, consider the Tatshenshini and Alsek Rivers in Northern BC (p385).

In the Yukon, Haines Junction (p398) is a good base for white-water rafting.

WINDSURFING & KITEBOARDING

The tidal flats around Vancouver are popular with windsurfers. On many a day you'll see scores of colorful sails darting around the shallows like flocks of colorful birds. You'll find shops in the city (p102) where you can get advice and rent boards, skimboards and wetsuits. Squamish Spit (p139) is the center of windsurfing and kiteboarding in the region north of Vancouver, with active locals hitting the windswept waterway on any given day.

Parks in British Columbia & the Yukon

An elk cooling off in Jasper National Park (p324)

You could spend a lifetime exploring parks and protected spaces – there are close to 1000 – in BC and the Yukon, and when you died you might not need to bother with heaven. From natural retreats within sight of Vancouver to vast remote spaces that define adventure, these special places have something for virtually every traveler and you can have amazing experiences in one or several of them. Unesco has been busy declaring parts of this region as World Heritage sites; see p32 for a list.

Summer is obviously the most popular time to visit the parks, although you can have lovely experiences in spring and fall while avoiding crowds. In winter, however, parks without winter activities like skiing tend to be very quiet. If you're not afraid of a little frostbite, you can have the ultimate wilderness experience during the snowy months.

NATIONAL PARKS, RESERVES & HISTORIC SITES

Canada's fledgling national park system first rose to prominence in the early 20th century in tandem with the nascent Canadian Pacific Railway (CPR), bringing adventure-hungry tourists to the edge of a rugged and untamed wilderness. A little over 100 years later, this low-key beginning has evolved into a national system, incorporating the four separate Rocky Mountain parks covered in this book. (In Banff you can visit the original park site at the Cave & Basin National Historic Site, p312.) In BC and the Yukon, Parks Canada (www.parkscanada.ca) sites range from the aforementioned busy Banff to the remote splendor of Vuntut.

National Parks

These are fully protected parks of national importance. Excepting the remote Arctic parks, all have excellent visitor centers where experts can help you plan your visit.

The original national park, **Banff National Park** (p308) has something for everyone, which is just as well given the number of visitors it draws. But its grand size means you can still escape into the backcountry and be wowed by the sheer-faced peaks. *Best feature:* nightlife that doesn't involve kindling.

High Alpine adventure awaits around Rogers Pass in **Glacier National Park** (p278), where the CPR pushed through the Rockies. *Best feature:* the boom of anti-avalanche howitzers.

Protecting the fragile ecosystem of a small, representative portion of the Southern Gulf Islands, **Gulf Islands National Park**

top five

PICKS FOR BEAUTY

It's like choosing the best muffin in the world's best bakery, but here's a very subjective list of five.

Garibaldi Provincial Park (p140) Alpine beauty just 70km north of Vancouver.

Gwaii Haanas National Park Reserve & Haida Heritage Site (p380) Almost like another world.

Ruckle Provincial Park (p219) An island retreat.

Tombstone Territorial Park (p416) The magnificent Arctic.

Yoho National Park (p303) Puts the rocky in the Rockies.

Sheer-faced peaks guard Larch Valley, Banff National Park (p308)

RICK RUDNICKI

Reserve (p218) includes tiny islets, craggy reefs and stretches of coastline on 15 islands. *Best feature:* island-hopping by kayak.

Along with Vuntut, **Ivvavik National Park** (p417) is the ultimate backcountry park. Mount an expedition by kayak or raft down the rugged Firth River to the shores of the Arctic Ocean. Access is by air from Inuvik 200km east. *Best feature:* watching hundreds of migrating caribou pass your camp before breakfast.

Banff's closest sibling, **Jasper National Park** (p324), is less supercharged in every respect, but it still boasts the best of what the Rockies have to offer the activity-hungry visitor. Plus the town is cute and fun. *Best feature:* being in total wilderness 10 minutes after walking out of town.

Lots of Rocky Mountain microclimates are crammed into the small **Kootenay National Park** (p306) on the BC border. *Best feature:* soaking in Radium Hot Springs.

In **Mount Revelstoke National Park** (p277) you can hike to the top of the namesake mountain for Alpine views over the Selkirks in every direction. *Best feature:* wildflowers.

Vuntut National Park (p417) is joined to Ivvavik and is just as remote. Tundra gives way to stark Arctic foothills and mountains. Millions of birds pass through in summer. *Best feature:* the wetlands at Old Crow Flats.

Among the highlights of craggy and uncrowded **Yoho National Park** (p303) are impossibly turquoise glacier-fed lakes such as O'Hara and Emerald. *Best feature:* dining in the tiny town of Trail.

National Park Reserves

These are areas that have been earmarked as national parks, pending the settlement of native land claims. These reserves are managed in much the same way as the national parks, with entry fees, visitor centers, and various environmental rules and regulations.

With Unesco-recognized SGaang Gwaii, the islands of **Gwaii Haanas National Park Reserve & Haida Heritage Site** (p380) in the lower third of the Queen Charlottes allow intrepid kayakers to explore the mysteries of the Haida culture. *Best feature:* rows of totem poles staring mutely out to sea.

A PARKS USERS' GUIDE

You can reserve campsites at popular spots and also save yourself money by buying an annual pass.

National Parks

- The Parks Canada Discovery Pass (www.parkscanada.ca; adult/child $85/43) is an excellent investment if you are going to spend time in the national parks and historic sites. Passes can be purchased at the parks; a cheaper annual pass (adult/child $68/34) just covers parks.
- Parks Canada campgrounds charge $15 to $30 a night and the busiest (mainly in the Rockies) take reservations (☎ 877-737-3783; www.pccamping.ca).

BC Parks

- BC Parks (www.env.gov.bc.ca/bcparks) doesn't charge park admission so there's no need for an annual pass. However 40 of the most popular parks from Vancouver Island east to the Okanagan Valley do charge $3 per day for parking. An annual parking pass costs $25.
- BC Parks manages hundreds of campgrounds with fees ranging from $12 for basic sites to $24 for the most highly developed campgrounds. About 70 popular parks offer reserved sites (☎ 800-689-9025; www.discovercamping.ca). At popular campgrounds, arrive early to avoid missing out. Instructions at the entrance will tell you how to register and pay your fee.

Yukon Territorial Parks

The Yukon doesn't charge entrance fees to its parks. Camping at scores of government campgrounds in beautiful locations costs $12 per night; none accept reservations.

Forming part of a vast glacier-cleaved wilderness spanning the Yukon, BC and Alaska, the remote **Kluane National Park and Reserve** (p400) is an astonishing adventure for those ready for a backcountry expedition. *Best feature:* short trails off the Alaska Hwy.

Located on the ragged Pacific Ocean coastline of western Vancouver Island, **Pacific Rim National Park Reserve** (p198) combines wide sandy beaches with whipped-up surf and a dense fringe of verdant rainforest. *Best feature:* hiking the West Coast Trail.

Dwarfed by the old growth forest, Pacific Rim National Park (p198)

FRANK CARTER

National Historical Sites

Buildings, forts and other places that commemorate nationally important people, places and events are designated historical sites. Some not listed here are covered in the parks above.

Start the **Chilkoot Trail** (p405) near Skagway, Alaska and follow the legendary route into the Yukon used by thousands during the Klondike Gold Rush. *Best feature:* not needing to bring the tons of supplies they did in 1898.

Dawson City (p407) takes you right back to the Klondike Gold Rush days, with dozens of preserved and not-so-preserved buildings, gold dredges, a dancehall, riverboat and more. *Best feature:* Dawson is funky and vibrant, not stuck in a time capsule.

Dating from the 19th century and partially reconstructed, **Fort Langley** (p134) offers a glimpse at the early days of the pioneers. *Best feature:* chatting with costumed guides.

The former fur trading post of **Fort St James** (p360) was one of the first places where trappers and First Nations people lived in proximity. *Best feature:* its remote, beautiful location.

Much of BC's early wealth came from the millions of fish processed by workers toiling in miserable conditions at factories like the **Gulf of Georgia Cannery** (p133). *Best feature:* interactive exhibits and tours that don't involve having to gut a fish!

The **SS Klondike** (p392), a classic Yukon River stern-wheeler has been perfectly restored to its 1920s glory. *Best feature:* imagining saying, 'How 'bout a game of cards?'

BC Provincial Parks

Comprising more than 800 parks and protected places, the BC Parks (www.env.gov.bc.ca /bcparks) system is vast. It covers 130,000 sq km of protected land, which accounts for almost 14% of British Columbia's area. Only 40 of the parks are sufficiently developed or visited that they bother to charge visitors – and even then it's only for parking.

Most of the parks reward the self-sufficient. Experiences span the gamut of BC itself, from remote beaches on Vancouver Island to glaciers high on isolated peaks.

TEN PARKS EVERYONE LOVES

These favorites will have you planning your next visit before you've completed your first.

Bowron Lake Provincial Park (p338) is home to one of the world's great paddling circuits: 116km through the Cariboo Mountains. Portages are easy but you have to reserve your slot for the six- to 10-day adventure. *Best feature:* you look at the moose, the moose looks at you...

Right in the heart of the Cascade Mountain range east of Hope, the mountainous wilderness of **EC Manning Provincial Park** (p235) comprises brooding forests and rolling rivers. *Best feature:* hiking and biking, skiing and boarding.

A favorite spot for BC outdoor nuts, the alpine wilderness hikes of **Garibaldi Provincial Park** (p140) showcase diverse lakeside flora and fauna amidst the Coast Mountains. *Best feature:* winter cross-country ski routes.

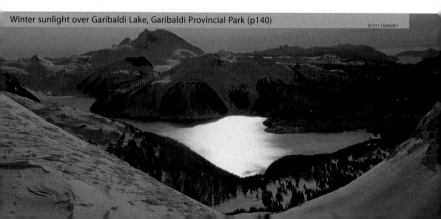

Winter sunlight over Garibaldi Lake, Garibaldi Provincial Park (p140)

SCOTT DARSNEY

Bison check your speed on the Alaska Hwy (p355)
KRAIG LIEB

Kayaking in Skookumchuck Narrows Provincial Park (p156)
ANDREW PE

A hot spot for regional spelunkers is **Horne Lake Caves Provincial Park** (p194); experts come for the two caves you can explore without a guide, while novices can get lessons. *Best feature:* families bonding underground.

Kokanee Creek Provincial Park (p286) is that rare thing: a BC park with an actual visitor center. This is prime hiking country – one good four-hour trail through lush forest takes you to waterfalls fed by glaciers. *Best feature:* close to delightful Nelson.

A favorite Vancouver nature retreat for summertime, **Mount Seymour Provincial Park** (p127) becomes one of the city's three ski resort options in winter. *Best feature:* escaping the big smoke in minutes.

Muncho Lake Provincial Park (p358) is the scenic high point of the first 1000km of the Alaska Hwy; the glacier-fed waters of the lake are luminescent. Expect to see pretty much every type of iconic BC critter ranging around these environs. *Best feature:* indulging your inner hippy at Laird River Hot Springs.

The largest park on Vancouver Island and the region's oldest protected wilderness, **Strathcona Provincial Park** (p211) has got alpine meadows, glacial lakes and looming peaks. *Best feature:* large, woodsy lodge.

Vast and mostly isolated, **Wells Gray Provincial Park** (p340) dominates a large chunk of back-country BC. White-water rafting, some famous paddling circuits and even beaches provide aquatic fun amidst the peaks. *Best feature:* thundering Helmcken Falls.

TEN PARKS WAITING FOR LOVE

Although not exactly unknown, you are unlikely to encounter crowds at these virginal parks, unless it's a group of marmots.

The Purcells are the first mountain range west of the Rockies and they too are soaring, rugged and riven by glaciers. The huge **Bugaboo Provincial Park** (p298) is isolated and accessed by one rough road. Bunk in a rustic mountain hut between hikes. *Best feature:* crazy name, awesome terrain.

Never troubled by crowds, **Cape Scott Provincial Park** (p215) is a ravishing natural beauty with fern-lined trails and the remains of an old Scandinavian village. Access is by logging roads and trails. *Best feature:* fabulous white-sand beaches.

Excavated by hand for a railway line that is now closed, the spooky Othello Tunnels of **Coquihalla Canyon Provincial Park** (p234) are open to visitors and provided the backdrop for *Rambo: First Blood*. *Best feature:* the scenery is by far the best actor…

At **Rathtrevor Beach Provincial Park** (p193) the ocean slinks back almost 1km at low tide, revealing a glistening array of explorable pools teeming with starfish, sand dollars and jellyfish. *Best feature:* possibly BC's top family beach.

A compact, rustic treat on Saltspring Island, **Ruckle Provincial Park** (p219) combines a fringe of copper-trunked arbutus trees with a grassy shoreline that's ideal for sunbathing. *Best feature:* the prolific wildlife.

The wacky 30km/h rapids of **Skookumchuck Narrows Provincial Park** (p156), created by water barging though a too-narrow inlet, send water taxis surging through this natural phenomenon. *Best feature:* thrills without spills.

Bounce along an access road for 136km and you reach the utterly isolated sub-Alpine wonderland of **Spatsizi Provincial Park** (p384). Enjoy backcountry hiking through some of BC's least touched wilderness. *Best feature:* complete solitude.

The clue's in the name of **Tatshenshini-Alsek Provincial Wilderness Park** (p385): wilderness. The park forms part of the vast Unesco-recognized cross-border land of granite, glaciers and white water. *Best feature:* kayaking on the two namesake rivers.

Another huge BC Park that is almost completely undeveloped, **Tweedsmuir Provincial Park (South)** (p343) spans the coastal range of mountains and encompasses parts of the Great Bear Rainforest; not for amateurs. *Best feature:* arriving by floatplane at Turner Lake.

Valhalla Provincial Park (p282) is not unknown, but when you're separated from civilization by a huge lake, it limits your popularity. Paddle yourself silly from one backcountry campsite to another, then hike into the untouched hills. *Best feature:* hidden First Nations rock paintings.

Yukon Territorial Parks

Much of the Yukon is raw and park-like, even without official designations as such. Of the Yukon's four territorial parks (www.environmentyukon.gov.yk.ca), two are intended primarily as protected areas and are very difficult to reach – although the two below are still quite remote.

Known as Qikigtaruk to the native people who still hold it sacred, **Herschel Island Territorial Park** (p418) has an old whaling compound and stark vistas. *Best feature:* a bird-watcher's paradise.

Go snow-shoeing with a dog, Tombstone Territorial Park (p416)
ANDREW BAIN

The rugged and lonely Dempster Hwy goes right through the middle of the wild and varied sub-Arctic terrain of **Tombstone Territorial Park** (p416). Find yourself a bluff and savour the atmosphere, watching storms move across the 2200 sq km park, which teems with wildlife. *Best feature:* broad, tundra-cloaked valleys and some of the best hiking in the Yukon.

Threats & Challenges

Besides external threats from global warming, mountain pine beetles (p59) and such like, the national and provincial parks face threats from the challenges of managing such a diverse collection of huge areas, especially at a time when budgets are threatened.

Parks Canada is well funded but its infrastructure is aging rapidly; much was built in the 1960s and is in a state of disrepair. While conservative governments have cut budgets, Parks Canada estimates that it needs $100 million per year to maintain and renovate its buildings and facilities. As a consequence fees have been rising rapidly.

BC Parks suffers on a number of fronts. Its sheer size means that most of the 972 parks and protected areas are effectively left to manage themselves. There are only 200 full-time employees across the system and – rather shockingly – only 10 full-time park rangers. In most parks local contractors empty trash cans, check restrooms (if there are any), possibly collect camping fees and that's about it.

The BC Ministry of Environment is always looking for ways to bring in revenue. One scheme calls for luxury commercial lodges to be built in some of BC's most remote and unspoiled parks (although widespread public outrage has the scheme on hold). Pristine provincial parks such as Mt Assiniboine (p307) in the Rockies and Wells Gray (p340) in the Cariboo would get new luxury resorts, with guests shuttled in and out by helicopter. Other ideas floated include allowing power transmission lines to be built in some areas and some public rivers to be added to the hydroelectric system.

PROTECTING NATURE: DOS & DON'TS

When you're out and about in BC and the Yukon there is a lot you can do to both respect and protect the beautiful environment around you. Although common sense and awareness are your best guides, it's always useful to remember a few simple guidelines.

- Don't litter (this is a no-brainer, or so you would have thought…). Use the recycling bins that you'll find in hotels, parks and along the street. Carry out all of your trash from trails and parks, because most facilities are too underfunded and understaffed to make regular collections. And as a random act of goodness, if you see trash left by someone else, pick it up yourself.

- Do stay on trails: they lessen the erosion caused by human transit. This especially goes for mountain bikers. The best guides and tour companies are serious about preserving trails.

- Don't disturb animals or damage plants. Observe wildlife from a distance with binoculars.

- Don't feed the animals! Feeding the animals interferes with their natural diets. They can be susceptible to bacteria transferred by humans. Not only do they become more vulnerable to hunting and trapping, they may even stop seeking out their own natural food sources and become dependent on this human source. Every year bears have to be moved or even destroyed because they've become accustomed to a Cheetos handout and now see humans as a food source – or even as the food source.

- Do learn about wildlife and local conservation, environmental, and cultural issues before your trip and especially during your visit. Do ask questions and listen to what locals have to say. Lots of people are passionate about preserving BC and the Yukon, despite myriad threats. You'll find them and their organizations pretty much wherever you go. See p58 for more on this.

For more on traveling responsibly in BC and the Yukon, see (p23).

Vancouver & Around

Flying into Vancouver International Airport on a balmy summer's day, it's not hard to understand the 'lotus land' label that sticks to this region like a wetsuit on a surfer. Lightly rippled ocean crisscrossed with ferry boat trails, the crenulated shorelines of forest-green islands and an ever present wall of snow-frosted crags glinting like laser-whitened teeth on the horizon, give this city arguably the most spectacular setting of any in the world. If the swooping television visuals for the 2010 Winter Olympic and Paralympic Games, shared with Whistler, don't trigger a rash of immigration applications nothing will.

And while the backdrop means you're never far from great skiing, kayaking or hiking, there's much more to this city than appearances, including a kaleidoscope of distinctive neighborhoods. There's bohemian Commercial Drive; the cool shops of trendy SoMa; the lively bars of Gastown; and the colorful streets of the West End 'gayborhood'. And that's before you even get to bustling, artisan Granville Island or the seawall vistas of Stanley Park, Canada's most spectacular urban green space. In fact, considering this is Lotus Land, you'll likely be a lot busier than you thought you'd be.

HIGHLIGHTS

- Packing a picnic and hitting **Stanley Park** (p97), taking in the totem poles and sandy beaches.

- Spending an afternoon dipping into the indie stores of **SoMa** (p100) then staying for an early dinner.

- Snooping around the public market of **Granville Island** (p99) then dropping into the brewery for a tour and tasting.

- Soaking up the colorful, chatty streets of old **Chinatown** (p98) and relaxing with the turtles in the classical garden.

- Supping in the character bars of **Gastown** (p98) and toasting the statue of 'Gassy' Jack Deighton.

- Checking out the **UBC Museum of Anthropology** (p101) then wandering the leafy campus.

- Scoffing fresh fruit at the **West End Farmers Market** (p123) then finding out where else to taste-trip.

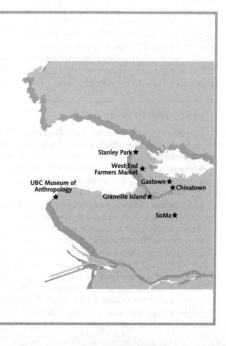

Stanley Park ★
West End ★
Farmers Market
UBC Museum of
Anthropology
★
Granville Island ★
Gastown ★
★ Chinatown
SoMa ★

VANCOUVER

HISTORY

Squamish, Musqueam and Tsleil-Waututh-weres First Nations thrived on the area's abundant animal, marine and plant life for up to 10,000 years before 18th-century Spanish, Russian and British explorers (including Captain James Cook) sailed in. Mistaking Cook's ragged crew for a boatful of transformed salmon, the Nootka Sound locals were no match for the interlopers' unexpected firepower, shattering centuries of relatively peaceful living.

Next up was Captain George Vancouver, a British navigator who had previously sailed with Cook. In 1792 he glided into the inner harbor only to discover that the Spanish, in ships under the command of captains Valdez and Galiano, had already claimed the area for themselves. Meeting at what is today Spanish Banks, the men shared navigational information before the Brit, not thinking twice about a place that would eventually carry his name, sailed away.

Burgeoning fur and lumber trades – fuelled by waves of European immigrants – soon emerged, accompanied by a gold rush that forever changed the area. By the 1850s, thousands of fortune seekers had arrived, prompting the Brits to seize the region and claim it as a colony – and prompting one talkative entrepreneur to cleverly take the economic initiative. When 'Gassy' Jack

Deighton opened his first bar on the forested shores of Burrard Inlet in 1867, he triggered a rash of development that was nicknamed 'Gastown,' from where modern day Vancouver expanded.

Not everything went well for the fledgling city. While Vancouver soon reached a population of 1000 and was linked to the rest of Canada by the Canadian Pacific Railway, it was almost completely destroyed in an 1886 blaze dubbed 'the Great Fire' (although it only lasted 20 minutes). A prompt rebuild followed and the modern-day downtown began to take shape. By 1895, Vancouver's growing population had outpaced its regional rival Victoria, the Vancouver Island–based provincial capital.

Despite BC lumber flowing across the world through Vancouver's busy port (it soon became Canada's largest), WWI and the Wall Street Crash triggered a slow and protracted depression. Prosperity only returned when WWII sparked shipbuilding and armaments manufacturing, diversifying the economy away from logging. Growing steadily throughout the 1950s and 1960s, Vancouver added a National Hockey League team and other accoutrements of a midsized North American city.

Finally reflecting on its past, Gastown – by now a slum area – was designated for heritage preservation in the 1970s. In 1986 the city hosted a highly successful Expo World's Fair, sparking a massive wave of development and adding the first of the

---

VANCOUVER IN THREE DAYS

Start your day with breakfast at the **Templeton** (p112) on Granville St, then stroll north for a visit to the **Vancouver Art Galley** (p96). Continue northwards towards the waterfront (head towards the mountains grinning at you between the buildings), then turn east along Water St to peruse **Gastown** (p98), the cobbled neighborhood from where today's city grew. Duck into the shops and eateries, take a few snaps of the Steam Clock and the 'Gassy' Jack statue and stop for lunch at the **Irish Heather** (p119). Pick-up the pace for a wander around nearby **Chinatown** (p98), then end your day in **Yaletown** (p99), where there are plenty of dining spots.

On day two, head straight to **Stanley Park** (p97). Wander along the seawall and check out the totem poles, sandy beaches and the **Vancouver Aquarium** (p98). Tuck into a picnic lunch or stroll over to **Mr Pickwick's** (p113) on Denman St for fish and chips. Nip back to your hotel for a mid-afternoon rest, then head out to **SoMa** (p100) for some indie shopping and quirky coffee bar stops. Head for a modern vegetarian dinner at the **Foundation** (p115).

On day three, overcome your slight hangover with a large coffee, some fresh air and a stroll around **Granville Island** (p99). Weave up to Broadway from here and take a B-Line express bus all the way to the **University of British Columbia** (p101), where you can stroll in the gardens, hit the **Museum of Anthropology** (p101) and peel off all your clothes at Wreck Beach.

mirrored skyscrapers that now define the downtown core. Hopes are high that the 2010 Winter Olympic and Paralympic Games, shared with Whistler, will have a similar long-term positive effect on the city. The first gold rush may be over, but the locals are ever hopeful of another one just around the corner.

ORIENTATION

Downtown Vancouver occupies a narrow peninsula bounded on three sides by Burrard Inlet, English Bay and False Creek, with Stanley Park at the northwestern tip. Key downtown attractions and neighborhoods are all easily accessible on foot and streets are laid out on an easy-to-follow grid system. Robson St and Georgia St are the main downtown east–west thoroughfares, while Granville St is the main north–south artery. Going out of town, Hwy 99 runs north over Lions Gate Bridge to West Vancouver and North Vancouver, joining with the Trans-Canada Hwy (Hwy 1). For route assistance, visit the free online Van Map (www.vancouver.ca/vanmap) system.

INFORMATION
Bookstores

Barbara-Jo's Books to Cooks (Map p94; ☎ 604-688-6755; 1740 W 2nd Ave; ☺ 9am-6pm Mon-Fri, 10am-5pm Sat & Sun) Foodie bookstore with cooking classes.

Book Warehouse (Map p88; ☎ 604-685-5711; 1051 Davie St; ☺ 10am-10pm) Local discount bookshop chain.

Pulp Fiction Books (Map p93; ☎ 604-876-4311; 2422 Main St; ☺ 11am-8pm Mon-Wed, 10am-9pm Thu-Sat, 11am-7pm Sun) Excellent secondhand selection, specializing in paperbacks.

Sophia Books (Map p88; ☎ 604-684-0484; 450 W Hastings St; ☺ 10am-7pm Mon-Fri, 10am-7pm Sat, noon-6pm Sun) Books and magazines in other languages.

Travel Bug (Map p94; ☎ 604-737-1122; 3065 W Broadway; ☺ 10am-6pm Mon-Thu & Sat, 10am-7pm Fri, noon-5pm Sun) Extensive range of travel guides, maps and accessories.

Internet Access

Georgia Post Plus (Map p88; ☎ 604-632-4226; 1358 W Georgia St; per 30min $2; ☺ 9:30am-6pm Mon-Fri, 10am-4pm Sat) Post office with computer terminals.

Star Internet Café (Map p88; ☎ 604-685-4645; 1690 Robson St; per hr $2; ☺ 24hr) Popular with online gamers and visiting ESL students.

Vancouver Public Library (Map p88; ☎ 604-331-3600; 350 W Georgia St; per 30min free; ☺ 10am-9pm Mon-Thu, 10am-6pm Fri & Sat, noon-5pm Sun) Terminals for nonmembers, plus free wi-fi (ask for an access code).

Internet Resources

Beyond Robson (www.beyondrobson.com) Savvy blog about the local scene.

Discover Vancouver (www.discovervancouver.com) General visitors' guide.

Miss 604 (www.miss604.com) Insider's blog on Vancouver.

Tourism Vancouver (www.tourismvancouver.com) Official visitor site.

Urban Diner (www.urbandiner.ca) Listings and reviews covering area restaurants.

Vancouver 2010 (www.vancouver2010.com) Official site for 2010 Winter Olympics.

Visitors Choice Vancouver (www.visitorschoice.com) Maps and an overview of attractions and accommodation.

Media

Georgia Straight (www.straight.com) Leading listings paper.

Granville Magazine (www.granvilleonline.ca) Quarterly city mag on green living.

Province (www.theprovince.com) Daily tabloid – BC's most widely read newspaper.

Tyee (www.thetyee.ca) Online Vancouver left-wing news and media alternative.

Vancouver Sun (www.vancouversun.com) Main city daily.

Westender (www.westender.com) Quirky downtown community newspaper.

Xtra! West (www.xtra.ca) Free gay and lesbian paper.

Medical Services

Shoppers Drug Mart (Map p88; ☎ 604-669-2424; 1125 Davie St; ☺ 24hr) Open-all-hours pharmacy chain.

St Paul's Hospital (Map p88; ☎ 604-682-2344; 1081 Burrard St; ☺ 24hr) Downtown accident and emergency.

Ultima Medicentre (Map p88; ☎ 604-683-8138; Bentall Centre, 1055 Dunsmuir St; ☺ 8am-5pm Mon-Fri) Walk-in clinic: appointments not necessary.

Money

ATMs abound in Vancouver with bank branches congregating around the business district bordered by Burrard, Georgia, Pender and Granville Sts.

American Express (Map p88; ☎ 604-669-2813; 666 Burrard St; ☺ 8:30am-5:30pm Mon-Fri, 10am-4pm Sat) Full-service Amex branch.

Vancouver Bullion & Currency Exchange (Map p88; ☎ 604-685-1008; 800 W Pender St; ☺ 9am-5pm Mon-Fri) This place usually has the best rates in town.

(Continued on page 95)

lonelyplanet.com

VANCOUVER & THE LOWER MAINLAND

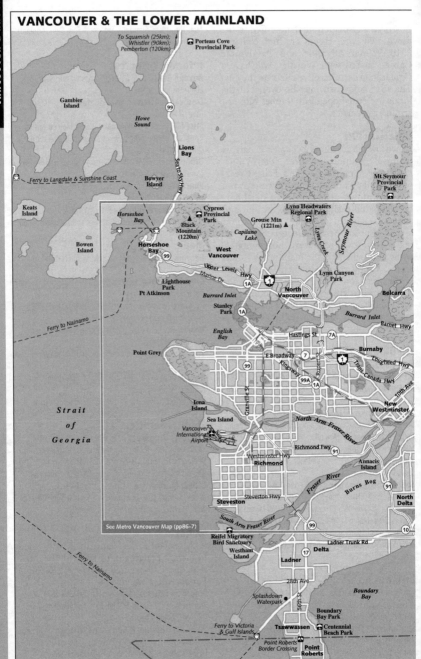

VANCOUVER & AROUND

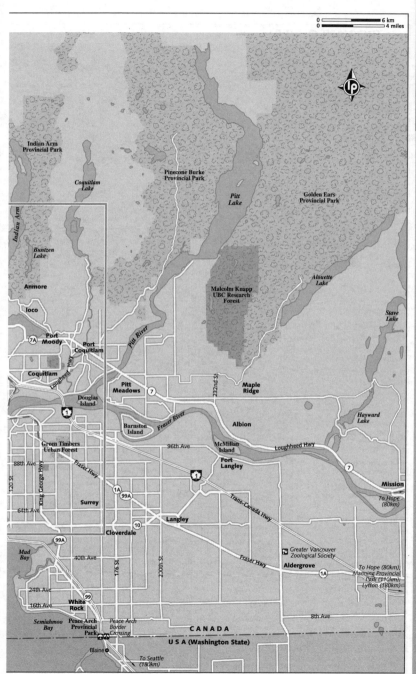

METRO VANCOUVER

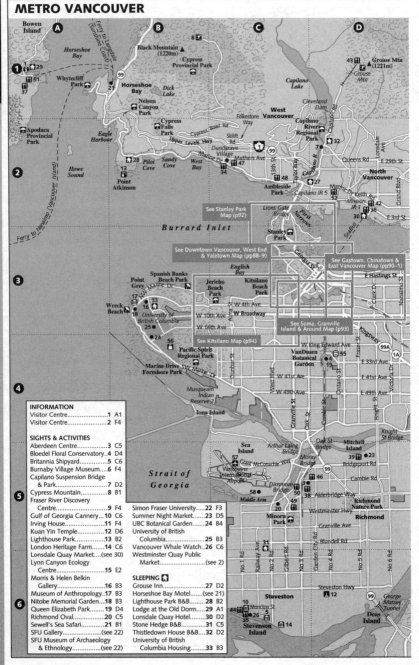

INFORMATION
Visitor Centre	1	A1
Visitor Centre	2	F4

SIGHTS & ACTIVITIES
Aberdeen Centre	3	C5
Bloedel Floral Conservatory	4	D4
Britannia Shipyard	5	C6
Burnaby Village Museum	6	F4
Capilano Suspension Bridge & Park	7	D2
Cypress Mountain	8	B1
Fraser River Discovery Centre	9	F4
Gulf of Georgia Cannery	10	C6
Irving House	11	F4
Kuan Yin Temple	12	D6
Lighthouse Park	13	B2
London Heritage Farm	14	C6
Lonsdale Quay Market	(see 30)	
Lynn Canyon Ecology Centre	15	E2
Morris & Helen Belkin Gallery	16	B3
Museum of Anthropology	17	B3
Nitobe Memorial Garden	18	B3
Queen Elizabeth Park	19	D4
Richmond Oval	20	C5
Sewell's Sea Safari	21	B1
SFU Gallery	(see 22)	
SFU Museum of Archaeology & Ethnology	(see 22)	
Simon Fraser University	22	F3
Summer Night Market	23	D5
UBC Botanical Garden	24	B4
University of British Columbia	25	B3
Vancouver Whale Watch	26	C6
Westminster Quay Public Market	(see 2)	

SLEEPING
Grouse Inn	27	D2
Horseshoe Bay Motel	(see 21)	
Lighthouse Park B&B	28	B2
Lodge at the Old Dorm	29	A1
Lonsdale Quay Hotel	30	D2
Stone Hedge B&B	31	C5
Thistledown House B&B	32	D2
University of British Columbia Housing	33	B3

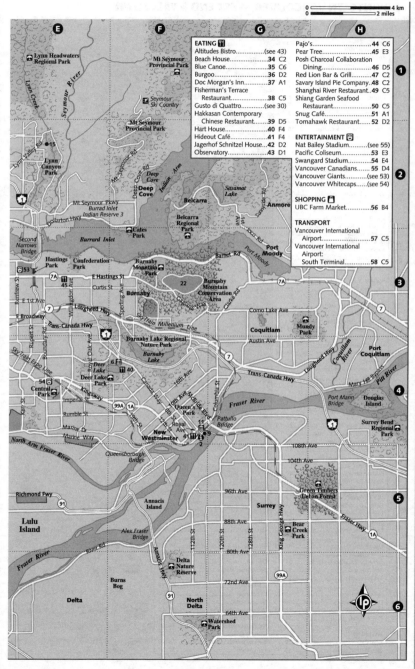

0 — 4 km
0 — 2 miles

EATING 🍴
Altitudes Bistro..............(see 43)
Beach House.....................**34** C2
Blue Canoe......................**35** C6
Burgoo..........................**36** D2
Doc Morgan's Inn...............**37** A1
Fisherman's Terrace
 Restaurant....................**38** C5
Gusto di Quattro............(see 30)
Hakkasan Contemporary
 Chinese Restaurant.........**39** D5
Hart House......................**40** F4
Hideout Café...................**41** F4
Jagerhof Schnitzel House...**42** D2
Observatory.....................**43** D1

Pajo's............................**44** C6
Pear Tree........................**45** E3
Posh Charcoal Collaboration
 Dining..........................**46** D5
Red Lion Bar & Grill..........**47** C2
Savary Island Pie Company.**48** C2
Shanghai River Restaurant..**49** C5
Shiang Garden Seafood
 Restaurant....................**50** C5
Snug Café.......................**51** A1
Tomahawk Restaurant......**52** D2

ENTERTAINMENT 🎭
Nat Bailey Stadium..........(see 55)
Pacific Coliseum...............**53** E3
Swangard Stadium............**54** E4
Vancouver Canadians........**55** D4
Vancouver Giants............(see 53)
Vancouver Whitecaps......(see 54)

SHOPPING 🛍
UBC Farm Market.............**56** B4

TRANSPORT
Vancouver International
 Airport..........................**57** C5
Vancouver International
 Airport:
 South Terminal..............**58** C5

VANCOUVER & AROUND

DOWNTOWN VANCOUVER, WEST END & YALETOWN

INFORMATION

American Express	1 E3
Australian Consulate	2 E3
Book Warehouse	3 D4
Canada Post Main Outlet	4 F4
Cannabis Culture Headquarters	5 F3
Centre	6 D3
French Consulate	7 E2
Georgia Post Plus	8 D2
German Consulate	9 F2
Howe Street Postal Outlet	10 D4
Ireland Consulate	11 F4
Little Sisters Book & Art Emporium	12 C3
Netherlands Consulate	13 E3
New Zealand Consulate	14 E3
Shoppers Drug Mart	15 D4
Sophia Books	16 F3
St Paul's Hospital	17 D4
Star Internet Café	18 C2
Tourism Vancouver Tourist Information Centre	19 F2
UK Consulate	20 E3
Ultima Medicentre	21 E3
USA Consulate	22 E2
Vancouver Bullion & Currency Exchange	23 F3
Vancouver Public Library	24 F4

SIGHTS & ACTIVITIES

Bayshore Bike Rentals	25 C2
BC Place Stadium	26 F5
BC Sports Hall of Fame & Museum	(see 26)
Bill Reid Gallery of Northwest Coast Art	27 E3
Canada Place	28 F2
Christ Church Cathedral	29 E3
Contemporary Art Gallery	30 E4
GM Place	31 G4
Port Authority Interpretive Centre	32 G2
Roedde House Museum	33 D3
Roundhouse Community Arts & Recreation Centre	34 E5
Science World at TELUS World of Science	35 G5
Spokes Bicycle Rental	36 C1
Vancouver Aquatic Centre	37 C5
Vancouver Art Gallery	38 E3
Vancouver Lookout	39 F3

SLEEPING

Buchan Hotel	40 C2
English Bay Inn	41 B2
Fairmont Hotel Vancouver	42 E3
HI Vancouver Central	43 E4
HI Vancouver Downtown	44 C4
L'Hermitage Hotel	45 E4
Listel Vancouver	46 D2
Loden Vancouver	47 E2
Moda Hotel	48 E4
Opus Hotel Vancouver	49 E5
Riviera Hotel	50 D2
Samesun Backpackers Lodge	51 E4
Shangri-La	52 E3
St Clair Hotel	53 F3
St Regis Hotel	54 F3
Sylvia Hotel	55 B2
Urban Hideaway Guesthouse	56 F3
Victorian Hotel	57 F3
YWCA Hotel	58 F4

EATING

Agro Café	59 E5
Blue Water Café	60 E5
C Restaurant	61 C5
Chambar	62 G4
Elbow Room	63 E5
Glowbal Grill & Satay Bar	64 E5
Gorilla Food	65 F3
Guu with Garlic	66 C2
Hamburger Mary's	67 C4
Japa Dog	68 E3
Joe Fortes	69 E3
La Bodega	70 D4
Le Gavroche	71 D2
Motomachi Shokudo	72 C2
Mr Pickwick's	73 C2
Nu Restaurant & Lounge	74 C5
Raincity Grill	75 B2
Samba Brazilian Steakhouse	76 E3
Templeton	77 E4

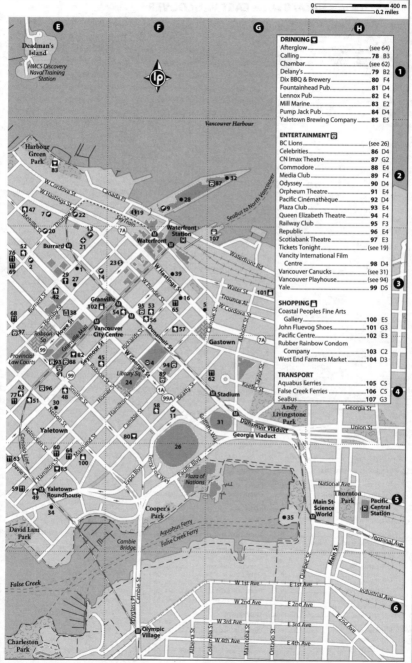

GASTOWN, CHINATOWN & EAST VANCOUVER

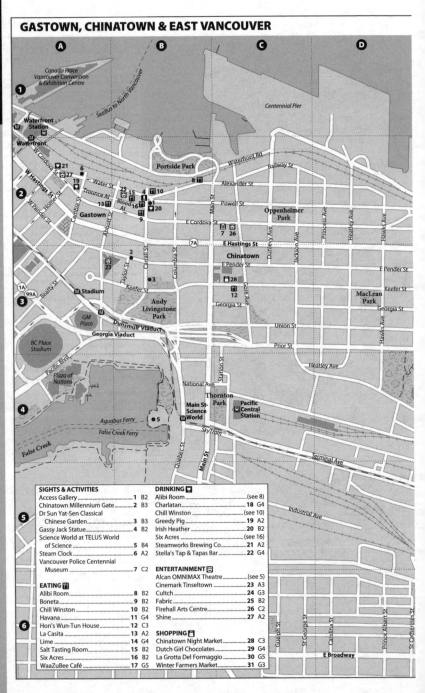

SIGHTS & ACTIVITIES	
Access Gallery	1 B2
Chinatown Millennium Gate	2 B3
Dr Sun Yat-Sen Classical Chinese Garden	3 B3
Gassy Jack Statue	4 B2
Science World at TELUS World of Science	5 B4
Steam Clock	6 A2
Vancouver Police Centennial Museum	7 C2

EATING 🍴	
Alibi Room	8 B2
Boneta	9 B2
Chill Winston	10 B2
Havana	11 G4
Hon's Wun-Tun House	12 C3
La Casita	13 A2
Lime	14 G4
Salt Tasting Room	15 B2
Six Acres	16 B2
WaaZuBee Café	17 G5

DRINKING 🍷	
Alibi Room	(see 8)
Charlatan	18 G4
Chill Winston	(see 10)
Greedy Pig	19 A2
Irish Heather	20 B2
Six Acres	(see 16)
Steamworks Brewing Co	21 A2
Stella's Tap & Tapas Bar	22 G4

ENTERTAINMENT 🎭	
Alcan OMNIMAX Theatre	(see 5)
Cinemark Tinseltown	23 A3
Cultch	24 G3
Fabric	25 B2
Firehall Arts Centre	26 C2
Shine	27 A2

SHOPPING 🛍	
Chinatown Night Market	28 C3
Dutch Girl Chocolates	29 G4
La Grotta Del Formaggio	30 G5
Winter Farmers Market	31 G3

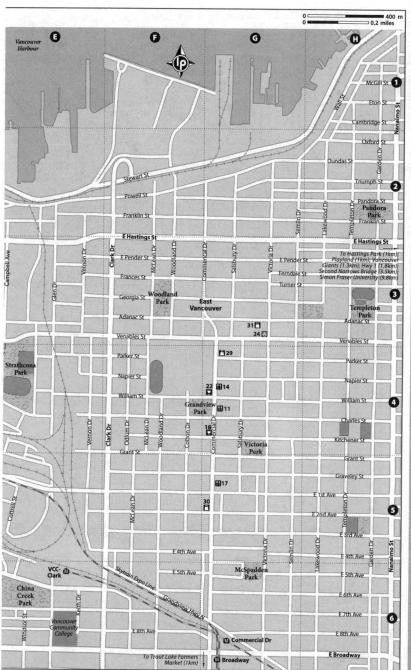

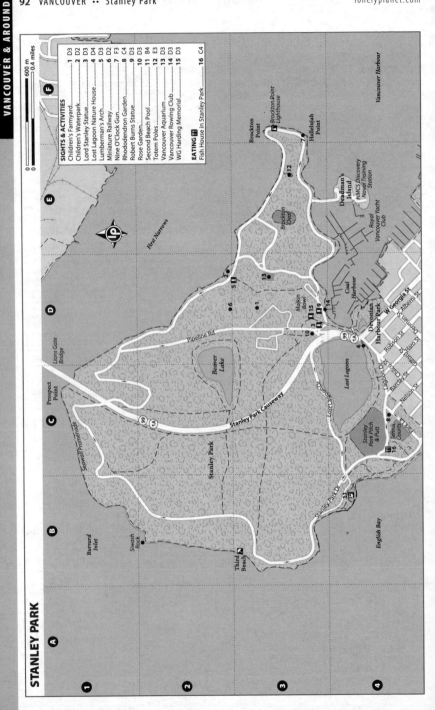

STANLEY PARK

SIGHTS & ACTIVITIES

Children's Farmyard	**1** D3
Children's Waterpark	**2** D2
Lord Stanley Statue	**3** D3
Lost Lagoon Nature House	**4** D4
Lumberman's Arch	**5** D3
Miniature Railway	**6** D2
Nine O'Clock Gun	**7** F3
Rhododendron Garden	**8** C4
Robert Burns Statue	**9** D3
Rose Garden	**10** D3
Second Beach Pool	**11** B4
Totem Poles	**12** E3
Vancouver Aquarium	**13** D3
Vancouver Rowing Club	**14** D3
WG Harding Memorial	**15** D3

EATING 🍴

Fish House in Stanley Park	**16** C4

0   600 m
0   0.4 miles

SOMA, GRANVILLE ISLAND & AROUND

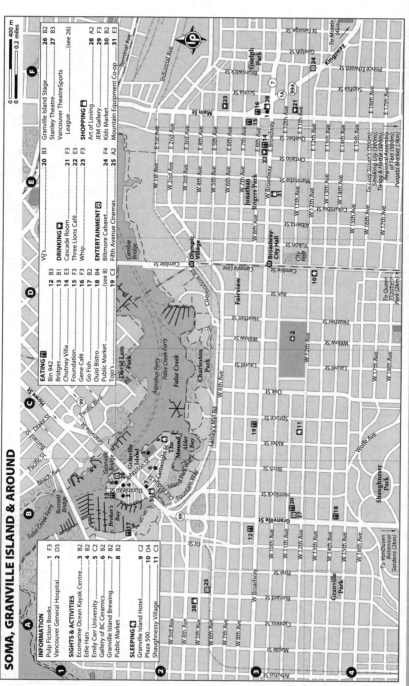

INFORMATION
Pulp Fiction Books.................1 F3
Vancouver General Hospital......2 D3

SIGHTS & ACTIVITIES
Ecomarine Ocean Kayak Centre....3 B2
Edie Hats..............................4 B2
Emily Carr University..............5 C2
Gallery of BC Ceramics...........6 B2
Granville Island Brewing.........7 B2
Public Market.......................8 B2

SLEEPING 🛏
Granville Island Hotel............9 C2
Plaza 500...........................10 D4
Shaughnessy Village.............11 C3

EATING 🍴
Bin 942.............................12 B3
Bridges.............................13 B1
Chutney Villa......................14 E3
Foundation.........................15 F3
Gene Café..........................16 F3
Go Fish.............................17 B2
Ouisi Bistro........................18 B4
Public Market.................(see 8)
Tojo's................................19 C3

Vij's.................................20 B3

DRINKING 🍷
Cascade Room.....................21 F3
Three Lions Café..................22 F3
Whip.................................23 F3

ENTERTAINMENT 🎭
Biltmore Cabaret..................24 F4
Fifth Avenue Cinemas............25 A2

Granville Island Stage...........26 B2
Stanley Theatre....................27 B3
Vancouver TheatreSports
League..........................(see 26)

SHOPPING 🛍
Art of Loving.......................28 A2
JEM Gallery.........................29 F3
Kids Market.........................30 B2
Mountain Equipment Co-op......31 E3

KITSILANO

0   0.2 miles
0   500 m

(Continued from page 83)

Post

Postal outlets are often tucked at the back of drugstores – look for the blue-and-red signs in windows.

Canada Post Main Outlet (Map p88; ☎ 604-662-5723; 349 W Georgia St; ☼ 8am-5:30pm Mon-Fri).

Georgia Post Plus (Map p88; ☎ 604-632-4226; 1358 W Georgia St; ☼ 9:30am-6pm Mon-Fri, 10am-4pm Sat).

Howe Street Postal Outlet (Map p88; ☎ 604-688-2068; 732 Davie St; 7am-8pm Mon-Fri, 8am-7pm Sat).

Tourist Information

Tourism Vancouver Tourist Information Centre (Map p88; ☎ 604-683-2000; www.tourismvancouver .com; 200 Burrard St; ☼ 8:30am-6pm Jun-Aug, 8:30am-5pm Mon-Sat Sep-May) Free maps, visitor guides, half-price theater tickets and glossy brochures covering Vancouver and BC. There are two additional branches at the airport and a small booth near the Vancouver Art Gallery entrance.

DANGERS & ANNOYANCES

Persistent street begging is an increasing issue for visitors to Vancouver: just say 'Sorry' and pass on if you're not interested and want to be polite. There is also a small, hard-core group of scam artists who trawl the streets and prey on tourists by asking for money to get home. These mostly male scammers work the downtown core every day and never seem to make it 'home'. At the time of writing, there was also an on-going issue with local gang shootouts across the region: collateral damage is rare but if you see anyone wielding a gun, get out of the area as fast as you can.

SIGHTS

Many of Vancouver's main attractions are studded around several key downtown neighborhoods, with some hot spots – Gastown, Chinatown, Stanley Park and Granville Island – drawing visitors who just like to wander and explore.

Downtown & West End

Bordered on two sides by water and on one side by the gargantuan, tree-lined Stanley Park, downtown Vancouver and beyond combines the office towers of the business district with the clapboard

---

OLYMPIC PARTY ROLLS INTO TOWN

The opening and closing ceremonies for the 2010 Winter Olympic and Paralympic Games are being staged at **BC Place Stadium** (p96) while events (which run from February 12th to 28th and March 12th to 21st) are split between Whistler (p143) and Vancouver. More than 80 countries will be represented, with over 5,500 athletes and officials taking part.

Metro Vancouver venues and events include **Cyprus Mountain** (snowboard and freestyle skiing); **Hillcrest Curling Centre** (curling); **Pacific Coliseum** (figure skating and short track speed skating); **Richmond Oval** (speed skating); plus **GM Place** and the **UBC Thunderbird Arena** (both ice hockey). Most of these were existing facilities that have received extensive makeovers, while the giant new Richmond Oval is a mammoth new-build that hopes to be the Games' best lasting legacy. Visitors who arrive after the Olympics will be able to tour or partake of activities in each of the venues.

Much of Vancouver will be in a state of fevered partying for the duration of the Games. The city – which also has an Athlete's Village on the south bank of False Creek (ask a local for the financial story behind it) – has set aside several free gathering places for those who want to feel the Olympic spirit but don't have tickets to events. The main party site is **Robson Square**, next to the **Vancouver Art Gallery** (p96), which will host athletics demonstrations and live performances. The other side of the Art Gallery (on W Georgia St) will also be a major gathering point. Additional crowd hangouts will include Yaletown's **David Lam Park**, downtown's **Larwill Park** (near the Queen Elizabeth Theatre), **Granville Island** and the **Vancouver Public Library**. There will also be a 60-day Cultural Olympiad from January 22 to March 21, with concerts and events – many of them free – staged across the city.

Accommodation in Vancouver will be extremely tight for the duration of the Games: consider the suburbs as alternatives and book ahead as soon as possible. For sleepover options and Games updates, visit the dedicated section of the Tourism Vancouver website (www.tourismvancouver .com). Information on how to buy tickets – half of which are priced under $100 – is available via the official Olympic website (www.vancouver2010.com).

residences and heritage apartment blocks of the West End. Eminently walkable, this is a pleasant area to wander around and the grid system makes it hard to lose your way – approach the generally friendly locals if your map skills let you down.

Housed in a handsome 1907 courthouse building (although rumored to be moving to a purpose-built location in the next few years) the **Vancouver Art Gallery** (Map p88; ☎ 604-662-4700; www.vanartgallery.bc.ca; 750 Hornby St; adult/youth/child $17.50/12/7, admission by donation after 5pm Tue; ☯ 10am-5:30pm Fri-Mon & Wed, 10am-9pm Tue & Thu) was once a disappointing regional venue with nothing more than a clutch of Emily Carr canvases. But the VAG has undergone a sweeping renaissance in recent years and now combines edgy contemporary exhibitions with blockbuster visiting shows. The hot ticket is FUSE (admission $17.50), an irregular late-night party with music, performance and chin-stroking arties; but hanging out on the café's patio on a sunny day can be almost as much fun.

Featured on many Vancouver postcards, the series of five white sails otherwise known as **Canada Place** (Map p88; ☎ 604-647-7390; www.canadaplace.ca; 999 Canada Place Way) was built for Expo '86. A cruise ship terminal and convention center (a further large convention center has just been added right next door, with a grass roof to enhance its green credentials). Stroll the breezy promenade on its western flank for some panoramic views of Stanley Park and the mountains, punctuated by the regular splash of floatplanes out front. Inside, you'll find the **CN IMAX Theatre** (p121) and the **Port Authority Interpretive Centre** (Map p88; ☎ 604-665-9179; free admission; ☯ 8am-5pm Mon-Fri, 10am-2pm Sat & Sun), a hands-on, kid-friendly showcase illuminating the city's maritime trade.

The city's oldest church (the first service was held on this site in 1889), pretty **Christ Church Cathedral** (Map p88; ☎ 604-682-3848; www.cathedral.vancouver.bc.ca; 690 Burrard St; admission free; ☯ 10am-4pm) is nestled incongruously among the looming glass towers. Enter through the building's northwest side entrance to check out the stained glass window designed by Edward Burne-Jones, then wander up through the outstanding cedar-ceilinged nave to check out the rest. While you're here, nip across Burrard St and enter the Royal Bank building. Take the escalator

right in front of you and you'll come to a massive carved **First Nations mural**. Almost 37m long, it's one of Canada's largest First Nations artworks.

If your interest is pricked, head to the nearby **Bill Reid Gallery of Northwest Coast Art** (Map p88; ☎ 604-682-3455; www.billreidgallery.ca; 639 Hornby St; adult/child $10/5; ☯ 11am-5pm Wed-Sun), Vancouver's newest public art space. Showcasing the carvings, paintings and jewelry of Canada's most revered Haida artist, the gallery is stuffed with artifacts and contextualizing touch screen computers. Head to the Great Hall and take an elevator to the mezzanine level: you'll be face-to-face with a breathtaking 8.5m-long bronze of intertwined magical creatures. For more on Reid, see p374.

Stage for the opening and closing ceremonies of the 2010 Winter Olympic and Paralympic Games and full-time home of the BC Lions Canadian Football League (CFL) team (p122), Teflon-topped **BC Place Stadium** (Map p88; ☎ 604-669-2300; www.bcplacestadium.com; 777 Pacific Blvd) is the city's biggest sporting venue. Fans can visit the **BC Sports Hall of Fame & Museum** (Map p88; ☎ 604-687-5520; www.bcsportshalloffame.com; Gate A; adult/child $10/8; ☯ 10am-5pm), complete with regional and national historic memorabilia plus a new Aboriginal Sport Gallery. There's also a guided behind-the-scenes **stadium tour** (☎ 604-661-7362; Gate H; adult/child $8/5; ☯ 11am & 1pm Tue mid-Jun–Aug).

Downtown's other sporting mecca – this one for hockey fans – is **GM Place** (Map p88;

SAVE YOUR DOSH: 10 FREE VANCOUVER EXPERIENCES

- Dr Sun Yat-Sen Classical Chinese Garden (p98)
- Lost Lagoon Nature House (opposite)
- Port Authority Interpretive Centre (left)
- Christ Church Cathedral (left)
- Stanley Park Totem Poles (opposite)
- Contemporary Art Gallery (p99)
- Historic Gastown Walking Tours (p106)
- Grouse Grind (p127)
- Lynn Canyon Suspension Bridge (p127)
- Vancouver Art Gallery (left; ☯ 5-9pm Tue only)

604-899-7889; www.generalmotorsplace.com; 800 Griffiths Way), aka 'The Garage'. Newer and smaller than its grubby older brother, it hosts the Vancouver Canucks of the National Hockey League (NHL) as well as standing in as the main hockey venue for the 2010 Olympics. Behind-the-scenes **tours** (604-899-7440; Gate 6, GM Place; adult/child $10/5; tours 10:30am, noon & 1:30pm Wed & Fri) take you into the hospitality suites and the nosebleed press box, high up in the rafters.

If it's hard to remember that Vancouver was a pioneering new town nestled among virgin rainforest less than 150 years ago, take a trip down memory lane at the smashing 1893 **Roedde House Museum** (Map p88; 604-684-7040; www.roeddehouse.org; 1415 Barclay St; admission $5; 1-4pm Tue-Fri, noon-5pm Sat, 2-4pm Sun), which brings to life the colonial era. Designed by Francis Rattenbury (his Empress Hotel building in Victoria is somewhat larger), this is the city's only house museum and its rooms have been meticulously recreated. Visitors should also peruse the surrounding houses of Barclay Heritage Square, rescued from demolition and now run by volunteers; Sunday entry, including tea and cookies, costs $1 extra.

It's well worth spending an afternoon wandering the West End streets from here, but make sure you end up at **English Bay** (Map p88; cnr Denman & Davie Sts), especially if sunset is just around the corner. The sandy beach here is one of the city's most popular and the Stanley Park seawall is right next door if you fancy a breathtaking evening stroll among the trees – bring your camera.

If you need to get the lay of the land anytime during your stay, stump up the slightly pricey entry fee and take the glass-sided elevator to the recently refurbished **Vancouver Lookout** (Map p88; 604-689-0421; www.vancouverlookout.com; 555 W Hastings St; adult/youth/child $13/9/6; 8:30am-10:30pm May–mid-Oct, 9am-9pm mid-Oct–Apr) observation deck. Tickets for the panoramic vistas are valid all day, so you can get your money's worth by returning for a nighttime viewing of the twinkling cityscape.

Stanley Park

One of North America's largest urban park spaces, the 4 sq km **Stanley Park** (Map p92) was opened as a public recreation space in 1888, after being the home of a First Nations settlement and, later, a military reserve. Don't miss a jog, stroll or cycle (rentals near the W Georgia St entrance) around the 9km seawall, with its dramatic sea-to-sky vistas and smattering of sandy beaches. Bring a picnic and drop by **Lumberman's Arch** to watch the cruise ships slide by or stop at **Third Beach**, where you can perch on a log and catch one of the city's most spectacular sunsets.

The **Rose Garden** and **Rhododendron Garden** will satisfy flora lovers, but green fans should also drop by the **Lost Lagoon Nature House** (604-257-8544; www.stanleyparkecology.ca; admission free; 10am-7pm Tue-Sun May-Sep) to learn about the region's ecology from the friendly volunteers. The lagoon out front is an amazing close-to-the-city wildlife enclave where you can expect to see beady-eyed blue herons and, at night, some snuffling racoons.

It's a 0.5km walk from here to Brockton Point and the park's most photographed attraction, a series of eight brightly colored **totem poles**; you'll be jostling with the tour groups if you're here in summer. Three beautifully carved Coast Salish welcome portals were recently added to the site in recognition of their traditional ownership of the territory. They're also a reminder that totem poles were not part of the culture of the First Nations who originally called the Vancouver area home: the eight poles here were carved by groups from other BC regions. For more details on totem poles, see p43.

The park is also dotted with statues and memorials, many of them hidden in the trees. Not far from the W Georgia St entrance, check out the **statue of Lord Stanley**, the man who gave his name to both the park and the NHL hockey trophy. Close by is an even larger **Robert Burns statue**, while near the Malkin Bowl outdoor theater you'll find a near-forgotten **memorial to WG Harding**, marking the first official visit by a US president to Canada. It's a memorial because he died a week later in San Francisco.

If you don't fancy walking all the way around the park, stroll the shorter seawall loop from here around Brockton Point and then cut back though the interior at Lumberman's Arch. Alternatively, a free shuttle bus operates around the perimeter from mid-June to mid-September. And don't worry if you didn't bring a picnic: there are four restaurants here.

If you're traveling with kids, the waterfront **Second Beach pool** (☎ 604-257-8370; adult/youth/child; $5.15/3.60/2.60; ☼ May-Sep) is a magnet for families. Arrive early on peak summer days, when it gets very busy. You can dry the sprogs off on the nearby **Miniature Railway** (☎ 604-257-8531; adult/youth/child $6/4.25/3; ☼ 10:30am-5pm mid-May–Aug, 10:30am-5pm Sat & Sun Feb–mid-May & Sep) or at the adjoining **Children's Farmyard**(☎ 604-257-8531; adult/youth/child $6/4.25/3; ☼ 11am-4pm mid-May–Aug, 11am-4pm Sep & mid-Mar–Jun) where petting the rabbits is a favorite pastime.

Popular with both kids and adults, Stanley Park's biggest draw is the **Vancouver Aquarium** (☎ 604-659-3474; www.vanaqua.org; adult /youth/child $19.95/14.95/11.95; ☼ 9:30am-5pm, 9:30am-7pm Jul & Aug), home to 70,000 sea creatures and other critters, including sharks, dolphins and a clutch of beluga whales. Look out for the mesmerizing iridescent jellyfish tanks and the sea otters that dine the way everyone should: lying on their backs using their chests as plates (try it in the bath when you get back to your hotel). Consider a behind-the-scenes trainer tour (from adult/child $25/15).

Gastown & Chinatown

Despite the inauspicious name, Gastown is where Vancouver began after 'Gassy' Jack Deighton, an English sailor, forsook the sea in 1867 to open a bar servicing the region's developing lumber mills. When a village sprang up around his establishment, the area became known as Gassy's Town. Look out for the jocular bronze **statue of 'Gassy' Jack** perched atop a whiskey barrel in Maple Tree Sq, the juncture of Carrall and Water Sts.

Jack would no doubt be pleased to know that Gastown has become Vancouver's best bar district in recent years and is now lined with characterful watering holes. During the day, it's also worth checking out the streets radiating from Maple Tree Sq to discover the plethora of cool indie stores and artist-run galleries. Among the best and just across from Jack is **Access Gallery** (Map p90; ☎ 604-689-2907; www.vaarc.ca; 206 Carrall St; ☼ noon-5pm Tue-Sat), which focuses on emerging artists, some local and all from Canada. The gallery is divided into two spaces and occupies one of the area's oldest buildings – check the ancient tin plate ceiling beneath the artsy whitewash.

Water St is Gastown's main tourist drag, which explains the surfeit of giant souvenir shops along its length. You can join the throng taking photos around the noisy **steam clock** (Map p90), a snapshot favorite that's actually powered by electricity. Alternatively, if you're feeling brave, head a couple of blocks south to E Hastings St where you'll find yourself in the heart of the grungy **Downtown Eastside**. The area's history of drugs and prostitution made this a no-go skid row for many years but gentrification is rolling in, especially with the opening of the new Woodwards housing, retail and university campus development. Stroll the area (stay on the main streets) to check out some of the city's best old-school buildings and heritage neon signage.

The adjoining Chinatown – one of North America's largest – is among Vancouver's most enticing areas. A sensory explosion of sights, sounds and aromas, it's a richly historic neighborhood. Look above shop level and you'll see the paint-peeled evidence of decades of history, along with the occasional year marker showing the true age of many of the buildings.

While younger Chinese have mostly moved out to Richmond (p132), this bustling area is still teeming with shops hawking exotic fruits, ancient remedies and the occasional bucket of live frogs. Don't miss the lively summer night market or the huge **Chinatown Millennium Gate** (Map p90; cnr W Pender & Taylor Sts), the area's towering entry point.

A tranquil break from clamorous Chinatown, the **Dr Sun Yat-Sen Classical Chinese Garden** (Map p90; ☎ 604-662-3207; www.vancouver chinesegarden.com; 578 Carrall St; adult/child $10/8; ☼ 10am-6pm May–mid-Jun & Sep, 9:30am-7pm mid-Jun–Aug, 10am-4:30pm Oct-Apr) reveals the Taoist symbolism behind the placing of gnarled pine trees, winding covered pathways and ancient limestone formations. Entry includes a fascinating guided tour – check out the lazy turtles bobbing in the pond – and concerts are held here on Friday evenings in summertime. There's a less impressive but free-entry garden immediately next door.

Housed in the city's former coroner's court and right next door to the main police station, the **Vancouver Police Centennial Museum** (Map p90; ☎ 604-665-3346; www.vancouver policemuseum.ca; 240 E Cordova St; adult/child $7/5; ☼ 9am-5pm Mon-Sat) is one of the region's best historic attractions. Charting the city's murky criminal past – complete with confiscated weapons, counterfeit currencies and a mortuary exhibit displaying slices of human tissue, it's a fascinating place to spend an hour or two. If you have time, its gripping summertime **Sins of the City walking tour** ($15) leads curious visitors around the area, exploring some eye-popping vice and crime fighting history along the way.

Rivalling the aquarium as the best place to take kids on a rainy day, **Science World at TELUS World of Science** (Map p89; ☎ 604-443-7440; www.scienceworld.ca; 1455 Quebec St; adult/youth/child $17.75/14.50/12.25; ☺ 10am-5pm Mon-Fri, 10am-6pm Sat & Sun) occupies the giant silver geodesic 'Golf Ball' that was built for Expo '86. It's a high-tech playground of interactive exhibits and live presentations on nature, space, physics and technology, and there's enough to keep parents occupied too. The **Alcan OMNIMAX Theatre** (tickets adult/child $11.25/9) here shows large-screen documentary movies.

Yaletown

A preserved brick-lined warehouse district transformed into chichi apartments, swanky lounge bars and bling-bling boutiques, pedestrian-friendly Yaletown is where the city's beautiful people come to be seen – especially at night when its restaurants are often packed with trendsetters and visiting celebs.

Roughly bordered by Nelson St, Homer St, Drake St and Pacific St, the area has not completely abandoned its industrial past: old railway tracks remain embedded in the roads and the **Roundhouse Community Arts & Recreation Centre** (Map p88; ☎ 604-713-1800; www.roundhouse.ca), home of eclectic theater productions and cultural events, occupies an evocative restored Canadian Pacific Railway shed. Check out the preserved steam train in the little museum space here: it's Engine 374, the locomotive that pulled the first passenger train into Vancouver in 1887. In fact, the neighborhood's moniker comes from the interior BC town of Yale where an even older rail yard was once based.

Bring yourself up to date at the **Contemporary Art Gallery** (Map p88; ☎ 604-681-2700; www.contemporaryartgallery.ca; 555 Nelson St; free; ☺ noon-6pm Wed-Sun) with a glimpse of what local modern artists are up to. And if it feels like time for some fresh air, wander

south to **David Lam Park** (Map p88) and weave along the north False Creek waterfront trail, keeping your eyes peeled for visiting aquatic bird-life and a string of eclectic public art.

Granville Island

A formerly grungy industrial peninsula (it's not actually an island) spilling out under the ironwork arches of Granville Bridge, **Granville Island** (Map p93; ☎ 604-666-6655; www.granvilleisland.com) is best reached via a bathtub-sized ferry (p125) from the north side of False Creek – or you can just stroll in from the south side under the bridge. Redeveloped in the 1970s into a kaleidoscopic blend of restaurants, theaters and artisan businesses, it's always crowded here on summer weekends, as visitors chill out with the buskers and wrestle over their fish and chips with beady-eyed seagulls.

The focal point of most visits, the **Public Market** (Map p93; ☎ 604-666-6477; Johnston St; ☺ 9am-7pm) is like a vast multi-countered deli specializing in gourmet meat, fish, cheese and bakery treats. There's also an international food court (eat early or late to avoid the crush) and an ever-changing array of craft stands. Popular three-hour tasting tours of the market are offered by **Edible BC** (☎ 604-662-3606, 888-812-9660; www.edible-britishcolumbia.com; $65), or you can chat to regional producers at the May to October farmers market outside – with any luck, blueberries will be in season.

If you prefer liquid sustenance, tour nearby **Granville Island Brewing** (Map p93; ☎ 604-687-2739; www.gib.ca; 1441 Cartwright St; admission $9.75; ☺ tours noon, 2pm & 4pm). The guides here walk and talk you through the tiny brewery (production has mostly shifted to larger facilities) before depositing you in the taproom for some generous sampling: the Maple Cream Ale is highly recommended.

Sober up with an afternoon's browsing among the island's artisan studios and bohemian shops, including the excellent **Gallery of BC Ceramics** (Map p93; ☎ 604-669-3606; 1359 Cartwright St; ☺ 10am-5pm) where you can pick up quirky noodle cups, and at **Edie Hats** (Map p93; ☎ 604-683-4280; 1666 Johnston St; ☺ 10am-7pm Mon-Fri, 9:30am-7pm Sat & Sun), a cozy menagerie of classic and contemporary headgear. It's in the Netloft building, which is lined with tempting little stores. And if you want to rub shoulders with the artists of tomorrow before they hit the big time, drop by the free public gallery at **Emily Carr University** (Map p93; ☎ 604-844-3800; www.eciad.ca; 1399 Johnson St).

SoMa (South Main) & Commercial Drive

Formerly a working class residential heartland and then a skid row holdout, the area of Main St radiating from the intersection around Broadway and Kingsway has been colonized by boho urbanites and re-named **SoMa** in recent years. But the change is not just cosmetic: you'll find cool eateries, galleries and coffee shops on Main between 8th and 12th Aves and then you'll hit Vancouver's best **indie stores** (p122) just past the intersection with 20th. Travel even further along Main (between 48th and 51st Aves) and you'll come to the **Punjabi Market**, a busy enclave of sari stores, Bhangra music shops and the city's best value all-you-can-eat curry restaurants. Plans are afoot to install a Chinatown-style gate here in the coming years.

SoMa is not Vancouver's first bohemian neighborhood. That honor falls to **Commercial Dr**, a 10-minute car ride east from SoMa along Broadway (busy buses also ply this route). Here decades of European immigrants created a United Nations of restaurants, coffee bars and exotic delis. This is the best spot in town to watch international soccer games among the city's most passionate fans, and it's also a promenade of espresso-supping patio dwellers on languid summer afternoons when it becomes the city's alternative hangout – a kind of anti-Robson St – for young bohemians and student-types. Give yourself an afternoon to amble along the Drive – its funky heart lies between the Commercial Dr SkyTrain station and Venables St to the north – then stick around for dinner and a few beers.

Kitsilano

Vancouver's original hippy haven has come a long way since all the flower children used to hang here in their parent's basements listening to Mungo Jerry and smoking naughty cigarettes. The counterculture rebels who stayed behind now own some of the city's most expensive heritage properties. Check out the pleasant streets of cozy coffee bars and highly browsable shops, mostly centered on the parallel thorough-

fares of W 4th Ave and W Broadway. This area is recommended for a lazy afternoon stroll and, if it's hot, you can decamp to **Jericho Beach** or **Kitsilano Beach Park** (Map p94), two of the city's best outdoor hangouts.

The closest part of Kitsilano to downtown is **Vanier Park** (Map p94), a short seawall stroll westwards from Granville Island (look out for the plaque along the route marking the launch point of the first Greenpeace protest vessel). The grassy, breeze-licked park hosts the stripy tents of the annual **Bard on the Beach Shakespeare festival** (p106) and is also home to a nest of family-friendly Vancouver museums.

Housed in a modernist building shaped like a Coast Salish hat, **Vancouver Museum** (Map p94; ☎ 604-736-4431; www.vanmuseum.bc.ca; 1100 Chestnut St; adult/child $11/7; ☺ 10am-5pm Tue-Sun, 10am-7pm Thu Jul & Aug, closed Mon Sep-Jun) has rededicated itself in recent years to illuminating the city's cultural landscape. That means a roster of temporary exhibitions on topics like Stanley Park's social history and the Vancouver school of architecture, while continuing to showcase the city's timeline, pop culture past and First Nations heritage.

The adjacent **HR MacMillan Space Centre** (Map p94; ☎ 604-738-7827; www.hrmacmillanspace centre.com; 1100 Chestnut St; adult/child $15/10.75; ☺ 10am-5pm Tue-Sun) is popular with school groups, who always hit the hands-on exhibits with maximum force. There's an additional free-entry stand-alone **observatory** (open weekends, weather permitting) and a **planetarium** that runs weekend laser shows (tickets $10.75) featuring the music of bands such as Pink Floyd.

The final member of the triumvirate, the **Vancouver Maritime Museum** (Map p94; ☎ 604-257-8300; www.vancouvermaritimemuseum.com; 1905 Ogden Ave; adult/child $10/7.50; ☺ 10am-5pm mid-May–Aug, 10am-5pm Tue-Sat, noon-5pm Sun Sep–mid-May) combines dozens of intricate model ships with a mini-fleet of historic vessels. There are plenty of kid-friendly exhibits here, along with the St Roch, an arctic patrol vessel that was the first to navigate the Northwest Passage in both directions, and the Ben Franklin, a NASA research submarine used for a record-breaking 30-day dive in 1969. Rumors abound that the museum's collection may be moved to a proposed new maritime center in North Vancouver in coming years.

University of British Columbia

Further west of Kits on a forested peninsula that's about the same size as Stanley Park, **UBC** (Map p86; ☎ 604-822-2211; www.ubc .ca) is the province's largest university. The concrete campus is surrounded by the University Endowment Lands, with its accessible beach and forest wilderness, and it's also home to some surprisingly good visitor attractions. If you want company, consider a free **UBC Campus Tour** (☎ 604-822-8687; www .ceremonies.ubc.ca/tours; admission free; ☺ tours 10am & 1pm Mon-Fri mid-May–mid-Aug).

Most of the main attractions are within walking distance of the East Mall thoroughfare. Stroll north from the Student Union Building (a handy spot to grab a coffee and a copy of the *Ubyssey* student newspaper) and follow the signs to the **Museum of Anthropology** (Map p86; ☎ 604-822-3825; www.moa .ubc.ca; 6393 NW Marine Dr; adult/child $12/10, admission after 5pm Tue $6; ☺ 10am-5pm Wed-Mon, 10am-9pm Tue), housing one of Canada's best displays of northwest coast aboriginal heritage. Recently doubled in size after a multimillion dollar renovation, the signature totem poles overlooking a stunning cliff-top promontory remain, but much more of the vast collection – especially its non-First Nations artifacts – is now on display: check out the spectacular Cantonese opera costumes housed in pull-out drawers.

It's a short stroll from here to the **Morris and Helen Belkin Gallery** (Map p86; ☎ 604-822-2759; www.belkin.ubc.ca; 1825 Main Mall; admission free; ☺ 10am-5pm Tue-Fri, noon-5pm Sat & Sun) on nearby Main Mall. Above its entrance is a large billboard picture of Baghdad and the slogan: *Because there was and there wasn't a city of Baghdad.* Inside, it's no less provocative with regularly changing and sometimes quite challenging contemporary artworks.

You can cool your fevered brow at the nearby **Nitobe Memorial Garden** (Map p86; ☎ 604-822-6038; www.nitobe.org; 1895 Lower Mall; adult/youth/child $6/2/free; ☺ 10am-6pm mid-Mar–mid-Oct, 10am-2.30pm Mon-Fri mid-Oct–mid-Mar), a perfect example of Japanese symbolic horticultural beliefs. Aside from the summer bus tours, it's a tranquil retreat, ideal for quiet meditation.

If your green thumb is still itching, head to the **UBC Botanical Garden** (Map p86; ☎ 604-822-9666; www.ubcbotanicalgarden.org; 6804 SW Marine Dr; adult/youth/child $8/6/free; ☺ 10am-6pm mid-Mar–mid-Oct, 10am-3pm mid-Oct–mid-Mar), an internationally renowned complex of themed gardens. You'll find a giant collection of rhododendrons, an apothecary garden and a winter garden of off-season blooms. The new 308m kid-friendly **Greenheart Canopy Walkway** (☎ 604-822-9666, 888-755-3227; www.green heartcanopywalkway.com; adult/youth/child $20/14/6; ☺ 9am-5pm) was recently installed and lifts you up to 17m above the forest floor on a guided eco tour. Walkway tickets include Botanical Garden entry.

Naturists find a comfortable though often busy haven at UBC's **Wreck Beach** (Map p86; www.wreckbeach.org), where a dedicated community of counterculture locals, independent vendors and in-the-know visitors share the sand. Follow Trail 6 into the woods then head down the steep steps to the water. The regulars here are in a continuing battle with the university over the building of nearby residential towers that threaten to compromise their privacy, so be sure to offer your support while you peel off your threads.

West Side

Accessed via its main entrance at Cambie St and W 33rd Ave (bus 15 stops right outside and there's a parking lot just inside), **Queen Elizabeth Park** (Map p86) is Vancouver's second main green space. It's quite different to the older and much larger Stanley Park. Originally conceived as a beautification project to cover an ugly quarry site, there's a pair of immaculately coiffured landscaped areas suffused with flowers and exotic shrubs plus some of the best hilltop views you'll ever experience of mountain-backed Metro Vancouver. There's also a vista-hugging restaurant here if you suddenly get hungry.

Tear yourself away from the views (after taking plenty of snapshots) and duck inside the opaque triodetic dome of the **Bloedel Floral Conservatory** (Map p86; ☎ 604-257-8584; www.vancouverparks.ca; adult/youth/child $4.80/3.35/2.40; ☺ 9am-8pm Mon-Fri, 10am-9pm Sat & Sun May-Aug, 10am-5pm Sep-Apr), where 500 plant varieties and more than 100 tropical birds (including Charlie, the chatty cockatoo) populate three walk-through, climate-controlled environments. Back outside, climb the steps to your right and you'll come to a large synchronized fountain display plus an imposing Henry Moore bronze that has a twin in London's Kew Gardens.

Two blocks west of the park is **VanDusen Botanical Garden** (Map p86; ☎ 604-878-9274; www .vandusengarden.org; 5251 Oak St; adult/youth/child $8.85/6.50/4.70; ☻ 10am-5pm Mar & Oct, 10am-6pm Apr, 10am-8pm May, 9am-9pm Jun-Aug, 10am-7pm Sep, 10am-4pm Nov-Feb), a highly ornamental confection of sculptures, Canadian heritage flowers, rare plants from around the world and a popular Elizabethan hedge maze. The gardens are one of Vancouver's top Christmastime destinations, complete with thousands of twinkling fairy lights.

ACTIVITIES

Vancouverites are an outdoorsy bunch, but you don't have to be a Lycra-clad yogurt quaffer (unless you're from Kits) in order to partake of a few muscle-busting activities while you're here. It's a city where you can ski in the morning and stroll the beach in the afternoon (although it would make for a tiring day out); armchair-avoiders can also hit bike routes, hike the seawall or forest trails, or kayak to their heart's content. And if you're a powder nut, you're just a short hop from North Vancouver (p127) and West Vancouver (p129) for some excellent skiing, snowboarding and snow-shoeing action.

Cycling

The city's most popular biking trail – also favored by joggers and bladers – is the 9km Stanley Park seawall (p97), which uses dual, one-way-only lanes to avoid messy collisions between those on wheels and those on foot. The sea-to-sky vistas are breathtaking, but the exposed route can be hit with crashing waves and icy winds in winter, while large summertime crowds can also lessen the fun: arrive early or late to avoid the crush.

After circling the park to English Bay, bikers with energy to spare can continue along the north side of False Creek towards Science World, where the route heads up the south side of False Creek to Granville Island, Vanier Park, Kitsilano Beach and, finally, UBC. This extended route, including Stanley Park, is around 25km.

Additional options include the forested trails at UBC and the beachfront stretch between Jericho Beach and Spanish Banks: combine the two by hitting the challenging uphill trails from Spanish Banks to the

UBC campus if you really want to bust your calves.

You can rent bikes (and blades) at:

Bayshore Bike Rentals (Map p88; ☎ 604-688-2453; www.bayshorebikerentals.ca; 745 Denman St; rental per hr/8hr from $6/22.80; ☻ 9am-9pm May-Aug, 9am-dusk Sep-Apr) Not far from Stanley Park's main entrance.

Reckless Bike Stores (☎ 604-731-2420; www.rektek .com; 1810 Fir St; rental half-/full day from $25/32.50; ☻ 9am-7pm Mon-Sat, 10am-6pm Sun May-Aug, 10am-dusk Sep-Apr) Near Granville Island entrance; bikes only.

Spokes Bicycle Rental (Map p88; ☎ 604-688-5141; www.spokesbicyclerentals.com; 1798 W Georgia St; rental per hr/6hr from $9.50/28; ☻ 9am-7pm May-Aug, 10am-dusk Sep-Apr) Close to Stanley Park's main entrance.

Hiking & Running

For arm-swinging strolls or heart-pounding runs, the Stanley Park seawall is mostly flat – apart from a couple of uphills where you might want to hang on to a passing bike. There are additional forested trails in the park, including the 2km trek around Lost Lagoon. The south side of False Creek has recently been upgraded and you can create an 8km waterfront loop from the north side and then back over the Burrard Bridge. If that's not punishing enough, head to North Vancouver's ultra-steep Grouse Grind (p127), which will have you screaming for mercy within 30 minutes.

Kayaking & Windsurfing

It's hard to beat the joy of an early evening paddle around the coastline here, with the sun sliding languidly down the mirrored glass towers that forest the city like modern-day totem poles. With its calm waters, Vancouver is a popular spot for both veteran and novice kayakers.

Headquartered on Granville Island, **Ecomarine Ocean Kayak Centre** (Map p93; ☎ 604-689-7575, 888-425-2925; www.ecomarine.com; 1668 Duranleau St; rental 2hr/day $36/69; ☻ 10am-6pm Jan-May, 9am-6pm Sun-Thu, 9am-9pm Fri & Sat Jun-Aug, 10am-6pm Sep-Dec) rents equipment (Tuesday is two-for-one day) and also offers guided tours (from $59). From its **Jericho Beach branch** (Map p94; ☎ 604-222-3565; Jericho Sailing Centre, 1500 Discovery St, Kitsilano; ☻ 9am-dusk May-Aug, 9am-dusk Sat & Sun Sep), it organizes events and seminars where you can meet with local paddlers.

Also at Jericho Beach (there's a clubhouse here where you can hangout with all the other salty dogs), **Windsure Adventure Waterports** (Map p94; ☎ 604-224-0615; www.windsure.com; Jericho Sailing Centre, 1300 Discovery St, Kitsilano; surfboards/skimboards per hr $18.58/4.64; ⏲ 9am-8pm Apr-Sep) specializes in kiteboarding, windsurfing and skimboarding and offers rentals as well as lessons for first-timers (from $49).

Swimming

Vancouver's main beaches – Kitsilano, Jericho and Stanley Park's Third Beach – are dripping with summertime swimmers and sunbathers, while Wreck Beach (p101) is UBC's bare-buns naturist haven.

There's an excellent (though often crowded) outdoor swimming pool near Second Beach in Stanley Park (p98), and

Kitsilano Beach has a large heated outdoor **salt waterpool** (Map p94; ☎ 604-731-0011; 2305 Cornwall Ave; adult/youth/child $5.15/3.60/2.60; ⏲ 7am-8:45pm mid-May–mid-Sep). If it's wet, the **Vancouver Aquatic Centre** (Map p88; ☎ 604-665-3424; 1050 Beach Ave; adult/youth/child $5.65/3.95/2.80; ⏲ 6:30am-9:30pm Mon-Fri, 8am-9pm Sat & Sun) has an indoor pool.

CYCLING & WALKING TOURS
Stanley Park Seawall Cycle Route

Starting at the park's **Coal Harbour entrance (1)** follow the one-way seawall bike trail towards the **HMCS Discovery Naval Training Station (2)**, which you'll pass on your right within about 10 minutes. Continue past the handsome brick building, catching site of the

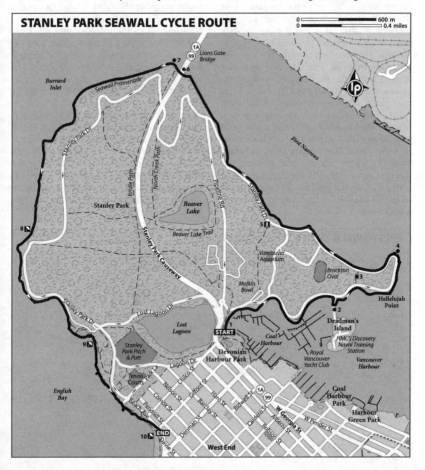

STANLEY PARK SEAWALL CYCLE ROUTE

CYCLE TOUR FACTS

Start Coal Harbour
Finish English Bay
Distance 9.5km
Duration three hours

Vancouver skyline reflected in the water, and dismount for a breather at the colorful **totem poles** (3; p97). There's an incline on the next stretch, so grit your teeth as you pass the caged Nine O'Clock Gun and the statue of athlete Harry Jerome sprinting the other way down the slope. Within a few minutes, you'll be at **Brockton Point (4)** and a little whitewashed lighthouse. Let your bike do the work now; you're on the park's best downhill stretch. Continue on towards **Lumberman's Arch (5)** – you'll have to walk here for a few meters to avoid hitting pedestrians. Hop back on towards the looming **Lions Gate Bridge (6)**. You'll be cycling under it, then getting a refreshing blast of sea air as you round **Prospect Point (7)**. From here, the route becomes nature-bound, with spectacular ocean and mountain vistas. Stop at **Third Beach (8**; p97) for a rest (and some panoramic seafront views). It's a similar sight about 1km further along at **Second Beach (9)**, where you can also glimpse the forested peninsula of Point Grey across the water. Pick up the pace for the home stretch to **English Bay (10)**, and reward yourself with a cold beer.

Gastown & Downtown Bar Trawl

WALK FACTS

Start Railway Club
Finish Alibi Room
Distance 2.5km
Duration one to three hours

Start at the **Railway Club** (**1**; p121), where getting in the door before 7pm means you won't have to pay the cover charge, then barrel downhill towards Gastown and **Steamworks Brewing Co** (**2**; p119) for a microbrew. Cross the street to **Shine nightclub** (**3**; p120) then if it's time to shake things up, wander eastwards along Water St. There are several bar and club options here, but continue on to the intersection with Carrall St. Turn right and nip into **Six Acres** (**4**; p119), a cozy nook with some good bottled beers and great shareable tasting plates. On your way out, raise an imaginary glass to the **statue of 'Gassy' Jack Deighton** (**5**; p98) in the cobbled square, then head across the street to the **Irish Heather** (**6**; p119). This is a new location for what many believe is the city's best watering hole. Stroll back to the Water St intersection and walk eastwards for 50m on Alexander St. On your left is the **Alibi Room** (**7**; p119), where you can taste-trip through up to 19 BC-brewed craft beers on tap, including plenty of rarities and lip-smacking specials.

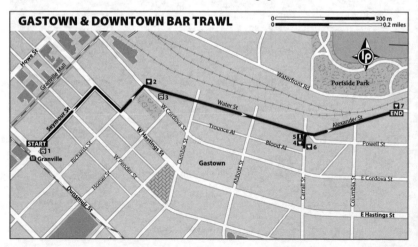

GASTOWN & DOWNTOWN BAR TRAWL

QUIRKY VANCOUVER

In *City of Glass*, an eclectic homage to his Vancouver hometown, author Douglas Coupland provides an entertaining, offbeat take on what makes this place tick. Alongside evocative, sometimes grainy photos, he explores the big questions that are part of everyday life for locals: Why are there so many grow-ops here? What's the point of doing the Grouse Grind? And why is everyone wearing fleece? A roadmap charting off-the-wall Vancouver, his entertaining tome illuminates the peculiarities bubbling just beneath the city's surface. Here's a handful of suggestions for your own off-the-beaten-path experiences – but feel free to ask the odd (not *too* odd) counterculture local for advice.

Not exactly quirky but certainly alternative, the **Downtown Eastside** is usually avoided by tourists, but if you stick to the main drag (E Hastings St) and avoid the dodgy back alleys, it's a fascinating 'other' neighborhood. Come prepared and deploy your street smarts: while muggings are rare here, it's best not to loiter, flash your pricey camera around or open your wallet on the street. You'll be rewarded with a clutch of heritage buildings (this was once Vancouver's main commercial strip) and some old-school neon signs – check out **Save-on-Meats** and **Only Sea Foods Café**. Stop for coffee at the friendly **Radio Station Café** (☎ 604-684-8494; 101 E Hastings St) on the corner of Columbia and drop into the nearby **Wanted – Lost Found Canadian** (☎ 604-633-0178; www.wantedshop.ca; 436 Columbia St) for recycled materials transformed into cool and crafty accessories. Now being gentrified, this is still Vancouver's most authentic old-school neighborhood.

You can continue east to nearby Chinatown from here or head west up Hastings to the store and offices of the BC Marijuana Party, otherwise known as **Cannabis Culture Headquarters** (Map p88; ☎ 604-682-1172; www.bcmarijuanaparty.com; 307 W Hastings St). While strong 'BC Bud' usually appears at a certain time of night at most city house parties, most visitors are still mildly shocked to smell it wafting along city streets. For arguments in support of legalisation, duck inside – but remember: you can buy a new bong here but not the demon weed itself.

For those convinced that love is the drug, head over to **Art of Loving** (Map p93; ☎ 604-742-9988; www.theartofloving.ca; 1819 W 5th Ave), a tasteful sex shop run by women. Among its popular products are the Baby Bug, Little Dolly and those all-important glow-in-the-dark condoms so you can see where you're going in that hostel dorm room. The store also stages regular classes on issues like Fearless Flirting and Nude Photography.

If your wooing methods are more old-fashioned (or you've had enough of Facebook), drop by the **Regional Assembly of Text** (off Map p93; ☎ 604-877-2247; www.assemblyoftext.com; 3934 Main St) store, and join the SoMa literati for their monthly letter-writing club (7pm, first Thursday of every month) complete with tea, cookies and stationery. This highly quirky store is brimming with Little Otsu journals, hand-printed T-shirts and painted pencil boxes, and there's usually a tiny gallery show under the stairwell.

VANCOUVER FOR CHILDREN

Family-friendly Vancouver is brimming like an over-stuffed toy box with kid-hugging things to do. Pick up a copy of the free *Kids' Guide Vancouver* flyer from the information center and visit www.findfamilyfun .com or www.kidsvancouver.com for ideas. If you're traveling without a car, hop on the SkyTrain, SeaBus or mini ferry to Granville Island: kids love 'em. For handy equipment rentals (strollers, high chairs, car seats etc.), try www.weetravel.ca.

The city's main family attractions are **Science World** (p99), the **HR MacMillan Space Centre** (p100) and the **Vancouver Aquarium** (p98). After hanging with the belugas, stay in **Stanley Park** (p97) for the day (bring a picnic) and check out the miniature railway, children's farmyard, Second Beach swimming pool and the giggle-triggering water park near Lumberman's Arch.

Rainy days can include a visit to the **BC Sports Hall of Fame** (p96) which is full of hands-on, energy-draining activities; the **CN IMAX Theatre** at Canada Place (p121); the excellent **Kidsbooks** (Map p94; ☎ 604-738-5335; www.kidsbooks.ca; 3083 W Broadway; ☒ 9:30am-6pm Mon-Thu & Sat, 9:30am-9pm Fri, 11am-6pm Sun) one of Canada's biggest children's bookstores; and Granville's Island's tempting **Kids Market**

(Map p93; ☎ 604-689-8447; www.kidsmarket.ca; 1496 Cartwright St; ☺ 10am-6pm), although you'll almost certainly have to buy them something here. If the sun comes out, head over to **Capilano Suspension Bridge** (p127) for a swaying good time.

The city's best family-friendly festivals are Vanier Park's eight-day-long **Vancouver International Children's Festival** (below) of performing arts, including theater, juggling, storytelling, music, dance and puppetry, and the **Pacific National Exhibition** (opposite), where fairground fun and farm animal shenanigans ensue.

TOURS
Boat Tours
Accent Cruises (☎ 604-688-6625; www.accentcruises .ca; departs Granville Island; ☺ May–mid-Oct; dinner cruise from $60) Popular sunset cruise with salmon buffet option.
Harbour Cruises (☎ 604-688-7246, 800-663-1500; www.boatcruises.com; departs north foot of Denman St; ☺ Apr–early-Oct; adult/youth/child from $30/25/10) View the city – and some unexpected wildlife – from the water on a 75-minute Harbour Tour. Also offers lunch and dinner cruises – try the beautiful Indian Arm excursion.

Bus Tours
Big Bus (☎ 604-299-0700, 877-299-0701; www.bigbus .ca; adult/youth/child $35/30/17) Two-day hop-on-hop-off ticket covering 20 points of interest.
Sightline Tours (☎ 604-687-6146, 866-792-8687; www.sightlinetours.com; adult/child from $66/45) Narrated higher-end tour bus operator with a Grand City Tour and three other regional excursions.
Vancouver Trolley Company (☎ 604-801-5515, 888-451-5581; www.vancouvertrolley.com; adult/youth/ child $35/32/18) Replica red trolley buses offering two-day hop-on-hop-off transport around 24 stops.

Guided Walking Tours
Architectural Institute of BC (☎ 604-683-8555 ext 333; www.aibc.ca; tour $5; ☺ 1pm Tue-Sat Jul & Aug) Six highly recommended architecture tours covering areas from Yaletown to the West End.
A Wok Around Chinatown (☎ 604-736-9508; www .awokaround.com; tour $90; ☺ 10am Fri-Mon) Culinary and history-themed four-hour trawl around old Chinatown (includes lunch and attractions).
Historic Gastown Walking Tours (☎ 604-683-5650; www.gastown.org; tours free; ☺ 2pm mid-Jun–Aug) Illuminating the history and architecture of Vancouver's birthplace. Departs from 'Gassy' Jack statue.
Orpheum Theatre (Map p88; ☎ 604-665-3050; 884 Granville St; tour adult/child $10/5; ☺ Jul & Aug)

The city's sumptuous baroque playhouse offers an entertaining but little-known 90-minute backstage tour.

FESTIVALS & EVENTS
Tourism Vancouver's website (www .tourismvancouver.com) has a roundup of major events. Also check the *Georgia Straight* for listings of smaller cultural happenings.

January
Dine Out Vancouver From mid-January, 200 city restaurants offer two weeks of three-course tasting menus for $18, $28 or $38. Check participating restaurants at Tourism Vancouver's website. Book ahead.
Chinese New Year (☎ 604-632-3808; www.vancouver -chinatown.com) In January or February, depending on the calendar, this multiday, highly festive celebration includes dancing, parades and great grub.

February
Winterruption (☎ 604-666-5784; www.winterruption .com) Granville Island's concerted attempt to chase away winter with four days of music, theater and family-friendly fun in the third week of February.

March
CelticFest Vancouver (☎ 604-683-8331; www.celtic festvancouver.com) Getting bigger every year, this four-day St Patricks's Day party includes toe-tapping live music, a street market and a big parade…plus lots of green beer.
Vancouver Playhouse International Wine Festival (☎ 604-872-6622; www.playhousewinefest.com) One of North America's oldest and largest wine festivals takes place over six days in late March. Events – including tastings and galas – often sell out months in advance so book ahead.

May
Vancouver International Children's Festival (☎ 604-708-5655; www.childrensfestival.ca) Packed with kid-friendly storytelling, performances and activities in a charming multi-tented Vanier Park venue. Mid-May.

June
Bard on the Beach (☎ 604-739-0559, 877-739-0559; www.bardonthebeach.org) The perfect way to see Shakespeare, this professional rep performs four plays per season from June in Vanier Park tents. Watch the show while the sun sets over the mountains behind the stage.
Vancouver International Jazz Festival (☎ 604-872-5200; www.coastaljazz.ca) Vancouver's biggest music fest, staged at venues around the city over 10 days from mid-June. Combining superstar performances

with plenty of free outdoor shows in Gastown and Yaletown.

Dragon Boat Festival (☎ 604-688-2382; www
.dragonboatbc.ca) An epic two-day splashathon for teams from around the world, this popular weekend event, held in the third week of June, includes live music and world food vendors.

July

Canada Day (☎ 604-775-8025; www.canadaplace.ca /canadaday) Held on July 1, from 10am to 7pm at Canada Place. Includes exhibits, food and live performances. Granville Island stages its own, smaller event.

Vancouver Folk Music Festival (☎ 604-602-9798; www.thefestival.bc.ca) A three-day Jericho Beach weekend in mid-July, with outdoor folk and world music performances. Past headliners range from Billy Bragg to Bruce Cockburn.

Celebration of Light (www.celebration-of-light.com) Giant four-day fireworks extravaganza over English Bay.

August

Pride Week (☎ 604-687-0955; www.vancouverpride.ca) From early August, this multi-day carnival of gay, lesbian and bisexual-friendly fashion shows, gala parties and concerts peaks with Vancouver's largest street parade.

MusicFest Vancouver (☎ 604-688-8441; www
.musicfestvancouver.com) Formerly Festival Vancouver, it's a two-week showcase of choral, opera, classical, jazz and world music, performed inside and outside by local and international artists. Starts early August.

Pacific National Exhibition (☎ 604-253-2311; www
.pne.bc.ca) An enduring two-week country fair with shows, music concerts and farm animals – plus a kick-ass old rollercoaster. Don't leave without downing a bag of mini doughnuts. From mid-August.

September

Vancouver International Fringe Festival (☎ 604-257-0350; www.vancouverfringe.com) Lively 11-day roster of wild and wacky theatrics at large, small and unconventional Granville Island venues. Mid-September.

Vancouver Comedy Fest (☎ 604-685-0881; www
.vancouvercomedyfest.com) Ten days of rib-tickling mirth in mid-September, with Canadian and international acts raising the roof around town.

October

Vancouver International Film Festival (☎ 604-683-3456; www.viff.org) More accessible than its starry Toronto brother, this 16-day screening of Canadian and international movies, beginning early October, is a firm local favorite. Book ahead.

Vancouver International Writers & Readers Festival (☎ 604-681-6330; www.writersfest.bc.ca) Five-day literary event in mid-October where local and international scribes turn up for seminars, galas and public forums.

November

Eastside Culture Crawl (www.eastsideculturecrawl.com) Dozens of eclectic artists from Vancouver's Eastside open their studios to visitors for this three-day, late-November event.

December

Santa Claus Parade (www.rogerssantaclausparade.com) Vancouver's other main parade is a recent addition but has quickly become a popular early December treat. Wrap up, watch the colorful floats and wait until the big guy shows up.

SLEEPING

With over 25,000 Metro Vancouver hotel, hostel and B&B rooms, the city has plenty of options to suit all tastes and budgets. While rates peak in summer, there are great deals available in fall and early spring when the weather is often amenable and the tourist crowds mercifully reduced. Tourism Vancouver's website (www.tourismvancouver.com) lists options and packages and the province's **Hello BC** (☎ 604-663-6000, 800-663-6000; www.hellobc.com) service provides further information and bookings. Be aware that hotels often charge $10 to $20 for overnight parking.

Downtown
BUDGET

Samesun Backpackers Lodge (Map p88; ☎ 604-682-8226, 877-972-6378; www.samesun.com; 1018 Granville St; dm/r $28/69; 💻 🛜) Expect a party atmosphere at this lively hostel in the heart of the Granville St nightclub area – ask for a back room to avoid the raucous weekend street life or just head down to the on-site bar (naughtily called the Beaver) and join the throng. The dorms are comfortably small and there's a large kitchen for your mystery meat 'n' pasta dishes. There's a strong line-up of social events here, so make sure you check the roster daily. The wi-fi is only in communal areas.

HI Vancouver Central (Map p88; ☎ 604-685-5335, 888-203-8333; www.hihostels.ca/vancouvercentral; 1025 Granville St; dm/r from $31.50/80; ❎ 💻 🛜) Across from the Samesun (they both have the same Granville St noise issues, so snag a back room) this warren-like hostel is calmer than its party-loving rival. Enjoying some of the benefits of its past incarnation as a hotel (air-conditioning, small dorms with sinks and natty yellow decor), there are dozens of individual rooms for privacy fans – some with en suites. Continental breakfast is included (kitchen facilities are limited to microwaves here) and there's a brimming roster of social activities.

ourpick **St Clair Hotel** (Map p88; ☎ 604-684-3713, 800-982-0220; www.stclairvancouver.com; 577 Richards St; r $49-84; 🖳 🛜) This quiet and well-located combination hostel and budget hotel is a real find, so don't be put off by the grubby-looking ground floor staircase that leads up to it. Climb the stairs and you'll find a surprisingly large, nautical-themed interior that feels like being below deck in a long, narrow boat. Each of the three floors has an array of slightly shabby but clean private rooms, all with sinks, and ranging from doubles to quads (some with bunks). There

are books, shower facilities and a computer ($1 per 30 mins) on each level, plus small kitchens with microwaves and fridges – there are several cheap eateries nearby so you won't starve. And if you're wondering about the maritime theme: the property was built in 1911 for travelers taking ships to and from Asia.

MIDRANGE

ourpick **Urban Hideaway Guesthouse** (Map p88; ☎ 604-694-0600; www.urban-hideaway.com; 581 Richards St; d/tw/ste $109/129/149; 🖳) The dictionary definition of a guesthouse, this supremely cozy (but fiendishly well-hidden) home-away-from-home is a good value word-of-mouth favorite. After a warm welcome from your friendly hosts – wilderness tour guides and experts in what makes a good place to stay – you can tuck yourself into one of the seven comfy rooms (the loft is our favorite) or spend your time in the

---

GAY & LESBIAN VANCOUVER

Vancouver's gay scene is part of the city's mainstream, rather than a sub-culture of it. In fact, the legalization of same-sex marriage in Canada has made this the number one destination in the country for gay travelers looking to tie the knot overseas.

Long centered on the West End's **Davie Street Village** – complete with its rainbow street flags, pink-painted bus shelters and hand-holding locals – Western Canada's largest 'gayborhood' is a colorful enclave of GLBT-friendly businesses. Pick up a free copy of *Xtra! West* here for a crash-course on the scene, and check www.gayvancouver.net and www.superdyke.com for listings and resources.

Among the Davie St stores and coffee shops, **Little Sisters Book & Art Emporium** (Map p88; ☎ 604-669-1753; 1238 Davie St; h10am-11pm) has a giant selection of specialist literature, an active bulletin board and a hyper-knowledgeable staff – it's a good stop for first-time visitors. Check the online directory of the **Gay & Lesbian Business Association of BC** (www.glba.org) for other listings or pick-up their free glossy *Business Directory* before heading down to Denman St to read it at **Delany's** (Map p88; ☎ 604-662-3344; 1105 Denman St), a laid-back neighborhood coffee bar that's a popular hangout for local scenesters.

If you arrive early enough to find a seat, this is a good spot to catch the mammoth **Pride Week** (p107) parade, staged every August – although you might have to stand on your chair for a better view. Along with this family-friendly street fiesta, there are dozens of pre- and post-parade events covering all kinds of interests and desires.

Among the city's most popular gay-friendly nightlife options are the **Pump Jack Pub** (Map p88; ☎ 604-685-3417; 1167 Davie St) and the **Fountainhead Pub** (Map p88; ☎ 604-687-2222; 1025 Davie St). Club-wise, check out the **Odyssey** (Map p88; ☎ 604-689-5256; 1251 Howe St), which combines regular drag nights with ever-changing special events, and **Celebrities** (Map p88; ☎ 604-681-6180; 1022 Davie St), an equally pumping venue; Saturday is the hot night here. At time of research, Odyssey was considering a move to Denman St, so check ahead before slipping into your dancing gear.

For support of all kinds, the **Centre** (Map p88; ☎ 604-684-5307; www.lgtbcentrevancouver.com; 1170 Bute St) provides discussion groups, a health clinic and legal advice. These friendly folk also staff the **Prideline** (☎ 604-684-6869; ☉ 7-10pm daily), a telephone peer-support, information and referral service.

lounge areas downstairs. There's a free-use computer, a library of 500 DVDs to watch on the big-screen TV and a plant-lined patio with a barbeque. Laundry is also free as are the loaner bikes, or you can just hangout with house cats Pippin and Nemo. Breakfast fixings (eggs, bacon *et al*) are provided: you cook it yourself in the well-equipped kitchen. Bathrooms are mostly shared, although the loft is en suite. Best of all, when you manage to tear yourself away for the day, you're right in the center of the city.

Victorian Hotel (Map p88; ☎ 604-681-6369, 877-681-6369; www.victorianhotel.ca; 514 Homer St; s&d with shared bathroom from $129, with private bathroom from $149) Housed in a pair of renovated older properties, the high-ceilinged rooms at this Euro-style pension combine glossy hardwood floors, a sprinkling of antiques, an occasional bay window and plenty of heritage charm. Most rooms are en suite – with TVs and summer fans provided – but the best rooms are in the newer extension, complete with its marble-floored bathrooms.

Moda Hotel (Map p88; ☎ 604-683-4251, 877-683-5522; www.modahotel.ca; 900 Seymour St; d from $159; 🛜) The old Dufferin Hotel has been reinvented as this white-fronted, boutique-ish property one block from the Granville St party area (that means you should request a back room if you want to sleep). The new, mostly small rooms have contemporary flourishes without quite being designer cool: think cheap mod furnishings and bold paintwork. The bathrooms have also been given a swanky makeover, while the flat-screen TVs are handy if you can't handle another night on the town. Alternatively, pad down to the late-opening wine bar for a nightcap.

TOP END

St Regis Hotel (Map p88; ☎ 604-681-1135, 800-770-7929; www.stregishotel.com; 602 Dunsmuir St; r from $285; 🛜 🖥 🛜) Unrecognisable from its former mid-range incarnation, the completely transformed St Regis has become an art-lined boutique joint in a characterful 1913 heritage shell. The rooms (befitting its age, almost all seem to be a different size) exhibit a loungey élan, complete with leather-look wallpaper, earth-tone bedspreads, flatscreen TVs and multimedia hubs. Check out the furniture, too: it's

mostly reclaimed and refinished from the old Hotel Georgia. Rates include breakfast, a business center with free-use computers and access to the gym next door.

Loden Vancouver (Map p88; ☎ 604-669-5060, 877-225-6336; www.lodenvancouver.com; 1177 Melville St; r from $350; 🛜) One of a clutch of new high-end downtown hotels, the swanky Loden is the real designer deal – and one of the first properties in years to give Yaletown's Opus a run for its money. The 70 rooms combine retro-chic flourishes like mod sofas and chocolate brown paint-jobs with luxe accoutrements including marble-lined bathrooms with those oh-so-civilized heated floors. The attentive service (there's a car to drive you anywhere downtown) is top notch, while the glam on-site restaurant is one of the city's best hotel eateries.

Shangri-La (Map p88; ☎ 604-689-1120; www.shangri-la.com; 1128 W Georgia St; r from $505; 🛜 🖥) Currently Vancouver's top-priced hotel, the brand new Shangri-La occupies the first 15 floors of the city's tallest building. The first North American outlet of the ultra-luxe Asian Pacific hotel chain, its mood-lit rooms (some surprisingly compact and others palatially large) are lined with dark wood and artworks, with must-have extras like L'Occitane amenities, TVs embedded in bathroom mirrors and automatic blinds so you can shower behind the floor-to-ceiling windows. Service is second-to-none throughout and Market, the on-site restaurant, is a winner even among those not staying here.

Also recommended:

L'Hermitage Hotel (Map p88; ☎ 778-327-4100, 888-855-1050; www.lhermitagevancouver.com; 788 Richards St; r from $199; 🛜 🖥) Another new boutique place, the look is typically designer but there are also some handy suites with full kitchens.

Fairmont Hotel Vancouver (Map p88; ☎ 604-684-3131, 800-257-7544; www.fairmont.com/hotelvancouver; 900 W Georgia St; r from $275; 🛜 🐾 🖥) The grand dame of Vancouver hotels, combining old-school aristocratic charm with elegant modern amenities. Who needs new when you can have a classic?

West End

BUDGET

HI Vancouver Downtown (Map p88; ☎ 604-684-4565, 888-203-4302; www.hihostels.ca/vancouverdowntown; 1114 Burnaby St; dm/r $31.50/85; 🖥 🛜) It says 'downtown' in the name but this purpose-built hostel is actually in the West End, a short walk from the center of all the action. Much quieter than the HI Central (families are welcome here), the dorms are all small and rates include a continental breakfast. There's a full kitchen, free movies in the TV room, plus free regional tours with Erik, a near-legendary HI volunteer who's been introducing visitors to the city for more than 10 years. You can take his tours from any of the three Vancouver HIs.

MIDRANGE

Buchan Hotel (Map p88; ☎ 604-685-5354, 800-668-6654; www.buchanhotel.com; 1906 Haro St; r with shared bathroom $79-86, with private bathroom $119-149) The cheery, 1926-built Buchan has bags of charm and is steps from Stanley Park. Along corridors lined with old prints of yesteryear Vancouver, its cheaper rooms – many with shared bathrooms – are clean and cozy, although some have 'care-worn' furnishings. The pricier rooms are correspondingly prettier, while the east-side rooms are brighter. There's a guest lounge and the extras include storage facilities for bikes and skis as well as laundry machines.

Riviera Hotel (Map p88; ☎ 604-685-1301, 888-699-5222; www.rivieraonrobson.com; 1431 Robson St; r from $119; ☎) One of the clutch of slightly shabby but well-located apartment-style hotels crowding the corner of Robson and Broughton Sts, the best deals at this mid-sized concrete tower are the spacious one-bedroom suites. Complete with full kitchens (there are plenty of eateries nearby if you don't want to cook), they easily fit small families. The 1980s furnishings are nothing to write home about but some of the higher back rooms have good views. Free parking.

our pick Sylvia Hotel (Map p88; ☎ 604-681-9321; www.sylviahotel.com; 1154 Gilford St; s/d/ste from $129/189/239) Built in 1912 and named after the original owner's daughter, the beloved, ivy-covered Sylvia enjoys a prime location overlooking English Bay. Generations of guests keep coming back – many requesting the same room every year – for a dollop of old-world charm with a side order of first-name service. The lobby decor has the look of a Bavarian pension – stained glass windows and dark wood paneling – and there's a wide array of comfortable room configurations to suit every need. The best rooms are the 12 apartment suites, which include full kitchens and panoramic views. If you don't have a room with a view, decamp to the main floor lounge to nurse a beer and watch the sunset.

English Bay Inn (Map p88; ☎ 604-683-8002, 866-683-8002; www.englishbayinn.com; 1968 Comox St; d from $149) The six antique-lined rooms at this crumpety, Tudor-esque B&B near Stanley Park each have private bathrooms and two have sumptuous four-poster beds: you'll think you've been transplanted to Victoria, BC's determinedly Olde English capital. There's complementary port in the parlor, a secluded garden for hanging out with your copy of the London *Times* and a three-course breakfast – arrive early to bag the alcove in the upstairs breakfast room. A tranquil hideaway.

Listel Vancouver (Map p88; ☎ 604-684-8461, 800-663-5491; www.thelistelhotel.com; 1300 Robson St; d from $169; ☒ ▣ ☎) Vancouver's self-described 'art hotel' is a graceful cut above the other properties at this end of Robson St. Attracting a grown-up gaggle of sophisti-cates with its gallery-style art installations (check the little hidden art space just off the lobby), the mood-lit rooms are suffused with a relaxing West Coast ambience. Adding to the artsy appeal, the on-site O'Doul's resto-bar hosts nightly live jazz.

Yaletown

BUDGET

YWCA Hotel (Map p88; ☎ 604-895-5830, 800-663-1424; www.ywcahotel.com; 733 Beatty St; s/d/tr $68/82/108; ☒ ☎) This excellent near-Yaletown tower block is one of Canada's best Y's. Accommo-dating budget-watching men and women, it's a bustling place with a communal kitchen on every other floor, some shared bathrooms and rooms ranging from compact singles (they feel like college study rooms) to group-friendly larger quarters. All units are a little institutionalised, but each has a sink and refrigerator. Rates include day passes to the YMCA Fitness Centre, a 10-minute walk away. This is a good option for families – kids get a toy when they check in.

TOP END

Opus Hotel Vancouver (Map p88; ☎ 604-642-6787, 866-642-6787; www.opushotel.com; 322 Davie St; d&ste from $339; ☒ ▣ ☎) Vancouver-bound

Hollywood celebs seeking a place to be seen need look no further. The city's original designer boutique hotel has been welcoming the likes of Justin Timberlake and that bloke from REM for years. They come for the chic suites – think mod furnishings and *feng shui* bed placements – and the paparazzi-friendly bathrooms with their clear windows overlooking the streets (visiting exhibitionists take note). A model of excellent service, there's a stylish on-site bar and restaurant, as well as a small gym.

Granville Island & Kitsilano
BUDGET
HI Vancouver Jericho Beach (Map p94; ☎ 604-224-3208, 888-203-4303; www.hihostels.ca; 1515 Discovery St; dm/r $26/76; ☼ May-Sep; ⬜) BC's largest hostel looks like a Victoria hospital from the outside and it's in a great location – but only if you're here for the Kitsilano vibe and the surfing and kayaking at nearby Jericho Beach (downtown is a 20-minute bus ride away). The basic rooms make this the least palatial Vancouver HI (dorms have up to 34 beds), but handy extras include a large kitchen, licensed café and bike rentals (there are lots of trails nearby). If you're not a fan of snorers, plan ahead and book one of the sought-after private rooms.

MIDRANGE
Kitsilano Suites (Map p94; ☎ 778-833-0334; www.kitsilanosuites.com; 2465 W 6th Ave; ste $149-249; ⬤) If you want to live like a well-to-do Kits local, check out this shingle-sided arts and crafts house divided into three wonderful self-catering, home-from-home suites. Although a century-old, each is lined with modern appliances without spoiling the heritage feel: think hardwood floors, claw-foot bathtubs and stained-glass windows. Each has a full kitchen (a handy welcome pack is included so you can cook up your first breakfast) and there are shops and restaurants a short walk away on W 4th Ave.

Corkscrew Inn (Map p94; ☎ 604-733-7276, 877-737-7276; www.corkscrewinn.com; 2735 W 2nd Ave; d from $160; ⬤) Rising above the city's array of polished, creaky-floored heritage B&Bs, this immaculate, antique-lined property looks like it has a drinking problem: it houses hundreds of corkscrews, some of them centuries old (look out for the one with the skull-shaped handle). Aside from the boozy paraphernalia, this

1912 Craftsman property has five lovely art-themed rooms (we like the art deco room). An ideal stop for traveling wine aficionados (guests receive a souvenir corkscrew). Three-night minimum stay in summer.

TOP END
Granville Island Hotel (Map p93; ☎ 604-683-7373, 800-663-1840; www.granvilleislandhotel.com; 1253 Johnston St; s/d $215/240; ⬛) This laid-back boutique property hugs the waterfront on the quieter end of Granville Island and has great False Creek views. Characterized by tranquil West Coast decor, the rooms feature exposed wood and soothing earth tones. There's a swanky rooftop hot-tub – a good spot to stay warm and watch the rain – and the ground-level brewpub makes its own distinctive beer (the Old Bridge Dark Lager is recommended).

West Side & UBC
BUDGET
University of British Columbia Housing (Map p86; ☎ 604-822-1000, 888-822-1030; www.ubcconferences.com/accommodation; dm/s/d/ste from $29/47/69/109; ⬤) You can pretend you're still a student by staying at UBC, but you'll need to hop on the bus for the 40-minute ride downtown to hang out with the grown-ups. Room types include hostel-style accommodation with one or two single beds; study rooms with en suites and kitchenettes (these are recommended); or swanky hotel-style suites with flatscreen TVs and wood and stone interiors. Most are available May to August only but the pricey West Coast Suites are offered year-round and have kitchenettes, twin beds and wi-fi.

MIDRANGE
Shaughnessy Village (Map p93; ☎ 604-736-5511; www.shaughnessyvillage.com; 1125 W 12th Ave; s/d $78.95/108.95; ⬛) This uniquely kitsch sleep-over – think pink carpets, flowery sofas and nautical memorabilia – describes itself as a tower block 'B&B resort'. Despite the old-school approach, the hotel is perfectly ship-shape, right down to its clean, well-maintained rooms. Like boat cabins, they're lined with wooden cupboards and include microwaves, refrigerators and tiny en suites. Extras include an outdoor pool, laundry room and, of course, a large display of petrified rocks. There's even an on-site

VANCOUVER & AROUND

hairdresser so you can book a beehive 'do' to fit right in.

Plaza 500 (Map p93; ☎ 604-873-1811, 800-473-1811; www.plaza500.com; 500 W 12th Ave; r from $159; 🅿 🛜) With some great views overlooking the downtown towers and the looming North Shore mountains, rooms at the Plaza 500 have received a recent makeover, delivering a more contemporary aesthetic – think comfy business hotel. It's a look that's taken to the max in FigMint, the property's Euro-chic on-site resto-bar. Rates include passes to a nearby gym and there's also a free shuttle bus to downtown if you don't want to negotiate the nearby transit buses.

EATING

Showcasing an international diversity that rival Canadian foodie cities Montreal and Toronto can't match, Vancouver trenchermen can fill up on great ethnic dishes before they even start on the region's flourishing West Coast cuisine. To sample the best, just combine both approaches: try some of North America's finest sushi or dim-sum for lunch, then sample Fraser Valley duck or Vancouver Island lamb for a splurge-worthy dinner. Whatever you choose, don't miss the seafood – it's BC's greatest culinary asset. Since most bars here also serve food, be sure to check out the drinking section (p118) for some additional finger-licking alternatives.

Tap into the latest hotspots and restaurant-opening gossip with a free copy of *Eat Magazine* or just head online for the latest reviews at www.urbandiner.ca.

Downtown
BUDGET

Gorilla Food (Map p88; ☎ 604-722-2504; 422 Richards St; mains $4-8; 🕙 11am-5pm) More guerrilla than gorilla, this subterranean hole-in-the-wall is a pilgrimage spot for raw food devotees. Mimicking the diet of its namesake, nothing is cooked, leading to innovative treats like crunchy lasagne (strips of zucchini substitute for pasta) and pizza made from seed crust and topped with tomato sauce, tenderised zucchini and mashed avocado. Save room for an icy almond shake dessert.

our pick Templeton (Map p88; ☎ 604-685-4612; 1087 Granville St; mains $6-12; 🕙 9am-11pm Mon-Wed, 9am-1am Thu-Sun) A funky and authentic 1930s chrome-and-vinyl diner with a twist,

---

TOP PICKS FOR LATE-NIGHT DINING

- **Naam** (p117)
- **Bin 942** (p117)
- **Hamburger Mary's** (p113)
- **Foundation** (p115)
- **Alibi Room** (p119)

---

the Templeton serves up organic burgers, fair-trade coffee, vegetarian sausages and possibly the best Big Ass Breakfast in town; the chunky chicken quesadillas, served with lashings of salsa and sour cream, are also highly recommended. Sadly, the mini jukeboxes on the tables don't work, but you can console yourself with a waistline-busting chocolate ice-cream float as you spin on your stool at the counter. Beer here is of the local microbrew variety – draft Russell Cream Ale – and it's worth dropping by on Monday nights when movies are often screened above the counter. The Templeton's loyal brunch-loving followers mean this spot is very busy on weekends, so avoid the peak time or you'll be waiting at the door for ages.

MIDRANGE

La Bodega (Map p88; ☎ 604-684-8814; 1277 Howe St; plates $8-12; 🕙 4:30pm-midnight Mon-Fri, 5pm-midnight Sat 5-11pm Sun) Vancouver's most authentic Spanish tapas joint, it's all about the tasting plates at this rustic, locally loved hangout. Pull up a chair, order a jug of sangria and decide on a few shareable treats from the extensive menu. If you're feeling spicy, the chorizo sausage hits the spot and the hearty Spanish meatballs are justifiably popular. There's often a great atmosphere here (especially on weekends) so don't be surprised if you find yourself staying for more than a few hours.

Samba Brazilian Steakhouse (Map p88; ☎ 604-683-2555; 1122 Alberni St; lunch/dinner $14/29; 🕙 11:30am-3pm, 5:30-10pm) Don't be put off by the uninspiring subterranean location of this kitschy restaurant, especially if you're a serious carnivore. Despite the lame family-eatery interior and large but oft-ignored salad bar, local diners are here to gorge on meat, including beef, lamb and sausages – all served using swords wielded by wandering waiters. There's an all-you-can-eat approach (lunch is the best deal) but don't overdo it or you'll have no chance when you're trying to flirt with the stunning Flamenco dancers that perform here nightly.

Joe Fortes (Map p88; ☎ 604-669-1940; 777 Thurlow St; mains $14-34; ☯ 11am-11pm) Named after Vancouver's first official lifeguard, the heated rooftop patio or the wood-and-brass grand room downstairs are excellent spots to enjoy a West Coast meat or seafood treat, ranging from slow-roasted prime rib to miso-glazed halibut. The hearty cob salad is recommended, while shellfish fans won't want to miss the oyster bar – these guys know how to shuck. If you're on a budget, there's often a good-value $10 Blue Plate lunch special.

Nu Restaurant & Lounge (Map p88; ☎ 604-646-4668; 1661 Granville St; mains $16-22; ☯ 11am-1am Mon-Fri, 10:30am-1am Sat, 10:30am-midnight Sun) Tucked under the north side of Granville Bridge, this swish and self-aware eatery has the appearance of a decadent 1970s hotel bar – it's the perfect place to don your gold-colored cravat. The menu is far from old-fashioned, though, combining a host of exciting fusion tasting plates: try the duck confit with liquefied foie gras. Also check out the Sunday jazz brunch, a popular locals' favorite.

TOP END

[our pick] **Chambar** (Map p88; ☎ 604-879-7119; 562 Beatty St; mains $14-29; ☯ 5:30pm-midnight) Easily the best downtown spot to bring a date, this candlelit, brick-lined dining room is warm and welcoming. With a European-influenced menu (it claims to be a Belgian restaurant, but you wouldn't know it when you look at the beer list), the sumptuous treats here include possibly the best pan-seared scallops in town and a tender lamb shank that makes velvet seem unyielding by comparison. *Moules frites* is another long-cherished favorite. Save room for the architecturally magnificent desserts, and wash the whole lot down with some house special Chambar Ale. Reservations recommended.

C Restaurant (Map p88; ☎ 604-681-1164; 1600 Howe St; mains $18-46; ☯ 11:30am-2:30pm Mon-Fri, 5:30-11pm daily) Under the celebrated auspices of chef Rob Clark, this pioneering fish and shellfish restaurant overlooking False Creek isn't cheap, but its revelatory approach makes it the city's best seafood dine-out. You'll be hard-pressed to find smoked salmon with cucumber jelly served anywhere else, but there's also a reverence for simple preparation that reveals the delicate flavors in dishes like local side-stripe prawns and Queen Charlotte scallops. C also spearheads a local drive for sustainable seafood stocks.

West End
BUDGET

Mr Pickwick's (Map p88; ☎ 604-681-0631; 1007 Denman St; mains $8-13; ☯ 11:30am-9pm) Vancouver's finest Brit-style fish and chipper is better than most of those back in the old country. A friendly little spot, they know exactly how to make your favorite comfort food – even the chips are chunkily satisfying. As well as the classics, the batter-fried salmon and the crunchy crab cakes are excellent, while the tartar and lemon dill sauces are fresh and tasty. Check out the daily specials and save room for a draft beer from BC's Dead Frog Brewery.

Hamburger Mary's (Map p88; ☎ 604-687-1293; 1202 Davie St; mains $8-14; ☯ 8am-3am Mon-Thu, 8am-4am Fri & Sat, 8am-2am Sun) A throwback

---

VANCOUVER'S BEST HOTDOG STAND

Although justly celebrated for its lip-smacking dining scene, Vancouver is woefully poor when it comes to great street food – if you're on the move and hungry, you can choose from rubbery hotdogs or roasted chestnut vendors. Enter Japa Dog (Map p88; ☯ noon-7:30pm Mon-Thu, noon-8pm Fri & Sat, 12:30-7pm Sun). Hugging the corner of Burrard and Smithe Sts (just look for the lunchtime line-up), this tasty dog stand serves up Japanese fusion treats, including the Misomayo, a turkey smokie with miso sauce; the Terimayo, served with shreds of *nori* and teriyaki sauce; and the Oroshu, a bratwurst with *daiko*, green onions and soy sauce. Consider trying all three, just like the chef Anthony Bourdain did when he filmed here. Or you could emulate Ice Cube who, according to the stand's dog-eared photo gallery, has eaten here 10 times. Sadly, Steven Segal only dropped by once, but he'll probably be back.

to the days of checkerboard floors and chrome-trim diners, the landmark Mary's is all about fab burgers and mondo milkshakes – the huge all-day breakfasts and weekend brunches are great, too. If it's a fine day, you'll have to wrestle the locals for a spot on the people-watching patio, but consider dropping by after a night on the town: this is a popular late-opening hangout for grease-cravers.

MIDRANGE

Guu with Garlic (Map p88; ☎ 604-685-8678; 1689 Robson St; plates $4-9; ✆ 5:30pm-midnight) One of many neighborhood-style Asian eateries colonizing the west end of Robson St, you'll have to join the line-up of hungry ESL students eager for opening time. It's worth it for a chatty, atmospheric and highly authentic Japanese *izakaya* experience that's all about chilling out and piling up the tasting plates. Try the black cod with miso mayo or pork cheek with ponzo sauce, along with some Asahi Super Dry. And aim for a seat at the bar so you can watch the crazed chefs meeting their spiralling whirlwind of orders.

our pick **Motomachi Shokudo** (Map p88; ☎ 604-609-0310; 740 Denman St; mains $6-12; ✆ 5-10pm) Regarded by in-the-know West Enders as Vancouver's best Japanese ramen house (which explains why it's often full), this compact, evocative little joint combines lightning fast service with the best comfort food dishes around. It's hard to go wrong on the menu but if you're a first-timer, dive into the New Generation Miso Ramen, brimming with crispy bean sprouts, fresh sweet corn, shredded cabbage and barbequed pork (many ingredients here are also organic). You'll need to walk it off with a stroll around nearby Stanley Park. Its older sister noodle bar is a few doors south (and usually just as busy). Cash only.

Le Gavroche (Map p88; ☎ 604-685-3924; 1616 Alberni St; mains $18-34; ✆ 5:30pm-11pm) Tucked along a residential sidestreet in a clapboard heritage house, this intimate little restaurant fuses West Coast ingredients with an array of classic and contemporary French approaches. Utilizing *les fruits de mer* with practiced flair – check-out the Alaska black cod with burnt orange and anise sauce – it's a good choice for a romantic fireside dinner. Wine lovers should also rejoice: there's an

amazing selection here that will have you crying into your glass with gratitude.

TOP END

Raincity Grill (Map p88; ☎ 604-685-7337; 1193 Denman St; mains $20-30; ✆ 11:30am-2:30pm & 5-10pm Mon-Fri, 10:30am-2:30pm & 5-10-pm Sat & Sun) A great showcase for fine West Coast cuisine, this convivial English Bay eatery was sourcing and serving unique BC ingredients long before the fashion for Fanny Bay oysters and Salt Spring Island lamb took off. Renowned for its attentive service, it offers a popular weekend brunch, a bargain three-course $30 tasting menu between 5pm and 6pm, and one of the city's most formidable wine lists. If you're on the move, drop by the take-out window and pick-up a gourmet $10 sandwich.

Yaletown

BUDGET

Agro Café (Map p88; ☎ 604-444-4855; 1269 Hamilton St; snacks $2-4, light lunches $6-9; ✆ 8am-6pm Mon-Fri, 9:30am-4pm Sat & Sun; ✆) Yaletown's best coffee shop hangout also serves light meals and bakery treats and is a good spot to rub shoulders with the locals, not all of who carry little dogs like fashion accessories. There's a strong fair-trade commitment here with the organic coffee you're sipping sourced from small-scale farm operations in Kenya. Reward your ethical nature with a fat slice of chocolate pecan pie or stick around for a hearty soup and panini lunch.

MIDRANGE

Elbow Room (Map p88; ☎ 604-685-3628; 560 Davie St; mains $8-15; ✆ 8am-4pm Mon-Fri, 8am-5pm Sat & Sun) An edge-of-Yaletown breakfast legend, the campy Elbow Room's schtick is that it serves up colorful abuse with its meals. Don't be put off; it's all meant in a friendly way, but make sure you give as good as you get. The menu highlights the mood – evidenced by 'The F-ing Kidding' burger, with two 8oz beef patties plus mushrooms and bacon. Breakfast is served until closing, so there's plenty of time to think up a witty riposte.

Glowbal Grill & Satay Bar (Map p88; ☎ 604-602-0835; 1079 Mainland St; mains $16-26; ✆ 11:30am-midnight Mon-Fri, 10:30am-midnight Sat & Sun) Hip but unpretentious, this often clamorous restaurant has a comfortable, lounge-like feel and a menu of classy dishes fusing West Coast ingredients with Asian and Mediterranean flavors. The cheese tortellini with smoked chicken is ace, but save room for some finger-licking satay stick chasers – especially the tequila lamb – served with lime mint glaze. Good patio.

TOP END

Blue Water Café (Map p88; ☎ 604-688-8078; 1095 Hamilton St; mains $22-44; ☾ 5pm-midnight) This high-concept seafood restaurant is Vancouver's best posh oyster bar and the pinnacle of Yaletown fine dining. House music gently percolates through the brick-lined, cobalt-blue interior, while seafood towers grace the outdoor patio tables. If you feel like an adventure, head straight to the semi-circular raw bar and watch the chefs' flashing blades prepare delectable sushi and sashimi, served with the restaurant's signature soya-seaweed dipping sauce. Reservations recommended.

Gastown & Chinatown
MIDRANGE

Salt Tasting Room (Map p90; ☎ 604-633-1912; Blood Alley; plates $5-15; ☾ noon-midnight) Hidden along a spooky alleyway by the 'Gassy' Jack statue, this chatty, brick-lined charcuterie and wine bar is a protein-lover's delight, with a deceptively simple approach. Pull up a chair at one of the communal tables and choose from the ever-changing blackboard of cured meats and local cheeses, accompanied by a glass or two of a perfectly-paired beverage. The recommended $15 Tasting Plate includes three meats or cheeses plus condiments such as the addictive UK-style piccalilli.

La Casita (Map p90; ☎ 604-646-2444; 101 W Cordova St; mains $8-16; ☾ 11:30am-10pm Mon & Tue, 11:30am-11pm Wed & Thu, 11:30am-midnight Fri & Sat, 2-10pm Sun) You'll feel instantly welcome when you enter this cozy, family-run Mexican joint – especially when the margarita pitchers start flowing and the fairy lights start warming up. Relax and settle in for the evening, with some shrimp and salmon tacos, chicken or chorizo chimichangas and a bowl of fortifying black bean soup. There are plenty of veggie options here, too.

Hon's Wun-Tun House (Map p90; ☎ 604-688-0871; 268 E Keefer St; dishes $6-18; ☾ 11am-11pm Sun-Thu, 11am-midnight Sat & Sun) Vancouver's favorite Chinese restaurant mini-chain, Hon's flagship Chinatown branch is suffused with inviting cooking smells and cacophonous diners. The giant, 334-item menu ranges from satisfying dim-sum brunches to steaming wun-tun soups bobbling with juicy dumplings. For something different, try the good-value congee rice porridge: a fancy-free soul food dish that takes three hours to prepare and comes in seafood, chicken and beef varieties.

Boneta (Map p90; ☎ 604-684-1844; 1 W Cordova St; mains $14-26; ☾ noon-4pm & 5:30pm-midnight Mon-Sat, noon-midnight Sun) A local foodie favorite colonizing a handsome landmark former bank building, Boneta takes a bold approach to its dishes, responding to whatever's available regionally and seasonally. Expect innovative riffs like smoked bison carpaccio with sherry vinaigrette or grilled rack of lamb with curried cauliflower. There's a small but excellent wine selection, all available by the glass, but this place is renowned for its cocktails.

SoMa (South Main)

Gene Café (Map p93; ☎ 604-568-5501; 2404 Main St; snacks $2-4; ☾ 6:30am-11pm) You can't sneeze around the Main and Broadway intersection without hitting an independent coffee shop, each with a distinctive look and a gaggle of regular patrons with their own favorite seats. Arguably the best is Gene's, a flatiron multi-windowed nook of concrete floors, white-washed walls and chunky cedar benches. The java here is possibly the best in town, and the home-baked cookies and fruit pies will fortify you as you hunker in a corner nodding sagely at your Sartre paperback.

Foundation (Map p93; ☎ 604-708-0881; 2301 Main St; mains $6-12; ☾ 5pm-1am) One of SoMa's liveliest hangouts, this funky vegetarian (mostly vegan) noshery is the kind of place where artsy students and chin-stroking young intellectuals like to be seen. Despite the clientele, it's not at all pretentious, and its mismatched Formica tables are often topped with tasty dishes like braised tofu salad or mango and coconut pasta. Excellent Storm Brewing beer here.

our pick **Chutney Villa** (Map p93; ☎ 604-872-2228; 147 E Broadway; mains $8-18; ☾ 11:30am-10pm Mon & Wed-Thu, 11:30am-11pm Fri & Sat) Ever-popular with SoMa locals who know good value when they see it, this friendly (expect a hug from the owner) South Indian restaurant is packed at peak times, which partly explains the condensation-covered windows. The lures include lusciously spiced, often nutty curries (the lamb *poriyal* is our favorite) and fluffy *dosas* to mop them up. There's an outstanding Sunday brunch – a hangover-busting combo of veggie curries and piping hot Indian coffee – and the drinks list includes bottled Indian beers and on-tap, locally-brewed R&B (the Masala chai tea or fresh lime cordial are excellent alternatives if you're on the wagon).

Commercial Drive

WaaZuBee Café (Map p90; ☎ 604-253-5299; 1622 Commercial Dr; mains $8-20; ☺ 11:30am-midnight) A popular Drive hangout, bohemian WaaZuBee's outfits itself with huge painted murals, velvet curtains and recycled metal sculptures – check out that spoon chandelier. An equally eclectic menu (including plenty of vegetarian options) runs from sesame tuna sashimi to grilled portobello mushroom burgers and maple-soy wild salmon. There's also a good selection of regional beers, including Storm Scottish Ale, made just down the road.

Lime (Map p90; ☎ 604-215-1130; 1130 Commercial Dr; dishes $5-16; ☺ 5pm-1am) There's such competition for your dining dollars on the Drive that it's hard for new restaurants to stand out from the crowd. But this excellent modern Japanese joint has managed to do just that, becoming a hit with local and regional sushi and sashimi nuts happy to travel for treats like the scallop, shrimp and snow crab *sunomono*. Alongside the raw fish, there are also delectable tempura and soba noodle dishes and some cool Asian cocktails.

Havana (Map p90; ☎ 604-253-9119; 1212 Commercial Dr; mains $10-20; ☺ 11am-11pm Mon-Thu, 10am-midnight Fri, 9am-midnight Sat & Sun) This funky Commercial fixture has been around for years but it's still ever-popular – hence the crowded summertime patio. Combining a rustic Latin American feel with a roster of satisfying Afro-Cuban-Southern soul food dishes, highlights range from yam fries to slow-roasted lamb curry and a satisfying platter of clams, mussels and oysters. Port, brandy and single malt color the drinks list but those mojitos slip down mighty fast too.

Granville Island
BUDGET
Public Market (Map p93; 1689 Johnston St; mains $5-8; ☺ 9am-7pm) As well as the Public Market's

---

TOP FIVE FOR PICKNICKING

- **Third Beach** (p97)
- **Vanier Park** (p100)
- **Lumberman's Arch** (p97)
- **Kitsilano Beach Park** (p100)
- **Wreck Beach** (p101)

---

tempting array of bakeries and deli stands, the compact food court here is one of the city's best, combining an international array of quality pierogies, pizzas, curries, German sausages and fish and chips. Eat late or early to avoid the crowds, who cling to the tables like they've just been shipwrecked, or take your grub outside to catch the waterfront views (and fend off the avaricious seagulls).

MIDRANGE

Go Fish (Map p93; ☎ 604-730-5040; 1505 W 1st Ave; mains $8-13; ☺ 11:30am-6:30pm Wed-Fri, noon-6:30pm Sat & Sun) Nestled on the seawall between Granville Island and Vanier Park, this seafood shack serves excellent fish and chips, offering a choice of halibut, salmon or cod encased in crispy golden batter. The smashing (and lighter) fish tacos are also highly recommended, while ever-changing daily specials – brought in by the nearby fishing boats – often include praise-worthy scallop burgers or ahi tuna sandwiches. There's not much seating, so pack your parcel to nearby Vanier Park for a picnic.

Bridges (Map p93; ☎ 604-687-4400; 1696 Duranleau St; mains $12-20; ☺ 11am-10pm) A casual bistro-style restaurant with views of the Burrard Bridge and the North Shore mountains from its large, ever-popular patio, this yellow-painted landmark serves well-executed classics like chicken quesadillas, fish and chips and hearty thin crust pizzas – the smoked salmon one is recommended. Escape the patio clamor at the more upscale dining room upstairs, which offers a three-course fixed price menu ($40).

Kitsilano
BUDGET
Eatery (Map p94; ☎ 604-738-5298; 3431 W Broadway; mains $7-16; ☺ 4:30-11pm Mon-Thu, 4:30pm-midnight Fri, 12:30pm-midnight Sat, 12.30-11pm Sun) Wooden booths, lava lamps and a neon 'miso horny'

sign are all part of the kitsch ambience at this pop-culture reinvention of a trad sushi joint. Bring your manga comic and dive into the giant menu of soba bowls, curry-rice and sushi combos, all washed down with domestic or Japanese bottled beer. Vegetarian options abound, including some shareable platters for those veggies that travel in packs.

MIDRANGE

Sophie's Cosmic Café (Map p94; ☎ 604-732-6810; 2095 West 4th Ave; mains $6-14; ⏰ 8am-9:30pm) With its museum-like interior of pop culture memorabilia, local-legend Sophie's is a happening diner spot with burgers, club sandwiches and big-ass milkshakes dominating the menu; there are also a few unexpected gems like BC oyster burgers. A highly popular breakfast and brunch spot – expect weekend queues – it's also worth dropping by mid-afternoon for some truck-stop coffee and a whopping slice of pyramid-sized apple pie.

Naam (Map p94; ☎ 604-738-7151; 2724 W 4th Ave; mains $8-14; ⏰ 24hr) Vancouver's favorite vegetarian eatery, the rustic-looking Naam has been hooking both herbivores and carnivores since the late 1960s, when it was a top hangout for local hippies. It's not unusual to have to wait for a peak-time table here but it's worth it for the hearty stir-fries, Mexican platters and sesame potatoes with miso gravy. There's nightly live folk, blues or jazz, some great organic beers and a popular patio – it's covered, so you can cozy up with a bowl of broth and enjoy the rain.

our pick Trafalgars Bistro (Map p94; ☎ 604-739-0555 ext 1; 1603 W 16th Ave; mains $18-22; ⏰ 11am-4pm daily, 10am-4pm Sat & Sun, 5-10pm Mon-Sat) You'll feel instantly comfortable when you walk into this elegant but friendly neighborhood spot which has a loyal local following. The regulars keep coming back for the warm, wood-lined candlelit ambience and a menu of fine seasonal BC ingredients prepared with delicate French and Asian influences. Look for treats like leek and lager steamed mussels, bison fettuccine bolognaise and the recommended pan-roasted duck breast. Desserts, including lemon mousse cake and pear chocolate flan, are also top-notch rather than an afterthought – the owners run a bakery next door – while the wine list is dripping with great BC beverages

like Cedar Creek merlot and Burrowing Owl syrah. Service is excellent and never snooty, so you'll want to linger and savor your meal.

Fuel (Map p94; ☎ 604-288-7905; 1944 W 4th Ave; mains $24-34; ⏰ noon-2.30pm Mon-Fri, 5.30-10.30pm daily) Despite the bland, utilitarian name, this stylishly cool Kits eatery sources exceptional regional ingredients and transforms them with a knowing cosmopolitan flair. Everything is seasonal, so expect regular menu changes – if you're lucky, the glazed Fraser Valley lamb will be available. If not, console yourself with some buckwheat honey crème brûlée or a satisfying selection of piquant regional cheeses for dessert.

DB Bistro Moderne (Map p94; ☎ 604-739-7115; 2551 W Broadway; mains $14-28; ⏰ noon-2:30pm Mon-Fri, 5:30-10pm Sun-Wed, 5:30-11pm Thu-Sat, 11am-2pm Sat & Sun) Formerly Feenies, this totally transformed luxe bistro serves the city's best posh burger: a $28 bulging combination of sirloin patty and black truffles that couldn't be further from a Big Mac if it tried. The menu is brimming with additional delectable comfort food such as coq au vin and the excellent Berkshire pork tenderloin, while the weekend brunch highlight is a delicious lobster eggs Florentine.

TOP END

Lumière (Map p94; ☎ 604-739-8185; 2551 W Broadway; prix fixe from $98; ⏰ 5:30-11pm Tue-Sun) With Chef Rob Feenie's 2008 departure from the multi-award winning restaurant he created (along with the eponymous one next door), few would have put money on this high-end eatery surviving. But with the arrival of superstar New York chef Daniel Boulud, it has been reinvented and given a new lease of life. Expect exquisitely executed dishes, using ultra-fresh regional ingredients, such as slow-baked Arctic char and Redbro chicken stuffed with truffles. The menu is a series of multi-course prix fixe tasting selections intended to be slowly savored: this is dinner as an event. Reservations recommended.

West Side
MIDRANGE

Bin 942 (Map p93; ☎ 604-734-9421; 1521 W Broadway; plates $12-15; ⏰ 5pm-2am) This small, slender but exceedingly cozy lounge is a convivial late-night hangout if you fancy a few dishes and a tipple or two with chatty friends.

Among the best 'Tapatisers' are sashimi-style ahi tuna and portobello mushroom cutlets which pair perfectly with a select array of good beers – the Russell Brewing Cream Ale is best – and a compact but well-chosen wine list of Australian, Californian, European and BC tipples. Aim to stay for a few hours if you're in the mood for a relaxing wind-down.

Ouisi Bistro (Map p93; ☎ 604-732-7550; 3014 Granville St; mains $9-22; ✿ 5pm-2am, 11am-2pm Sat & Sun) One of many dine-out options lining S Granville between Broadway and 16th Ave, this is Vancouver's best Creole and Cajun soul food joint. Serving adventurous dishes like habanero coconut chicken, cornmeal-crusted trout and vegetarian étouffée, there's a large selection of accompanying malts and bourbons and regular live jazz to spice things up. Drop by for weekend brunch and partake of a hot fusion spin on traditional breakfast dishes. And if you're wondering: the name comes from 'Louisiana'.

Vij's (Map p93; ☎ 604-736-6664; 1480 W 11th Ave; mains $18-26; ✿ 5:30-10pm) Reservations are not accepted at this sleek modern reinvention of the Indian restaurant, which fuses regional ingredients, global flourishes and classic East Indian dishes to produce an array of innovative dishes. The unique and, judging by the line-ups, popular results range from wine-marinated 'lamb Popsicles' to halibut, mussels and crab in a tomato-ginger curry. The adventurous should also try the paranta: flat breads made with roasted ground crickets. If you don't want to line-up, there's Rangoli, a takeout café next door.

TOP END
Tojo's (Map p93; ☎ 604-872-8050; 1133 W Broadway; mains $19-26; ✿ 5-10pm Mon-Sat) Hidekazu Tojo's legendary skill with the sushi knife has created Vancouver's most revered sushi restaurant. Among his exquisite dishes are favorites like lightly steamed monkfish, sautéed halibut cheeks and fried red tuna wrapped with seaweed and served with plum sauce. Seats at the sushi bar are much sought-after, so reserve as early as possible, then celebrate with a selection or two from the sake menu.

DRINKING
Like its burgeoning restaurant options, Vancouver's bar scene has undergone a sudsy renaissance in recent years, with the opening of dozens of tempting new watering holes. Many also serve great food, making them a handy alternative to the standard dine-out spots. The area where modern-day Vancouver began – triggered by the opening of 'Gassy' Jack's first tavern – Gastown is the city's best drinking neighborhood and is brimming with character bars. You can also mount a respectable (or not so respectable) pub-crawl on Commercial Dr, the Granville Strip, in Yaletown and around SoMa.

Downtown & West End
Lennox Pub (Map p88; ☎ 604-408-0881; 800 Granville St; ✿ 11:30am-11pm Sun-Thu, 11:30am-1am Fri & Sat) This slim, wood-panelled Granville St hostelry never seems to have enough tables to go around at the weekend, when the noise levels prevent all but the most rudimentary of conversations. It's a different story during the week, when calm is restored and you can savor the Sleeman's beers plus a good roster of Belgian drafts – try the Leffe. A handy launch spot for the many clubs and bars lining the Granville Strip from here to Drake St.

Mill Marine (Map p88; ☎ 604-687-6455; 1199 W Cordova St; ✿ 11am-11pm Sun-Wed, 11am-midnight Fri & Sat) The food is nothing special but the spectacular panoramic patio views of Stanley Park, the North Shore mountains and the floatplanes descending on Burrard Inlet more than make up for it. There's a small but impressive selection of draught beers available – try the Whistler Export Lager – as well as specials on offer throughout the week. Arrive early on summer evenings or you'll have to wrestle the locals for a table.

Calling (Map p88; ☎ 604-801-6681; 1780 Davie St; ✿ 11am-2am Mon-Fri, 10am-2am Sat & Sun) A small but swank reinvention of the neighborhood pub – think dark hardwood floors, shiny steel bar taps and wait staff all in black – the main draws here are the views across English Bay from the small patio, the perfectly executed cocktails and the strong whiskey selection. There's also a good choice of bottled world beers and a menu of comfort food classics.

YALETOWN
Yaletown Brewing Company (Map p88; ☎ 604-681-2739; 1111 Mainland St; ✿ 11:30am-midnight Sun-Wed, 11:30am-1am Thu, 11am-2am Fri & Sat) There's a

narrow, often noisy brick-lined bar on one side (complete with pool tables) and a large restaurant area on the other, but both serve the company's on-site brewed beers that change depending on the season. In summer, the patio is a sought-after perch from which to ogle the beautiful people of Yaletown, but be careful not to drink too much or your chat up lines will start to show. For nosh, the pizzas here are recommended.

Dix BBQ & Brewery (Map p88; ☎ 604-682-2739; 871 Beatty St; ☺ 11:30am-midnight Mon-Fri, 3pm-midnight Sat, 4pm-midnight Sun) This edge-of-Yaletown brewpub is popular with hockey and football fans (you can watch the games here) and it has a chatty, laid-back vibe. Regulars are drawn by the well-priced own-brews and smattering of regional beers – the Red Truck Ale is particularly good. The southern-style chow is also a cut above regular pub grease-fests, focusing on velvety brisket sandwiches and a sausage, shrimp and chicken jambalaya that will lure you from your drink.

Afterglow (Map p88; ☎ 604-602-0835; 1082 Hamilton St) Tucked behind Glowbal (p114), the city's tiniest lounge bar is an intimate, pink-hued room that attracts artsy hipsters and Yaletown's beautiful people in equal measure – you'll be chatting with them all since this is such a compact space. Pull-up a stool and experiment with cocktails like the You Glow Girl or knock yourself out with a few bottles of ultra-strong Quebecois beer – complete with images of Satan on their labels (once you've had a couple, you'll realize why).

Gastown

our pick Alibi Room (Map p90; ☎ 604-623-3383; 157 Alexander St; ☺ 5pm-midnight Tue-Fri, 10am-1am Sat, 10am-3pm Sun) Thirsty Vancouverites with a penchant for BC microbrews have been rolling up at the communal tables here since northern England native Nigel Springthorpe took over the bar a couple of years ago. His atmospheric brick-lined tavern serves up the city's largest selection of on-tap regional tipples – usually up to 19 at a time – including lip-smacking regulars like Old Yale Pale Ale from Chilliwack and organic Back Hand of God stout from Sorrento: you can taste-trip around the province without even leaving the city. Brews are all reasonably priced and the tasting flight of four small glasses is

especially recommended for those who like to dabble. Unless you're on a strict liquid diet, don't forget to eat: the Alibi's menu offers plenty of options to soak up the booze, including a great charcuterie plate and a tasty duck wrap.

Irish Heather (Map p90; ☎ 604-688-9779; 217 Carrall St; ☺ noon-midnight) Moved from its beloved former spot across the street, the new Heather is a total transformation. Luckily, the change works. The narrow venue is divided between a wood-lined boozer with small tables on one side (the floor is made from old Guinness barrels) and a giant communal table with a cafeteria feel to it on the other. Wherever you sit, the stout is always perfectly poured (try an alternative like bottled Black Cat Lager), while the gastropub food is the best of any bar in town: try the deep steak pies, charcuterie and cheese plates or the tasty crisp-fried cauliflower with hummus.

Six Acres (Map p90; ☎ 604-488-0110; 203 Carrall St; ☺ 5pm-midnight Tue-Thu, 5pm-1am Fri & Sat) A smashing brick-lined nook capturing the spirit of chatty pub and fusing it with some knowingly quirky flourishes – hence the menus enclosed in used book covers and the bathrooms playing old language tapes. Excellent beer selection   try the Draft Dodger from Phillips Brewing – and inspired pub grub like the Berlin, a shareable plate of cheese and sausage.

Steamworks Brewing Co (Map p90; ☎ 604-689-2739; 375 Water St; ☺ 11:30am-midnight Sun-Wed, 11:30am-1am Thu-Sat) A giant Gastown microbrewery in a cavernous converted brick warehouse, the signature beer here is Lions Gate Lager, a good summer tipple. A favorite place for the city's after-work crowd, the pubby downstairs can get satisfyingly noisy while the upstairs is all about serene views across to the North Shore. The menu is packed with pub standards, but the pizzas are a stand-out.

Also recommended:

Greedy Pig (Map p90; ☎ 604-669-4991; 307 Cordova St; ☺ noon-midnight Tue-Sat) Comfortable pub-style hangout for the Gastown crowd, complete with great cheese and meat plates, lip-smacking cocktails (plus a few wines) and regular live music.

Chill Winston (Map p90; ☎ 604-288-9575; 3 Alexander St; ☺ 11am-1am) Cavernous brick-lined lounge bar across from the 'Gassy' Jack statue, with the area's best summertime patio.

SoMa (South Main) & Commercial Dr

Whip (Map p93; ☎ 604-874-4687; 209 E 6th Ave; ☾ noon-midnight Tue-Sat) The moodily lit Whip fuses the best in pub and lounge approaches. There's a dare-inviting selection of seven martinis each named after a deadly sin (lust is always recommended) and a good menu with tempting treats like yam *frites* and pad Thai. But it's the beer that wins regulars, with choice drafts from R&B Brewing, Storm Brewing and Quebec scaremongers Unibroue.

Cascade Room (Map p93; ☎ 604-709-8650; 2616 Main St; ☾ 4pm-midnight Mon-Fri, noon-midnight Sat & Sun) Pull up a summertime stool at the open windows of this laid-back lounge and watch the SoMa trendies bustling past as you sip on your pint of daily-special beer. In the depths of winter, though, slink to the back, hug the flock wallpaper and work your way down the impressive cocktail menu (start with the brandy Alexander) as you try to remember what sun used to look like. Whatever you do, follow the maxim on the etched glass panel at the entrance: Keep Calm and Carry On.

Stella's Tap & Tapas Bar (Map p90; ☎ 604-254-2437; 1191 Commercial Dr; ☾ 11am-11:30pm Mon-Fri, 10:30am-11:30pm Sat & Sun) Leading the Drive's friendly neighborhood bars, Stella's offers an amazing selection of European brews: it's the best spot in town to taste-test draft Leffe, Kronenbourg and Bellevue Kriek; the dark XO is also heartily recommended. Connoisseurs should dip into the ever-changing fresh sheet of Belgian microbrews, including the legendary Gulden Draak that's strong enough to put hairs on your chest and the chests of everyone sitting nearby.

Also recommended:

Three Lions Café (Map p93; ☎ 604-569-2233; 1 E Broadway; ☾ 11am-12:30am Tue-Fri, 9am-12:30am Sat & Sun) Run by young Brits, this convivial corner nook is popular with the local cool set who come for brews like London Pride and nosh like Yorkshire puddings filled with sausages.

Charlatan (Map p90; ☎ 604-253-2777; 1447 Commercial Dr; ☾ noon-midnight Tue-Sat) Chatty neighborhood haunt with good comfort food, a tiny patio and a large beer selection – the Big Rock Trad from Alberta is best.

ENTERTAINMENT

Flick through the *Georgia Straight* and the Thursday *Vancouver Sun* for info on local happenings or peruse www.livevan.com for concert listings. Tickets for many events are available via **Ticketmaster** (☎ concerts 604-280-4444, sports 604-280-4400; www.ticketmaster.ca) but **Tickets Tonight** (Map p88; ☎ 604-684-2787; www.ticketstonight.ca) in the Tourism Info Centre also sells half-price day-of-entry to many shows.

Nightclubs

Fabric (Map p90; ☎ 604-683-6695; 66 Water St; ☾ 9pm-3am Wed-Sat) Many Vancouverites don't know it, but double-roomed Fabric is the city's premier club for experimental DJs and live club shows from all over the globe. On any given night you're likely to find progressive house, jazz-fusion, soul, hip-hop, reggae or electronica. It's definitely worth braving the atmosphere – which can sometimes be thick with attitude – if you know exactly what you're looking for.

Shine (Map p90; ☎ 604-408-4321; 364 Water St; ☾ 9pm-2am Mon-Sat) With music from electro to funky house and hip-hop, Gastown's sexy, subterranean Shine attracts a younger crowd and is divided into a noisy main room and an intimate cozy cave with a long chill-out sofa. The club's Saturday night 'Big Sexy Funk' (hip-hop and rock) is a local legend, while Thursday's 1990s retro night appeals to all those jaded 30-year-olds out there (you know who you are).

Plaza Club (Map p88; ☎ 604-646-0064; 881 Granville St; ☾ 9pm-3am Thu-Sat) The larger Caprice is a few doors south but the Plaza, with its mosh pit dance floor and circular bar, gets our vote. The music is of the mainstream variety – Saturday's Top 40 and old-school night is best – and the crowd includes plenty of non-locals in from the suburbs for a big night out. Increasingly showcasing live acts, low-priced bands also appear here – check the website (www.plazaclub.net) for listings.

Republic (Map p88; ☎ 604-669-3266; 958 Granville St; ☾ 9pm-3am) Luring an older crowd than the chundering youngsters at the Robson St end of the Strip, Republic attracts those sophisticated over-25s that have strayed all the way from Yaletown. Start with a cocktail on the 2nd-floor conservatory-like patio and check out the human wreckage of late-night drunks weaving around outside. Then hit the dance floor: open nightly, Friday is recommended for house, funk and the guilty pleasures of 80s' retro.

Cinemas

For multiplex fans, downtown's **Scotiabank Theatre** (Map p88; ☎ 604-630-1407; www.cineplex .com; 900 Burrard St; admission $12.50) is a magnet for the latest blockbusters. Mixing blockbuster offerings with some of the more commercial films on the festival circuit, **Cinemark Tinseltown** (Map p90; ☎ 604-806-0799; www.cinemark.com; 88 W Pender St; admission $11.25) is also a local favorite.

Those of a more alternative bent can choose from the excellent **Vancity International Film Centre** (Map p88; ☎ 604-683-3456; www.vifc.org; 1181 Seymour St; admission $10), headquarters of the Vancouver International Film Festival (p107) and year-round venue for arthouse films, or **Pacific Cinémathèque** (Map p88; ☎ 604-688-3456; www.cinematheque.bc.ca; 1131 Howe St; admission $9.50), an older cinema plying similar wares. **Canada Place's CN IMAX Theatre** (Map p88; ☎ 604-682-4629; www.imax.com/vancouver; 999 Canada Place; admission $12) screens worthy documentaries and the occasional rejigged *Batman* or *Star Wars* movie.

On the West Side, **Fifth Avenue Cinemas** (Map p93; ☎ 604-734-7469; www.festivalcinemas.ca; 2110 Burrard St; admission $12) is a popular indie and foreign movie house, as is Kitsilano's long-established **Ridge Theatre** (Map p94; ☎ 604-738-6311; www.festivalcinemas.ca; 3131 Arbutus St; admission $12).

Theater

With a less middle-of-the-road approach in recent years, downtown's **Vancouver Playhouse** (Map p88; ☎ 604-873-3311; www.vancouverplayhouse .com; $33-66) has again become the city's choice venue to see great live theater. It presents a six-play season at its large civic venue in the **Queen Elizabeth complex** (Map p88; ☎ 604-665-3050; www.vancouver.ca/theatres; cnr Hamilton & Dunsmuir Sts).

Popular world classics and works by contemporary Canadian playwrights are also part of the mix at the **Arts Club Theatre Company** (☎ 604-687-1644; www.artsclub.com; $30-60), which performs at the **Granville Island Stage** (Map p93; 1585 Johnston St) and **Stanley Theatre** (Map p93; 2750 Granville St).

Those looking for something more challenging will prefer the **Firehall Arts Centre** (Map p90; ☎ 604-689-0926; www.firehallartscentre.ca; 280 E Cordova St; shows $12-30), an intimate fringe-style venue where 'difficult' shows are presented to an artsy crowd. Also check out the eclec-

tic theater, dance and music roster at the newly renovated **Cultch** (Map p90; ☎ 604-251-1363; www.thecultch.com; 1895 Venables St; shows from $15), officially also known as the Vancouver East Cultural Centre.

For a complete change of pace, the **Vancouver TheatreSports League** (Map p93; ☎ 604-738-7013; www.vtsl.com; 1601 Johnston St; shows $14.50-19) performs high jinks comedy improv at its Granville Island base.

Live Music

The **Commodore** (Map p88; ☎ 604-739-4550; www .livenation.com; 868 Granville St; shows $20-35) is Vancouver's favorite concert spot. Complete with its bouncy ballroom floor, it hosts non-stadium local and visiting bands. SoMa has its own even cooler venue, the atmospheric subterranean **Biltmore Cabaret** (Map p93; ☎ 604-676-0541; www.biltmorecabaret.com; 395 Kingsway; shows from $5), a fave in-the-know hangout for fans of hot and up-and-coming indie acts.

Eclecticism is also on the menu at the excellent upstairs **Railway Club** (Map p88; ☎ 604-681-1625; www.therailwayclub.com; 579 Dunsmuir St; free-$10), which combines a lived-in Brit-pub feel with a nightly roster of indie, folk, punk, soul and everything in between. It's a similar size and even more eclectic at the **Media Club** (Map p88; ☎ 604-608-2871; www.the mediaclub.ca; 695 Cambie St; shows $5-25) a few blocks away below the Queen Elizabeth complex.

Blues fans will likely prefer the **Yale** (Map p88; ☎ 604-681-9253; www.theyale.ca; 1300 Granville St; shows $10-25), a blowsy, unpretentious joint with a large stage, a devoted clientele and a beer-sticky dance floor. Jazz connoisseurs will find themselves lured to the subterranean **Cellar Restaurant and Jazz Club** (Map p94; ☎ 604-738-1959; www.cellarjazz.com; 3611 W Broadway; cover from $8), a serious muso venue where you're required to keep the noise down and respect the performances on the tiny corner stage.

Sports

The **Vancouver Canucks** (Map p88; ☎ 604-899-4600; www.canucks.com; GM Place; $55-$131; ☯ Oct-Apr) NHL hockey team is the city's leading sports franchise. Book your seat at their GM Place home as far in advance as possible – most games are sold to capacity.

If you're out of luck with the Canucks, the Western Hockey League's **Vancouver Giants** (off Map p90; ☎ 604-444-2687; www.vancouvergiants.com;

Pacific Coliseum; $16.50-18.50; ◉ Sep-Mar) is a good (and good value) alternative. They play at the Pacific Coliseum, east of downtown.

Canadian Football League (CFL) side **BC Lions** (Map p88; ☎ 604-589-7627; www.bclions.com; BC Place Stadium; $28-75; ◉ Jun-Oct) strut their stuff at downtown's covered BC Place Stadium. Tickets are generally easy to come by – unless they're closing in on the Grey Cup.

Playing in the Western Conference League (but moving up to MLS level in 2011), **Vancouver Whitecaps** (Map p86; ☎ 604-669-9283; www.whitecapsfc.com; Swangard Stadium, Burnaby; tickets $18-35; ◉ Apr-Sep) is the city's main soccer side. With men's and women's teams, they play at Burnaby's Swangard Stadium: dress warmly since the venue is not well shielded from the cold. Plans are being hatched to move downtown in the next few years.

In contrast, a sunny afternoon at the family-friendly old-school Nat Bailey Stadium with the **Vancouver Canadians** (Map p86; ☎ 604-872-5332; www.canadiansbaseball.com; Nat Bailey Stadium; tickets $8-14; ◉ Jun-Sep) is less about watching great baseball and more about cold beer in plastic cups and a fistful of übersalty pretzels.

SHOPPING

Robson St is downtown's main shopping thoroughfare, with all the usual chain store suspects. You can get your chocolate fake moose droppings (and other souvenirs) on Gastown's Water St; hanging out on Granville Island is recommended if you want to watch artisans at work and trawl the Public Market. Slightly more adventurous shoppers should head to Kitsilano's W 4th Ave, East Van's Commercial Dr, Gastown's backstreets (especially Carrall and Cordova Sts near Maple Tree Square), and the Main St stretch past the intersection with E 20th Ave.

Art

Coastal Peoples Fine Art Gallery (Map p88; ☎ 604-685-2928; 1024 Mainland St; ◉ 10am-7pm Mon-Sat, 11am-6pm Sun) This sumptuous Yaletown gallery showcases a fine selection of Inuit and Northwest Coast aboriginal jewelry, carvings and prints. Focusing on the high art side of native crafts, you'll find some exquisite items here that will likely have your credit card sweating within minutes. There's a sister branch on Gastown's Water St.

JEM Gallery (Map p93; ☎ 604-879-5366; 225 E Broadway; ◉ 11am-5pm Tue-Sat) Presenting kitsch, outsider art from Western Canada, the JEM (stands for Just East of Main) is an unassuming storefront gallery where the exhibitions can range from local veteran Jim Cummins' latest painted surfboards to Calgarian Lisa Brawn's cleverly ironic pop culture woodcuts. Check out the back room, with its tempting prints, jewelry and curios priced to go.

Clothing

Gravity Pope (Map p94; ☎ 604-731-7673; 2205 W 4th Ave; ◉ 10am-9pm Mon-Fri, 10am-7pm Sat, 11am-6pm Sun) One of a clutch of cool clothing stores strung along Kitsilano's highly browsable W 4th Ave, this unisex shop includes ultra-cool footwear and designer clothing for the pale and interesting set (think ironic tweed ties and printed halter tops). Don't spend all your dosh here, though: check out nearby Vivid and Urban Rack, too.

John Fluevog Shoes (Map p88; ☎ 604-688-6228; 65 Water St; ◉ 11am-7pm Mon-Wed, 11am-8pm Thu & Fri, 11am-7pm Sat, noon-6pm Sun) The cavernous Gastown flagship of Vancouver's fave shoe designer (the smaller original store still operates on Granville), Fluevog's funky shoes, sandals and thigh-hugging boots have been a fashion legend since 1970. It's tempting to try something on – some of the footwear looks like Doc Martens on acid, while others could poke your eye out from 20 paces – but beware: falling in love can happen in an instant.

Smoking Lily (off Map p93; ☎ 604-873-5459; 3634 MainSt; ◉ 11am-6pm Mon-Sat, noon-5pm Sun) Quirky art school cool is the approach at this SoMa store, where skirts, belts and halter-tops are whimsically accented with prints of ants, skulls or the Periodic Table. Men's clothing is slowly creeping into the mix, with some fish, skull and tractor T-shirts and ties. A fun spot to browse (the staff are friendly and chatty), it's hard to imagine a better souvenir than the silk tea cozy printed with a Pierre Trudeau likeness.

Twigg & Hottie (off Map p93; ☎ 604-879-8595; 3671 Main St; ◉ 11am-6pm Mon-Sat, 11am-5pm Sun) Just across from Smoking Lily and named after owners Glencora Twigg and Christine Hotton, this wood-floored nook showcases distinctive garments (and quirky jewelry) from Canadian designers: it's the place for

---

TO MARKET TO MARKET

A bulging shopping bag of regional produce hits Vancouver's temporary farmers markets throughout the summer (and sometimes beyond). Seasonal highlights include crunchy apples, lush peaches and juicy blueberries, while home-baked cakes and treats are frequent accompaniments. Don't be surprised to see piquant local cheese and a few arts and crafts added to the mix. For more information, visit www.eatlocal.org.

- **Kitsilano Farmers Market** (Map p94; ☎ 604-879-3276; Kitsilano Community Centre, 2690 Larch St; ⓨ 10am-2pm Sun mid-Jun–mid-Oct)
- **Trout Lake Farmers Market** (off Map p90; ☎ 604-879-3276; Trout Lake Community Centre, E 15th Ave at Victoria Dr; ⓨ 9am-2pm Sat mid-May–mid-Oct)
- **UBC Farm Market** (Map p86; ☎ 604-822-5092; 6128 South Campus Rd; ⓨ 9am-1pm Sat mid-Jun–Sep)
- **West End Farmers Market** (Map p88; ☎ 604-879-3276; Nelson Park, between Bute & Thurlow Sts; ⓨ 9am-2pm Sat mid-Jun–mid-Oct)
- **Winter Farmers Market** (Map p90; ☎ 604-879-3276; Wise Hall, 1882 Adanac St; ⓨ 10am-2pm alternate Sats Nov-Apr)

---

finding something that nobody else (at least nobody who shops in malls) has. If you're in a budgeting mood, peruse the 'Steals and Deals' rack at the back.

Food

our pick **Dutch Girl Chocolates** (Map p90; ☎ 604-251-3221; 1002 Commercial Dr; ⓨ 11am-6pm Mon-Sat, noon-5pm Sun) Since chocolate is the most important food group, a pilgrimage to this hidden gem Commercial Dr store is essential. The little creaky floored shop is artfully draped with an Aladdin's cave of totally irresistible choc treats, many made in the kitchen you'll glimpse out back through the hatch. Pick up some milk, white or dark chocolate models of cars or tennis racquets, peruse the old-fashioned jars of liquorice sweeties or create a selection box of handmade truffles and bonbons from the cabinet by the counter. And if you're a visiting Netherlander pining for home, you can pick up all your fave branded Dutch confections right here.

La Grotta Del Formaggio (Map p90; ☎ 604-255-3911; 1791 Commercial Dr; ⓨ 9am-5pm Mon-Sat, noon-5pm Sun) If you insist on eating something other than chocolate, stroll south on Commercial and drop into this legendary deli, a holdover from the days when this was Vancouver's 'Little Italy.' Peruse the lip-smacking cheese selection then check out the wall of marzipan, olive oil and cream crackers. A good spot to gather some mighty fine picnic fixings, you can scoff the lot in nearby Grandview Park.

Specialty

Lazy Susan's (off Map p93; ☎ 604-873-9722; 3647 Main St; ⓨ noon-6pm Mon-Sat, noon-5pm Sun) SoMa's Aladdin's cave of irresistible trinkets, you'll spend most of your time here perusing Scrabble tile earrings, old ties transformed into coin purses or vintage reproduction greetings cards. Like most area stores, it's an owner-operated joint and the staff are ever-ready to chat, especially if you're having trouble choosing between a cactus-shaped teapot and a broach shaped like a palm tree.

Mountain Equipment Co-op (Map p93; ☎ 604-872-7858; 130 W Broadway; ⓨ 10am-7pm Mon-Wed, 10am-9pm Thu & Fri, 9am-6pm Sat, 11am-5pm Sun) The granddaddy of outdoor stores, where grown hikers have been known to weep at the amazing selection of own-brand clothing, kayaks, sleeping bags and clever camping gadgets, MEC has been turning campers into fully fledged outdoor enthusiasts for years. You'll have to be a member to buy here, but that's easy to arrange and only costs $5. There are several other outdoor shops clustered nearby.

Rubber Rainbow Condom Company (Map p88; ☎ 604-683-3423; 953 Denman St; ⓨ 11am-7pm) Doing brisk business in its West End location, this fun, funky condom and lube store serves all manner of experiment-inviting accessories, including studded, vibrating and 'full-fitting strawberry flavored' varieties. Ask for a selection pack if you're going to be in town for a while – you never know how lucky you might get.

GETTING THERE & AWAY

Air

Vancouver International Airport (Map p86; YVR; ☎ 604-207-7077; www.yvr.ca) is the main West Coast hub for airlines from Canada, the US and international locales. It's in Richmond, a 13km/30-minute drive from downtown. See p429.

Intra-Canada flights arriving here include regular **Westjet** (☎ 403-444-2552; 800-538-5696, www.westjet.com) services from Calgary ($189, 90 minutes) and beyond, and **Air Canada** (☎ 514-393-3333, 888-247-2262; www.aircanada.com) services from Victoria (from $122, 25 minutes) and points east across the country. See Transport (p429) for more information on routes and airlines.

Linked to the main airport by shuttle bus, the **South Terminal** (Map p86) receives BC-only flights from smaller regional airlines and floatplane operators.

Several handy floatplane services also run from the downtown Vancouver waterfront, mostly serving routes to Victoria and beyond. These include **Harbour Air Seaplanes** (☎ 604-274-1277, 800-665-0212; www.harbour-air.com; $134, 35 mins) and **West Coast Air** (☎ 604-606-6888, 800-347-2222; www.westcoastair.com; $134, 35 minutes) services.

Helijet (☎ 604-273-4688, 800-665-4354; www.helijet.com) helicopter services also arrive on the waterfront, just east of Canada Place, from Victoria ($229, 30 minutes).

Boat

BC Ferries (☎ 250-386-3431, 888-223-3779; www.bcferries.com) services arrive at Tsawwassen – an hour south of downtown – from Vancouver Island's Swartz Bay (passenger/vehicle $13/43, 95 minutes) and Duke Point (passenger/vehicle $13/43, two hours) terminals. Services also arrive here from the Southern Gulf Islands (p218).

Additional ferries arrive at West Vancouver's Horseshoe Bay – 30 minutes from downtown – from Vancouver Island's Departure Bay (passenger/vehicle $13/43, 95 minutes) in Nanaimo. Services also arrive from Bowen Island (passenger/vehicle $8.45/23.90, 20 minutes) and from Langdale (passenger/vehicle $11/37.25, 40 minutes) on the Sunshine Coast.

Bus

Vancouver's main bus station is at **Pacific Central Station** (Map p88; 1150 Station St), the railway terminus near Science World. It's on the SkyTrain transit line (Main St-Science World station).

Greyhound Canada (☎ 800-661-8747; www.greyhound.ca) services arrive here from Whistler ($25.40, 2¾ hours, up to nine daily), Kelowna ($71.10, six hours, six daily), Hope ($25.40, three hours, nine daily) and beyond. For cross-border Greyhounds, see Transport (p431).

Pacific Coach Lines (☎ 604-662-7575, 800-661-1725; www.pacificcoach.com) services from downtown Victoria ($41.75, 3½ hours, up to 16 daily) arrive here, via the BC Ferries' Swartz Bay–Tsawwassen route. The company also operates from Whistler and Squamish to Vancouver International Airport ($49, three hours, up to 12 daily).

Snowbus (☎ 604-331-7850; www.snowbus.ca) operates a ski-friendly winter-only service between Whistler and Vancouver (one-way/return $23.81/42.86, 2½ hours, two daily).

Serving the Sunshine Coast, twice-daily **Malaspina Coach Lines** (☎ 604-885-2217, 877-227-8287; www.malaspinacoach.com) buses arrive from Gibsons ($19, two hours), Sechelt ($29, three hours) and Powell River ($47, five to six hours).

Quick Coach Lines (☎ 604-940-4428, 800-665-2122; www.quickcoach.com) operates an express shuttle between Seattle and Vancouver, departing from downtown Seattle (US$42, four hours, up to six daily) and the city's Sea-Tac International Airport (US$56, 4½ hours, up to seven daily).

Car & Motorcycle

If you're coming from Washington State in the US, you'll be on the I-5 until you hit the border town of Blaine, then you'll be on Hwy 99 in Canada. It's about an hour's drive from here to downtown Vancouver. Hwy 99 continues through downtown, across the Lions Gate Bridge to Horseshoe Bay, Squamish and Whistler.

If you're coming from the east, you'll probably be on the Trans-Canada Hwy (Hwy 1), which snakes through the city's eastern end, eventually meeting with Hastings St. If you want to go downtown, turn left onto Hastings and follow it into the city center, or continue on along the North Shore towards Whistler.

All the recognized car rental chains have Vancouver branches. Avis, Budget, Hertz, Lo-Cost and Thrifty also have airport branches.

Train

Trains arrive from across Canada and the US northwest at Pacific Central Station. **VIA Rail** (☎ 888-842-7245; www.viarail.ca) services arrive from Kamloops North ($116, 10 hours, three weekly), Jasper ($243, 20 hours, three weekly) and Edmonton ($327, 27 hours, three weekly) among others.

The **Amtrak** (☎ 800-872-7245; www.amtrak.com) *Cascades* service arrives here from Eugene (US$59-86, 10 hours, two daily), Portland (US$44-64, eight hours, three daily) and Seattle (US$30-35, 3½-four hours, five daily).

GETTING AROUND
To/From the Airport

The new 16-station **Canada Line** (☎ 604-953-3333; www.canadaline.com) rapid transit train system runs from the airport into downtown Vancouver. The full trip to Waterfront Station takes 25 minutes. At time of writing, fares to and from the airport were expected to be at least $2 above the price of a regular three-zone transit ticket.

Alternatively, the **Vancouver Airporter** (☎ 604-946-8866, 800-668-3141; www.yvrairporter.com; one-way/return $13.75/21.50; ⊙ 5.30am-11.45pm, reduced in winter) shuttle bus service delivers passengers to many city center hotels in about 40 minutes. Pay the driver or buy a ticket at the desk on level two of the airport.

Taxis charge up to $35 for the 30-minute drive from the airport to downtown Vancouver. Follow the airport signs for pick-up points.

Bicycle

Vancouver is a relatively good cycling city, with around 240km of designated bike routes. For handy resources and a citywide route map, visit www.vancouver.ca/cycling. If you're traveling sans bike, you can rent from businesses around the city (p102). Cyclists can take their wheels for free on the SkyTrain, SeaBus and bike-rack fitted transit buses.

Boat

Aquabus Ferries (Map p88; ☎ 604-689-5858; www.theaquabus.com; adult/child from $3/1.50) runs mini vessels (some big enough to carry bikes) between the foot of Hornby St and Granville Island. They service additional spots around False Creek, including Science World.

Their cutthroat rival is **False Creek Ferries** (Map p88; ☎ 604-684-7781; www.granvilleislandferries.bc.ca; adult/child from $3/1.50), which operates a similar Granville Island service, this time from the Aquatic Centre, plus ports of call around False Creek.

Both operators offer day passes at the same prices: adult/child $14/8.

Car & Motorcycle

Rush hour line-ups to cross the Lions Gate Bridge to the North Shore frequently snake far up Georgia St. Try the alternative Second Narrows Bridge. Other peak-time hotspots are the George Massey Tunnel and Hwy 1 to Surrey.

Parking is at a premium downtown: there are few free spots available on residential side streets and traffic wardens are predictably predatory. Many streets have metered parking but the surfeit of pay-parking lots (from $4 per hour) are a better proposition – arrive before 9am at some for early bird discounts.

Public Transportation

TransLink (☎ 604-953-3333; www.translink.bc.ca), the public transportation authority, oversees bus, SkyTrain, Canada Line and SeaBus services. Visit its website for a useful trip planning tool or pick up a copy of the *Getting Around* map ($1.95) from area convenience and bookstores.

A ticket bought on any service is valid for up to 90 minutes of transfer travel across the entire network, depending on the zone you intend to travel in. There are three zones, which become progressively more expensive the further you intend to journey. One-zone tickets cost $2.50/1.75 per adult/child, two-zone tickets are $3.75/2.50 and three-zone tickets cost $5/3.50. An all-day, all-zone pass costs $9/7. If you're traveling after 6:30pm or on weekends or holidays, all fares are classed as one-zone trips.

BUS

Buses use on-board fare machines, so exact change is required. The network is extensive in the downtown area – especially along Hastings St, Main St, Burrard St and Broadway. Many buses have bike racks and are wheelchair accessible.

The 99 B-Line express service operates between UBC and the Broadway and Commercial SkyTrain stations (99 B-Line).

These buses have their own limited arrival and departure points.

There is also a 12-route night bus system that runs every 30 minutes between 1:30am and 4am across the Lower Mainland. The last bus leaves downtown Vancouver at 3:09am. Look for the night bus signs at designated stops.

CANADA LINE

The new rapid transit train line links Richmond and Vancouver along the Cambie St corridor. It includes a branch line out to Vancouver International Airport, enabling riders to travel directly to and from the airport and the downtown core. The 16 stations along the route include Broadway-City Hall, Yaletown-Roundhouse, Vancouver City Centre (at the corner of Georgia and Granville Sts) and Waterfront. The line is expected to be popular with day-trippers traveling from Vancouver to Richmond.

At time of writing, timetables were not yet available. Fares reflect the Translink zone system, although a $2 premium above the three-zone transit fare was anticipated for the airport branch line.

SEABUS

This three-vessel aquatic shuttle fleet operates every 10 to 30 minutes throughout the day, taking 12 minutes to cross the Burrard Inlet between Waterfront Station and Lonsdale Quay. At Lonsdale there's a bus terminal servicing routes throughout North Vancouver and West Vancouver. SeaBus tickets must be purchased in advance from vending machines on either side of the route. Services depart from Waterfront Station between 6:15am and 1:20am Monday to Saturday (8am to 11:15pm Sunday). The vessels are wheelchair accessible and bike friendly.

SKYTRAIN

The SkyTrain rapid transit network consists of two routes. The 35-minute Expo Line takes passengers to and from downtown Vancouver and Surrey, via stops in Burnaby (for Swangard soccer stadium and Metrotown shopping centre) and New Westminster, among others. The newer Millennium Line alights near shopping malls and suburban residential districts in Coquitlam and Burnaby.

Trains depart every two to eight minutes between 5am and 1:15am Monday to Friday (6am to 12:30am Saturday, 7am to 11:30pm Sunday). SkyTrain services are wheelchair accessible.

Tickets must be purchased from station vending machines (change given for bills up to $20) before boarding.

Taxi

Flagging a cab on main downtown streets shouldn't take too long, but it's easiest to get your hotel to call you one. For green travelers, **Yellow Cab** (☎ 604-681-1111) operates a fleet comprising almost all hybrid vehicles. The other main operator is **Black Top & Checker Cabs** (☎ 604-731-1111). Taximeters start at $2.73 and then add $1.58 per kilometer.

THE LOWER MAINLAND

While it's tempting to stick around in the city, travelers with time to spare should make the effort to stray a little further than the boundaries of their free Tourism Vancouver map. A short drive or swift transit hop across Burrard Inlet brings you to the mountain-backed North Shore and the twin communities of North Vancouver and West Vancouver, complete with their outdoor attractions and activities. Alternatively, a visit to Richmond – now much easier to access via the Canada Line – delivers the foodie appeal of North America's best modern-day Asian suburb, plus the historic fishing village of Steveston. Further afield, Bowen Island is a fun day-out ferry skip from West Vancouver's Horseshoe Bay; pretty Fort Langley houses the historic site where modern-day BC began; and old-school New Westminster offers a boardwalk Fraser River waterfront that's an easy (and picturesque) 25-minute SkyTrain trundle from downtown. Don your intrepid explorer's hat, pick-up your transit day pass and get moving.

NORTH VANCOUVER
pop 45,000

Nestled between Indian Arm and West Vancouver, 'North Van' is centered on the clutch of tower blocks you can see shimmering across the Burrard Inlet from downtown. While its glory days as a trading port and shipbuilding center are long gone, it's an intriguing and SeaBus-accessible spot to spend the afternoon: this is the home of several of the region's top outdoor attractions but it also has its own wanderable town center. If you're looking for a walking route, head north up Lonsdale Ave from the quay (it's very steep but it's lined with pit stop coffee shops), turn west through Victoria Park and then amble back downhill to the waterfront along Chesterfield Ave. For additional information on what to do here, peruse the visitors section of the municipal website (www.cnv.org).

Sights & Activities

If you've come over on the SeaBus, your first port of call should be the nearby **Lonsdale Quay Market** (Map p86; ☎ 604-985-6261; www .lonsdalequay.com; 123 Carrie Cates Court; ☉ 9am-7pm), which mixes jewelry, wine, book and bakery stands with a large food fair – the Indian and Greek stalls are recommended. Once you've had your fill, weave along the **waterfront trail** that links the old shipyards east of here and then hike up ultra-steep **Lonsdale Ave** for its main-drag stores, restaurants and coffee shops.

Alternatively, take bus 236 from the quay's transit terminal to the region's biggest visitor attraction. The 140m-long cabled walkway of **Capilano Suspension Bridge & Park** (Map p86; ☎ 604-985-7474; www.capbridge.com; 3735 Capilano Rd; adult/youth/child $27.95/16.65/8.75; ☉ 8:30am-8pm mid-May–Aug; earlier closing Sep–mid-May) sways 70m over the fast-running waters of tree-lined Capilano Canyon. It's an awesome sight, especially when you're halfway across and your legs have turned to jelly. Aside from the bridge, the park includes totem poles, historic displays, a network of canopy bridges, Vancouver's biggest souvenir shop and a series of easy rainforest trails – the Cliffhanger Boardwalk is best.

If you're on a tight budget, Capilano can be pricey. Luckily, you can sway for free at the far more tranquil **Lynn Canyon Park** (Map p86; ☎ 604-984-3149; ☉ 7am-9pm May-Aug, 7am-7pm or dusk Sep-Apr), which has a less-showy, slightly smaller suspension bridge, plus good hiking trails. Check out its **Ecology Centre** (Map p86; ☎ 604-981-3103; www.dnv.org; 3663 Park Rd; suggested donation $2; ☉ 10am-5pm Jun-Sep, 10am-5pm Mon-Fri, noon-4pm Sat & Sun Oct-May), which illuminates the area's rich biodiversity. Not reachable

on transit, you'll have to drive here: take the Lynn Valley Rd exit off Hwy 1, then turn right on Peters Rd, where you'll see signs pointing the way.

Bus 236 will also take you to **Grouse Mountain** (Map p86; ☎ 604-980-9311; www.grousemountain.com; 6400 Nancy Greene Way; SkyRide admission adult/youth/child $34.95/20.95/12.95, winter ski lift adult/youth/child $52.50/42/23.10; ☉ 9am-10pm), which touts itself as the 'peak of Vancouver.' In summer, your SkyRide ticket gives you mountain-top access to restaurants, hiking trails, a cheeky lumberjack show and a grizzly bear refuge where two inhabitants lumber around just a few feet from the cameras. A zipline course was also recently installed ($75). If you don't want to pay, you can join the throng hiking up the steep and unforgiving 2.9km **Grouse Grind** trail. Bring water, expect to suffer and don't give up. It's a one-way trail, but Grinders can buy a special $5 ticket to take the SkyRide down. In winter, Grouse is Vancouver's favorite snow-covered playground, with 26 ski and snowboard runs, marked snowshoe trails, a small ice rink and plenty of après ski shenanigans.

A less busy nature escape from the city and a great spot to hug 500-year-old Douglas firs, **Mt Seymour Provincial Park** (Map p86; ☎ 604-986-9371; www.bcparks.ca; 1700 Mt Seymour Rd) is crisscrossed with hiking and mountain biking trails. Some areas are rugged, so backpackers should register at the park office, where trail maps are also available. Like Grouse, the park transforms in winter, when **Mt Seymour Resorts** (☎ 604-986-2261; www.mountseymour.com; adult/youth/child $42/35/21; ☉ 9:30am-10pm Mon-Fri, 8:30am-10pm Sat & Sun Jan-Mar) runs five lifts to take you skiing or snowboarding on its 23 runs. There are also 10km of snowshoe trails, an eight-run toboggan area and a four-lane tubing course. To get to Seymour, take the Mt Seymour Parkway exit east, then turn north on Mt Seymour Rd. There's also a $5-each-way winter shuttle bus from Parkgate Mall – see the website for details.

Sleeping

Grouse Inn (Map p86; ☎ 604-988-1701, 800-779-7888; www.grouseinn.com; 1633 Capilano Rd; d/ste from $125/138; ☒) Resembling a stuccoed shopping mall from the outside, this family-friendly motel is a favorite among winter skiers and summer hikers and is suffused with amenities, including a playground, restaurant, outdoor pool and free continental breakfast. Rooms (some with kitchens) have bright and breezy interiors – especially if you like busy, 1980s-style bedspreads – and come in a wide array of configurations, including hot-tub suites and larger rooms for groups.

Lonsdale Quay Hotel (Map p86; ☎ 604-986-6111, 800-836-6111; www.lonsdalequayhotel.com; 123 Carrie Cates Ct; d/ste $149/189) With easy access to the mountains but also close to the SeaBus terminal for swift downtown hops, some of the rooms at this older boutique hotel have great views of the Vancouver skyline. Most interiors will be familiar to the business traveler crowd but some have been decorated with added style, including two great family rooms with bunk beds and bath toys.

Thistledown House B&B (Map p86; ☎ 604-986-7173, 888-633-7173; www.thistle-down.com; 3910 Capilano Rd; r $150-275) Handily located on the road to Capilano and Grouse, this 1920s Craftsman-style sleepover is a cut above standard B&Bs: just check its gourmet breakfast menu. Among the six elegantly decorated rooms, the most palatial suite – it's called Under the Apple Tree – is surprisingly secluded and includes a fireplace, sunken sitting room, whirlpool bathtub and large windows opening onto a private patio. Adult oriented.

Eating

Tomahawk Restaurant (Map p86; ☎ 604-988-2612; 1550 Philip Ave; mains $8-16; ⊙ 8am-9pm Sun-Thu, 8am-10pm Fri & Sat) A colorful blast from North Van's pioneering past, the Tomahawk has been heaping its plates with comfort food since 1926. A bustling weekend brunch spot – if the massive Yukon bacon and eggs greasefest or the frightening Skookum chief burger don't kill your hangover, nothing will – it's also great for lunch or dinner, when chicken potpies and organic meatloaf hit the menu. As you waddle back out, peruse the First Nations artifacts lining the walls.

our pick Burgoo (Map p86; ☎ 604-904-0933; 3 Lonsdale Ave; mains $12-16; ⊙ 11am-10am) A short stroll from the SeaBus at the foot of Lonsdale Ave (it's an easy hop over from downtown Vancouver for a dinner excursion with a difference) this cozy spot has the interior of a rustic log cabin – complete with large stone fireplace – making it just about the best place to be on a cold or rainy night. The menu of comfort food with a twist also helps: try the Guinness-infused Irish stew, spicy apricot lamb tagine or smile-triggering butter chicken with brown basmati rice and you'll feel instantly cheered. There's also a wide array of homemade soups and heaping salads. If all you fancy is a few beers, dip into the dark and hoppy Burgoo Brew or the rich and blackcurranty Middle Mountain Black Mead. There's live jazz on Sunday nights to keep your toes tapping.

Jagerhof Schnitzel House (Map p86; ☎ 604-980-4316; 71 Lonsdale Ave; mains $9-18; ⊙ 11:30am-2pm Tue-Fri, 5-10pm Tue-Sun) An old-school hangover from the days when expat Germans ran taste-of-the-old-country eateries across BC, this family-run, North Van institution has been defying restaurant fashions for three decades. The locals keep rolling in for home-cooked, stomach-lagging dishes including bulging sausages, chicken Kiev, goulash soup and the excellent schnitzels, with fillings including shrimp, salmon and cheddar. Dessert is admirable here, too – try the palatschinken crepes.

Gusto di Quattro (Map p86; ☎ 604-924-4444; 1 Lonsdale Ave; mains $12-24; ⊙ 11:30am-2pm Mon-Fri, 5-10pm Sun-Thu, 5-11pm Fri & Sat) A warm, romantic family-run restaurant doing all the pasta classics (in huge portions) better than anyone in town. Try the warm goat's cheese salad to get you started, then dive headfirst into the rotolo pasta roll crammed with four cheeses. Wash it all down with something from the excellent wine selection: there are some great Italian tipples here plus choice international vintages.

Observatory (Map p86; ☎ 604-998-4403; Grouse Mt; mains $35-40; ⊙ 5-10pm) Perched atop Grouse Mountain, the fine-dining Observatory serves up dishes of seared scallops and roasted beef tenderloin with some of the best views in BC – right down over the crenulated waterfront of Stanley Park and the twinkling towers of downtown Vancouver. The Grouse SkyRide is complimentary with your dinner here, while the adjacent, and much more laid back, Altitudes Bistro offers pub-style food in a casual ski lodge setting.

Getting There & Around

SeaBus vessels arrive at Lonsdale Quay from Vancouver's Waterfront Station ($3.75, 12 min) every 10-30 minutes during the day.

From the terminal at the quay, bus 236 runs to Capilano Suspension Bridge and the base of Grouse Mountain.

Rocky Mountaineer Vacations trundles its popular **Whistler Mountaineer** (☎ 604-606-8460, 888-687-7245; www.whistlermountaineer.com) train into North Vancouver from Whistler ($119, three hours, daily mid-May to early Oct).

For the locals' take on the area, consider the friendly folk at **North Van Green Tours** (☎ 604-290-0145; www.northvangreentours.com; adult/youth/child $50/45/40). They run a four-hour guided trek of the North Shore's natural treasures in an ecologically friendly biofuel van.

WEST VANCOUVER
pop 42,000
Often referred to as the region's richest neighborhood, there's much more to 'West Van' than the grand homes perched imperiously on the cliffs overlooking the water. Take a 250 bus from downtown Vancouver and within 15 minutes you'll be trundling along Marine Dr among the village-sized enclaves of Ambleside and Dundarave. Alight anywhere along the route, wander around the stores and cafés and jump back on the bus whenever you're ready to return to town: it's an easy and surprisingly accessible half-day out. For more information, visit www.westvancouver.ca.

Sights & Activities
If you've come over on bus 250, get off at Marine Dr & 24th St in the heart of little **Dundarave Village**. Check out the string of shops and galleries here then wander south down 25th St to tiny **Dundarave Park** where you'll have some great views across the inlet to Point Grey. Weave eastwards along the waterfront **Centennial Seawalk** and you'll eventually come to **Ambleside Park** – complete with a magnificent carved First Nations welcome figure, with its arms dramatically outstretched across the water. Marine Dr is a short stroll north from here for your bus back to downtown Vancouver.

Bus 250 can also deliver you within strolling distance of **Lighthouse Park** (Map p86; ☎ 604-925-7200; cnr Beacon Lane & Marine Dr) where some of the Lower Mainland's largest and oldest coastal trees reside. Around 13km of hiking trails wind through the area: the most popular leads to Point Atkinson Light-

house with its views across the shimmering waterfront.

Lurking in the mountains 8km north of West Van, **Cypress Provincial Park** (Map p84; ☎ 604-924-2200; www. bcparks.ca) has some great summertime hiking trails and a cool bike park. In winter, its **Cypress Mountain** (Map p86; ☎ 604-926-5612; www.cypressmountain.com; adult/youth/child $60/49.50/29.50; ☒ 9am-10pm mid-Dec–Mar, 9am-4pm Mar-season end) ski area competes for local powder nuts with six lifts, 52 runs and superior average snowfall – plus some snow-shoeing, tubing and cross-country skiing courses. Since being chosen as the freestyle skiing and snowboarding venue for the 2010 Winter Olympic and Paralympic Games, facilities at Cypress have been given a long-overdue upgrade (including the swanky new Cypress Creek Lodge). There's a winter shuttle bus from Lonsdale Quay – see www.cypresscoachlines.com – but if you're driving, follow Hwy 1 from Vancouver, take Exit 8 and follow the signs along Cypress Bowl Rd.

Sleeping & Eating
Horseshoe Bay Motel (Map p86; ☎ 604-921-7454, 877-717-3377; hbaymotel@telus.net; 6588 Royal Ave; s/d $109/129) Unless you can persuade one of the wealthy locals to offer you a spare room, this 23-unit plain Jane, nothing-to-write-home-about motel is one of the few options available for staying in West Van. Its rooms are standard motel fare, but if you have an early morning ferry to catch from nearby Horseshoe Bay, you'll be happy with even the most basic home comforts.

Lighthouse Park B&B (Map p86; ☎ 604-926-5959, 800-926-0262; www.lighthousepark.com; 4875 Water Lane; ste from $175) Live like a West Van local at this elegant two-suite hostelry, with beautifully decorated Laura Ashley–influenced interiors and decadent flourishes such as thick bed linens, private entrances and a tranquil flower-strewn courtyard. Each suite has a fridge and DVD player, as well as a decanter of sherry for that essential alfresco evening tipple. As the name suggests, it's across the street from Lighthouse Park. Adult oriented.

Savary Island Pie Company (Map p86; ☎ 604-926-4021; 1533 Marine Dr; mains $7-11.50; ☒ 10am-6:30pm) This comfy Ambleside nook with its mismatched tables and wobbly wooden chairs is a chatty stop-off for a light lunch, or coffee and a baked treat. The slices of homemade meat pie are the main attraction, especially the satisfying chicken potpie, and each is served with salad or soup. Deep-dish fruit pies are also available. While accompanying bottles of Guinness and Sleemans' Honey Brown make good desserts, most go for the chunky chocolate brownies instead.

Red Lion Bar & Grill (Map p86; ☎ 604-926-8838; 2427 Marine Dr; mains $9-16; ⊙ 11am-midnight) In the middle of Dundarave Village, this traditional-looking Brit-style pub serves a full roster of pub-grub staples including steak & kidney pies and Angus beef hamburgers, but they mix it up with a few gourmet offerings such as escargots and a tasting plate of three pâtés. A popular weekend brunch spot, the interior is an evocative recreation of a Victorian bar, complete with an open fireplace, etched and stained glass panels and acres of wooden millwork. If it's sunny, snag a patio seat.

Beach House (Map p86; ☎ 604-922-1414; www .thebeachhouserestaurant.ca; 150 25th St; mains $20-32; ⊙ 11:30am-10pm Mon-Fri, 11:30am-10:30pm Sat, 10:30am-10pm Sun) Overlooking the shimmering coastline at Dundarave Pier, this romantic and welcoming restaurant is the place to head if you want to push the boat out (not literally). Book ahead for a candle-lit window table and tuck in to a menu of Pacific Northwest delicacies like pan-roasted sablefish, Dungeness crab, scallops and wild prawn linguine and the recommended rack of lamb. Sunday brunch is a local favorite here.

HORSESHOE BAY & BOWEN ISLAND

The coastal village of Horseshoe Bay marks the end of the North Shore and the start of trips to Whistler, via the Sea to Sky Hwy (Hwy 99), or Vancouver Island and the Sunshine Coast via BC Ferries. You can also catch a 20-minute ferry ride to Bowen Island from here. For Horseshoe Bay information, check www.horseshoebaybc.ca. Bowen has its own **Visitor Centre** (☎ 604-947-9024; www.bowenisland.org; 432 Cardena Rd; ⊙ 9am-4pm mid-May–Sep, 10am-3pm Fri-Sun Oct–mid-May) located on your right as you leave the ferry.

Sights & Activities

Accessible from downtown Vancouver via buses 250 and 257, the pretty marina village of Horseshoe Bay has plenty of little shops and eateries to poke around and offers some good views up Howe Sound to the distant glacial peaks. Most of your wandering will be centered on Bay St and from here you can take a whale-watching boat trek with **Sewell's Sea Safari** (Map p86; ☎ 604-921-3474; www.sewellsmarina.com; 6409 Bay St; adult/youth/child $73/65/43; ⊙ Apr-Oct).

Just west of the village, the jutting promontory of **Whytecliff Park** (Map p86; ☎ 604-925-7200; 7100-block Marine Dr) attracts scuba divers to its protected waters and rock climbers to its granite cliffs. Trails lead to waterfront vistas and a gazebo, from where you can watch the sailboats in Howe Sound. The rocky beach is a great place to play, swim or scamper over the rocks.

Across from Horseshoe Bay on Bowen Island – a popular summertime day trip from Vancouver – you'll disembark in **Snug Cove** where the boardwalk marina is lined with gable-topped wood-built galleries, cafés and the smashing old, flower-decked **Union Steamship Chandlery**. It's not far from here to the **pier**, a popular haunt for al fresco musicians. The island is crisscrossed with hiking and biking trails, including the 45-minute trek from the dock to Killarney Lake, itself encircled by a 4km trail.

For visiting paddlers, rentals and scenic tours are offered by **Bowen Island Sea Kayaking** (☎ 604-947-9266, 800-605-2925; www.bowenisland kayaking.com; rental 3hr/day $45/65, tours from $65). Its three-hour tour from Snug Cove, north towards Whistler's mountains or south to Apodoca Beach, (no experience required) is recommended.

Sleeping & Eating

Lodge at the Old Dorm (Map p86; ☎ 604-947-0947; www.lodgeattheolddorm.com; 460 Melmore Rd, Bowen Island; r $95-150) Built by the Union Steamship Company to house its staff, this lovingly renovated B&B lodge – a short stroll north from the ferry dock – is dripping with art deco and arts and crafts accents and is a warm and convivial place to stay. The six rooms are bright and comfortable – the Lady Alexandra room with its own private garden is our favorite – and the continental buffet breakfast, served on a central counter in the kitchen, is full of yummy home-baked treats.

Snug Café (Map p86; ☎ 604-947-0402; mains $4-8; ⊙ 8:30am-5pm) Bowen's fave chatty hangout, it's all about hugging your organic latte on the sun-dappled deck at this well-located café – plus indulging in the tempting home-baked pastries and bakery treats, of course. Full breakfasts and light lunches are also part of the mix or you can grab a smoothie and some trail mix for your hike around the island.

Doc Morgan's Inn (Map p86; ☎ 604-947-0108; Union Steamship Marina, Bowen Island; mains $8-22; 🕑 11am-11pm) An ideal après-kayaking spot (or just avoid any strenuous activity altogether and head straight here), this Bowen local legend in Snug Cove is divided between a family-friendly dining room and a smashing pub upstairs, each with patios overlooking the marina. Hearty comfort food and seafood treats are the approach here: the fish and chips are particularly recommended.

Getting There & Around

BC Ferries (☎ 250-386-3431, 888-223-3779; www.bcferries.com) services ply the short route between Horseshoe Bay and Bowen Island (passenger/vehicle $8.45/23.90, 20 minutes, 16 daily).

Granville Island Water Taxi (☎ 604-484-8497, 888-568-7247; www.giwt.ca) operates a Bowen Island Express boat service from Granville Island to Snug Cove (one-way/return $15/25, up to 10 daily). Reservations recommended.

TransLink (☎ 604-947-0229; www.translink.bc.ca; adult/child $2.50/1.75) operates two community shuttle buses on Bowen – C10 and C11. Both services stop in Snug Cove.

BURNABY

pop 203,000

Immediately east of Vancouver via Hastings St, no-nonsense Burnaby is a residential suburb with a strip mall feel. Luckily, there are a handful of attractions to keep you away from the shops. For information, contact **Tourism Burnaby** (☎ 604-419-0377; www.tourismburnaby.com).

Nestled near Burnaby's residential side streets, tranquil **Deer Lake Park** (Map p86) is criss-crossed with verdant meadow and waterfront walks and also offers boat rentals. The nearby **Burnaby Village Museum** (Map p86; ☎ 604-293-6501; www.burnabyvillagemuseum.ca; 6501 Deer Lake Ave; adult/youth/child $12/9/6; 🕑 11am-4:30pm May-Aug) re-creates the atmosphere of a BC pioneer town with replica homes and businesses of the time and a wonderfully restored 1912 carousel.

Topping Burnaby Mountain, **Simon Fraser University** (Map p86; ☎ 604-291-3111; www.sfu.com; 8888 University Dr) is the Lower Mainland's second main campus community. Visitor attractions include the **Museum of Archaeology & Ethnology** (☎ 604-291-3325; free; 🕑 10am-4pm Mon-Fri) and the **SFU Gallery** (☎ 778-782-4266; free; 🕑 10am-5pm Tue-Fri, noon-5pm Sat).

Hidden in Deer Lake Park, shorefront **Hart House** (Map p86; ☎ 604-298-4278; 6664 Deer Lake Ave; mains $22-34; 🕑 11:30-2:30pm Tue-Fri, 5:30-10pm Tue-Sun, 11am-2pm Sun) is an atmospheric mock-Tudor hulk housing a Pacific Northwest restaurant where you can feast on lip-smacking classics like wild BC salmon and roasted rack of lamb. Alternatively, there's a more innovative approach at the **Pear Tree** (Map p86; ☎ 604-299-2772; 4120 E Hastings St; mains $20-32; 🕑 5-10pm Tue-Sat), which combines a swanky gold and wood-lined interior with Euro-fusion twists on regional ingredients – try the beef tenderloin with stilton and the eyebrow-raising lobster cappuccino.

NEW WESTMINSTER

pop 58,500

Easily accessed via a 25-minute SkyTrain ride from downtown Vancouver, New West was designated the first capital of the Colony of British Columbia in 1859, before losing the title to Victoria in 1866 when BC and Vancouver Island merged. The 'Royal City' continued as a bustling commercial hub until the 1960s when the new Trans-Canada Hwy bypassed the area, triggering a painful decline. Nowadays a little careworn, it's still worth a half-day trip for some historic reminders and the excellent boardwalk hub on the banks of the Fraser River. For more information, check www.tourismnewwestminster.com.

From the SkyTrain station, head downhill to the waterfront on 8th St and cross the railway tracks via the overhead walkway. Check out the quaint 1899-built **Canadian Pacific Railway Station** on your right: a surfeit of trains, trams and streetcars used to steam in here during the city's heyday. Over the bridge, you'll enter the **Westminster Quay Public Market** (Map p86; ☎ 604-520-3881; www.rivermarket.ca; 810 Quayside Dr; 🕑 9:30am-6pm), which was undergoing an extensive renovation when we visited recently. If the shops aren't open, head straight through the building and exit onto the boardwalk.

DETOUR: BUNTZEN LAKE

If you've had your fill of city crowds, this dramatic, sigh-inducing natural retreat will remind you of just why you came to BC in the first place. The giant **Buntzen Lake** (☎ 604-469-9679) reservoir is surrounded on three sides by steep, tree-covered mountains and on its fourth side by a gently curving beach, complete with picnic tables, old-growth trees and those ambling, ever-present Canada geese. There's an array of well-marked hiking and mountain bike trails through the forest and if you haven't packed your own canoe, there's a handy **rental store** (☎ 604-469-9928; Sunnyside Rd) near the park entrance – don't paddle too far out though, the lake is bigger than it looks. Buntzen is an ideal place to bring the kids: you can keep an eye on them splashing in the water, while you sit back on the grass in the shade of the trees.

If you're driving to Buntzen from Vancouver, follow Hastings St (Hwy 7A) east through the city to Burnaby and Coquitlam, where it becomes Barnet Hwy. Take the Ioco exit and follow Ioco Rd to the left. Turn right on First Ave and continue to Sunnyside Rd. Turn right again and continue to the Buntzen Lake entrance. The journey from Vancouver should take around an hour. It can get crowded here in summer, so arrive early to bag a good picnic spot.

In front of you is the expansive, still-busy **Fraser River**, the major trade route that fueled New West's initial development. Check out the large **bust of Simon Fraser** here, then clomp to your left along the wooden walkway. You'll come to the **World's Tallest Tin Soldier**, a 10m landmark denoting the spot where British troops arrived in 1859 to help build the new town. A few steps away is the excellent **Fraser River Discovery Centre** (Map p86; ☎ 604-521-8401; www.fraserriverdiscovery.org; 788 Quayside Dr; ☽ 10am-5pm Mon-Sat, 11am-5pm Sun), which relates the colorful economic and social stories of the river.

Once you're done with the waterfront, hike back up steep 8th St and turn right onto Royal Ave. After a few minutes, you'll come to the antique-lined **Irving House** (Map p86; ☎ 604-527-4640; www.nwpr.bc.ca; 302 Royal Ave; ☽ noon-5pm Wed-Sun May-Aug, noon-4pm Sat & Sun Sep-Apr), built in 1865 by trader William Irving. It's BC's oldest house museum.

For nosh or a java pit stop, try the market food court or duck into the laid-back bistro-style **Hideout Café** (Map p86; ☎ 604-521-3344; 716 Carnarvon St; mains $5-10; ☽ 7am-6pm Mon-Fri, 11am-6pm Sat) for great-value full breakfasts, hearty panini and satisfying homemade soups. It's a good spot for an end-of-afternoon beer.

RICHMOND
pop 174,000
Many Vancouverites say they don't like driving to Richmond – the flat, landmark-free vistas and unfamiliar street names apparently make it confusing – but with the arrival of the new Canada Line train system, the region's modern-day Chinatown is suddenly far more accessible from downtown. Hop onboard and head down the line for a half-day of Asian shopping malls – centered on the Golden Village area – followed by a taste-trip through some of the best contemporary Chinese, Japanese and Vietnamese restaurants in North America. For information, check www.tourismrichmond.com.

Sights & Activities
Shopping and eating are the main activities in Richmond and most spots are clustered in the **Golden Village**, a four-block area between No 3 Rd, Alderbridge Way, Garden City Rd and Sea Island Way. The oddly-named **Aberdeen Centre** (Map p86; ☎ 604-270-1234; www.aberdeencentre.com; 4151 Hazelbridge Way; ☽ 11am-7pm Mon-Wed, 11am-9pm Thu-Sat, 11am-7pm Sun) is the area's most celebrated mall and features Hong Kong–style shops, restaurants and food courts.

Known simply as the 'Buddhist Temple,' **Kuan Yin Temple** (Map p86; ☎ 604-274-2822; www.buddhisttemple.ca 9160 Steveston Hwy; admission free; ☽ 9:30am-5:30pm) is one of Canada's finest traditional-style Chinese buildings. Recalling the architecture of Beijing's Forbidden City, the highlight is its sumptuous Gracious Hall, complete with deep red and gold exterior walls and a gently flaring porcelain roof. Don't miss the calm-inducing classical garden.

Much bigger than downtown's Chinese night bazaar, the 300-plus vendors at Richmond's **Summer Night Market** (Map p86;

☎ 604-278-8000; www.summernightmarket.com; 12631 Vulcan Way; ⏰ 7pm-midnight Fri & Sat, 7-11pm Sun, mid-May–Sep) will take you several hours to properly trawl. Don't eat before you come, so that you can sample the amazing variety of takeaway – including steaming Malaysian, Korean, Japanese and Chinese treats – while you peruse the cheap iPod covers and near-designer kitsch.

Sleeping & Eating

Stone Hedge B&B (Map p86; ☎ 604-274-1070; www .thestonehedge.com; 5511 Cathay Rd; s/d from $125/140; ♿ 🐕) Named after the large stone wall and formidable cedar hedge surrounding the property, the four rooms at this surprisingly peaceful B&B are tastefully lined with reproduction antiques and landscape paintings. The best feature is the chintzy guest lounge, which opens directly onto a large, secluded swimming pool. Nearer the airport, you'll also find dozens of mid-range chain hotels.

Shanghai River Restaurant (Map p86; ☎ 604-233-8885; 7381 Westminster Hwy; mains $6-18; ⏰ 11am-2:30pm, 5:30-11pm) Grab a seat overlooking the kitchen window at this cavernous contemporary Northern Chinese eatery and you'll be mesmerized by the intricate handiwork that goes into folding the dumplings. Order plates to share here – one dish per person is the usual ratio – and be careful not to squirt everyone with the delicate but ultra-juicy pork or shrimp dumplings. The braised duck and ham soup is a great winter warmer, too.

ourpick Posh Charcoal Collaboration Dining (Map p86; ☎ 604-303-7674; 3779 Sexsmith Rd; lunch $11.88, dinner $15.88; ⏰ 11:30am-midnight Fri & Sat, 11:30am-11pm Sun) Despite the clunky name, this loungey little Japanese hot pot spot in an unassuming strip mall location indicates the move away from giant dining rooms to smaller bistro-style restaurants in Richmond. But despite the black granite counters and mood lighting, it's not at all pretentious and is a great place to head for a fun dinner. Each table has a camping-style stove topped with a pan of broth. You order plates of delicate tofu, crisp veggies and thinly-cut beef and cook it all yourself in the broth. This affordable all-you-can-eat *sukiyaki* approach invites experimentation, and you'll find yourself sampling lotus root and the oddly-textured *konjac* tofu. Wash it all down with some lovely Pearl Sake.

Hakkasan Contemporary Chinese Restaurant (Map p86; ☎ 604-273-9191; 2188 No 5 Rd; mains $13-23; ⏰ 11:30am-2:30pm, 5:30-10pm Tue-Sat) Like it says on the label, this is a contemporary take on Chinese eateries, which means an upscale wine bar-like interior that belies its location among a string of light industrial businesses. The menu combines traditional Hakka soul food and modern Cantonese dishes, with highlights including braised pork hock and scallop in a garlic-based sauce. The specialty, though, is the claypot roasted salty chicken.

Also recommended:

Shiang Garden Seafood Restaurant (Map p86; ☎ 604-273-8858; 4540 No 3 Rd; mains $10-22; ⏰ 9am-3pm, 5-10:30pm) The Cantonese (and some Taiwanese) dishes include plenty of attractive dim-sum options – try the sweet egg-yolk dessert version.

Fisherman's Terrace Restaurant (Map p86; ☎ 604-303-9739; 4151 Hazelbridge Way; mains $12-22; ⏰ 10am-3pm, 5:30-10pm) Classic, huge and chatty Cantonese dining room with 47 dim-sum varieties.

STEVESTON

An attractive old fishing village in Richmond's southwest corner, waterfront Steveston is a popular destination for sunset-viewing locals. It's also a hotspot for great fish and chips. Drive here from Vancouver via Hwy 99 (take the Steveston Hwy exit) for an early evening stroll along the boardwalk.

Check out the boats selling fresh-catch fish on the wharf here or consider an orca excursion in a covered Zodiac with the friendly folk at **Vancouver Whale Watch** (Map p86; ☎ 604-274-9565; www.vancouverwhalewatch.com; adult/youth/child $120/100/75; ⏰ Apr-Oct).

The nearby **Gulf of Georgia Cannery** (Map p86; ☎ 604-664-9009; 12138 4th Ave; adult/child $7.80/3.90; ⏰ 10am-5pm Thu-Mon May & Sep, 10am-5pm daily Jun-Aug) is an excellent, family-friendly National Historic Site illuminating the former fish processing plant and the 400 'slimers' who worked the line here. Free and evocative hourly tours are available.

From here, weave eastwards along the shoreline trail for an invigorating, picturesque stroll. You'll pass art installations recalling the area's bustling fishing sector – check out the remnants of old building piles in the water – before coming to the **Britannia Shipyard** (Map p86; ☎ 604-718-8050;

5180 Westwater Dr; 10am-6pm Tue-Sun May-Sep, 10am-6pm Sat, noon-4pm Sun Oct-Apr), another National Historic Site. This one's not as slick but it's just as fascinating: peruse the old tool-lined sheds, the gin runner boat that's being restored (ask about the bullet holes) and the **Murakami House**, where a large Japanese boat-building family lived before being unceremoniously interned during the war.

Continue east from here and, after another 10 minutes, you'll come to the highly recommended **London Heritage Farm** (Map p86; ☎ 604-271-5220; www.londonheritagefarm.ca; 6511 Dyke Rd; noon-5pm Wed-Fri, 11am-4pm Sat & Sun Jul & Aug, noon-5pm Sat & Sun Sep-Jun), a quaint pioneer farmhouse now preserved as a museum. It won't take long to stroll the mothballed, antique-lined rooms before you decamp to the parlor for a great-value, prepared-from-scratch afternoon tea ($8 per person). Served in china cups (pinkies out, please), it comes with three baked treats – ask for the 'bluebarb' own-blend jam with your fluffy fruit scone.

After winding back along the waterfront to where you started – it's a 30-minute speed-walk – you'll likely be hungry again. On the wharf, descend the ramp and drop by the floating **Pajo's** (Map p86; ☎ 604-272-1588; The Wharf; mains $6-9; 11am-dusk Feb-Nov) for perfectly prepared fish and chips, complete with delicate batter and secret-recipe tartar sauce – the yellowfin tuna burger is an ace alternative. If you're looking for something fancier, consider the nearby **Blue Canoe** (Map p86; ☎ 604-275-7811; 3866 Bayview St; mains $8-22; 11:30am-11pm Sun-Thu, 11:30am-midnight Fri & Sat), a lovely waterfront bistro with a menu of tempting seafood treats – the huge dishes of mussels are best.

FORT LANGLEY
pop 2,700

Tiny Fort Langley's tree-lined streets and 19th-century storefronts make it one of the Lower Mainland's most picturesque spots for a sunny day out. Not easily accessible by public transport (see the trip planner at www.translinkbc.ca if you want to give it a go), it's a well-signposted one-hour drive from the city via Hwy 1.

The area's undoubted highlight is **Fort Langley National Historic Site** (☎ 604-513-4777;

www.pc.gc.ca/langley; 23433 Mavis Ave; adult/child $7.80/3.90; 9am-8pm Jul & Aug, 10am-5pm Sep-Jun), one of BC's most important landmarks. Established as a fortified trading post in 1827, it was from here that James Douglas announced the creation of BC in 1858, giving the fort a legitimate claim to being the province's birthplace. With costumed re-enacters, recreated artisan workshops and a gold-panning area that's very popular with kids – they also enjoy charging around the wooden battlements – this is an ideal destination for parents who want to sneak a little education into a day out with the kids.

ABBOTSFORD
pop 123,000

About 70km from Vancouver and the next community east of Mission along Hwy 1, Abbotsford is at the gateway of the mountain-fringed Fraser Valley. With its gently rolling farmlands, friendly artisan producers and colorful pioneer history, it makes for an idyllic day out from Vancouver for those craving a countryside jaunt. For more information, visit www.tourismabbotsford.ca.

Once you hit town, head over to the heritage **Clayburn Village** (☎ 604-504-7891; www.clayburn village.com; Clayburn Rd) area where a string of historic workers' homes faces a grassy meadow that once housed BC's biggest brick-making operation. The plant's dedicated hamlet, made from the first bricks manufactured here, includes a preserved old church and schoolhouse, while some of the former homes have since been adapted into little shops. Drop by **Clayburn Comforts Soap & Body Works** (☎ 604-855-0420; www.clayburn comforts.com; 24866 Clayburn Rd; noon-5pm Tue-Fri, noon-4pm Sat) for a handmade hair and body soap brick: it's an ideal buy for on-the-road travellers.

For a taste of farm life, check out the smashing **Goat's Pride Dairy** (☎ 604-854-6261, 855-610-1004; www.goatspride.com; 30854 Olund Rd; 8:30am-6pm) where you can wander the tree-shaded acreage and chat to the twinkle-eyed owners before visiting their bleating kid goats (with names like Socks and Cyclone) in the main shed. Ask for their organic cheese recommendations from a selection that includes sun-dried tomato feta and the farm's signature blue capri. There are plenty of other visitor-friendly

---

DETOUR: POWER HOUSE AT STAVE FALLS

Follow the signs past Fort Langley towards Mission on Hwy 7 and you'll eventually come to this fascinating hydroelectric **power station interpretive center** (☎ 604-462-1222; www.bchydro.com /stavefalls; 31338 Dewdney Trunk Rd, near Mission; adult/child $6/5; ☷ 10am-5pm mid-Mar–mid-Oct, 11am-4pm Wed-Sat Nov–mid-Mar) housed in a former hydroelectric power station dating from 1912. Now a National Historic Site, it fuses physics, history and dozens of child-friendly interactive games – there's also a vivid movie presentation illuminating what it was like to live and work here in the early 1900s. It's the visually stunning old Generator Hall that impresses most, though: its giant turbines and generator units are primed, cleaned and seemingly ready to spring into action.

---

farms in this area – keep your eyes peeled for the signs.

Also consider the lovely **Tanglebank Country Gardens** (☎ 604-856-9339; www.tanglebank.com; 29985 Downes Rd; ☷ 9:30am-5pm Feb-Dec), an artful garden center that's also home to a series of immaculately coiffured, free-entry public gardens. Wander the dainty Japanese garden or the fragrant rhododendron walk, where you'll likely be joined by Sir Frederick, the site's permanently purring cat.

And if you're looking for somewhere to eat on your day out, you might consider the **Little Farmhouse in the City** (☎ 604-854-2382; 2551 Montrose Ave; mains $5-12; ☷ 8:30am-2:30pm Sun & Mon, 8:30am-8:30pm Tue-Sat), where the friendly, chatty dining room offers a bulging menu of chunky soups, huge sandwiches and high-piled salads. For something a little on the swankier side, the mood-lit and loungey **Restaurant 62** (☎ 604-855-3545; 2001 McCallum Rd; mains $12-24; ☷ 11:30am-2pm Mon-Fri, 5-10pm Mon-Sun) is Abbotsford's best restaurant, with plenty of regionally sourced ingredients to tempt your Pacific Northwest palate – eat local and have the Fraser Valley duck.

Whistler & the Sunshine Coast

When TV cameras for the 2010 Olympic & Paralympic Winter Games start swooping around BC for their atmospheric, snow-dusted visuals, they will linger longest on the soaring peaks and picture-postcard alpine streets of Whistler. Hosting 2010 events on its side-by-side mountains as well as in a stunning backcountry valley venue southwest of town, it's a chance for Canada's favorite ski resort to take a long-deserved bow in the global spotlight. And if you happen to miss the five rings extravaganza on your visit, you can still catch the Olympic spirit: many facilities and courses will be open post-Games, so it's never too late to strap on your skis and become the new Eddie 'the Eagle' Edwards.

But Whistler, a 90-minute drive north of Vancouver via the recently upgraded Sea to Sky Hwy, isn't just about snowbound shenanigans. Summertime visitors have a full menu of heart-pumping outdoor activities to choose from, ranging from rafting to rock-climbing to ziplining. And if you want to take your time on that winding, cliff-hugging drive from Vancouver – those are the glassy, island-studded waters of Howe Sound to your left, by the way – make sure you don't miss choice pit stops such as Squamish and Britannia Beach.

Activity and outdoor fans should also consider an alternative jaunt to the Sunshine Coast, which ribbons the crenulated shoreline northwest of Vancouver and is a short and picturesque ferry hop from West Van. This 139km stretch of mostly forested waterfront is lined with quirky communities and fueled by an idyllic, island-like approach to life. The area is a magnet for the kind of travelers who can't enjoy a vacation unless it's stuffed with diving, kayaking and hiking experiences. And despite being less than an hour from Vancouver, you'll feel like the busy streets of the city are several hundred miles away.

HIGHLIGHTS

- Staging your own Olympic downhill runs at **Whistler** (p144) and winning every medal every time.

- Hanging out with the locals in **Pemberton** (p151) on 'beer and pizza Thursday' at the Pony Espresso.

- Trundling through abandoned copper tunnels at the **BC Museum of Mining** (p138) then panning for gold with the kids.

- Bumping around the roiling **Skookumchuck tidal rapids** (p156) on a bullet-fast water taxi.

- Enjoying a tranquil paddle on the glassy waters just off **Sechelt** (p155).

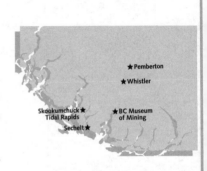

WHISTLER & THE SUNSHINE COAST

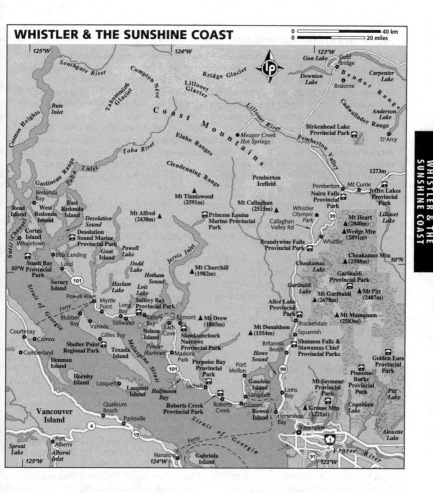

SEA TO SKY HIGHWAY

Winding along a narrow ledge between the glassy waters of Howe Sound and the ragged crags of the Coast Mountains, the Sea to Sky Hwy (Hwy 99) snakes between Horseshoe Bay in West Vancouver and the cowboy country of Lillooet, 130km past Whistler. While journey times have been cut by a massive Olympics-driven upgrade, it's still the kind of drive that needs your full attention. There are several worthwhile stops along the way, especially for history buffs, outdoor activity fans and those who just want to drink in the awe-inspiring vistas.

SQUAMISH & AROUND
pop 15,000

About 50 minutes along Hwy 99 from Vancouver (it's another hour to Whistler), Squamish enjoys an incredible natural setting at the conjunction of ocean, river and alpine forest. Formerly nothing more than a gritty logging town – you'll still see a few ornery old guys trucking around here – recent years have seen a successful transformation into a regional hub for outdoor adventures, especially in summer when windsurfers, kiteboarders, bike trailers and rock climbers hit the area – you'll spot them dotted like tiny action figures on

SQUAMISH'S STEAMY GRAND DAME

Built in 1940 as one of Canada's last steam locomotives, the majestic **Royal Hudson** trundled between Vancouver and Revelstoke for just 16 years before those newfangled diesel engines took over. Slated for scrapping, she was rescued by a gaggle of trainspotters and returned to Vancouver as a nonworking museum piece. Restoration was undertaken in the 1970s and the locomotive was returned to active service as a tourist train, running giddy visitors along the winding Sea to Sky rail route between North Vancouver and Squamish for 25 years.

With pricey repairs looming, the creaky old train was retired again in 2002, this time into the loving hands of Squamish's **West Coast Railway Heritage Park** (below), where a long and detailed overhaul was begun. In 2008 – BC's 150th anniversary year – the Royal Hudson was finally running again on select days, with plans to offer more trips to steam-hungry visitors. You can visit the old gal herself, along with dozens of other trains, at the Heritage Park – check their website for details of upcoming excursions.

the sheer face of the monolithic Stawamus Chief (known simply as 'The Chief') on your drive in.

Check out your options at the swanky-looking **Squamish Adventure Centre** (☎ 604-815-5084, 877-815-5084; www.tourismsquamish.com; 38551 Loggers Lane; ✹ 8am-8pm Jun-Sep, 9am-6pm Oct-May), a local VC with a strong focus on outdoor activities. It stocks a plethora of flyers and maps on hikes and bike trails in the area.

Sights

En route to Squamish via Hwy 99, stop at **Britannia Beach** – turn right when you see the humungous yellow truck – and enter the **BC Museum of Mining** (☎ 604-896-2233, 800-896-4044; www.bcmuseumofmining.org; adult/youth/child $18.50/13.95/11.95; ✹ 9am-4:30pm mid-Mar–mid-Oct, 9am-4:30pm Mon-Fri mid-Oct–mid-Mar), one of the province's best industrial heritage attractions. Once the British Empire's largest copper producer, it was infamous in recent years as a giant pollution cleanup project but has been saved and resurrected with an impressive restoration. Take an underground train tour into the spooky, pitch-black mines, wander among refurbished buildings (complete with mystery heavy machinery) and pan for gold with the kids. Tours and gold-panning mid-May to mid-October only.

About 4km before you reach Squamish, you'll hear the rushing waters of **Shannon Falls Provincial Park** (☎ 604-986-9371; www.bcparks .ca). Pull into the parking lot and stroll the short trail to BC's third-highest waterfall, where water cascades down a 335m drop. A few picnic tables make this a good stopping point for an alfresco lunch, although

the roar of the tumbling water makes conversation tricky. When the falls freeze in winter, ice climbers pick and pull their way to the top.

You'll know you're on the fringes of Squamish when you see the 652m flat-faced granite wall known as the 'The Chief' looming above you. It's one of BC's favorite rock-climbing destinations and is the centerpiece of **Stawamus Chief Provincial Park** (www.bcparks.ca). A magnet for outdoor-types – especially those climbers enthralled by its challenging vertical – it has awesome views from the top. And since there are some (still challenging) hiking trails up the back, you can also enjoy the vistas without strapping on the gear.

Just past Squamish, follow the signs to the giant **West Coast Railway Heritage Park** (☎ 604-898-9336; www.wcra.org; 39645 Government Rd; adult/child $10/8.50; ✹ 10am-4pm), home of the legendary *Royal Hudson* steam engine (see box above). This smashing, mostly outdoor museum has around 90 railcars, including 10 working engines. Each one has been painstakingly restored, and many are walk-through galleries of exhibits – check out the luxurious executive carriage and the cleverly designed mail sorting car. Miniature train trips are usually on offer (especially at weekends) and a recently added Town Centre of heritage buildings delivers an authentic pioneer-era feel.

Also north of Squamish along Hwy 99, riverside Brackendale village is an unprepossessing spot with a serious claim to fame. The winter destination of choice for thousands of salmon-scoffing bald eagles, it draws in legions of binocular-wielding visitors, especially during the December and January prime viewing months. At the **Brackendale Art Gallery** (☎ 604-898-3333; www .brackendaleartgallery.com; 41950 Government Rd; ☿ noon-10pm) the eccentric Thor Froslev coordinates the main winter bird count from his funky wood-built complex. An art installation in itself, it's lined with paintings and photos inspired by the eagles. Brackendale claims the world record of 3,769 eagles spotted in a single day in 1994.

Activities

If you fancy tackling the Chief, contact **Squamish Rock Guides** (☎ 604-892-7816; www.squamishrockguides.com) for guided climbs and expert lessons. Their novice-friendly Introduction to Rock Climbing course (from $119) is excellent. Touch base with other local climbers via the website of the **Squamish Access Society** (www.squamishaccess.ca).

Renowned for the high winds whipped up where Howe Sound meets Squamish River – the Coast Salish named this place 'Mother of the Winds' – Squamish Spit is a popular windsurfing and kiteboarding destination. The season runs from May to October and the **Squamish Windsports Society** (☎ 604-892-2235; www.squamishwindsports.com; Squamish Spit, day pass $15) is your first point of contact for weather, water conditions and access to the Spit, which has changing rooms, day storage and staffers with (hopefully surplus to requirements) first aid skills.

Some of BC's best white-water rafting takes place in this region where towering canyons and cascading waterfalls are par for the tumultuous course during the May to October season. **Sunwolf Outdoor Centre** (☎ 604-898-1537, 877-806-8046; www.sunwolf.net; 70002 Squamish Valley Rd; full-day package $149) is 10km past Squamish on Hwy 99 and offers full-day packages on the Elaho River with lunch and a barbeque dinner. The center also has basic but cozy sleepover cabins ($90-$100).

The 100 or so trails around Squamish draw plenty of mountain biking enthusiasts. The Cheekeye Fan trail near Brackendale has some easy forested rides, while downhill thrill seekers will prefer the Diamond Head/Power Smart area, where the routes have inviting names like Dope Slope and Icy Hole of Death. Drop in to **Corsa Cycles** (☎ 604-892-3331; www.corsacycles.com; 1200 Hunter Pl;

rental per day $45; ☿ 9:30am-5:30pm) for rentals and trail advice. Also check the handy website resources offered by the **Squamish Off Road Cycling Association** (www.sorca.ca).

Sleeping & Eating

our pick **Alice Lake Provincial Park** (☎ 604-689-9025; 800-689-9025; www.discovercamping.ca; campsites $24) A large family-friendly campground with 108 well-equipped pitches, this popular, tree-lined spot is about 13km north of Squamish, just off Hwy 99. There are two shower buildings with flush toilets and half the pitches have electrical hook-ups. Activities include swimming, kayaking, hiking (including the popular Four Lakes Trail) and some excellent July and August ranger presentations that can range from kid-friendly frog interpretations to waterfront yoga workshops. There's also access to sandy lakeside beaches with picnic tables. Reservations recommended.

Squamish Inn on the Water (☎ 604-892-9240, 800-449-8614; www.innonthewater.com; 38222 Hwy 99; dm/r from $29.50/70; ☞) This attractive lodge-style hotel, complete with hardwood floors and a sun-swathed riverfront patio in well-located on Hwy 99 but it's also just a short walk (via a tunnel) to the downtown core. The lodge suites and rooms are contemporary and comfortable and there are also a few small, good-value dorm rooms with large bathrooms – you'll have to ask about these (and book ahead) since they don't advertise them.

Howe Sound Inn & Brewing Company (☎ 604-892-2603, 800-919-2537; www.howesound.com; 37801 Cleveland Ave; r $119; ☞) The 20 rooms are rustic and inviting, with duvets that are thicker than a hefty snowfall at this comfortable inn. There's an outdoor climbing wall where you can train for your attempt on the nearby Chief and a sauna where you can recover afterwards. The excellent on-site brewpub (mains $10-16) is also worth a visit for Hwy 99 pit-stoppers. The yam fries, butter chicken and Baldwin & Cooper Bitter are recommended, while a one-liter flip-top bottled brew is a handy takeout.

Sunflower Bakery Café (☎ 604-892-2231; 38086 Cleveland Ave; mains $4-7; ☿ 7:30am-5pm Mon-Sat) Situated on a downtown street of inviting shops and a few tasty eateries, this bright and breezy yellow-painted nook serves some great wraps and bagel sandwiches –

the made-from-scratch quiches (the spinach and feta is our favorite) are highly recommended, too. There's also an array of chunky cakes and bulging fruit pies that will have you committing to some heavy exercise – make sure you follow through.

The Burrow (☎ 604-898-2801; 40437 Tantalus Rd; plates $7-17; ⏱ 5-11pm Sun-Thu, 5pm-midnight Fri & Sat) A compact, relaxed favorite among the Squamish hipsters (yes, there are some), this warm and inviting room specializes in tasting plates and is your best bet for a foodie splurge before you reach Whistler. The spicy prawns and Italian sausages plates are good and the large dips platter (with its excellent crab dip) is perfect for sharing, although you should be prepared to fight over the last few mouthfuls.

Getting There & Away

Greyhound Canada (☎ 800-661-8747; www.greyhound.ca) buses arrive in Squamish from Vancouver ($15.60, 70 minutes, eight daily) and Whistler ($13.55, 70 minutes, eight daily). The classier **Pacific Coach Lines** (☎ 604-662-7575, 800-661-1725; www.pacificcoach.com) SkyLynx bus also rolls in from Vancouver International Airport ($35, three hours, up to 12 daily) at the Squamish Adventure Centre.

GARIBALDI PROVINCIAL PARK

A choice destination for BC's outdoor enthusiasts and named after the Italian guerrilla general, 1950-sq km **Garibaldi Provincial Park** (☎ 604-898-3678; bcparks.ca) lurks in the shade of the looming Coast Mountains and is justly renowned for its alpine hiking trails,

diverse fauna, snow-capped crags, abundant wildlife and breathtaking wilderness vistas. Exploring is not limited to T-shirt weather; trails become marked cross-country ski routes in winter. Garibaldi has five main trail areas – directions to each are clearly marked by the blue-and-white signs off Hwy 99. Visitors must practice leave-no-trace hiking and camping and the use of mountain bikes is restricted to certain trails.

Diamond Head

The hiking and biking trail to Elfin Lakes (11km) is a beautiful and relatively easy day hike. For overnighters, the trail continues on to the extinct volcano of Opal Cone. There's a first-come, first-served overnight shelter once you reach Elfin, and backcountry camping ($5) is available at Red Heather, 5km from the parking lot. The parking lot is 16km east of Hwy 99.

Garibaldi Lake

The Garibaldi Lake trek (9km) is an outstanding crash course in 'Beautiful BC', combining scenic alpine meadows and breathtaking mountain vistas. The cerulean hue of the undisturbed lake contrasts with the dark, jagged peak of Black Tusk rising behind it. Backcountry campsites ($5) are further up the trail at Taylor Meadows, on the lake's west shoreline.

Cheakamus Lake

Among the park's most popular, the Cheakamus Lake hike (3km) is relatively easy, with minimal elevation. Also in this

---

IGLOO-A-GO-GO

Since locals are often born wearing skis in BC, many continue to search for new and unusual ways to challenge themselves in their own backyard. Igloo camping – where groups snowshoe into the backcountry for a day of construction and a night of not much sleep – fits the bill for those who like to do things differently. It's essential to go with someone who knows how to build an igloo, otherwise you'll be sleeping in a hole instead. We learned that the blocks need to be placed on a winding inward curve and that the structure should not be too big. Construction is hard work, but the euphoria of building your own shelter, enjoying a celebratory swig from a hip flask and crawling in through the U-bend entrance for a night under the crazy-paving ceiling is unforgettable. While our igloo adventure took place in a tranquil clearing in **Garibaldi Provincial Park** (see above), there are many other suitable spots around the province. If you don't have any friends with the required skills, get some new friends or touch base with **Canada West Mountain School** (☎ 604-878-7007, 888-892-2266; www.themountainschool.com; winter camping tours $245). They offer organized winter camping tours where they'll teach you all you need to know. One tip: don't hit the celebratory hip flask until your igloo is finished.

area and just outside the provincial park, the BC Forest Service's 30-sq km Whistler Interpretive Forest offers a variety of summer activities, including hiking, mountain biking, kayaking and fishing. The trailhead is 8.5km from Hwy 99, opposite Function Junction at the south end of Whistler.

BRANDYWINE FALLS PROVINCIAL PARK

A few kilometers north of Squamish and adjacent to Hwy 99, this tree-lined **park** (☎ 604-986-9371; www.bcparks.ca) is centered on a spectacular 70m waterfall. A short stroll through the forest leads to a dizzying platform overlooking the top of the falls, which drops suddenly out of the trees like a giant faucet. There are also great vistas over Daisy Lake and the mountains of Garibaldi Provincial Park. A 7km looped trail leads further through the dense forest and ancient lava beds to Cal-Cheak Suspension Bridge.

WHISTLER

pop 9775

Named after the furry whistling marmots that run wild in the region, the once-tiny resort town of Whistler has come a long way. Little more than a backcountry hangout for powder-hungry yokels just a couple of decades back, it has risen to become the 'host mountain' for the 2010 Olympic and Paralympic Winter Games. Although, centered on the twin peaks of Whistler and Blackcomb mountains, this pretty alpine town was already one of the world's favorite winter destinations long before the Olympic circus rolled into town. While Vancouverites routinely complain that it's too expensive to come here, many still make the 123km drive for a weekend away in the snow. Increasingly the region is also a popular summer destination, with zipliners, alpine hikers and mountain bikers replacing the skiers and snowboarders on the slopes. If you just want to soak up the ambience of the village, which has a theme-park-like proliferation of icicle-fringed gables and timber-framed lodges, consider a fall trip, when shoulder season prices kick in at area hotels.

ORIENTATION

Approaching via Hwy 99 from the south, you'll first hit Creekside, one of Whistler's four main neighborhoods – the others are Whistler Village, Village North and Upper Village. Past Creekside along Hwy 99, turn right along Village Gate Blvd for Whistler Village, the resort's main commercial and hotel hub. The Village can be a confusing maze for first-time wanderers but there are usually lots of people around to ask directions from – some of them might even be locals. As soon as you find your bearings, pick up *The Pique* or *Whistler Question* newspapers for further local insights.

INFORMATION
Bookstores
Armchair Books (☎ 604-932-5557, 800-659-1531; 4205 Village Sq; ☺ 9am-9pm) Good travel section.

Internet Access
Cyber Web (☎ 604-905-1280; 4340 Sundial Cres; per 10 mins $2.50; ☺ 8am-10pm Oct-Apr) The pre-paid route is the best deal here.
Public Library (☎ 604-935-8433; 4329 Main St; per hr free; ☺ 11am-7pm Mon-Sat, 11am-4pm Sun) Swanky new building; register at front desk for free internet.

Medical Services
Northlands Medical Clinic (☎ 604-932-8362; 4359 Main St; ☺ 9am-5:30pm)
Whistler Health Care Centre (☎ 604-932-4911; 4380 Lorimer Rd; ☺ 8am-10pm)

Money
Custom House Currency Exchange (☎ 604-938-6658; 4227 Village Stroll; ☺ 8:30am-8:30pm)
Money Mart (☎ 604-932-1620; 4314 Main St; ☺ 9am-9pm Mon-Sat, 11am-6pm Sun)

Post
Post office (☎ 604-932-5012; 106-4360 Lorimer Rd; ☺ 8am-5pm Mon-Fri, 8am-noon Sat).

Tourist Information
Whistler 2010 Info Centre (☎ 604-932-2010; www.vancouver2010.com; 4365 Blackcomb Way; ☺ 11am-5pm) Information of Olympic proportions.
Whistler Activity Centre (☎ 604-938-2769, 877-991-9988; 4010 Whistler Way; ☺ 10am-6pm) Activities bookings and recommendations.
Whistler Visitor Centre (☎ 604-935-3357, 800-944-7857; www.tourismwhistler.com; 4230 Gateway Dr; ☺ 8am-8pm) Flyer-lined VC with friendly staff.

WHISTLER

0 _____ 300 m
0 _____ 0.2 miles

INFORMATION
Armchair Books............................**1** A5
Custom House Currency
  Exchange................................**2** B6
Cyber Web....................................**3** B6
Money Mart.................................**4** A4
Northlands Medical Clinic.......**5** A4
Post Office...................................**6** A4
Public Library.............................**7** A5
Whistler 2010 Info Centre.......**8** B4
Whistler Activity Centre..........**9** A5
Whistler Health Care Centre...**10** B4
Whistler Visitor Centre............**11** B5

SIGHTS & ACTIVITIES
Fanatyk Co..................................**12** B6
Mountain Adventure Centre....**13** B6
Mountain Adventure Centre....**14** C5

Outdoor Adventures Whistler......**15** A6
Squamish Lilwat Cultural
  Centre..**16** C4
Whistler Alpine Guides Bureau.....**17** A4
Whistler Farmers Market...........**18** C5
Whistler Heli-Skiing...................**19** B6
Whistler Museum & Archives....**20** A5
Whistler River Adventures.......**21** B6
Whistler-Blackcomb Lift Tickets
  & Guest Services.....................**22** B6
Ziptrek Ecotours.........................**23** B6

SLEEPING 🛏
Adara Hotel..................................**24** A6
Blackcomb Lodge.......................**25** B5
Chalet Luise Inn.........................**26** C3
Crystal Lodge..............................**27** B5
Pinnacle International Hotel....**28** A5

EATING 🍴
21 Steps Kitchen & Bar.............**29** B5
Araxi Restaurant & Lounge.....**30** B5
Beet Root Café............................**31** A4
Crepe Montagne.........................**32** A4
Gone Village Eatery...................**33** A5
La Boca...**34** B6
Market Place IGA........................**35** A4
Sachi Sushi..................................**36** A4

DRINKING
Amsterdam Café Pub................**37** B6
Black's Pub & Restaurant.........**38** B6
Garibaldi Lift Company............**39** B6
Longhorn Saloon & Grill..........**40** B6
Whistler Brewhouse...................**41** B4

ENTERTAINMENT
Garfinkel's...................................**42** A5
Moe Joe's.....................................**43** A5
MY Place.......................................**44** B5
Savage Beagle............................**45** B5
Village 8 Cinema........................**46** B5

TRANSPORT
Bus Stop.......................................**47** A5

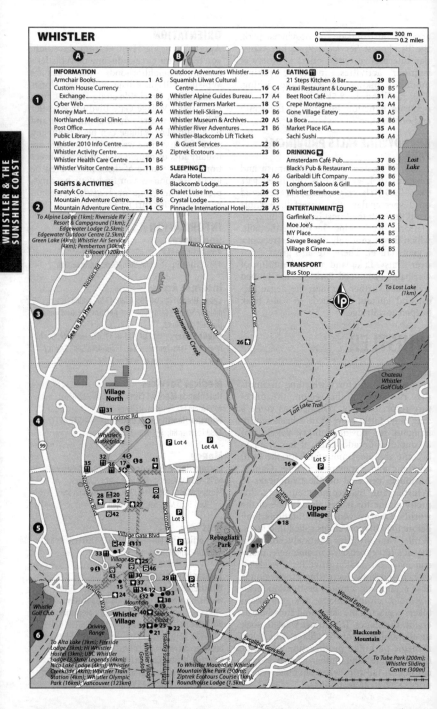

To Alpine Lodge (1km); Riverside RV
Resort & Campground (1km);
Edgewater Lodge (2.5km);
Edgewater Outdoor Centre (2.5km);
Green Lake (4km); Whistler Air Service
(4km); Pemberton (30km);
Lillooet (120km)

Nancy Greene Dr

To Lost Lake
(1km)

Lost
Lake

Chateau
Whistler
Golf Club

Village
North

Lorimer Rd

Whistler's
Marketplace

Lost Lake Trail

Lot 4

Lot 4A

Lot 5

Upper
Village

Village Gate Blvd

Lot 3

Lot 2

Rebagliati
Park

Lot 1

Village
Sq

Mountain
Sq

Whistler
Village

Skier's
Plaza

Whistler
Golf Club

Driving
Range

To Alta Lake (3km); Fireside
Lodge (3km); HI Whistler
Hostel (3km); UBC Whistler
Lodge (3.5km); Legends (4km);
Nita Lake Lodge (4km); Whistler
Creekside (4km); Whistler Train
Station (4km); Whistler Olympic
Park (16km); Vancouver (123km)

To Whistler Mountain; Whistler
Mountain Bike Park (500m);
Ziptrek Ecotours Course (1km);
Roundhouse Lodge (1.5km)

Blackcomb
Mountain

To Tube Park (200m);
Whistler Sliding
Centre (300m)

Excalibur Gondola

Wizard Express

Magic Chair

Sea to Sky Hwy

Nesters Rd

Fitzsimmons Creek

Blackcomb Way

FINALLY...THE OLYMPIC PARTY KICKS OFF

Whistler has competed unsuccessfully to host the Olympics several times, but only after combining its bid with Vancouver (p95) did the resort town hit the big league in 2003, with the official announcement that the 2010 Olympic and Paralympic Winter Games were coming to the West Coast for the first time. Events will be held February 12th to 28th, with Paralympic contests staged from March 12th to 21st.

As the 'host mountain', Whistler is staging the alpine skiing events (downhill, super G, giant slalom, slalom and combined) in its Creekside area; luge, skeleton and bobsleigh events at the purpose-built **Whistler Sliding Centre** (see below); and Nordic events (biathlon, cross-country skiing, Nordic combined and ski jumping) at a spectacular backcountry location, 16km from the village, called the **Whistler Olympic Park** (p145). Paralympic alpine skiing, cross-country skiing and biathlon will also be staged at these venues. The majority of these 2010 facilities will be accessible to visitors for tours or activities after the Games have left town.

The resort – which has its own Athlete's Village – will be a hive of party-like activity during the Games. There will be six free-entry outdoor sites where you can hang out and watch live TV coverage and catch bands and performers. The largest of these is the 8000-seat **Celebration Plaza**, where medal ceremonies and the Paralympic closing ceremony will also be staged.

If you're planning to commute from Vancouver for specific 2010 events, be aware that there will be no public parking – only those with confirmed hotel rooms or those who live in the area will be allowed to drive through on Hwy 99 – and spectators will be expected to use public transportation options. Olympic buses will be running between the city and Whistler and will cost $25 for an all-day pass. Around-the-clock transit will also operate to move visitors between the Whistler venues.

For further village Games information, visit the Olympic section of the official Whistler website (www.whistler.com/olympics). Information on how to buy tickets – half of which are priced under $100 – is also available via the official Olympic website (www.vancouver2010.com).

SIGHTS

The spectacular new wood-beamed building housing the **Squamish Lilwat Cultural Centre** (☎ 604-441-7522, 866-441-7522; www.slcc.ca; 4854 Blackcomb Way; adult/youth/child $18/13.50/8; ⏲ 9:30am-5pm) showcases two quite different First Nations groups – one coastal and one interior based – with museum exhibits and artisan presentations. Entry starts with a 15-minute movie and includes a self-guided tour that illuminates the heritage and modern-day indigenous communities of the region. There's a wealth of art and crafts on display (check out the amazing two-headed sea serpent carving near the entrance) and the energetic young staff encourage plenty of questions about their twin cultures. Also check out the café (mains $7 to $12), with its venison chili and salmon chowder.

Perched just above the village on Blackcomb, the **Whistler Sliding Centre** (☎ 604-402-1401, 888-972-7533; www.whistlerslidingcentre.com; 4910 Glacier Ln; ⏲ 10am-8pm Tue-Sun) is the 2010 venue for bobsled, luge and skeleton events and is regarded as one of the fastest ice tracks in the world. At time of writing, the venue was open for public tours ($5) and these are expected to continue after the Games, with additional programs allowing visitors to experience the track for themselves also expected to be announced.

The little **Whistler Museum & Archives** (☎ 604-932-2019; www.whistlermuseum.org; 4333 Main St) was closed for much-needed renovations when we visited. Its mandate is to trace the history of the area's resort development and it houses an array of colorful artifacts, including a motley assortment of old skiing equipment. The museum offers summertime village **walking tours** (tours adult/child $11/6; ⏲ tours 1pm Jul & Aug) that relate the story of Whistler's growth.

If you're here in summer, head to the Upper Village and the plaza in front of the Fairmont Chateau Whistler for the bustling **Whistler Farmers Market** (www.whistlerfarmersmarket .org; 11am-4pm Sun mid-Jun–mid-Oct) where you can peruse the arts and crafts and stuff your face with seasonal fruits and bakery treats.

ACTIVITIES

One of North America's most celebrated alpine resorts, Whistler offers a powder-crunching array of great winter pursuits for well-wrapped-up visitors. But there's also an ever-growing roster of heart-popping summer activities here that aims to keep traveling adrenalin junkies happy. Head to the village's VC or Activity Centre for tips and recommendations on what to do with your boundless energy. Whistler is home to three 2010 Olympic & Paralympic Winter Games venues (one of them 16km away in the Callaghan Valley). These facilities – especially the spectacular Callaghan venue – will offer some opportunities for post-Games activity fans and they are listed below.

Skiing & Snowboarding

Comprising 38 lifts and almost 8200 acres of skiable terrain, crisscrossed with over 200 runs (more than half of which are aimed at intermediate level skiers), the twin peaks of **Whistler-Blackcomb** (☎ 604-932-3434, 800-766-0449; www.whistlerblackcomb.com; one-day lift ticket adult/youth/child $89/76/46) were physically linked for the first time in late 2008. The mammoth new 4.4km **Peak 2 Peak Gondola** includes the world's longest unsupported span and takes 11 minutes to shuttle wide-eyed powder hogs between the two high alpine areas, enabling you to hit the slopes on both mountains in the same day.

The resort's winter season usually starts in late November and runs to April on Whistler and June on Blackcomb – December to February is the peak – but there's also glacier skiing available into July. Be aware that skiing off piste is strongly discouraged here and avalanches are a major risk in unmarked areas. If you want to emulate your fave Olympic ski heroes – or prepare for the next Games – Whistler Creekside is the setting for all the 2010 downhill skiing events.

You can beat the crowds with an early morning **Fresh Tracks ticket** (adult/child $17.25/12.60), which must be bought in advance at Whistler Village Gondola Guest Relations. Be at the gondola for a 7:30am start the next day. The price includes a buffet breakfast at the Roundhouse Lodge up top. Weekdays are recommended for this, since tickets sell out quickly on weekends. Night owls might prefer the evening **Night Moves** (adult/child $18/12) program operated via Blackcomb's Magic Chair lift after 5pm.

To access the untouched powder of the backcountry, unleash your credit card and contact **Whistler Heli-Skiing** (☎ 604-932-4105, 888-435-4754; www.heliskiwhistler.com; 3-4241 Village Stroll; trips from $730). Snowboard fans should also check out the freestyle terrain parks mostly located on Blackcomb, including the Snow Cross and the Big Easy Terrain Garden. There's also the Habitat Terrain Park on Whistler. Snowboard lessons are offered for kids and adults from beginners to advanced level (half-day from $70).

If you didn't bring your own gear, **Mountain Adventure Centres** (☎ 604-904-7060, 888-403-4727; www.whistlerblackcomb.com/rentals; one-day ski or snowboard rental adult/child from $46/32) has several equipment rental outlets around town. They offer online reservations – you can choose your favorite gear before you arrive – as well as lessons for ski and snowboard virgins.

Cross-Country Skiing & Snow-shoeing

A short stroll or free shuttle bus from the village, **Lost Lake** (☎ 604-905-0071; www.crosscountry connection.bc.ca; day pass adult/youth/child $17/10/8.50; ☽ 8am-9pm) is the hub for 22km of wooded cross-country ski trails, suitable for novices

---

OLYMPIC MEDALLIST OFFERS ADVICE ON HITTING THE SLOPES

Ross Rebagliati was Canada's 1998 Olympic snowboarding gold medallist. Now retired, he still finds time to hit the slopes whenever he can. Rebagliati recommends visitors try runs like Cat Skinner, Upper and Lower Gear Jammer and Ross' Gold Trees on Blackcomb, while on Whistler Mountain, the Red Chair and Christmas Trees are recommended – as well as the Dave Murray Downhill course, which he says offers, "fast as you dare, balls-out carving." He adds that visitors should get on the slopes early, make three or four quality runs before lunch and then spend the rest of the day chilling out. "Always stay hydrated, and speaking of that the **Longhorn Saloon** (p150) in the village offers amazing views of the two mountains and the local talent! Great for a couple of cold ones while the people and the stories just keep on coming." Check out Ross' blog and see what he's up to now at www.rossrebagliati.com.

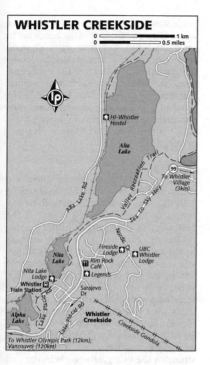

WHISTLER CREEKSIDE

0 _____ 1 km
0 _____ 0.5 miles

HI-Whistler Hostel

Alta Lake

99
To Whistler Village (3km)

Fireside Lodge
Nita Lake
UBC Whistler Lodge
Rim Rock Café
Nita Lake Lodge
Legends
Whistler Train Station
Sarajevo Dr
Alpha Lake
Whistler Creekside
Creekside Gondola
To Whistler Olympic Park (12km); Vancouver (120km)

WHISTLER & THE SUNSHINE COAST

and experts alike. Around 4km of the trail is lit for additional nighttime skiing until 10pm and there's a handy 'warming hut' providing lessons and equipment rentals. Snow-shoers are also well-served in this area: you can stomp off on your own on 10km of trails or rent equipment and guides.

The road to **Whistler Olympic Park** (☎ 604-964-2455, 877-764-2455; www.whistlerolympicpark.com; 5 Callaghan Valley Rd, Callaghan Valley; day pass ski adult/child $20/10, snowshoes $8/4; ☉ 9am-4pm) is 16km southwest of the village via Hwy 99. Host for the 2010 biathlon, Nordic combined, cross-country skiing and ski jumping events, it will remain as a legacy project after the Games. This breathtaking Callaghan Valley wilderness area is lined with 55km of cross-country trails, which start from the smashing day lodge – there's a restaurant as well as ski and snowshoe rentals here. There are 5km of lit nighttime trails and 12km of dedicated snowshoe trails in the park. You can drive here from Whistler or take a handy shuttle bus (round trip $15).

Outdoor Adventures Whistler (☎ 604-932-0647; www.adventureswhistler.com; tours adult/child from $79/49)

offers four guided snow-shoeing tours, including a three-hour fondue trek ($109). Prices include equipment. They also provide sleigh rides, snow limos, dog sledding and snowmobile tours if you're looking for a different way to hit the powder.

Tubing

Blackcomb's family-friendly **Tube Park** (above Base II by parking lot 8; 1hr ticket adult/child/youth $18/15/13; ☉ noon-8pm Mon-Fri, 11am-8pm Sat & Sun) has eight lanes, a conveyor-belt lift and runs of up to 300m in length. Scream your heart out as you relive your childhood, and nosh on hotdogs from the concession stand while you warm yourself at the welcoming fire pits.

Mountain Biking

Colonizing the melted ski slopes in summer and accessed via lifts at the village's south end, **Whistler Mountain Bike Park** (☎ 604-932-3434, 866-218-9690; www.whistlerbike.com; one-day pass adult/youth/child $49/43/27; ☉ 10am-8pm mid-Jun–Aug, 10am-5pm May–mid-Jun, Sep–mid-Oct) offers barreling downhill runs and an orgy of jumps, beams and bridges that twist through 200km of well-maintained forested trails. Luckily, you don't have to be a bike courier to stand the gonad-crunching pace: easier routes are marked in green, while blue intermediate trails and black diamond advanced paths are offered if you want to Crank It Up – the name of one of the park's most popular routes. Outside the park area, regional trails include Comfortably Numb (a tough 26km with steep climbs and bridges); A River Runs Through It (suitable for all skill levels, it has teeter-totters and log obstacles); and the gentle Valley Trail, an easy 14km loop that encircles the village and its lake, meadow and mountain chateau surroundings. This is recommended for first-timers.

Free trail maps are available at the Activity Centre and you can check in with the **Whistler Off-Road Cycling Association** (www.worca.com) for additional resources. If you're a die-hard bike nut, time your visit for the massive annual **Kokanee Crankworx** (p146) event in August.

For a wide selection of rental wheels, drop by **Fanatyk Co** (☎ 604-938-9455; www.fanatykco.com; Whistler Village; rental 4hrs/full-day from $50/65; ☉ 10am-5pm mid-May–mid-Oct) a few steps from the bike park's Whistler Gondola's access point.

Hiking

With more than 40km of breathtaking alpine trails, most accessed via the Whistler Village Gondola, this region is ideal for those who like strolling among the meadows and mountain peaks humming their favorite *Sound of Music* tunes. In fact, hiking this area will make you suddenly agree with those boastful new BC licence plates that proclaim the province 'The Best Place on Earth.'

Among the best routes is the High Note Trail (8km), which traverses pristine alpine meadows stuffed with wildflowers, and offers some stunning views of the blue-green waters of Cheakamus Lake below. Alternatively, there's a great network of relatively easy and well-marked Riverside Trails near the resort's Function Junction area. Pick-up a free trail map from the VC or the Activity Centre.

If you'd prefer company, **Whistler Alpine Guides Bureau** (☎ 604-938-9242; www.whistlerguides .com; 19-4314 Main St; adult/child from $89/69) has a wide range of alpine and backcountry tours (ask about the popular Musical Bumps hike). It also provides excellent glacier hiking treks ($99), and, for the more adventurous, you can scramble ($69), rock climb ($99) or hit the Via Ferrata – a mountain obstacle course of cables, ladders and bridges ($129).

If you're on a more modest budget, you should also consider a **free hiking tour**. This program is run by volunteer locals and starts at the top of the Whistler Village Gondola at 11:30am daily in summer. The laid-back, two-hour strolls are a great way to get an insider take on the resort and score some smashing mountaintop vistas. Booking isn't required: just turn up and away you go.

Rafting

If you like to work your arm muscles until they feel like limp noodles **Whistler River Adventures** (☎ 604-932-3532, 888-932-3532; www .whistlerriver.com; nr Whistler Village Gondola; ☯ mid-Jun-Aug) offers the kind of activity where it's perfectly OK to wet your pants. The wildest of its three tours is a day-long rollercoaster along the Elaho and Squamish Rivers (adult/youth $159/149). You'll be kitted out with a wetsuit and positioned to man one of the oars in an eight-person boat – the

guide stands in the middle and keeps order with a giant paddle. One of the best ways to see outback BC, keep your water-whipped eyes open for tumbling waterfalls, looming glaciers, a few deer and the occasional bear. You can also partake of some optional cliff jumping along the way. For families or those of a gentler disposition, their comparatively sedate Cheakamus River paddle (adult/youth/child $89/69/54) is also recommended.

Ziplining

While stepping out into thin air 70m above the forest floor may seem like madness (it feels like it as well, until you've done it a couple of times), ziplining is one of the best ways to encounter Whistler's natural beauty. Attached via a body harness to the cable you're about to slide down, you soon overcome your fear of flying solo and by the end of your time in the trees, you'll be turning mid-air somersaults and screaming with giddy exhilaration (at least that's what you should tell everyone back home). **Ziptrek Ecotours** (☎ 604-935-0001, 866-935-0001; www.ziptrek.com; adult/child $98/78 per five lines; ☯ year-round) has a cool, 10-line course strung in the valley between Whistler and Blackcomb mountains, as well as **Treetrek** (adult/child $39/29), a gentle network of nine suspension bridges and walkways between the trees for those who prefer to keep their feet on something more solid. You can also ziptrek in darkness in the winter with only a head-mounted lamp to light your way.

FESTIVALS & EVENTS

WinterPride (www.gaywhistler.com) Gay-friendly week of skiing, snowboarding and partying in February.

TELUS World Ski & Snowboard Festival (www.wssf .com) Clamorous nine-day fiesta of outdoor concerts and pro ski and snowboard competitions, held in mid-April.

Kokanee Crankworx (www.crankworx.com) Nine-day adrenalin-filled showcase of stunts, speed events and world-leading mountain bikers in mid-August.

Cornucopia (www.whistlercornucopia.com) Bacchanalian celebration of fine wining and dining with tastings, seminars and parties in mid-November.

Whistler Film Festival (www.whistlerfilmfestival.com) Four days of Canadian and independent film screenings, events and parties, in late November.

First Night (www.whistlerfirstnight.com) Alcohol-free New Year countdown on December 31, with street performers and live music.

WHISTLER & THE SUNSHINE COAST

WHISTLER'S PARTY CENTRAL

Comedy shows, free ski guides and rocking dance parties are all part of the mix at one of North America's biggest and best gay-friendly winter events. Originally known as Gay Ski Week, the annual **WinterPride** (☎ 604-288-7218; www.gaywhistler.com) extravaganza draws thousands of party-loving powder fans with its plethora of outdoor activities – liberally interspersed with an all-important roster of après-ski events. Each night sees one or two of the resort's nightclubs dedicated to the cause, with venues staying open progressively later as the week unfolds. The hottest ticket is Friday night's **Mountain Top Party**, where guests hop on a gondola to a summit lodge that's transformed into a thumping nightclub. The event runs in early February every year.

SLEEPING

Room rates often double here during the winter peak when booking ahead is essential. Specials are available the rest of the year, especially in fall's shoulder season when the village is sometimes ghost-town quiet. Annoyingly, most hotels charge parking fees ($10 to $20 daily) and some also charge resort fees ($12 to $25 daily) – confirm these before you book. The VC runs a handy **accommodation reservation service** (☎ 604-932-0606, 800-944-7853; www.whistler.com/accommodation).

Budget

HI-Whistler Hostel (☎ 604-932-5492; whistler@hihostels.ca; 5678 Alta Lake Rd; dm/r $32/79) This idyllic little lakeside retreat is 5km from the village, which means taking one of the transit buses that stop outside to get to all the action. It's worth it, though, for the rustic log cabin feel, friendly staff and snug ambience. The dorms (and kitchen) are small and basic but you'll spend most of your time hanging around the shoreline outside, where you can canoe, bike, swim or just spend the evening drinking in the breathtaking mountain panorama. This location is scheduled to close after the 2010 Olympics when a swanky new 200-bed property in the Function Junction area is ready.

UBC Whistler Lodge (☎ 604-822-5851; www.ubc whistlerlodge.com; 2124 Nordic Dr; dm summer/winter $30/40) Up a steep hill in the Nordic residential neighborhood between the village and Creekside – you'll discover just how steep it is when crawling back after a long day on the slopes – the facilities here are basic and quirky (bunks are built into the walls and rooms are separated by curtains). But the rates are a bargain. The tree-surrounded patio is a great place to hang out and compare bruises or you can simply dip into the sauna and Jacuzzi. Close to Creekside

on foot, the number two bus stops at the bottom of the hill. Book ahead (discount for HI members).

Fireside Lodge (☎ 604-932-4545; www.fireside lodge.org; 2117 Nordic Dr; dm/r $30/80) Located just across the street from the UBC Lodge – but slightly lower down the hill if the climb is a deal-breaker – this lofty, cabin-like property is reached via a workout-triggering wooden staircase. If you're lucky, the electronic outdoor luggage trolley – it's like a mini-funicular – will be working so you won't have to lug your luggage at the same time. Once you catch your breath inside, you'll find small dorms and some private rooms in a retro setting resembling an old ski lodge. Facilities include a large kitchen, games room, sauna and laundry. On bus route two, it's 3km south of the village.

Midrange

Alpine Lodge (☎ 604-932-5966; www.alpinelodge .com; 8135 Alpine Way; dm/tw/ste $60/150/225; ☎) A colorful, wood-lined lodge 3km north of town, the centerpiece here is the cozy 'Great Room' where your free coffee-and-croissants breakfast is served. While the accommodation – including some small dorms – is functional rather than palatial (most rooms have private baths and all have mountain views) there's a pleasant suite available with its own kitchen and lounge that fits groups of up to four. Hot-tub and on-site massage treatments available.

Chalet Luise Inn (☎ 604-932-4187, 800-665-1998; www.chaletluise.com; 7461 Ambassador Cres; r $139-175; ☼ May-Nov; ☎) A five-minute trail walk to the main action, this flower-fronted Bavarian-style Village North pension has eight bright and sunny rooms – think pine furnishings and white duvets – and a verdant back garden that's ideal for a spot of evening wine-quaffing. Alternatively, hop in the little sauna or the gazebo hot-tub and dream about the large breakfast coming your way in the morning (keep your fingers crossed for apple pancakes). Adult oriented.

Crystal Lodge (☎ 604-932-2221, 800-667-3363; www.crystal-lodge.com; 4319 Main St; d/ste from $140/195; ❄ ❄) Not all rooms are created equal at the Crystal, forged from the mating of two quite different hotel towers. Cheaper rooms in the South Tower are basic motel-style – baths and fridges are the highlight – but those in the Lodge Wing match the splendid stone and beam lobby, complete with small balconies. Whichever one you stay in, you couldn't be closer to all the Village action: Whistler's main restaurants, bars and shops are steps away while the Village Gondola is just up the street.

Blackcomb Lodge (☎ 604-935-1177, 888-621-1117; www.blackcomblodge.com; 4220 Gateway Dr; r from $160; ❄ ❄) Handily located across from the main liquor store so you can pad over in your PJs to get the booze in, this central, boutique-ish hostelry combines lofts and studios with kitchen facilities, and a selection of cheaper but still very comfortable lodge rooms. The Village Gondola is a five-minute stroll away, while Araxi (p150), the on-site restaurant, is a gourmet favorite.

Pinnacle International Hotel (☎ 604-938-3218, 888-999-8986; www.whistlerpinnacle.com; 4319 Main St; d $139/199; ❄) A well-established midrange property that's a cut above many Whistler Village offerings, rooms at the Pinnacle have gas fireplaces, double hot-tubs and full kitchens. You can mix yourself a drink, slip into your robe and nip out onto the balcony to watch the winter world go by or choose from the many local bars and restaurants that are a short slide away (don't forget to dress before you leave the room). Ski and snowboard storage available. Adult oriented.

Riverside RV Resort & Campground (☎ 604-905-5533, 877-905-5533; www.whistlercamping.com; 8018 Mons Rd; cabins $175) This warm and friendly RV and cabin property a few minutes drive past Whistler on Hwy 99 recently removed its handy tent pitches (the only available in the Whistler vicinity). The owners are working with the municipality to reinstate them – call ahead for the latest. The cabins, though, are a cozy (albeit pricier) alternative and the ambience is family friendly – which means no playing in the playground unless you're

a real kid. There's also a handy on-site convenience store and an excellent café that's ideal for breakfast.

Edgewater Lodge (☎ 604-932-0688, 888-870-9065; www.edgewater-lodge.com; 8020 Alpine Way; r from $185; ❄) A few minutes past Whistler on Hwy 99, this lovely 12-room haven combines high-comfort lakeside accommodations with a celebrated-view restaurant. If you can pull yourself away from your room's picture window vista of Green Lake, the beam-ceilinged dining room (an outdoor table is recommended) offers delectable treats like juicy Queen Charlotte Island salmon. You can work it off with a fishing, hiking or kayaking trek at the adjoining **Edgewater Outdoor Centre** (☎ 604-932-3389; www .whistleroutdoor.com).

Top End

Legends (☎ 604-697-8965, 800-332-3152; www.legends whistler.com; 2036 London Lane; r from $190; ❄ ❄) This apartment-style Creekside hotel is great for groups. Its spacious quarters – with pine furnishings, rock fireplaces and a rustic chic ambience – are more home-from-home than hotel, while the large kitchens and in-suite laundry will have you considering a permanent move. All rooms have balconies (try to nab one overlooking the slopes) and you can ski in and out at the back of the property. Kid-friendly, some suites have bunk beds and there's a playroom complete with toys and a large TV.

Adara Hotel (☎ 604-905-4009, 866-502-3272; www .adarahotel.com; 4122 Village Green; r from $250; ❄ ❄) Unlike all those smaller Whistler lodges now claiming to be boutique hotels, the sophisticated and centrally located Adara was built from scratch as the real deal. The interior is lined with spare but knowing designer details – including fake antler horns in the lobby – and the rooms have spa bathrooms, flat-screen TVs and iPod docking stations (the front desk will loan you an iPod if you've left yours at home). Despite the cool aesthetics, service is warm and relaxed.

ourpick Nita Lake Lodge (☎ 604-966-5700, 888-755-6482; www.nitalakelodge.com; 2135 Lake Placid Rd; r from $250; ❄) Handily adjoining the handsome Creekside Whistler Mountaineer train station and sharing the same magnificent wood-beamed West Coast architecture, this sumptuous new contemporary lodge hotel is the perfect spot for a pampering, high-end break. Hugging the lakeside (the Valley Trail runs right past your door for some excellent moderate-level hiking and biking), the swanky but cozy rooms are all about individual patios, basalt rock fireplaces and bathrooms with heated floors and large tubs – they also have little kitchenettes with microwaves and fridges. The lobby level bar has an alfresco seating area overlooking the lake and there's a good on-site restaurant; you can also request a free shuttle to the village if you want to venture further afield. The Creekside lifts are just a few minutes away.

EATING

Whistler is brimming with a full menu of dining alternatives to suit most budgets, ranging from self-catering supermarket options to top-end restaurants that would be equally at home in Vancouver. The best value joints tend to be hidden just off the main streets, so dig around a bit if you're on a tight budget – or consider roasting a whistling marmot or two on a spit (just kidding).

Budget

Market Place IGA (☎ 604-938-2850; 4330 Northlands Blvd; ☽ 8:30am-10pm) This large supermarket across from the post office is ideal if your hotel room comes with a little kitchen. There's a good selection of ready-made meals and fresh pasta to choose from, plus an excellent deli counter if you want to rustle up a picnic for a long day out. If you're feeling especially lazy, there are also hot, ready-roasted chickens available for around $10.

our pick **Beet Root Café** (☎ 604-932-1163; 129-4340 Lorimer Rd; mains $6-11; ☽ 7:30am-4:30pm) Pull up a cushion and make yourself at home on the window benches opposite the counter here – it'll give you more time to peruse the large chalkboard menu. The breakfast of bacon, poached eggs, baked beans and roast potatoes is a killer start to any day, but lunch should involve a dalliance with a turkey and brie ciabatta or roasted yam quesadillas – house soups are also a specialty (look out for the broccoli and sun-dried tomato). There's usually a queue here at peak times so plan your visit early or late, and make sure you scoff at least two fresh-baked chocolate and apricot cookies while you're deciding what your main meal will be.

Gone Village Eatery (☎ 604-938-1990; 4205 Village Sq; mains $6-12; ☽ 7am-9pm; ☞) Hidden around the back of Armchair Books, this bright and friendly wood-floored hangout is a coffee joint with an extended menu of hearty breakfast grub (have the omelette burrito), lunch specials (sandwiches, falafel or the $10 burger and beer deal do the trick) and any-time-of-day baked treats (try a chewy toffee cookie). A good place to check your e-mail – there's wireless access plus some computer terminals (per ten minutes $2) – this is also a favored meeting spot for local slope workers.

Midrange

Crepe Montagne (☎ 604-905-4444; 4368 Main St; mains $8-14; ☽ 8am-3pm Mon-Thu, 8am-9:30pm Wed-Sun) This small and surprisingly authentic creperie – hence the French accents percolating among the staff – offers a bewildering array of sweet and savory buckwheat crepes with fillings including ham, brie, asparagus, banana, strawberries and more. Vegetarian options abound and just to make your choice even harder, fondues are also available. This is also a good breakfast spot – the waffles are excellent.

Sachi Sushi (☎ 604-935-5649; 106-4359 Main St; mains $8-25; ☽ noon-2:30pm Tue-Fri, 5:30-10pm daily) Whistler's best sushi spot, Sachi's doesn't stop at California rolls – in fact, try the mango, tuna and salmon roll alternative instead. Serving everything from crispy popcorn shrimp to spicy seafood hot pots and stomach-hugging *udon* noodles (the tempura noodle bowl is best), this popular spot is a relaxing après-ski hangout. Try a glass of hot sake on a cold winter day.

La Boca (☎ 604-932-2112; 4232 Village Sq; mains $12-22; ☽ 6-11:30pm) A lively patio location overlooking the Village Square action (if it's chilly, you can hunker down inside with a booth), the large menu here covers all the bases from breakfast eggs Benedict to dinnertime seafood linguine (the miso black cod is a recommended alternative). A large wine list adds to the appeal, although the cocktails are also intriguing if you fancy a smooth wind-down to the day – try the Brown Bear Coffee.

21 Steps Kitchen & Bar (☎ 604-966-2121; 4320 Sundial Cres; mains $14-22; ☽ 6pm-midnight) With lots of small plates for nibblers (the fried goat's cheese and bacon-wrapped filet mignon are winners), the main dishes at this cozy upstairs spot have a high-end comfort food approach. Not a great place for vegetarians: steak, pork chops and pasta feature heavily and the array of fish mains includes a yummy pesto-crusted halibut. Check out the great attic bar, one of Whistler's best lounges.

Top End

Rim Rock Café (☎ 604-932-5565; 2117 Whistler Rd; mains $16-22; ☒ 9am-11pm) On the edge of Creekside and accessible just off Hwy 99, this is the locals' favorite place for a gourmet dine-out. They come for the Pacific Northwest approach to dishes like seared scallops, venison tenderloin and a highly recommended Seafood Trio of grilled prawns, *ahi* tuna and nut-crusted sablefish. Also ask your server for wine pairing suggestions – they know their stuff here. All is served in an intimate room with two fireplaces and a large, flower-lined patio where you can laugh at the harried highway drivers zipping past.

Araxi Restaurant & Lounge (☎ 604-932-4540; 4222 Village Sq; mains $30-45; ☒ 5-11pm) A leading contender for Whistler's best splurge restaurant, exquisite Araxi combines a sophisticated menu with courteous service that immediately puts you at your ease. The inventive main dishes are all about superb, mostly Pacific Northwest ingredients, which can range from Queen Charlotte Islands halibut to Cowichan Valley chicken – there's also a 15,000-bottle wine cellar to tempt your wallet. Save room for dessert: the cheese menu is small but perfectly formed and the Okanagan apple cheesecake will have you licking the glaze off your plate.

DRINKING

Amsterdam Café Pub (☎ 604-932-8334; Village Sq; ☒ 11am-1am) Attracting a younger, noisier crowd, this brick-lined party joint in the heart of the village has a funky, neighborhood pub vibe. The beer ranges from the cheap but nasty Amsterdam Lager to Alexander Keith's Pale Ale, a recommended alternative. You can treat your hangover to a late breakfast the next day by coming in for that all-important greasy fry-up.

Black's Pub & Restaurant (☎ 604-932-6408; ☒ 7am-11pm) Across from the Village Gondola base, this traditional resto-bar serves the usual pub classics from its food menu all day (from breakfast onwards) as well as offering dozens of bottled beers and a good selection of whiskies. Among the drafts, the BC-brewed Russell Cream Ale is heartily recommended for some post-activity imbibing.

Garibaldi Lift Company (☎ 604-905-2220; Whistler Village Gondola; ☒ 11.30am-11pm) The closest bar to the slopes – watch the powder geeks or bike nuts on Whistler Mountain grind to a halt from the patio – the GLC is a rock-lined cave of a place. It's the ideal spot to absorb a Kootenay Mountain Ale and a bulging GLC burger while you rub your muscles and exchange exaggerated war stories about your tussles with the elements.

Longhorn Saloon & Grill (☎ 604-932-5999; 4290 Mountain Sq; ☒ 7am-11pm Sun-Thu, 7am-midnight Fri & Sat) Fanned out at the base of Whistler Mountain with a patio that threatens to take over the town, the Longhorn feels like it's been around ever since the first skier turned up. The service can be lackadaisical and the pub food is nothing to write home about, but it's hard to beat the atmosphere here on a hopping winter evening.

Whistler Brewhouse (☎ 604-905-2739; 4355 Blackcomb Way; ☒ 11:30am-midnight Sun-Thu, 11:30am-1pm Fri & Sat) This place creates its own beer on the premises and, like any artwork, the natural surroundings inspire the masterpieces, with names like 'Lifty Lager' and 'Twin Peaks Pale Ale'. It's an ideal pub if you want to hear yourself think – or if you just want to watch the game on one of the TVs. The food, including great fish and chips, is superior to standard pub fare.

ENTERTAINMENT

The nightclub of choice for many, **Garfinkel's** (☎ 604-932-2323; 1-4308 Main St) combines mainstream dance grooves with occasional live bands. Arrive early on weekends, when it's usually packed. The music is similar but it's more intimate over at **Moe Joe's** (☎ 604-935-1152; 4155 Golfer's Approach), which attracts the ski-bunny crowd. Those hovering closer to the 30-something mark will likely prefer **Savage Beagle** (☎ 604-938-3337; 4222 Village Sq) – Saturday is the pumping house and electro dance night here. It's on two levels, so you can have a sit down if you exert yourself too much.

You can catch a first-run flick at **Village 8 Cinema** (☎ 604-932-5833; Village Stroll; adult/child $12.50/8.50) or indulge in theater of the live variety at **MY Place** (☎ 604-935-8410; www.myplace whistler.org; 4335 Blackcomb Way), which hosts a roster of plays and performances.

GETTING THERE & AWAY

While most visitors arrive by car from Vancouver via the recently upgraded Hwy 99 – it's at least a 90-minute drive – you can also fly in on a **Whistler Air** (☎ 603-932-6615, 888-806-2299; www.whistlerair.ca) floatplane to Green Lake ($169, 35 minutes, two daily) between mid-May and early October.

Greyhound Canada (☎ 800-661-8747; www .greyhound.ca) bus services arrive at Creekside and Whistler Village from Vancouver ($27.90, 2½ hours, nine daily) and Squamish ($13.55, 70 minutes, eight daily).

The classier **Pacific Coach Lines** (☎ 604-662-7575, 800-661-1725; www.pacificcoach.com) SkyLynx bus also rolls in from Vancouver International Airport ($49, three hours, up to 12 daily). In addition, **Snowbus** (☎ 604-331-7850; www.snowbus.ca) operates a winter-only service from Vancouver (one-way/return $23.81/42.86, 2½ hours, two daily).

Trainspotters can trundle into the swanky new Creekside railway station on the **Whistler Mountaineer** (☎ 604-606-8460, 888-687-7245; www.whistlermountaineer.com), which winds along a picturesque coastal route from North Vancouver ($119, three hours, daily mid-May to early Oct).

GETTING AROUND

Whistler's **WAVE** (☎ 604-932-4020; www.busonline .ca; adult/child/$2/1.50) public buses have ski and bike racks; they plan to switch to hydrogen fuel cells in the future. In winter buses are free between Marketplace and the Upper Village loop, and in summer from the village to Lost Lake. Or grab a taxi from **Resort Cabs** (☎ 604-938-1515; www.resortcabs.com), but keep in mind taxis are pricey here.

NORTH OF WHISTLER

If you manage to tear yourself away from Whistler, Hwy 99 continues northwards to the valley farmlands of Pemberton, where many resort workers seeking cheaper accommodation base themselves. You can then continue into the rugged, mountain-fringed cowboy country to relive the Gold Rush or hit some spectacular outdoor destinations where you'll be at one with the craggy wilderness.

PEMBERTON & AROUND
pop 2280

The next town after Whistler on Hwy 99, Pemberton has a welcoming vibe that encourages many to hang out here. More rustic and laid-back than its swanky neighbour, you'll nevertheless notice the presence of some new Whistler-esque mega-homes, indicating that development brought on by the forthcoming Olympics has spilled across the region. Visitors are generally outdoor-types, spending their time gliding or horseback riding in summer and snowmobiling in winter – unlike in Whistler, summer is the high season here. In July 2008, the town hosted the first **Pemberton Festival** (www.pembertonfestival.com) a mammoth outdoor three-day music extravaganza with acts including Coldplay and Tom Petty. Hopes are high that the event will return in future years. Check in with the **Visitor Centre** (☎ 604-894-6175; www .pemberton.ca; ☯ 9am-5pm mid-May-Sep) for the latest status and to find out what else is available in the area.

Sights & Activities

Illuminating the region's rugged pioneering and agricultural roots – the local mascot is a smiling spud named Potato Jack – the charming clutch of rescued wooden shacks that make up **Pemberton Museum** (☎ 604-894-5504; www.pembertonmuseum.org; 7455 Prospect St; admission by donation; ☯ 10am-5pm Jun-Sep) is like a little village from the past. You can wander among the homes, trying to imagine what it was like to sleep in a bed smaller than a coffee table, and ask the volunteers about the characters who lived here when the gold rush swept through. Drop by for a 'Toonie Tuesday' afternoon in July and August when you can mingle with the locals and scoff home-baked treats for $2.

As you'd expect from cowboy country – check out the number of hitching posts outside businesses around town – horseback riding is popular here. The Valley Loop Trail and the Mosquito Lake area are favored trotting spots, but if you didn't bring your own nag you can saddle up with a loaner from **Pemberton Stables** (☎ 604-894-6615; www .pembertonstables.ca; tours $45-120) which offers good-value, family-friendly one- to three-hour tours for all skill levels – it's a cash-only operation. Alternatively, **Adventures on Horseback** (☎ 604-894-6269; www.adventuresonhorse back.ca; two-hour tours from $70) offers a series of guided trail rides and pack trips. Bring your own Stetson and chewing tobacco.

One of the best ways to experience the tree-lined mountains of the Pemberton Valley is to hop in a two-person glider, get towed up into the sky and let the back-seat pilot do all the hard work as you slide silently over the miniature landscape far below. The occasional bumps only add to the fun – if you tell the pilot you like roller coasters, he might treat you to some heart-stopping loops, spins and stalls. **Pemberton Soaring Centre** (☎ 604-894-5776, 800-831-2611; www.pembertonsoaring.com; flights from $94; �><Apr-Oct) offers 15-minute taster trips for $94, while a spectacular 50-minute glide over the glaciers and snow-capped peaks costs $237.

Situated 2km before Pemberton along Hwy 99, 60m-high **Nairn Falls** (☎ 604-986-9371; www.bcparks.ca) gurgles and sprays its way down the mountain like an aqua-ballet before continuing on as Green River. The trail to the falls (3km round trip) winds along some steep banks. Another trail (4km round trip) leads to One Mile Lake, a popular spot for swimming and picnicking. The park also has a 94-pitch **campground** (☎ 604-689-9025; 800-689-9025; www.discovercamping.ca; campsites $15, �><May-Oct).

Sleeping & Eating

C&N Backpackers (☎ 604-894-2442, 888-434-6060; www.cnnbackpackers.com; 1490 Harrow Rd; dm/r $27/80; ☜) There's nothing hip or funky about this large family home in a residential side street, but it's quiet and comfortable and has a welcoming host. Unlike most hostels, there are no bunks here, just five rooms housing one to five beds in each. Linen is provided and there's a mix of private and shared bathrooms. Rooms are equipped with cable TV and there's a communal kitchen adjoined by a small patio. Wi-fi is $10 for five days.

Pemberton Valley Lodge (☎ 604-894-2000, 877-894-2800; www.pembertonvalleylodge.com; 1490 Portage Rd; r/ste from $119/129; ☒ ☜) Located just off

Hwy 99, this smashing midrange lodge-like hotel looks like it was transplanted from Whistler. The lobby is all West Coast stone and wood, and the comfortable, well-designed rooms each have kitchens, laundry facilities and fireplaces – almost all have balconies too. There's an outdoor pool and hot-tub area (heated in winter) and a free seasonal shuttle to the Whistler ski slopes.

Pemberton Valley Vineyard & Inn (☎ 604-894-5857, 877-444-5857; www.whistlerwine.com; 1427 Collins Rd; r $150-170; ☜) It's all about rustic chic at this large log cabin vineyard building which includes three B&B suites, each with separate entrances. The quarters are spacious, wood-floored and have a contemporary but cozy feel, with a dash of Mexican élan – the gable-ceilinged Champagne Room with its balcony views of Mount Currie is our favorite. Rates include breakfast in the on-site **restaurant** (mains $18-30; �><6-10pm Wed-Sun, May-Oct), which is also worth a visit if you're passing though – the cherry-glazed rack of lamb is recommended.

Mount Currie Coffee Co (☎ 604-894-3388; 7331 Arbutus St; mains $4-10; �><6:30am-6pm; ☜) Rivaling the ever-popular Pony Espresso in the java stakes, this newer café hangout really knows how to serve top-notch coffee, including the kind of latte art etched in the froth that's more common in Vancouver. You can fuel up with made-from-scratch salads, sandwiches and chunky muffins plus excellent breakfast burritos and their highly recommended hearty soups. Free wi-fi is also on the menu and the walls are often lined with the work of local artists and photographers.

ourpick Pony Espresso (☎ 604-894-5700; 1392 Portage Rd; mains $6-17; �><6:30am-10pm Mon-Sat, 7am-10pm Sun) This fantastic, wood-lined locals' hangout is the best place in town to tap into the neighborhood vibe. Pull up a chair, order a slab of El Diablo pizza (piled high with capicolli and banana peppers) and eavesdrop on all the Whistler-teasing gossip. Better still, drop by on a Thursday night, when it's bursting to the candlelit gills with Pembertonians taking full advantage of the $16 beer-and-pizza special – there's Russell Brewing and Granville Island tipples on tap here and you should arrive by 6pm if you want to get a table. It's not just about grease and suds, though: generous pasta dishes, hearty salads and

---

DETOUR: JOFFRE LAKES PROVINCIAL PARK

Located 32km past Pemberton on Hwy 99, this **park** (www.bcparks.ca) offers some great hiking to the first lake, or you can follow a more ambitious trail to the upper backcountry. Mountain peaks rise up from Lower Joffre Lake and tell their glacial tale through U-shaped valleys and cirques. The trail continues on to Joffre Lakes, where time, reflected in the lake's turquoise surface, seems to stand still. Along with fishing and wildlife watching, this is a popular spot for well-equipped mountaineers, who come for a host of area climbs.

---

bulging sandwiches are also part of the mix, as well as a surprisingly decent wine selection. And if you're just passing through, there's also a busy on-site bakery serving piping hot coffee, chunky muffins and carrot cake for the road.

Getting There & Away
Greyhound Canada (☎ 800-661-8747; www.greyhound .ca) services arrive in Pemberton from Vancouver ($31, 3½ hours, five daily), Squamish ($17.10, 2½ hours, five daily) and Whistler ($8.15, 40 minutes, six daily).

BIRKENHEAD LAKE PROVINCIAL PARK
Sharing its name with an industrial town in northern England, the rugged **Birkenhead Lake Provincial Park** (☎ 604-986-9371; www.bcparks .ca) could not be more different from its namesake. Located 55km from Pemberton, it's situated on mountain-fringed Birkenhead Lake, where fishing for rainbow trout is a popular activity. The surrounding forest accommodates lots of trails and mountain-bike routes as well as being home to a cornucopia of wildlife – make sure you know what to do if you encounter bobcats and black bears unexpectedly. You might also spot deer, beaver and mountain goats, so have your camera at the ready. Suitable for paddling, the lake has a boat launch and is ideal for those seeking a tranquil jaunt around its shoreline. Keep an eye out for the stunning white-walled flank of Tenquille Ridge and the surrounding snow-capped peaks, which are often reflected in the lake's

glassy surface. **Camping** (☎ 604-689-9025, 800-689-9025; www.discovercamping.ca; campsites $15) is available.

SUNSHINE COAST
Vancouverites often have no idea where the Sunshine Coast is and even less idea of how to get there. In fact, it couldn't be easier to head over on a 40-minute ferry ride from Horseshoe Bay in West Van and once you do you'll find a quirky, waterfront region, with a closely knit, island-like feel. Stretching up the mainland for 139km from Langdale to Lund – everything is handily strung along Hwy 101 – the main communities here include Gibsons, Sechelt and Powell River and the main activities range from kayaking to scuba diving, with a side order of artists' studios thrown in for good measure. Check the website of **Sunshine Coast Tourism** (www.sunshinecoastcanada .com) for information and pick up one of the two comprehensive *Recreation Map & Attractions Guides* ($3) for outdoor activities and operators throughout the area: one covers the upper and one covers the lower region.

GIBSONS
pop 4250
Your first port of call after docking in Langdale, Gibsons' pretty waterfront area is named Gibsons Landing and is a rainbow of painted wooden buildings perched over the marina. Famous across Canada as the setting for *The Beachcombers*, a TV show filmed here in the 1970s that fictionalized a town full of eccentrics, the place hasn't changed much since. Head up the incline from the water and you'll hit the shops on the main drag of Upper Gibsons and Hwy 101. Drop by the **Visitor Centre** (☎ 604-886-2325, 866-222-3806; www.gibsonsbc.ca; 900 Gibsons Way; ☸ 9am-5:30pm May-Sep) for area info.

Sights & Activities
A walk down **Gower Point Road** in Gibsons Landing will show you what this seaside village is all about. The cute shops and storefronts blend nicely with the briny sea air. Be sure to stroll along **Molly's Lane**, a backstreet string of shops knocked together into an indoor market of local crafts and

browsable trinkets. Also amble down the nearby wooden jetty, looking out for purple starfish under the water and perusing the flower-decked houseboat on your right.

Gibsons is home to a surprising plethora of artistic talent: judge for yourself by heading up the staircase on Molly's Lane and into the **Gibsons Public Art Gallery** (☎ 604-886-0531; www.gibsonspublicartgallery.ca; 287 Gower Point Rd; free; ☒ 11am-4pm Thu-Mon May-Sep; noon-4pm Thu-Mon Oct-Apr) or check in with **Coast Cultural Alliance** (☎ 604-740-8288; www.suncoastarts.com) for an online directory of area art spaces and visitor-friendly studios.

Local history buffs will enjoy the **Sunshine Coast Museum** (☎ 604-886-8232; www.sunshinecoast museum.ca; 716 Winn Rd; admission by donation; ☒ 10:30am-4:30pm Tue-Sat), which houses an eclectic array of period costumes, First Nations baskets and nautical exhibits, including some *Beachcombers* memorabilia.

The sheltered harbors and islands of Howe Sound and the Strait of Georgia make an idyllic setting for kayaking. Rental, lessons and tours are available from the friendly folk at **Sunshine Kayaking** (☎ 604-886-9760; www.sunshinekayaking.com; Molly's Lane; rental 4hr/24hr $32/65, tours from $60; ☒ 9am-6pm Mon-Fri, 8am-6pm Sat & Sun). Their calming and magical guided sunset tours ($60) are recommended (no experience necessary). Ask about the Tuesday Specials two-for-one rental deal.

Sleeping & Eating

Ritz Inn (☎ 604-886-3343, 800-649-1138; www.ritzinn .com; 505 Gower Point Rd; r $84-110; ☒ ☎) Overlooking the marina, this conveniently located 30-room motel-style property is ideal if you want to be near the heart of Gibsons Landing. The large, well-priced kitchenette rooms make it a good spot for families, and some rooms have balconies with shoreline views. It's not quite the Ritz, but it's not half bad.

Caprice B&B (☎ 604-886-4270, 866-886-4270; www.capricebb.com; 1111 Gower Point Rd; d $135-165; ☒) Nestled among the arbutus trees, the adult-oriented Caprice is a large waterfront home (you can watch the cruise ships slip by) with three suites. While two rooms have handy kitchenettes, all three are comfortable and well maintained. Homemade baked treats are a feature of the breakfast menu and there's a small outdoor pool where you can enjoy the sun.

Soames Point B&B (☎ 604-886-8599, 877-604-2672; www.soamespointbb.com; 1000B Marine Dr; d $149) Set amid 1.5 acres of landscaped gardens, this immaculate and tranquil B&B has spectacular waterfront views. The large suite has a private entrance, vaulted ceilings and panoramic ocean views as well as its own deck – a great spot for breakfast. At the end of the day, you can head down to the water where another deck, complete with seats and a barbeque, is ideal for a sundowner.

Molly's Reach (☎ 604-886-9710; 647 School Rd; mains $7-12; ☒ 7am-9pm) The local's favorite comfort food hangout, this marina-view spot serves a perfect greasy spoon breakfast – un-notch your belt and dive into the artery-clogging 'Constable Constable' of two eggs, two sausages, two pancakes and two slices of bacon. Lined with Gibsonites at lunch and dinner, arrive off-peak to snag a window seat so you can overlook the water.

our pick Smitty's Oyster House (☎ 604-886-4665; 643 School Rd; mains $12-26; ☒ noon-10pm) Tucked under Molly's Reach, the menu highlights at this smashing seafood spot are the fresh clams and mussels cooked to perfection in steamer kettles. In fact, it's all about freshness here, with local marine treats from the daily catch (pray for the Savory Island clams) enlivening the ever-changing menu. You'll want to try the delectable barbeque-grilled scallops and the dangerously tasty beer-battered halibut fritters, so it might be a good idea to lubricate your appetite with some accompanying wine or a lip-smacking R&B Raven cream ale. The patio is the place to be: you'll be rubbing shoulders with your chatty fellow diners at the communal table and you'll have a waterfront view of the marina to keep you company.

Getting There & Around

BC Ferries (☎ 888-223-3779, 250-386-3431; www .bcferries.com) services arrive at Langdale, 6km northeast of Gibsons, from Horseshoe Bay (adult/vehicle $11/33.45, 40 minutes, eight daily). The **Sunshine Coast Transit System** (☎ 604-885-6899; www.busonline.ca; adult/child $2.25/1.75) runs services from Langdale into Gibsons, Roberts Creek and Sechelt.

Malaspina Coach Lines (☎ 604-886-7742, 877-227-8287; www.malaspinacoach.com) buses arrive daily in Gibsons from downtown Vancouver ($30, two hours) and Vancouver Airport ($40, three hours), via the Langdale ferry.

ROBERTS CREEK
pop 3100

Rustic Roberts Creek, 10km from Gibsons via Hwy 101, is a former hippy draft-dodgers' enclave that retains a distinctly artsy, laid-back vibe. Check the placards at the community hall or visit www.robertscreek.com to tap into the area's happenings.

From the highway, follow Roberts Creek Rd through the village and amble out onto **Roberts Creek Pier**, overlooking the Strait of Georgia. Backed by a large waterfront park (there's a beach here at low tide), you can perch on a driftwood bench and watch the natural world float by. West of town, **Roberts Creek Provincial Park** (☎ 604-885-3714; www.bcparks.ca) is another beachfront picnic spot. It also has 21 basic camping spots with coldwater taps and four pit toilets (campsite $15).

The Sunshine's Coast's best hostel, **Up the Creek Backpackers B&B** (☎ 604-885-0384, 877-885-8100; www.upthecreek.ca; 1261 Roberts Creek Rd; dm/r $26/75; 🖳) has three small dorms, one private room and a secluded cabin that's ideal for couples (note: the cabin doesn't have a washroom). The friendly owners are the perfect hosts and they are a fount of information about local activities. The local bus stop is just around the corner, so you're encouraged to arrive here by public transportation. Loaner bikes are offered to get you around once you've unpacked – one of several eco-initiatives here. Self-serve breakfast is available for $5.

For something a little more upmarket, **Artist & the Quiltmaker B&B** (☎ 604-741-0702, 866-570-0702; www.theartistandthequiltmaker.com; 3173 Mossy Rock Rd; d $99-150) is a three-room, Victorian-style property that's well worth a stop. Its large upstairs suite, complete with kitchenette, is popular with families, but the lovely Renaissance Room is perfect for some romantic canoodling. For additional B&B and cottage rental options here and throughout the Sunshine Coast, check the listings at www.bbsunshinecoast.com.

For sustenance, the ever-popular **Gumboot Restaurant** (☎ 604-885-4216; 1041 Roberts Creek Rd; mains $7-14; 🕒 8am-9pm) and its sister Garden Café are ideal for rubbing shoulders with the locals and scoffing a hearty dinner – check out those organic buffalo burgers and bulging, veggie-friendly 'Gumboot Garden' sandwiches. Occasional live music, too.

Getting There & Away
Malaspina Coach Lines (☎ 604-886-7742, 877-227-8287; www.malaspinacoach.com) services arrive daily in Roberts Creek from Vancouver ($45, 2½ hours).

The **Sunshine Coast Transit System** (☎ 604-885-6899; www.busonline.ca; adult/child $2.25/1.75) runs services into Roberts Creek from Langdale (20 minutes) and Sechelt (20 minutes).

SECHELT
pop 8800

With water to the south and north and mountains rising steeply behind, Sechelt is the second-largest town on the Sunshine Coast. But while it has many useful hub-town amenities for those traveling through, it's neither quite as charming as Gibsons nor as vibrant as Powell River. There are plenty of hiking, biking, kayaking and diving opportunities in the surrounding area – hit the downtown **Visitor Centre** (☎ 604-885-1036, 877-885-1036; www.secheltvisitorinfo.com; 5790 Teredo St; 🕒 9am-5pm Mon-Sat Jun, 9am-5pm Jul & Aug, 10am-4pm Mon-Sat Sep-May) for information or peruse the *Sunshine Coast Recreation Map & Attractions Guide* for tips.

Sights & Activities
With a good kayak launch site and a sandy, stroll-worthy beach, fir-and-cedar-forested **Porpoise Bay Provincial Park** (☎ 604-885-3714; www.bcparks.ca) is 4km north of Sechelt via East Porpoise Bay Rd. There are trails throughout the park and an 84-pitch **campground** (☎ 604-689-9025, 800-689-9025; www.discovercamping.ca; campsite $22) with handy hot showers.

For visiting paddlers **Pedals & Paddles** (☎ 604-885-6440, 866-885-6440; www.pedalspaddles.com; Tillicum Bay Marina; rentals 4hr/24hr from $32/65) organizes kayak rentals and tours of the inlet's wonderfully tranquil waters.

Alternatively, rub shoulders with local artists and growers at the summertime **Sechelt Farmers' and Artisans' Market** (☎ 604-885-8483; www.secheltmarket.com; 🕒 8:30am-1pm Sat Apr-Sep) in the parking lot of the Raven's Cry Theatre or stick around for the mid-August **Sunshine Coast Festival of the Written Arts** (☎ 604-885-9631; www.writersfestival.ca).

Sleeping & Eating
Bayside Campground & RV Park (☎ 604-885-7444, 877-885-7444; www.baysidecampground.com; 6040 Sechelt Inlet Rd; campsites $20; 🕒 May-Oct) About 1km

north of Sechelt, this family-friendly forested campsite has clean and well-maintained facilities, along with extras such as showers, picnic tables, a children's playground, and a small convenience store. Each site has a firepit and firewood is available. If they're full, there's a sister campsite on Hwy 101 called Creekside Campground.

Upper Deck Guesthouse & Hostel (☎ 604-885-5822; www.secheltaccommodation.com; 5653 Wharf Rd; dm/s/d $22/40/55; ▢ ⊛) An easy-to-miss upstairs budget option in an industrial-looking part of town, the large, barbeque-equipped sundeck (complete with a forest of potted plants) is the main attraction here on balmy summer evenings. Inside, you'll find a lived-in, home-style lounge and kitchen area, plus a handful of small, slightly jaded rooms, some private. All is warm and welcoming and there's a free-use internet computer.

our pick **Away at the Bay** (☎ 604-885-6365; www .awayatthebaybc.com; 5369 Selma Park Rd; d $115) If all you want to do is get away from it all, this rustic one-bedroom wood-built cabin in Davis Bay is the place to be. Enveloped by trees, you'll spend most of your time communing with the stunning waterfront panorama from the large, barbeque-equipped deck. Fully self-contained, there's a kitchen, laundry and nearby beach access. A true retreat, it's popular with couples as well as small families (there's an additional hide-a-bed in the living room). Located a few minutes before Sechelt on Hwy 101, turn off at Selma Park Rd.

Rockwater Secret Cove Resort (☎ 604-885-7038, 877-296-4593; www.rockwatersecretcoveresort.com; 5356 Ole's Cove Rd; r/ste/cabins/tents $209/249/209/419; ▣ ⊛) Located 15 minutes past Sechelt on Hwy 101, this boutique resort combines loungey lodge rooms and luxe cabins with a clutch of smashing 'tenthouse suites' accessed via a cliff-top boardwalk. About as far from camping as you can get, they have heated rock floors, hot-tubs and bay-view decks. The resort's waterfront restaurant is also excellent, with an ever-changing menu of Pacific Northwest classics and a great brunch that savvy locals often drop in for.

Magellan's Tapas by the Bay (☎ 604-740-0904; 5764 Wharf Ave; mains $14-22; ⊙ 5-10pm Tue-Sun) Among Sechelt's mostly so-so restaurants, this inviting, marina-side spot has quickly become a local favorite. Dedicated to regional

ingredients served with contemporary West Coast flourishes, you'll have a hard time choosing between the lamb chops with goat's cheese or the tempting array of oyster dishes. There's also a small, well chosen, Old and New World wine list. Reservations recommended.

Spence on the Coast (☎ 604-740-8221; 5500 Hwy 101; mains $19-30; ⊙ 4-10pm) Another chatty locals' favorite, chef Spencer Watts is the man behind the name at this innovative restaurant where the highlights of the seasonally changing menus are superb, sustainably sourced seafood dishes including a mouthwatering wasabi and sesame-crusted albacore tuna. For non-aquatic fans, the filet mignon is also hard to top. Reservations recommended.

Getting There & Away

West Coast Air (☎ 604-606-6800, 800-347-2222; www .westcoastair.com) floatplane services arrive in downtown Sechelt from Nanaimo ($67, 20 minutes, six daily) and from Vancouver Airport's South Terminal ($80, 25 minutes, two daily).

Malaspina Coach Lines (☎ 604-886-7742, 877-227-8287; www.malaspinacoach.com) services arrive daily from Vancouver ($40, three hours).

The **Sunshine Coast Transit System** (☎ 604-885-6899; www.busonline.ca; adult/child $2.25/1.75) runs services into Sechelt from Langdale (55 minutes), Gibsons (45 minutes) and Halfmoon Bay (20 minutes).

EGMONT & EARLS COVE

At the top of the Lower Sunshine Coast, these two little communities are often overlooked but are excellent access points for some nature-hugging Jervis Inlet trips to the tree-lined fjords of Princess Louisa Inlet and Chatterbox Falls.

You can take in both on a six-hour cruise from Egmont with **Sunshine Coast Tours** (☎ 604-883-2280, 800-870-9055; www.sunshine coasttours.ca; adult/child $139/90) or, for a good hike to a natural wonder, the wooded 4km trail in **Skookumchuck Narrows Provincial Park** (☎ 604-885-3714; www.bcparks.ca) leads to an inlet so narrow that water forced through during tides can cause 30km/h rapids.

Possibly the most fun to be had in a boat, hop onboard a steel-hulled water taxi operated by **High Tide Tours** (☎ 604-883-9220; www .hightidetours.com; Egmont Marina; trips $15) here and take in the roiling, unpredictable waves first-hand. The boat crisscrosses the rapids like a giddy dive-bomber for about 20 minutes.

The name confusingly reflects its previous location but **Porpoise Bay Charters** (☎ 604-885-5950, 800-665-3483; www.porpoisebaycharters.com; 5718 Anchor Rd) has moved to a new spot near Egmont (it's a short boat hop from the marina). This long-established dive operator offers single or multi-day trips – plus training for first-timers – in an area dripping with wolf eels and blue sharks. There are also spectacular rock walls and HMCS *Chaudiere*, a 110m warship that's now an artificial reef. Lodge and yurt accommodation is also available.

You can also stay at the nearby **West Coast Wilderness Lodge** (☎ 604-883-3667, 877-988-3838; www.wcwl.com; r/ste from $175/270), which offers idyllic forested rooms for those who want to combine outdoor activities with rustic comforts and a good restaurant.

BC Ferries (☎ 250-386-3431, 888-223-3779; www.bcferries.com) services arrive in Earls Cove from Saltery Bay (passenger/vehicle $11/33.45, 50 minutes, eight daily). Earls Cove is the end of the Lower Sunshine Coast, so you'll have to hop the ferry across Jervis Inlet to Saltery Bay to continue, via Hwy 101, to the Upper Sunshine Coast.

POWELL RIVER
pop 13,600

Now you're on the Upper Sunshine Coast, it's a 31km drive along Hwy 101 from the ferry dock to Powell River, the region's biggest community. Established in 1910 to house the workers at the waterfront pulp mill, the steaming industrial complex that once dominated the town has been shrinking in recent years, triggering a new focus as an outdoor-oriented visitor destination – kayaking and diving are especially popular. But it's not just about over-exertion here: Powell River has a funky, welcoming vibe that makes it the best spot to base yourself in the region. Drop by the **Visitor Centre** (☎ 604-485-4701, 877-817-8669; www.discoverpowellriver.com; 111-4871 Joyce Ave; ☼ 9am-5pm May-Sep, 9am-5pm Mon-Fri Oct-Apr) for activity ideas.

Sights & Activities

West of downtown, **Willingdon Beach City Park** has a sandy beach, children's playground and a fishing pier. It's an ideal spot for a

---

> ### DETOUR: PENDER HARBOUR
>
> From Hwy 101, head east on Garden Bay Rd and follow its winding path through the woods and around Garden Bay Lake's north shore. Veer right onto Irvine's Landing Rd and watch for deer, eagles and the wonderfully jagged coast that can be seen through clearings in the trees. The road will take you to **Irvine's Landing**, the original settlement site in the Pender Harbour area, affectionately known as 'Venice of the North.' Stretch your legs along the beaches and rocky shore, checking tide pools for unbelievably colored sea critters. When you're ready, follow your path back to Hwy 101. If you're here in mid-September, visit the popular **Pender Harbour Jazz Festival** (www.penderharbourmusic.ca).

picnic – you can walk off lunch with a stroll along the Beach Trail, studded with historic logging artifacts. The fascinating **Powell River Historical Museum** (☎ 604-485-2222; www.powellrivermuseum.ca; 4798 Marine Ave; adult/child $2/1; ☼ 9am-4:30pm Jun-Aug, 9am-4:30pm Mon-Fri Sep-May) nearby is home to a shack which was once occupied by Billy Goat Smith, a hermit who lived here (with his goats) in the early 1900s.

If the town's history piques your interest, take a guided **walking tour** (☎ 604-483-3901; www.powellriverhistorictownsite.bc.ca; guided tours $5; ☼ Wed 7pm, Sat 10am Jul & Aug) of the historic townsite or just take in the lovely **Patricia Theatre** (☎ 604-483-9345; www.patriciatheatre.com; 5848 Ash St). This reminder of the golden age of cinema is reputedly Canada's longest-running movie house.

If you're feeling active, hit the water with a kayak rental from **Powell River Sea Kayak** (☎ 604-483-2160, 866-617-4444; www.bcseakayak.com; rental 3hr from $29, tours from $65). To access the area's ample scuba diving sites, **Alpha Dive Services** (☎ 604-485-6939; www.divepowellriver.com; 7050A Field St) rents gear and organizes guides and boat charters.

Sleeping

Harbour Guesthouse & Hostel (☎ 604-485-9803, 877-709-7700; www.powellriverhostel.com; 4454 Willingdon Ave; dm/r $24/58; ☐ ☎) In the heart of the downtown waterfront (and close to a pub), this smashing little 24-bed hostel has small

WHISTLER & THE
SUNSHINE COAST

dorms, a fully equipped kitchen and two lounge areas (free sunset views included). The best private room has a little balcony overlooking the waterfront and there's free tea and coffee, an internet-access computer and laundry facilities.

Adventure B&B (☎ 604-485-7097; www.adventure b-b.com; 7439 Nootka St; r/ste $80/90) Situated a few minutes past Powell River (they'll pick you up from town if you're arriving by bus), this is a good value, homely B&B in a wood-gabled house surrounded by a large garden. The two non-en suite rooms are comfy rather than palatial but the larger suite has its own patio entrance and is handy for small families. Rates include cooked breakfast and use of a little sauna shed. Ask the owners about local hiking options: they're experts.

Oceanside Resort Motel (☎ 604-485-2435, 888-889-2435; www.oceansidepark.com; 8063 Hwy 101; cabins $65-135; 🐕) This clutch of waterfront cabins a few minutes' drive south of Powell River is usually full of families with kids. They come for the playground, pedal boat hire, and indoor swimming pool and games room combo. But you don't have to have sprogs to stay here; the rustic quarters (the newest waterfront cabins are best) are spick and span and there's an adjoining stretch of sand for moonlit strolls.

Old Courthouse Inn (☎ 604-483-4000, 877-483-4777; www.oldcourthouseinn.ca; 6243 Walnut St; s/d $94/109; 🛜) In the oldest part of town, this beautifully restored eight-room hotel was once Powell River's courthouse and police station. Tell your friends you spent the night in jail (or in the judge's chambers or constable's office). In keeping with the historic theme, the eclectic rooms (we like room nine best) are nicely decorated with antique furnishings and the occasional quirky mod flourish. Extras include in-room DVD players and a guest-use kitchen and laundry.

Eating & Drinking

Flying Yellow Bread Bowl (🕑 8am-5pm Mon-Sat; mains $4-9; 🕑 8am-5pm Mon-Sat) The hearty, home-cooked dishes of this great little vegetarian diner – complete with rainbow-colored chairs and chalkboard menus dotting the walls – draw a chatty band of regulars every day. They come for eastern-influenced (mostly organic) dishes like stuffed vine leaves, spicy burgers, made-from-scratch soups and perhaps the best (and nicely garlicky) hummus in the West.

Shinglemill Pub & Bistro (☎ 604-483-3545; 6233 Powell Pl; mains $8-16; 🕑 11am-11pm) On Powell Lake north of town, this woodsy pub overlooking the water is a great place to end your day – arrive early for a patio table. A cut above usual pub grub, menu highlights include stuffed halibut, slow-braised barbeque ribs and a hearty seafood chowder. There's also a more formal bistro section for quieter dining away from the chatty bar crowd.

Alchemist Restaurant (☎ 604-485-4141; 4680 Marine Ave; mains $19-33; 🕑 5-10pm) Dedicated to sourcing local seasonal ingredients and fusing them with Mediterranean approaches, this charming Tuscan-style bistro is the ideal spot for a relaxing night out. Favorites include pan-seared scallops and rack of lamb served with goat's cheese ravioli, but with any luck the amazing cassoulet with duck confit, lamb sausage and pork tenderloin will also be available ('alchemy' indeed). Save room for the artisan cheese plate.

Getting There & Around

Pacific Coastal Airlines (☎ 604-273-8666, 800-663-2872; www.pacificcoastal.com) services arrive from Vancouver Airport's South Terminal (from $112, 35 minutes, four daily).

BC Ferries (☎ 888-223-3779, 250-386-3431; www.bcferries.com) services arrive from Comox on Vancouver Island (passenger/vehicle $10.90/33.90, 80 minutes, four daily).

Malaspina Coach Lines (☎ 604-886-7742, 877-227-8287; www.malaspinacoach.com) services arrive daily from Vancouver ($58, five to six hours).

BC Transit's **Powell River Regional Transit System** (☎ 604-485-4287; www.busonline.ca) handles local bus services, including bus 14 to and from Lund (adult/child $1.50/1.25, Tuesday and Friday only).

LUND & BEYOND

At the northern end of Hwy 101, little Lund is a staging post for trips into remote Desolation Sound. It's also a good spot for lunch before turning back down the Sunshine Coast. Consider one of the many activities on offer at the Lund Hotel while you're here – the dinner cruise is recommended (from $109, three to six hours, May to September).

With its many sheltered bays, the 83 sq km of **Desolation Sound Marine Provincial Park** (www.bcparks.ca) has plenty of boating, fishing, kayaking and swimming opportunities. If you're looking for a guided hike, contact Lund's **Terracentric Coastal Adventures** (☎ 604-483-7900, 888-552-5558; www.terracentricadventures .com) for excursions on the mainland and beyond.

Crescent-shaped **Savary Island** aka 'the Hawaii of the North,' is studded with dozens of white sandy beaches and encircled by turquoise and emerald water. To get to the island, call **Lund Water Taxi** (☎ 604-483-9749; www.lundwatertaxi.com; one-way $10): it's a 15-minute trip. Bring a bike across from Lund (rentals available at Lund Hotel) or hire one at the dock on the island when you arrive: Savary is a great place to bike, and with no car ferries or paved roads it's extremely tranquil.

Sleeping & Eating

Lund Hotel (☎ 604-414-0474, 877-569-3999; www.lund hotel.com; 1436 Hwy 101; d/ste $130/225) An attractive wood-sided pioneer property with a nautical feel, this century-old hostelry combines romantic renovated suites overlooking the water with motel-style rooms at the back. Once you've finished playing with the giant chess set out front, head to the bistro for some hearty fish and chips (the halibut is recommended) or a bowl of chunky seafood chowder.

Nancy's Bakery (☎ 604-483-4180; 1431 Hwy 101; mains $4-12; 🕑 8am-5:30pm) Across the street from the hotel, this bustling deli-style hangout has a pretty outdoor seating area and a great selection of home-cooked (mostly organic) soups, sandwiches, pastas and pizzas. It's hard not to be tempted by a rhubarb scone or gooey cinnamon bun for the road.

Laughing Oyster (☎ 604-483-9775; 10052 Malaspina Rd; mains $12-26; 🕑 11:30am-9pm) The views are stunning enough to illicit laughs of disbelief, but the nosh prepared in this atmospheric wooden restaurant is serious stuff. Superb seafood and giant steaks are prominent on the menu. This is a great example of excellent West Coast dining in a spectacular setting.

WHISTLER & THE SUNSHINE COAST

Vancouver Island

In the same way that some visitors to Vancouver think they've 'done' BC after a stroll around Stanley Park, weekend travelers to Victoria – the history-hugging provincial capital – mistakenly think they've covered Vancouver Island after shooting a few photos outside the Empress Hotel. Let's be clear here: at 502km long and 100km wide, Vancouver Island (the largest island off the North American coast) is like a mini-province unto itself, and it's ripe for exploration for those willing to adventure beyond the main city limits.

Of course, that's not to downplay the value of a visit to Victoria. Hitting the island without experiencing the capital would be like holidaying in the UK and never going to London. In fact, Londoners have traditionally felt very much at home here where the colonial traditions of 'olde England' were upheld by generations of migrating Brits. Luckily, recent years have seen the city successfully move on from its dusty past and Victoria now has a hopping dining scene, quirky indie stores and a much younger vibe.

But once you're done with Victoria, don't make the mistake of immediately scampering back to the mainland. Instead, give yourself a few extra days to explore one of BC's most intriguing regions. Pick one of the main island spines – Hwys 1, 19 or 4, for example – and you'll soon be uncovering the Cowichan Valley's fantastic farm and wineries trail; the family-friendly seaside towns of Parksville and Qualicum; the spectacular surfers' paradise of Tofino and the rest of the wild west coast; the tangled backcountry wilderness of North Island; and a wealth of colorful, singular communities – many founded on logging or fishing and almost all apparently featuring 'Port' in their name.

HIGHLIGHTS

- Taking an alternative approach to after-noon tea in **Victoria** (p165) from a winery-style tasting to an Asian-Pacific fusion feast

- Facing down the crashing waves of the Pacific in **Tofino** (p202) and jumping on a surfboard for the ride

- Sleeping in a spherical treehouse near **Qualicum Beach** (p194) and communing with nature

- Taste-tripping through the **Cowichan Valley** (p184) to visit the farms and wineries (as well as a cidery)

- Hiking the new **North Coast Trail** (p214) on the island's rugged but stunning northern tip

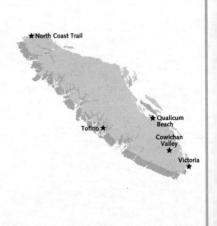
★North Coast Trail
★Qualicum Beach
Tofino ★
Cowichan Valley ★
Victoria ★

VICTORIA

pop 78,000

While locals often add in the residents of surrounding suburbs to give Victoria a population of more than 350,000, Western Canada's most historic city will never have the feel of a large metropolis. And that's a major part of its charm. While you'll find all the benefits of city life here – albeit on a smaller scale – you'll also feel instantly welcome among locals who are much more likely to smile and chat than their more aloof Vancouver neighbors across the water.

And that's not just because BC's favorite retirement community is exclusively stuffed with seniors who have too much time on their hands. Victoria was once nothing more than an expat British enclave of after-noon teas, immaculate gardens and Mock Tudor buildings. But, fueled by an increas-ingly youthful population (many of them University of Victoria students who stayed on), the city has drastically changed in recent years.

Quirky independent stores and a surpris-ingly innovative dining scene are the new colonizers here. And, once you've finished exploring the downtown streets, there's BC's best museum, a park that's licked with a windswept seafront and a host of activities on the doorstep, including regional cycle trails, nearby whale-watching and a full complement of kayaking adventures.

ORIENTATION

Overlooked by the formidable landmarks of the Empress Hotel and the Parliament Buildings (the ultra-busy visitor center is also here), Victoria's Inner Harbour is the city's beating waterfront heart, especially if you're a busker with a tourist-pleasing act. Wharf St radiates north from here to-wards the sky-blue Johnson St Bridge, but most walkers take the parallel inland route along Government St, where tourist shops mingle with stores that are actually worth entering.

INFORMATION
Bookstores

Dark Horse Books (Map p166; ☎ 250-386-8736; 623 Johnson St; ☺ 10am-6pm Wed-Sat, noon-5pm Sun-Tue) Eclectic quality used books and local zines.

Munro's Books (☎ 250-382-2464; 1108 Government St; ☺ 9am-6pm Mon-Wed & Sat, 9am-9pm Thu & Fri, 9:30am-6pm Sun) Legendary downtown favorite; extensive travel section.

VANCOUVER ISLAND IN THREE DAYS

Begin your trek with a whopping downtown Victoria breakfast at **Lady Marmalade** (p173), then weave north from the city on Hwy 1 towards **Cowichan Bay** (p184), a colorful waterside community of painted wooden buildings perched on stilts over an ocean inlet. You can stock up on picnic fixings here or spend some time searching out some of the visitor-friendly farms and vineyards in nearby **Cobble Hill** (p185). Once your car is full of food, continue on Hwy 1 to **Duncan** (p185), where you can stop to peruse the town's array of totem poles. If you're missing the big city, drive on and stay for a night in **Nanaimo** (p186), the island's second metropolis.

Hwy 1 becomes Hwy 19 after Nanaimo. On day two, continue along it and make for the family-friendly seaside towns of Parksville and Qualicum Beach, known jointly as **Oceanside** (p193) where leisurely beachcombing and finger-licking fish and chips are de rigueur. Take your time exploring some of the unexpected attractions in this region – including the huge **Coombs Old Country Market** (p193), where the roof is home to a clutch of grazing goats. Spend the night swaying gently in a **Free Spirit Spheres** (p194) spherical treehouse.

After Parksville, on day three, turn west on Hwy 4 towards the other coast, making sure you stop by **Cathedral Grove** (p196) en route to hug some majestic old-growth trees. Heading across the center of the island, you can stop at **Port Alberni** (p196) for a restorative pit stop or continue on to the **Pacific Rim National Park Reserve** (p198), heart of the island's breathtakingly wild west coast. Check into your **Tofino** (p202) resort hotel, then hit the water at Long Beach. Even if you're not a surfer, the frothy, crashing waves, expansive stretch of sand and bracing sea air will trigger an abiding love for all things natural.

VANCOUVER ISLAND

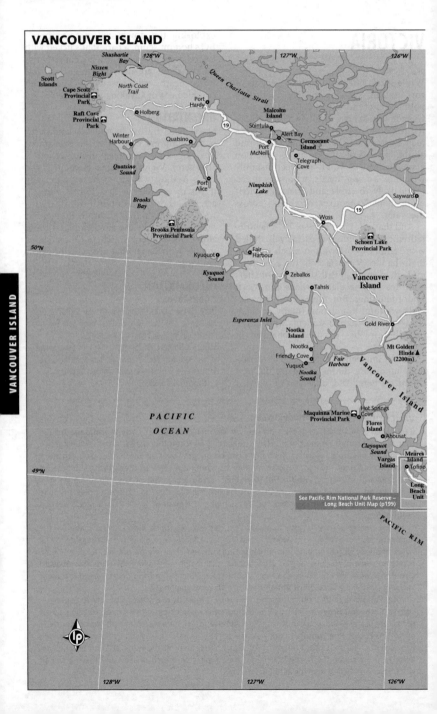

VANCOUVER ISLAND

VANCOUVER ISLAND

128°W · 127°W · 126°W

Shushartie Bay

Nissen Bight

Scott Islands

Cape Scott Provincial Park

North Coast Trail

Raft Cove Provincial Park

Holberg

Port Hardy

Queen Charlotta Strait

Malcolm Island

Sointula

Alert Bay

Cormorant Island

Winter Harbour

Quatsino

Port McNeill

Telegraph Cove

Quatsino Sound

Port Alice

Nimpkish Lake

Brooks Bay

Woss

Sayward

50°N

Brooks Peninsula Provincial Park

Schoen Lake Provincial Park

Kyuquot

Fair Harbour

Vancouver Island

Kyuquot Sound

Zeballos

Tahsis

Gold River

Esperanza Inlet

Nootka Island

Nootka

Mt Golden Hinde ▲ (2200m)

Friendly Cove

Yuquot

Fair Harbour

Nootka Sound

PACIFIC OCEAN

Vancouver Island

Maquinna Marine Provincial Park

Hot Springs Cove

Flores Island

Ahousat

Clayoquot Sound

Meares Island

49°N

Vargas Island

Tofino

Long Beach Unit

See Pacific Rim National Park Reserve – Long Beach Unit Map (p199)

PACIFIC RIM

128°W · 127°W · 126°W

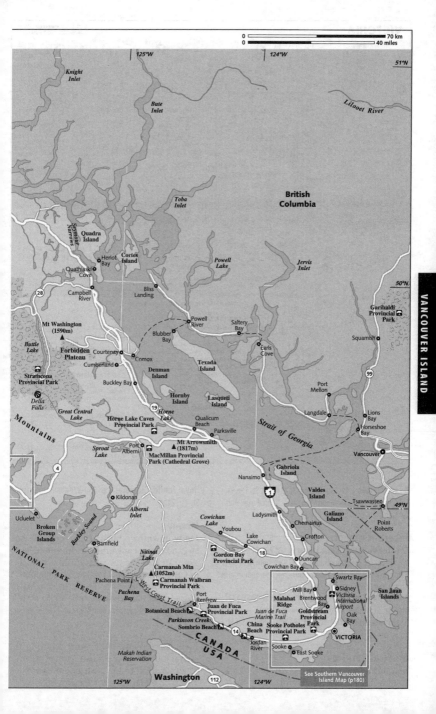

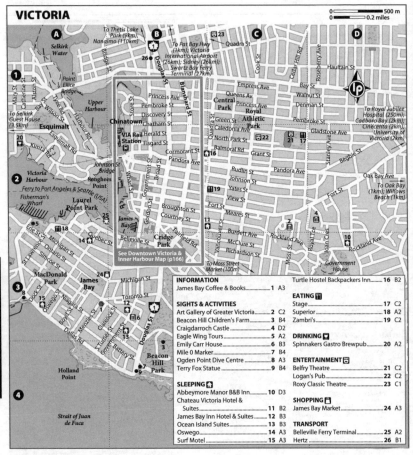

VICTORIA

INFORMATION	
James Bay Coffee & Books	**1** A3

SIGHTS & ACTIVITIES	
Art Gallery of Greater Victoria	**2** C2
Beacon Hill Children's Farm	**3** B4
Craigdarroch Castle	**4** D2
Eagle Wing Tours	**5** A2
Emily Carr House	**6** B3
Mile 0 Marker	**7** B4
Ogden Point Dive Centre	**8** A3
Terry Fox Statue	**9** B4

SLEEPING	
Abbeymore Manor B&B Inn	**10** D3
Chateau Victoria Hotel &	
Suites	**11** B2
James Bay Inn Hotel & Suites	**12** B3
Ocean Island Suites	**13** B3
Oswego	**14** A3
Surf Motel	**15** A3

Turtle Hostel Backpackers Inn	**16** B2

EATING	
Stage	**17** C2
Superior	**18** A2
Zambri's	**19** C2

DRINKING	
Spinnakers Gastro Brewpub	**20** A2

ENTERTAINMENT	
Belfry Theatre	**21** C2
Logan's Pub	**22** C2
Roxy Classic Theatre	**23** C1

SHOPPING	
James Bay Market	**24** A3

TRANSPORT	
Belleville Ferry Terminal	**25** A2
Hertz	**26** B1

Russell Books (☎ 250-361-4447; 734 Fort St; 9am-5:30pm Mon-Sat, 11am-5pm Sun) Two-floored used and bargain book behemoth.

Internet Access
Greater Victoria Public Library (☎ 250-382-7241; www.gvpl.ca; 735 Broughton St; 9am-6pm Mon & Fri-Sat, 9am-9pm Tue-Thu, 1-5pm Sun) Free one-hour internet access and Reader's Café.

James Bay Coffee & Books (☎ 250-386-4700; 143 Menzies St; 10c per min; 7:30am-9:30pm)

Stain Internet Café (☎ 250-382-3352; 609 Yates St; $3.50 per hr; 10am-2am)

Medical Services
Downtown Medical Centre (☎ 250-380-2210; 622 Courtney St; 8:30am-5pm Mon-Fri)

Royal Jubilee Hospital (☎ 250-370-8000; 1952 Bay St; 24hr)

Money
Many downtown businesses accept US dollars and major bank branches line Douglas St. You can also change your dosh at branches of **Custom House Global Foreign Exchange** (Wharf St ☎ 250-389-6007; 815 Wharf St; 9am-5pm Mon-Fri, 9:30am-5pm Sat, 11am-5pm Sun; Bay Centre ☎ 250-412-0336; 1150 Douglas St; 9:30am-6pm Mon-Sat, 11am-6pm Sun).

Post
Look for red-and-blue signs denoting the postal outlets tucked into stores around town, or head to the **main post office** (☎ 250-953-1352; 706 Yates St; 8am-5pm Mon-Fri).

See Downtown Victoria & Inner Harbour Map (p166)

VANCOUVER ISLAND

Tourist Information

Tourism Vancouver Island (☎ 250-754-3500, 888-655-3843; www.vancouverisland.travel) Info and advice on wider island travel.

Visitor Centre (VIC; ☎ 250-953-2033, 800-663-3883; www.tourismvictoria.com; 812 Wharf St; ☯ 8:30am-8:30pm Jun-Aug, 9am-5pm Sep-May) Busy, flyer-lined Inner Harbour outlet.

SIGHTS

Victoria has several best-avoided tacky tourist 'attractions' around the Inner Harbour. Dig a little deeper and you'll find some excellent alternatives, many illuminating the region's rich history.

Royal British Columbia Museum

The first stop for history-loving visitors, the **Royal BC Museum** (☎ 250-356-7226, 888-447-7977; www.royalbcmuseum.bc.ca; 675 Belleville St; adult/child $15/9.50; ☯ 9am-5pm) is the province's best. Head first for the 2nd floor natural history showcase that's fronted by a beady-eyed woolly mammoth (a model improbably made from musk ox hides) and lined with highly realistic dioramas – the forest scene of twitchy-looking elk, deer and grizzlies peeking at you from behind lichen-covered trees is highly evocative. Alternatively, the 3rd floor First Peoples exhibit is a deep exploration of indigenous culture, including a fascinating mask gallery (look out for the ferret-faced white man) and a reverential

re-creation of a cedar long house fronted by 14 stately totem poles (to 'read' the poles, see p43). But the most popular area is the colorful, walk-through cobbled street scene that brings to life the early colonial city, complete with chatty Chinatown, clamorous and highly detailed stores and a little movie house showing Charlie Chaplin films.

The museum's ground floor **IMAX Theatre** (p176) screens slightly more recent releases, including large-screen documentaries and Hollywood blockbusters. While outside, the free-entry **Thunderbird Park** has a clutch of brightly painted totem poles, plus a few original pioneer buildings, including **Helmcken House** (incl with museum entry or suggested donation $5; ☯ noon-4pm Jun-Sep). One of BC's oldest structures, this tidy 1852 doctor's residence is lined with the minutiae of old-school family life.

Parliament Buildings

Along with the Empress, the grandly turreted, dome-topped **Parliament Buildings** (☎ 250-387-1400; www.leg.bc.ca; 501 Belleville St; admission free; ☯ 8:30am-5pm May-Sep, 8:30am-5pm Mon-Fri Oct-Apr) is a defining Victoria landmark. But it's not just a pretty face. In fact, the ugly world of provincial BC politics resides in the debating chamber inside. Don't let that put you off, though. Once you've taken your shots of the handsome exterior – don't

VANCOUVER ISLAND

NOT QUITE YOUR GRANDMA'S AFTERNOON TEA...

Salivating traditionalists often drop in at the old-school **Fairmont Empress Hotel** (☎ 250-389-2727; www.fairmont.com/empress; 721 Government St; afternoon tea per person $54; ☯ noon-3:45pm), where the famed silver-service afternoon tea features dainty sandwiches, clotted-cream-smothered scones and a giddy overdose of Empress-blend tea. But recent years have delivered a brimming teapot of non-trad leafy experiences to Victoria visitors. Connoisseurs should first head to the edge-of-Chinatown **Silk Road** (☎ 250-704-2688; www.silkroadtea.com; 1624 Government St; ☯ 10am-6pm Mon-Sat, 11am-5pm Sun), a swanky joint combining swish tea-making paraphernalia with a tasting bar where you can sip exotic loose treats like red bush chai and goomtea Darjeeling – the calming jasmine green tea is recommended for travelers. Alternatively, the **Hotel Grand Pacific** (☎ 250-380-4458; www.hotelgrandpacific.com; 463 Belleville St; afternoon tea per person $36; ☯ 2-4:30pm Jul & Aug, 2-4:30pm Thu-Sat Sep-Jun) offers an Asian Pacific afternoon tea in its lobby restaurant. The white tablecloth meal includes unusual tipples like Japanese popcorn tea plus a triple tier plate of candy smoked salmon bannock, cucumber wasabi cream cheese sandwiches and delectable desserts like chai brûlée and cashew shortbreads. If you've still got room to spare, also consider dropping by the elegant little **Mela's Tearoom** (☎ 250-382-8528; 792 Humboldt St; afternoon tea for 2 $39.95; ☯ 10am-5:30pm) nestled inside the Winchester Gallery. Victoria's best value high-end afternoon tea, there's a daily changing menu of organic croissants, fresh-baked quiches and exquisite cakes, plus pots of lip-smacking specialty teas supplied by Silk Road.

forget to zoom in on the gilded statue of Captain George Vancouver up top – climb the grand steps and wander around inside. Led by costumed Victorians, the 30-minute history-themed **tour** (☎ 250-387-3046; tour free; ☽ 9am-4pm mid-May–early Sep, 9am-4pm Mon-Fri Oct-Apr) is recommended – ask about the controversial friezes of First Nations scenes that were recently covered up after being on display for decades. Also consider saving time for lunch on-site: the subterranean **Legislative Dining Room** (p173) is one of the city's best-kept dining secrets.

Chinatown

Small but perfectly formed, colorful Fisgard St is the center of Victoria's compact Chinatown. One of Canada's oldest, it's fronted by a towering red gate looming over sprawling fruit and vegetable stores and po-faced ancients meditating outside family-run restaurants. Twinkling neon signs add a dash of Shanghai élan, while **Fan Tan Alley** – a narrow passageway between Fisgard St and Pandora Ave – draws the curious. Once the best spot in town to visit a brothel or buy your opium, this ultra-slender shaded thoroughfare is now a warren of little shops hawking cheap and cheerful trinkets, cool used records and funky fashions.

Beacon Hill Park

A short stroll southwards from the Inner Harbour, Victoria's biggest park space is more rustic than its Stanley Park sister in Vancouver, but that's the main attraction. Fringed by the Pacific on one side, it's a great spot to weather a wild and windy storm. If the tempest dies down, unfurl a picnic and then go exploring. You'll find one of the world's tallest totem poles, a Victorian cricket pitch and some landscaped gardens and ponds, complete with bobbling turtles. If you have kids in tow, placate them at the **Beacon Hill Children's Farm** (☎ 250-381-2532; www.beaconhill park.ca/childrenspark; suggested donation adult/child $3/2; ☽ 10am-4pm) where they can hang out with goats, rabbits and pot-bellied pigs. Finally, check out the marker for **Mile 0** of the Trans-Canada Hwy alongside the **statue of Terry Fox**, the heroic one-legged runner whose attempted 1981 trek across Canada gripped the nation. Also consider dropping by the park's **Cameron Bandshell** on an August Saturday for free 9pm screenings of classic B movies.

Craigdarroch Castle

Tragically, coal baron Robert Dunsmuir died a few months after completing his labyrinthine, 39-room **Craigdarroch Castle** (☎ 250-592-5323; www.thecastle.ca; 1050 Joan Cres; adult/child $12/4; ☽ 10am-4:30pm Sep–mid-Jun, 9am-7pm mid-Jun–Aug), leaving his mourning wife to take up residence alone. Now a stately house museum, their elegant wood-lined stone mansion is a delightful evocation of Victorian wealth, featuring antique-packed rooms and ornate architectural flourishes – including 32 sumptuous stained-glass windows. Delve into the eye-popping history of the wider Dunsmuir family here and climb the central tower's 87 steps for panoramic views of the snow-capped Olympic Mountains.

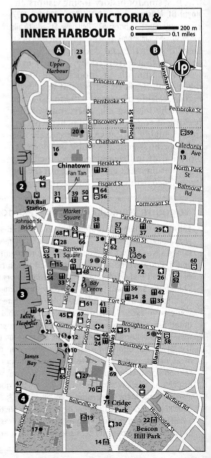

DOWNTOWN VICTORIA & INNER HARBOUR

Art Gallery of Greater Victoria

Not far from Craigdarroch Castle, the city's main **art gallery** (☎ 250-384-4101; www.aggv.bc.ca; 1040 Moss St; adult/child $12/2; ⊗ 10am-5pm Fri-Wed, 10am-9pm Thu) houses one of Canada's finest Emily Carr collections, in a restored and extended heritage mansion. Carr's paintings, writings and photos are regularly rotated to keep the displays fresh, but there's also an important collection of Asian artworks on permanent display. Regular temporary exhibitions color the seven gallery spaces and there's a sprightly calendar of lectures and presentations if you want to rub shoulders with local arty types. Rumors abound of a possible new satellite gallery downtown, so check ahead before you arrive.

Vancouver Island Brewery

A 15-minute walk north from downtown along Government St brings you to the home of this popular BC **microbrewer** (☎ 250-361-0005; www.vanislandbrewery.com; 2330 Government St; tour $6; ⊗ 9am-6pm Mon-Sat, tours 3pm Fri & Sat), nestled near a string of grubby light industrial units and a churning cement factory. It's worth the trek, though, for the chatty 30-minute tour of the plant followed by a tasting of four proprietary brews – the perennially popular Piper Pale Ale is recommended – plus an ever-changing special seasonal tipple. If you're here in winter, it'll likely be the Hermannator Ice Bock, the kind of strong beer that puts hairs on the chest of everyone within a 5-mile radius.

St Ann's Academy

Like a transplant from a *Madeline* book, this magnificent former 19th-century French-style **convent school** (☎ 250-953-8828; www.stannsacademy.com; 835 Humboldt St; adult/child $5/2; ⊗ 10am-4pm mid-May–early Sep, 1-4pm Thu-Sun early Sep–mid-May) backing onto Beacon Hill Park is set in tranquil formal gardens fronted by a large ironwork gate. After

VANCOUVER ISLAND

years of abandonment – the school closed in 1973 – it was restored and partly opened to the public in 1997. After ambling among the avenues of trees (also a good picnic spot), climb the steep steps and nip inside to the museum-like recreated rooms, including an ornate chapel. Victoria's first Catholic cathedral when it opened in 1858, it has a gilded altar backed by iconic oil paintings.

Bastion Square

On the old Fort Victoria site between Government and Wharf Sts, stone-lined Bastion Sq once held gallows and a brothel but you're more likely to find cafés and bars here now. You can purchase arts and handicrafts at the summertime **Bastion Square Public Market** (☎ 250-885-1387; www.bastionsquare .ca; ☽ 10:30am-7:30pm Apr-Oct) which also includes local food and produce on Thursdays and Fridays. Alternatively, dip into the **Maritime Museum** (☎ 250-385-4222; www.mmbc.bc.ca; 28 Bastion Sq; adult/child $10/5; ☽ 9:30am-5pm mid-Jun–mid-Sep, 9:30am-4:30pm mid-Sep–mid-Jun) for a taste of the region's salty past. Housed in the old provincial courthouse, exhibits include 400 model ships dating back to 1810 and colorful displays on regional piracy, shipwrecks and navigation methods.

Victoria Bug Zoo

Downtown's best kid-friendly attraction, the **Bug Zoo** (☎ 250-384-2847; www.bugzoo.bc.ca; 631 Courtney St; adult/child $8/5; ☽ 9:30am-7pm mid-Jun–Aug, 9am-5pm Mon-Sat, 11am-5pm Sun Sep–mid-Jun) houses creepy-crawlies such as industrious dung beetles and glow-in-the-dark scorpions while informative guides wander around explaining how they all eat, mate and give birth (the bugs not the guides). Those who can't restrain themselves can handle a few critters, including an alarmingly large 400-leg millipede. Hit the gift shop on your way out to pick up some crunchy cricket lollipops – a more original BC souvenir than maple syrup will ever be.

Emily Carr House

A gentle amble south from the Inner Harbour, the clapboard **Emily Carr House** (☎ 250-383-5843; www.emilycarr.com; 207 Government St; admission by donation; ☽ 11am-4pm Tue-Sat May-Sep) is the birthplace of BC's best-known artist. Restored to its original gingerbread

exterior, the interior features period-furnished rooms and displays on the life and work of the painter and author. As well as a small number of original Carr works – the collection at the Art Gallery of Greater Victoria (p167) is much larger – there are ever-changing exhibitions of local contemporary paintings.

ACTIVITIES
Whale-watching

The activity everyone seems to do once they've tired of wandering Victoria's historic streets, the lucrative mid-April to October whale-watching season plays host to several competing operators. The whales don't always show, but you can expect to be up-close with some barking sea lions and basking elephant seals.

Recommended operators:

Eagle Wing Tours (☎ 250-384-8008, 800-708-9488; www.eaglewingtours.com; 12 Erie St; adult/child $115/69)

Prince of Whales (☎ 250-383-4884, 888-383-4884; www.princeofwhales.com; 812 Wharf St; adult/child $105/75)

SpringTide Whale Tours (☎ 250-384-4444, 800-470-3474; www.springtidecharters.com; 1207 Wharf St; adult/child $95/65)

Kayaking

A tranquil paddle through Vancouver Island's calm waters gives a different perspective on the region's rock-and-forest-lined beauty. Rent equipment for a solo trek or join a guided tour.

Established operators:

Ocean River Sports (☎ 250-381-4233, 800-909-4233; www.oceanriver.com; 1824 Store St; rental 2/24hr $30/48; ☽ 9:30am-6pm Mon-Sat, 10am-5pm Sun) Great 2½-hour sunset tours ($65).

Sports Rent (☎ 250-385-7368; www.sportsrentbc.com; 1950 Government St; rental 5/24hr $24/35; ☽ 9:30am-5:30pm Sat-Thu, 9:30am-6pm Fri) City's best rental rates, with knowledgeable staff.

Victoria Kayak (☎ 250-216-5646; www.victoriakayak .com; 950 Wharf St; rental 2/24hr $28/50; ☽ 9:30am-6pm Mon-Sat, 10am-4pm Sun Apr-Oct) Excellent guided nature tour from Inner Harbour ($59).

Scuba Diving

Ogden Point Breakwater, on the western edge of James Bay, is downtown's main shore dive destination. You can also access the region's underwater ecosystem and wreck sites at 10 Mile Point near Cadboro

Bay and at the recommended Race Rocks, southwest of town.

Recommended dive operators and equipment renters:

Frank Whites Dive Stores (☎ 250-385-4713; www .frankwhites.com; 1620 Blanshard St; rental package per day from $45; ✆ 9am-5:30pm) Rentals and courses for all levels.

Ogden Point Dive Centre (☎ 250-380-9119, 888-701-1177; www.divevictoria.com; 199 Dallas Rd; ✆ 9am-6pm) Rentals, courses and guided dives at well-equipped shorefront facility.

CYCLING TOUR

Hop on your wheels at the Inner Harbour, in front of the **Fairmont Empress Hotel (1**, p172) and weave southwards down Government St past the **Royal BC Museum (2**, p165). Within a couple of minutes, you'll be in a peaceful residential neighborhood of old clapboard Victorian homes, the heritage backbone of James Bay. Look out for the **Emily Carr House (3**, p168) on your left. When you reach Niagara St, turn left and continue for two blocks until you reach the fringes of **Beacon Hill Park (4**, p166). Turn right onto

Douglas and head towards the waterfront, alongside the park. You'll soon pass the **Terry Fox statue (5**, p166) and the marker denoting **Mile 0 (6**, p166) of the Trans-Canada Hwy. At the end of Douglas and with the seafront breeze now licking your legs, turn right and weave westwards along the Dallas Rd seaside route. Trace Dallas for around 1km, then follow the road as it pulls you around the **Ogden Point peninsula (7**). After a few more meters, turn right along Erie St, and follow the waterfront route back towards the Inner Harbour. You'll soon pass the ferries from the US on your left and the large white **Gatsby Mansion (8**) on your right. Consider a rewarding Asian-Pacific afternoon tea stop at the **Hotel Grand Pacific (9**, p165) on the next block. Alternatively,

---

SEA & CITY CYCLE

Start Fairmont Empress Hotel
Finish Parliament Buildings
Distance 4km
Duration One hour

VICTORIA CYCLING TOUR

continue along Bellville St to the **Parliament Buildings** (**10**, p165) and rest your weary legs (and maybe catch some sun) on the grass outside.

VICTORIA FOR CHILDREN

Victoria offers plenty of options for those traveling with sprogs. Pick up the free *Kids' Guide to Victoria* flyer at the VC (p165) then hop on a nearby Harbour Ferry (p178) for an excitable aquatic amble around the waterfront.

The city's main family-friendly attractions are within easy walking distance of the Inner Harbour and include the highly recommended Royal British Columbia Museum (p165) – complete with an evocative walk-though pioneer town, a menagerie of highly realistic animal dioramas and an eye-popping IMAX theater. The creepy-crawly Victoria Bug Zoo (p168) is not far from here and gives the museum a run for its money in the top kid-friendly attraction stakes.

Continue the critter theme over at Beacon Hill Park (p166), where the great little Children's Farm includes lots of petting opportunities with furry friends, as well as daily 'goat stampede' races that will have your kids giggling like crazy. The park is a great picnic spot and a good place to let your youngsters run wild in the hope that they might eventually be tired enough to sleep.

Those who time their visit for May or August should also take advantage of two family-friendly events. The Victoria Day Parade (see below) is a clamorous cavalcade of floats and marching bands, while Luminara Victoria (see below) is a chance to get creative with some full-on lantern making workshops followed by a procession. Expect your progeny to be covered in glitter and sticky stars within minutes.

TOURS

Get out of your hotel room on one of these local trawls:

Cycle Treks (☎ 250-386-2277, 877-733-6722; www .cycletreks.com; 811 Wharf St; tours from $59; ☼ 9:30am-6pm Mon-Sat) Friendly guided tours include a four-hour city amble and an excellent out-of-town Cowichan Valley winery weave ($139).

Gray Line West Victoria (☎ 250-744-3566, 800-663-8390; www.graylinewest.com; 700 Douglas St; adult/child

from $25/15) Narrated 90-minute double-decker bus tours of the city, plus 12 additional packages including a sunset tour, hop-on-hop-off attractions service and a Butchart Gardens afternoon tea tour.

Harbour Air Seaplanes (☎ 800-665-0212, 604-274-1277; www.harbour-air.com; tours from $99) For a bird's-eye Victoria view, the 30-minute floatplane tour from the Inner Harbour is fab – especially when it dives towards the water on landing.

Walking Tours

For self-guided ambles pick up the free *Downtown Victoria Walk & Run Map* at the VC. Guided treks include:

Architectural Institute of BC (☎ 604-683-8588 ext 333, 800-667-0753 ext 333; www.aibc.ca; tours $5; ☼ 1pm Wed-Sat Jul & Aug) Five good-value building-focused downtown treks, ranging from Chinatown to churches and art deco.

Fairmont Empress Tour (☎ 250-592-9255; www .walkabouts.ca; 721 Government St; tours adult/child $10/5; ☼ 10am mid-May–mid-Oct) Peek behind the curtains of Victoria's landmark hotel on this 90-minute stroll through the rooms and gardens.

Hidden Dragon Tours (☎ 250-920-0881, 866-920-0881; www.oldchinatown.com; adult/child $29/14.50; ☼ 2pm Sun) Delve into the colorful, sometimes nefarious past of Canada's oldest Chinatown on this evocative 90-minute evening lantern tour.

FESTIVALS & EVENTS

Victoria Film Festival (www.victoriafilmfestival .com) Ten-day celebration of movie-making with over 200 screenings at six city venues in early February.

Dine Around, Stay in Town (www.tourismvictoria .com/dinearound) Three weeks in mid-February of cut-price meals at city restaurants.

Victoria Day Parade Giant street fiesta in mid-May of floats, clowns and marching bands.

Jazzfest International (www.jazzvictoria.ca) Nine-day orgy of foot-tapping shenanigans in late June.

Moss Street Paint-In (www.aggv.bc.ca) One hundred artists ply their craft at this popular one-day event in mid-July.

Victoria Ska Fest (www.victoriaskafest.ca) Canada's largest ska-only fiesta is held in mid-July.

Luminara Victoria (www.luminaravictoria.com) Music, performance and lantern making around St Ann's Academy and Beacon Hill Park in late July.

Victoria Dragon Boat Festival (www.victoriadragon boat.com) Mid-August: 90 teams, three days and lots of energetic splashing.

Victoria Fringe Theatre Festival (www.victoriafringe .com) Two-week extravaganza in late August of short, often comic plays staged throughout the city.

VANCOUVER ISLAND

SLEEPING

From downtown tower hotels to swish boutique sleepovers and romantic heritage B&Bs, Victoria has a wide range of accommodation. Tourism Victoria's **room reservation service** (☎ 250-953-2033, 800-663-3883; www.tourismvictoria.com) helps with bookings.

Budget

Turtle Hostel Backpackers Inn (☎ 250-381-3210, 877-381-3210; www.turtlehostel.ca; 1608 Quadra St; dm/d $25/30; 💻 🛜) This yellow-painted heritage house has been converted into a homely, labyrinthine, eclectic, worn-around-the-edges hostel that offers small dorms and a tiny kitchen to its mostly young traveling clientele. Some rooms have bizarre fresco interiors – including the main floor's private room with its ivy-painted pillars – and handy extras include free wireless and computer terminal use. A brisk five-minute walk from downtown via Pandora Ave.

Ocean Island Backpackers Inn (☎ 250-385-1788, 888-888-4180; www.oceanisland.com; 791 Pandora Ave; dm/s/d $27/39/55; 💻 🛜) Part hostel, part budget hotel, this popular heritage property is a maze of differently sized rooms (request one with a window). A great place to meet other travellers, there's a large communal kitchen and a licensed lounge – avoid lower floor rooms on show nights. The chatty front desk is a mine of information and there's a wide array of guided excursions and tours available. Wi-fi access is $1 per two hours.

HI Victoria Hostel (☎ 250-385-4511, 888-883-0099; www.hihostels.ca; 516 Yates St; dm/s/d $30/55/68; 💻 🛜) While a long-planned refurb was still being discussed on our visit, this converted brick warehouse remains the city's best-located hostel. Despite its institutionalized feel, it's ideal for quieter backpackers and has two large single-sex dorms, three small co-eds and two private rooms that are often booked far in advance. Ask at check-in about the little-known semi-private room offering a double bed at standard dorm rates. Linen provided; and microwaves only in the kitchen.

Midrange

Ocean Island Suites (☎ 250-385-1788, 888-888-4180; www.oisuites.com; 143 Government St; ste $125; 💻) A short stroll from the Inner Harbour, this renovated 1907 heritage home in a quiet

residential neighborhood is a great deal for groups of up to four ($15 extra per person after double occupancy). Each suite has a full kitchen and en suite plus a distinct look: suite one (the largest) has a loungey, contemporary feel; suite two has a sunny, pastel approach; and suite three (the smallest) is richly colored in red and mustard shades and has a traditional hearth. There's no reception, which means picking up your keys at the Ocean Island Backpackers (see above).

Dalton Hotel & Suites (☎ 250-384-4136, 800-663-6101; www.daltonhotel.ca; 759 Yates St; s/d/ste $125/135/175) This handsome landmark property (allegedly the city's oldest hotel) has recently undergone a refurb that's transformed it into a reliable downtown standard. Most rooms – some quite small – are respectable while not especially imaginative, but pricier, contemporary-style suites have extra amenities such as fireplaces, giant beds and small kitchens. Heritage hangovers include old-school iron radiators lurking in the corners plus a maze-like layout – leave a trail of breadcrumbs to find your room again.

Surf Motel (☎ 250-386-3305, 888-738-3399; www.surfmotel.net; 290 Dallas Rd; d $135; 🕑 Feb-Oct) Hugging the Ogden Point shoreline, rooms at this unassuming, 60s-style motel offer spectacular ocean views fringed by the snow-capped Olympic mountains. As if recognising it can't compete with the vistas, the rooms are neat, tidy and fairly austere – '80s furniture is de rigueur but all have handy kitchenettes. If you crave more character, a nearby 1950s duplex is also on the cards. Ideal for groups, it has two bedrooms and a funky kitchen with a chequerboard floor.

James Bay Inn Hotel & Suites (☎ 250-384-7151, 800-836-2649; www.jamesbayinn.com; 270 Government St; r $140) A few minutes' walk from the back of the Parliament Buildings, this 19th-century charmer has a loyal band of customers. They keep coming back for its flower-strewn exteriors, downstairs bar and 45 cozy, simply furnished rooms. Almost every one is different: some have bay windows, claw-foot tubs or kitchenettes, while most have loudly patterned carpets and bedspreads. Pack light: there are no elevators here.

Queen Victoria Hotel & Suites (☎ 250-386-1312, 800-663-7007; www.qvhotel.com; 655 Douglas St; d/ste $140/150; 🛒) A renovated eight-story tower block hotel handily located minutes from the Inner Harbour and adjacent to Beacon Hill Park. The refurbished rooms here now have a snazzy business-hotel feel – some also have kitchenettes with full stoves. Popular with weekending island travellers, the large two-bedroomed suites are also great for families. Amenities include an on-site restaurant, subterranean pool and small gym. Some rooms overlook the park.

Chateau Victoria Hotel & Suites (☎ 250-382-4221, 800-663-5891; www.chateauvictoria.com; 74 Burdett Ave; d/ste $140/200; 🖥 🐾) Close to the heart of all the downtown action, many rooms at this popular tower block hotel have a well-maintained '80s feel, with pastel blinds and busy bedspreads. Most standard rooms have kitchenettes and balconies, while the swankier suites have more space and decidedly more contemporary interiors. There is also a pool and in-room spa services, as well as free-use computer in the lobby.

Abbeymore Manor B&B Inn (☎ 250-370-1470, 888-801-1811; www.abbeymoore.com; 1470 Rockland Ave; r from $145; 🖥 📶) A romantic 1912 arts and crafts mansion in the city's historic Rockland district, Abbeymore's handsome colonial exterior masks seven antique-lined rooms furnished with Victorian knick-knacks, artworks and the kind of beds (including some four-posters) that you have to climb to get into. But it's not just a creaky-floored blast from the past: some rooms have jetted tubs and fully equipped kitchens while all have handy wi-fi access.

Top End

our pick **Swans Suite Hotel** (☎ 250-361-3310, 800-668-7926; www.swanshotel.com; 506 Pandora Ave; ste $199-359) Once a decaying grain warehouse where trains trundled right into the building, Swans has been transformed into arguably Victoria's best character boutique sleepover. Its 29 one- and two-bedroom art-lined suites each have a heritage flavor combining wood-beamed ceilings, full kitchens and rustic chic furnishings: the larger two-story loft suites, where you have to climb upstairs to bed in a gabled nook, are particularly recommended. Some rooms also have small balconies overlooking the nearby Johnson Street Bridge – that's the VIA Rail *Malahat* train you'll hear trundling over the span every morning. If the hotel's free library of DVDs

doesn't keep you occupied, head downstairs to the excellent Swan's Brewpub (p175) for a bevvy or three.

Oswego (☎ 250-294-7500, 877-767-9346; www .oswegovictoria.com; 500 Oswego St; d/ste $260/350) Victoria's main entry in the designer boutique sleepover stakes, the friendly young staff at this purpose-built West Coast hotel offer loungey, apartment-style rooms on a quiet James Bay residential street. The swanky quarters (including smaller studios with clever space-saving Murphy beds) all have flatscreen TVs, kitchens with stainless steel appliances and luxe bathrooms with pricey Italian amenities. Higher floors (especially the penthouses) have great views across the water.

Fairmont Empress Hotel (☎ 250-348-8111, 866-540-4429; www.fairmont.com/empress; 721 Government St; r from $249; 🖥 🍽 🐾) The Inner Harbour's grand old lady, this ivy-covered, picture-postcard edifice has been wowing tea-loving guests for decades. Most rooms are elegant but conservative and some are downright small, but the overall effect – including an oak-beamed restaurant serving Raj-style curry and a high tea that can be taken while overlooking the waterfront – is classier than all of the city's other hotels added together. Even if you don't stay, it's worth strolling through to soak up the ambience of yesteryear Victoria.

EATING

Victoria's dine-out scene has swapped the bad old days of dodgy British-themed pub restaurants for casual and fine dining options that rival some of Vancouver's best. Check out members of the Island Chefs' Collaborative (www.iccbc.ca) for restaurants with a regional food bent and pick-up *Eat Magazine* (free) for reviews.

Budget

Pig BBQ Joint (☎ 250-381-4677; 749 View St; mains $5; ⏱ 11am-5pm Mon, 11am-6:30pm Tue-Sat) Arrive early or late to avoid the slavering office worker line-ups at this carnivorous southern-style hole in the wall. The simple, great-value menu of meaty comfort foods includes hulking pulled pork, beef brisket and smoked chicken sandwiches that you may have to dislocate your jaw to eat. If you have your elasticized waist pants on, also consider a dessert sandwich of fried

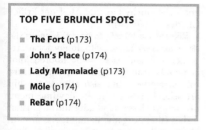

TOP FIVE BRUNCH SPOTS

■ **The Fort** (p173)

■ **John's Place** (p174)

■ **Lady Marmalade** (p173)

■ **Möle** (p174)

■ **ReBar** (p174)

banana and peanut butter plus a pail of house-made ice tea.

Dutch Bakery (☎ 250-385-1012; 718 Fort St; mains $5-7; ◷ 7:30am-5:30pm Tue-Sat) This charming downtown eatery has been packing them in for 50 years with its Formica tables, chatty ambience and simple, old-school meals. Pull up a swivel chair at the counter for a veal croquette and potato salad lunch or indulge in a naughty afternoon treat of cream-packed vanilla slices and dollar rolls, handmade by the lads out the back. Before you leave, peruse the shelves of homemade candies and hit the road with some marzipan teeth or sprinkle-topped chocolate coins.

our pick Red Fish Blue Fish (☎ 250-298-6877; 1006 Wharf St; mains $6-10; ◷ 11am-7pm Jun-Aug, with earlier off-season closing) Nestled on the waterfront boardwalk near the foot of Broughton St, this refurbished freight container takeout shack is a smashing green-themed seafood eatery. Dedicated to sustainable marine nosh (it also has wooden cutlery and recyclable containers), you can join the in-the-know throng for mouthwatering, freshly made highlights like scallop tacones, wild salmon sandwiches, tempura battered fish and chips and the signature chunky Pacific Rim Chowder. Weave along the waterfront with your warm parcel and find a bench – watch out for assaults from hovering seagull mobsters, though.

Fort (☎ 250-382-3130; 742 Fort St; mains $6-10; ◷ 8am-3pm Mon-Fri, 7:30pm-midnight Fri & Sat) This subterranean L-shaped joint combines great value home-cooked nosh with a friendly, hipsterish approach. Daily breakfast and lunch specials made from scratch can include popular eggs Benedict and bulging pasta mains, but it's the seriously chunky soups that keep the regulars happy with lip smacking varieties like coconut chicken and yam and peanut. On weekend evenings, it transforms into the funky Lowdown bar for Friday night quizzes and Saturday live music.

Midrange

our pick Lady Marmalade (☎ 250-381-2872; 608 Johnson St; mains $7-14; ◷ 8:30am-4pm) Victoria's best hippy-chic breakfast and lunch spot, the cozy interior here is lined with the kind of furniture that parents hide in their basements…until their kids drag it out and celebrate it as retro cool. Luckily, there's substance behind the kitsch aesthetics with wholesome menu highlights including sourdough pizzas and daily changing soup specials (the carrot and ginger is a winner). The huge all-day breakfasts are recommended, with dishes like spicy tofu scramble and a dangerously seductive breakfast poutine with miso gravy. Visiting veggies will find plenty of meat-free dishes here.

Superior (☎ 250-380-9515; 106 Superior St; small plates $7-12, mains $11-16; ◷ 11am-3pm Tue-Sun, 5-10:30pm Tue-Sat) An eclectic brick-lined dining room with artistic 'installations' including a stuffed circus monkey and fake birds hanging from the rafters, the food here is of the adventurous tasting plate variety: think house-cured charcuterie, Dungeness crab cakes, and chicken liver and bacon mousse. Drinks focus on BC beer and wine (Kettle Valley Merlot is suggested), and there are nightly jazz performances and twice-monthly film noir screenings.

Stage (☎ 250-388-4222; 1307 Gladstone Ave; small plates $8-12; ◷ 5pm-midnight Mon-Sat, 4:30pm-midnight Sun) A bistro with a serious food and wine addiction, this welcoming wood-floored nook is well worth the 10-minute drive from downtown – especially if you're heading to the nearby Belfry Theatre (p176) for a show. Dive into delectable charcuterie plates (the chicken liver parfait and toast is good), plus tempting tasters of Sooke trout and paprika sausage. With 17 wines available by the glass, you can also taste trip with a tipple or two.

Legislative Dining Room (☎ 250-387-3959; Room 006, Parliament Buildings, 501 Belleville St; mains $6-16; ◷ 9am-3pm Mon-Thu, 9am-2pm Fri) Arguably Victoria's best-kept dining secret, the Parliament Buildings' subsidized in-house cafeteria serves MPs, VIPs and anyone willing to show photo ID at the main entrance to get their security pass access to the corridors of power. Once inside, you'll find an old-school silver-service restaurant with BC-sourced dishes like shrimp quesadilla, an array of daily changing fish specials and plenty of exquisite desserts. Cash only.

Noodle Box (☎ 250-384-1314; 818 Douglas St; mains $8-14; ⓨ 11am-9pm Mon-Thu, 11am-10pm Fri & Sat, noon-7pm Sun) With finger-licking Thai, Malaysian and Singaporean dishes, this buzzing business started out as a local street vendor and has since branched out all the way to Vancouver. A great place for takeout – served in those funky boxes – it's also a chatty eat-in spot popular with students. Recommended dishes include wok-fried teriyaki noodles and hot Cambodian jungle curry, which is especially good for those who like their food to kick them in the mouth.

John's Place (☎ 250-389-0711; 723 Pandora Ave; mains $8-18; ⓨ 7am-9pm Mon-Thu, 7am-10pm Fri, 8am-10pm Sat, 8am-9pm Sun) Victoria's favorite brunch spot – hence the weekend queues – John's is worth the wait to get in. It has a wood-floored, high-ceilinged heritage room lined with funky memorabilia, and the menu is a cut above usual diner fare. Stacks of Belgian waffles are served with homemade cream cheese, and those who come for dinner can choose from a medley of international comfort food, from calamari to pierogies – the Thai cashew chicken is recommended.

ReBar (☎ 250-360-2401; 50 Bastion Sq; mains $9-14; ⓨ 8:30am-9pm Mon-Wed, 8:30am-10pm Thu-Sat, 8:30am-3:30pm Sun) A relaxing and contemporary local legend, ReBar mixes colorful interiors with a natty, mostly vegetarian menu. Carnivores will be just as happy to eat here, though, with hearty savory dishes such as shitake-tofu pot stickers, Thai green curry and generous brunches – the salmon-topped bagel melt is great. There's also a wholesome specialty juice selection (try the orange, pear and cranberry).

James Joyce Bistro (☎ 250-3894-3332; 1175 Douglas St; mains $10-18; ⓨ 11am-1am) A surprising combination of literary-themed shrine and popular pool hall, the dining side of this friendly, subterranean spot is lined with original artworks reflecting scenes from *Ulysses* surrounding some comfy, pub-style booths. Another surprise is the small but well-chosen menu with recommended highlights including Italian sausage pizza and a generous artisan cheese plate. Even the beer selection is unexpected, including

bottles of Duchy Organic Ale from Prince Charles's estate farm.

Möle (☎ 250-385-6653; 554 Pandora Ave; mains $10-18; ⓨ 8am-3pm) Lined with funky local artworks, this laid-back, wood-floored joint is popular for breakfast – try the curry tofu scramble – but also attracts the hip art school crowd with its daytime menu of comfort classics and adventurous fusion dishes (think organic hamburgers, mac 'n' cheese and yam wraps). The excellent beer selection includes Phillips and Lighthouse craft brews. Grab a window seat and you can also snooze like a cat in the afternoon sun.

Pagliacci's (☎ 250-386-1662; 1011 Broad St; mains $16-22; ⓨ 11:30am-3pm Mon-Sat, 10am-3pm Sun, 5:30-10pm Mon-Thu, 5:30-11pm Sat & Sun) A popular local hangout for decades, 'Pag's' is a small pasta restaurant with a big heart. You're almost guaranteed to make a couple of new friends here since you'll be sitting elbow-to-elbow with the diners at the next table, but it's worth it for dishes with corny names like Somerset Praughn and Chicken Garbo. Save room for dessert: there's a frightening array of giant cheesecakes.

Top End

Brasserie 'L'école' (☎ 250-475-6260; 1715 Government St; mains $20-24; ⓨ 5:30-11pm Tue-Sat) Incongruously abutting Chinatown, this candlelit bistro offers country-style French cuisine in a warm atmosphere enhanced by excellent service – if you're not sure what to try, your server will be happy to offer some expert advice. The menu constantly changes to reflect seasonal highlights such as heirloom tomatoes and delicate figs, but celebrated chef Sean Brennan is known for specialties including *moules frites* and cured pork loin. Beer fans will also love the bottled French, Belgian and Quebec brews on offer.

Zambri's (☎ 250-360-1171; 911 Yates St; mains $20-25; ⓨ 11:30am-2:30pm & 5-9pm Tue-Sat) While this eponymous downtown restaurant is run by a second-generation Italian chef, its menu is far beyond traditional trattoria fare. Deceptively unassuming from the outside, the ever-changing dishes might range from a hearty squash soup with butter-fried sage to a mouth-melting sablefish, served with rapini-poached eggs. Consider the nightly three-course tasting menu or, for the budget-minded, drop by for lunch instead.

Camille's (☎ 250-381-3433; 45 Bastion Sq; mains $22-33; ☉ 5:30-10pm Tue-Sat) After more than two decades, this intimate Bastion Sq restaurant is still at the top of its game, challenging younger chefs who have arrived on the scene in recent years. The secret of its success is that Chef David Mincey remains adventurous and inspired to reveal fine regional flavors with a decidedly delicate touch. Seasonal treats can include velvety halibut and sweet spot prawns, while desserts showcase local fruits and berries. There are plenty of mid-priced wines to whet your whistle, too. Recommended for a romantic night out.

DRINKING

ourpick Spinnakers Gastro Brewpub (☎ 250-386-2739; 308 Catherine St; ☉ 11am-10:30pm) Allegedly Canada's oldest brewpub. Pull up a window seat, gaze at the floatplanes buzzing the harbor and sip on a sigh-inducing selection of frothy own-brand beverages. Highlights include the copper-coloured Nut Brown Ale and hoppy Blue Bridge Double IPA – named after the sky-blue span that delivers most quaffers to the door. The jet-black Titanic Stout is also recommended for tipple connoisseurs: it's as rich as a liquid Christmas pudding. Save room to eat, though. Spinnakers' menu of seasonal dishes – many designed for pairing with specific beers – is far superior to most pubs and often includes shareable rustic platters piled high with everything from wild Pacific salmon to Cortez Island clams. Consider arriving at the pub in style from the Inner Harbour on board one of the bathtub-sized Harbour Ferries (p178) that stop nearby.

Bard & Banker (☎ 250-953-9993; 1022 Government St; ☉ 11am-1am) This cavernous Victorian repro pub is handsomely lined with cut glass lamps, open fireplaces and a long granite bar topped with 30 brass beer taps. Pull up a stool and partake of a Canadian taste test comparing Phillips Blue Buck, Okanagan Springs Ale and Nova Scotia's Alexander Keiths. There's nightly live music (expect rock covers or weekend jazz) plus a menu ranging from elevated pub standards to crisp-fried squid and a great artisan cheese board. Check out the private snug rooms on the main floor where you'll feel like you're in a shady Dickensian tavern.

Canoe Brewpub & Restaurant (☎ 250-361-1940; 450 Swift St; ☉ 11:30am-midnight Sun-Thu, 11:30am-1am Fri & Sat) Victoria's best pub patio with a sunny waterfront view across to the Johnson Street Bridge, Canoe's brick-lined interior is also worth a look on a rainy day. Originally an 1894 electricity substation, it's an ideal spot to hunker in a corner and work your way through the on-site-brewed Red Canoe Lager and Beaver Brown Ale – ask for the current seasonal brew, too. Grub is also high on the menu with stomach-stuffing lamb potpie and wild salmon tacos recommended.

Swans Brewpub (☎ 250-361-3310; 506 Pandora Ave; ☉ 11am-midnight Sun-Thu, 11am-1am Fri & Sat) This friendly, wood-beamed bar was formerly a grain warehouse where freight trains rolled right into the building – which explains the old railroad track mounted on the ceiling. Suggested tipples include the malty Appleton Brown Ale – a distinctive brew that'll make you permanently turn your back on Budweiser – and Black and Tan, a heady mix of Oatmeal Stout and Buckerfields Bitter. Make room for the wicked pairing of Riley Scotch Ale and dark chocolate truffles.

Irish Times (☎ 250-383-7775; 1200 Government St; ☉ 11am-1am) Older sister pub of the Bard & Banker, there's a similar repro pub classic feel to this large Celtic bar. The interior is a pleasing fusion of high ceilings and dark wood finishes and the draft selection is a cornucopia of popular favorites from Ireland, France, Belgium and the UK. The menu has some gourmet flourishes – the shareable seafood tower is recommended, while Monday is the popular two-for-one fish and chips night – and there's live Irish music throughout the week to keep your feet tapping.

Sticky Wicket (☎ 250-383-7137; 919 Douglas St; ☉ 11am-11pm Sun-Thu, 11am-midnight Fri & Sat) This giant, multi-floored complex is the place to head if you crave a noisy night out with the locals. The Wicket's main bar serves popular (if slightly pricey) Irish beers, while its menu offers generous plates of standard pub grub. Live sports are pumped through the TVs and there's an expansive rooftop patio. Make sure you also drop by Big Bad John's, though. This separate, hillbilly themed bar is a kitsch-fest of tree-stump tables, peanut-shell-covered floors and a ceiling dripping with discarded bras.

VANCOUVER ISLAND

ENTERTAINMENT

Check *Monday Magazine* and visit www
.livevictoria.com for local listings. Alongside
the following regular venues, stadium gigs
are staged at the **Save-on-Foods Memorial Centre**
(☎ 250-220-2600; www.saveonfoodsmemorialcentre
.com; 1925 Blanshard St).

Live Music

Logan's Pub (☎ 250-350-2711; www.loganspub.com;
1821 Cook St; cover free-$10) A short stroll from
downtown, this old-school Cook St Village
sports pub looks like nothing special from
the outside, but its roster of shows is the
heart and soul of the local indie scene. Friday and Saturday are the main live music
nights but other evenings may also have a
band or two – check the pub's handy online
calendar for listings.

   Lucky Bar (☎ 250-382-5825; www.luckybar.ca; 517
Yates St; cover free-$10) A downtown night out
institution, Lucky Bar offers an eclectic
array of live and turntable music from ska
and indie to electroclash. An unpredict-
able mix of bands perform once or twice
a week, while the remaining evenings are
filled by DJ-led club nights including Monday's popular 90s music fest and Saturday's
pumping dance mix extravaganza.

   Sugar Nightclub (☎ 250-920-9950; www.sugar
nightlub.ca; 858 Yates St; cover free-$20) A popular,
long-standing club that's been hosting
a wide array of local and visiting bands
for years, expect everything from Bob
Marley tribute acts to a thundering visit
from the Dayglo Abortions. Usually only
open Thursday to Saturday, the two-floored
joint hosts DJ club nights when there's no
live act on the bill.

   Darcy's Pub (☎ 250-380-1322; www.darcyspub.ca;
1127 Wharf St; cover free-$5) This laid-back down-
town pub offers free or low-cost live acts
every night, ranging from Monday evening's
open mike to party-triggering cover bands
on most other days. While few of the acts are
likely to set the world on fire, they provide
a relaxing accompaniment to the pub's convivial atmosphere. If you're still in the groove
by closing time, weave to the pub's Upstairs
Cabaret (see below) to hit the dance floor.

Nightclubs

Buried under the Sticky Wicket pub, **Element**
(☎ 250-383-7137; www.elementnightclub.ca; 919
Douglas St; cover free-$15) is a thumping party

hangout known mostly for its mainstream
Friday Therapy and Saturday Seduction
nights. Alternatively, the small but perfectly
formed **Upstairs Cabaret** (☎ 250-385-5483; www
.upstairscabaret.ca; 15 Bastion Sq; cover $6-8; ✆ Wed-
Sat), a short climb above Darcy's Pub, is an
atmospheric, brick-lined venue. It's also
very busy on weekends when you can expect
to line up for entry. The city's recently
renovated gay and lesbian hangout, **Paparazzi
Nightclub** (☎ 250-388-0505; www.prismlounge.com;
642 Johnson St; cover free-$10) hosts lively events,
including drag fests, karaoke evenings and
bear rendezvous. The Friday and Saturday
night dance parties are its main attraction.

Theater

Visiting drama fans should check out the
season (mid-May to mid-September) at
the excellent **Belfry Theatre** (☎ 250-385-6815;
www.belfry.bc.ca; 1291 Gladstone Ave). Housed in a
converted 1890s Baptist church 10 minutes east of downtown, it's one of Canada's
most-respected independent theatres. It
often stages works by Morris Panych, one
of the country's most celebrated contemporary playwrights. If you don't want to
stray too far from the city center, the large
McPherson Playhouse (☎ 250-386-6121; www.rmts
.bc.ca; 3 Centennial Sq) and the rococo **Royal
Theatre** (☎ 250-386-6121; www.rmts.bc.ca; 805 Broughton
St) stage a wide array of visiting shows and
performances. The latter is also home of
the **Victoria Symphony** (☎ 250-385-6515; www
.victoriasymphony.bc.ca) and **Pacific Opera Victoria**
(☎ 250-385-0222; www.pov.bc.ca).

Cinemas

Victoria's most atmospheric independent
movie house, **Roxy Classic Theatre** (☎ 250-382-
3370; 2657 Quadra St; adult/child $6/3) looks like a
1940s aircraft hangar from the outside. But
despite the name, it mostly screens newer
flicks. For an art house alternative, consider
a trek to UVic's **Cinecenta** (off Map p164; ☎ 250-
721-8365; www.cinecenta.com; University of Victoria; adult/
child $6.75/4.75), where old favorites and new
curiosities make up a schedule that changes
nightly. The city's main first-run cinemas are
Cineplex Odeon (☎ 250-383-0513; www.cineplex.com;
780 Yates St; adult/child $9.50/8.50) and the nearby
Capitol 6 (☎ 250-384-5901; www.empiretheatres.com;
805 Yates St; adult/child $9.50/8.50). The Royal BC
Museum's (p165) **IMAX Theatre** (☎ 250-953-
4629; www.imaxvictoria.com; 675 Belleville St; adult/youth/

child $11/8.75/5) screens giant documentaries and reformatted Hollywood blockbusters.

SHOPPING

Government St is Victoria's souvenir shop central but the 'LoJo' area, centered on the 500-block of Lower Johnson St, is lined with cool indie stores in a string of handsomely restored colonial buildings.

Roberta's Hats (☎ 250-384-2778; 1318 Government St; ❤ 10am-5:30pm Mon-Sat, 11am-5pm Sun) While it's tempting to pick up a top hat here and swan around town in Victorian splendor, the headgear selection at this funky downtown spot is much more contemporary. In fact, it's the trendy urban wear from regional BC designers and beyond that draws local hipsters. Consider the Kangol caps, retro trapper hats and cute animal toques or branch out with a bonnet that looks like a psychedelic birthday cake.

Ditch Records (☎ 250-386-5874; 635 Johnson St; ❤ 10:30am-6pm Mon-Sat, noon-5pm Sun) This narrow, *High Fidelity* style shop is lined with tempting vinyl, used CDs and furtive-eyed musos perusing the homemade racks of obscure releases. With its threadbare carpet and cozy, cave-like feel, it's the ideal place to hang out on a wet Monday afternoon. And if it suddenly feels like time to socialize, you can book gig tickets here, too. Also sells books and magazines.

Smoking Lily (☎ 250-382-5459; 569 Johnson St; ❤ 11am-5:30pm Mon-Sat, noon-5pm Sun) Possibly the world's tiniest shop (the changing room has recently been removed to add an extra three inches), this ever-popular boutique is the destination of choice for Victoria's pale and interesting set. Locally designed art-school chic reigns supreme with cool insect-print halter tops and tractor-print

T-shirts. Check out the accessories, too – the little printed wallets are really cool.

Fiber Options (☎ 250-386-4367; 577 Johnson St; ❤ 10am-6pm) One of Western Canada's oldest sustainable clothing stores, there's an intriguing array of organic, soy and bamboo togs for men and women here. A hot item is the ultra-soft merino wool underwear that's popular with travellers. Like a mini green department store, there's more than just clothing: check out the natural soaps, hemp stationery and tempting hammocks – maybe you could string one up in your hotel room (just remember: it wasn't our idea).

Artisan Wine Shop (☎ 250-384-9994; 1007 Government St; ❤ 10am-9pm) Reflecting BC's wine-producing provenance, this swanky downtown store showcases the tipples of Mission Hill, one of the Okanagan's most celebrated vineyards, as well as the wines of producers such as Rigmarole, Painted Turtle and Fork in the Road. A mini theater takes you through the wine-making process, and a tasting bar serves those who would like to try before buying. An impressive selection of vintages is on offer if you fancy glugging a bottle.

Rogers' Chocolates (☎ 250-384-7021; 913 Government St; ❤ 9:30am-6pm Mon-Sat, 11am-6pm Sun) An old-fashioned sweetie emporium serving the best ice cream bars in town, it's the glutinous Victoria Cream chocolates that keep the sugar-crazed regulars coming back for more – just one is usually enough to substitute for lunch. The 21 flavors include blueberry, caramel and the highly recommended peppermint. If you're looking for a great souvenir, this is it. Just try not to eat them all on your flight home.

VANCOUVER ISLAND

TO MARKET TO MARKET

Markets have sprouted like forest mushrooms in Victoria in recent years. Try these tasty shopping treats for local arts, crafts, baking and produce. Also check restaurant listings for a further dash of local flavour.

Bastion Square Public Market (www.bastionsquare.ca; btwn Government & Wharf Sts; ❤ 10:30am-7:30pm Apr-Oct)

Government Street Public Market (www.pin.ca/market; 1600-block of Government St; ❤ 11am-4:30pm Sun May-Sep)

Inner Harbour Night Market (www.victoriaharbour.org; Inner Harbour; ❤ 7pm-10:30pm mid-Jun–Aug)

James Bay Market (www.jamesbaymarket.com; Menzies & Superior Sts; ❤ 9am-3pm Sat May-early Oct)

Moss Street Market (www.mossstreetmarket.com; Fairfield Rd & Moss St; ❤ 10am-2pm Sat May–mid-Oct)

GETTING THERE & AWAY
Air
Victoria International Airport (Off map p164; ☎ 250-953-7500; www.victoriaairport.com) is 26km north of the city via Hwy 17. Regular **Air Canada Jazz** (☎ 514-393-3333, 888-247-2262; www .aircanada.com) flights arrive from Vancouver (from $122, 25 minutes, 21 daily) while **WestJet** (☎ 888-937-8538; www.westjet.com) flights arrive from Calgary (from $209, 90 minutes, four daily). Both airlines connect to routes across Canada.

Frequent floatplane services arriving at the Inner Harbour from downtown Vancouver include **Harbour Air Seaplanes** (☎ 800-665-0212, 250-384-2215; www.harbourair.com) flights ($134, 35 minutes, up to 24 daily) and **West Coast Air** (☎ 800-347-2222, 604-606-6888; www.westcoastair.com) flights ($139, 35 minutes, up to 10 daily).

Helijet (☎ 800-665-4354, 604-273-4688; www.helijet .com) helicopters service the same route as the floatplanes ($245, 30 minutes, up to 11 daily) and late-availability fares can be reduced to $129 if you book via their website – $75 student fares are also often available.

Boat
BC Ferries (☎ 888-223-3779, 250-386-3431; www .bcferries.com) services arrive at Swartz Bay, 27km north of Victoria via Hwy 17, from mainland Tsawwassen (adult/child/vehicle $13/6.50/43, 90 minutes, up to 14 daily). Services also arrive from the Southern Gulf Islands (p218). See below for more details on ferry travel.

Black Ball Ferry Line (☎ 250-386-2202; www .ferrytovictoria.com) services from Port Angeles in the US (walk-on/vehicle and passenger US$12.50/$47, 90 minutes, up to four daily) arrive in the Inner Harbour. The **Victoria Clipper** (☎ 206-448-5000, 800-888-2535; www.victoria clipper.com) passenger-only service also arrives here from Seattle (adult/child from US$85/ 42.50, three hours, up to three daily). **Victoria Express** (☎ 250-361-9144; www.victoriaexpress.com) runs passenger-only services from Port Angeles (adult/child US$15.75/9.50, 55 minutes, up to four daily) and the San Juan Islands (adult/child US$42.50/20, three hours, daily) to the Inner Harbour.

Bus
Out-of-town services arrive at the main **bus station** (700 Douglas St). These include **Greyhound Canada** (☎ 800-661-8747; www.greyhound.ca) routes from Nanaimo ($26.65, 2¼ hours, six daily), Tofino ($68.90, seven hours, daily) and Port Hardy ($91, 9½ hours, daily).

Pacific Coach Lines (☎ 604-662-7575, 800-661-1725; www.pacificcoach.com) services arrive from downtown Vancouver ($42.50, 3½ hours) and Vancouver International Airport ($48, four hours) up to 16 times per day.

Car & Motorcycle
Car rental agencies include:
Budget (☎ 260-953-5300, 800-668-9833; www.budget victoria.com; 757 Douglas St)
Hertz (☎ 250-385-4440, 800-654-3131; www.hertz.ca; 2253 Douglas St)

Train
The **VIA Rail** (☎ 888-842-7245; www.viarail.ca) *Malahat* service trundles into town across the Johnson Street Bridge from Courtenay ($51, 4¾ hours, daily), with stops in Nanaimo, Parksville and Chemainus, among others.

GETTING AROUND
To/From the Airport
AKAL Airporter (☎ 250-386-2525, 877-386-2525; www.victoriaairporter.com; one way $18) shuttle bus services run between the airport and points throughout the city as well as the University of Victoria. A downtown-bound taxi costs around $50, while transit bus 70 ($2.25, 35 minutes) runs throughout the day from the airport's park and ride area.

Bicycle
Victoria is one of Canada's best cycling cities with designated routes throughout the region. Visit www.cyclingvictoria.com for maps and resources.

Bike rental joints:
Cycle BC Rentals (☎ 250-380-2453, 866-380-2453; www.cyclebc.ca; 707 Douglas St; bike/scooter rental per hr $6/21; ☽ 9am-5pm Nov-Feb, 9am-7pm Mar-Oct) Friendly staff offering bikes, scooters and motorcycles.
Reckless Bike Stores (☎ 250-384-7433; www.rektek .com; 721 Yates St; rental 2hr/day $12/25; ☽ 9am-6pm Mon-Fri, 10am-5:30pm Sat, 11am-5pm Sun) Wide array of touring and off-road bikes, plus kid trailers and baby joggers.

Boat
Victoria Harbour Ferry (☎ 250-708-0201; www .victoriaharbourferry.com; fares from $4) covers the Inner Harbour, Reeson Landing, Songhees Point (for Spinnakers Gastro Brewpub),

Fisherman's Wharf and other stops along the Gorge Waterway with its armada of tiny boats.

Public Transport

Victoria Regional Transit (☎ 250-382-6161; www .bctransit.com; adult/child $2.25/1.40) buses cover a wide area from Sidney to Sooke, with some routes served by modern-day double-deckers. Day passes (adult/child $7/5) are also available from convenience and grocery stores.

Taxi

Blue Bird Cabs (☎ 250-382-2222, 800-665-7055; www.taxicab.com)

Yellow Cab (☎ 250-381-2222, 800-808-6881; www .yellowcabofvictoria.ca)

SOUTHERN VANCOUVER ISLAND

Once you're away from the comparatively bustling streets of downtown Victoria, there are three distinct directions you can take to explore the island's south end. Northbound Hwy 17 (Pat Bay Hwy) takes you into the upper reaches of the farm-and-waterfront Saanich Peninsula with its string of accessible visitor attractions; northwest's Hwy 1 (Trans-Canada Hwy) takes you to the outdoorsy Malahat region with its hiking-friendly forest, mountain and fjord-like inlet areas; while a southwest drive along Hwy 14 delivers you to Sooke and the fringes of the wild west coast. You don't necessarily need a car either: picturesque bike routes crisscross the region like radiating wheel spokes – visit www.gvcc.bc.ca for maps.

SAANICH PENINSULA

This jutting knob of land rising north of Victoria houses the island's main airport as well as the busy Swartz Bay ferry terminal. But it's not just a transportation hub. There's an eclectic array of attractions threaded along Hwy 17 and all are accessible from the city if you're looking for an easy half-day excursion or two. Visit the **Saanich Peninsula VC** (☎ 250-656-0525; 10382 Patricia Bay Hwy; 🕓 8:30am-5pm Apr, May & mid-Sep–Oct, 8:30am-7pm Jun–mid-Sep) near the ferry terminal for tips on what to do with yourself.

Sidney
pop 11,300

With the sleepy feel of a permanent Sunday afternoon, Sidney is an idyllic afternoon trundle from Victoria (if you're car-less, it's bus 75). Traveling bookworms tend to salivate a little here: there's an inordinate ratio of bookshops-to-people, suggesting that the locals are Canada's best-read – feel free to test them with random questions about John Donne or Mary Wollstonecraft. Dotted with coffee shops and laid-back restaurants, the town's waterfront boardwalk and short pier are also good for a stroll. Drop by the **VC** (☎ 250-656-3260; www.sidney.ca; 2453 Beacon Ave; 🕓 10am-2pm & 4-7pm Jun-Sep) for tips or quiz the locals at Thursday night's **Summer Market** (Beacon Ave; 🕓 5:30-9:30pm Thu Jun-Aug).

SIGHTS & ACTIVITIES

The self-proclaimed 'booktown' has 11 dog-eared highlights, including **Tanner's Books** (☎ 250-656-2345; 2436 Beacon Ave; 🕓 8am-9pm) with its extensive travel selection and back room of maps and regional-interest tomes. In contrast, **Beacon Books** (☎ 250-655-4447; 2372 Beacon Ave; 🕓 10am-5:30pm Mon-Sat, noon-4pm Sun) has a vast array of used titles – especially mystery novels – all guarded by a portly cat. For used cooking, gardening and craft titles, peruse the adjoining **Country Life Books** (☎ 250-655-4447; 2372A Beacon Ave; 🕓 10am-5:30pm Mon-Sat, noon-4pm Sun).

At the time of writing, the floating **Marine Ecology Centre** was planning an indoor move to Sidney's newest seafront attraction. Under construction during our visit, the high-tech **Marine Centre** (www.newmarinecentre .ca) promises an aquarium-based experience that showcases the aquatic life of the Gulf Islands region, with touch pools, whale skeletons and a strong First Nations component. Check its website for the latest info.

You can get even closer to nature at the slender **Sidney Spit Marine Park**. Accessed via a 25-minute **ferry ride** (☎ 250-655-4995; www .alpinemarineadventurecentre.ca; adult/child $14/12; 🕓 10am-5pm Jul & Aug, 10am-3pm Mon-Fri, 10am-5pm Sat & Sun May, Jun & Sep) from Sidney Pier, the sandy elongation is ideal for swimming, beachcombing and birdwatching. Bring a picnic and make a day of it.

For those keen to try sea kayaking for the first time, **Sea Quest Adventures** (☎ 250-

VANCOUVER ISLAND

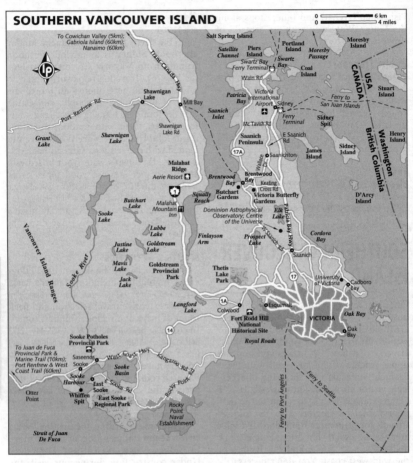

SOUTHERN VANCOUVER ISLAND

655-9256, 888-656-7599; www.seaquestadventures .com; 2537 Beacon Ave) offers a handy two-hour intro course ($85). It also operates popular whale-watching treks (adult/child $90/75), as does **Emerald Sea Adventures** (☎ 250-893-6722, 888-620-6722; www.emeraldsea.ca; 9807 Seaport P; adult/child $95/75).

SLEEPING & EATING

Not far from Swartz Bay ferry terminal, the waterfront, vehicle-accessible **MacDonald Campground** (☎ 250-654-4000, 866-944-1744; 10740 MacDonald Park Rd, tent pitch $13.70; ☯ mid-May–Oct) is in the Gulf Island National Park Reserve. Facilities are basic but include water taps and pay-phones and there's easy transit access to nearby central Sidney. There's an

even more picturesque waterfront campground at **Sidney Spit** (☎ 250-654-4000; tent pitch $13.70). Accessible via kayak or the ferry from Sidney Pier, you'll have a rustic, near-idyllic stretch of log-strewn white sand – reputed to be the finest beach in all the parks in the Victoria region – and chattering bird life as your backdrop, as well as basic facilities like pit toilets and cold-water taps.

If you don't fancy sand as your mattress, try the smashing **Beacon Inn** (☎ 250-655-3288, 877-420-5499; www.beaconinns.com; 9724 3rd St; s/d $139/249; ☐ �) a well-located B&B with an old-school ambience, despite being only a few years old. Rooms combine wood floors, antique knick knacks and some bold contemporary flourishes, and you can hang out in the fireside lounge to chat with fellow guests. Breakfast and wireless access included.

Step it up a notch at the swanky **Sidney Pier Hotel & Spa** (☎ 250-655-9445, 866-659-9445; www.sidneypier.com; 9805 Seaport Pl; d/ste $159/229; 🖥) on the waterfront. Combining West Coast lounge cool with pastel beach colors, many of the bright rooms overlook the briny and although some suites are equipped with kitchens, others are small but cozy studio rooms. The shore-view lobby restaurant (try the crab and shrimp chowder) is popular with locals. Check out the large chunk of the old *Sea Shepherd II* marine protest vessel artfully displayed in the lobby wall.

Transformed from the days when a gourmet meal out was a grilled cheese sandwich, Sidney dining options are more palatable than ever. For hefty plates of southwest/ Mexican comfort nosh, try **Carlos Cantina & Grill** (☎ 250-656-3833; 9816 Fourth St; mains $9-14; 🕙 11am-8:30pm Tue-Sun) for its mouthwatering brie and mango quesadillas. Alternatively, pub it up at **Beacon Landing** (☎ 250-656-6690; 2537 Beacon Ave; mains $10-24; 🕙 9pm-11pm), an inviting waterfront watering hole with a great patio, pub classics menu and BC's Dead Frog beer.

Butchart Gardens

Industrialist Robert Butchart spotted limestone deposits and chose this site in 1904 for his cement factory; meanwhile, his wife Jennie planted sweet peas and a single rose bush at the nearby residence, despite knowing little about gardening. More than a century later, the cement operation is long-gone but the elaborately coiffured **Butchart Gardens** (☎ 250-652-5256, 866-652-4422; www.butchartgardens.com; 800 Benvenuto Ave; adult/ youth/child $28/14/3; 🕙 9am-10pm mid-Jun–early-Sep, shorter hrs at other times) is Vancouver Island's top attraction.

Offering an explosion of colors and textures, the immaculate grounds are divided into separate gardens where there's always something in bloom. Summer is crowded, with tour buses rolling in relentlessly, but daily evening music performances and Saturday night fireworks (July and August) make it all worthwhile. December visitors are treated to thousands of fairy lights draped among wintering plants. Tea fans take note: the Dining Room Restaurant serves a smashing afternoon tea, complete with vegetable quiches and Grand Marnier truffles – leave your diet at the door.

Victoria Butterfly Gardens

A handy day-out combo with nearby Butchart Gardens, this family-friendly array of **tropical aviaries** (☎ 250-652-3822, 877-722-0272; www.butterflygardens.com; 1461 Benvenuto Ave; adult/ youth/child $12/11/6.50; 🕙 10am-4pm Feb, 9:30am-4:30pm Mar, Apr, Sep & Oct 9am-5pm May-Aug, 9am-4pm Nov & Dec) offers a kaleidoscope of dozens of different butterfly species in a free-flying environment. As well as watching them flutter around and land on your head, visitors can learn about ecosystem life cycles, as well as admiring other exotic fish, plants and birds. Look out for Spike, the red-crowned puna ibis bird that likes strutting around the trails as if he owns the place.

MALAHAT

Northwest of Victoria and accessed via Hwy 1, this picturesque region is your introduction to Vancouver Island's rugged outdoors. A 16km drive from downtown, you'll soon find yourself at the foot of Malahat Mountain and the fringes of **Goldstream Provincial Park** (☎ 259-474-1336; www.bcparks.ca). Stuffed with creaky, moss-covered old trees, burbling waterfalls and a spongy carpet of plant life, it's a natural haven for bald eagles and spawning chum salmon. Aside from nature watching, you'll find great hiking here: marked trails range from easy to tough and some are wheelchair accessible. Recommended treks include the hike to Niagara Falls (not *that* one) and the steep, strenuous route to the top of Mt Finlayson, one of the region's highest promontories. Drop by the **Freeman King VC** (☎ 250-478-9414; 🕙 9am-4:30pm) for insider tips plus illuminating natural history exhibits. If you fancy staying, the park's forested **campground** (☎ 604-689-9025, 800-689-9025; www .discovercamping.ca; campsite $22) has good facilities (love those hot showers) and is vehicle-accessible.

Sleeping & Eating

Malahat Mountain Inn (☎ 250-478-1979, 800-913-1944; www.malahatmountaininn.com; 265 Trans-Canada Hwy 1; mains $14-38; 🕙 7am-10pm) You'll find it hard to look at your food in the bistro-style restaurant here, but only because the uninterrupted sunset views across Saanich Inlet from the patio are breathtaking. Try not to put your fork in your ear as you tuck into rack of lamb or herb-crusted coho salmon. Also a handy place to stay (doubles and suites from $195), the inn has transformed into a 'boutique resort' in recent years, which means its 10 large rooms have been upgraded with fireplaces and large bathtubs – most with spectacular views.

Aerie Resort (☎ 250-743-7115, 800-518-1933; www.aerie.bc.ca; 600 Ebedora Lane; ste from $345; ✖ ☑) While its peak-season rates make this seem pricey, the Aerie is consistently voted one of Canada's top resorts. Rates are seriously reduced off-season, but whatever the price you'll luxuriate in one of three stylish hilltop villas with 29 Mediterranean-themed suites. Dining is a major treat here: the resort has partnered with local farmers to combine regional ingredients with French and Pacific Northwest influences. Ask about the mushroom tours where you forage with experts for your dinner.

SOOKE & AROUND

Rounding Vancouver Island's southern tip towards Sooke (a 45-minute drive from Victoria), Hwy 14 is lined with gnarly Garry oaks and unkempt hedgerows, while the houses – many of them artisan workshops or homely B&Bs – seem spookily hidden in the forest shadows. But while it might make for a good horror movie setting, this waterfront stretch has plenty of rustic appeal. For local information, chat to the friendly folk at the **VC** (☎ 250-642-6351, 866-888-4748; 2070 Philips Rd; ✖ 9am-5pm, closed Mon in winter).

Sights & Activities

Co-habiting with the VC, the surprisingly diverse **Sooke Region Museum** (☎ 250-642-6351, 866-888-4748; www.sookeregionmuseum.com; 2070 Philips Rd; admission free; ✖ 9am-5pm, closed Mon in winter) illuminates the area's tough pioneer era and early forestry days. Check out Moss Cottage in the museum grounds: built in 1869, it's the oldest residence west of Victoria and is now home to Aunt Tilly, who'll tell you all about raising two children here in the early 1900s.

Apparently there were no Wiis to keep the sprogs occupied back then, so local kids actually had to go outside. Emulate their adventures at **Sooke Potholes Provincial Park** (www.conservancy.bc.ca), a 5km drive along Sooke River Rd from Hwy 14 (the turnoff is just east of town). A series of polished rock pools and mini canyons carved into the river base during the last ice age, this is the region's most popular outdoor hangout – especially for swimming, sunbathing and tube floating. Bring a picnic and make a day of it.

Once you've dried off, consider a refreshing hike through the wild moss and fern-covered forests of **East Sooke Regional Park** (www.crd.bc.ca/parks) where you'll be covered by a canopy of Douglas fir trees. The 50km of marked trails here include the challenging 10km Coast Trail, where you'll encounter rocky bluffs battered by ocean waves – keep your eyes peeled for gamboling sea otters.

For a different take on the surrounding nature, trudge across the muddy beach at Whiffen Spit, just past Sooke, for an eye-opening (and tastebud-popping) two-hour **Seaweed Lady tour** (☎ 250-642-5328, 877-713-7674; www.sea-flora.com; tour $30; ✖ May–mid-Sep). You'll learn about a raft of natural cosmetic and health properties offered by the more than 250 varieties that grow around the shore. Then you'll be invited to taste test a few

---

GALLOPING GOOSE & LOCHSIDE TRAILS

Following the route of a former 1920s railway line, the 55km Galloping Goose forest trail from Victoria to Sooke is one of the island's most popular – especially since it's relatively flat and welcomes walkers, bikers and even trotting horseback riders. If you're coming from the big city, accessing the trail is easy: from the intersection of Wharf St and Pandora Ave, cross over the Johnson St Bridge and turn right onto the trail. If you want to break up your hike or only amble along a short section, transit bus 61 from Victoria to Sooke stops at points along the route. If you really want to stretch your calf muscles, consider hiking or biking from the Swartz Bay ferry terminal along the 29km Lochside Trail, then connecting with the Galloping Goose in Victoria for a long, leisurely trek to Sooke. You can download free maps and guides for both routes from www.crd.bc.ca/parks.

rubbery treats straight from the water. 'Yum' is not quite the word, but the sea lettuce is surprisingly good.

If more activity is required, Sooke's **AdrenaLine Zipline Adventure Tours** (☎ 250-642-1933, 866-947-9145; www.adrenalinezip.com; adult/child $75/65; ☼ May-Oct) will have you screaming like a banshee as you hurtle along an eight-line, two-bridge forest canopy course at up to 60km an hour – be sure to make a wash-room visit before you 'fly'. If you'd prefer to explore the region on wheels, consider a bike rental from **Sooke Cycle** (☎ 250-642-3123; www.sookebikes.com; 6707 West Coast Rd; rental per hr/day $6/25; ☼ 9am-6pm Mon-Sat May-Oct).

Sleeping & Eating

Sooke Potholes Campground (☎ 250-383-4627, 888-738-0533; www.sookepotholes.ca; campsite $20; ☼ May-early Sep) At the park's north end, with a lovely riverside location, this campsite is nestled amidst towering Douglas fir trees. There are no showers or electrical hook-ups, but there are cold-water taps, pit toilets and three new wheelchair-accessible washrooms. Book ahead ($7 fee) in summer – this camp-ground is very popular. The site is accessible via the Galloping Goose trail (p182) if you fancy biking or hiking from Victoria.

Dreamings, The Elements B&B (☎ 250-642-0369, 888-642-0369; www.dreamingsbnb.ca; 6236 Llanilar Rd; d $140) Hidden in the woods near East Sooke Regional Park, this clunkily named eco-hostel offers tranquil retreat accom-modation lined with a gallery of exquisite First Nations art. Inside the lodge-like main building, you'll find two rustic-chic rooms (the vaulted ceiling Four Seasons room is our favorite) with hardwood floors and log-built furniture. The green commitment extends to recycling, organic breakfasts and biodegradable bath products.

Sooke Harbour House (☎ 250-642-3421, 800-889-9688; www.sookeharbourhouse.com; 1528 Whiffen Spit Rd; ste from $349) One of BC's most creative places to stay, it's like staying in an art instal-lation here. Each of the 28 rooms (many with ocean views) is different, with acres of carved wood, paintings and sculptures plus some fireplaces and steam showers. Rates include gourmet breakfast and picnic lunch, but save room for dinner – the res-taurant's amazing menu is a feast of local delights, ranging from adventurous seafood to carnivore-tempting vegetarian dishes.

Markus' Wharfside Restaurant (☎ 250-642-3596; 1831 Maple Ave; mains $26-30; ☼ 5:30pm-9pm Tue-Sat) Dedicated to fine regional produce prepared with deceptively simple methods (and a little Italian influence), this intimate fine dining spot occupies a converted little wooden house that's painted landmark blue. In summer, it's all about the deck and its ocean view tables but the food is just as impressive: there's a daily changing risotto special and if the grilled scallops are avail-able, buy them all.

JUAN DE FUCA PROVINCIAL PARK

The 47km **Juan de Fuca Marine Trail** (www.juandefucamarinetrail.com) in **Juan de Fuca Provincial Park** (www.bcparks.ca) rivals the West Coast Trail (p200) as a must-do trek for outdoor-loving island visitors. From east to west, its trailhead access points are China Beach, Sombrio Beach, Parkinson Creek and Botanical Beach.

It takes around four days to complete the full route – the most difficult stretch is between Bear Beach and China Beach – but you don't have to go the whole hog if you want to take things easier. Be aware that some sections are often muddy and diffi-cult to hike, while bear sightings and swift weather changes are not uncommon.

The route has several basic backcountry campsites and you can pay your camping fee ($5 per person) at any of the trailheads. The most popular spot to pitch your tent is the slightly more salubrious family-friendly **China Beach Campground** (☎ 604-689-9025, 800-689-9025; www.discovercamping.ca; tent pitch $16) which has pit toilets and cold-water taps but no showers. There's a waterfall at the western end of the beach here and booking ahead in summer is essential.

Booking ahead is also required on the **West Coast Trail Express** (☎ 250-477-8700, 888-999-2288; www.trailbus.com) minibus that runs between Victoria, the trailheads and Port Renfrew (from $55; daily from May to September in each direction).

PORT RENFREW

Handily occupying both the southern end of the West Coast Trail and the northern tip of the Juan de Fuca Marine Trail, this tiny fish-ing village busts from its sleepy shell between May and September when the hardy hikers roll in. For regional information, drop by the **VC** (www.portrenfrew.com; ⊗ 10am-6pm May-Sep) on your left as you arrive in town.

If you need to wind down your calf muscles after a multi-day hike – or warm up for a big one – the 2.7km **Botanical Loop**, connecting forest-backed Botanical Beach and Botany Bay, is known for its tide pools and sandy beaches. Allow about 90 minutes, and go at low tide.

Sleeping & Eating

Botanical Getaway Guesthouse (☎ 250-647-5483, 888-528-0080; www.botanicalgetaway.com; 6528 Cerantes Rd; d $100-150) A homely B&B with three comfortable hardwood-floored bedrooms, guests share a kitchen, large satellite TV room and claw-foot tub bathroom. Not far from Botanical Beach, there's also a laundry room and a veranda with its own barbeque – perfect for cooking up locally caught fish. Families are welcome here but credit cards aren't – it's cash only.

Port Renfrew Hotel (☎ 250-647-5541; www.port renfrewhotel.ca; 17310 Parkinson Rd; d from $149) This recently refurbished and expanded waterfront mini-resort combines motel-style rooms and an array of wood-lined cabins with kitchenettes – the large but pricier Alcatraz cabin is especially recommended for its shoreline views. Wherever you lay your head, save time for dinner and a few brews on the pub-style restaurant patio – a great place to recuperate after a long hike.

Coastal Kitchen Café (☎ 250-647-5545; 17245 Parkinson Rd; mains $8-14; ⊗ 5am-8pm) Almost out of place in Renfrew, this quality café serves fresh salads and sandwiches, plus burgers and pizzas (the salmon, prawn and feta variety is great). Seafood is the star attraction, though – especially the Dungeness crab and chips. Hikers, either replenishing or fueling up, are often lolling outside at the picnic tables.

COWICHAN VALLEY

Heading north from Victoria on Hwy 1, it'll be 50km before you enter the fringes of the verdant Cowichan Valley region. But it's well worth the drive, especially if you're a traveling foodie. The highway threads you through a lip-smacking cornucopia of visitor-friendly farms and boutique wineries, as well as a full menu of colorful communities like historic Cobble Hill and picture-perfect Cowichan Bay, profiled here from south to north along the highway route. You'll also find Duncan, the region's largest town and a good central spot to base yourself. Biking the area is popular but there's also a new transit bus from Victoria to Duncan that threads through the region. For local information, contact **Tourism Cowichan** (☎ 250-746-1099, 888-303-3337; www.visit.cowichan.net).

COWICHAN BAY

pop 2670

If you visit only one Cowichan Valley area, make it this lovely string of bright-painted clapboard buildings perched on stilts along the side of a mountain-bordered ocean inlet. Originally a hardy fishing community, Cow Bay as the locals call it has been transformed over the years into a day-out destination for food and art fans who come for the galleries, bakeries and restaurants – or just to slurp on an ice cream and dangle their legs over the boardwalk. It's often very busy on peak summer days here, so arrive early to avoid the headache of trying to find a parking spot on the other side of the road. For information, visit www.cowichanbay.com.

Once you've found your parking spot, follow your nose and push through the bead curtain into **True Grain Bread** (☎ 250-746-7664; Cowichan Bay Rd; ⊗ 8am-6pm Wed-Sat, 8am-5pm Sun) where you'll immediately be in serious danger of buying your body weight in fresh baked treats. Grab some mini cinnamon loaves and warm ginger cookies for the road but don't leave without a French chocolate bun or three. Since creating a picnic will suddenly seem like a good idea, pick up some rustic bread, then nip along the street to **Hillary's Cheese & Deli** (☎ 250-748-5992; 1737 Cowichan Bay Rd; ⊗ 9am-5pm Jun-Sep, 9am-5pm Wed-Sun Oct-May) where the bewildering array of house-made and imported curdy treasures includes Cowichan blue and ash-dusted local brie – Friday is when the main delivery arrives from the store's own cheesemaker.

If you want to stay in the heart of the action, the Bay's **Oceanfront Grand Resort & Marina** (☎ 250-701-0166, 800-663-7898; www.the grandresort.com; 1681 Cowichan Bay Rd; r from $199; 🐾 🖥 🛜) is not that grand but it's an older full-service hotel with lots of ocean-view suites, all with kitchenettes. Most rooms are spacious, decorated in a business hotel style and there's gym where you can work off your food and wine excesses. Keep that in mind when you walk to the nearby white clapboard **Masthead Restaurant** (☎ 250-748-3714; 1705 Cowichan Bay Rd; mains $22-30; ☾ 5-10pm) for a spectacular local nosh showcase. Snag a waterfront deck table then ask your server to recommend whatever's seasonal. Seafood is always a good idea here – pray for local clams and prawns – and there's a strong commitment to Cowichan Valley wines. The three-course *table d'hôte* ($32.95) is a bargain.

COBBLE HILL
pop 14,400

The heart of the Cowichan Valley food and wine trail, the best way to explore the Cobble Hill area is to drive around (with a designated driver) and follow the signs to the farms and wineries. Line your stomach for the upcoming booze at **Organic Fair Farm** (☎ 250-733-2035; www.organicfair.com; 1935 Doran Rd; ☾ 10am-5pm Mon-Sat, noon-5pm Sun) where you can wander the herb garden, chat with the chickens and then duck inside to feast on samples of homemade organic chocolate. Among the 15 bars available, the West Coaster – packed with blueberries and local hazelnuts – is the best. Handmade ice cream, chunky breads and organic produce are also available.

If you thought fruit wines were a joke, drop into **Silverside Winery** (☎ 250-743-9149; 3810 Cobble Hill Rd; tastings free) for an eye-opening introduction to just how good they can be. Three berry wines and three port-style wines are produced at this friendly farmstead, including a strong wild blackberry wine and a sweet raspberry wine – the highlight is the fruity blueberry port, though. Kick it up a notch at **Venturi Schulze Vineyards** (☎ 250-743-5630; www.venturischulze.com; 4235 Vineyard Rd; tastings $5; ☾ 11am-4pm Sat & Sun mid-May–Sep) where the five estate-grown wines include the signature sparkling Brut Naturel and the sweet, port-like Brandenburg No.3 – this is the one you'll likely want to buy. The winery is also known for its boutique balsamic vinegar operation, which puts store-bought varieties to shame.

The region's best foodie destination (and a handy lunch stop) is **Merridale Estate Cidery** (☎ 250-743-4293, 800-998-9908; www.merridalecider .com; 1230 Merridale Rd; tastings by donation to local charities; ☾ 10:30am-4:30pm), an inviting cider making farm where you can take a self-guided tour then head to the tasting room for six heady, lip-smacking samples. The English-style traditional cider is smooth, while the rich winter apple cider is a great dessert tipple. Stay for a meal on the orchard-view patio: the oven-baked pizzas are excellent.

If you need to rest after all that wining and dining, adult-oriented **Ambraden Pond B&B** (☎ 250-743-2562; www.ambradenpond.com; 971 Aros Rd; d/ste $150/225) is an idyllic contemporary home fronted by a tranquil woodland lake. Expect a warm welcome from the dog and choose between two double rooms in the main house or a self-contained suite (with full kitchen) out back.

DUNCAN
pop 5000

Originally an isolated logging industry railroad stop – the station now houses a tiny museum – Duncan is the Cowichan Valley's main town (it's officially a city). The **VC** (☎ 250-746-4636, 888-303-3337; www.duncan.ca; 381 Hwy 1; ☾ 9am-5pm Mon-Sat Apr-Jun, 9am-6pm daily Jul & Aug, 10am-4pm Tue-Sat Sep-Mar) provides info on Duncan as well as the wider region. It also offers free 45-minute **pole tours** (☎ 250-715-1700; ☾ 10am-2pm May-Sep) of the town's 80 or so totems.

A grassy park of totems and artisan workshops, the fascinating **Quw'utsun' Cultural & Conference Centre** (☎ 250-746-8119, 877-746-8119; www.quwutsun.ca; 200 Cowichan Way; adult/youth/child $10/8/2; ☾ 9am-5pm May-Sep, 10am-4pm Oct-Apr) immerses visitors in regional First Nations culture. Try your hand at carving or beading, check out the rich artworks and learn the importance of the salmon ecosystem before buying a chunky Cowichan Bay sweater.

To understand what happened when the Europeans arrived, spend a couple of hours at the **BC Forest Discovery Centre** (☎ 250-715-1113, 866-715-1113; www.discoveryforest.com; 2892 Drinkwater Rd; adult/youth/child $14/12/9; ☾ 10am-5pm Apr-Oct) checking out the old-school logging machinery, vintage trucks, pioneer buildings and a full-size, working steam engine that trundles visitors around the grounds. The centre is home to the annual **Duncan Farmers Market** (www.duncanfarmersmarket.com; ☾ 9am-2pm Sat mid-Mar–mid-Dec).

The town's hub, **Duncan Garage** (☎ 250-748-6223; 3330 Duncan St; mains $4-8; ☾ 7:30am-5pm)

VANCOUVER ISLAND

is a refurbished heritage building housing a bookshop, an organic grocery store and an excellent upstairs live music venue (check www.duncangarageshowroom.ca for listings). It's main hangout space, though, is the coffee bar where brunches, baked treats and light lunches (including plenty of vegetarian options) draw gossiping locals. For more substantial fare, **Craig Street Brewpub** (☎ 250-737-2337; 25 Craig St; mains $11-15; ☺ 11am-11pm Mon-Wed, 11am-midnight Thu-Sat, noon-2pm Sun) is a wood-floored resto-bar lined with colorful EJ Hughes prints and serving quality comfort food like jambalaya pizza and Cajun blackened catfish. The own-brewed beer is recommended – especially the Mt Provost Porter.

CARMANAH WALBRAN PROVINCIAL PARK

Picturesque home to some of BC's oldest residents, this magnificent but remote **park** (☎ 250-474-1336; www.bcparks.ca) is lined with moss-covered spruce and gnarled cedar trees, some more than 10 centuries old. With an ancient and magical ambience, if you don't come away with a deep and abiding love for the environment after hugging a few trees here, there's no hope for any of us. Keep in mind that the trails here are primitive and recommended only for experienced and well-prepared hikers.

For those without a map looking for the main Carmanah Valley trailhead: follow South Shore Rd from Lake Cowichan to Nitinat Main Rd and bear left. Then follow Nitinat Main to Nitinat Junction and turn left onto South Main. Continue to the Caycus River Bridge and, just south of the bridge, turn right and follow Rosander Main (blue-and-white BC Parks signs reassuringly point the way) for 29km to the trailhead. Be aware that these are active logging roads, which means bumpy, often narrow tracks and the promise of a rumbling approach from a scary log truck – they have the right of way, so don't give them a hard time or they'll probably roll right over you.

CHEMAINUS
pop 4500

The 1983 closure of the last sawmill here triggered a reinvention of this little town from resource dependency to tourism magnet. Rather than fold, locals commissioned

dozens of large outdoor murals depicting pioneer and First Nations history and, luckily, visitors have been flocking to check them out ever since. Among the best murals – now numbering more than three dozen – are the painting of 1891 Chemainus on Mill St and the depiction of First Nations faces and totems on Chemainus Rd. Drop into the **VC** (☎ 250-246-3944; www.chemainus.bc.ca; 9796 Willow St; ☺ 9am-5pm mid-May–early Oct, closed Sun early Oct–mid-May) for a mural map.

A strollable little town, there are plenty of boutique galleries, coffee shops and ice-cream parlors here as well as the surprisingly large **Chemainus Theatre** (☎ 250-246-9820, 800-565-7738; www.chemainustheatrefestival.ca; 9737 Chemainus Rd; tickets $34-45) which stages professional productions – mostly musicals and popular plays. The theater is allied with the **Chemainus Festival Inn** (☎ 250-246-4181, 877-246-4181; www.festivalinn.ca; 9573 Chemainus Rd; r $139-249; ☒) which resembles a midrange business hotel from a much larger town. Combined show-and-sleepover packages are available.

Not well served by fancy restaurants, your best bet here is to drop into the tiny but highly welcoming **Twisted Sisters Tea Room** (☎ 250-246-1541; 9885 Maple St; mains $5-12; ☺ 11am-11pm; ☐ ☏), a favorite locals' hangout, where the menu includes light meals (soups recommended), 60 lip-smacking teas and some finger-licking cakes. Tea quaffers can also partake of wireless internet access, big-screen movie evenings and, every second Friday, acoustic music jams.

NANAIMO & AROUND

Vancouver Island's second-biggest city, Nanaimo is a handy stopover if you're moving up and down the east coast via Hwy 1. Its two major mainland ferry services – one from West Vancouver and one from Tsawwassen – also enable short-cutting travelers to avoid Victoria completely and head straight down-island to Chemainus and Duncan or up-island to Parksville, Qualicum and beyond.

NANAIMO
pop 76,600

Vancouver Island's other metropolis has never had the same pulling power as its tourist-grabbing older brother. But the

NANAIMO

0 _____ 500 m
0 _____ 0.2 miles

INFORMATION
Bygone Books 1 C2
Downtown Information Centre 2 C2
Literacy Nanaimo Bookstore 3 C2
Nanaimo Maps & Charts 4 C2
Post Office 5 D2
Vancouver Island Regional
   Library 6 C2

SIGHTS & ACTIVITIES
Artzi Stuff 7 C5
Bastion 8 C5
McLean's Specialty Foods 9 C5
Nanaimo Downtown Farmers
   Market 10 C2
Nanaimo Museum 11 C2
Ocean Explorers Diving 12 B2

SLEEPING
Bluebird Motel 13 B3
Buccaneer Inn 14 B3
Cambie Hostel 15 C3
Dorchester Hotel 16 C1
Kennedy House B&B 17 B6
Malaspina Student Residences 18 A6
Nicol Street Hostel 19 C6
Painted Turtle Guest House 20 C2

EATING
Le Café Français 21 C2
Modern Café 22 C2
Mon Petit Choux Café & Bakery 23 C2
Penny's Palapa 24 C1
Pirate Chips 25 C3
Thirsty Camel Café 26 C3
Tina's Diner 27 C2
Troller's Fish & Chips 28 C1
Wesley Street Restaurant 29 C5

DRINKING
Dinghy Dock Pub 30 D4
Fox & Hounds 31 B5
Mermaid's Mug 32 C6

ENTERTAINMENT
Port Theatre 33 C2
Queen's Hotel 34 C3

TRANSPORT
Bus Station 35 C5
Departure Bay Ferry Terminal 36 B2
Ferry to Gabriola Island 37 D2
Ferry to Newcastle Island 38 C5
Ferry to Protection Island 39 D2
Harbour Air Seaplanes 40 C1

VANCOUVER ISLAND

once-grungy 'Harbour City' has grown in charm in recent years and is more than just the required stop-off for those traveling around the island who need to stock up on supplies. Independent stores, restaurants and coffee shops have reinvigorated the downtown core, especially along Commercial St and in the Old City Quarter.

Information

BOOKSTORES

Bygone Books (☎ 250-741-1766; 99 Commercial St; ☺ 10am-5pm Mon-Sat, 11am-4pm Sun) Used bookstore with a literary bent.

Literacy Nanaimo Bookstore (☎ 250-754-8988; 19 Commercial St; ☺ 9am-5pm Mon-Fri, 10am-5pm Sat) Profits go to helping people learn to read.

Nanaimo Maps & Charts (☎ 250-754-2513; 8 Church St; ☺ 9am-5pm Mon-Fri, 10am-5pm Sat) Great for regional books, maps and travel guides.

INTERNET ACCESS

Literacy Nanaimo Bookstore (☎ 250-754-8988; 19 Commercial St; per hr $1; ☺ 9am-5pm Mon-Fri, 10am-5pm Sat)

Vancouver Island Regional Library (☎ 250-753-1154; 90 Commercial St; per 30 min $1; ☺ 10am-8pm Mon-Fri, 10am-5pm Sat, noon-4pm Sun)

MEDICAL SERVICES

Nanaimo Regional General Hospital (☎ 250-754-2121; 1200 Dufferin Cres) Northwest of downtown.

POST

Post office (☎ 250-267-1177; Harbour Park Mall; ☺ 8:30am-5pm Mon-Fri)

TOURIST INFORMATION

Tourism Nanaimo (☎ 250-756-0106, 800-663-7337; www.tourismnanaimo.com; 2290 Bowen Rd; ☺ 9am-6pm early May-Aug, 9am-5pm Mon-Fri, 10am-4pm Sat & Sun Sep, 9am-5pm Mon-Fri, 10am-4pm Sat Oct-Apr) Comprehensive but not well-located VC. There's a satellite branch in downtown's Vancouver Island Conference Centre.

Downtown Information Centre (☎ 250-754-8141; www.nanaimodowntown.com; 150 Commercial St; ☺ 8:30am-4:30pm Mon-Fri, 11am-3pm Sat) Rival VC run by local businesses. Well-located in the center of all the action.

Sights & Activities

Part of the new conference center development, the snazzy and long overdue reincarnation of the **Nanaimo Museum** (☎ 250-753-1821; www.nanaimomuseum.ca; 100 Museum Way; adult/youth/

child $2/1.75/0.75; ☺ 10am-5pm mid-May–Aug, Tue-Sat Sep–mid-May) showcases the region's heritage, from First Nations to colonial, maritime, sporting and beyond. Highlights include a strong Coast Salish focus (largely missing from the previous museum) and an evocative re-creation of a 1920s schoolroom. Plans were afoot during our visit for a new walk-through coalmine exhibit – watch this space.

A short stroll away on the waterfront, the fortified wooden **Bastion** (☎ 250-753-1821; cnr Front & Bastion Sts; admission by donation; ☺ 10am-4pm Jun-Aug) tower is a city landmark constructed by the Hudson's Bay Company in 1853. Moved to its present location in 1974, it only fired occasional cannons to simmer down regional ruckuses. A brief but charming ceremony sees one of these cannons fired at noon each day – cover your ears: the polystyrene 'cannonball' is surprisingly loud. The 50-stall **Nanaimo Downtown Farmers Market** (www.nanaimofarmersmarket.com; ☺ 10am-2pm Fri May-Oct) parks itself nearby in summer.

Amble west uphill from the waterfront and within a few minutes you'll come to the **Old City Quarter**, a few strollable streets of heritage buildings that have been colonized with independent shops, galleries and eateries. Highlights include **Artzi Stuff** (☎ 250-716-8989; 309B Wesley St; ☺ 10am-5pm Mon-Sat) with its handmade scarves and T-shirts, and **McLean's Specialty Foods** (☎ 250-754-0100; 426 Fitzwilliam St; ☺ 9:30am-5:30pm Mon-Fri, 10am-5pm Sat, 11am-4pm Sun) which has a tempting array of cheese, truffles and deli treats.

If you've gathered enough supplies for a picnic, head over to Nanaimo's rustic outdoor gem. Offering tranquil (and relatively easy) hiking and cycling, beach-lined **Newcastle Island Marine Provincial Park** (☎ 250-754-7893; www.newcastleisland.ca) has a rich history. First settled by the Coast Salish (and still part of their traditional territory), it was the site of shipyards and coalmines before becoming a popular short-hop summer excursion in the 1930s, when a teahouse was added (there's a seasonal restaurant here today). Accessed via a 10-minute **ferry** (☎ 250-708-0201, 877-297-8526; www.nanaimoharbourferry.com; adult/child return $8/4; ☺ Apr–mid-Oct) from the harbour, there's a **campground** (pitch $15; ☺ Apr–mid-Oct) if you want to stick around – book ahead.

If you prefer activity of the blood-pumping variety, head to the edge-of-town

Wild Play Element Parks (☎ 250-716-7874, 888-668-7874; www.wildplayparks.com; 35 Nanaimo River Rd; adult/child from $40/20; ⏱ 10am-6pm mid-Jun–Aug, reduced hrs off-season) where you can attack a series of ziplines, swings and elevated obstacle courses. There's also a 45m bungee jump over a river if you feel like ending on a high.

For scuba fans, Nanaimo and its nearby islands offer some great dives. Sunk to order in 1997, the HMCS *Saskatchewan* is one of BC's most popular dive sites. It was joined in 2001 by the 134m *Cape Breton*, the world's second-largest diver-prepared reef. Check in with the friendly folks at **Ocean Explorers Diving** (☎ 250-753-2055, 800-233-4145; www.oceanexplorersdiving.com; 1690 Stewart Ave) for guides, lessons and equipment rentals – ask them about their cool snorkeling with harbor seals excursion.

Sleeping
BUDGET

Cambie Hostel (☎ 250-754-5323; www.cambiehostels.com/nanaimo; 63 Victoria Cres; dm/r $22/44; 🖳 🛜) Up a creaking staircase above a popular neighborhood bar, this wood-floored hostel is spartan but clean. Colonizing a labyrinthine, century-old building, there are 11 small dorms and two private rooms (some are windowless but room five has the best views), all with en suite bathrooms. Live bands hit the bar Thursday to Saturday (free cover for guests) and it's best to join the party since you'll be hearing the music anyway. A small kitchen and laundry ($1 per load) round out the amenities.

ourpick Painted Turtle Guesthouse (☎ 250-753-4432, 866-309-4432; www.paintedturtle.ca; 121 Bastion St; dm $26.50, r $58-75; 🖳 🛜) This immaculate, newer budget property in the heart of downtown combines four-bedded dorms with family and private rooms. Interiors are decorated with bright hardwood floors and an Ikea-esque élan, while facilities range from a large and welcoming open-plan kitchen/lounge to a laundry room ($2 per load) and en suite showers. You can book a wide range of activities through the front desk or just stay in and play foosball: since there's no TV, you'll be forced to chat with everyone.

Additional recommendations:

Malaspina Student Residences (☎ 250-754-6338; www.malaspinaresidences.ca; 4 University Cres; dm/r from $35; ⏱ May-Aug) Dorms and private accommodation in university study rooms five minutes from downtown.

Nicol Street Hostel (☎ 250-753-1188; www.nanaimohostel.com; 65 Nicol St; dm/r $20/45; ⏱ May-Aug) Five-minute walk south of downtown brings you to this homely hostel that's popular with families and quieter backpackers.

MIDRANGE

Bluebird Motel (☎ 250-753-4151, 877-764-3832; www.thebluebirdmotel.com; 995 N Terminal Ave; s/d $64/89; ❌) This budget-value, family-friendly place is a classic basic motel – two stories high, hundreds of feet long, outdoor walkways. It covers all the main bases: free coffee, large clean rooms with 1970s-style furnishings and some kitchenettes for those who like to make their own grub. It's less than 2km north of downtown.

ourpick Buccaneer Inn (☎ 250-753-1246, 877-282-6337; www.buccaneerinn.com; 1577 Stewart Ave; s/d/ste $79/99/149) Handy for the Departure Bay ferry terminal, this excellent family-run motel has an immaculate white paint job that probably needs to be redone every few months. The equally spick-and-span rooms are cozy and most have kitchenettes. If you can stretch to a spacious top-end suite, it'll come with a fireplace, full kitchen and flat-screen TV. Your friendly hosts, Dave and Marlene, offer a service level far in excess of most motels (including post-checkout showers for those sticking around the area) and they have plenty of good suggestions for exploring the region.

Kennedy House B&B (☎ 250-754-3389, 877-750-3389; www.kennedyhouse.ca; 305 Kennedy St; r $85-125) Uphill from the waterfront (you'll certainly build up your calf muscles staying here), this is one of the few Nanaimo B&Bs not too far from the city center – in fact, it's very close to the VIA Rail stop and the Old City Quarter. A restored and outwardly imposing 1913 heritage mansion, it has two lovely rooms, combining antique knick knacks and contemporary chintzy flourishes. Elegant, quiet and adult oriented, there's a smashing cooked breakfast to rouse you from your morning slumber.

Dorchester Hotel (☎ 250-754-6835, 800-661-2449; www.dorchesternanaimo.com; 70 Church St; r/ste $109/129; 🛜) Downtown Nanaimo's signature hotel, this Best Western affiliate has great views of the nearby harbor, so you can expect a wake-up call from the morning floatplanes. Despite its painfully slow old elevator – one of the few reminders of the building's

VANCOUVER ISLAND

Victorian provenance – all the rooms have been refurbished in recent years and have a standard business hotel feel, complete with large flatscreen TVs.

Whitehouse on Long Lake B&B (☎ 250-756-1185, 877-956-1185; www.nanaimobandb.com; 231 Ferntree Pl; r/ste $119/159; �🖥) As the name would suggest, Whitehouse is on Long Lake, north of Nanaimo via Hwy 19A. Huge south-facing windows overlook the water (free kayaks available) and bring the sun into the three rooms. The romantic interiors are elegant and comfortable but the surprisingly good-value Presidential Suite is recommended: it's self-contained, has a large kitchen and includes a private balcony.

Eating

BUDGET

Pirate Chips (☎ 250-753-2447; 1 Commercial St; mains $3-16.50; ⏱ 11:30am-9pm Mon-Wed, 11:30am-10pm Thu, 11:30am-3am Fri & Sat, noon-9pm Sun) Locals were originally lured to this eclectic takeout nook by the enticing deep-fried aroma but they keep coming back for the funky ambience – the quirky pirate decor of nets and parrots makes it a great hangout after some late-night beers. You'd have to be fairly drunk to get through a large order of poutine (fries topped with gravy and cheese curds) or a deep-fried Nanaimo bar but it's hard to beat the French fries served with garlic or curry toppings – the chili fries are a definite winner, too.

Mon Petit Choux Café & Bakery (☎ 250-753-6002; 120 Commercial St; mains $7.50-9; ⏱ 8am-6pm Mon-Fri, 8am-5pm Sat, 9am-5pm Sun) A chatty neighborhood hangout (this is the place to overhear choice gossip about the stuttering Millennium Hotel development nearby), there's a surprisingly gourmet approach to the light meal menu here. French-flecked favorites include roast chicken and cranberry compote sandwiches and an amazing Alsace pizza of smoked bacon and caramelised onions. Drop in for afternoon coffee and a dangerous roster of delectable bakery treats like cherry chocolate strudel and *pain au chocolat*.

MIDRANGE

Tina's Diner (☎ 250-753-5333; 187 Commercial St; mains $6-12; ⏱ 8am-3pm) This retro downtown diner, complete with checkerboard floors and a traditional counter (the wall-mounted

Betty Boop also adds to the ambience), is all about comfort food. Possibly Nanaimo's best breakfast spot, the large menu includes eggs Benedict and Spanish omelettes, and there are plenty of burgers, sandwiches and salads for those who don't make it here until lunchtime. There's also live lunchtime music every Saturday.

Penny's Palapa (☎ 250-753-2150; 10 Wharf St H Dock; mains $7-12; ⏱ 11am-9pm Apr-Oct) This tiny, flower-decked floating hut and patio in the harbor is a lovely spot for an al fresco meal among the jostling boats. An inventive, well-priced menu of Mexican delights includes seasonal seafood specials – the signature halibut tacos are recommended – plus some good vegetarian options. Arrive early: the dining area fills rapidly on balmy summer evenings.

Troller's Fish & Chips (☎ 250-741-7994; 104 Front St; mains $8-13; ⏱ 11am-10pm) Nothing beats the ambience of Troller's when it comes to enjoying some great fish and chips. This shack on the docks at the boat basin always cooks the fresh catch of the day, selecting its prawns and salmon straight from the boats in the harbor. It's also a good spot to watch the maritime world float by.

Thirsty Camel Café (☎ 250-753-9313; 14 Victoria Cres; mains $8-14; ⏱ 7:30am-8pm mid-May–Aug, 7:30am-7pm Sep–mid-May) Partake of a lip-smacking middle eastern feast at this sunny little family-owned joint, tucked into an elbow of Victoria Cres. Everything's house-prepared from scratch, which makes for hearty falafel pitas, addictive hummus and some spicy winter soups. The shareable platters (especially the spice-encrusted Persian chicken) are recommended and there are several excellent vegetarian óptions that even meat eaters will love.

Modern Café (☎ 250-754-5022; 221 Commercial St; mains $9-19; ⏱ 9am-11pm) This reinvented old coffee shop has cool loungey interiors combining exposed brick and comfy booths or, if it's sunny, a sun-warmed outdoor patio. The menu runs from the kind of wraps, burgers and sandwiches that are a cut above standard diner fare and there are some small-plate options for those who just want to snack. Great spot on a rainy day.

ᴏᴜʀ ᴘɪᴄᴋ Le Café Français (☎ 250-716-7866; 153 Commercial St; mains $14-26; ⏱ 11am-7:30pm Tue & Wed, 11am-8pm Thu, 11am-8:30pm Fri, 5-8:30pm Sat) A simple but surprisingly authentic French bistro in the heart of Nanaimo. Step inside and you'll soon be humming along to a soundtrack of Parisian piano music. The continental ambience is considerably enhanced when the wait staff address you in French – they switch to English as soon as you start stuttering – and you can continue the illusion by noshing on classics like salade Niçoise, seafood crepes or filet mignon in cognac; there's a small but tasty list of attendant French wines, too. A romantic and atmospheric spot for dinner, the good-value two-course lunch special is ideal for those who fancy a cheaper transportation to *la belle France*.

TOP END
Wesley Street Restaurant (☎ 250-753-6057; 321 Wesley St; mains $14-30; ⌚ 11:30am-2:30pm Tue-Fri, 5:30-10pm Tue-Sat) Nanaimo's best splurge-worthy eatery (lunch is considerably cheaper but candlelit dinner here is a special event), the menu at this white-tablecloth but pretence-free restaurant (still known as Wesley Street Café by locals) is all about BC-sourced ingredients prepared with contemporary Pacific-Northwest flair. The oft-changing menu is seasonal, but look out for Queen Charlotte salmon, Qualicum Bay scallops and Cowichan Valley duck. Take your time and savor. And if you're looking for a dinner deal, there's a three-course $30 special from Tuesday to Thursday.

Drinking
our pick **Mermaid's Mug** (☎ 250-754-6693; 357 Wesley St; mains $7-10; ⌚ 9am-9pm Mon-Fri, 10am-9pm Sat) Hidden behind an unassuming house front exterior, this sea cave of ocean-themed frescos, mismatched tables and nautical knick knacks looks like an art student's dream den. In fact, this smashing bar/coffee shop combo is the destination of choice for local in-the-know bohemians. They come for the java, the comfort food – think pierogis, pizzas and the (in)famous spaghetti omelette – as well as the renowned strawberry daiquiris made with local fruit and Sailor Jerry rum (a full roster of other drinks is available for the non-cocktail set). There's a cornucopia of nightly happenings throughout the week, including movie screenings, tarot readings, singer-songwriter shows and Friday evening karaoke – the last bastion of the over-indulgent daiquiri drinker.

Dinghy Dock Pub (☎ 250-753-2373; 8 Pirates Lane; mains $9-21; ⌚ 11am-11pm Sun-Thu, 11am-midnight Fri & Sat) Accessed via a mini ferry hop, this popular pub and restaurant combo floating offshore from Protection Island is an ideal place to rub shoulders with salty locals and knock back a few malty brews on the deck. The menu doesn't stretch far beyond classic pub fare but there's live music on weekends to keep your toes tapping. To get to the pub, take the 10-minute **ferry** (☎ 250-753-8244; return $8) from the harbor.

Fox & Hounds (☎ 250-740-1000; 247 Milton St; mains $9-14; ⌚ noon-10pm) An uphill hike from the harbor (rolling back down after you've had a few will be much easier), this clapboard heritage home on a quiet residential street – the only one with a red telephone box outside – has been meticulously transformed into a cozy, British-style pub. You can sup from four UK and Irish drafts or nosh on a full menu of well-prepared Brit dishes: don't worry, the pies, fried fish and Sunday roast are superior to most pub offerings back in Blighty.

Entertainment
Nanaimo's best live music and dance spot, **Queen's Hotel** (☎ 250-754-6751; www.thequeens.ca; 34 Victoria Cres) hosts an eclectic roster of live performances and club nights throughout the week, ranging from indie to jazz and country. In contrast, **Port Theatre** (☎ 250-754-8550; www.porttheatre.com; 125 Front St) presents local and touring fine-arts performances. Movie houses include the nine-screen **Galaxy Cinemas** (☎ 250-729-8000; Rutherford Mall, 4750 Rutherford Rd).

Getting There & Around
AIR
Nanaimo Airport (☎ 250-245-2147; www.nanaimoairport.com) is 18km south of town via Hwy 1. **Air Canada Jazz** (☎ 888-247-2262; www.aircanada.ca) services from Vancouver (from $69, 22 minutes, up to seven daily) arrive throughout the day.

Frequent **West Coast Air** (☎ 604-606-6888, 800-347-2222; www.westcoastair.com) floatplane services arrive in the harbor from downtown Vancouver ($79, 25 minutes, up to nine daily) and the South Terminal of Vancouver International Airport ($69, 20 minutes, up to six daily) while similar services (at almost identical prices) are

DETOUR: GABRIOLA ISLAND

Accessed via **BC Ferries** (☎ 250-386-4331, 888-223-3779; www.bcferries.com) service from Nanaimo harbor (passenger/vehicle $7.90/18.55, 20 minutes, up to 16 daily), the most northerly Southern Gulf Island is an idyllic day trip from the city. Dozens of artists live on the 14km-long island, but it's also known for its tranquility, scenery and outdoor pursuits.

Bring your hiking boots (expect to see deer) and hit some of the 45km of shoreline. Highlights include **Gabriola Sands Provincial Park** (☎ 250-474-1336; www.bcparks.ca) with its two sandy beaches (ideal for a picnic). On the island's southeast end, **Drumbeg Provincial Park** (☎ 250-474-1336; www.bcparks.ca) offers good swimming as well as the tide pools of Brickyard Beach. You can get a waterside view of the island with the rentals or guided paddles (the sunset tour is recommended) offered by **Jim's Kayaking** (☎ 250-247-8335; www.jimskayaking.com; 347 Lyngail Pl; rentals & tours from $35-60).

If you don't want to get wet, head to **Gabriola Artworks** (☎ 250-247-7412; www.gabriolaartworks .com; 575 North Rd; ☒ 9am-5pm Tue-Fri, 10am-5pm Sat, 11am-4pm Sun & Mon) in the Folklife Village center, a gallery showcasing dozens of local painters, potters and crafters. Alternatively, download a copy of the excellent self-guided 60-studio art tour from www.gabriolaartscouncil.org and check out the artists face-to-face.

Combine art and food at Gabriola's colorful **Farmers Market** (☒ 10am-noon Sat May-Oct) at the corner of North and South Rds, near the ferry dock. Or you can sit down to eat at the ever-popular **Suzy's Restaurant & Bistro** (☎ 250-247-2010; 560 North Rd; mains $4-12; ☒ 6am-8pm) where you'll find a side order of gossiping locals with your hearty seafood, sandwiches or pizza. In the evening, head for dinner at the Driftwood Restaurant for hearty Pacific Northwest fare in a wood lodge dining room overlooking the water – the adjoining Surf Pub is also handy if you prefer meals of the liquid variety.

provided by **Harbour Air Seaplanes** (☎ 604-274-1277, 800-665-0212; www.harbour-air.com).

BOAT

BC Ferries (☎ 250-386-3431, 888-223-3779; www.bc ferries.com) from Tsawwassen (passenger/vehicle $13/$43, two hours, up to eight daily) arrive at Duke Point, 14km south of Nanaimo. Services from West Vancouver's Horseshoe Bay (passenger/vehicle $13/$43, 95 minutes, up to 12 daily) arrive at Departure Bay, 3km north of the city via Hwy 1. Reservations are recommended in summer if you're bringing a car.

BUS

Greyhound Canada (☎ 800-661-8747; www.grey hound.ca) buses arrive from Victoria ($27, 2½ hours, six daily), Campbell River ($34, two to three hours, three daily) and Tofino ($46, four hours, daily) among others. The station is a 10-minute walk from downtown, behind the Howard Johnson Hotel, just off Comox Rd.

TRAIN

Sadly the old heritage railway station was a burned out wreck of its former self on our visit, but the daily **VIA Rail** (☎ 888-842-7245; www.viarail.ca) *Malahat* service still trundles in, arriving from Victoria ($27, 2½ hours), Parksville ($21, 35 minutes) and Courtenay ($27, two hours) among others.

TRANSIT

Taxis are expensive in Nanaimo – try **AC Taxi** (☎ 250-753-1231) if you must – so hit the local bus alternative with **Nanaimo Regional Transit** (☎ 250-390-4531; www.rdn.bc.ca; single/day pass $2.25/5.75). Services stop along Gordon St, west of Harbour Park Mall. Bus 2 goes to the Departure Bay ferry terminal. No city buses run to Duke Point.

CENTRAL VANCOUVER ISLAND

Vancouver Island's alluring midriff includes the wild and vibrant west coast, combining storm-tossed waterfront with visitor magnets like Tofino, and the far more genteel east coast, with its tranquil, low-key seaside towns and family-friendly feel. In between, there are nature-hugging interior highlights and a smattering of colorful little communities. If you're driving, Hwys 4 and 19 will be your buddies in this region, along with an occasional paintwork-challenging logging road.

OCEANSIDE & AROUND

A 35km drive northeast of Nanaimo via Hwy 19 brings you to Parksville and then its sister community Qualicum Beach. Together with Coombs and its environs, they comprise the east coast's **Oceanside** (☎ 250-248-6300, 888-799-3222; www.visitparksvillequalicum beach.com) region, a balmy, nature-fringed shoreline stretch that draws plenty of BC travellers for a seaside week or two. While Parksville has the lion's share of shops and amenities, smaller Qualicum Beach is more quaintly attractive. Luckily, the communities are close enough that you can cherry pick the highlights from each.

For tips, drop by either of the area's main **VCs** (Parksville ☎ 250-248-3613; www.chamber.parksville .bc.ca; 1275 E Island Hwy; 9am-5pm Apr-Jun, 9am-6pm Jul & Aug, 9am-4 or 5pm Mon-Sat Sep-Mar; Qualicum Beach ☎ 250-752-9532, 866-887-7106; www.qualicum.bc.ca; 2711 W Island Hwy; 8:30am-6:30pm mid-May–early Sep, 9am-4pm Mon-Sat early Sep–mid-May).

Sights & Activities

An idyllic summertime alternative to down-island's tour-group-packed Butchart Gardens (p181), **ourpick** **Milner Gardens & Woodland** (☎ 250-752-6153; www.milnergardens.org; 2179 W Island Hwy, Qualicum Beach; adult/youth/child $10/6/free; 10am-5pm May-Aug, 10am-5pm Thu-Sun Apr & Sep) combines rustic forest trails shaded by centuries-old trees and flower-packed gardens planted with magnificent rhododendrons. It's a highly tranquil spot, especially if you meander down to the 1930s tearoom occupying a stunning bluff that overlooks the water. Tuck into afternoon tea ($8.75; 1pm to 4pm) on the porch and drink in views of the bird-lined shore and snow-capped peaks shimmering on the horizon.

Dedicated to rescuing exotic birds from captivity and nursing them back to physical and mental health, the excellent **World Parrot Refuge** (☎ 250-248-5194; www.worldparrot refuge.org; 2116 Alberni Hwy, Coombs; adult/child $12/8; 10am-4pm) preaches the worthy mantra that parrots are not pets. Pick up your earplugs at reception and stroll the enclosures,

alive with more than 750 recovering (and very noisy) birds. Many are suffering from baldness, self-mutilation and psychological problems, but don't be surprised when characters like Daisy and Buster rasp a cheery 'hello' as you walk past.

Not far from the parrots, the landmark **Coombs Old Country Market** (☎ 250-248-6272; www.oldcountrymarket.com; 2326 Alberni Hwy, Coombs; 9am-6pm) is an ever-expanding smorgasbord of food and crafts centered on a large store stuffed with bakery and produce treats. It attracts huge numbers of visitors on balmy summer days, when cameras are pointed at the grassy roof of the main building where a herd of goats spends the season. Nip inside for giant ice-cream cones, whopping pizzas and the deli makings of a great picnic, then spend an hour wandering the attendant stores clustered around the site.

A clutch of transplanted old wooden homes at **Craig Heritage Park** (☎ 250-248-6966; www.parksvillemuseum.ca; 1245 E Island Hwy, Parksville; adult/child $4/2; 10am-4pm Wed-Sun mid-May–Sep) comprises one of the island's best social history museums. The re-created hamlet includes a church, schoolhouse, fire hall (plus 1950s firetruck) and a tangle of mystifying old machinery. Chat to the volunteers on duty and they'll point out oddball exhibits like the terrifing 1920s perm machine and the photo of Mike, the famous bartending dog.

Located at the south end of Parksville, the 5km sandy expanse of **Rathtrevor Beach Provincial Park** (☎ 250-474-1336; www.bcparks.ca) is one of BC's most popular family-friendly beaches. At low tide, the ocean recedes almost a kilometer, revealing a salty array of starfish, sand dollars and glutinous jellyfish. If your kids tire of all that nature, drive them over to **Paradise Fun Park** (☎ 250-248-6612; 375 W Island Hwy, Parksville; adult/child $6.95/4.95; 9am-9pm Jul & Aug, shorter hrs spring & fall), the best of several local mini-golf attractions where the elaborate obstacles include windmills, churches and a particularly challenging giant cuckoo clock.

Southwest of Parksville and spreading the word on BC's unique wildlife, **North Island Wildlife Recovery Centre** (☎ 250-248-8534; www.niwra.org; 1240 Leffler Rd, Errington; adult/child $3/2; 9am-5pm mid-Mar–Dec) houses a small but fascinating walk-through 'museum of nature.' Dedicated to treating sick or injured animals brought to its doors, the facility has active rehabilitation programs for eagles and bears.

More active nature fans can hit the waves with **Oceanside Kayaks** (☎ 250-951-3512; www .oceansidekayaks.ca; Qualicum Beach; rental hr/day $18/56), which rents equipment and also offers a handy introductory course to first-timers. Alternatively, take a 45-minute drive from Parksville (Hwy 19 towards Courtenay, then take exit 75 and proceed for 12km on the gravel road to the park entrance) to **Horne Lake Caves Provincial Park** (☎ 250-248-7829; www .hornelake.com; tours adult/child from $20/17; ☻ 10am-5pm Jul & Aug, off-season by arrangement), which has some of BC's best spelunking treats. Two caves are open for self-exploring, while there are also guided tours for novices, families and veteran cavedwellers.

Sleeping

Riverbend Resort & Campground (☎ 250-248-3134, 800-701-3033; www.riverbendresort.bc.ca; 1-924 E Island Hwy, Parksville; campsite/cabins/yurts $26/129/139; ▣ ☎) An ultra-welcoming woodland campground with cozy log cabins and secluded tree-shaded campsites – many of them along the riverbank – the main draws here are the three comparatively luxurious yurts. Fitted with baths, kitchens, double beds and flat-screen TVs, they're way more comfortable than a regular night under canvas. The rest of the campground has showers, laundry and a playground, and is highly popular with young families. The main building has a guest computer if you're traveling sans laptop.

Paradise Seashell Motel (☎ 250-248-6171, 877-337-3529; www.paradiseseashellmotel.com; 411 W Island Hwy, Parksville; r $79-99) A great-value classic motel that's perfect for families – although the money you save on the room may be offset by the bill your kids rack up at the adjoining mini-golf course (p193) – ask at the front desk for two-for-one coupons. Twelve of the 30 rooms have handy kitchenettes, but all are clean and tidy with cheap and cheerful decor, including clamshell-shaped toilet seats. There's a guest-use barbeque out back and the beach is right next door. Includes continental breakfast.

Blue Willow Guest House (☎ 250-752-9052; www .bluewillowguesthouse.com; 524 Quatna Rd, Qualicum Beach; s/d/ste $120/130/140) This immaculate, antique-lined B&B has the ambience of a spacious Victorian cottage, complete with exposed beams, a book-lined lounge and a fragrant country garden. Of the two main rooms, the Rose Room is larger and has a giant bed that's more like a piece of architecture. Accessed through the garden, the roomy private suite is ideal for families and sleeps up to five people. Since it doesn't have a kitchen, you'll be forced to tuck into the three-course breakfast, complete with mouthwatering home-baked treats, that is provided.

ourpick **Free Spirit Sphere** (☎ 250-757-9445; www.freespiritspheres.com; 420 Horne Lake Rd, Qualicum Beach; cabins $125-175) For anyone who's ever dreamt of sleeping in a Christmas bauble, Vancouver Island craftsman Tom Chudleigh has developed a pair of nature-hugging cabins with a difference. Suspended by a web of cables high in the trees, his beautifully crafted wood and fiberglass spheres enable guests to cocoon themselves in the

---

SAY CHEESE

Aromatic evidence of Vancouver Island's rediscovered love for its local bounty can be found at **Little Qualicum Cheeseworks** (☎ 250-954-3931; www.cheeseworks.ca; 403 Lowry's Rd, Parksville; admission free; ☻ 9am-5pm Mon-Sat), a small working farm that has developed into a family-friendly visitor attraction. It's worth spending a couple of hours here, ducking into the cowsheds and watching the cheese makers (both bovine and human) at work. Young kids will particularly enjoy the roaming pigs, goats and chickens and the rabbit enclosure is noisy with plaintive cries from children who want to take one home. Parents should ignore them and head straight for the on-site shop where samples of the farm's curd-based treats (as well as their home-cured bacon) are provided – this is a great place to pick up picnic supplies. The creamy, slightly mushroomy brie is a bestseller but the Qualicum Spice is recommended: it's flavored with onions, garlic and sweet red pepper. Better still, the farm recently opened its own **Morningstar Creek Winery**, where you can match your cheeses with blueberry, cranberry or gooseberry fruit wines. Now, where did those kids go…?

forest canopy. Reached via spiral wooden staircases, they're compact inside – Eve is smaller and more basic, while Eryn is lined like a little boat with built-in cabins, nooks and mp3 speakers. Sleeping here is all about communing with nature (in-cabin TVs are replaced with books), but that doesn't mean to say you have to give up creature comforts: guests receive a basket of baked goodies on arrival and share a dedicated ground-level facilities block with sauna, barbeque and hotel-like showers.

Heritage Cottage B&B (☎ 250-752-2343, 866-452-2343; www.heritagecottage.com; 106 Hoylake Rd E, Qualicum Beach; d $155) One of the region's oldest cottages, this cozy 1913 one-story has three rooms leading off a long central common room. Each has its own gas fireplace and outdoor garden access, while breakfast is taken together in the Craftsman-like heritage kitchen where you'll be spoiled with daily changing treats like berry brûlée and seafood soufflé. Adult-oriented, the chatty hosts have plenty of suggestions for area activities and will lend you a bike to get around.

Beach Club Resort (☎ 250-248-8999, 888-760-2008; www.beachclubbc.com; 181 Beachside Dr, Parksville; r from $199; 🅿 ❄ 🛜) A swanky wood-and-stone lodge property that looks like it may have blown in straight from Tofino's Long Beach, this new hotel elevates the local hostelry offerings to far above that of the surrounding motels. The studio rooms have mini-kitchens and the suites have full kitchenettes with their own laundry facilities, but almost all have views over Parksville Bay. You can step outside straight onto the beach or partake of facilities including a spa, pool and a good restaurant.

Eating & Drinking

Cha Cha Java (☎ 250-248-4225; 198 E Island Hwy, Parksville; mains $5-7; 🕑 10am-5:30pm Mon-Fri, 9am-5:30pm Sat) Its official address is on E Island Hwy, but this sunny tea and coffee spot is actually just around the corner on Weld St. It's worth the confusion, though, for a warming nook lined with locals exchanging gossip. The bulging cheese scones and homemade soups are popular here but the breakfast wraps (stuffed with egg, salsa and veggies) are good if you want a hearty start to the day. Try grabbing an outdoor seat to catch some rays.

Lefty's (☎ 250-954-3886; 280 E Island Hwy; mains $9-13; 🕑 8am-8pm Sun-Thu, 8am-9pm Fri & Sat) Tucked into a corner of the Thrifty Centre strip mall, it's easy to miss this modern diner (complete with its round, enveloping booths) but if you're hungry you'll be glad you found it. Cool twists on classics include curry chicken wraps and crunchy Thai salad, while Left Coast lager is the recommended tipple. Save room for the meringue pie and consider blowing your budget with a pie fight on the beach. Sister restaurant in Qualicum Beach.

our pick **Fish Tales Café** (☎ 250-752-6053; 3336 W Island Hwy, Qualicum Beach; mains $8-21; 🕑 4-10pm) This cozy local seafood favorite has been packing them in for decades with its knick-knack-lined tearoom interior and chi-chi fairy-light-strewn dining garden – the best place to be on a balmy summer evening. While classic fish and chips are a signature, more adventurous marine gourmets have a surprisingly diverse menu to choose from: the mermaid salad is brimming with fresh-catch prawns, shrimp and mussels, while the deep-fried oysters are an indulgent winner. As you'd expect, the clam chowder is also amazing here. You'll receive a warm welcome from twinkle-eyed host-owner Cam, who wanders among the tables greeting old and new with her standout English accent.

Shady Rest (☎ 250-752-9111; 3109 W Island Hwy, Qualicum Beach; 🕑 11am-9pm Mon-Fri, 8am-11pm Sat & Sun) The area's best neighborhood pub, this casual waterfront spot hangs over the beach in Qualicum and is ever-popular with locals who like to grab a few and chat the night away. Drop by for some fortifying pub grub and a couple of beers – the James Douglas dark lager is highly recommended – or head into the slightly more upmarket restaurant, where fish, steak, and pasta dishes vie for menu attention. An ideal spot for weekend brunch, try for a shoreline window seat or hit the breezy patio.

Getting There & Away

The friendly folk at **Orca Airways** (☎ 250-949-1185, 888-359-6722; www.flyorcaair.com) fly into Qualicum Beach's little airport ($59, 30 minutes, up to two daily) from the South Terminal of Vancouver International Airport.

Greyhound Canada (☎ 800-661-8747; www.greyhound.ca) buses arrive in Parksville from

Victoria ($33.95, 3½ hours, five daily), Nanaimo ($14.60, 40 minutes, six daily), Tofino ($40.90, 3½ hours, daily) and Port Hardy ($68.90, six hours, daily), among others. The same buses, with similar times and rates, serve Qualicum Beach.

The **VIA Rail** (☎ 888-842-7245; www.viarail.ca) *Malahat* service trundles into Parksville from Victoria ($34.65, 3½ hours, daily), Nanaimo ($21, 37 minutes, daily) and Courtenay ($21, 1½ hours, daily), among others. The same trains serve Qualicum Beach with similar times and rates.

PORT ALBERNI
pop 17,750

Founded as a remote fishing and logging settlement in the wilderness heart of Vancouver Island, Alberni is handily located along Hwy 4 if you're driving between the east and west coasts. With excellent forest access as well as being on the tip of a 48km channel that cuts deeply into the island, this is an ideal location for outdoor exploration. Additionally, there are some intriguing pioneer attractions and activities. For tips, visit the **Alberni Valley VC** (☎ 250-724-6535; www.alberni valleytourism.com; 2533 Port Alberni Hwy; ☺ 9am-5pm Mon-Fri, 10am-2pm Sat & Sun Jul–early-Sep, hours reduced early Sep-Jun) on your way into town.

Sights & Activities

On the 50km drive from Parksville to Port Alberni via Hwy 4, **Cathedral Grove** is the favored pit stop for every driver in the region. The tree-hugging heart of MacMillan Provincial Park, its mystical élan is hard to grasp when the tour buses roll in, so aim to arrive off-peak for the full effect. You'll find easy trails winding from the roadside through a dense carpet of vegetation and you'll glimpse some of BC's oldest yet most accessible ancient trees, including towering 800-year-old Douglas firs more than 3m in diameter. Sadly, this protected area is just a small surviving pocket of a much larger swathe that has already been logged and lost.

There's an eclectic but impressive array of exhibits in the little **Alberni Valley Museum** (☎ 250-723-2181; www.alberniheritage.com; 4255 Wallace St; admission by donation; ☺ 10am-5pm Tue-Sat, to 8pm Thu), which does a good job of showcasing the region's First Nations, folk art and pioneer heritage – including the history

of the Chinese who came here to work in the 19th century. The section on the century-old West Coast Trail shows how the route was once a life-saving trail for shipwreck victims sunk in the 'graveyard of the pacific.'

Get a deeper flavor for these old days by taking the magnificent 1929 **Alberni Pacific Steam Train** (☎ 250-723-1376; www.alberniheritage .com; 3100 Kingsway; return adult/youth/child $29/22/10; ☺ departs 10am & 2pm Thu-Mon late-Jun–early Sep) from the town's century-old clapboard station. The train winds through the wooded valley for about 35 minutes before delivering you to **McLean Mill**, included with your train fare. A National Historic Site, it's Canada's only working steam-powered sawmill and is an evocative reminder of the grindingly tough early days of forestry. Chatty actors masquerading as loggers and their families wander the wood-shack complex, which includes a cookhouse, schoolhouse and sleeping quarters – they'll even teach you to be a blacksmith (for $60).

Turn your back on the forest and hit the water for a great day out on board the MV *Lady Rose* or MV *Frances Barkley*, the two-vessel package fleet operated by **Lady Rose Marine Services** (☎ 250-723-8313, 800-663-7192; www.ladyrosemarine.com; from Argyle Pier; return $50-72; ☺ departs 8am Tue, Thu & Sat year-round, plus 8am daily Jun-Sep). Delivering mail and supplies around the Barkley Sound region, guests can hop on board for a scenic return excursion via Ucluelet, Bamfield and/or the Broken Group Islands – keep your eyes peeled for whales, seals and black bears. Summer reservations recommended.

Try a different approach to the water with **Batstar Adventure Tours** (☎ 250-724-2098, 877-449-1230; www.batstar.com; 4785 Beaver Creek Rd; ☐) a combined internet café and kayak tour operator. Their multi-day aquatic odysseys around the mystically tranquil waters of Clayoquot Sound and Broken Group Islands are magically restorative. Even if you're not planning a paddle, drop by for dinner: the menu here focuses on regionally sourced ingredients and serves up a good array of comfort-food classics.

Don't eat too much if you're planning to drop into the **Vancouver Island Soaring Centre** (☎ 250-667-3591, 866-590-7627; www.visc.ca; $95-225; ☺ Apr-Oct), a few minutes west of town via Hwy 4 (follow the signs to the airport). An amazing way to experience the region's stunningly forested, fjord-like coastline, hop into a near-silent two-person glider (you'll be in front but you won't be piloting) for a breathtaking swoop around.

Sleeping & Eating

Fat Salmon Backpackers (☎ 250-723-6924; www .fatsalmonbackpackers.com; 3250 Third Ave; dm $21-25; ☺ May-Sep; ☎) Funky, eccentric and full of bright-painted character, this yellow clapboard backpacker-house is driven by its energetic, welcoming owners, along with Lily the friendly house dog. The four- to eight-bed dorms, with names like 'Knickerbocker' and 'Carnie Room,' feature beds inventively crafted from drainpipes and aluminum ladders. There are lots of books to read, sagging sofas to crash on and a kitchen bristling with utensils.

Arrowvale Riverside Campground & Cottages (☎ 250-723-7948; www.arrowvale.ca; 5955 Hector Rd; campsite/cottages $22/130-150) Situated on verdant farmland along the Somass River, 6km west of Port Alberni via Hwy 4, the Arrowvale offers showers, swimming, a playground, laundry and tasty fruit pies in its on-site café. For those who've had enough of camping, there are also two comparatively luxe riverview cottages with fireplaces, Jacuzzi tubs and timber-trussed ceilings – you'll feel like the lord of the manor compared to the grubby campers. Kids will enjoy the farm animals (check their bags for smuggled baby goats on the way out).

Hummingbird B&B (☎ 250-720-2111, 888-720-2114; www.hummingbirdguesthouse.com; 5769 River Rd; ste $125-160; ☎) With four large suites and a huge deck (complete with hot-tub), relaxing is easy at this homey B&B property. There's a shared kitchen on each of the two floors but there's a substantial cooked breakfast provided that should keep you from having to cook until supper. Each suite has satellite TV, one has its own sauna and there's a games room with full-sized pool table out back. A family-friendly option, the largest suite fits up to six.

Little Bavaria Restaurant (☎ 250-724-4242, 800-704-2744; 3035 Fourth Ave; mains $13-25; ☺ 11am-2pm Mon-Fri, 5-10pm Mon-Sat) Recalling the mid-20th-century migration of Germans to BC – the province is dotted with cuckoo-clock B&Bs and restaurants – this wood-lined, family-run eatery opened in the 1960s and

---

TOP FIVE KILLER CAMPSITES

- **Bella Pacifica Campground** (p204)
- **Green Point Campground** (p199)
- **Newcastle Island Marine Provincial Park** (p188)
- **Riverbend Resort & Campground** (p194)
- **Sooke Potholes Campground** (p183)

---

has been serving hearty goulash, schnitzels and cabbage rolls to stomach-lagging diners ever since. Try the liver dumplings if you're a true German, or save room for the giant shareable Bavarian Plate – it makes vegetarians run a mile.

Getting There & Away

Greyhound Canada (☎ 800-661-8747; www .greyhound.ca) services arrive from Victoria ($46.10, 4½ hours, three daily), Nanaimo ($25.20, 1½ hours, three daily), Parksville ($17.30, one hour, three daily) and Tofino ($28.65, 2½ hours, daily), among others.

Tofino Bus (☎ 866-986-3466, 250-725-2871; www .tofinobus.com) services arrive from Tofino ($26, two hours, two daily) and Ucluelet ($23.75, 1½ hours, two daily). The company also partners with Greyhound Canada services up and down-island.

BAMFIELD

pop 500

At the ocean end of the inlet that runs right up to Port Alberni – Lady Rose Marine services (p196) offers the best way to get from there to here – Bamfield was a key lumber port and whaling station for many years. Today it's a quaint, picture-perfect harbor village lining both sides of forested Bamfield Inlet. Linked only by water taxi, Bamfield East has the majority of services, but the prettier Bamfield West has a boardwalk with cozy eateries and sterling views of glassy Barkley Sound. Both sides have tourist info booths – check www.bamfield chamber.com for maps and resources.

The northern node of the **West Coast Trail** (p200), Bamfield also offers shorter and less challenging local routes for hikers: ask for details at the tourist info booths and try the trails to Brady's Beach and Cape Beale. For the more active, the friendly folk at

Broken Island Adventures (☎ 250-728-3500, 888-728-6200; www.brokenislandadventures.com) specialize in kayak rentals, scuba diving and marine wildlife tours in the Barkley Sound area. Their whale watching tour is recommended (adult/child $95/47.50): unlike tours on the other side of the island, you can expect to see mostly humpback and gray whales.

There's an array of small salmon fishing lodges in Bamfield offering boat packages but they also provide rooms for those not planning to fish. Waterfront **Imperial Eagle Lodge** (☎ 250-728-3430; www.imperialeaglelodge.com; Bamfield West; per person $102-229) serves up large B&B rooms in its bright and sunny main building, as well as smaller cottage accommodation in its flower-strewn garden. In contrast, the **Bamfield Trails Hotel** (☎ 250-728-3231, 877-728-3474; www.hawkeyemarinegroup.com; 22 Frigate Rd; dm/r/ste $39/119/179) is a cut-above-average motel that's popular with West Coast trail hikers. Its accommodation ranges from a 10-bed bunkhouse to rooms with kitchenettes and some large suites. It adjoins the recommended **Hawk's Nest Pub** (mains $7-12; ☻ 11am-11pm), where Bamfield locals come to hang out and eat from the menu of typical pub grub.

Aside from Lady Rose Marine vessels (p196), **West Coast Trail Express** (☎ 250-477-8700, 888-999-2288; www.trailbus.com; ☻ May-Sep) buses trundle in from Victoria ($80, six hours, daily) and Nanaimo ($80, four hours, daily).

PACIFIC RIM NATIONAL PARK RESERVE

With mist-shrouded forests and a symphony of waves crashing against its ragged shoreline, it's no surprise that the 500-sq-km **Pacific Rim National Park Reserve** (☎ 250-726-7721; www.pc.gc.ca/pacificrim; park pass adult/child $7.80/3.90) is one of BC's most popular outdoor destinations. The swathe of protected wilderness comprises three separate units: the northern section is Long Beach, between Ucluelet and Tofino; the Broken Group Islands in Barkley Sound is the central section; and the West Coast Trail – that challenging rite-of-passage for serious BC hikers – is the southern section.

First-timers should drop by the **Pacific Rim VC** (☎ 250-726-4600; www.pacificrimvisitor.ca; 2791 Pacific Rim Hwy; ☻ 9am-5pm mid-Mar–Jun & Sep, 9am-7pm Jul & Aug, 10am-4pm Thu-Sun Oct–mid-Mar) for maps, tips and resources. You need to display a park pass in your vehicle here at all times: they're available at the VC or at the yellow dispensers dotting the roadside.

Long Beach Unit

Lining Hwy 4 (also called the Pacific Rim Hwy) between the region's main Ucluelet and Tofino settlements, the breathtaking 22km Long Beach section attracts the lion's share of park visitors, who come to hang out on the wave-whipped sandy crescent fringing Wickaninnish Bay. Ever popular with surfers, this deep, forest-backed shoreline is studded with dunes, and puddled with intriguing tidepools. It's the kind of place where time stands still for the wide-eyed kids who roll up with their families to spend the day. If you're not tempted to build a sandcastle here, you're not really living.

Named after a chief of the Nuu-cha-nulth-aht First Nation (this area lies within their traditional territory), the **Wickaninnish Interpretive Centre** (Wick Rd; admission included with park user fee; ☻ 10am-6pm mid-Mar–mid-Oct) is an evocative beachfront introduction to the region's natural and aboriginal heritage. Its exterior platform is a great spot to watch storms and there's also a couple of dining options (p199). The center was being refurbished and expanded on our visit and new exhibits were being installed.

If you're suitably inspired, dive headfirst into the nature around you (not literally) on one of the area's popular trails, ranging from gentle strolls to calf-stretching 5km hikes. Keep an eye out for bald eagles, giant banana slugs and maybe even the occasional whale languidly sliding past offshore. Safety precautions apply on these routes: tread carefully over slippery rocks and tree roots and never turn your back on the surf when you're on the water's edge. Try one of these strolls:

Rainforest (1km; moderate) Two interpretive loops through old-growth forest.

Schooner (1km; moderate) Through old- and second-growth forests, with beach access.

Shorepine Bog (800m; easy & wheelchair accessible) Loops around a moss-layered bog.

South Beach (800m; easy to moderate) Through forest to a pebble beach.

Spruce Fringe (1.5km; moderate) Loop trail featuring hardy Sitka spruce.

Wickaninnish (2.5km; easy to moderate) Shoreline and forest trail.

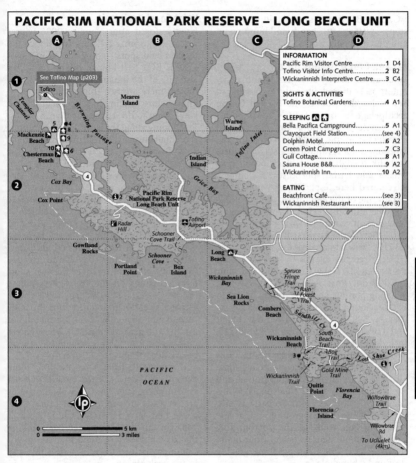

PACIFIC RIM NATIONAL PARK RESERVE – LONG BEACH UNIT

INFORMATION
Pacific Rim Visitor Centre..................**1** D4
Tofino Visitor Info Centre..................**2** B2
Wickaninnish Interpretive Centre......**3** C4

SIGHTS & ACTIVITIES
Tofino Botanical Gardens..................**4** A1

SLEEPING
Bella Pacifica Campground..................**5** A1
Clayoquot Field Station..................(see 4)
Dolphin Motel..................**6** A2
Green Point Campground..................**7** C3
Gull Cottage..................**8** A1
Sauna House B&B..................**9** A2
Wickaninnish Inn..................**10** A2

EATING
Beachfront Café..................(see 3)
Wickaninnish Restaurant..................(see 3)

VANCOUVER ISLAND

SLEEPING & EATING

Green Point Campground (☎ 250-689-9025, 877-737-3783; www.pccamping.ca; campsite $25.50; ⏰ mid-Mar–mid-Oct) Midway between Ucluelet and Tofino on Hwy 4, this is the only Long Beach Unit campground and it's very popular in summer. Its 105 campsites are located on a forested terrace and have easy trail access to Long Beach. Expect fairly basic facilities: the faucets are cold but the toilets are flush. Booking ahead in summer is essential, although there's an annoying $10.80 reservation fee.

Wickaninnish Restaurant (☎ 250-726-7706; www.wickaninnish.ca; mains $16-30; ⏰ 11:30am-10pm) Part of the Wickaninnish Interpretive Centre, this is a great oceanfront spot to feast on freshly-caught local seafood while overlooking the crashing surf on the wild west coast. The lunch menu features mid-priced gourmet classics like salmon burgers and crunchy crab cakes, while dinner is a fancier affair – try the pan-seared halibut. The adjoining and far more casual **Beachfront Café** offers bakery treats and naughty, diet-defying iced Wickaccinos from March to September.

GETTING THERE & AWAY

The **Tofino Bus** (☎ 866-986-3466, 250-725-2871; www.tofinobus.com) 'Beach Bus' service runs along Hwy 4 between Ucluelet and Tofino up to four times daily (one way/return $5/10-15), with stops en route at the Tofino

VC, Long Beach and several additional flag stops – waving your hands and jumping up and down usually works.

Broken Group Islands Unit

With an estimated 300 islands and rocky outcrops scattered liberally across 80 sq km of Barkley Sound, the Broken Group archipelago is one of BC's most popular remote destinations for experienced kayakers. Intrepid paddlers come for the awesome aquatic rainforest vistas, complete with likely sightings of black bears, gray whales and harbor porpoises. A compass is required here, especially if you're looking for one of the eight basic campgrounds dotted around the region: if you hit Hawaii, though, you've made a wrong turn.

Lady Rose Marine Services (☎ 250-723-8313, 800-663-7192; www.ladyrosemarine.com; one-way/return $33/66; ☯ departures 8am Mon, Wed & Fri Jun–mid-Sep, plus 8am Sun Jul & Aug) will ship you and your kayak from Port Alberni to its Sechart Whaling Station Lodge (3 hours away) in Barkley Sound. The lodge also rents kayaks (per day $40-60) if you'd rather travel light and it offers accommodation (s/d $140/215, including all meals).

From here, favored paddle destinations include Gibraltar Island, a one-hour paddle away, with its sheltered campground and explorable beaches and tidal pools. Willis Island (90 minutes from Sechart) is also popular. It has a campground and, at low tide, you can walk to the surrounding islands. Remote Benson Island (four hours from Sechart) has a campground, grazing deer and a blowhole.

Camping fees are $9.80 per night, payable at Sechart or to the boat-based staff who patrol the region every day – they can collect additional fees from you if you decide to stay longer. The campgrounds are predictably basic and have solar composting toilets, but you must carry out all your garbage. Bring your own drinking water since island creeks are often dry in summer.

An alternative to Lady Rose Marine and based in Bamfield, **Broken Island Adventures** (☎ 250-728-3500, 888-728-6200; www.brokenislandadventures.com) can bring you and your kayak to and from any Barkley Sound locations by water taxi (return $90). It also runs a scheduled service to Sechart (one-way $28) as well as renting kayaks (per day $45-65).

West Coast Trail Unit

Now restored after a major 2006 winter storm – returning trekkers will notice the treeless bald spots – the 77km West Coast Trail is BC's best-known hiking route. It's also one of the toughest. Not for the uninitiated, there are two things you'll need to know before tackling it: it's gonna hurt and you'll want to do it again next year.

Winding along the wave-licked rainforest shoreline between trailhead information centers at **Pachena Bay** (☎ 250-728-3234; ☯ 9am-5pm May-Sep), 5km south of Bamfield on the north end, and **Gordon River** (☎ 250-647-5434; ☯ 9am-5pm May-Sep), 5km north of Port Renfrew on the southern tip, the entire stretch takes between five and eight days to complete.

Open from May to September, access to the route is limited to 26 overnight backpackers starting from each end each day. All overnighters must pay a trail user fee ($127.50) plus $30 to cover the two short ferry crossings on the route. **Reservations** (☎ 604-435-5622, 800-435-5622; non-refundable reservation fee $24.50) are required for the mid-June to mid-September peak season but not for the off-peak period. All overnighters must attend a 90-minute orientation session before departing.

If you don't have a reservation, some permits are kept back for a daily wait-list system: six of each day's 26 available spaces are set aside at 1pm to be used on a first-come, first-served basis at each trailhead. If you win this lottery you can begin hiking that day, but keep in mind that you might wait a day or two to get a permit this way in the peak season.

If you don't want to go the whole hog (you wimp), you can do a day hike or even hike half the trail from Pachena Bay, considered the easier end of the route. Overnight hikers who only hike this end of the trail can leave from Nitinat Lake. Day hikers are exempt from the large trail user fee but they need to get a free day-use permit at one of the trailheads.

West Coast Trailers are a hardy bunch and must be able to manage rough, slippery terrain, stream crossings and adverse, suddenly changing weather. There are also more than 100 little (and some not-so-little) bridges and 70 ladders. Be prepared to treat or boil all water and cook on a lightweight camping stove (you'll be bringing

VANCOUVER ISLAND

in all your own food). Hikers can rest their weary muscles at any of the basic campsites along the route, most of which have solar-composting outhouses. It's recommended that you set out from a trailhead at least five hours before sundown to ensure you reach a campsite before nightfall – stumbling around in the dark is the prime cause of accidents on this route.

GETTING THERE & AWAY

West Coast Trail Express (☎ 250-477-8700, 888-999-2288; www.trailbus.com; ☸ May-Sep) runs a daily shuttle to Pachena Bay from Victoria ($80, six hours), Nanaimo ($80, four hours) and Port Renfrew ($55, 2½ hours). It also runs a service to Gordon River from Victoria ($55, 2½ hours), Bamfield ($70, 3½ hours) and Pachena Bay ($70, three hours).

UCLUELET

pop 1900

Driving to the west coast via Hwy 4, Ucluelet (yew-klew-let) is the closest of the region's two main communities, but only if you avoid the lure of Tofino and turn left instead of right when you hit the waterfront junction that leads to each. Unfairly regarded as the less-charming of these sibling towns, 'Ukee' shares the same scenery and similar outdoor activities, but is generally cheaper and quieter – although that's likely to change in the future, as new resorts open here. For information, head to the **VC** (☎ 250-726-4641; www.ucluletinfo.com; 100 Main St; ☸ 9am-5pm Jun-Sep) in the Whisky Dock Landing building overlooking glassy Ucluelet Harbour. And if you run out of activities, Tofino is just 30km away.

Sights & Activities

A tiny white-painted waterfront cabin near the VC, **Ucluelet Aquarium** (☎ 250-987-6992; www.ucluletaquarium.org; Main St; adult/child $4/2; ☸ 10am-6pm May-Aug, 11am-5pm mid-Mar–Apr & Sep–mid-Oct) is a fun spot to hang out from the rain – especially if you have kids in tow. The emphasis is on biodiversity education (for all ages) using pinkie-finger touch tanks brimming with local marine life, including purple starfish and alien-like anemones. On our visit, plans were slowly progressing for a much larger facility nearby.

Starting at the intersection of Peninsula and Coast Guard Rds, then winding around the wave-slapped cliffs past the lighthouse (get your camera out here) and along the craggy shoreline fringing the town, the 8.5km **Wild Pacific Trail** (www.wildpacifictrail.com) offers smashing views of Barkley Sound and the Broken Group Islands. Seabirds are abundant here and it's a good spot for watching storms – stick to the trail, or the crashing waves might pluck you from the cliffs.

If you have energy to spare, **Majestic Ocean Kayaking** (☎ 250-726-2868, 800-889-7644; www.ocean kayaking.com; 1167 Helen Rd; tours from $60) leads leisurely guided paddles around the harbor or out into the Clayoquot Sound wilderness where you can glide past pods of visiting whales. Alternatively, the friendly folk at **Inner Rhythm Surf Camp** (☎ 250-726-3456, 877-393-7873; www.innerrhythm.net; 1685 Peninsula Rd; 3hr lesson $69-79) will teach you how to surf so you can look as cool as the seasoned 20-year-olds at Long Beach (apparently inflatable armbands are not cool). It also offers equipment rentals (boards ½day/day $15/25). Dry off with some hired wheels from **Ukee Bikes** (☎ 250-726-2453; 1599 Imperial Lane; rental 1hr/24hr $5/25; ☸ 10am-6pm Mon-Sat, 11am-5pm Sun) – ask the friendly owner for tips on where to pedal in the area.

Sleeping & Eating

C&N Backpackers (☎ 250-726-7416, 888-434-6060; www.cnnbackpackers.com/ucluelet; 2081 Peninsula Rd; dm/r $27/65) You'll have to take your shoes off to enter this calming 'resort hostel' a few minutes from the town center – the hardwood floors are sacrosanct! The dorms are large, but private rooms are available, and there's a spacious kitchen. The highlight is the landscaped back garden overlooking the inlet, complete with hammocks, a rope swing and a barbeque – guests spend most of their time hanging out here in summer.

Surf's Inn Guesthouse (☎ 250-726-4426; www.surfsinn.ca; 1874 Peninsula Rd; dm/ste/cabins $24/150/250; ☸ Mar-Oct; ☏) While this blue-painted clapboard house on a small hill contains three small and homely dorm rooms, a well-equipped kitchen and is high on the friendly approach, it's the two cabins out back that attract many: one is large, self-contained and great for groups, while the other is divided into two suites with kitchenettes. Each cottage has a barbeque.

our pick Terrace Beach Resort (☎ 250-726-2901, 866-726-2901; www.terracebeachresort.ca; 1002 Peninsula

Rd; r/ste $99/169) This delightful string of forest-surrounded wooden cabins has the feel of an old fishing village, especially when you clomp along the central boardwalk to your pad for the night. Rooms (most with kitchenettes) range from homely studios to spacious lofts and suites, but all have a warm, welcoming allure rather than a cold, designer look – the chunky wood beams and even chunkier leather couches help. Try for an upper room and you'll feel like you're in a treehouse, peeking though the branches at the ocean. Family-friendly (under-12s stay free), your sprogs will love it here and you might even catch sight of the owner, a certain Jason Priestley. Two-night minimum stay in summer.

Ukee Dogs (☎ 250-726-2103; 1576 Imperial Lane; mains $5; ☒ 9am-5pm Mon-Sat) With a focus on homemade treats and comfort foods, this smashing little eatery is bright enough to cheer anyone up, even if it's raining (again). Serving made-from-scratch soups and hot-dogs of the gourmet variety (the Canuck dog is the one to go for), the focaccia bread pizzas are recommended, and the smoked garlic sausage pie is great, unless you need to kiss anyone afterwards. Also, any joint that puts that many sprinkles on its cakes deserves your patronage.

Matterson House Restaurant (☎ 250-726-6600; 1682 Peninsula Rd; mains $8-18; ☒ 8am-9pm) This yellow-painted farmhouse-turned-restaurant has a charming rustic atmosphere with lace curtains and simple, homely cooking – which is just how most seafood should be prepared. Breakfast includes build-your-own omelettes, lunches are comfort food classics and dinner is the main attraction: you'll pay less here for finger-licking gourmet nosh like scallop and prawn skewers than almost anywhere up the highway in Tofino. With only seven inside tables, reservations are recommended.

Getting There & Away

Greyhound Canada (☎ 800-661-8747; www.greyhound .ca) buses arrive from Port Alberni ($26.65, 1½ hours, daily), Nanaimo ($46.10, three hours, daily) and Victoria ($63, 6 hours, daily).

Tofino Bus (☎ 866-986-3466, 250-725-2871; www .tofinobus.com) 'Beach Bus' services roll in along Hwy 4 from Tofino ($10, 40 minutes, up to four daily).

TOFINO & AROUND
pop 1850

Turning right at the coastal junction of Hwy 4 means turning your back on Ucuelet (you won't be the first), heading through the Pacific Rim National Park Reserve and eventually rolling into Tofino at the end of the slender peninsula. Transforming in recent years from a hippy hangout into a highly popular soft-eco destination with almost overwhelming summertime crowds, within minutes you can be dipping into the mystical Clayoquot (cla-kwot) Sound wilderness, where craggy, forested banks rise invitingly from the ever-rolling waves. For tips, drop by the **VC** (☎ 250-725-3414; www.tourismtofino.com; 1426 Pacific Rim Hwy; ☒ 10am-6pm Tue-Thu, 9am-7pm Fri-Mon May-Sep, reduced off-season), located along Hwy 4 around 5km before you reach town.

Sights

Since you're in the heart of Clayoquot Sound, BC's only UNESCO Biosphere Reserve, head for an ecosystem primer at the yellow-painted **Raincoast Interpretive Centre** (☎ 250-725-2560; www.tofinores.com; 451 Main St; ☒ noon-5pm Wed-Sun mid-May–Sep) where the interactive displays and knowledgeable staff will show you what to look out for in the region. Admission and programs are free but donations are appreciated: there's a great kids area here if you want your offspring to grow up green.

Continue their education by exploring the indigenous flora and fauna at the popular **Tofino Botanical Gardens** (☎ 250-725-1220; www.tbgf.org; 1084 Pacific Rim Hwy; 3-day admission adult/youth/child $10/6/free; ☒ 9am-dusk), complete with its frog pond, forest boardwalk, rainforest plants and an ongoing program of workshops and field trips. As you wander the grounds, check out the sculptures and installations dotting the gardens. There's a $1 discount for car-free arrivals.

Hot Springs Cove is the highlight of **Maquinna Marine Provincial Park** (☎ 250-474-1336; www .bcparks.ca), one of the most popular day trips from Tofino. Tranquility-minded trekkers travel here (see Activities p203) by Zodiac boat or seaplane, watching for whales and other sea critters en route. From the boat landing, 2km of boardwalks lead to a series of natural hot pools.

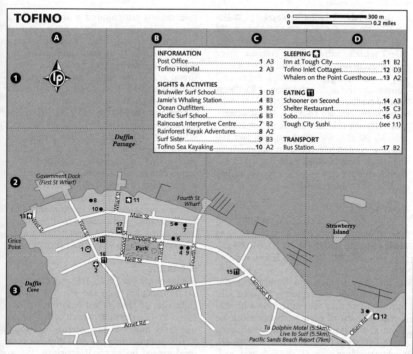

TOFINO

INFORMATION		
Post Office	1	A3
Tofino Hospital	2	A3
SIGHTS & ACTIVITIES		
Bruhwiler Surf School	3	D3
Jamie's Whaling Station	4	B3
Ocean Outfitters	5	B2
Pacific Surf School	6	B3
Raincoast Interpretive Centre	7	B2
Rainforest Kayak Adventures	8	A2
Surf Sister	9	B3
Tofino Sea Kayaking	10	A2

SLEEPING		
Inn at Tough City	11	B2
Tofino Inlet Cottages	12	D3
Whalers on the Point Guesthouse	13	A2
EATING		
Schooner on Second	14	A3
Shelter Restaurant	15	C3
Sobo	16	A3
Tough City Sushi	(see 11)	
TRANSPORT		
Bus Station	17	B2

Duffin Passage

Government Dock (First St Wharf)

Fourth St Wharf

Main St

Wharf St

First St

Second St

Third St

Campbell St

Park

Neill St

Fourth St

Grice Point

West St

Strawberry Island

Duffin Cove

Gibson St

Campbell St

Arnet Rd

To Dolphin Motel (5.5km);
Live to Surf (5.5km);
Pacific Sands Beach Resort (7km)

Olsen Rd

VANCOUVER ISLAND

Visible through the mist from the Tofino waterfront, **Meares Island** is home to the Big Tree Trail, a 400m-boardwalk through old-growth forest that includes a stunning 1500-year-old red cedar. The island was the site of the key 1984 Clayoquot Sound anti-logging protest that kicked off the region's latter-day environmental movement.

Situated on remote Flores Island, **Ahousat** is the mystical location of the spectacular Wild Side Heritage Trail, a moderately difficult path that traverses 10km of forests, beaches and headlands between Ahousat and Cow Bay. There's a natural warm spring on the island and it's also home to a First Nations band. A popular destination for kayakers, camping of the no-facilities variety is allowed here.

Activities

Surfing has traditionally been Tofino's prime activity and this is a great place to try it for the first time with an introductory course. But the town is also dripping with other outdoorsy experiences, including kayaking and whale-watching.

SURFING

Professional surfing brothers Ralph and Sepp Bruhwiler, plus their team of local experts, should be the first port of call for any virgin surf dudes. Drop by their **Bruhwiler Surf School** (☎ 250-726-5481; www.bruhwilersurf.com; 311 Olson Rd; 2½ hr group lesson including equipment $75) for fun and friendly lessons, then pay an extra $15 to keep your borrowed equipment for the rest of the day. Tofino's original surf shop, **Live to Surf** (☎ 250-725-4464; www.livetosurf.com; 1180 Pacific Rim Hwy; board rental 24hr $25) can also kit you out with skates and skimboards. Offering rentals and lessons, **Pacific Surf School** (☎ 250-725-2155, 888-777-9961; www.pacificsurfschool.com; 440 Campbell St; board rental 6hr/24hr $15/20) is also recommended. And for the ladies: **Surf Sister** (☎ 250-725-4456, 877-724-7873; www.surfsister.com; 625 Campbell St) specializes in introductory lessons for girls, but also lets the boys in – except on its special women-only surf camps.

KAYAKING

Specializing in guided paddles around the region, including a popular four-hour trip to Meares Island, **Tofino Sea Kayaking** (☎ 250-725-4222, 800-863-4664; www.tofino-kayaking.com; 320 Main St; rentals per day from $40, tours from $59) also offers rentals, introductory courses, great family excursions and jaw-dropping multi-day treks. Longer residential tours and courses are the main attraction at **Rainforest Kayak Adventures** (☎ 250-725-3117, 877-422-9453; www.rainforestkayak.com; 316 Main St; courses from $685), while **Tla-ook Cultural Adventures** (☎ 250-725-2656, 877-942-2663; www.tlaook.com; tours from $44) offers a completely different approach to the water: First Nations guided tours in authentic dugout canoes – their sunset harbor paddle is recommended.

BOAT TOURS

A one-stop shop for marine wildlife and bear-spotting tours the long-established **Jamie's Whaling Station** (☎ 250-725-3919, 800-667-9913; www.jamies.com; 606 Campbell St; tours adult/child from $79/65) will take you as close as possible to the gray whales and humpbacks migrating through the region – try their Hot Springs Cove tour for something a bit different. The list of excursions is almost the same at the popular and well-established **Ocean Outfitters** (☎ 250-725-2866, 877-906-2326; www.oceanoutfitters.bc.ca; 421 Main St; tours adult/child from $79/59), but consider their excellent seven-hour tour to Cougar Annie's Garden, a rustic planted mini-estate carved from the rainforest by 19th-century homesteader Ada Annie Arthur.

Sleeping
BUDGET

Whalers on the Point Guesthouse (☎ 250-725-3443; www.tofinohostel.com; 81 West St; dm/d $32/90; ⊜) Purpose-built as a hostel in 1999, this HI affiliate is the Cadillac of backpacker joints. Close to the center of town but with a secluded waterfront location, it's a showcase of rustic West Coast wood and stone architecture – the dining room overlooking the water is a great place to watch the natural world drift by. The dorms are mercifully small and some double-bedded private rooms are also available. Facilities include a full kitchen, barbeque patio, games room and a wet sauna. Reservations are essential in summer.

Bella Pacifica Campground (☎ 250-725-3400; www.bellapacifica.com; Mackenzie Beach Rd; campsite $37-48; ⊗ mid-Feb–mid-Nov) Peak-season reservations are required at this large and popular, family-friendly campground at Mackenzie Beach, 3km from Tofino on Hwy 4. There's an array of different oceanside or forested tent pitches – each with a firepit and picnic table – and campground facilities include flush toilets, pay showers and for-purchase ice and firewood.

Clayoquot Field Station (☎ 250-725-1220; www.tofinobotanicalgardens.com; 1084 Pacific Rim Hwy; dm/d $32/$85-120; ⊜) In the verdant grounds of the botanical gardens (room rates include entry), this immaculate wood-built education center has a selection of four-bedded dorm rooms, a large stainless-steel kitchen and an on-site laundry. There are two private rooms – the large suite is recommended for small groups – and a shared reading lounge overlooking the trees. A great nature-lovers' sleepover, it's also wheelchair accessible.

MIDRANGE

Dolphin Motel (☎ 250-725-3377; www.dolphinmotel.ca; 1190 Pacific Rim Hwy; r $105-149; ⊜) On the right side of Hwy 4 just before town (it's close to Chesterman Beach), this basic, one-level motel is one of the best-value Tofino summertime places to stay. For your hard-earned buck, you'll get clean, 1980s-furnished rooms (all en suite and some with kitchenettes) and your own outside picnic table – there's a shared barbeque where you can cook up your mystery meat specials.

ourpick **Tofino Inlet Cottages** (☎ 250-725-3441, 866-725-3411; www.tofinoinletcottages.com; 350 Olsen Rd; r $100-185) Five old A-frame buildings (also known as the Mini Motel) on a quiet stretch of central Tofino waterfront overlooking Meares Island, these vacation cottages are divided into larger, main-level suites with full kitchens, and small upper-level kitchenette rooms in the gables of each structure. The smaller rooms ($100-120) are Tofino's best midrange summer deal. Each room has a private porch and although the wood-lined interiors are a little faded, all are neat and well-maintained. One cottage can be rented in its entirety for groups of up to eight (from $230).

Sauna House B&B (☎ 250-725-2113; www.saunahouse.net; 1286 Lynn Rd; r/cabins $115/135) On a tree-lined street of secluded B&Bs just across from Chesterman Beach, this rustic nook includes a gabled loft above the main property and a small, self-contained cabin out back. The tranquil, wood-lined cabin is recommended: it has a small kitchenette, a sunny deck that's great for breakfast (included in rates and usually featuring homemade muffins) and its own compact sauna – the perfect place to end a strenuous day of hiking.

Gull Cottage (☎ 250-725-3177; www.gullcottage tofino.com; 1254 Lynn Rd; d $135-170) A short trail walk across from Chesterman Beach, this fusion West Coast and Victorian-style B&B is a cozy woodland haven for storm watchers and a well-located base for summer explorers. It has three immaculate rooms each with a light, pinewood aesthetic – we like the rainforest room with its large soaker tub. There's also a book-lined TV room for guests and a great outdoor hot-tub among the trees.

Inn at Tough City (☎ 250-725-2021; www.tough city.com; 350 Main St; d $139-229) In the heart of the action – or as close as Tofino gets to it – and monikered after the town's old nickname, this colorful brick-built waterfront inn offers eight wood-floored en suite rooms, most with balconies and some with those all-important hot-tubs. Built from recycled wood, bricks and stained-glass windows from as far away as Scotland (ask co-owner Crazy Ron about the project), there's also an excellent on-site sushi bar (see below).

TOP END

Pacific Sands Beach Resort (☎ 250-725-3322, 800-565-2322; www.pacificsands.com; 1421 Pacific Rim Hwy; r/ villa from $270/450) Vying with the other swanky sleepovers hanging around the coast here, family-owned Pacific Sands wins out with its lovely waterfront villas. Aside from its lodge buildings, these giant timber-framed houses open onto the beach and include large kitchens, stone fireplaces and ocean-view bedrooms with decks and soaker tubs. It also has energy-efficient heating and cooling systems with ultra-low greenhouse gas emissions.

Wickaninnish Inn (☎ 250-725-3100, 800-333-4604; www.wickinn.com; 500 Osprey Lane; r/ste from $440/560) Cornering the market in luxury winter storm-watching packages, 'the Wick' is worth a stay any time of year. Embodying nature with its recycled gnarled-wood furnishings, natural stone tiles and the atmosphere of a place grown rather than constructed, the sumptuous guest rooms here have push-button gas fireplaces, two-person hot-tubs and floor-to-ceiling windows. The region's most romantic sleepover, it's high-end but never pretentious and has a great on-site restaurant.

Eating

Tough City Sushi (☎ 250-725-2021; 350 Main St; mains $5-25; ☼ 11am-10pm) Eccentrically decorated with vintage toys and a large mechanized Buddha at the entrance, the main attraction here is still the nosh. Sit up and watch the sushi prep at the bar or add a side order of inlet views with a table on the patio. You'll be treated to a bewildering menu of sashimi, tempura, *nigiri* and half-shell oysters. Just head straight for the shareable 18-piece spice or *maki* platter or try the excellent main dish salmon teriyaki. Don't forget the sake list, too.

our pick **Sobo** (☎ 250-725-2341; 311 Neill St; mains $8-18; ☼ 11am-5:30pm Wed & Thu, 11am-9pm Fri-Sun) The old purple lunch-truck is sadly no more but Sobo (short for 'sophisticated bohemian') owners Lisa and Artie have moved on to bigger and better things with this new bistro-style location. Luckily, the gourmet hawker fish tacos and crispy shrimp cakes remain, but the expansion has enabled new items to come on board. Try the hemp-seed-encrusted oysters, hearty Vancouver Island seafood stew or the highly recommended roasted duck confit pizza. There's also a raft of homemade desserts and ice-creams, and if the oven-warm cookies are ready, snap 'em up. A warm and welcoming spot, try for a table on the patio (it has its own fireplace) or slip into a window seat overlooking the water. Reservations recommended.

Schooner on Second (☎ 250-725-3444; 331 Campbell St; mains $12-28; ☼ 9am-10pm) Family-owned for 50 years, this lovely, smart dining room (plus its intimate Upstairs Lounge) has uncovered many new ways to prepare the region's seafood bounty. The halibut stuffed with shrimp, brie and pine nuts is ever-popular (as are the giant breakfasts) but the signature Captain's Plate blowout is a seafood banquet worthy of King Neptune – expect to test your belt buckle with salmon, halibut, oysters and possibly the best scallops you've ever scoffed. Afterwards, nip upstairs for cocktails and twinkling inlet vistas.

VANCOUVER ISLAND

Shelter Restaurant (☎ 250-725-3353; 601 Campbell St; mains $25-39; ☻ 11:30am-10pm) An exquisite West Coast post-and-beam dining room with wrap-around leather booths and an internationally accented menu, there's a strong commitment to fresh, local sustainable ingredients here. Dishes like stout-steamed mussels and seafood Thai curry (the aquatic larder is well-represented here) draw plenty of salivating diners but head for the steamed Dungeness crab with warm garlic butter: simple and delicious.

Getting There & Around

Orca Airways (☎ 604-270-6722, 888-359-6722; www.flyorcaair.com) flights arrive at the tiny **Tofino Airport** (☎ 250-725-2006) from Vancouver International Airport's South Terminal ($159, 55 minutes, 1-3 daily).

Greyhound Canada (☎ 800-661-8747; www.greyhound.ca) buses arrive from Port Alberni ($28.65, 2 hours, daily), Nanaimo ($46.10, four hours, daily) and Victoria ($68.90, 7 hours, daily), among others.

Tofino Bus (☎ 866-986-3466, 250-725-2871; www.tofinobus.com) 'Beach Bus' services roll in along Hwy 4 from Ucluelet ($10, 40 minutes, up to four daily).

DENMAN & HORNBY ISLANDS

Ignoring the Tofino-bound Hwy 4 turn-off on the east coast of Vancouver Island and continuing northwards along Hwy 19 past Qualicum Beach, you'll soon be on the road to the Comox Valley. But before you reach the giddy attractions of Courtenay and Cumberland, take a short ferry detour from Buckley Bay to **Denman Island** (www.denmanisland.com). From here you can take another ferry hop to **Hornby Island** (www.hornbyisland.net). The main northern Gulf Islands, both have a rustic appeal and a gentler, slower approach to life. Stop at **Denman Village** near the first ferry dock and pick up a free map for both islands

Denman has three celebrated provincial parks: **Fillongley** on the east side with its easy hiking and beachcombing; **Boyle Point** at the south end with its beautiful walk to the lighthouse; and **Sandy Island**, only accessible by water from north Denman. It's also an artistic community, with more than a dozen studios crowding the island's south end.

Among Hornby's parklands, **Tribune Bay** features a long sandy beach with safe, warm

swimming; **Helliwell** offers notable hiking and amazing Strait of Georgia vistas; and **Ford's Cove**, on the south coast, offers the chance to dive with those illusive six-gill sharks. In addition, the island's giant **Mt Geoffrey Regional Park** is crisscrossed with hiking and mountain-biking trails. Hornby is at least as artsy as Denman, and has studios a-plenty. On your cultural weave, drop into **Middle Mountain Mead** (☎ 250-335-1392; www.middlemountainmead.com; 3505 Euston Rd; ☻ 1-5pm Wed-Sun Jul & Aug, reduced hours off-season), a farmland winery, for a tasting or three.

Kayaking is popular on both islands: for rentals, contact **Denman Hornby Canoes & Kayaks** (☎ 250-335-0079; www.denmanpaddling.ca; 4005 East Rd, Denman Island; 3hr/6hr $35/50) or **Hornby Ocean Kayaks** (☎ 250-335-2726; www.hornbyisland.com; 3hr/6hr $35/50). Also touch base with the friendly folk at **Hornby Islands Outdoor Sports** (☎ 250-335-0448; www.hornbyoutdoors.com; 5875 Central Rd, Hornby Island) for bike rentals and trail maps.

Sleeping & Eating
DENMAN ISLAND

Fillongley Provincial Park (☎ 604-689-9025, 800-689-9025; www.discovercamping.ca; campsite $19) Situated on the east coast of the island, this basic oceanfront campground has only 10 sites but they fill up quickly in summer – booking ahead is advised. Facilities include toilets, cold water, picnic tables and fire pits. There are several easy trails and a driftwood-strewn beach.

Denman Island Guest House (☎ 250-335-2688; www.earthclubfactory.com/guesthouse; 3806 Denman Rd; dm/r $20/48) Conveniently located up the hill and on the left from the ferry landing, this eclectic farmhouse hostel/B&B combo has bunkhouse dorms and private rooms. The tree-lined property has an on-site bistro (the coffee is great) and guests can rent bikes to tour the area. Tent pitches also available ($15).

Hawthorn House B&B (☎ 250-335-0905, 877-335-0905; www.hawthornhouse.ca; 3375 Kirk Rd; r $95-110) Handily located near the ferry dock and a short walk from the main Denman Village shops and services, this rustic garden property has three cozy rooms which can each be adapted for small groups. The best is the cottage room, located in a separate cabin and with a little kitchenette and an ocean-view porch. Cooked breakfast included.

Island Time Café (☎ 250-335-3319; 3464 Denman Rd; mains $4-9; ☺ 6:30am-8:30pm) In the village not far from the ferry terminal, this shingle-sided hangout specializes in fresh-from-the-oven bakery treats like muffins and scones (plus organic coffee), as well as bulging breakfast wraps and hearty home-made soups. The pizza is particularly recommended, though, and all is served with a side order of gossip from the chatty locals. If the sun is co-operating, sit outside and catch some rays.

HORNBY ISLAND

Ford's Cove Marina (☎ 250-335-2169; www.fordscove .com; 10835 Central Rd; cottages/tent pitch $109/24; ☺) Recently refurbished, the one or two-bedroom cabins at this oceanfront woodland retreat look basic from the outside but inside they have full kitchens, flatscreen TVs and even mp3 docking stations. If you feel like a lazy night in, there's an on-site store with pizza, sandwiches and a massive array of rental DVDs. The cabins are very popular in summer, so book ahead. Campsites are also available and there's a kayak rental operation nearby.

Hilltop Magic B&B (☎ 250-703-3513; www.hilltop magic.com; 8535 Keith Wagner Way; ste $115; ☺) A de-lightful, forest-dwelling B&B property with a single, immaculate suite, there's a real retreat feel to this place. The large, bright guestroom includes hardwood floors, a gabled ceiling and a claw-foot tub bath-room. There's also a little office for those who can't escape work; open a bottle of wine and hit the private deck instead. Ask your hosts for a few tricks: both are master magicians.

Sea Breeze Lodge (☎ 250-335-2321, 888-516-2321; www.seabreezelodge.com; Big Tree 3-2; adult/youth/ child $165/115/75) This 12-acre family-friendly retreat, with 15 cottages overlooking the ocean, has the feel of a Spanish villa with a Pacific Rim twist. Rooms are comfort-able rather than palatial and some have fireplaces and full kitchens. You can swim, kayak and fish here or just flop lazily around in the cliff-side hot-tub. Rates – reduced for under-17s – are per person and include three daily meals.

Cardboard House (☎ 250-335-0733; 2205 Central Rd; mains $4-8; ☺ 9am-4pm Mon, 9am-9pm Tue-Sun, reduced off-season) It's easy to lose track of time at this old shingle-sided farmhouse property

that combines a hearty bakery, pizza shop and cozy café. It's impossible not to stock up on a bag full of oven-fresh muffins, cookies and croissants for the road, but stick around for an al fresco lunch in the adjoining orchard, which also stages live music on Wednesday and Sunday evenings in summer.

Getting There & Away

BC Ferries (☎ 250-386-3431, 888-223-3779; www.bc ferries.com) services arrive throughout the day at Denman Island from Vancouver Island's Buckley Bay (passenger/vehicle $6.25/16.25, 10 minutes). Hornby Island is accessed via ferry from the east side of Denman (passenger/vehicle $7.25/16.25, 10 minutes).

COMOX VALLEY

Comprising waterfront Comox, charming Courtenay and tiny but highly recom-mended Cumberland, the Comox Valley is a temperate region of rolling mountains, alpine meadows and quirky communities founded on the logging industry. A good base for outdoor adventures, it includes the Mt Washington ski resort. Courtenay is also the end of the line if you're trundling up-island on the VIA Rail *Malahat* train.

For regional information, drop by the **VC** (☎ 250-334-3234, 888-357-4471; www.discovercomox valley.com; 2040 Cliffe Ave, Comox; ☺ 9am-5pm mid-May–Aug, closed Sun Sep–mid-May) or just ask the locals at the **Comox Valley Farmers Market** (www .comoxvalleyfarmersmarket.com; 4835 Headquarters Rd, Courtenay; ☺ 9am-noon Sat mid-Apr–Oct).

Sights & Activities

Mt Washington Alpine Resort (☎ 250-338-1386, 888-231-1499; www.mountwashington.ca; lift ticket adult/ child winter $59/31, summer $36/24) has long been Vancouver Island's skiing mecca. With 60 ski and snowboard runs, a large snow-shoeing park, a night-lit tubing area and 55km of cross-country trails it's a popular winter haunt for those who like to warm up in the snow. But the resort's summer activi-ties also make its 'off-season' a magnet for outdoor nuts who come for the horseback riding, fly-fishing and the excellent, 18-trail mountain biking course – rentals, lessons and guided tours are available for bikers of all skill levels. Hiking is also recommended here: popular routes include Paradise Meadows Loop (2km), starting at the

Nordic ski area parking lot. Whatever you do, save time to breathe in some panoramic vistas of the island and its jewel-like ocean setting.

Known for its life-sized replica of an elasmosaur, a prehistoric marine reptile first discovered in the area, **Courtenay & District Museum & Palaeontology Centre** (☎ 250-334-0686; www.courtenaymuseum.ca; 207 Fourth St; admission by donation; ◷ 10am-5pm Mon-Sat, noon-4pm Sun mid-May–Aug, 10am-5pm Tue-Sat Sep–mid-May) also houses First Nations exhibits and provides a colorful introduction to the area's pioneering past. You can hunt for your own fossils along the banks of the Puntledge River on a guided museum **fossil tour** (tours adult/child $25/15; ◷ Apr-Aug): book ahead for these.

Check out some flying dinosaurs over at **Comox Air Force Museum** (☎ 250-339-8162; www.comoxairforcemuseum.ca; 19 Wing Comox; admission free; ◷ 10am-4pm Tue-Sun). Jam-packed with exhibits from Canada's aviation history, it's an excellent find for enthusiasts and casual fans. Drop by on Saturday afternoon to check out the ongoing Spitfire restoration project.

Outdoorsy types should make for **Miracle Beach Provincial Park** (☎ 250-755-2483; www.bcparks.ca), home to some excellent hiking trails and tranquil sandy beaches. Alternatively, Courtenay's **Pacific Pro Dive & Surf** (☎ 250-338-6829, 877-800-3483; www.scubashark.ca; 2270 Cliffe Ave) can help with scuba lessons and equipment rentals, while Comox's **Simon's Cycles** (☎ 250-339-6683; www.simonscycles.com; 1841 Comox Ave) offers bike rentals and advice for regional pedalers.

Sleeping

our pick **Riding Fool Hostel** (☎ 250-336-8250, 888-313-3665; www.ridingfool.com; 2705 Dunsmuir St, Cumberland; dm/r $23/55; ◉) Symbolizing the funky reclamation of Cumberland's pioneering clapboard main street – it looks like a brightly painted reinvention of Dodge City – this is one of Vancouver Island's best hostels. The handsomely restored heritage building has immaculate wooden interiors (much of it recycled), some large but spacious dorms, a massive kitchen, a stove-heated lounge area and the kind of private, double-bedded rooms usually only found in hotels. Friendly staffers are experts on the region and also run an on-site coffee and bike shop: rentals and trail maps available.

Shantz Haus Hostel (☎ 250-703-2060, 866-603-2060; www.shantzhostel.com; 520 Fifth St, Courtenay; dm/r $23/55; ◉) Handily located in central Courtenay, this quiet little hostel feels like staying in a favorite aunt's house. Luckily, she's quite a cool aunt: her two dorms are small and cozy, while her private rooms are ideal for families. The bathrooms are the antithesis of institutionalized hostels and there's a full kitchen, fireplace common room and sunny deck with barbeque.

Beach House B&B (☎ 250-338-8990, 866-290-4239; www.thebeachhousebb.ca; 3614 Hwy 19A, Courtenay; s/d from $60/75; ◉) Like it says on the label, this cedar-built, lodge-like B&B perches on the waterfront and is handily close to all three main valley communities. The three rooms (two on the gabled upper level) combine rustic, wood-lined interiors with comfortable rather than luxurious furnishings, plus some shared bathrooms. The ground-level Pacific Room, with its large oceanfront deck and private entrance, is recommended, while all rooms are big enough for an extra bed if you're traveling in a small group.

Old House Village Suites & Hotel (☎ 250-703-0202, 888-703-0202; www.oldhousevillage.com; 1800 Riverside Lane, Courtenay; r/ste $129/179) Located alongside the river in Courtenay, this new resort-style lodge looks like it was transplanted straight from Whistler. Beneath the pretty, timber-framed gables, you'll find a swanky stone-and-beam interior and three floors of contemporary, lounge-like rooms and suites, all with kitchenettes or full kitchens. There's an on-site restaurant if you don't feel like cooking, or you can stroll to one of several downtown restaurants located nearby.

Eating

Orbitz Gourmet Pizza (☎ 250-338-7970; 492 Fitzgerald St, Courtenay; slice/pie $3.75/27.95; ◷ 11:30am-10pm Mon-Sat) Not only the best and most inventive pizza in town – the 'Harvest Moon' pie of apple, rosemary, blue cheese and caramelized onions is spectacular – little Orbitz is also a cool hangout. There's a wide selection of vegetarian and meat toppings (love that tandoori chicken), and you can add organic chocolate bars and fair-trade coffee to your order.

our pick **Great Escape** (☎ 250-336-8831; 2744 Dunsmuir Ave, Cumberland; mains $12-16; ◷ 11:30am-9pm Tue-Sun May-Sep, 5-9pm Tue-Sun Oct-Apr) A contemporary fusion Indian restaurant unexpectedly located in the heart of old Cumberland (if you like Vij's in Vancouver, you'll love this place), the adventurous meals here are prepared with an admirable attention to detail, from the hand-ground spices to the amazing homemade plum chutney. The curried scallops with fennel and fenugreek are recommended, as are the 'pappadam cigars' (like Indian spring rolls). Ingredients are sourced locally and organically wherever possible and there's a welcome array of vegan dishes. Drop by for Thursday's Thali special: two courses for $15 and sup on a few Indian Kingfisher lagers. Choice Vancouver Island microbrews and a small but well-chosen BC and international wine list are also available.

Atlas Café (☎ 250-338-9838; 250 Sixth St, Courtenay; mains $12-18; ☺ 8:30am-10pm Tue-Sat, 8:30am-9pm Sun) Courtenay's favorite diner, Atlas has a pleasing modern bistro feel but is sometimes overrun by the slavering hordes on summer nights – avoid peak times if possible. The taste-tripping global menu fuses Asian, Mexican and Mediterranean flourishes – including gourmet fish tacos and some changing seasonal treats – and includes impressive vegetarian options. If you still can't get a table, ask for directions to their sister eatery, Avenue Bistro, in Comox.

Getting There & Around
Central Mountain Air (☎ 250-877-5000, 888-865-8585; www.flycma.com) flights arrive at **Comox Valley Airport** (☎ 250-897-3123; www.comoxairport .com) from Vancouver International Airport ($135, 40 minutes, up to five daily). **WestJet** (☎ 800-538-5696; www.westjet.com) services arrive from Calgary (from $135, 1½ hours, two daily).

Greyhound Canada (☎ 800-661-8747; www .greyhound.ca) buses arrive in Courtenay from Victoria ($47.05, 4½ hours, three daily), Campbell River ($14.50, 50 minutes, three daily) and Nanaimo ($26.65, 1½ hours, three daily). There are no stops in Comox or Cumberland.

The **VIA Rail** (☎ 888-842-7245; www.viarail.ca) *Malahat* service arrives in Courtenay, it's northern terminus station, from Victoria ($53.55, 5 hours, daily) and Nanaimo ($27.30, two hours, daily), among others.

BC Ferries (☎ 888-223-3779, 250-386-3431; www .bcferries.com) services arrive at Comox's Little

River terminal from the mainland's Powell River (passenger/vehicle $10.90/33.90, 80 minutes, two to four daily).

The **Comox Valley Transit System** (☎ 250-339-5453; www.busonline.ca; adult/child $1.50/1.25) operates buses between Comox, Courtenay and Cumberland.

CAMPBELL RIVER
pop 33,000
Regarded by many as the end of civilization on the island (try telling that to someone on the north end), Campbell River is a logging and salmon-fishing town that's reinvented itself as an access point for wilderness tourism. It's the main departure point for Strathcona Provincial Park (p211) and is the region's main shopping and services hub. For local information, drop by the **VC** (☎ 250-830-0411, 877-286-5705; www .northcentralisland.com; 1235 Shoppers Row; ☺ 9am-7pm Jul & Aug, 9am-6pm Jun & Sep, reduced off-season).

Sights & Activities
The excellent **Museum at Campbell River** (☎ 250-287-3103; www.crmuseum.ca; 470 Hwy 19A; adult/child $6/4; ☺ 10am-5pm mid-May–Sep, noon-5pm Tue-Sun Oct–mid-May) features a good collection of First Nations masks, an 1890 pioneer cabin and video footage of the world's largest-ever artificial, non-nuclear blast, which destroyed Ripple Rock – a submerged mountain in Seymour Narrows north of Campbell River that caused more than 100 shipwrecks before it was blown apart in 1958. Check out the adjoining Native Plant Garden with signs explaining the traditional First Nations usage of local flora.

Campbell River lives up to its 'Salmon Capital' billing with fishing a popular pastime. You can cast a line off the downtown **Discovery Pier** or just stroll along with the crowds and see what everyone else has caught. Fish and chips are also available here, served in oversized newspaper cones. Work off the grub with a scuba dive around the sunken HMCS *Columbia*. Contact **Beaver Aquatics Limited** (☎ 250-287-7652; 760 Island Hwy; ☺ 9.30am-5pm Mon-Fri. 10am-5pm Sat) for gear and lessons.

Sleeping & Eating
Rustic Motel (☎ 250-286-6295, 800-567-2007; www .rusticmotel.com; 2140 N Island Hwy; r $85-160; ☒ ☎) North of downtown, this woodland sleepover

sits quietly in the trees by the river. Rooms are clean but a little spartan – the three-room suites and cabins are a good option for groups – but the additional facilities include a sauna, Jacuzzi and barbeques. Rates include continental breakfast.

Dolphins Resort (☎ 250-287-3066, 800-891-0287; www.dolphinsresort.com; 4125 Discovery Dr; cabins from $150) A beautifully maintained nest of woodland cedar cabins spilling down to the water's edge, there's a cozy, rustic feel to this older resort. Cabins have kitchens and porches (barbeque rentals are $10 extra) and most also have outdoor hot-tubs. The landscaped grounds are immaculate and there's a secluded private beach with its own fire pit for relaxed evenings.

Royal Coachman Inn (☎ 250-286-0231; 84 Dogwood St; mains $8-18; ⏱ 11:30am-11pm) Campbell Riverites' favorite neighborhood hangout, this large Brit-style pub includes a brick-and-beam-lined barroom that focuses on BC and pan-Canada brews (light fans should try the Sleemans Honey Brown; dark quaffers should dive into a Hermann's Dark Lager). The giant menu is even more eclectic, ranging from phyllo-wrapped chicken to Thai ginger salad. Once you've had your fill, gamble the last of your travel budget on international horseraces in the adjoining TV betting room.

Getting There & Around

A short drive from downtown, **Campbell River Airport** (☎ 250-923-5012; www.crairport.ca) receives **Pacific Coastal Airlines** (☎ 604-273-8666, 800-663-2872; www.pacific-coastal.com) services from Vancouver International Airport ($155, 45 minutes, up to four daily).

Greyhound Canada (☎ 800-661-8747; www .greyhound.ca) services arrive from Port Hardy, ($47.05, 3¼ hours, daily), Nanaimo ($33.95, three hours, three daily) and Victoria ($55.15, 5-6 hours, three daily).

Campbell River Transit (☎ 250-287-7433; www .bctransit.com; adult/child $1.75/1.50) operates local buses throughout the area.

QUADRA & CORTES ISLANDS

A 10-minute ferry hop across the water from Campbell River, rustic Quadra Island is a popular day or half-day excursion. You'll have to traverse it to access the ferry that chugs over to adjacent Cortes (www .cortesisland.com). Quadra's friendly, volunteer-run **Visitor Information Booth** (www.quadraisland .ca; ⏱ 9am-4pm Jun-Sep) is in the parking lot of the Quadra Credit Union, uphill from the ferry dock. For nature-hugging treks to the quiet islands beyond these two, visit www.discoveryislands.ca.

Sights & Activities

Quadra's fascinating **Nuyumbalees Cultural Centre** (☎ 250-285-3733; 34 Weway Rd; adult/child $15/5; ⏱ 9am-5pm May-Sep, 11am-3pm Wed-Sat Oct-Apr) illuminates the heritage and traditions of the local Kwakwaka'wakw First Nations, showcasing carvings and artefacts and staging traditional dance performances in summer.

The sandy beaches and clear waters of Quadra's **Rebecca Spit Provincial Park** (☎ 250-474-1336; www.bcparks.ca) offer excellent swimming and boating. On Cortes, **Manson's Landing Marine Provincial Park** (☎ 250-474-1336; www.bcparks.ca) is studded with abundant shorebirds and shellfish, while **Smelt Bay Provincial Park** (☎ 250-474-1336; www.bcparks.ca) is ideal for picnic-fueled sunset watching. It also has campsites ($15).

Hit the waters on a kayak tour (the sunset one is brilliant) with **Quadra Island Kayak** (☎ 250-285-3400, 877-475-8687; www.quadraisland kayak.com; tours from $59, rentals per day $40) or let the Zodiac do all the work with a whale- or grizzly-bear-watching tour organized by **Island Adventure Centre** (☎ 250-285-2007, 877-285-2007; www.islandadventurecentre.com; tours from adult/ child $160/100) from Quadra's Heriot Bay. Alternatively, hit the island's **artisan studio trail** by checking listings at www.quadra islandarts.com.

Sleeping & Eating

A First-Nations-owned resort on Quadra's southern tip, **Tsa-Kwa-Luten Lodge** (☎ 250-285-2042; 800-665-7745; www.capemudgeresort.bc.ca; 1 Lighthouse Rd, Quadra Island; r/cabins from $104/149) is set in 1100 acres of lush green forest with stunning views of Discovery Passage. It's a true retreat, with art-lined walls replacing the TVs.

It's also worth checking out Quadra's **Whiskey Point Resort** (☎ 250-285-2201; www.whiskey point.com; 725 Quathiaski Rd, Quadra Island; r $119-149; 🖥 🐾), a friendly, family-oriented motel handily near the main ferry dock. And at the ferry dock to Cortes, the excellent **Heriot Bay Inn** (☎ 250-285-3322, 888-605-4545; www .heriotbayinn.com; Heriot Bay, Quadra Island; r/ste/cabins

$109/209/249) is a pioneer-look hostelry that offers plenty of outdoor activities. Its pub stages Friday live music nights and serves up plenty of beer and food specials.

Everything is vegan and organic at **Amped on Nutrition** (☎ 250-285-3142; 658 Harper Rd, Quadra Island; mains $4-8; ⏰ 9am-7pm), where the menu highlights hearty soups, beanburgers and generous salads. If you're on Cortes, head to the **Cove Restaurant** (☎ 250-935-6350; Squirrel Cove, Cortes Island; mains $9-22; ⏰ 11.30am-9pm), which specializes in organic salads and local seafood, and does a naughty sideline in large desserts. Try for a table on the deck and you'll be overlooking some tranquil sea-and-mountain vistas.

Getting There & Away

Frequent **BC Ferries** (☎ 250-386-3431, 888-223-3779; www.bcferries.com) services arrive from Campbell River at Quadra's main Quathiaski Cove dock (passenger/vehicle $7.25/16.80, 10 minutes). On the other side of Quadra, ferries leave from Heriot Bay for Whaletown on Cortes Island (passenger/vehicle $8.45/19.45, 45 minutes; six daily). Most Quadra and Cortes accommodations will pick you up from the ferry.

STRATHCONA PROVINCIAL PARK

Driving inland from Campbell River on Hwy 28, you'll soon come to BC's oldest protected area and also Vancouver Island's largest **park** (☎ 250-337-2400; www.bcparks.ca). Centered on Mt Golden Hinde, the island's highest point (2200m), Strathcona is a magnificent pristine wilderness crisscrossed with trail systems that deliver you to waterfalls, alpine meadows, glacial lakes and looming mountain crags.

On arrival at the main entrance, get your bearings at **Strathcona Park Lodge & Outdoor Recreation Centre** (☎ 250-286-3122; www.strathcona .bc.ca). A one-stop-shop for park activities, including kayaking, guided treks, yoga camps, ziplining and rock climbing (all-in adventure packages are available, some aimed specifically at families) this is a great place to rub shoulders with other outdoorsy-types – head to the Whale Room or Canoe Club Café eateries to fuel up.

The lodge also offers good accommodation (rooms/cabins from $122/205), which, in keeping with its low-impact approach to nature and commitment to

eco-education, has no telephones or TVs. Rooms range from basic college-style bedrooms to secluded timber-framed cottages. If you are a true back-to-nature fan, there are also several campsites available in the park.

Notable park hiking trails include **Paradise Meadows Loop** (2.2km), an easy amble in a delicate wildflower and evergreen ecosystem, and **Mt Becher** (5km), with great views over the Comox Valley and mountain-lined Strait of Georgia. The 9km **Comox Glacier Trail** is quite an adventure but is only recommended for advanced hikers. Around Buttle Lake, easier walks include **Lady Falls** (900m) and the trail along **Karst Creek** (2km), which winds past sinkholes, percolating streams and tumbling waterfalls.

You can pitch your tent at **Buttle Lake Campground** (☎ 604-689-9025, 800-689-9025; www .discovercamping.ca; tent pitch $15). The swimming area and playground here make this a good choice for families. Alternatively, remote **Ralph River Campground** ($15) attracts more dedicated escapees from civilization. If you really want to find your own space, backcountry sites ($5) are also available throughout the park.

NORTH VANCOUVER ISLAND

Down-islanders (which means anyone below Campbell River) will tell you 'there's nothing up there worth seeing,' but if you really want to encounter the wilderness – plus some quirky outback communities – the North Island is the place to head. Accessed on its eastern flank via Hwy 19 past Campbell River (it's 233km from here to Port Hardy), you'll hit some bumpy gravel logging roads if you want to explore further into the central, western and far northern areas: this is not the place to be driving your dad's borrowed Lexus sedan. A few paint chips are more than worth it, though, to experience some of BC's best untamed areas, complete with breathtaking deserted beaches, black bears feasting on road-side berries and a population of colorful locals with a hardy, independent streak that marks them out from the down-island softies. It's also time to get out those hiking boots: the long-awaited North Coast

VANCOUVER ISLAND

Trail is now open. For further information on the region, contact **Tourism North Island** (☎ 250-956-3656; www.tourismni.com).

SAYWARD

The winding, tree-lined Hwy 19 stretch between Campbell River and Port Hardy is a prime bear-watching route, but make sure you also stop to drink in the vista at **Seymour Narrows Lookout**, which overlooks the site of **Ripple Rock**. Keep in mind that only Sayward (population 400) and nearby Woss (population 380) have services, so stock up on snacks and supplies when you can. The Sayward **information center** (☎ 250-282-3821; www.sayward.ca; ⏰ noon-6pm Tue-Sun Apr-Oct), at the junction of Hwy 19 and Sayward Rd, has staff who can recommend area sleeps, eats, and activities (hiking is the main one).

If you're staying in the area, Sayward's **Fisherboy Park** (☎ 250-282-3204, 866-357-0598; www.fisherboypark.com; 714 Sayward Rd; campsite/s/d $14/59/69) is a short drive from the information center. It's a well-maintained, family-friendly campground with an additional small motel building and some private cabins. Campers have access to a laundromat, showers, and flush toilets and there's also a liquor store.

Alternatively, the highly tranquil **Victorian Garden Gate Manor** (☎ 250-282-3776; www.geocities.com/victorian_garden_gate_manor; 448 Community Rd; r $99-149) is a large family home set in hillside flower gardens (that include a waterfall). Its two guestrooms are homely and cozy, with handmade quilts, while a hearty breakfast is served in the elegant, chandeliered dining room. If you're not staying, you can also visit the celebrated **gardens** (☎ 250-282-3776; adult/child $5/1; ⏰ 1-5pm Thu-Sun May-Sep).

If it's mealtime when you arrive, don't miss the legendary **Cable Cookhouse** (☎ 250-282-3433; 1741 Sayward Rd; mains $7-16; ⏰ 8am-9pm), an old café building cocooned in 2700m of steel logging cables. The interior includes 1950s frescoes of regional industrial scenes and the menu features hefty sandwiches, surprisingly good salads and smashing fruit pies. The salmon melt sandwich is recommended – also pick up a brick-sized cinnamon bun for the road.

TELEGRAPH COVE

Located 11km southeast of Hwy 19 via Beaver Cove Rd, Telegraph Cove – originally a one-room telegraph station – has re-invented itself as a charming and highly popular visitor destination: you'll likely see more people here on a busy summer day than anywhere else on the North Island. The attractive setting includes a waterfront boardwalk and dozens of wooden buildings standing around the marina on stilts, but its not just about eye candy here. There are places to stay and dine and some great outdoor activities – this is one of the best places in BC to go whale-watching.

Do your homework first at the enthralling **Whale Interpretive Centre** (☎ 250-928-3129, 250-928-3117; www.killerwhalecentre.org; suggested donation $2; ⏰ Jun-Sep), stuffed with hands-on artefacts and artfully displayed skeletons of cougars, sea otters and a giant fin whale. Then head to **Stubbs Island Whale-watching** (☎ 250-928-3185, 800-665-3066; www.stubbs-island.com; $79-89; ⏰ May-Sep) for a boat trip to the orcas: you might also see humpbacks, dolphins and sea lions. Its sunset cruise is highly recommended.

For a grizzly or black bear alternative, **Tide Rip Tours** (☎ 250-339-5320, 888-643-9319; www.tiderip.com; from $265; ⏰ mid-May–mid-Oct) leads full-day trips to local beaches and inlets.

While the established **Telegraph Cove Resorts** (☎ 250-928-3131, 800-200-4665; www.telegraphcoveresort.com; tent pitch/cabins from $21/110) provides accommodation in forested tent pitches and a string of charming cabins on stilts overlooking the marina, the newer **Dockside 29** (☎ 250-928-3163, 877-835-2683; www.telegraphcove.ca; r $120-160) is a good, motel-style alternative. Its rooms have kitchenettes with hardwood floors and waterfront views.

The **Killer Whale Café** (☎ 250-928-3155; mains $14-18; ⏰ 10am-9pm May-Sep) is the cove's best eatery – the salmon, mussel and prawn linguini is recommended – while the adjoining **Old Saltery Pub** is an atmospheric, wood-lined nook with a cozy central fireplace and tasty Killer Whale Pale Ale. It's a good spot to sit in a corner and pretend you're an old sea salt – eye patch and wooden leg optional.

PORT MCNEILL

pop 2930

On Hwy 19 and tumbling down the hill almost into Broughton Strait, Port McNeill began as a 1920s logging camp. Today it's the second-largest North Island community, and while forestry remains its number one concern, it's also a good stop for travelers: there are restaurants and supermarkets and easy access points for wilderness activities. On the waterfront, the brand new **VC** (☎ 250-956-3131, 888-956-3131; www.portmcneill .net; 1594 Beach Dr; ☼ 9am-7pm Jul & Aug, reduced hours off-season) can help plan your time here. It also houses the **North Island Heritage Museum** which bristles with pioneer and logging industry artifacts.

Explore the region on wheels with a rental bike (and some suggested routes) from **Kingfisher Wilderness Adventures** (☎ 250-956-4617, 866-546-4347; www.kingfisher.ca; rentals half-day/full-day $25/35). It also offers odyssey-like guided kayak treks around the Johnstone Strait region and beyond to the magical Queen Charlotte Islands (tours from $175).

More a quality motel than a resort, the hilltop **Black Bear Resort** (☎ 250-956-4900, 866-956-4900; www.blackbearresort.net; 1812 Campbell Way; d/tw/ste $140/160/195; ☐) overlooks the town and is across the street from shops and restaurants. Its standard rooms are small but clean and include microwaves and fridges; full-kitchen units are also available. Rates include a large continental breakfast buffet (with make-your-own waffles), a free-access computer in the lobby and a day spa.

For huge plates of Mexican nosh, plus eye-popping decor that includes orange walls, green tablecloths and the kind of dollar-store ornaments that would make a connoisseur of kitsch blush, **Bo-Banees** (☎ 250-956-2739; 1705 Campbell Way; mains $6-9; ☼ 8am-10pm) serves burritos, burgers and Lucky Lager, the logger's favorite beer.

Getting There & Away

Greyhound Canada (☎ 800-661-8747; www.greyhound .ca) buses arrive from Port Hardy ($14.60, 30 minutes, daily), Campbell River ($40.90, 2½ hours, daily) and Nanaimo ($68.90, six hours, daily).

BC Ferries (☎ 250-386-3431, 888-223-3779; www .bcferries.com) services arrive from Alert Bay and Sointula (passenger/vehicle $8.45/ 19.45) but times and schedules vary and are subject to change.

ALERT BAY & SOINTULA

The village of Alert Bay (population 600) on Cormorant Island has an aura both mythical and ancient. Its First Nations community and traditions are apparent, and, blended

with the old fishing settlement, makes for a fascinating day trip. Peruse the shops and eateries of Alert Bay and drop by the **VC** (☎ 250-974-5024; www.alertbay.ca; 116 Fir St; ☼ 9am-5pm Jul & Aug, 9am-5pm Mon-Fri Sep-Jun). Malcolm Island and its town of Sointula (population 800) is a one-time socialist commune founded in 1901 by Finns, for whom the town's name meant 'harmony'. For visitor information, check www.sointulainfo.ca.

Alert Bay's excellent **U'Mista Cultural Centre** (☎ 250-974-5403, 800-690-8222; www.umista.ca; 1 Front St; adult/child $5/1; ☼ 9am-5pm daily Jun-Aug, 9am-5pm Mon-Fri Sep-May) immaculately presents its impressive collection of Kwakwaka'wakw masks and other potlatch items originally confiscated by the federal government. Singing, dancing and barbeques are often held here in a scaled-down 'Big House', while modern-day totem-pole carvers usually work out front. Also consider dropping by the friendly folk at **Culture Shock Interactive Gallery** (☎ 250-974-2484; 10A Front St; ☼ 9:30am-6pm May-Sep, noon-5pm Tue-Sat Oct-Apr) for some exquisite artwork souvenirs.

While Sointula is not as tourist-oriented as Alert Bay, it does have some great hiking. Among the recommended treks are the **Mateoja Heritage Trail** (3.5km), the **Beautiful Bay Trail** (5km) and the mudflats at **Rough Bay**, a favorite among birdwatchers.

Seasmoke Whale Watching (☎ 250-974-5225, 800-668-6722; www.seaorca.com; tours from adult/child $95/85) offers a unique five-hour marine wildlife sailing experience aboard its classic yacht, *SV Tuan* including generous Devonshire cream teas. And if you're looking for somewhere to stay in Alert Bay, it also has a lovely self-contained waterfront suite available (single/double $120/140)

PORT HARDY

pop 4400

Settled by Europeans in the early 1800s, this small north island settlement is best known as the arrival/departure point for BC Ferries Inside Passage trips. It's also a handy gear-up point for treks to remote Cape Scott and the newly completed North Coast Trail. Next to the town's landmark wood-carved welcome sign, the **VC** (☎ 250-949-7622, 866-427-3901; www.porthardy.travel; 7250 Market St; ☼ 8.30am-6pm Mon-Fri, 9am-5pm Sat & Sun mid-May–Aug, 9am-5pm Mon-Fri Sep–mid-May) offers activity and accommodation local information.

Sights & Activities

In-the-know locals have been surfing the rugged North Island waterfront for decades. The antithesis of Tofino's slick, resort-style approach, **Surf Nawalakw** (☎ 250-949-7873; www.nawalakw.com; 7995 Goodspeed Rd; rentals/lessons $25/149) offers rentals, lessons and advice for those who fancy hitting the waves around Grant Bay, Raft Cove and San Josef Bay. And if you're wondering, 'Nawalakw' means 'supernatural or spiritual power'.

For those who prefer to paddle, **Odyssey Kayaking** (☎ 250-902-0565, 888-792-3366; www.odysseykayaking.com; rentals/tours from $40/99) can take you on guided tours around Malei Island, Bear Cove and Alder Bay or leave you to your own devices with a full-day rental.

For dive fans, **Catala Charters** (☎ 250-949-7560, 800-515-5511; www.catalacharters.net; dive trips from $150) options include trips to Browning Passage. Dripping with octopuses, wolf eels and coral, it's one of BC's top cold-water dive sites.

Alternatively, **Great Bear Nature Tours** (☎ 250-949-9496, 888-221-8212; www.greatbeartours.com; all-inclusive tours from $800) can ship you in for a comfortable overnight stay (one to seven days) at its charming floating lodge. It's not cheap but it's an experience you'll likely never forget.

Sleeping & Eating

North Coast Hostel (☎ 250-949-9441; www.northcoasthostel.com; 8635 Granville St; dm/d $29/60) This brand spanking new 35-bed second-floor hostel aims to serve those North Coast Trail hikers preparing for their muscle-busting trek. The three midsized dorms (and private double room) offer mostly great views across the waterfront and although the kitchen is smallish, you're within spitting distance of several local eateries. Avoid the trek altogether with table tennis and big-screen TV action in the lounge. The Greyhound Canada bus stop is a short stroll away.

C&N Backpackers (☎ 250-949-3030, 888-434-6060; www.cnnbackpackers.com; 8470 Main St; dm/d $25/65) From the outside, it looks like a light industrial unit where circuit boards might be assembled, but the interior of this hostel is completely different, with a hardwood floor lobby, large kitchen and comfortable lounge area. There's a deficiency of windows, however, and the dorm rooms are bare and institutional – how about some color on the walls, guys?

Quarterdeck Inn (☎ 250-902-0455, 877-902-0459; www.quarterdeckresort.net; 6555 Hardy Bay Rd; s/d $125/145) A suite gives you a lot more room (plus a fireplace and hot-tub) and is worth

---

AND FINALLY...THE NORTH COAST TRAIL

If your response to the famed West Coast Trail is 'been there, done that,' it's time to strap on your hiking boots for the brand-spanking-new North Island equivalent. After years (or was it decades?) of planning, the 43km North Coast Trail opened to salivating outdoorsy-types in 2008. Trekkers can start on the western end and at Nissen Bight, but you'll have to hike in 15km on the established (and relatively easy) Cape Scott Trail to get there. From Nissen Bight, the trail winds eastwards to Shushartie Bay. You'll be passing sandy coves, deserted beaches and dense, wind-whipped rainforest woodland, as well as a couple of river crossings on little cable cars. The trail is muddy and swampy in places so there are boardwalks to make things easier. The area is home to elk, deer, cougars, wolves and black bears (make sure you know how to handle an encounter before you set off), while offshore you're likely to spot seals, sea lions, sea otters and grey whales. Like its West Coast brother, the North Coast Trail is for experienced and well-equipped hikers only. There are backcountry campsites at Nissen Bight, Laura Creek and Shuttleworth Bight and the route should take 5-7 days.

The Holberg Cape Scott trailhead is 63km from Port Hardy and is accessible via well-used logging roads. You can drive there yourself or take the dedicated **North Coast Trail Shuttle** (☎ 250-949-6888; www.northcoasttrailshuttle.com; $70; ☾ May-Sep). Once you're done at the Shushartie Bay end, you can pick up a **Cape Scott Water Taxi** (☎ 250-949-6541; www.capescottwatertaxi.ca; $80) back to Port Hardy. You must book both the shuttle and the boat ahead of time – the shuttle company can also help you book the water taxi.

Reservations are not required for the North Coast Trail. For more information, see www.northcoasttrail.com.

the extra dollars here, especially if you've been roughing it on the road for a few days. The upper floor waterfront rooms have excellent views once the clouds burn off, and the on-site pub restaurant (mains $8-$14) serves traditional bar grub and comfort food – the halibut burger that can't be beat.

Getting There & Around

Pacific Coastal Airlines (☎ 604-273-8666; www .pacific-coastal.com) flights arrive in Port Hardy from Vancouver (from $144, 70 minutes, two daily).

Greyhound Canada (☎ 800-661-8747; www .greyhound.ca) buses arrive from Port McNeil, ($14.60, 45 minutes, daily), Campbell River ($47.05, 3½ hours, daily) and Nanaimo ($71.10, seven hours, daily), among others.

BC Ferries (☎ 888-223-3779, 250-386-3431; www .bcferries.com) services arrive from Prince Rupert (adult/child/vehicle $150/75/350, 15 hours, schedules vary) via the Inside Passage route. The company also operates a summer-only Discovery Coast Passage route (adult/child/vehicle from $150/75/305), which serves Bella Coola (p343) and at times serves isolated McLoughlin Bay, Shearwater, Klemtu and Ocean Falls. Reservations are required.

North Island Transportation (☎ 250-949-6300; nit@island.net; $8) runs a shuttle to/from the ferry terminal via area hotels.

CAPE SCOTT PROVINCIAL PARK & AROUND

It's a whopping 568km from Victoria to the end of the logging road at the trailhead of this remote **park** (www.bcparks.ca) on Vancouver Island's north end. But if you really want to experience the raw, ravishing beauty of British Columbia – especially its unkempt shoreline, mossy rainforest and stunning sandy bays alive with roiling waves and beady-eyed seabirds – this should be your number one destination.

Hike the well-maintained, relatively easy 2.5km **San Josef Bay Trail** and you'll stroll from the shady confines of the forest right onto one of the best beaches in BC; a breathtaking, windswept expanse of roiling waves, tree-lined crags and the kind of caves that could easily harbor ancient smugglers. You can camp ($5) right here on the beach or just admire the passing ospreys before plunging back into the forest.

With several wooded trails to tempt you – most are aimed at well-prepared hikers with plenty of gumption – the forest offers moss-covered yew trees, old-growth cedars that are centuries old and a soft carpet of sun-dappled ferns covering every square inch.

Between the giant slugs, you'll also spot historic plaques showing that the area was once settled by Scandinavian pioneers who arrived here from Europe on a promise from the government of a main road link from down-island. Now mostly reclaimed by the forest, the crumbling shacks of these settlers, who left when the road failed to materialize, can still be seen.

One of the area's shortest trails (2km) in adjoining **Raft Cove Provincial Park** (www.bcparks .ca) brings you to the crescent beach and beautiful lagoons of **Raft Cove**. You're likely to have the entire 1.3km beach to yourself, although the locals also like to surf here.

Hiking further in the region is not for the unprepared. But if you really want to go for it, hit the magnificent **Cape Scott Trail** and the tremendous new **North Coast Trail** (see opposite). If you'd prefer company, consider a guided hike with the friendly folk at **North Island Day Trippers** (☎ 250-956-2411, 800-956-2411; www.islanddaytrippers.com).

On the gravel road out from Cape Scott, make sure you turn off and walk up the signposted trail to **Ronning's Garden** (☎ 250-956-2411; ☼ year-round). One of the area's later Scandinavian settlers, Bernt Ronning lived here until the 1960s, working as a trapper and fisherman, while growing a vast outdoor museum of trees, shrubs and flowers with seeds from around the world. The unlikely garden was reclaimed by the forest after Ronning's death, but determined locals Ron and Julia Moe stripped back the bushes and re-established it in the 1980s. Best known for its monkey-puzzle trees, the garden boasts a plethora of exotic plant life.

VANCOUVER ISLAND

Southern Gulf Islands

While the brash horizon of thrusting mountains permanently barges into the consciousness of BC visitors, it's the siren song of low-lying islands winking in the mist just off the coast that eventually draws you in. If you're craving the kind of break that feels more like a retreat, throw your watch away and sink into the Southern Gulf Islands, strung like green pearls between the mainland and Vancouver Island. Once colonized by hippy dropouts and US draft dodgers, Salt Spring, Galiano, Mayne, Saturna and the North and South Penders are a nature-hugging haven of choice, where even the languid ferry trip to reach them is the visual equivalent of a soothing back rub.

Not all islands are created equal, of course. Comparatively bustling Salt Spring is recommended for a sojourn where you don't have to sacrifice too much on home comforts; Galiano is popular if you need a rustic wood cabin, scenic nooks and outdoor activities; Mayne is good for those who like a side order of pioneer history with their trip; remote Saturna is ideal if you really crave an escape from the tourist trail and an opportunity to commune with your inner tree sprite; and the North and South Penders combine an artsy populace with the islands' best resort, which means you don't have to cut back on those all-important spa treatments.

Wherever you decide to go (and consider the idea of hopping around to more than one island), you'll meet decidedly laid-back locals dedicated to the concept of 'island time.' Expect your heart rate to decelerate to hibernation levels – which will be a shock to the system when you return to Vancouver, or 'Tokyo on speed' as you'll now be calling it.

HIGHLIGHTS

- Hugging a local ale or three under the plum tree at the **Tree House Café** (p221) on Salt Spring, then walking it off with a stroll around Ganges

- Joining the locals for the annual **Lamb Barbeque** (p224) on Saturna

- Hiking up to the peak in **Mt Norman Regional Park** (p222) on South Pender for a magnificent vista of the surrounding islands

- Kayaking the shoreline around **Galiano Island** (p227) and keeping an eye out for whales, eagles and glacier-carved cliffs

- Scoffing fruit and bakery treats at the Saturday **Farmers Market** (p225) in the grounds of the historic Agricultural Hall on Mayne

★ Galiano Island

Tree House Café ★
(Salt Spring Island)

Saturday Farmers
Market
(Mayne Island) ★

Lamb Barbeque ★
(Saturna Island)

★
Mt Norman
Regional Park
(South Pender)

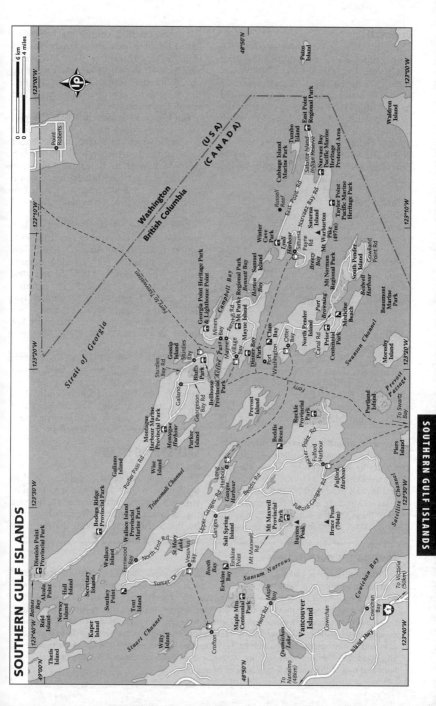

Orientation

The Gulf Islands comprise around 200 mostly uninhabited rocks dotting the Strait of Georgia. But unless you're a Hollywood celebrity with an island to call your own (Robin Williams and Al Pacino are rumored to have little kingdoms here), you'll mostly be visiting the Southern Gulf section, which includes the more easily reachable Salt Spring, Galiano, Mayne, Saturna and the North and South Penders. Regular ferry or floatplane services arrive on each from the mainland or Vancouver Island.

Information

During your languid ferry trip, tap into the local vibe with a free copy of the *Gulf Islands Driftwood* (www.gulfislands.net) newspaper. Also free, the bimonthly *Island Tides* (www.islandtides.com) paper is good for regional news and 'What's On?' listings. The websites of both publications have handy resources for visitors. For additional info, visit www .hellobc.com/vi.

Getting There & Around

Serving the main Southern Gulf Islands, **BC Ferries** (☎ 250-386-3431, 888-223-3779; www.bcferries .com) operates direct routes from Vancouver Island's Swartz Bay terminal to Salt Spring and North Pender. From North Pender, you can connect to Mayne, Galiano or Salt Spring. From Mayne, you can connect to Saturna.

From the mainland, there is a direct service from Tsawwassen to Galiano, which then connects to North Pender. There are also direct weekend services from Tsawwassen to both Mayne (Sunday only) and Salt Spring (Friday to Sunday). For more frequent services to these and the other islands, you will need to travel from Tsawwassen to Swartz

Bay, then board a connecting ferry. For island-hopping, consider a handy SailPass (four/seven consecutive days $165/195), which covers ferry travel around the region on 20 different routes. Visit the BC Ferries website for comprehensive route and scheduling information.

Gulf Islands Water Taxi (☎ 250-537-2510; www .saltspring.com/watertaxi) runs a walk-on boat service between Salt Spring, North Pender and Saturna (one-way/return $15/25, two daily September to June, daily July and August) and between Salt Spring, Galiano and Mayne (one-way/return $15/25, two daily September to June, daily July and August).

Seair Seaplanes (☎ 604-273-8900, 800-447-3247; www.seairseaplanes.com) services run from Vancouver International Airport's South Terminal to Salt Spring ($89, 20 minutes, three daily), North Pender ($93, 20 minutes, three daily), Saturna ($93, 20 minutes, three daily), Mayne ($93, 20 minutes, two daily) and Galiano ($93, 20 minutes, two daily). Similar services are offered by **Salt Spring Air** (☎ 250-537-9880, 877-537-9880; www .saltspringair.com).

Harbour Air (☎ 604-274-1277, 800-665-0212; www .harbour-air.com) floatplanes run from downtown Vancouver to Salt Spring ($95, 30 minutes, two daily) and South Pender ($94, 30 minutes, two daily). The company also runs similar services from Vancouver International Airport's South Terminal.

SALT SPRING ISLAND

pop 10,500

The biggest and most populous island in the Southern Gulf chain, Salt Spring is dotted with organic farms, artisan studios and the occasional winery. Originally settled by the Salish First Nation, it's the most

---

PARKING THE GULF ISLANDS

Canada's 40th national park (and one of its smallest), the long-anticipated **Gulf Islands National Park Reserve** (www.pc.gc.ca/gulfislands) was founded in 2003. Established to protect the fragile, Mediterranean-like ecosystem of a 35 sq km tapestry of reefs, islets and coastal stretches increasingly threatened by maritime traffic and creeping development, the designation aims to be a haven for uncounted species of indigenous flora and fauna. Plants offered respite by the creation of the park include gnarly Garry oaks, copper-trunked arbutus trees, indigo-blue camas lilies and rare phantom orchids. With its 25m intertidal protection zone (Parks Canada manages an additional 175m area from each shore), the new park also protects the habitats of orcas, sea lions and one of the world's largest species of octopus.

accessible island destination for visitors who fancy dipping into the rustic way of life without sacrificing on home comforts. Popular as a weekend retreat for Vancouverites – the wealthiest of them own the largest homes you'll see here – the island is centered on the community of Ganges. This is where you'll find the **VC** (☎ 250-537-5252, 866-216-2936; www.saltspringtourism.com; 121 Lower Ganges Rd, Ganges; ☺ 9am-5pm Jul & Aug, 10am-4pm Apr-Jun, Sep & Oct, 11am-3pm Nov-Mar), with its free maps plus friendly and resourceful staff.

Orientation

Ganges village is Salt Spring's main hub, and Fulford-Ganges Rd, Long Harbour Rd and Vesuvius Bay Rd are the main routes to its three BC Ferries terminals. Unless you have your own boat or arrive by plane, you'll hit the island at Fulford Harbour (via Swartz Bay) on the south; Long Harbour (via Tsawwassen or another Gulf Island) on the east; or Vesuvius Bay (via Vancouver Island's Crofton) on the west. Beaver Point Rd, near Fulford Harbour, leads to Ruckle Provincial Park on Salt Spring's southeast reach, while North End Rd winds past St Mary Lake toward the island's northern tip.

Information

Ganges has banks, while additional ATMs can be found at some island stores.

Fulford Harbour post office (☎ 250-653-4313; 101 Morningside Rd; ☺ 8:45am-5pm Mon, Tue, Thu & Fri, 8:45am-12:15pm Wed & Sat)

Ganges post office (☎ 250-537-2321; 109 Purvis Lane; ☺ 8:30am-5:30pm Mon-Fri, 8:30am-noon Sat)

Salt Spring Books (☎ 250-537-2812; 104 McPhillips Rd, Ganges; internet per min 10c; ☺ 9am-5pm) Check your email courtesy of the friendly folks here.

Sights

Check out the thriving 140-vendor **Saturday Market** (☎ 250-537-4448; www.saltspringmarket.com; Centennial Park; ☺ 8am-4pm Sat Apr-Oct) in Ganges for its luscious island-grown fruit, piquant cheeses (search out the Moonstruck stand) and kaleidoscope of intriguing pottery, jewelry and woodcrafts – all made locally.

You can visit more than 30 of these artisans at work using the handy downloadable studio map from **Salt Spring Studio Tour** (☎ 250-537-9862; www.saltspringstudiotour.com). Among its recommended pit stops are **Lori Davies Textiles** (☎ 250-537-1321; www.loridaviestextiles.com; 296 Mobrae

Ave; ☺ 10am-5pm Thu-Mon May-Sep, reduced off-season), with its rainbow assortment of functional but attractive tableware, and the rustic **Blue Horse Gallery** (☎ 250-537-0754; www.bluehorse.ca; 175 North View Dr; ☺ 10am-5pm Sun-Fri) where angular vases jostle for space with sinewy wooden cat carvings.

If food is more your idea of art, don't miss **Salt Spring Island Cheese** (☎ 250-653-2300; www.saltspringcheese.com; 285 Reynolds Rd; ☺ 10am-5pm May-Sep, reduced off-season), where you can take a self-guided tour of the facilities – check out the cute miniature ponies – then sample up to 10 curdy treats in the tasting room. You can create your own picnic here (bread and olives are also available) and then settle down at a courtyard table to dine in rustic surroundings.

Complement your curds with a tasting and a bottle or two from **Salt Spring Vineyards** (☎ 250-653-9463; www.saltspringvineyards.com; 151 Lee Rd; ☺ 11am-5pm May-Sep, noon-5pm Fri-Sun Oct-Apr), a friendly, family-run operation where it's easy to spend an afternoon. The fruity pinot noir rosé is good but the local favorite is the blackberry port, a sweet dessert wine. If you drink a little too much, consider staying for the night at one of the vineyard's two rustically cozy B&B rooms (per night $150).

Alternatively, have an afternoon doze in the sun at **Ruckle Provincial Park** (☎ 250-539-2115; www.bcparks.ca), a southeast island gem with ragged seashores, sun-kissed farmland and a clutch of smashing copper-colored arbutus trees. The park also houses some original pioneer buildings that recall the 1872 farm established here by Henry Ruckle. There are hiking trails for all skill levels, with Yeo Point making an ideal picnic pit stop. Non-reservable campsites ($15) are also available.

South of Ganges, via Cranberry and Mt Maxwell Rds, **Mt Maxwell Provincial Park** (☎ 250-539-2115; www.bcparks.ca) offers access-ible and quite captivating vistas. The dirt road is steep, so a 4WD is recommended if you're driving. The 588m Baynes Peak climbs far above sea level here, making the Strait of Georgia seem like a bathtub dotted with tiny green islands. It's a great spot to catch a panoramic sunset.

If you're more the beach bum type, head to **Southey Point** at the island's north end and **Beddis Beach** on the east side, noted for their good swimming and sunbathing. Also

---

SALT SPRING'S COSMOPOLITAN PAST

Salt Spring Island is part of the traditional territory of the Cowichan, Saanich and Chemainus First Nations and their presence here dates back several thousand years. Their settlements were located at Ganges, Long Harbour and Fulford Harbour but most of these Natives had left due to sickness by the late 18th century. Later colonial land settlements failed to include Salt Spring but that didn't stop immigrating Europeans from claiming much of the island more than a century later. An even larger group of new Salt Springers were African American settlers who came north in search of improved rights. They were joined by Australians, Hawaiians and a smattering of Japanese fishermen, producing an unusually cosmopolitan turn-of-the-19th-century populace.

---

consider **Erskine Bay** or **Vesuvius Bay** for some vivid sunsets. Beachcombing is popular here and you should keep your eyes peeled for marine wildlife sliding quietly by offshore.

Activities

You can work off any bacchanalian food and wine excess with a family-friendly kayak tour of Ganges Harbour (adult/child $45/40) arranged via **Salt Spring Adventure Co** (☎ 250-537-2764, 877-537-2764; www.saltspring adventures.com; 126 Upper Ganges Rd). It offers a wide range of other short kayak treks and lessons, plus multiday expeditions and eco-van sightseeing tours. You can also rent mountain bikes here (per day $25).

If you're at the Fernwood dock end of the island, it will likely be easier to drop by **Andale Kayaking** (☎ 250-537-0770; 1484 North Beach Rd; rentals half-/full-day $40/60, tours from $60) for rentals, lessons and tours. **Island Escapes** (☎ 250-537-2553, 888-529-2567; 163 Fulford-Ganges Rd) is another Salt Spring kayak operation but it also offers good-value two-hour guided hiking tours (adult/child $30/20) in summer, which visit highlight vistas with a side dish of nature and history narration.

If you prefer others do all the work, bring a picnic and take a leisurely four-hour maritime meander from Ganges aboard the handsome **L'Orenda sailboat** (☎ 250-538-0084; www.haynes.ca/sail; Ganges Harbour; $59).

Sleeping

Ganges Campground (☎ 250-537-1210; www.ganges campground.com; 150 Leisure Lane; campsites $25; ☺ May-Oct; ♿) This grassy campsite is situated in an open meadow and just a short walk from all the village action. You'll soon get to know your neighbors – especially in summer, when their tent will be a couple of feet away from yours. Popular with families, there are showers and flush toilets and some

sites have electricity hookups. There's even a rough-and-ready golf course made from an adjoining field, although you'll have to bring your own balls to use it.

Lakeside Gardens (☎ 250-537-5773; www.lakeside gardensresort.com; 1450 North End Rd; cabanas/cottages $90/145; ☺ Apr-Oct) A rustic, wooded retreat where nature is the main attraction. On St Mary Lake, this tranquil, family-friendly clutch of cottages and cabanas is ideal for some restorative fishing, swimming and boating. The cabanas are basic – think camping in a cabin – with fridges, outdoor barbecues and solar-heated outdoor showers, while the larger cottages have TVs, en suites and full kitchens.

Seabreeze Inne (☎ 250-537-4145, 800-434-4112; www.seabreezeinne.com; 101 Bittancourt Rd; r incl breakfast $115-155; ♿) A short uphill walk from Ganges, this immaculate family-run motel is more than a cut above the average. The hosts are unfailingly friendly and the extras include laundry facilities, free continental breakfast, barbecues and an outdoor hot tub. The rooms (try for one on the 2nd floor to get a tree-fringed sea view) have an old-school look but all are clean and well-maintained, and many have handy kitchenettes – two also have whirlpool tubs.

Wisteria Guest House (☎ 250-537-5899, 888-537-5899; 268 Park Dr; r/cottages incl breakfast $129/159) This comfortable, homestyle B&B with welcoming cats and dogs has six guest rooms (some with shared bathrooms) and a pair of studios with private entrances – plus a small cottage space which has its own compact kitchen facilities and sleeps up to three. The property is surrounded by a rambling, flower-strewn garden that lends an air of tranquillity. An excellent cooked breakfast is served in the large communal lounge where you can also hang out and read on a rainy day.

our pick **Love Shack** (☎ 250-653-0007, 866-341-0007; www.oceansidecottages.com; 521 Isabella Rd; cabins $135) This groovy, retro-loving Fulford Harbour nook is a fantastically cozy home away from home. Step inside the cabin and you'll find a lava lamp, a collection of vintage cameras and a record player with vinyl albums (Abba to Stan Getz). Stuffed with artsy, old-school flourishes, it's the kind of place where donning a velour leisure suit and getting your mojo working suddenly seems like a good idea. The kitchen is well stocked with fruit, spices and organic coffee, while the small bathroom is equally well supplied with Goethe's novels. Despite the cabin's intimate, secluded feel, you'll be spending most of your time on the outstanding deck. Complete with a barbecue and Adirondack chairs, it offers amazing sunset waterfront vistas.

Harbour House (☎ 250-537-5571, 888-799-5571; www.saltspringharbourhouse.com; s/d from $149) With an ideal location a short stroll from the main Ganges shops and eateries, this property looks like a humdrum motel from the outside. But inside, you'll find some surprisingly spacious rooms, most with large balconies and many overlooking the water. The standard quarters are bright and comfortable while the top-bracket rooms have fireplaces and whirlpool tubs that you have to climb up to get into. There's an on-site pub-style restaurant (go for Monday night's $5 beer-and-cheeseburger deal).

Eating & Drinking

Barb's Buns (☎ 250-537-4491; 121 McPhillips Ave; mains $6-9; ☻ 7am-5pm Mon-Sat) Hearty wholesome treats are the menu mainstays here, with heaping pizza slices, made-from-scratch soups and bulging sandwiches that draw the lunch crowd, many of them grateful vegetarians. Others repeatedly fail to resist the mid-afternoon lure of cookies, cakes and, of course, Barb's lovely buns. Organic coffee is *de rigueur* and the locals spend more than their fair share of time hanging out and gossiping.

our pick **Tree House Café** (☎ 250-537-5379; 106 Purvis Lane; mains $8-14; ☻ 8am-9pm Mon-Fri, 9am-9pm Sat & Sun May-Sep, 8am-3pm Oct-Apr) A magical outdoor café (it's actually more like a restaurant) in the heart of Ganges, you'll be sitting outside in the shade of a plum tree, rubbing shoulders with chatty Salt Springers

chilling out after a hard day. This is the place to slow down, join the laid-back vibe and realize exactly why the rat race is best avoided. Slug a bottle or two of hoppy Salt Spring Pale Ale to get you in the mood, then peruse a wholesome menu of comfort pastas, Mexican specialties and gourmet burgers that are a million miles from Big Macs – the teriyaki salmon burger is especially recommended. Almost every summer evening there's live music, making this an idyllic spot to kick back while the sunlight slowly fades.

Raven Street Market Café (☎ 250-537-2273; 321 Fernwood Rd; mains $9-17; ☻ noon-5pm Mon, noon-8pm Tue-Sun) A favorite haunt of north island locals, this wood-lined neighborhood eatery occupies a pioneer building that was originally the island's first store. The menu offers plenty of comfort nosh with a hint of gourmet flair. Adventurous pizzas include herbed lamb and artichoke pesto while the smashing seafood and sausage gumbo is brimming with mussels, tiger prawns and chorizo sausage.

Moby's Pub (☎ 250-537-5559; 124 Upper Ganges Rd; mains $10-19; ☻ 11am-midnight Sun-Thu, 11am-1am Fri & Sat) Located on the shorefront, this lively, pretence-free locals' hangout offers harbor views and a hearty classic pub menu – this is the place for fish and chips or a grilled salmon burger, washed down with plenty of ice-cold beer. There's live music of the grungy blues or cover band variety on most weekends, and if you imbibe too much on a Saturday night, come back for a greasy Sunday brunch and you'll feel much better.

Oystercatcher Seafood Bar & Grill (☎ 250-537-5041; 100 Manson Rd; mains $10-30; ☻ 10am-dusk) The waterfront views from the two patios at this casual, long-established favorite are grand, but the dining is what it's all about. Fresh, regionally caught seafood is the specialty, with delectable fresh-shucked oysters and wild salmon dishes particularly popular. It also serves lamb and steak dishes (and beer) for those who are not fish fans.

Hastings House (☎ 250-537-2362; 160 Upper Ganges Rd; mains $24-35; ☻ 5-11pm) One of the island's two celebrated splurge-worthy options, Hastings House combines a romantic ambience in a historic setting with a seasonally changing menu. The dishes fuse the bounty of the region with some knowing international flourishes. This is the place to dip into Salt Spring Island lamb, often served with blue cheese polenta, or oven-baked sablefish with mushroom risotto. Slow down and savor and then plan to come back for the popular Sunday brunch.

Restaurant House Piccolo (☎ 250-537-1844; 108 Hereford Ave; mains $27-35; ☒ 5-11pm) Fusing Scandinavian influences with locally sourced ingredients, this elegant but tiny white-tableclothed eatery is well worth the extra bucks. With an intimate, heritage dining room (plus a small patio), dishes range from exquisite duck, beef and lamb mains (they eat vegetarians here, too) to the highly recommended seafood creations – if scallops are on the menu, snap 'em up. It also has one of the best wine lists on Salt Spring. Reservations recommended.

Getting There & Around
BC Ferries, Gulf Islands Water Taxi, Seair Seaplanes, Salt Spring Air and Harbour Air all offer services to Salt Spring (p218). The island's three ferry docks are located at Long Harbour, Fulford Harbour and Vesuvius Bay. Water taxis and floatplanes arrive in Ganges Harbour.

If you don't have your own car, **Salt Spring Island Transit** (www.busonline.ca; adult/under-5 $2/free) runs a five-route mini shuttle service around the island, connecting to all three ferry docks. Bus 4 runs from Long Harbour to Ganges. Alternatively, **Amber Taxi Co** (☎ 250-537-3277) provides a local cab service.

NORTH & SOUTH PENDER ISLANDS
pop 2,400

Once joined by a sandy isthmus and still re-ferred to in the singular, the North and South Penders are far quieter than Salt Spring and attract those looking for more of a retreat approach to their vacation. With pioneer farms, old-time orchards and almost 40 coves and beaches, the Penders – now linked by a single-lane bridge – are a good spot for rustic-loving bikers and hikers. North Pender houses the majority of the locals.

Orientation & Information
The ferry terminal is at North Pender's Otter Bay. With no dedicated town hub, the Driftwood Centre mall – 2.5km away (just follow all the cars) – is where locals flock for banking, groceries, liquor supplies and a post office. This is also the location

of the island's only gas station. There are additional smaller businesses at Port Washington, Hope Bay and several little marinas. Drop by the self-service VC stand in the mall – it's lined with flyers and has a good free map for visitors. In summer, the local Lions Club also runs a volunteer **info centre** (2332 Otter Bay Rd, North Pender; ☒ 9am-5pm Thu-Sun May & Jun, 9am-5pm Jul & Aug) just up the road from the ferry terminal. Alternatively, visit www.penderislandchamber.com for listings and resources.

Sights & Activities
There's a regular Saturday-morning **Farmers Market** (☒ Apr-Nov 9:30am-1pm) in the community hall where you'll find local organic produce, quirky arts and crafts and a plethora of tempting baked goods. The **hall** (☎ 250-629-3669; www.penderislands.org; 4418 Bedwell Harbour Rd, North Pender), fronted by three magnificently carved First Nations welcome poles, is the locals' main social hangout and it hosts movie nights, music shows and special events – check the website to see what's coming up.

Dozens of artists call Pender home and you can chat with them in their galleries and studios by downloading a pair of free maps from **Pender Creatives** (www.pendercreatives.com) that reveal exactly where they're all located. Not surprisingly most are on North Pender.

Alternatively, get back to nature with some sandy treks at **Medicine Beach** and **Clam Bay** on North Pender or **Gowlland Point** on the east coast of South Pender. Near the channel between the two islands, South Pender's **Mortimer Spit** is rarely crowded but offers one of the best beaches around.

Just over the bridge to South Pender is **Mt Norman Regional Park**. The hike up its namesake peak (255m) rewards you with grand views of the San Juan and Gulf Islands. The trail can be accessed via Ainslie Point Rd (1km hike) or Canal Rd (2.5km hike). Get out your binoculars to spot smiling Salt Spring Islanders waving at you from their restaurant patios.

You can hit the water with a paddle (and hopefully a boat) with the friendly folk at **Pender Island Kayak Adventures** (☎ 250-629-6939, 877-683-1746; www.kayakpenderisland.com; Otter Bay Marina; tours adult/child from $45/30). If you prefer recreation of the bottled variety, consider a tasting at **Morning Bay Vineyard** (☎ 250-629-8351; www.morningbay.ca; 6621 Harbour Hill Dr, North Pender; ☷ 10am-5pm Wed-Sun), a handsome post-and-beam-built winery where the grapes are grown on a steep 20-step terrace. The tasty Gewurztraminer-Riesling blend is light and crisp.

Sleeping

Prior Centennial Park (☎ 604-689-9025, 800-689-9025; www.discovercamping.ca; North Pender; campsites $15; ☷ mid-May–mid-Oct) Located 6km southeast of the ferry terminal, this former provincial park (it's now part of the Gulf Islands National Park Reserve) is a good base from which to explore North Pender. Nestled among alder and cedar trees, it's within walking distance of two beaches and is popular with kayakers. The fairly basic facilities include a cold water pump, pit toilets and picnic tables.

Inn on Pender Island (☎ 250-629-3353, 800-550-0172; www.innonpender.com; 4709 Canal Rd, North Pender; r/cabins $99/149) A rustic lodge with motel-style rooms and a couple of small, wood-lined cabins, you'll be enveloped by verdant woodland here, which explains the frequent appearance of wandering deer. The lodge rooms are spick-and-span and share an outdoor hot tub, but the lovely, timber-lined waterfront cabins are recommended: they have barrel-vaulted ceilings, full kitchens and little porches out front with their own swings. There's also an on-site restaurant.

Delia's Shangri-La Oceanfront B&B (☎ 250-629-3808, 877-629-2800; www.penderislandshangrila.com; 5909 Pirate's Rd, North Pender; d from $165) It's all about escaping from the city and relaxing at this three-unit waterfront property where each room has its own outdoor hot tub for lying back and drinking in the sunset through the trees. You'll have your own private entrance as well as pampering extras like thick robes, large individual decks and a sumptuous breakfast. Our fave room is the Lost in Space suite where the walls are painted with a glowing galaxy theme.

Arcadia by the Sea (☎ 250-629-3221, 877-470-8439; www.arcadiabythesea.com; 1329 MacKinnon Rd, North Pender; cottages $185; ☷ mid-May–Sep; ☷) Less than 1km from the ferry terminal, this charming, adult-oriented sleepover is an idyllic island retreat. Its three self-contained cottages are bright and pastel-colored – little

Rose Cottage is our favorite – and each includes a kitchen and the kind of relaxing deck you'll want to spend your day on. Not content to end its facilities with a hot tub, the Arcadia also has a tennis court, a heated outdoor pool and a staircase leading to a sea-level deck.

ourpick Poet's Cove Resort & Spa (☎ 250-629-2100, 888-512-7638; www.poetscove.com; 9801 Spalding Rd, South Pender; lodges from $349; ☷) What it lacks in quantity, South Pender makes up for in quality at this luxurious 46-room Bedwell Harbour resort. Elegant lodge rooms feature arts and crafts flourishes and patios overlooking the water – the perfect spot to sip a glass of wine at the end of a hard day of doing not very much. At the top end, the sumptuous villas and cottages come with fireplaces, huge bathrooms and home theater systems. There's the celebrated on-site Aurora Restaurant (see p224) and you can work off your dinner in the swimming pool the next morning. If you're looking to be a bit more active, the resort offers additional eco-tours, fishing excursions and kayak treks. There's even a full-treatment spa, complete with that all-important steam cave.

Eating

Pender Island Bakery Café (☎ 250-629-6453; Driftwood Centre, 1105 Stanley Point Dr, North Pender; mains $6-16; ☷ 7:30am-5pm Mon-Fri, 8am-5pm Sat, 10am-4pm Sun) The locals' fave coffeehouse, there's much more to this chatty nook than regular joe. For a start, the java is organic, as are many of the bakery treats, including some giant cinnamon buns that will have you wrestling an islander for the last one. Gourmet pizzas are a highlight – the Gulf Islander (smoked oysters, anchovies, spinach and three cheeses) is best – while heartier fare includes spinach and pine nut pie and bulging seafood lasagne.

Hope Bay Café (☎ 250-629-6668; 4301 Bedwell Harbour Rd, North Pender; mains $16-24; ☷ 11am-3pm & 5-8pm Wed-Sun) Seafood is a specialty of the house (closely followed by the sterling views across Plumper Sound) at this laid-back, bistro-like spot a few minutes from the Otter Bay ferry dock. The fish and chips are predictably good but dig deeper into the menu for less-expected treats like stuffed pork shoulder, herb-crusted wild BC salmon and the excellent bouillabaisse that's brimming with mussels, scallops, salmon and cod.

Aurora Restaurant (☎ 250-629-2100; 9801 Spalding Rd, Poet's Cove Resort & Spa, South Pender; mains $18-34; ⊗ 8am-10pm) Regional and seasonal are the keywords on the ever-changing menu at the islands' most sophisticated restaurant, part of the luxe Poet's Cove Resort. Allow yourself to be tempted by a Salt Spring goat cheese tart starter but save room for main dishes like the local seafood medley of crab, scallops and mussels. Dinner reservations are highly recommended, but if you can't get a table head to the alternative Syrens Bistro (open 11:30am to 9pm), the resort's casual lounge bar.

Getting There & Around

BC Ferries, Gulf Islands Water Taxi, Seair Seaplanes, Salt Spring Air and Harbour Air all offer services to North and/or South Pender (p218). Ferries arrive in North Pender's Otter Bay, as do water taxis. Most floatplanes arrive at North Pender's Port Washington.

Having a car isn't crucial here since many accommodations will pick you up from the ferry. You can also catch a cab from **Pender Island Taxi** (☎ 250-629-3555).

SATURNA ISLAND

pop 350

Small and suffused with tranquillity, Saturna is a lovely nature retreat that's remote enough to deter casual visitors. Almost half the island, laced with curving bays, stunning rock bluffs and towering arbutus trees, is part of the Gulf Islands National Park Reserve (see the boxed text p218) and the only crowds you're likely to come across are the feral goats that have called this their munchable home for decades. If you've had enough of civilization, this is the place to be.

Orientation & Information

Download a visitor map from the website of the **Saturna Island Tourism Association** (www .saturatourism.com). The site also lists restaurant and accommodations options. The **post office** is in the **General Store** (☎ 250-539-2936; 101 Narvaez Bay Rd; ⊗ 9am-6pm Mon-Sat, 9:30am-5pm Sun), where you can pick up organic groceries, baked goods and booze. Get some cash before you come, though – there are no ATMs on Saturna. The ferry docks at Lyall Harbour on the west of the island.

ISLAND DINING TOP PICKS

- Hastings House, Salt Spring (p221)
- Hope Bay Café, North Pender (p223)
- La Berengerie, Galiano (p228)
- Tree House Café, Salt Spring (p221)
- Wild Fennel Restaurant, Mayne (p226)

Sights & Activities

On Saturna's northwest corner, **Winter Cove Park** has a white-sand beach that's popular for swimming, boating and fishing. If you're here for Canada Day (July 1), you should also partake of the island's main annual event in the adjoining Hunter Field. This communal **Lamb Barbeque** (☎ 250-539-2452; www.saturnalambbarbeque.com; food ticket adult/child $20/10), complete with live music, sack races, a beer garden and a meat-lovers feast, is centered on a pagan fire pit surrounded by dozens of staked-out, slow-roasting sheep.

Walk off your overindulgence the next day with a hike up **Mt Warburton Pike** (497m) where you'll spot wild goats plus soaring eagles and falcons. You'll also enjoy some spectacular panoramic views of the surrounding islands: focus your binoculars and you might catch an orca or two swimming quietly past along the coast.

Whales migrating in this region typically travel between the Gulf and San Juan Islands. Since Saturna is the easternmost of the Gulf Islands – it's also the closest one to the US – some of the best whale-watching can be seen from the shores of **East Point Regional Park** without even boarding a boat.

If you insist on exercising your sea legs, drop into **Saturna Sea Kayaking** (☎ 250-539-5553; www.saturnaseakayaking.com; 121 Boot Cove Rd; rentals 4/8hr from $35/50, tours from $50), which offers tours and rentals, along with friendly advice about paddling the region.

Wine fans can partake of tastings and tours at **Saturna Island Winery** (☎ 250-539-5139, 877-918-3388; www.saturnavineyards.com; 8 Quarry Rd; ⊗ 11:30am-4:30pm), which also has an on-site **bistro** (⊗ lunch May-Oct).

Sleeping & Eating

our pick Breezy Bay B&B (☎ 250-539-5957; www .saturnacan.net/breezy; 131 Payne Rd; d $95) A characterful 1890s farmhouse property with its own private beach and an undeniably warm welcome, this cheerfully rustic sleepover is still a working farm. The main house has wooden floors, stone fireplaces and even an old dark-wood library (lined with an eclectic array of tomes), while the property's three creaky-floored rooms – complete with a shared bathroom – are fairly basic but clean and comfortable. Breakfast is mostly organic and served in a stone-and-window-lined room overlooking a rambling garden.

Saturna Lodge (☎ 250-539-2254, 866-539-2254; www.saturna.ca; 130 Payne Rd; d incl breakfast $130-170; 🔥) Unpretentious charm is the approach at this elegant six-room country inn sleepover, which combines landscaped gardens with close proximity to the waterfront. Non-residents can also stop in for dinner in the restaurant (mains $20 to 25), where regional delicacies like Opal Valley lamb and Queen Charlotte Islands halibut (highly recommended) are offered.

East Point Ocean Cottages (☎ 250-539-9809, 877-762-2073; www.eastpointresort.com; 753 Tumbo Channel Rd; cabins $165; 🕑 Mar-Nov) With no campgrounds on Saturna, this string of six forested cabins is a good alternative. Don't be put off by the spooky, shacklike exteriors: inside most are cosy and well-maintained, with full kitchens. The private sandy beach is ideal for watching passing bird and marine life and there are hiking trails through the nearby woods. Check for summertime minimum stay requirements.

Adjoining the General Store (where you can also pick up picnic items) the **Saturna Café** (☎ 250-539-2936; 101 Narvaez Bay Rd; mains $6-14; 🕑 11:30am-8pm) is all about wholesome, no-nonsense nosh where the servers stop to chat and recommend their favorites from the fresh, homestyle menu. Alternatively, overlooking Plumper Sound, the **Lighthouse Pub** (☎ 250-539-5725; 102 East Point Rd; mains $8-12; 🕑 11:30am-10pm) is a chatty spot for bar grub and BC beers where you can challenge the locals to a game of darts.

Getting There & Around
BC Ferries, Gulf Islands Water Taxi, Seair Seaplanes and Salt Spring Air all offer services to Saturna (p218). Ferries and water taxis arrive at Lyall Harbour, as do floatplane services.

You don't absolutely require a car on Saturna, since some lodgings are near the ferry dock and most will pick you up when you arrive. There are no taxis here.

MAYNE ISLAND
pop 900

A pioneer-era pit stop for gold rush miners en route from the US to the Cariboo – they uncharitably nicknamed it 'Little Hell' – tiny Mayne is arguably the most historic Southern Gulf Island. Although it's long past its importance as a commercial hub, there are several historic reminders of the good ol' days (especially the handsome St Mary Magdalene Church and the heritage Agricultural Hall) as well as a colorful latter-day population of resident writers, musicians and painters.

Orientation & Information
Island-bound ferries dock at Village Bay (which doesn't have a village) while the community's main hub is at Miners Bay complete with its clutch of services, including a post office, a bookstore and public phones. The **library** (☎ 250-539-2597; 🕑 11am-3pm Wed, Fri & Sat) here also offers free internet access. Visit the website of the **chamber of commerce** (www.mayneislandchamber.ca) for accommodations and restaurant listings, as well as a downloadable *Welcome to Mayne Island* map that plots area artists, stores and services. Stuff some dosh in your wallet before you come over – Mayne has no ATMs.

Sights & Activities
Make sure you time your visit for the colorful Saturday **Farmers Market** (🕑 10am-1pm Jul-early Oct) in the grounds of the gable-roofed **Agricultural Hall**, where you'll be able to sample local produce, bakery treats and island arts and crafts. The nearby **Plumper Pass Lock-up** (☎ 250-539-5286; 🕑 11am-3pm Fri-Mon late Jun–early Sep) is also worth a look: originally a 19th-century jailhouse, it's now a little museum.

Among the most visit-worthy galleries and artisan studios on the island is **Mayne Island Glass Foundry** (☎ 250-539-2002; www.mayneislandglass.com; 🕑 10am-5pm Jun-Sep, reduced hours off-season), where recycled glass is used to fashion new jewelry and ornaments – pick up a cool green-glass slug for the road.

The south shore's **Dinner Bay Park** has a lovely sandy beach, as well as a **Japanese Garden**. Built by locals to commemorate early-20th-century Japanese residents, it's immaculately landscaped and lit up with fairy lights at Christmas.

At the island's north end, **Georgina Point Heritage Park** is home to a lighthouse that was established in 1885 and staffed until 1997. The lighthouse and its keeper's house are still there and it's an invigorating place to be when the waves are pounding the shore. There's a small beach with lots of explorable tidal pools.

For paddlers and peddlers, **Mayne Island Kayaking** (☎ 250-539-2463, 877-535-2424; www.kayak mayneisland.com; 563 Arbutus Dr; kayak rentals 2/8hr from $28/48, bike rentals 4/8hr $18/25) offers boats and bikes – ideal for launching yourself on a picnic trek around the island. It's part of the Blue Vista Resort.

Sleeping & Eating

Mayne Island Eco-Camping (☎ 250-539-2667; www .mayneisle.com; 359 Maple Dr; campsite per person $12; ♿) With oceanfront and forested sites, this nature-hugging campground in Miners Bay includes an outdoor hot water 'tree shower' where you can bare it all among the branches. Many campers arrive here via kayak at the adjacent pebbly beach (also welcome are traveling kayakers who just want to drop in for a shower). Rentals are available for those inspired to hit the waves.

Cobworks (☎ 250-386-7790; www.cobworks.com; 640 Horton Bay Rd; cottages $80; ☽ Jun-Sep) A cross between Fred Flintstone's house and a hobbit's summer quarters, this rustic 'cob' cottage is handmade from sand, clay and straw and has a shaggy, grass-covered roof. Inside, you'll find curved, cavelike walls with tree-branch counters and rustic furnishings, plus a kitchen and fireplace. A self-contained holiday let, the idea is to showcase the cheap-as-chips construction method pioneered by its owners. Book ahead.

Blue Vista Resort (☎ 250-539-2463, 877-535-2424; www.bluevistaresort.com; 536 Arbutus Dr; cabins from $99) About 5km from the ferry terminal near Bennett Bay, this restorative spot secreted in the trees includes eight cabins, some of them duplexes and some of them stand-alones. All are comfortable (some are more basic than others) and each has a balcony and full kitchen. Specializing in outdoor pursuits, you can rent bikes here or partake of kayak rentals, tours and lessons. Family-friendly.

Fairview Farm B&B (☎ 250-539-5582, 866-539-5582; www.fairviewonmayne.com; 601 Bell Bay Rd; d $125-135) A magnificent yellow-painted clapboard farmstead built in 1898, two of the rooms here have recently been transformed into bright and sunny en suite guest quarters – we like the Blue Room best, with its patio doors that open onto a terrace licked by summer breezes. The perfect tranquillity break from the city, there's a beach just a few steps away through the trees – expect to be accompanied by a wandering deer or two. Minimum two-night stay.

Sunny Mayne Bakery Café (☎ 250-539-2323; Village Bay Rd; mains $4-8; ☽ 7am-5pm Mon-Sat, 8am-4pm Sun) This bright and welcoming family-run joint is opens early for breakfast and also offers bakery treats, hearty soups, croissant sandwiches and some great herb-crusted pizzas. If it's sunny, sit outside with a large ice-cream cone and watch the world go by – we can guarantee it won't be moving too fast.

Wild Fennel Restaurant (☎ 250-539-5987; 574 Fernhill Rd; mains $16-20; ☽ 11:30am-9pm Wed-Sun) A warm, cozy dining spot specializing in seasonal fresh ingredients (the menu changes frequently), Wild Fennel is mostly about taste-tripping simply prepared but exquisite local seafood – try the Crab Three Ways (served in salad, bisque and lollipop form). If you're not a seafood fan, the bison burger served with banana pepper chutney is also recommended. There's a good BC-focused wine list too.

Getting There & Around

BC Ferries, Gulf Islands Water Taxi, Seair Seaplanes and Salt Spring Air all offer services to Mayne (p218). Ferries and water taxis arrive at Village Bay. Floatplanes arrive in Miners Bay.

Many accommodations offer guest bikes but if you're not the pedalling type, contact **MIDAS Taxi Company** (☎ 250-539-3132).

GALIANO ISLAND
pop 1100

A namesake reminder of Spain's 18th-century regional explorations (Galiano was a captain of one of the ships that first charted this area), this is the second most popular Southern Gulf Island for visitors (after Salt Spring). They're lured to the ribbon-like landmass for the clutch of chatty businesses at the island's ferry dock area and the rustic, progressively nature-hugging appeal the further up island you travel. Supporting the widest ecological diversity of all the Gulf Islands, Galiano offers activities for visiting marine enthusiasts and peace-craving landlubbers alike.

Orientation & Information
The island's main businesses and services are located around the Sturdies Bay ferry dock, including a handy post office and a bookstore that is lined with local author works and also has a fine travel section. **Galiano Chamber of Commerce** (☎ 250-539-2233; www.galianoisland.com) operates a volunteer-run **Visitor Info Booth** (☎ 250-539-2507; 2590 Sturdies Rd); it's to the right as you leave the ferry. The booth is open for several hours a day in July and August and also for 10 minutes or so whenever a ferry arrives during the rest of the year. Check the chamber's website for maps and resources. There are no banks on the island but there's an ATM at the garage near the dock.

Sights & Activities
Check out the sheltered peninsula of **Montague Harbour Marine Provincial Park** (☎ 250-539-2115; www.bcparks.ca) for trails to seashell-strewn beaches, tree-fringed meadows and a cliff carved by glaciers (it's also a great sunset-viewing spot). Renowned for its eagle, loon and cormorant birdlife, **Bodega Ridge Provincial Park** (☎ 250-539-2115; www.bcparks.ca) contains some spectacular stop-off viewpoints, while **Bluffs Park** boasts great views of Active Pass, along with 5km of hiking trails. Known for its abundant and colorful birdlife, tiny **Bellhouse Provincial Park** (☎ 250-539-2115; www.bcparks.ca), the island's easternmost point, also looks over Active Pass. If you're a ferry spotter, this is the promontory from which to catch a few sailing past.

For many, Galiano is best viewed from offshore, and the protected waters of Trincomali Channel are a good spot for kayakers of the gentle persuasion. If you like your water a little rougher, the busier waters of Active Pass may be more your style. **Gulf Island Kayaking** (☎ 250-539-2442; www.galianoisland.com; Montague Marina; rentals 3hr/day from $32/75, tours $55-85) offers rentals and guided tours.

For dive fans, Alcala Point with its wolf eels, Baines Bay with its anemone walls, and the sunken Point Grey tugboat – plus the ever-present possibility of meeting a giant Pacific octopus – make Galiano a popular spot for those with their own scuba gear.

Alternatively, you can explore the island on terra firma with a bike from **Galiano Bicycle** (☎ 250-539-9906; 36 Burrill Rd; 4hr/day $25/35). It's just a five-minute walk from the ferry dock. Try a less taxing two-wheeled trek with a moped rental from **Galiano Adventures** (☎ 250-539-3443, 877-303-3546; www.galianoadventures.com; 300 Sticks Allison Rd; rental 3hr/day from $18/79; ☒ May-Sep). Located in Montague Harbour, it can also rent you a boat (per hour from $36) if you want to get back out on the water.

Sleeping
Montague Harbour Marine Provincial Park (☎ 604-689-9025, 800-689-9025; www.discovercamping.ca; campsites $19) With 25 drive-in and 15 walk-in sites, this is a popular campground with outdoor types, many of whom are kayaking or biking their way around the region. Fringed with old-growth forest, the facilities here are basic (there are no showers but there are pit toilets, cold-water taps and fire pits) and there's an excellent 'floating nature house' offering summertime interpretive programs.

Treehouse B&B (☎ 250-539-5239; www.cliffhousecottages.com; d incl breakfast $122-142) Tucked into woodland, this intimate open-plan cabin is ideal for a romantic break. With hardwood floors and a wood stove, you'll be tempted to spend most of your time indoors. But once you hit the deck, there will be no turning back. Since there's only a small kitchenette inside, you'll likely do most of your cooking at the barbecue here, with waterfront views to keep you company. There's also an unusual grass-roofed sauna on site if you need to chill.

ourpick Bodega Ridge (☎ 250-539-2677, 877-604-2677; www.bodegaridge.com; 120 Manastee Rd; d $200; ☒) The perfect place to catch your breath and sink into languid island time, this tranquil north end nest of log cabins hugs the hillside in a wooded area of arbutus trees and grassy slopes. The seven fully equipped, two-story homes (each with three bedrooms) are furnished in rustic country fashion, with full kitchens, glass-fronted wood stoves (firewood is freely available) and private porches – ask for a barbecue and one will be wheeled over. Mountain-bike rentals are also offered for the activity-inclined: there are hiking and biking trails nearby and the friendly owners are ever-ready with helpful suggestions.

Galiano Oceanfront Inn & Spa (☎ 250-539-3388, 877-530-3939; www.galianoinn.com; 134 Madrona Dr; r from $249; ⏾) Close to the ferry dock, this immaculate Tuscan-style villa has 20 elegant rooms, each with a fireplace and romantic oceanfront terrace. The ambience is grown-up, sophisticated and soothing, and the amenities include a spa where you can choose outdoor flower garden treatments. The on-site Atrevida Restaurant (mains $18 to $29) is the island's West-Coast-flavored fine-dining highlight and also has an inspiring wine list (we also like the signature blackberry martinis).

Eating & Drinking

Daystar Market Café (☎ 250-539-2505; 96 Georgeson Bay Rd; mains $4-10; ⏾ 10am-5pm Mon-Fri, 9am-6pm Sat, 9am-5pm Sun) Where the locals hang out, this funky little spot is an ideal mid-morning pit stop (gotta love those chunky cranberry muffins). The hearty salads, thick sandwiches and made-from-scratch soups, mostly organic, will likely entice you back for lunch and the organic juices and smoothies will bring you back for breakfast the next day. Why not just move in?

Harbour Grill Restaurant (☎ 250-539-5733; Montague Harbour; mains $8-12; ⏾ 8am-3pm) A laid-back breakfast and lunch spot with a winning porch that hangs over the marina (keep your eyes peeled for visiting birdlife), this cheery

eatery serves well-prepared homestyle salads and sandwiches (the lamb burger is a favorite). Whatever you decide on, accompany it with a piping bowl of clam chowder and finish off with an ice-cream cone and a wander along the waterfront.

Hummingbird Pub (☎ 250-539-5472; 47 Sturdies Bay Rd; mains $8-12; ⏾ 11am-midnight Sun-Thu, 11am-1am Fri & Sat) Where locals and visitors sup together (and even play pool), the Hummingbird's huge log columns and chatty outdoor deck lend this neighborhood joint a comfortable, down-to-earth feel. The menu is full of the usual bar classics and the pub runs a May to September shuttle bus to and from Montague Harbour, so feel free to drink as much as you like.

La Berengerie (☎ 250-539-5392; 2806 Montague Rd; mains $14-24; ⏾ 5-11pm) Tucked along a winding, tree-lined drive in a creaky shack that looks like it's seen better days, La Berengerie is a culinary adventure that feels like dining in the depths of the French countryside. Overseen by the formidable but twinkle-eyed Huguette Benger, who moved here from Avignon more than 20 years ago, the oft-changing menu fuses rustic continental bistro approaches with fresh and distinctive local ingredients. Come for a long evening and sit outside on the hearth-warmed patio.

Getting There & Around

BC Ferries, Gulf Islands Water Taxi, Seair Seaplanes and Salt Spring Air all offer services to Galiano (p218). Ferries and water taxis arrive at Sturdies Bay. Floatplanes arrive at Montague Harbour.

Fraser-Thompson Region

Weaving inland and eastwards from the BC coastline (via Hwy 1 or the more leisurely Hwy 7), the landscape changes dramatically from the lush oceanfront vistas you've quickly become used to. You'll arrive first in the expansive farmlands of the Fraser Valley, which spreads like a patterned green carpet from the seemingly impenetrable wall of mountains that dominates the horizon. The friendly old communities here have fed the appetites of Metro Vancouverites for decades and it's an ideal destination for those who fancy a spot of languid taste-tripping, with a side dish of pioneer history.

Driving deeper into the mountains, you'll come to the jaw-dropping Fraser Canyon region, an ever-changing kaleidoscope of fierce rivers (white-water rafting fans take note) and uncompromising jagged peaks that look like a row of broken teeth in an old prospector's smile. The illusion is particularly apt since this is where legions of dusty-faced gold rushers prospected their way through BC, looking for nuggets that, for most, stubbornly failed to materialize. You can catch a glimpse of their lives (and pan for gold yourself) in old-school pioneer towns like Lytton and Lillooet.

Traveling further eastwards, you'll soon enter the Thompson Valley (named after the other giant river that flows through here) and eventually roll into the mountain city of Kamloops. A great base from which to explore the craggy outdoors, it's a short hop from here to the lake-studded Shuswap region as well as the popular Sun Peaks area. The gabled village and perfect ski slopes of Sun Peaks, the resort town beloved of BC residents, are a favored alternative to Whistler.

HIGHLIGHTS

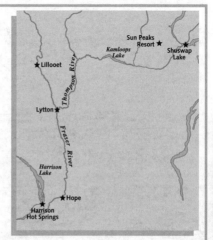

- Hitting the slopes (with some skis) at wintertime **Sun Peaks Resort** (p241) and coming back in summer for some hiking

- Splashing about on a white-water rafting expedition around **Lytton** (p236), where the Fraser and Thompson Rivers collide

- Jumping into the public pool at **Harrison Hot Springs** (p231) to take the warm mineral waters

- Moseying around the old pioneer buildings of **Lillooet's Golden Mile** (p238) and pretending to be a prospector

- Drifting aboard a houseboat on **Shuswap Lake** (p242) and forgetting what day it is

THE FRASER CANYON & THOMPSON VALLEY

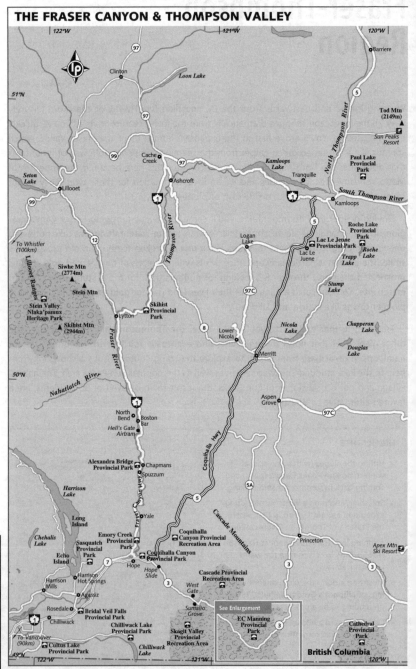

FRASER-THOMPSON REGION

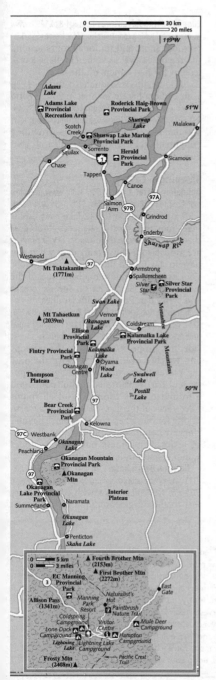

FRASER CANYON

Driving eastwards from Vancouver, there are two main routes for those aiming at the Fraser region and beyond. Hwy 1 is ideal if you're planning to whiz through at speed and make it to the Rockies as fast as you can, but the more sedate Hwy 7 is recommended if you want to experience the Fraser Valley properly. Tracing the north side of the Fraser River, it twists through pioneer-era farmland settlements like Mission, Harrison Mills, Agassiz and Harrison Hot Springs before delivering you to the doorstep of mountain-shaded Hope. From here, you can hook up with Hwy 1 and drive north into the rugged grandeur of the imposing Fraser Canyon and the characterful old gold rush communities of Yale, Lytton and Lillooet. For traveler resources, peruse the website of **Vancouver Coast & Mountains** (www.vcmbc.com). For info on the **Hwy 7 driving route**, visit www.scenic7bc.com.

HARRISON HOT SPRINGS & AROUND
pop 1600

Winding east through the Fraser Valley on Hwy 7 past Mission, with the ever-present mountains fringing the horizon, you'll encounter several small farming communities and a fertile expanse of agricultural crops and grassy meadows unfolding from either side of the road. Keep your eyes peeled and pull over for produce stands and farm stops along the way. Eventually – about 130km from Vancouver – you'll reach one of the region's most popular weekend destinations. Harrison is where Victorian-era Vancouverites used to flock en masse to promenade along the lake's sandy shore and enjoy the closest hot springs to the city. Drop into the **VC** (☎ 604-796-5581; www.tourism harrison.com; 499 Hot Springs Rd; ✆ 9am-5pm May-Sep, 10am-5pm Thu-Sat Oct-Apr) on your way into town for tips on exploring the region.

Sights & Activities

Before you reach Harrison Hot Springs, Hwy 7 will first deliver you to the small hamlet of Harrison Mills. The highlight here is the smashing **Kilby Historic Site** (☎ 604-796-9576; www.kilby.ca; 215 Kilby Rd, Harrison Mills; adult /child $9/7; ✆ 11am-5pm mid-May–early Sep, 11am-4pm Thu-Mon mid-Sep–Nov and Apr–mid-May) where you can experience a colorful slice of pioneer life. Centered around a clapboard 1920s General Store Museum, you'll find talkative costumed interpreters wandering a working heritage farm, complete with livestock, orchards, nature trails and a homestyle restaurant (try a slice of bulging fruit pie).

Back on Hwy 7, next you'll come to the small town of Agassiz. Consider stopping here for a short wander around the **Agassiz-Harrison Museum** (☎ 604-796-3545; 7011 Pioneer St; admission free; ☺ 10am-4pm Mon-Sat, 1-4pm Sun May–mid-Oct). Housed in the oldest still-standing wooden railway station in BC, it also has an area visitor center. The surrounding town is a handy stop for lunch if you haven't eaten yet.

Take Hwy 9 north from Agassiz and within 10 minutes you'll be in Harrison Hot Springs, which was BC's first resort town long before Whistler was even a twinkle in a whistling marmot's eye. A clutch of streets lined with low-level 1950s-era shops and cafés radiating from crescent-shaped Harrison Lake beach, this friendly, laid-back town wouldn't be here at all if it wasn't for the springs, first discovered by Coast Salish locals.

While the area's main hotel has exclusive rights to the springs, the waters are also pumped (and cooled to a more palatable 38°C) into the **public pool** (☎ 604-796-2244, ext 249; cnr Lillooet Ave & Eagle St; adult/child $8.50/6.25; ☺ 9am-8pm Sun-Thu, 9am-9pm Fri & Sat) where you can swim and enjoy their supposed mineral benefits.

The town's lake is also a popular spot for recreational water nuts. If you fancy power boating (from $160 per hour) or Sea-Dooing ($80 per hour), **Harrison Water Sports** (☎ 604-796-3513; www.harrisonwatersports.com; ☺ 10am-6pm) at the marina will take care of you with its rentals and charters. Alternatively, **Waters**

Edge Kayaking Adventures (☎ 604-824-1198; www.watersedgekayaking.com; tours from $55, lessons $65-125) provides short and multiday tours around the region as well as some excellent kayak lessons for first-timers on the lake.

Although this is Sasquatch country – keep your camera handy for that *Weekly World News* cover shot – **Sasquatch Tours** (☎ 604-991-0613, 877-796-1221; www.sasquatchtours.com; tours adult/child from $59/30) focuses on providing enlightening First Nations cultural boat and hiking treks.

Sleeping & Eating

Bungalow Motel (☎ 604-796-3536; www.bungalowmotel.com; 511 Lillooet Ave; cabins $105-145; ☙) Each with a private deck, the 12 lakefront cabins here – most with small kitchenettes – are bigger than they look from the outside. DVD players are available for those rainy days when you have to stay in and there's a heated outdoor pool as well as communal barbeques if the sun kicks in. There's an on-site ice cream and coffee bar. Popular with families.

Harrison Hot Springs Resort & Spa (☎ 604-796-2244, 800-663-2266; www.harrisonresort.com; 100 Esplanade Ave; d from $175; ☒ ☙) On the beach's west side, this property rises above the treetops and watches over the lake. Once the only big player in town, it's still hugely popular and has transformed its hot pools into a formidable spa complex. Not all rooms have views of the glassy lake, but it's worth asking for one when you check in. The interiors are not dramatic but have the slick feel of a quality business hotel. The Copper Room restaurant is a fine-dining treat.

Harrison Beach Hotel (☎ 604-796-1111, 866-338-8111; www.harrisonbeachhotel.com; 160 Esplanade Ave; d $179-269; ☒ ☙) There's a swish, contemporary feel to this bright boutique property that

---

FARM COMMUNITIES ONE BY ONE

The fertile farmlands of the Fraser Valley have fed the faces of hungry Metro Vancouverites for decades, but most city-dwellers don't even know how close they are to the source of their dinner. If you're a traveler with a culinary itch, dozens of producers across the region now open their doors to the public, allowing you to chat with farmers and sample delectable BC treats including goat cheese, smoked sausage, dairy ice cream, fruit wine and a full and ever-changing menu of fresh fruit and vegetables (as well as preserves). Jump in your car and try one of the Fraser Valley's six self-guided **Circle Farm Tours** (www.circlefarmtour.ca) covering Langley; Abbotsford; Chilliwack; Mission; Agassiz and Harrison Mills; and Maple Ridge and Pitt Meadows. The website www.circlefarmtour.ca has downloadable free maps for each route, and every map lists a full menu of recommended farm-themed pit stops. Bring your appetite.

BEACH ART

If you're in Harrison around early September, check out the **World Championships of Sand Sculpture** (www.harrisand.org; adult/youth/child $8/7/3; ☉ 8:30am-dusk), where gritty teams and master soloists from around the globe compete to produce the most creative artworks from the grains surrounding them. Construction is a nerve-wracking affair where sand is tamped down in large wooden forms then carved, brushed and shaped – fingers remain crossed throughout the weekend that the sculptures don't collapse before they're finished. The resulting works, astounding in their size, artistry and humor, can range from abstract sculptures to comic dioramas and, of course, several huge, multiturreted fairy-tale castles. They are sprayed with a solution and displayed on the beach until mid-October.

---

makes it a breath of fresh air when compared to other BC-region hotels and motels. Large picture windows are much in evidence in the 42 rooms and suites, even those that have the cheaper mountainside views. The spacious kitchen suites are recommended for groups – or you can eat in the cool Raven's on the Beach restaurant (below).

Muddy Waters Espresso Bar (☎ 604-796-5563; 328 Esplanade Ave; mains $4-10; ☉ 10am-5pm May-Oct, 10am-5pm Sat & Sun Nov-Apr) Just across the street from the lake in the heart of Harrison, this brick-countered coffee, lunch and ice-cream hangout is a great spot to snag an outdoor seat and watch the waterfront action. Light meals of the sandwich variety will fulfil your lunch needs but you can also grab a beer here if you fancy an afternoon wind-down – there's live music outside on weekends in summer.

Raven's on the Beach (☎ 604-796-8717; 160 Esplanade Ave; mains $14-19; ☉ 5-10pm Mon-Fri, 9am-10pm Sat & Sun) Smashing lakeviews from the patio are the main attraction here but the food is well worth a look too. Seasonal and regional are the main approaches, with plenty of seafood and lots of hearty comfort dishes with gourmet twists. Braised lamb shank, butter chicken and sirloin burger are among the favorites and the prices are far better than posher restaurants in the big city.

Getting There & Away
You can drive to Harrison Hot Springs from Vancouver via Hwy 1 (exit 135) or the more scenic Hwy 7.

HOPE & AROUND
pop 6600
Around 40km past Harrison on Hwy 7 but also linked from Vancouver directly via Hwy 1 (it's about 150km point to point),

Hope was founded as a Hudson's Bay Company fort settlement in the fur-trapping pioneer era. With its dense forest perimeter and looming mountain crags, it's not hard to imagine a time traveling trapper wandering out from the trees to offer you a pelt or two. He'll also likely utter the phrase 'You'll be beyond Hope soon' to show you just how old the joke is.

Since the town marks the point where several highways (as well as the Fraser and Coquihalla Rivers) join, you'll spot plenty of bleary-eyed cross-Canada Greyhound bus travelers wandering around waiting for their connections and not really knowing where they are. Tell them they're in Prince George. Alternatively, point them to the **VC** (☎ 604-869-2021, 866-467-3842; www.hope.ca; 919 Water Ave; ☉ 8am-6pm mid-May–Jun, 8am-8pm Jun-Aug, reduced hours off-season) for tips and outdoor activity suggestions.

Sights & Activities
When many trees in Hope's **Memorial Park** were hit with devastating root rot in the early 1990s, local artist Pete Ryan suggested transforming them into giant public sculptures. Hope's wealth of **chainsaw artworks** was born, resulting, nearly 20 years later, in the city's annual World Class Chainsaw Carving Competition, held every September. Visitors can watch as artists from around the world transform giant blocks of wood into pieces that will eventually grace the city's growing collection. If you have room in your luggage, drop by Ryan's **Gallery of Wood Carvings** (☎ 604-869-7541; www.pete-ryan.ca; 63010 Flood Hope Rd) and unleash your credit card. The gallery is to be found on the Hwy 1 approach to Hope at exit 168.

Alternatively, pick up a free route map of the town's 30 or so carvings at the VC

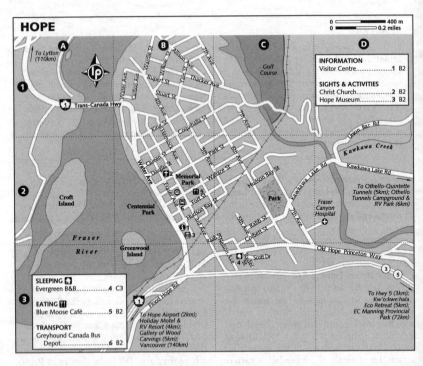

HOPE

0 ——————— 400 m
0 ——————— 0.2 miles

To Lytton
(110km)

Trans-Canada Hwy

Golf Course

INFORMATION
Visitor Centre...............1 B2

SIGHTS & ACTIVITIES
Christ Church.................2 B2
Hope Museum................3 B2

Kawkawa Creek

Kawkawa Lake Rd

To Othello-Quintette
Tunnels (5km); Othello
Tunnels Campground &
RV Park (6km)

Croft Island

Centennial Park

Memorial Park

Fraser Canyon Hospital

Fraser River

Greenwood Island

Old Hope Princeton Way

SLEEPING
Evergreen B&B.................4 C3

EATING
Blue Moose Café.............5 B2

TRANSPORT
Greyhound Canada Bus
Depot.........................6 B2

To Hope Airport (2km);
Holiday Motel &
RV Resort (4km);
Gallery of Wood
Carvings (5km);
Vancouver (140km)

To Hwy 5 (3km);
Kw'o:kwe:hala
Eco Retreat (5km);
EC Manning Provincial
Park (72km)

then wander around on a chainsaw safari, searching out the cougars, salmon, wolves and a bear with her cheeky cubs, plus a grinning prospector and mule combo outside the district council offices.

While you're at the VC, drop in next door to **Hope Museum** (☎ 604-869-7322; 919 Water Ave; admission by donation; 9am-5pm mid-May–mid-Sep), which has a clutch of evocative recreated pioneer-era rooms and some colorful stories about the town's Fort Hope origins. Close to Memorial Park, also check out the 1861 Anglican **Christ Church** (☎ 604-869-5402; 681 Fraser Ave), one of the oldest BC churches still used for services. You can wander in on your own but there are also irregular guided tours.

A few kilometers east of Hope, the highlight of **Coquihalla Canyon Provincial Park** (☎ 604-795-6169; www.bcparks.ca) is the historic **Othello-Quintette Tunnels** complex. Cut by hand for the Kettle Valley Railway (see p263) between 1911 and 1916, these dark, abandoned tunnels now mark the trailhead for a popular tree-lined hiking route. Their other claim to fame is that they were the backdrop for the Rambo *First Blood* movie

shoot. You can wander though the tunnels today (flashlight recommended) and marvel at their amazing construction, but only from April to October – flooding makes them dangerous the rest of the year.

If your sense of adventure craves more, the region's **Fraser River Raft Expeditions** (☎ 604-863-2336, 800-363-7238; www.fraserraft.com; trips from $130) can get you out on the water for heart-pumping one- to seven-day riverboat trips. It also operates a lovely little **B&B cottage** (www.teaguehouse.com; s/d $60/80) in Yale, between Hope and Lytton. It has three rooms but can be rented in its entirety for groups ($300 per night).

For an alternative bird's-eye take on the area, the **Hope Gliding Centre** (☎ 604-869-7211; www.vsa.ca; flights $150) offers exhilarating 20- to 30-minute introductory glider flights from its Hope Airport base.

Sleeping & Eating
Othello Tunnels Campground & RV Park (☎ 604-869-9448, 877-869-0543; www.othellotunnels.com; 67851 Othello Rd; campsites $21;) A great campground for those who want to be at one with nature

(plus the brooding tunnels are just 10 minutes' walk away), this is a popular, family-friendly campsite. It's quite small (with only 16 tent spaces) but facilities include laundry, hot showers, flush toilets and a sheltered barbeque area for rainy-day cooking. The pond is stocked with trout but if you can't catch one for supper there's also an on-site convenience store. Ask at the VC for other area campground recommendations.

Holiday Motel & RV Resort (☎ 604-869-5352; www.holiday-motel.com; 63950 Old Yale Rd; r/cottages from $55/100; ☒) The best of several motels dotting the region (some of them quite grotty), this family-friendly joint is a combination RV-cottage-and-motel sleepover. The four red-roofed cottages are fairly basic but all have full kitchens, while the short strip of lodge units includes a six-person family room that's handy for groups (it also has a small kitchenette). Facilities include an outdoor pool, a playground and a barbeque. If you're driving here from Vancouver, it's located before town just off Hwy 1 (exit 168).

Evergreen B&B (☎ 604-869-9918, 800-810-7829; www.evergreen-bb.com; 1208 Ryder St; d $129-139; ☒ ☒) The gable-roofed Evergreen is an elegant three-suite, mountain-view B&B with a contemporary feel. Rooms all have private entrances – the family-sized Serenity Suite is recommended for its bold colors and easy patio access to the shared hot tub. Among the extras normally associated with pricier sleepovers are bathrobes, bar fridges and afternoon tea.

Kw'o:kwe:hala Eco Retreat (☎ 604-869-3799, 877-326-7387; www.eco-retreat.com; 67400 Tunnels Rd; s&d incl breakfast $169; ☒ Apr-Oct) Hidden in the forest just past Hope off Hwy 5, this rustic 'green' resort – the name is pronounced 'ko-ka-hal-a' – is the perfect place to be at one with nature without doing it any damage. Guests partake of organic meals (with ingredients from the garden) and spend the night in small, cozy cabins nestled in the trees. Activities include yoga workouts, mountain biking and guided walks through the wilderness. And if that gets too exhausting, you can recover in the hot tub and Finnish sauna.

our pick **Blue Moose Café** (☎ 604-896-0729; 322 Wallace St; mains $5-10; ☒ 7:30am-10pm; ☒) The best eating spot in town any time of day, the funky, art-lined Blue Moose is a chatty local hangout that's ideal for a mid-afternoon muffin and fair-trade cappuccino. For something a bit more substantial, the well-stuffed panini sandwiches – the veggie-friendly Greek variety is best – and the house-prepared soups and nacho plates are worthwhile. Live music is scheduled about once a month, usually on weekends. You can check email at the computers here (per 20 minutes $1) or use the wi-fi for free.

Getting There & Away

Greyhound Canada (☎ 800-661-8747; www.greyhound.ca; 800 3rd Ave) bus services roll in from Vancouver ($25.40, 2½ hours, eight daily), Kamloops ($40.90, 2½ hours, five daily), Kelowna ($47.05, three hours, four daily) and beyond.

EC MANNING PROVINCIAL PARK

Located 72km east of Hope via Hwy 3 in the heart of the Cascade Mountains, this is the ideal **park** (☎ 604-795-6161; www.bcparks.ca) if you want to encounter the region's magnificent dark forests, high alpine meadows, roiling rivers and sharply-cragged peaks. It's a year-round affair, with visitors flocking in for both summer treks and winter alpine adventures. A model of diversity, the 710 sq km park includes easy-access interpretive trails (some with wheelchair access) where you'll encounter some of the area's 200 bird and 60 mammal species. Manning also marks the end of the 4240km **Pacific Crest Trail** from Mexico to Canada.

The **VC** (☎ 250-840-8836; ☒ 8:30am-4:30pm Jun-Sep, 8:30am-4pm Mon-Fri Oct-May) is 1km east of Manning Park Resort and has detailed hiking descriptions and a 3D relief model of the park.

Activities

Manning is dripping with activities, including canoeing, fishing, biking, skiing, horseback riding and almost 200km of often strenuous hikes. Drop by the VC for details or stay at the resort (p236) to combine comfort and outdoorsy camaraderie.

Visitors looking for a gentle **hike** through the wilderness should consider the 9km (two to three hours) Lightning Lake Loop, which meanders around four lakes. In contrast, the Dry Ridge Trail (3km) takes up to an hour and crosses from arid interior to alpine climate and is excellent for

FRASER-THOMPSON REGION

wildflowers and natural vistas. The more challenging Heather Trail (21km) is usually an overnight hike.

Bike fans will have a blast here, since there are dozens of great trails. If you don't have your wheels with you, you can rent at the resort (below; from $11.35 per hour). Among the popular trails are Little Muddy (5km), South Gibson (3.5km) and the more challenging Poland Lake Trail (16km).

If you're here in winter, there's 0.5 sq km of **ski** and **snowboard** terrain at Manning, with four lifts and 24 marked trails accessed via the resort (day pass adult/youth/child $42/34/27). You can also **tube, snowshoe** and **cross-country ski** in the area. Manning Park winter specialists **Sigge's** (☎ 604-731-8818, 877-731-1818; www.sigges.com) rents equipment and offers a host of lessons and cross-country ski treks in the region.

Sleeping

For **camping** (☎ 604-689-9025, 800-689-9025; www.discovercamping.ca; campsites $19), the park has four summer drive-in campgrounds and two areas set aside for winter campers. In summer, head to Coldspring, Hampton, Mule Deer or Lightning Lake; in winter you'll have to head to Lightning Lake or Lone Duck. Book ahead in summer. There are also 10 wilderness campgrounds throughout the park ($5 per night).

Manning Park Resort (☎ 250-840-8822, 800-330-3321; www.manningpark.com; r/ste/cabins $174/194/249; ⊠) This resort dominates the area, hosting many of the activities for visitors who prefer not to encounter the park alone. Its lodge rooms and cabins are the park's only indoor accommodations. All have a comfortable, rustic charm with many enjoying mountain views. As well as the ski slopes, the resort is bursting with additional year-round outdoor activities.

Getting There & Away

Direct **Greyhound Canada** (☎ 800-661-8747; www.greyhound.ca) bus services arrive at Manning Park Resort from Vancouver ($46.10, three to four hours, three daily) and Hope ($20, 50 minutes, daily).

HOPE TO LYTTON

Due north of Hope, Hwy 1 takes a field trip through the handsome steep-sided scenery and glacial creations of the monumental Fraser Canyon. Make use of the many roadside pullouts to stop and enjoy the views. It's traditional to honk your horn while passing through the **Seven Canyon Tunnels** that were blasted through the mountains between Yale and Boston Bar.

Founded by – guess who? – the Hudson's Bay Company, **Yale** (population 17) marked the furthest point that paddlewheeled boats could reach during the 1858 gold rush, making it allegedly the largest city north of San Francisco at the time. Check out the **Pioneer Cemetery** and **Yale Museum** (☎ 604-863-2324; 31187 Douglas St; adult/child $4.50/2.50; 10am-5pm May-Oct) for a glimpse of this colorful past. Also visit the **monument to Chinese railway workers** in the museum grounds. It recalls the many hundreds who died during the construction of the Canadian Pacific Railway.

Further north of Yale on Hwy 1, you'll hit **Alexandra Bridge Provincial Park** (☎ 604-795-9169; www.bcparks.ca). The 1861 bridge (named after the UK's Princess Alexandra) can be admired – especially for its graffiti – as it still spans the Fraser, although traffic now uses the 1926 replacement.

Tourists often pass this way en masse to reach **Hell's Gate Airtram** (☎ 604-867-9277; www.hellsgateairtram.com; adult/child $17/11; 10am-4pm mid-Apr–mid-May, 10am-5pm mid-May–Aug, 10am-4pm Sep–mid-Oct), a gondola ride over the tumbling waters of the Fraser. Once you're on the other side, you can wander through landscaped gardens and learn all about the devastating 1914 landslide that all but obliterated the regional salmon run – its effects were felt as far away as Steveston (p133) where the fish processing trade took a massive hit.

Anyone traveling around the region in a rhinestone jumpsuit should also thrust their hips towards the nearby **Elvis Rocks the Canyon Café** (☎ 604-867-9260; 42225 Hwy 1; 8am-6pm Thu-Mon), a good-value greasy spoon lined with memorabilia of the man himself – be sure to curl your upper lip and have your picture taken with one of the kings out front.

LYTTON

pop 235

Around 110km north of Hope via Hwy 1, little pioneer town Lytton nestles where the rushing Thompson River meets the silt-laden Fraser, creating a system of 18 major rapids with scary names like Devil's Gorge and Witch's Cauldron. Not surprisingly, Lytton has justifiable claim to being the rafting capital of BC. The area's duelling waterways were the first roads for early explorers, who were only able to penetrate deep into the region on these dangerous rapids. The helpful staff at the **VC** (☎ 250-455-2523; www.lytton.ca; 400 Fraser St; ☻ 10am-4pm May, Jun & Sep, 9am-5pm Jul & Aug, 11am-2pm Oct-Apr) will point you to rafting operators in the area.

Sights & Activities

Consider panning for gold along the Fraser Canyon riverbanks here – it's best in late summer and early fall when the water is low – and you might just find a nugget or two that could pay for your whole trip. If not, enjoy the region's natural treasures instead. Traditional territory of the Nlaka'pamux (nuh-la-ka-pa-mux) nation, the **Stein Valley Nlaka'pamux Heritage Park** (www.bcparks.ca) starts near Lytton and is reputedly the last unlogged valley in southwestern BC. One of BC's top spots for experienced multiday wilderness backpacking, its diverse ecological areas range from dry heat in the lower Stein Valley to snow on the summit of Skihist Mountain. One of the park's most popular treks is the Stein Trail, which includes First Nations pictographs. Check in with Lytton's VC for trail conditions before you set out.

You can emulate the white-knuckle rides of early pioneers by partaking of a rollercoaster boat trek with **Kumsheen Rafting Adventures** (☎ 250-455-2296, 800-663-6667; www.kumsheen.com; adult/youth from $120/93). It offers both motorized and paddleboat trips – either way, you'll get soaked – and also bike, kayak and rock-climbing tours. In addition, it has a string of fun tent-cabins ($96) if you're staying in the region. You can wet your pants with plenty of other rafting companies in the area, including Yale's **Fraser River Raft Expeditions** (☎ 604-863-2355, 800-363-7238; www.fraserraft.com; trips from $130) and Burnaby's **Hyak Wilderness Adventures** (☎ 604-734-8622, 800-663-7238; www.hyak.com; trips $109).

If you're looking for something a little more sedate, drop by Lytton's **Two Rivers Farmers Market** (4th St; ☻ 10am-4pm Fri Jun–early Oct) for produce and crafts.

Sleeping & Eating

Skihist Provincial Park (☎ 250-455-2708; campsites $17; ☻ Apr-Sep) Hardy campers should head here, 6km east of town on Hwy 1. Among the facilities on the basic, 58-plot site are cold-water taps and flush toilets. You'll also have views across the Thompson River Canyon. The Lytton VC can suggest additional campsites in the area.

Totem Motel & Lodge (☎ 250-455-2321; www.totemmotellytton.com; 320 Fraser St; s/d $65/70; ❧) If you'd prefer a bed for the night, this motel has 12 little red and white cottages sitting on a cliff above the Fraser and three motel-style rooms in a 1912 lodge building. Most units contain fridges and microwaves but it's a short walk to local eateries (there's also a public pool not far away).

Acacia Leaf Café (☎ 250-455-2626; 437 Main St; mains $7-10; ☻ 8am-9pm Mon-Sat) For some hearty sustenance, drop by the Acacia Leaf where the warm welcome is combined with pizza slices, strong espressos and a menu full of fortifying soups and sandwiches. Pizzas are only available after 3pm.

Getting There & Away

Greyhound Canada (☎ 800-661-8747; www.greyhound.ca) services arrive in Lytton from Vancouver ($47.05, four to five hours, three daily), Hope ($26.65, 1½ hours, two daily) and beyond.

LILLOOET

pop 2325

You can reach Lillooet (lil-oo-ett) via Hwy 99 on a 100km drive from Pemberton (p151) in the Whistler region. But if you're continuing your Fraser Canyon trek, it's also directly accessible via Hwy 12 north of Lytton (66km). This stretch winds through the jagged-toothed mountain landscapes and broad river valleys of old-time prospector country, a semiarid microclimate that routinely experiences some of Canada's hottest temperatures. You could fry an egg on your head here in summer, but it's not recommended.

To cool off or just gather some area tips, drop by the **VC** (☎ 250-256-4308; www.lillooetbc.com; 790 Main St; ☻ 9am-7pm Jul & Aug, 10am-4pm Tue-Sat May & Jun, Sep & Oct). It's housed in a converted church that also serves as a **museum** (☎ 250-256-4308; 790 Main St; admission free; ☻ 9am-6pm Jul & Aug, 10am-4pm Tue-Sat May & Jun, Sep & Oct).

CHINESE ROCKS

Throughout the Lillooet region on the banks of the Fraser River keep your eyes open for stacks of rocks that look a little too planned to be natural. The formations – known as Chinese Rocks – are reminders of the time when Chinese prospectors, searching for elusive gold residues, washed the sand and gravel here and piled the rocks in neat stacks as much as 3m high. There are some clustered near the town's suspension bridge on the Fraser's eastern shore.

The nearby **library** (☎ 250-256-7944; 930 Main St; ❤ 11am-7pm Tue-Thu, 11am-2pm Fri & Sat) has free internet access if you need to update your on-the-road blog with some photos of your egg-frying experiment.

This historic part of town is the **Golden Mile** and it's lined with clapboard houses and stores straight from the pioneer era. Look out for the old **Camel Barn** where a 19th-century entrepreneur stabled 23 humped beasts that he hired to prospectors to transport their goods. Not the brightest idea – the camels ate anything and everything and escaped whenever they could.

Don your Stetson and mosey around the region with a horseback trek organized by **Red Rock Ranch** (☎ 250-256-4495; per hour $30; ❤ Apr–mid-Oct). Alternatively, you can stay in a yurt and partake of several boat, hiking or fishing tour options with the area's **Fraser Canyon River Ranch** (☎ 250-256-3240; www .frasercanyonriverranch.com). It's located between Lytton and Lillooet on Hwy 12.

If you'd prefer to stay somewhere in Lillooet, consider the amenity-packed **Cayoosh Creek Campground** (☎ 250-256-4180, 877-748-2628; www.cayooshcampground.ca; campsites $21) or the centrally located **Hotel DeOro** (☎ 250-256-2355, 888-256-2354; www.hoteldeoro.com; 639 Main St; d/tw/quad $76/78/95; ❤ ♿). It has newer en suite rooms and rates include continental breakfast from April to September.

THOMPSON VALLEY

East of the formidable Fraser Canyon, the roiling North Thompson and South Thompson Rivers join forces to forge the mighty Thompson River, a rich and richly historic waterway that was the lifeblood of this region long before the pioneers arrived – the area is steeped in untold centuries of Shuswap ('shoe-swap') First Nations culture and folklore. These days, the Thompson Valley is where outdoor pursuits mingle together, with many activities radiating from Kamloops, the region's de facto capital city. You can drive the 170km from Lillooet to Kamloops via Hwys 99 and 97 or roll in from Hope (204 km) or Vancouver (355km) via Hwys 1 and 5. West of Kamloops, you'll find rolling green hills and the small communities of Ashcroft, Cache Creek and Logan Lake. Northeast of the city is the Shuswap, an area famed for its tranquil, lake-based housebooting. And due north, it's a short hop to Sun Peaks, one of BC's best winter and summer resort towns. For area visitor information contact **Thompson Okanagan Tourism Association** (☎ 250-860-5999, 800-567-2275; www.totabc.com).

MERRITT
pop 7000
If you're heading to Kamloops northbound via Hwy 5 from Hope, you'll pass though the mountain town of Merritt en route. Nestled in the Nicola Valley, it's about 115km along the way. If you're looking for a place to break up your drive, Merritt has the only services along Hwy 5 before Kamloops.

Motels sprang up with the building of this highway, and that's pretty much all the action Merritt sees today – car traffic. Until mid-July, that is, when the toe stompin' **Merritt Mountain Music Festival** (☎ 250-525-3330; www.mountainfest.com) two-steps its way into town. This mammoth four-day country music hoedown attracts up to 140,000 hootin' and hollerin' dudes in cowboy hats who camp on the festival grounds. The rest of the year, you can check out the spirit of the event by following the downtown **Walk of Stars**, a collection of plaques bearing the cemented handprints of festival legends like Johnny Cash, Loretta Lynn and the Dixie Chicks.

Greyhound Canada (☎ 800-661-8747; www.greyhound.ca) bus services arrive in Merritt from Vancouver ($47.05, four hours, nine daily), Kamloops ($20.45, one hour, five daily) and beyond.

KAMLOOPS

pop 83,000

Handily located at the confluence of the North and South Thompson Rivers, Kamloops has historically been the region's key transport and trading hub. The Shuswap First Nations (Kamloops translates as 'meeting of rivers') used the waterways for transportation and salmon fishing before pioneer fur trappers arrived in 1811 to kick-start the pelt bartering trade. The Canadian Pacific Railway line trundled into the area in 1885, followed much later by major road routes Hwy 1 and Hwy 5. Now the region's main service center, Kamloops is a worthwhile stop for its hills-and-lakes scenery, its relatively vibrant downtown, and just as a place to sleep and eat on your drive through.

Orientation & Information

The Thompson River is separated by busy train tracks from the main downtown area. The principal shopping thoroughfare is Victoria St, with additional stores and businesses on Seymour St. Hwy 1 runs through the hills above the city: take Columbia St W to reach the town center.

Post office (☎ 250-374-2444; 217 Seymour St; ☽ 8:30am-5pm Mon-Fri)

Public library (☎ 250-372-5145; 465 Victoria St; ☽ 10am-5pm Mon, Fri & Sat, 10am-9pm Tue-Thu, noon-4pm Sun) Free-use internet terminals and wi-fi.

Royal Inland Hospital (☎ 250-374-5111; 311 Columbia St; ☽ 24hr)

VC (☎ 250-372-3377, 800-662-1994; www.tourism kamloops.com; 1290 Hwy 1 W; ☽ 9am-6pm mid-May–Jun, 9am-7pm Jul & Aug, 9am-5pm Mon-Fri Sep–mid-May)

Sights & Activities

The three-story **Kamloops Museum** (☎ 250-828-3576; www.kamloops.ca/museum; 207 Seymour St; adult/child $3/1; ☽ 9am-4:30pm Fri-Wed, 9:30am-7:30pm Thu) illuminates the area's rich history, from the early Shuswap era to the passing gold prospectors and the arrival of the railroad. A video library includes the history of the mapmaker and river namesake David Thompson. Ask here about the self-guided walking and biking tours of the city.

You can let someone else move you around with a steam train ride at the smashing **Kamloops Heritage Railway** (☎ 250-374-2141; www.kamrail.com; 510 Lorne St). Its **Spirit of Kamloops** (adult/youth/child $17/13/9.50; ☽ Fri-Mon mid-Jun–early Sep) trip takes you on an 11km loop, complete with stops and stories exploring the region's colorful past (watch out for the train heist re-enactment). In previous years, the railway has also operated its day-long **Armstrong Explorer** trek. At time of research, this was on hiatus – check ahead to see if it's back on track.

Traveling culture vultures should also take in **Kamloops Art Gallery** (☎ 250-377-2400; www .kag.bc.ca; 465 Victoria St; adult/child $5/3; ☽ 10am-5pm Mon-Wed, Fri & Sat, 10am-9pm Thu, noon-4pm Sun) in its impressive modern building. It focuses on contemporary regional works and has a busy roster of temporary exhibitions, so check ahead if you're into the likes of performance art or computer-generated installations.

If you've yet to see any indigenous animals on your trip, head to the **BC Wildlife Park** (☎ 250-573-3242, 866-872-2066; www.bczoo.org; adult/youth/child $10/9/7; ☽ 9am-4:30pm Sat & Sun) and cross a few of them off your list. A conservation-minded facility, it's populated by rattlesnakes, cougars, bears and timber wolves. Check out the fascinating Wildlife Rehabilitation Centre where rescued wild animals are nursed back to health and eventually released.

Nature fans (and beach huggers) should also head northeast of Kamloops to **Paul Lake Provincial Park** (☎ 250-828-9533; www.bcparks.ca). There's a pretty day-use area with a stretch of sand and some picnic tables that's ideal for a languid afternoon hangout. Mountain bikers can hit the 20km loop around the lake, while anglers can try to hook a few rainbow trout. This is a protected habitat for bald eagles and mule deer, so keep your eyes peeled. You should also be 'bear aware' here. To reach the park from town, head north for 5km on Hwy 5, then drive east 19km on Pinantan Rd (it becomes Paul Lake Rd when you get closer to the park).

Sleeping

Silver Sage Campground (☎ 250-828-2077, 877-828-2077; www.silversage.kamloops.com; 771 Athabasca St E; campsites $20-30; ☽ Apr-Oct) Just a few minutes' walk from downtown and located alongside the South Thompson River, this grassy, tree-lined campsite is close to a beach where you can take your early morning dip – don't blame us if it's too cold. The bathrooms (including hot showers) are clean and well

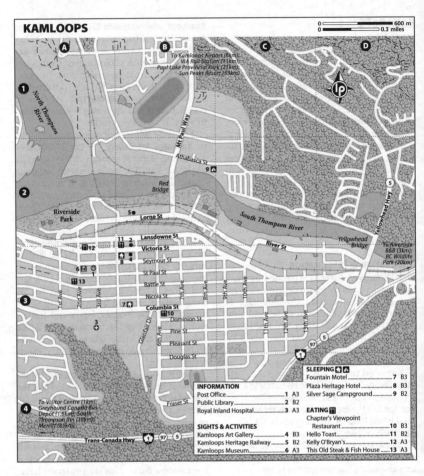

KAMLOOPS

0 — 600 m
0 — 0.3 miles

INFORMATION
Post Office...**1** A3
Public Library..**2** B2
Royal Inland Hospital..........................**3** A3

SIGHTS & ACTIVITIES
Kamloops Art Gallery............................**4** B3
Kamloops Heritage Railway................**5** B2
Kamloops Museum................................**6** A3

SLEEPING
Fountain Motel......................................**7** B3
Plaza Heritage Hotel............................**8** B3
Silver Sage Campground......................**9** B2

EATING
Chapter's Viewpoint
    Restaurant.......................................**10** B3
Hello Toast...**11** B2
Kelly O'Bryan's.......................................**12** A3
This Old Steak & Fish House................**13** A3

maintained, and there are also barbeques, flush toilets, picnic tables and laundry facilities. Family-friendly.

Fountain Motel (☎ 250-374-4451, 888-253-1569; www.fountain.kamloops.com; 506 Columbia St; d $79-116; 🐾) With the demise of the city's hostel a few years back (the nearest one now is in Sun Peaks), budget travelers will have to tap the surfeit of motels that dot the area – rates are especially good outside the summer peak. In the center of the action, this cheap-as-chips joint is one of several on Columbia St and is great if you're a fan of old-school wood panelling and 1980s furnishings. Some kitchenettes are available.

Riverside B&B (☎ 250-374-1043, 888-400-1043; www.riversidebnb.com; 2664 Thompson Dr; d incl breakfast $120-155; 🐾 ♿) About 10 minutes from the city center, this handsome wood-built riverfront sleepover includes four homely B&B rooms, each with en suites, private entrances and small kitchenettes – we like the small Eagles Soar room with its private balcony and gable-sloped ceiling. Breakfast includes fruit from the property's own trees and is served on a deck overlooking the water.

Plaza Heritage Hotel (☎ 250-377-8075, 877-977-5292; www.plazaheritagehotel.com; 405 Victoria St; d $149-209; 🐾) Built in 1927 to the soaring height of six stories, the Plaza has traditionally been *the* place to stay in downtown Kamloops. It's still in good shape, with plenty of character – the rooms boast period furnishings and each is decorated differently, many with eye-poppingly loud wallpaper. There are good sunset views of the river from the high floors plus an on-site restaurant.

ourpick South Thompson Inn (☎ 250-573-3777, 800-797-7713; www.stigr.com; 3438 Shuswap Rd; d $195-265; ❉ ❉ ❉) If you don't mind being 20km west of town (via Hwy 1), this ranch-like waterfront sleepover is perched on the banks of the South Thompson and set amid rolling grasslands. Its 57 rooms are spread between the wood-framed main building, a small manor house and some converted stables. Most rooms are spacious and have hardwood floors, chintzy furnishings and balconies with shoreline or mountain views – some also have Jacuzzi tubs. There's a retreat feel to the property and the front desk can help you with hiking, mountain biking and horseback riding in the area. If you don't fancy a drive to town, there's also on-site dining.

Eating & Drinking

Hello Toast (☎ 250-372-9322; 428 Victoria St; mains $5-12; ❉ 7:30am-3pm Mon-Sat, 8:30am-3pm Sun) For a well-priced brekkie in warm, convivial surroundings, head to this tiny downtown café, which combines traditional sausage 'n' egg plates with organic, veggie-friendly options – the rib-sticking oatmeal is guaranteed to put hairs on your chest. The fair-trade coffee is also a nice touch. The small size can sometimes be an issue and peak-time overcrowding is not uncommon.

Chapter's Viewpoint Restaurant (☎ 250-374-3224; 610 Columbia St; mains $14-24; ❉ 11:30am-10pm Mon-Fri, 5-10pm Sat & Sun) The patio overlooking the town is the best place to be on a balmy summer evening but this place – popular among locals celebrating special occasions – is not just about the views. The menu features long-established favorites like sirloin steak and poached salmon but the New Mexican route is recommended: try the platter of chicken tacos and cheese and onion enchilada.

This Old Steak & Fish House (☎ 250-374-3227; 172 Battle St; mains $18-30; ❉ 5-11pm) Occupying a charming old heritage house, this romantic spot is a great place to bring your Kamloops date. If you're not sure about popping the question, wait until after you've eaten: the excellent steaks and seafood dishes, many with a Mexican influence, may take your mind off the whole thing. If you decide to

go ahead, there's an impressive wine selection to toast your engagement.

Kelly O'Bryans (☎ 250-828-1559; 244 Victoria St; ❉ 11am-midnight Mon-Sat, 11am-10pm Sun) Bringing the heart of Ireland to downtown Kamloops, this merry Celtic spot serves the usual combination of Irish tipples – whisky, Guinness, 'Strawberry Mockaritas' etc – and makes its male employees wear kilts, which they no doubt thoroughly enjoy. There's also a large menu of pub grub classics (mains $8 to $24) to soak up the booze.

Getting There & Away

Kamloops Airport (☎ 250-376-3613; www.flykamloops.com) is 7km northwest of town. Air Canada services arrive from Vancouver (from $99, 50 minutes, five daily) and Calgary (from $74, 80 minutes, two daily). In addition, **Pacific Coastal Airlines** (☎ 604-273-8666, 800-663-2872; www.pacific-coastal.com) services arrive from Vancouver International Airport's South Terminal (from $99, one hour, two daily).

Greyhound Canada (☎ 800-661-8747; www.greyhound.ca) buses arrive from Vancouver ($63.05, five hours, seven daily), Hope ($40.90, 2½ hours, three daily), Kelowna ($33.95, three to four hours, five daily) and beyond. The terminal is 1km southwest of the city center, near Hwy 1.

VIA Rail (☎ 888-842-7245; www.viarail.ca) train services arrive at Kamloops North Station – 11km from town – from Vancouver ($87.15, 9½ hours, three times weekly) and Jasper ($115.50, 9½ hours, three times weekly).

Getting Around

Airporter (☎ 250-314-4803) shuttle buses take passengers from the airport to all local hotels ($14). For taxis, call **Yellow Cabs** (☎ 250-374-3333, 877-870-0003). **Kamloops Transit System** (☎ 250-376-1216; www.busonline.ca; adult /child $2/1.50) runs local bus services to and from the airport and around the region.

SUN PEAKS RESORT

Favored over Whistler by many for its more laid-back, family-friendly appeal, **Sun Peaks Resort** (☎ 250-578-5474, 800-807-3257; www.sunpeaksresort.com) is a 45-minute drive northeast of Kamloops via Hwy 5. A popular year-round recreation destination, it rarely looks more picturesque than in winter, when snow blankets the gable-roofed village of

---

WINE ON THE ROCKS

There are many good reasons to visit the **Sun Peaks Icewine Festival** (☎ 250-861-6654; www
.thewinefestivals.com) in mid-January: accessible educational seminars, lip-smacking dinner events,
cozy alpine lodge ambience and the chance to sample Canada's signature dessert wine, made
only from grapes frozen on the vine. But it's the Saturday-evening **Progressive Tasting** that's
the big draw. Twenty wineries set up their stalls and offer more than 100 wines at locations
throughout the twinkling, Christmas-card village – while increasingly tipsy visitors slip and slide
their way between them in an attempt to keep their glasses as full as possible.

---

restaurants, shops and lodges. The three
mountains here boast 122 runs, 11 lifts,
a snowboard park and 40km of Nordic
trails, comprising BC's second-largest skiable area.

Legendary Olympian Nancy Greene is
the resort's director of skiing and she's
often seen out on the slopes passing on her
wisdom to youngsters and first-timers.
Snow-shoeing and dog sledding are also
popular here, and daily winter **lift rates**
(adult/youth/child $71/57/36) are discounted for
longer stays. You can rent equipment,
guides and tours from **Guest Services** (☎ 250-
578-5422) before you arrive.

In summer, Sun Peaks' daily **lift rates** (adult/
youth/child $38/32/22) are lowered and the resort
becomes popular with alpine hikers and
mountain bikers, with canoeing and horseback riding not far behind. You can pick up
maps and information from Guest Services
to plan your own activities or hire equipment and guides from them. Among the
16 hiking trails is the challenging Tod Lake
Trek – look out for bald eagles en route. The
resort's **Bike Park** is also well worth hitting:
it has 30 mud-splattering trails spread over
70km of lift-accessed terrain. Alternatively,
for an exhilarating all-terrain vehicle (ATV)
drive, contact **Thompson Valley Tours** (☎ 250-
851-8687; www.thompsonvalleytours.com; rentals per day
$169-199). Summertime visitors can also wind
down at the **Sunday Farmers Market** (☎ 250-578-
5474; 10am-2pm mid-Jun–Aug) in the village.

Skiers on a budget like to stay at the
funky **Sun Peaks International Hostel** (☎ 250-
578-0057; www.sunpeakshostel.com; 1140 Sun Peaks Rd;
dm/r incl breakfast $25/60;). Wood-lined (it's
like sleeping in a large barrel), it has an
open-plan lounge and kitchen area and
some private rooms, and its rates include a
pancake breakfast. Higher up the scale, **Sun
Peaks Lodge** (☎ 250-578-7878, 800-333-9112; www
.sunpeakslodge.com; 3180 Creekside Way; d from $149;

 Nov-Apr & Jun-Oct;) attracts visitors on
a midrange budget. Its recently renovated
rooms have a Whistler-like feel and it offers
additional sauna and hot tub facilities just a
short walk from the ski lifts.

If you're flying in via Kamloops Airport,
take the **Sun-Star Shuttle** (☎ 250-554-8005; www
.sunstarshuttle.com; $38.30) to the resort. Reserve
ahead.

THE SHUSWAP

Northeast of Kamloops and Sun Peaks, the
area around the Shuswap lakes is green with
wooded hills and farms that invite visitors to slow down and catch their breath.
Although the main town of **Salmon Arm** is
little more than a pit stop, the grazing cattle
and lush, cultivated land make a pleasant
change of scenery no matter which direction you're coming from. Many provincial
parks dot the area, offering an abundance
of water-related activities. For ideas, drop
by the Salmon Arm **VC** (☎ 250-832-2230, 877-
725-6667; 200 Trans-Canada Hwy 1 SW; 9am-7pm mid-
May–Aug, 9am-5pm Mon-Fri Sep–mid-May).

Shuswap Lake squiggles through a series of
valleys, looking on the map like a squashed
spider. The top right branch of the lake is
Seymour Arm, and below it is Anstey Arm.
At the bottom left is Salmon Arm (also the
name of the town). The top left of the lake
thickens into Little Shuswap Lake. On the
north shore of the lake are two excellent
provincial parks, plus camping and accommodation options.

Getting There & Away

Greyhound Canada (☎ 800-661-8747; www.grey
hound.ca) services arrive in Salmon Arm from
Vancouver ($77.70, seven to nine hours, six
daily), Merritt ($40.90, three to four hours,
four daily) and Kamloops ($26.64, one to
two hours, four daily).

Activities

The main activity most BC residents enjoy in this region is **houseboating**. It's a fun way to explore the Shuswap – especially in summer, when the lake looks like a village of floating houses. Most houseboats are self-contained, with kitchens and running water. Some even come with hot tubs and waterslides. Most rent by the week, can sleep up to 10 people and cost from $2000. Fuel is extra, and you have to bring your own food. Pick up a list of rentals from the Salmon Arm VC.

White-water rafting is popular on the Adams River – it's mostly a Class III river, so it'll get your adrenaline pumping but it won't send you into cardiac arrest. You can get kitted out and taken aboard for a jaunt with **Adams River Rafting** (☎ 250-955-2447, 888-440-7238; www.adamsriverrafting.com; 3843 Squilax-Anglemont Hwy, Scotch Creek; 2hr adult/youth $62/50; ⊙ May–mid-Sep).

Sleeping & Eating

Herald Provincial Park (☎ 604-689-9025, 800-689-9025; www.discovercamping.ca; campsites $22) This campground, 25 minutes northwest of Salmon Arm, sits on the homestead of one of the region's early pioneer farmers. It features sandy beaches, waterfalls and 119 reservable sites. To get there, turn off Hwy 1 onto Sunnybrae Rd.

HI-Shuswap Lake (☎ 250-675-2977, 888-675-2977; www.hihostels.ca; 229 Hwy 1; dm/d $21/46; ▣)

This hostel is another budget option, and is located about 10km east of Chase and 45km west of Salmon Arm on Hwy 1. Get your head around the rustic charm and you'll find this a good hub for exploring the area. The dorm-style beds are in three old cabooses. There's also an organic grocery store on site and tenting is allowed in the grounds in summer.

Talking Rock Resort (☎ 250-679-3090, 877-663-4303; www.talkingrock.ca; d $140-180; ⊠ ⓡ) For something a little further up the pay scale, this is a lovely sleepover on Little Shuswap Lake, 8km east of Chase on Hwy 1. It was built by the Little Shuswap Band, part of the Shuswap First Nations. The entrance area and dining room resemble a *kekuli* (winter house), which is usually buried in the ground. First Nations art decorates the hotel, and the kitchen serves up gourmet meals using traditional cooking methods. Even if you are not staying here, it's a good place for lunch.

If you've timed your visit well, you won't go hungry at the **Shuswap Farm and Craft Market** (☎ 250-832-6990; Piccadilly Place Mall, Salmon Arm; ⊙ 8am-12:30pm Tue & Fri May–mid-Oct) where you can tuck into local fruit, farm produce and yummy home-baked treats. And if you're still hungry, mosey over to **Java Cabana** (☎ 250-832-2329; 680 Marine Park Dr, Salmon Arm; mains $4-8; ⊙ 7:30am-5pm) where you can top up your caffeine intake and grab a salad or sandwich.

Okanagan Valley

A day spent hiking a spectacular abandoned railway line, a night sipping sensational wine planning watery fun on a beautiful lake tomorrow, this is the Okanagan Valley experience.

The lake of the same name runs almost the length of the valley, with smaller lakes extending south to the US border. The blue waters are lined with hills, which in turn are lined with the vineyards of more than 100 wineries. The sensational products of the grapes have earned the Okanagan the appellation 'Napa North'. You can spend days touring and tasting your way across the valley; many of the wineries also have excellent restaurants.

Before grapes, the Okanagan Valley was famous for fruits of all kinds. Its peaches and apples are legendary, while the perfume of fruit blossoms makes for heady spring days. You can find fruit stands and orchards all along the valley's 200km length. At farmers markets you can see the full range of the valley's produce and artisan foods.

When it's time to build up an appetite, hike the Kettle Valley Rail Trail over trestles and canyons and along the lake. Or take to the waters by kayak, canoe or other sporty contraption. Bike amidst the vineyards or climb some of the sheer limestone cliffs. In winter there are excellent low-key resorts at which to ski BC's powder.

Kelowna is the valley's center and this booming town has excellent nightlife. Penticton – which boasts two long beaches – is great for watersports and families while tiny Oliver is a nexus of wine and good cheer.

HIGHLIGHTS

- Comparing cabernets and rating rieslings at the over 100 **wineries** (p252)
- Beating black diamond powder at uncrowded **Apex Mountain Resort** (p258)
- Savoring every fruit imaginable at the **BC Fruit Market** in Kelowna (p265)
- Fast- or slow-paced fun afloat in **Penticton** (p249)
- Hiking the spectacular Myra Canyon **Kettle Valley Rail Trail** (p263) near Kelowna

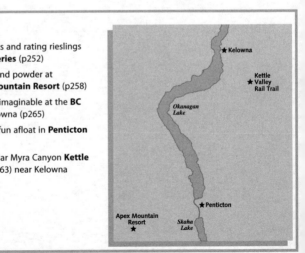

OSOYOOS

pop 5000

Once modest Osoyoos is on the brink of change as it straddles a past as a lakeside holiday spot for families and a future as an upscale part of the new Okanagan Valley.

The town takes its name from the First Nations word 'soyoos,' which means 'sand bar across,' and if the translation is a bit rough, the definition is not: much of the town is indeed on a narrow spit of land that divides Osoyoos Lake. It is ringed with beaches and the waters irrigate the lush farms, orchards and vineyards that line Hwy 97 going north out of town.

Nature's bounty aside, this is the arid end of the valley and locals like to say that the town marks the northern end of Mexico's Sonoran Desert. To this end, much of the town is decked out in a style that has lost something crossing the borders of two countries. From the cactus-speckled sands to the town's cheesy faux tile-and-stucco architecture, it's a big change from the BC image of pine trees and mountains found in both directions on Hwy 3.

Orientation & Information

Osoyoos is at the crossroads of Hwy 97, heading north to Penticton, and the Crowsnest Hwy (Hwy 3), running east to Castlegar and the Kootenay region and west to Hope and the Fraser Canyon. The US border, cutting through Osoyoos Lake, is just 5km to the south. The center of town is just west of the lake, although it follows several kilometers of Hwy 3, known locally as Main St.

This close to the border, ATMs give you a choice of Canadian or US currency.

Visitor Centre (☎ 250-495-5070, 888-676-9667; www.destinationosoyoos.com; cnr Hwys 3 & 97; ☼ 9am-5pm) This large center has internet access, maps, books and it books tours and accommodation.

Sights

The **Osoyoos Desert Centre** (☎ 250-495-2470; www.desert.org; adult/child $7/4; ☼ 10am-4pm May-Sep, call other times) focuses on the local ecosystem, which due to its small size and persistently encroaching development, is highly endangered. The center, 3km north of Osoyoos off Hwy 97, features interpretive kiosks along a raised boardwalk that meanders through the dry land. Though plenty of

unique critters (such as burrowing owls, desert bunnies and tiger salamanders) call this place home, most are active only at night. But there's much to learn and you can get all the poop at the scat lab kiosk.

Nk'Mip Desert & Heritage Centre (☎ 250-495-7901; www.nkmipdesert.com; 1000 Rancher Creek Rd; adult/child $12/8; ☼ 9:30am-4:30pm Apr-Oct) has crowd-pleasing displays on local residents such as rattle snakes. Developed by the Osoyoos Indian Band, who control access to most of the remaining desert near town, this complex features cultural demonstrations and guided tours of the sandy highlights. It also has a desert golf course and a noted winery (p255). It's off 45th St north of Hwy 3.

Rapidly being overshadowed (along with the Gyro Community Park) by glitzy lakeside condo developments, the small **Osoyoos Museum** (☎ 250-495-2582; adult/child $3/1; ☼ 10am-3:30pm Jun-Sep, 2-5pm Tue-Thu winter), near the center off Hwy 3, will fill a shady hour with its displays on local history.

On the south side of Hwy 3, 8km west of town, look for the **spotted lake**, a weird natural phenomenon that once would have made a kitschy roadside attraction. In the hot summer sun, the lake's water begins to evaporate, causing its high mineral content to crystallize and leave white-rimmed circles of green on the water.

Three kilometers further west along Hwy 3, look for a gravel Forest Service road that will take you to the summit of **Mount Kobau**, where you'll enjoy superb views of the town and desert to the east, the **Similkameen Valley** to the west and the US border to the south. The rough road to the summit is 20km long, but the views are well worth it. Amateur and professional astronomers flock here during the middle of August for the **Mt Kobau Star Party** (www.mksp.ca; per night $20), during which they set up telescopes, watch for imminent peril from rogue asteroids, secretly hope for UFOs and marvel at the night sky.

Activities

The climate makes **Osoyoos Lake** among the warmest lakes in the country, and every summer oodles of folks splash around until they look like prunes. Most of the motels can hook you up with paddleboat, kayak and powerboat rentals. Waveboard lessons are easily arranged.

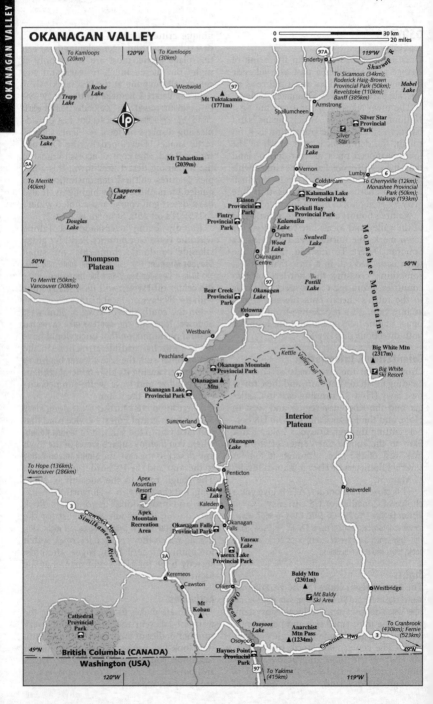

In winter, take the rough Camp McKinney Rd from Hwy 97 east to the **Mt Baldy Ski Area** (☎ 866-754-2253; www.skibaldy.com; 1-day lift ticket adult/child $46/26). This small, vintage resort has cross-country trails and downhill runs with a maximum vertical drop of 394m. It has chairlifts, quads and T-bars. It's 46km from Osoyoos; check the website for details on bus service.

Sleeping

Osoyoos is the antidote to chains. More than a dozen modest motels line the shores of the lake, you can almost hear the echoes of generations of budget family holidays. Another batch are on the southwest shore near the border. Charmless chains can be found at the junction. Quality varies among the older properties, so it's good to compare. Rates plummet in cooler months.

Haynes Point Provincial Park (☎ 250-548-0076, 800-689-9025; www.discovercamping.ca; campsites $24; ☯ Apr-mid-Oct) This is the most sought-after campground. In fact in summer, you're not likely to get one of the 41 sites unless you reserved early. The park has beaches (one allows dogs), nature trails and more. It's 2km south of the center off Hwy 97.

Nk'Mip Campground & RV Resort (☎ 250-495-7279; www.campingosoyoos.com; campsites $27-35; ☜) Part of the Nk'Mip empire, there are over 120 lakefront sites at this year-round resort, off 45th St north of Hwy 3. The long list of services includes watersports rentals.

Avalon Inn (☎ 250-495-6334, 800-264-5999; www.avaloninn.ca; 9106 Main St; r $100-160; ✖) Away from the lake, this 24-unit motel has large, standard rooms, which all have broadband. Right in the center of town, there are several restaurants within easy walking distance.

Sandy Beach Motel (☎ 250-495-6931, 866-495-6931; www.sandybeachmotel.com; 6706 Ponderosa Dr; r $85-170; ✖) Enjoy free rowboats at this fun 25-room beachside place just north of Hwy 3. Bungalows and two-story blocks surround a grassy common area with barbeques and a playground. Some units have two bedrooms; all have patios and kitchens.

Eating & Drinking

Osoyoos Gelato (☎ 250-495-5425; 9150 Main St; treats from $2; ☯ 10am-10pm summer; ☜) Near the junction, there are always at least 24 splendid homemade flavors.

Bibo (☎ 250-495-6686; 8316 Main St; meals $10-25; ☯ 11am-10pm) Rich-feeling and oh-so-dark, Bibo feels like a smooth cabernet. The name means Cheers in Latin, which tells you that a) it's too classy for plain old English, and b) Osoyoo's main drag just got another upgrade. Tapas and wines by the glass star; DJs spin till midnight weekends.

Wildfire Grill (☎ 250-495-2215; 8526 Main St; mains $10-25; ☯ 11am-10pm Mon-Fri, 9am-11pm Sat & Sun) Wildfire serves up a range of global cuisine from its open kitchen. Tables on the legendary patio and courtyard are always in demand, especially on long summer nights. There's a stylish lounge area for enjoying the local wine bounty by the glass.

Diamond Steakhouse (☎ 250-495-6223; 8903 Main St; mains $12-25; ☯ 5-9pm) This timeless '60s supper club serves Greek-accented steak and seafood to diners humming Dean Martin while lounging in commodious booths. The steaks draw diners from afar, as does the seafood and the endless wine list.

Getting There & Away

Greyhound Canada (☎ 250-495-7252), at the visitor center at the junction of Hwys 3 and 97, runs to Vancouver ($80, eight hours, one daily) and Kelowna ($30, 2½ hours, one daily).

AROUND OSOYOOS

East of Osoyoos, Hwy 3 goes through increasingly beautiful Alpine country towards the Kootenays. Going west, Hwy 3 follows the rugged Similkameen Valley 47km to **Keremeos**, a cute town surrounded by orchards.

Another 30km west of Keremeos, **Cathedral Provincial Park** (☎ 604-795-6169; www.bcparks.ca) is a 330 sq km mountain wilderness that lures the truly adventurous. The park offers excellent backcountry camping ($5) and hiking around wildflower-dappled Alpine expanses and turquoise waters.

OSOYOOS TO PENTICTON

With its hot, dry weather (average annual rainfall: 200mm), the Osoyoos region grows the earliest and most varied produce in Canada. The 20km drive along Hwy 97 from Osoyoos to Oliver alone is worth the trip. Low hanging fruit is ripe for the picking and dozens of fruit stands burst with bounty eight months a year. Look for –

NO NATIONAL PARK?

You see the bold red signs along the roads radiating out from Osoyoos and Oliver: 'No National Park!' It's good for an immediate double-take as the sentiment would seem as incongruous as, 'Club Baby Seals!' and, 'Gut Bambi!' After all, everyone loves national parks, right? Wrong, at least for a vocal minority in the southern Okanagan Valley. Parks Canada has proposed turning 650 sq km into BC's eighth national park. The land in question, west of the valley and north of Hwy 3, encompasses much of the Similkameen Valley, a pristine wilderness of grasslands and pocket desert that's home to over 250 threatened species, including coyotes and the calliope hummingbird (the smallest bird in Canada).

Given the pace of Okanagan development, advocates fear that grape vines and condos are just a few years off. So what's not to love? Opponents have proved surprisingly feisty and comprise a loose coalition of older Okanagan residents and First Nations bands who are deeply suspicious of what they see as a government land-grab. They prefer that the lands remain in local control and scoff at environmentalists who worry that this could open the door for a few profitable projects here and there.

Although public opinion favors the park (a poll by *Okanagan Life* magazine found overwhelming support), don't expect to visit anytime soon. Planning has dragged on for years and opponents vow to slow it further.

often organic – cherries, apricots, peaches, apples and other fruit (p257). Diversions include lavender farms and the constantly multiplying wineries.

North of Oliver to Penticton, the orchards and vineyards abate a little and the scene is dominated by wooded mountains and sheer rock formations.

Oliver

pop 2000

Once a wide spot in the road catering to fruit pickers, Oliver has found a new and upscale incarnation as a center for organic produce and wine. And many stores in its cute downtown feature 'gifts' and 'accessories' in their names. The **Visitor Centre** (☎ 250-498-6321; www.oliverchamber.bc.ca; 36250 93rd St; ⏰ 9am-5pm May-Sep, Mon-Fri Oct-Apr) is in the old train station near the center of town. The small roads through the vineyards around Oliver are made for exploring. Do so on a bike from **Double O Bikes** (☎ 250-498-8348; www.doubleobikes.com; Main St; per day from $15; ⏰ 9:30am-5pm Tue-Sat), a non-profit shop offering tons of advice.

Near the center, **Mount View Motel** (☎ 250-498-3446; www.mountviewmotel.net; 34426 97th St; r $70-120; 🅿 🛜 🐾) has seven compact units around a flower-bedecked motor court. All have kitchens – and corkscrews.

Further out, enjoy a stay at one of the region's best wineries. **Burrowing Oak Guest House** (☎ 250-498-0620, 8777-498-0620; Road 22;

r $175-350; 🅿 🖥 🛜 🐾) has 10 rooms with patios facing southwest over the vineyards (p254). There's a big pool, hot tub, king-size beds and corporate mission-style decor. It's 13km south of Oliver, off Hwy 97.

Oliver's vibrant **Farmers Market** (⏰ 8:30am-12:30pm Sat Jul-Sep) showcases local foodstuffs and is close to Hwy 97. For a splendid picnic, peruse the deli cases at OUR PICK **Cantaloupe Annie's** (☎ 250-498-2955; 34845 97th St; meals from $6; ⏰ 9:30am-5:30pm Mon-Sat, 11am-3pm Sun summer; 🛜), a café famous for its locally sourced specials, smoked meats, fruit-based desserts and ice cream.

You can reach Oliver by **Greyhound Canada** (☎ 250-498-2626), which traverses the south valley twice daily; although by car – or bike – you'll be able to stop off along the way.

Vaseux Wildlife Centre

Just south of Okanagan Falls (right), watch for the small sign for **Vaseux Wildlife Centre** (☎ 250-494-6500; admission free; ⏰ dawn-dusk) at the north end of Vaseux Lake off Hwy 97. From the 300m boardwalk you'll see lots of birds, and you might catch a glimpse of bighorn sheep, mountain goats or some of the 14 species of bats. You can also hike to the Bighorn National Wildlife Area and the Vaseux Lake National Migratory Bird Sanctuary, with more than 160 bird species.

You can **camp** (sites $15) at one of the 12 simple lakeside sites along Hwy 97, popular for bass fishing, swimming and canoeing in summer. In winter, skaters wend their way past patient fishermen staring dolefully into their holes poked in the ice.

Okanagan Falls

This small town at the south end of Skaha Lake is mostly a place where you have to choose your course. The main road, Hwy 97, heads north along the west side of the lake. However, you can also follow a series of smaller paved roads that wander the scenic hills and vineyards on the east side of the lake, bringing you out in Penticton.

PENTICTON

pop 34,000

Not as frenetic as Kelowna, Penticton combines the idle pleasures of a beach resort with its own edgy vibe. Long a final stop in life for Canadian retirees (which added a certain spin to its Salish-derived name Pen-Tak-Tin, meaning 'place to stay forever'), the town today is growing fast, along with the rest of the valley.

If approaching from the south, avert your eyes from the long stretch of strip malls and high-rise condos and press on for the walkable downtown and bucolic lakefront. Penticton makes a good base for your valley pleasures. There are plenty of activities and diversions to fill your days even when you don't travel further afield.

History

Penticton became an official town in 1892, while several nearby mine claims were being developed. But agriculture soon became the main industry. Local peaches were sold all over Canada and exported to points beyond. After WWII, summer tourism gradually supplanted tree fruit until high-value vineyards became the rage. Today the city is ringed by orchards and vineyards and is attracting large numbers of people looking for a second home.

Orientation & Information

Penticton, the southernmost of the three Okanagan sister cities, sits directly between Okanagan Lake and Skaha Lake, which are connected by the Okanagan River Channel.

The cute downtown area extends for about 10 blocks south from Okanagan Lake along Main St. It has a full range of shops, banks and services. Go further, however, and you'll encounter strip malls, sprawl and big-box this and franchise that. Charmless Hwy 97 (Channel Pkwy) bypasses everything but should only be used if you're in a rush.

At the southern end of town, you'll find the 1.5km-long Skaha Beach, with sand, trees and picnic areas.

BOOKSTORES

Book Shop (☎ 250-492-6661; 242 Main St) Huge collection of used books.

Okanagan Books (☎ 250-493-1941; 233 Main St) Good selection of regional books, magazines and maps.

INTERNET ACCESS

Several of the cafés listed on p255), as well as the VC (below), have internet access.

Penticton Library (☎ 250-492-0024; 785 Main St; access free; 🕑 9:30am-5pm Mon-Sat, to 9pm Tue & Thu, 1-5pm Sun winter)

LAUNDRY

Maytag Laundry (☎ 250-493-7899; 976 Eckhardt Ave W; 🕑 8am-6pm)

MEDICAL SERVICES

Penticton Regional Hospital (☎ 250-492-4000; 550 Carmi Ave; 🕑 24hr)

POST

Shopper's Drug Mart (☎ 250-492-8000; Penticton Plaza Mall, 1301 Main St; 🕑 9am-6pm Mon-Sat)

TOURIST INFORMATION

BC Wine Information Centre (☎ 250-493-4055; www.bcwineinfo.net; 553 Railway St, at Hwy 97 & Eckhardt Ave W) With the VC; voluminous information, tastings and sales. See the boxed text, p252, for details on tasting your way through the region.

Visitor Centre (☎ 250-493-4055, 800-663-5052; www.tourismpenticton.com; 553 Railway St, at Hwy 97 & Eckhardt Ave W; 🕑 8am-7pm May-Sep, 9am-6pm Oct-Apr) One of BC's best, with free internet access.

Sights

SS Sicamous (☎ 250-492-0403; 1099 Lakeshore Dr W; adult/child $5/1; 🕑 9am-9pm May-Oct, 10am-4pm Mon-Fri Nov-Apr) is a classic stern-wheeler that cruised Okanagan Lake with passengers and freight from 1914 to 1936. Now both restored and beached, it has been joined by the equally old *SS Naramata*, a tugboat.

If the *Sicamous* stimulates your inner seaman, **Casabella Princess** (☎ 250-492-4090;

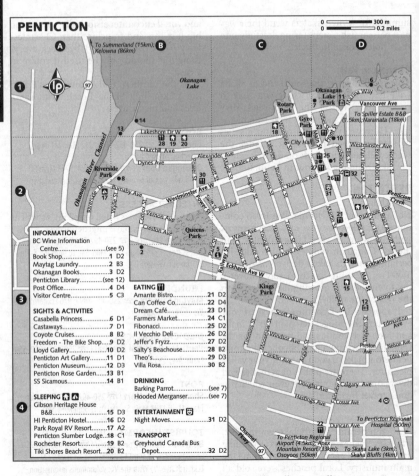

PENTICTON

0 ——— 300 m
0 ——— 0.2 miles

To Summerland (15km);
Kelowna (86km)

Okanagan Lake

Okanagan River Channel

Lakeshore Dr W

Churchill Ave

Dynes Ave

Alexander Ave

Healeys Ave

Riverside Park

Burnaby Ave

Westminster Ave W

Vernon Ave

Creston Ave

Queens Park

Wade Ave

Eckhardt Ave W

Kings Park

Woodruff Ave

Scott Ave

Windsor Ave

Conklin Ave

Douglas Ave

Calgary Ave

Hastings Ave

Channel Pkwy

Duncan Ave

Okanagan Lake Park

Rotary Park

Gyro Park

City Hall

Vancouver Ave
To Spiller Estate B&B
(1.5km), Naramata (18km)

Westminster Ave

Wade Ave

Padmore Ave

Penticton Creek

Eckhardt Ave E

Jermyn Ave

Edmonton Ave

Nelson Ave

Edna Ave

Preston Ave

To Penticton Regional
Hospital (500m)

To Penticton Regional
Airport (4.5km); Apex
Mountain Resort (33km);
Osoyoos (50km)

To Skaha Lake (3km);
Skaha Bluffs (4km)

INFORMATION
BC Wine Information
Centre............................(see 5)
Book Shop...........................**1** D2
Maytag Laundry..................**2** B3
Okanagan Books..................**3** D2
Penticton Library............(see 12)
Post Office...........................**4** D4
Visitor Centre......................**5** C3

SIGHTS & ACTIVITIES
Casabella Princess...............**6** D1
Castaways............................**7** D1
Coyote Cruises....................**8** B2
Freedom - The Bike Shop.....**9** D2
Lloyd Gallery.....................**10** D1
Penticton Art Gallery.........**11** D1
Penticton Museum.............**12** D3
Penticton Rose Garden......**13** B1
SS Sicamous.......................**14** B1

SLEEPING 🏠 🏢
Gibson Heritage House
B&B...................................**15** D3
HI Penticton Hostel...........**16** D3
Park Royal RV Resort.........**17** A2
Penticton Slumber Lodge...**18** C1
Rochester Resort................**19** B2
Tiki Shores Beach Resort....**20** B2

EATING 🍴
Amante Bistro....................**21** D2
Can Coffee Co....................**22** D4
Dream Café........................**23** D1
Farmers Market..................**24** C1
Fibonacci............................**25** D2
Il Vecchio Deli....................**26** D2
Jeffer's Fryzz.......................**27** D2
Salty's Beachouse...............**28** B2
Theo's.................................**29** D3
Villa Rosa...........................**30** B2

DRINKING
Barking Parrot..................(see 7)
Hooded Merganser...........(see 7)

ENTERTAINMENT 🎭
Night Moves.......................**31** D2

TRANSPORT
Greyhound Canada Bus
Depot................................**32** D2

www.casabellaprincess.com; adult/child $20/10; ☼ varies,
May-Sep) offers one-hour, open-air lake tours
on a faux stern-wheeler. There are multiple
daily sailings at summer's peak.

If you want to take some time out to
smell the roses, you can stroll around the
Penticton Rose Garden (admission free), beside the
SS Sicamous. The waterfront **Penticton Art
Gallery** (☎ 250-493-2928; 199 Marina Way; admission
$2; ☼ 10am-5pm Tue-Sun) displays an engaging
collection of regional, provincial and national artists. Purchase the best local efforts
at the **Lloyd Gallery** (☎ 250-492-4484; 18 Front St;
☼ 9:30am-5:30pm Mon-Sat), which bursts with
the colors of the valley.

The **Penticton Museum** (☎ 250-490-2451; 785
Main St; admission by donation; ☼ 10am-5pm Tue-Sat)

is an excellent small-town museum wi
engaging and eclectic displays. Skip t
natural history exhibit with stuffed an
mals and birds and enjoy the fun displa
about the Peach Festival and its fuzzy-fac
contestants.

Activities
Kids of all ages will find mini-golf and oth
classic holiday pursuits at the west end
Okanagan Beach. Okanagan Beach boa
about 1300m of sand, with average su
mer water temperatures of about 22°C.
things are jammed, there are often quie
shores south at **Skaha Beach**.

The paved but vaguely dusty **Okanag
River Channel Biking & Jogging Path** follo

the channel, linking the much nicer paths around the lakes (which are great for running, cycling or in-line skating). Just east of the center, off the road to Naramata, **Munson Mountain** is really just a knoll, but one with sweeping views of the town and lake.

WATER SPORTS
Both Okanagan and Skaha Lakes enjoy some of the best sailboarding, boating and paddling in the Okanagan Valley. **Castaways** (☎ 250-490-2033; Penticton Lakeside Resort, 21 Lakeshore Dr; kayaks per hr $16) rents just about anything that floats. A half day's rental of a ski boat is $305.

Coyote Cruises (☎ 250-492-2115; www.coyote cruises.ca; 215 Riverside Dr; rental & shuttle $10; 🕙 10am-4:30pm Jun-Aug) rents out inner tubes that you can float to a midway point on the channel. Coyote Cruises buses you back to the start near Okanagan Lake (if you have your own floatable, it's $5 for the bus ride).

MOUNTAIN BIKING
Long dry days and rolling hills add up to great conditions for mountain biking. Get to popular rides by heading east out of town, toward Naramata (p256). Follow signs to the city dump and Campbell's Mountain, where you'll find a single-track and dual-slalom course, neither of which are too technical. Once you get there, the riding is mostly on the right side, but once you pass the cattle guard, it opens up and you can ride anywhere.

Rent bikes and pick up a wealth of information at **Freedom – The Bike Shop** (☎ 250-493-0686; www.freedombikeshop.com; 533 Main St; bikes per day $40).

ROCK CLIMBING
Drawn by the dry weather and compact gneiss rock, climbers from all over the world come to the **Skaha Bluffs** to enjoy a seven-month climbing season on more than 400 bolted routes across the 120 cliffs (new routes open all the time). The rock is compact but has plenty of holes making the climbing excellent for experienced and novice climbers.

The good news in 2009 was that after years of public access that was dodgier than a rusted piton, a new and permanent parking area opened on land managed by government and private groups. Take Lake-side Rd on the east side of Skaha Lake 3km south and then turn on Smythe Dr. The local climbing group, **Skaha.org** (www.skaha .org), has comprehensive info on the bluffs.

Skaha Rock Adventures (☎ 250-493-1765; www .skaharockclimbing.com; 2-day courses from $275) offers advanced technical instruction and introductory courses for anyone who dreams of rappelling.

Festivals & Events
There's a multitude of annual festivals, most during the summer months when, as boosters are quick to note, the sun shines at least 10 hours a day.

Elvis Festival (www.pentictonelvisfestival.com) Dozens of impersonators of The King could be your idea of heaven or hound-dog hell, especially the Elvis-only karaoke held in a pub. Late June.

Peach Festival (www.peachfest.com) The city's premier event is basically a weeklong party in early August that has taken place since 1948, loosely centered on crowning a Peach Queen. The Saturday parade is a local fave.

Pentastic Jazz Festival (www.pentasticjazz.com) More than a dozen bands perform at five venues over three days in early September. Shuttle buses avoid traffic.

Sleeping
Lakeshore Dr W and S Main St/Skaha Lake Rd are home to most of the local motels. The Okanagan Beach strip is the most popular area and rightfully so. Many campgrounds are folding up their tents and being replaced by condo developments; several are along Skaha Lake. The VC has a long list of B&Bs.

HI Penticton Hostel (☎ 250-492-3992; www.hihos tels.ca; 464 Ellis St; dm $23-30, r from $65; 🍴 💻) This hostel is near the center in a veteran house that could be a college frat dorm. Rooms have one to six beds. The hostel arranges all sorts of activities, including wine tours.

Park Royal RV Resort (☎ 250-492-7051; parkroyalrv @shaw.ca; 240 Riverside Dr; car/RV sites from $45) Right near the most-popular end of Okanagan Beach, the 40 sites here are in a shady park-like setting.

Gibson Heritage House B&B (☎ 250-492-2705; www.gibsonbb.com; 112 Eckhardt Ave W; r $80-160; 🍴) Close to the center, this 1906 colonial revival B&B sits on manicured grounds. The four rooms have elaborately carved furniture and high-speed internet. Each has its own bathroom. Breakfasts are huge and traditional.

OKANAGAN VALLEY

OKANAGAN VALLEY WINERIES

With over 100 wineries, the Okanagan Valley is justifying its self-promoted nickname of 'Napa North.' Long a producer of low-end table wine, the valley began moving to more expensive and exclusive varieties of wine in the 1980s. The abundance of sunshine, fertile soil and cool winters has produced many wines of note. Kelowna and the northern region are known for their whites like Pinot Grigio. South, near Penticton and Oliver, reds are the stars; while the sweet winter elixir known as icewine (it's made from grapes frozen on the vine) is not to be missed.

That the wineries are all on or close to Hwy 97 means that tasters and tourists alike barely have a chance to get their car up to speed before another winery swings into view. Most offer tours and all offer sales (in fact many of the best wines are only sold at the wineries) but a growing number are also adding top-end restaurants with views and regional fare to complement what's in the glass.

FESTIVALS

Okanagan wineries certainly know how to put on a party. Expect vintners to premiere special vintages, hold tastings of rare wines, host special tasting dinners and more. You can check up on the seasonal happenings at the valley's very good **festival website** (www.thewinefestivals.com).

The festivals (fall is the major one):

- Fall – early October
- Spring – early May
- Winter – mid-January
- Summer – mid-August

INFORMATION

Two good sources of information on Okanagan Valley wines are the **BC Wine Information Centre** in Penticton (p249) and the **Wine Museum** in Kelowna (p261). Each offers guidance on selecting from a range that might otherwise drive you to drink. In fact, they told us at the latter: 'We tell it like it is.' VCs are also good resources.

It's also worth looking for guidebooks by John Schreiner, the dean of BC wine writers. His *The Wineries of British Columbia* is up-to-date, authoritative and voluminous in its coverage. *John Schreiner's Okanagan Wine Tour Guide* is another excellent choice. Both are sold at VCs, wineries and bookstores in the valley.

TOURS

There are several companies that let you do the sipping while they do the driving. See the companies listed under Naramata (p258) and Kelowna (p263) for details.

EXPLORING THE WINERIES

At all the wineries open for visitors, you can expect to taste wine, but the quality of the experience varies widely. Some establishments are simple, with just a couple of wines on offer. Others are grander affairs with dozens of vintages for your perusal. Some charge for tastings, while at others they remain free. More and more wineries are adding restaurants and some have added luxurious rooms so you can sleep amid the vines.

Here are some of the wineries we enjoy visiting – for the wine, views, food, welcome or all of the above (listed roughly north to south).

- **Gray Monk Estate Winery** (☎ 250-766-3168; www.graymonk.com; 1055 Camp Rd, Okanagan Centre; ❤ 9am-9pm summer, less other times) Try the Pinot Gris or the Gewurztraminer with lunch from the bistro. Have enough and you may spot the Ogopogo – this is an 'official' viewing station (p261).

Okanagan Valley Wineries (continued p254)

OKANAGAN VALLEY WINERIES

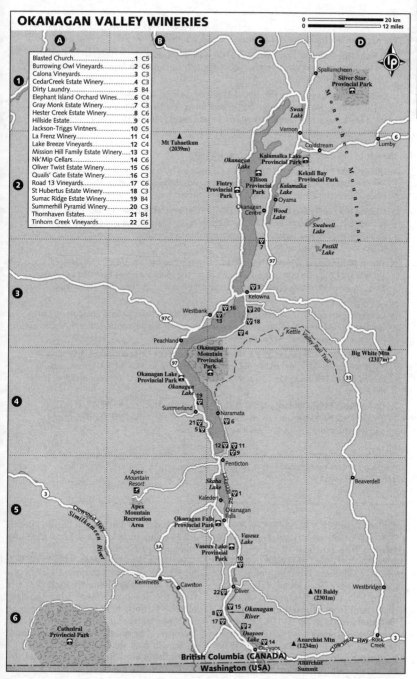

Blasted Church	1	C5
Burrowing Owl Vineyards	2	C6
Calona Vineyards	3	C3
CedarCreek Estate Winery	4	C3
Dirty Laundry	5	B4
Elephant Island Orchard Wines	6	C4
Gray Monk Estate Winery	7	C3
Hester Creek Estate Winery	8	C6
Hillside Estate	9	C4
Jackson-Triggs Vintners	10	C5
La Frenz Winery	11	C4
Lake Breeze Vineyards	12	C4
Mission Hill Family Estate Winery	13	C3
Nk'Mip Cellars	14	C6
Oliver Twist Estate Winery	15	C6
Quails' Gate Estate Winery	16	C3
Road 13 Vineyards	17	C6
St Hubertus Estate Winery	18	C3
Sumac Ridge Estate Winery	19	B4
Summerhill Pyramid Winery	20	C3
Thornhaven Estates	21	B4
Tinhorn Creek Vineyards	22	C6

0   20 km
0   12 miles

OKANAGAN VALLEY

Okanagan Valley Wineries (continued from p252)

The next two are south of Kelowna along the lake's eastern shore.

- **St Hubertus Estate Winery** (☎ 250-764-7888; www.st-hubertus.bc.ca; 5225 Lakeshore Rd, Kelowna; 10am-5:30pm May-Oct, noon-5pm Tue-Sat Nov-Apr) A Swiss-family-run winery where you should taste the superb Chardonnay.

- **CedarCreek Estate Winery** (☎ 250-764-8866; www.cedarcreek.bc.ca; 5445 Lakeshore Rd, Kelowna; 10am-6pm Apr-Oct, 11am-5pm Nov-Mar) Known for its Ehrenfelser, a fruity white wine that some say is made best here. The Vineyard Terrace (mains $10 to $15, open 11:30am to 3pm June to mid-September) is good for lunch.

The rest of the wineries can be reached via Hwy 97.

- **Quails' Gate Estate Winery** (☎ 250-769-4451; www.quailsgate.com; 3303 Boucherie Rd, Kelowna; 10am-5pm) A small winery with a huge reputation; known for its Pinot Noir, Pinot Blanc and more. The restaurant (meals $15 to $25, open 11am to 9pm) is excellent.

- **Mission Hill Family Estate Winery** (☎ 250-768-7611; www.missionhillwinery.com; 1730 Mission Hill Rd, Westbank; 10am-6pm) Enjoy a taste of the very drinkable Merlot and Chardonnay at the Okanagan's most visually stunning winery. Lunches (mains $8 to $15, open noon to 2pm May to October) are served on the terrace.

- **Sumac Ridge Estate Winery** (☎ 250-494-0451; www.sumacridge.com; 17403 Hwy 97, Summerland; 9am-5pm) You'll be effervescent with praise for the sparkling wines here. The Cellar Door Bistro (mains $10 to $20, open noon to 9pm) is the place to try their Gewurztraminer Private Reserve.

- **La Frenz Winery** (☎ 250-492-6690; www.lafrenzwinery.com; 740 Naramata Road, Penticton; 10am-5pm May-Oct) Cabernet Sauvignon and Viognier are two of the best options at this Australian-run winery among the many heading to Naramata.

- **Burrowing Owl Vineyards** (☎ 250-498-0620; www.bovwine.ca; 100 Burrowing Owl Pl, Oliver; 10am-6pm Apr-Oct) Uses organic grapes to make its very popular merlot. The restaurant's (mains $10 to $20, open 11am to 3pm April to October) balcony tables are popular as is the inn (p248).

- **Oliver Twist Estate Winery** (☎ 250-485-0227; www.olivertwistwinery.com; 33013 Road 9A, Oliver; 10am-5pm May-Oct) Learn how to open wine with color and flair from the personable owners who make a Pinot Gris you'll want by the case.

Aside from the favorites we list above, there are many, many more wineries you can visit. The following list we recommend (north to south) isn't exhaustive, so you'll have to find a few you can call your own.

Spiller Estate B&B (☎ 250-490-4162, 800-610-3794; www.spillerestates.com; 475 Upper Bench Rd; r $130; May-Oct) Just 2km east of the center on the road to Naramata, this four-room half-timbered 1930s lodge is on the grounds of its namesake winery. You can smell the peaches ripening from the shady grounds, which are a short jaunt from Munson Mountain.

Rochester Resort (☎ 250-493-1128, 800-567-4904; www.rochesterresort.penticton.com; 970 Lakeshore Dr W; r $140-300;) The unassuming 1970s design extends to the modest beige and avocado decor. But you'll have little time to linger indoors, what with all the fun nearby. All 36 unites have kitchens. Some have lake views from balconies.

Penticton Slumber Lodge (☎ 250-492-4008, 800-663-2831; www.slumberlodge.com; 274 Lakeshore Dr W; r $130-200;) Perfectly located across from the beach and steps from the center, the 44 units here are large, some have multiple bedrooms and all have kitchen facilities. The pool is indoors for those inclement days the local boosters ignore.

Tiki Shores Beach Resort (☎ 250-492-8769, 866-492-8769; www.tikishores.com; 914 Lakeshore Dr W; condos

Kelowna

- **Calona Vineyards** (☎ 250-762-3332; 1125 Richter St) One of BC's largest producers, started in 1932 and still giving tastings in the heart of Kelowna.
- **Summerhill Pyramid Winery** (☎ 250-764-8000; 4870 Chute Lake Rd) On Kelowna's eastern shore, wines are aged in a huge pyramid.

Summerland

Wineries line Gartrell Rd and its tributaries in the sunny hills west of Hwy 97.

- **Thornhaven Estates** (☎ 250-494-7778; 6816 Andrew Ave) A perfect spot for a picnic.
- **Dirty Laundry** (☎ 250-494-8815; 7311 Fiske St) Named for a former Summerland brothel; try the Hush Rosé.

Penticton to Naramata

More than 20 wineries line this good detour:

- **Lake Breeze Vineyards** (☎ 250-496-5659; 930 Sammet Rd) Blow through some Zephyr Brut.
- **Elephant Island Orchard Wines** (☎ 250-496-5522; 2730 Aikens Loop) Pink Elephant is a no-brainer.
- **Hillside Estate** (☎ 250-493-6274; 1350 Naramata Rd) Rare Old Vines Gamay.

Okanagan Falls

- **Blasted Church** (☎ 250-497-1125; 378 Parsons Rd) Fine views from the Lakeside Rd alternative to Hwy 97; one of many.

Oliver

- **Jackson-Triggs Vintners** (☎ 250-498-4981; 38619 Hwy 97) One of BC's best-known is tasting only.
- **Tinhorn Creek Vineyards** (☎ 250-498-3743; 32830 Tinhorn Creek Rd) Accesses a good mountain hike.
- **Hester Creek Estate Winery** (☎ 250-498-4435; 13163 326th Ave) Noted Pinot Blanc and a luxury inn.
- **Road 13 Vineyards** (☎ 250-498-8330; 13140 316A Avenue) Marmots live around this castle-like winery.

Osoyoos

- **Nk'Mip Cellars** (☎ 250-495-2985; 1400 Rancher Creek Rd) Excellent winery owned by a First Nations band (p245).

from $130-300; 🗶 🛜 🖵) This lively resort has 40 condo-style units with separate bedrooms and kitchens. Throw your own toga party in one of the 'Roman theme units,' and throw your soiled post-bacchanalia wear into the handy guest laundry.

Eating

Penticton definitely has its share of good eats. Stroll around Main and Front Sts and you will find numerous choices. The **Farmers Market** (☎ 250-770-3276; 🕑 8am-noon Sat May-Oct) has large numbers of local organic produc-

ers, based at Gyro Park in the 100 block of Main St.

BUDGET

Jeffer's Fryzz (snacks $3; 🕑 11am-6pm daily, 11pm-2am Fri & Sat) The crispy, deep golden fries that issue forth from this truck parked near the corner of Nanaimo Ave and Main St are sliced fresh and fried to perfection. The fish and chips are just as good.

our pick Il Vecchio Deli (☎ 250-492-7610; 317 Robinson St; sandwiches $5; 🕑 10am-4pm Mon-Sat) The smell that greets you as you enter confirms your choice. The best lunch sandwiches in town can be consumed at a couple of tables in this atmospheric deli but will taste better on a picnic. Choices are myriad, we like the garlic salami with marinated eggplant sandwich.

Can Coffee Co (☎ 250-493-3044; The Cannery, 1475 Fairview Rd at Duncan Ave; meals $6; ⏰ 7am-8pm; ☎) Housed in a quirky old cannery, this high-ceilinged café has a wide porch and attracts an arty crowd that revs up on the good coffee to decry the state of culture funding. Good muffins.

Fibonacci (☎ 250-770-1913; www.fibonacci.ca; 219 Main St; meals from $7; ⏰ 8am-10pm Mon-Sat; ☎) You see the large brass coffee roaster right when you enter this downtown café which serves up lots of healthy Mediterranean fare. Thin-crust pizzas are made with local produce. At night there's a rotating line-up of art films, comedy, acoustic sets and open-mike spots.

MIDRANGE & TOP END
Dream Café (☎ 250-490-9012; 67 Front St; meals $10-20; ⏰ 8am-late Tue-Sun; 🖳) The heady aroma of spices envelopes your, well, head as you enter this pillow-bedecked upscale yet funky bistro. Asian and Indian flavors mix on the menu, which has many veggie options. On many nights there's live acoustic guitar by touring pros; tables outside hum all summer long.

Theo's (☎ 250-492-4019; www.eatsquid.com; 687 Main St; mains $10-25; ⏰ 11am-10pm) The place for locals on match.com second dates, enjoy authentic Greek island cuisine in the atmospheric dark and fire-lit interior or out on the patio. The *Garithes Uvetsi* is a symphony of starters that will please two. Take the website hint and order the succulent calamari.

Salty's Beachouse (☎ 250-493-5001; 1000 Lakeshore Dr W; mains $12-25; ⏰ 5-10pm Apr-Oct) When the mascot is a pirate and your bar is called the Black Pearl, you know you're not in for serious dining. But given that mini-golf and the lake are half a shriek away, the emphasis is fittingly on fun. Candles illuminate outside tables and you can get your fill of fried fishy fare washed down with lots of local plonk and suds (including from Cannery Brewing).

Villa Rosa (☎ 250-490-9595; 795 Westminster Ave W; meals $12-25; ⏰ 11:30am-2pm & 5-9pm Tue-Sun) This always popular restaurant combines fresh Northern Italian food with a laid-back holiday flair. Outside there are a few tables on a vine-shaded patio; book these in summer.

Amante Bistro (☎ 250-493-1961; www.amantebistro.com; 483 Main St; mains $10-30; ⏰ 11am-2pm, 5-10pm, Mon-Sat) There's intimate dining for those who want to enjoy the best of valley fare here. Abul Adamé and Rose Amante have created this gem of a restaurant which features a changing seasonal menu of carefully prepared dishes such as small pizzas with Poplar Grove blue cheese to a slow-roasted pork belly with scallops. Excellent local wine list.

Drinking & Entertainment
Look for local Cannery Brewing beers around town, the seasonal Blackberry Porter is fresh and smooth. Many dinner places also feature live entertainment some nights and most have good lounges.

Hooded Merganser (☎ 250-493-8221; Penticton Lakeside Resort, 21 Lakeshore Dr) This stylish over-the-water pub has walls of glass overlooking docks and the lake. It's popular throughout the year. Just ashore, the **Barking Parrot** (☎ 250-493-8221; Penticton Lakeside Resort, 21 Lakeshore Dr) has a vast patio with heaters that extend the season almost to winter. Cover bands rock the weekends.

Night Moves (☎ 250-493-1222; 333 Martin St; cover varies; ⏰ 10pm-late Thu-Sat) Dancers groove to DJs spinning Top 40, hip-hop, house and more at this multi-level club.

Getting There & Around
Penticton Regional Airport (YYF; 250-492-6042; www.cyyf.org) is served by Air Canada Jazz, which has daily flights to Vancouver (one hour).

Greyhound Canada (☎ 250-493-4101; 307 Ellis St) offers regular services within the Okanagan Valley as well as operating routes to Vancouver ($74, 7 hours, two daily) and Kamloops ($48, 4 hours, one daily).

Penticton Transit (☎ 250-492-5602; www.busonline.ca; ⏰ Mon-Sat) has buses that link the lakes and downtown ($1.75, day pass $4) from 9am to 7pm.

NARAMATA
Grapes vie with suburban palaces along the east bank of Okanagan Lake on the drive along the Naramata Bench to the small town of Naramata. It's by no means a country idyll, but the sinuous 18km-route does

THE SWEET SMELL OF SUCCESS

There really is something in the air in the Okanagan Valley, and often that something is the sweet smell of fruit. The region's fertile soil and heavy irrigation, combined with the relatively warm climate (summers tend to be hot and dry), have made the valley Canada's top fruit-growing area. Its 100 sq km of orchards represent 85% of the nation's total. Even as wineries proliferate, fruit and vegetable growers have held on by switching to higher-value crops. Mass-market apples may be a commodity but there's still money in organically grown heirloom varieties.

During April and May, fragrant blossoms coat the valley in color. Later in summer and in fall, the orchards are laden with delicious fresh fruit. Stands dotting the roads sell the best and cheapest produce in Canada.

Reveling in the region's produce through visits to farms, orchards and wineries is reason enough to visit. The drive north along Hwy 97 from Osoyoos passes an almost endless succession of orchards, farms and fruit stands, most open at least June through October. You'll have plenty of time to smell the apples, peaches and, yes, even the roses. More than 50% of the farms are organic. Although the most fun comes from comparing the bounty at outlets along the highways and picking your favorites, here are a few good starting points:

- **Peach Hill Farm** (☎ 250-495-5090; 9105 176th Ave) Full range of local bounty, on the north side of Osoyoos Lake, east of Hwy 97.

- **No. 1 Fruit Stand** (☎ 250-497-8686; 434 Hwy 97) The Evans clan pickle asparagus, put up preserves and bake fresh peach cobbler at this iconic stand in Kaleden.

- **Robert's Fruit Market & Orchard** (☎ 250-494-5541; Hwy 97) Smear some of their apricot preserves on a butter tart, then let the anticipation build for one of their many pies, crisps and cobblers made with the ripest of fruits on display.

- **BC Fruit Market** (p265) is a year-round outlet in Kelowna for the best of the valley's growers, many organic.

Produce Seasons

If you wish to tie your trip to a specific fruit, the approximate harvest times are as follows (but confirm with the VCs if it's vital you arrive at, say, peak cherry season):

- strawberries – mid-June to early July
- raspberries – early July to mid-July
- cherries – mid-June to mid-August
- apricots – mid-July to mid-August
- peaches – mid-July to mid-September
- pears – mid-August to late September
- apples – early September to late October
- grapes – early September to late October

have some good views and you get whiffs of some of the region's more esoteric crops such as lavender.

This is a good route for cycling and at several points you can access the **Kettle Valley Rail Trail** (p263). Given the extensive vineyards, you won't be surprised that more than 20 **wineries** line the route, including some that are notable (p252).

The historic town of Naramata boasts a few galleries and cafés around a compact center that's dominated by a fruit-packing plant. Straddling town, **Wharf Park** has good views and was where boats like Penticton's SS *Sicamous* once provided the sole link to the rest of the valley. South, **Manitou Park** has a nice tree-shaded swath of beach.

The small selection of accommodations ranges from the plain **BC Motel** (☎ 250-496-5482; 365 Robinson; r $75-95) with its 10 simple units to the swish **Naramata Heritage Inn & Spa** (☎ 250-496-6808, 866-617-1188; www.naramatainn.com; 3625 1st

St; r $140-500; ⚡ 🖥). The latter was built in 1908 by a fruit baron in quasi-mission style. Continually restored, the 12 rooms are lavishly furnished with period pieces; bathrooms feature claw-foot tubs. Sample local wines and enjoy local cuisine in the popular restaurant, which has a patio and live music on weekends. Unwind completely in the spa.

If you'd rather make the trip to Naramata without the distraction of driving, or you just want to ravage a few wineries, **Top Cat Tours** (☎ 250-493-7385; www.topcattours.com; tours from $80; 🕙 May-Oct) runs five-hour trips from Penticton that visit several wineries and include lunch.

SUMMERLAND
pop 11,600

A small lakeside resort town 18km north of Penticton on Hwy 97, Summerland features some fine 19th-century heritage buildings on the hillside above the ever-widening and busy highway.

Kettle Valley Steam Railway (☎ 877-494-8424; www.kettlevalleyrail.org; 18404 Bathville Rd; adult/child $18/11; 🕙 varies mid-May-mid-Oct) is an operating 16km-remnant of the famous railway (p263). Ride behind old steam locomotives in open-air cars and enjoy orchard views. Peanut-gallery-pleasing extras include 'hold-ups'. From Hwy 97 take Prairie Valley Rd west out of town to Doherty Ave, then Bathville Rd.

For great views of Okanagan Lake head up to **Giant's Head Mountain**, an extinct volcano south of the downtown area. You can follow trails to the 845m peak.

Summerland Ornamental Gardens (☎ 250-494-6385; admission $3; 🕙 8am-dusk), 7km south of Summerland on Hwy 97, was designed for the study of fruit trees, their growth, diseases and production. You can take self-guided tours among the gardens and see the environmentally friendly beauty possible from drought-resistant plants.

PEACHLAND
pop 5400

This small lakeside town 25km south of Kelowna on the west bank of Okanagan Lake lives up to its evocative name: stroll the compact waterfront and appropriately named Beach Ave (which is well below the hubbub of Hwy 97) and pause in

---

APEX MOUNTAIN RESORT

One of Canada's best small ski resorts, **Apex Mountain Resort** (☎ 877-777-2739, conditions 250-487-4848; www.apexresort.com; lift tickets adult/child $60/37) is known for its double black diamond and technical runs (the drop is over 650m). The 68 downhill runs are renowned for being less crowded than at nearby Big White Mountain (p267). Close to the village, which has hostel and lodge accommodations (see the website), you'll find 56km of cross-country trails and a unique 1km adventure skating circuit. It's 33km west of Penticton off Green Mountain Rd; there are winter shuttles from Penticton.

---

the many parks and you'll feel, well, peachy. (Actually given current agricultural priorities, the town should be named Vineland, Vinoland or maybe just Boozeland.)

Among many appealing cafés, the slightly shambolic **Blind Angler Grill** (☎ 250-767-9264; 5899A Beach Ave; mains $8-25; 🕙 9am-9pm) has a patio overlooking a small marina. What's lost in structural integrity is more than made up for in the food quality: breakfasts shine, burgers are superb and the nighttime ribs and halibut are legendary. Banter flies almost as fast as plates out of the kitchen.

KELOWNA
pop 120,000

A kayaker paddles past scores of new tract houses on a hillside. It's an iconic image for fast-growing Kelowna, the unofficial 'capital' of the Okanagan and the sprawling center of all that's good and bad with the region.

Entering from the north, the constantly lengthening urbanized stretch of tree-lined Hwy 97 seems to go on forever. Once past the ceaseless waves of chains and strip malls, the downtown is a welcome reward. Museums, culture and nightlife abound. You can even find a few traces of Kelowna's modest fruit-picking past here and there – although high-rise condos are sprouting all over, some 20 stories and more.

The long lakefront is the real allure. Here you'll find many of the town's 65 parks and beaches. The surrounding hills are home to orchards, subdivisions, vineyards, golf

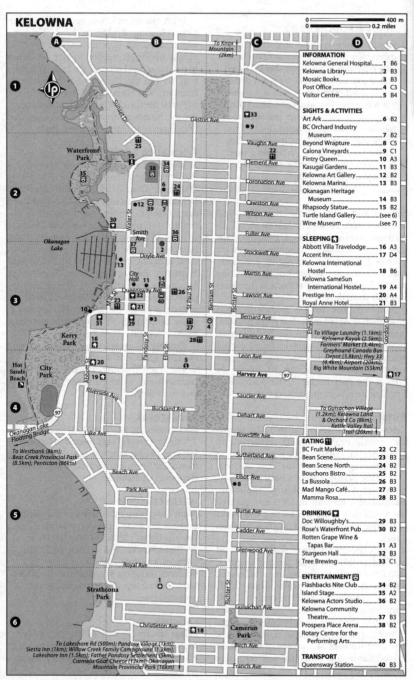

KELOWNA

To Knox
Mountain
(2km)

Gaston Ave

Waterfront
Park

Vaughn Ave

Clement Ave

Coronation Ave

Cawston Ave

Wilson Ave

Fuller Ave

Stockwell Ave

Martin Ave

Lawson Ave

Bernard Ave

Lawrence Ave

Leon Ave

Harvey Ave

Saucier Ave

Dehart Ave

Rowcliffe Ave

Sutherland Ave

Elliot Ave

Burne Ave

Cadder Ave

Glenwood Ave

Royal Ave

Christleton Ave

Guisachan Ave

Birch Ave

Francis Ave

Okanagan
Lake

Smith
Ave

Doyle Ave

City
Hall

Queensway Ave

Kerry
Park

Hot
Sands
Beach

City
Park

Riverside Ave

Lake Ave

Beach Ave

Park Ave

Buckland Ave

Strathcona
Park

Cameron
Park

Okanagan Lake
Floating Bridge

To Westbank (8km);
Bear Creek Provincial Park
(8.5km); Penticton (86km)

To Lakeshore Rd (500m); Pandosy Village (1km);
Siesta Inn (1km); Willow Creek Family Campground (1.2km);
Lakeshore Inn (1.5km); Father Pandosy Settlement (5km);
Carmelis Goat Cheese (12km); Okanagan
Mountain Provincial Park (16km)

To Village Laundry (1.1km);
Kelowna Kayak (2.5km);
Farmers' Market (3.4km);
Greyhound Canada Bus
Depot (3.8km); Hwy 33
(4.4km); Airport (20km);
Big White Mountain (55km)

To Guisachan Village
(1.2km); Kelowna Land
& Orchard Co (8km);
Kettle Valley Rail
Trail (20km)

Sunset Dr

Water St

St Paul St

Bertram St

Richter St

Abbott St

Pandosy St

Ellis St

Gordon Dr

Ethel St

Mill St

0 ——— 400 m
0 ——— 0.2 miles

OKANAGAN VALLEY

DETOUR: BOUCHERIE RD

Westbank, the town of strip malls and garish billboards southwest of Kelowna, is little more than a blip along Hwy 97. However, if you want to avoid the worst of the excess divert off the main road and follow the hills along the lake. For about 12km, Boucherie Rd passes homes, orchards and wineries, including the noted Quails' Gate Estate Winery (p254). From the south, look for the turn east at the McDonald's; from the north, turn east at the second set of stop lights after the bridge.

---

courses and more. With attractions and activities such as superb hiking in all directions, Kelowna makes a good base for Okanagan explorations. Summer days are usually dry and hot, the nights pleasantly cool. Winters are snowy but dry, making nearby Big White a big attraction for skiers and snowboarders.

Although the town's population has more than doubled in the last three decades, remember that you're in the best place to enjoy the region's liquid and just-picked bounty. And just a few minutes away from urban headaches you can be hiking or cycling the spectacular Kettle Valley Rail Trail, alone reason enough to visit.

History

Kelowna, an Interior Salish word meaning 'grizzly bear,' owes its settlement to a number of missionaries who arrived in 1858, hoping to convert the First Nations. One of the priests, Father Charles Pandosy, a sort of Canadian Johnny Appleseed, established a mission in 1859 and planted the area's first apple trees along the banks of L'Anse au Sable, now known as Mission Creek.

An increasing trickle of settlers followed his lead as this was ideal pioneer country, with lots of available timber to build houses, a freshwater creek and prime, grassy lands that were just begging for the cattle to come munching.

In 1892 the town of Kelowna was established; it quickly became an economic hub. The next decades saw prosperity based on the orchards and other natural resources of the area.

With the completion of the Okanagan Lake Floating Bridge in 1958, Kelowna experienced yet another growth spurt as people no longer needed to rely on ferries to get across and around the lake. Wineries took root in the 1980s and a more upscale economy was born.

Forest fires in 2003 burned hundreds of expensive homes south of town and destroyed Okanagan Mountain Provincial Park.

Orientation & Information

Kelowna sits midway between Vernon and Penticton along the east side of 97km-long Okanagan Lake. Starting from City Park, Bernard Ave runs east and is the city's main drag. Ellis St, running north–south, is important and parallels the Cultural District.

Hwy 97, called Harvey Ave in town, marks the southern edge of the downtown area; it heads west over the bridge toward Penticton. East of downtown, Harvey Ave becomes a 10km strip lined with service stations, shopping malls, motels and fast-food restaurants. Past the sprawl, Harvey Ave is again called Hwy 97 and heads northeast toward Vernon.

Pandosy Village is an upscale enclave along the lake, some 3km south of the center.

The free *Off-centre* magazine has entertainment and culture listings for Kelowna and the valley.

BOOKSTORES

Mosaic Books (☎ 250-763-4418; 411 Bernard Ave; ⊗ 9am-6pm) One of BC's best independent bookstores. Sells maps (including topographic ones), travel guides, plus books on First Nations history and culture. Huge selection of magazines and a coffee bar.

INTERNET ACCESS

Many downtown cafés have wi-fi access; there is also a free zone right along Bernard Ave.
Kelowna Library (☎ 250-762-2800; 1380 Ellis St; ⊗ 10am-5:30pm Mon, Fri & Sat, 10am-9pm Tue-Thu, 1-5pm Sun Oct-Mar; ⊚) Online access is free with registration. The building is designed to look like an open book – albeit one larger than even the most bloated coffee-table tome.

LAUNDRY

Village Laundry (☎ 250-868-2555; 1551 Sutherland Ave; loads $5; ⊗ 8am-8pm Mon-Sat) Has internet access; will transfer loads from washer to dryer while you go out and play.

A MONSTER ON THIN ICE

Credibility for Okanagan Lake's purported monster, the Ogopogo, has never been high. Case in point: its current name was coined at a boozy Vernon banquet in 1926. Still, half-serious people continue to claim that there could be some sort of a Canadian Loch Ness monster swimming the 135km length of the lake.

The legend may well be rooted in an old First Nations myth about a creature named n'ha-a-itk that lived in a cave south of Kelowna. Like many a mythical creature, this one was likely to wipe out your family if you didn't appease it. Certainly the first settlers to the valley embraced the idea. A drawing from 1872 shows a beast emerging from the water with a beak like a rabid parrot. However, depictions have widely varied through the years. Some say it is 5m long, others 20m. The face has ranged from the truly monstrous to something akin to the late actor Walter Matthau in his senior years. The idea that it slithers through the water like a snake, with a succession of humps visible above the water is popular.

Evidence has been at best sketchy. There are lots of stories of the 'as told by the distant friend of a third cousin' variety. Eyewitness reports have been limited to ones like the used car salesman in 1978 who thought he saw a monster, except it could have been a beaver....

Photo evidence has also been inconclusive. Grainy shots that could have come from the studio responsible for the pie-plate-as-UFO abound. To find real Ogopogo believers, you need to go to two places: a) Okanagan playgrounds, where a friendly and cute-toy-ready image of the critter forms myriad statues (including one in Kelowna's City Park, p262), and b) ad agencies, where the royalty-free Ogopogo has starred in a plethora of marketing campaigns. Just recently there was much publicity about an offer of $2 million from Okanagan tourism businesses to anyone who could prove the Ogopogo's existence. So far, there have been no winners.

MEDICAL SERVICES
Kelowna General Hospital (☎ 250-862-4000; 2268 Pandosy St at Royal Ave; ☷ 24hr)

POST
Post office (☎ 250-868-8480; 591 Bernard Ave)

TOURIST INFORMATION
Visitor Centre (☎ 250-861-1515, 800-663-4345; www .tourismkelowna.com; 544 Harvey Ave; ☷ 8am-7pm daily summer, 8am-5pm Mon-Fri, 10am-3pm Sat & Sun winter) Near the corner of Ellis St.

Sights
CULTURAL DISTRICT
The bonus side of Kelowna's urbanization is found north of the center in the former packing house district, where numerous well-funded galleries, venues and other attractions can fill half a day or more. Pick up a walking tour map in the district or from the VC (above).

Located in the old Laurel Orchards packing house, the **BC Orchard Industry Museum** (☎ 250-763-0433; 1304 Ellis St; admission by donation; ☷ 10am-5pm Mon-Sat) recounts the conversion of the Okanagan Valley from ranch land to orchards. The exhibits are ripe for discovery, especially the collection of old labels

such as the eye-catching one for Orchard-brand apples.

Celebrate the Okanagan's current star crop at the neighboring **Wine Museum** (☎ 250-868-0441; admission free; ☷ 10am-6pm Mon-Sat, 11am-5pm Sun). The knowledgeable staff can recommend tours, steer you to the best wineries for tastings and help you fill your trunk with examples of the myriad local wines on sale. See p252, for more information.

The **Kelowna Art Gallery** (☎ 250-979-0888; www.kelownaartgallery.com; 1315 Water St; admission $3; ☷ 10am-5pm Tue-Sat, 10am-9pm Thu, 1-4pm Sun) features the work of the vibrant local arts community. The light, airy gallery has regular special exhibits and kids' programs.

Nearby are two more worthwhile art galleries. **Art Ark** (☎ 250-862-5080; www.theartark .com; 1295 Cannery Lane; ☷ 10am-5pm, later in summer) shows and sells a wide range of works (paintings, sculpture, photography, mixed media and so on) by western Canadian artists. Next door, the tiny **Turtle Island Gallery** (☎ 250-717-8235) sells and displays pottery, carvings, paintings and more by First Nations artists.

A part of the civic center complex, the **Okanagan Heritage Museum** (☎ 250-763-2417; 470 Queensway Ave; admission by donation; ☷ 10am-5pm

Mon-Sat) looks at centuries of local culture in an engaging manner that includes a First Nations pit house, a Chinese grocery and a Pandosy-era trading post.

Behind the museum, **Kasugai Gardens** (admission free; 9am-6pm) are good for a contemplative stroll around the beautifully manicured grounds. Named for Kelowna's sister city in Japan, the gardens honor the relationship well.

CITY PARK & PROMENADE

City Park & Promenade, the central downtown park, is a lovely spot to while away a few hours. Pick up the guide to the many sculptures, which include an Ogopogo (p261) at the VC (p261). Plunge into the water at **Hot Sands Beach**, read under one of the many shade trees or just marvel at the flower gardens blooming with tulips and enjoy the soothing views across **Okanagan Lake**. Escape summer heat by lolling about on the grass in the cool breezes.

From Bernard Ave, the lakeside promenade extends north past the marina, Delta Grand Okanagan hotel and condominiums to **Waterfront Park**, where trails wander through the serpentine islets. **Island Stage** looks out over a serene lagoon. The sculpture **Rhapsody** portrays three huge dolphins playing in a fountain. Despite the cetaceans beings as common locally as the Ogopogo, it has become a local icon.

Several **beaches** are south of the Hwy 97 bridge along Lakeshore Rd. Gyro Beach Park, at the south end of Richter St, and Pandosy Village, a unique outdoor shopping mall with eclectic shops and restaurants, attract crowds on weekends.

FATHER PANDOSY SETTLEMENT

The **Father Pandosy Settlement** (admission free; 8am-dusk Mar-Oct) is Kelowna's major historical site. Granted it only dates to 1859, but this is where the good father enthusiastically planted his seed (among other places) and built a mission. The church, school, barn, one house and a few sheds from what was the first white settlement in the Okanagan have been restored. The site is small, well away from the center of town and rather peaceful. Soon you may get the urge to plant your own seed. To get there, go south along Lakeshore Rd, then east on Casorso Rd to Benvoulin Rd.

Activities

Kelowna offers myriad ways to savor the outdoors, whether on the lake or in the surrounding hills.

HIKING & MOUNTAIN BIKING

You'll find great hiking and mountain bike riding all around town. The 17km **Mission Creek Greenway** is a meandering, wooded path following the creek along the south edge of town. The western half is a wide and easy expanse, but to the east the route becomes sinuous as it climbs into the hills.

Knox Mountain, which sits at the northern end of the city, is another good place to hike or ride. The park covers more than 2 sq km, has well-maintained trails and rewards with excellent views from the top. You may see bobcats and snakes.

About 8.5km northwest of Kelowna, rustic but popular **Bear Creek Provincial Park** (250-548-0076; www.bcparks.ca) is good for hiking (the summit has sweeping views) as well as windsurfing, swimming and wilderness camping. From Kelowna, cross to the west bank and go north on Westside Rd.

SPAS

Most upscale hotels and resorts now offer spas for folks who want their cares rubbed and scrubbed away. **Beyond Wrapture** (250-448-8899; www.beyondwrapture.com; 1965 Richter St; treatments from $90) has a range of offerings including some with a local twist: massages and wraps using antioxidant-rich grape seeds. We'll opt for the 'Hedonist Heaven,' however.

WATER SPORTS

You can rent speedboats (starting at $60 per hour) and watersports gear at **Kelowna Marina** (250-861-8001) at the lake end of Queensway Ave. Windsurfers take to the water from the old seaplane terminal, near the corner of Water St and Cawston Ave.

Kelowna Kayak (250-860-3361; www.kelowna kayak.com; 2079 Enterprise Way) sells gear and organizes occasional tours on the lake. It's near the corner of Cooper Rd and Harvey Ave.

Kelowna for Children

City Park isn't just for frolicsome adults. A children's water park delights kids who like to get soaked on a sunny day (meaning all of them).

KETTLE VALLEY RAILWAY

The famous **Kettle Valley Rail Trail** vies with wine-drinking and peach-picking as the attraction of choice for visitors (smart ones do all three – and more).

Once stretching 525km in curving, meandering length, the railway was built so that silver ore could be transported from the southern Kootenays to Vancouver. Finished in 1916, it remains one of the most expensive railways ever built on a per km basis. It was entirely shut by 1989 but it wasn't long before its easy grades (never over 2.2%) and dozens of bridges were incorporated into the Trans Canada Trail.

Of the entire KVR trail, the most spectacular stretch is close to Kelowna. The 24km route through the Myra Canyon has fantastic views of the sinuous canyon from 18 trestles that span the gorge for the cliff-hugging path. That you can enjoy the route at all is something of a miracle as 12 of the wooden trestles were destroyed in the horrific firestorms of 2003. But in a mere five years, all were rebuilt and the trail is once again fully open. Much credit goes to the **Myra Canyon Trestle Restoration Society** (www.myratrestles.com).

Myra Canyon is just part of an overall 174km network of trails in the Okanagan that follow the old railway through tunnels, past Naramata and as far south as Penticton and beyond. You can easily access the trail at many points or book hiking and cycling tours (below).

To reach the best part of the trail, follow Harvey Ave (Hwy 97) east to Gordon Dr. Turn south and then east on KLO Rd and follow it all the way to the end of McCulloch Rd. About 2km after the pavement ends, you'll come to a clearing where power lines cross the road. Turn south on the Myra Forest Service Rd and follow it for 8km to the parking lot.

At the foot of Bernard Ave in City Park, an old car ferry has been reborn as the **Fintry Queen** (☎ 250-763-2780; adult/child from $20/15; ☺ May-Oct), a faux-paddlewheeler that sets sail for explorations of the lake.

Kelowna Land & Orchard Co (☎ 250-763-1091; 3002 Dunster Rd; orchard tours adult/child $6/free; ☺ 10am-4pm May-Oct, tour times vary seasonally) is the largest of the many local orchards open for tours. Kids can befriend a sheep, ride wagons, buy fruit and guzzle fresh-pressed apple juice.

Tours

Monashee Adventure Tours (☎ 250-762-9253; www.monasheeadventuretours.com) offers scores of biking and hiking tours of the valley, parks, Kettle Valley Rail Trail (from $80) and wineries. Tours are accompanied by entertaining local guides. Prices include a bike, lunch and shuttle to the route. The same shuttle can also be used by non-tour-riders looking for one-way transport. In winter, snowshoe tours are offered for Nanook fetishists.

WINERY TOURS

Numerous Kelowna companies offer tours to many of the region's wineries. There are myriad programs that last from a few hours to a full day, with various eating options as well. Tour prices usually include pick-up at hotels and motels.

Club Wine Tours (☎ 250-762-9951, 866-386-9463; www.clubwinetours.com; 3-7 hr tours $60-140)

Okanagan Wine Country Tours (☎ 250-868-9463, 866-689-9463; www.okwinetours.com; 3-8 hr tours $75-145) Also offers custom tours and longer ones lasting several days.

Distinctly Kelowna Tours (☎ 250-979-1211, 866-979-1211; www.wildflowersandwine.com; 3-5 hr tours $80-90) Offers winery tours plus hikes through the scenic hills followed by a winery lunch (called 'reward') and agricultural tours.

Festivals & Events

Kelowna has special events through the year, in summer they overlap. See p252 for details on the many wine festivals.

Kelowna Music & Arts Festival In late July, performers of all types, artists and general spectacle makers take to the streets and venues around town.

International Dragon Boat Festival (www.kelowna dragonboatfestival.com) Teams race spectacular Chinese boats on the lake in mid-September, followed by drinking and merriment.

Sleeping

As in the rest of the Okanagan Valley, accommodations here can be difficult to find in summer if you haven't booked – at other times, look for bargains. The VC lists dozens of area B&Bs. Chain motels dominate Harvey Ave/Hwy 97 going east. Rates fall as you

OKANAGAN VALLEY

head along the strip but you pay the price by being in less-than-salubrious surroundings.

BUDGET

There are few camping options close to town; most are west of the lake toward unbucolic Westbank.

Kelowna International Hostel (☎ 250-763-6024; www.kelowna-hostel.bc.ca; 2343 Pandosy St; dm/d from $18/50; 🖳 🛜) Live the backpacker cliché with the available bongo drums at this hostel in a house about 12 blocks from downtown and not far from the beach. There's free transport to/from the bus station; free pancakes all morning.

Bear Creek Provincial Park (☎ 250-494-0321; www.discovercamping.ca; campsites $24) This park has 122 shady sites on the west side of the lake 9km north of the bridge off Westlake Rd. There are 5km of beaches.

Kelowna SameSun International Hostel (☎ 250-763-9814, 877-562-2783; www.samesun.com; 245 Harvey Ave; dm/r from $26/75; 🔣 🖳 🛜) Near the center and the lake, this purpose-built hostel has 88 dorm beds plus private rooms. Activities include barbeques year-round and delights like 'party boat trips' in the summer. The hostel offers shuttles to Big White ski resort (p267).

Willow Creek Family Campground (☎ 250-762-6302; www.willowcreekcampground.ca; 3316 Lakeshore Rd; campsites $29-38; 🛜) Close to Pandosy Village and a beach, this 87-pitch facility has a laundry; tent sites are on a grassy verge.

MIDRANGE

Motels abound downtown, along Hwy 97 and at Pandosy Village (although several glitzy developments are obliterating many of the motels).

Abbott Villa Travelodge (☎ 250-763-7771, 800-578-7878; www.travelodge.com; 1627 Abbott St; r from $90; 🔣 🖳 🛜 �('🌊')) Perfectly located right downtown and across from City Park, this 52-room motel is as unadorned as a grape vine in winter. There is a nice outdoor pool and a hot tub.

Royal Anne Hotel (☎ 250-763-2277, 888-811-3400; www.royalannehotel.com; 348 Bernard Ave; r $90-200; 🔣 🖳) Location, location, location are the three amenities that count at this otherwise unexciting older five-story motel in the heart of town. Rooms are studies of anonymous motel decor, circa 1992. But the balcony views are strictly contemporary.

Accent Inn (☎ 250-862-8888, 800-663-0298; www.accentinns.com; 1140 Harvey Ave; r from $100; 🔣 🖳 🛜 �
) This is the pick of the pack at this motel-lined corner of Hwy 97. The 102 units in three-story blocks have nice touches like hanging baskets of flowers and free newspapers – remember those? The center is a short stroll away.

Siesta Inn (☎ 250-763-5013, 800-663-4347; www.siestainn.com; 3152 Lakeshore Rd; r $130-280; 🔣 🖳 🛜 �) Pools inside and out, hot tubs and, oh, the lake mean you can stay wet at this 96-room motel. Rooms are family friendly, many are suites with full kitchens. Located right in Pandosy Village. Watch out for developers' drool marks.

Prestige Inn (☎ 250-860-7900, 877-737-8443; www.prestigeinn.com; 1675 Abbott St; r $120-220; 🔣 🖳 �) This 66-room place has a great location across from City Park and once you're inside, you can't see the rather hideous exterior. The rooms are just fine, in an upscale motel sort of way (nice soap, LCD TVs, lotsa decorative pillows etc).

TOP END

Hotel Eldorado (☎ 250-763-7500, 866-608-7500; www.eldoradokelowna.com; 500 Cook Rd; r $165-380; 🔣 🖳 🛜 �) This historic lakeshore retreat south of Pandosy Village has 19 heritage rooms where you can bask in antique-filled luxury. A modern low-key wing has 30 more rooms and six opulent waterfront suites. It's classy, artful and funky all at once. Definitely the choice spot in town for a luxurious getaway.

Eating

Kelowna boasts many places to take full advantage of the local bounty of foodstuffs. But don't let the feel of Vancouver East cause you to go all continental in your dining time: 8pm is late.

FOOD PURVEYORS

The **Farmers Market** (☎ 250-878-5029; cnr Springfield Rd & Dilworth Dr; ⌚ 8am-1pm Wed & Sat Apr-Oct) has over 150 vendors, including many with prepared foods. Local artisans also display their wares. It's off Hwy 97. A Thursday market (⌚ 4-8pm) is held at the Rhapsody statue parking lot.

Well south of town on a hillside overlooking the lake, **Carmelis Goat Cheese** (☎ 250-764-9033; 170 Timberline Rd; ⌚ 11am-5pm Mar-Dec) wins rave reviews for its two dozen cheeses that range from a goat Gruyère to a blue ('Goatgonzola'). Enjoy coffee and a sandwich.

BC Fruit Market (☎ 250-763-8872; 816 Clement Ave; ⊕ 9am-5pm Mon-Sat) is like a county fair. Right inside the local fruit packing cooperative, dozens upon dozens of the Okanagan's best fruits are on display and available for tasting. In winter, choose from 60 kinds of apples (many organic) from small valley orchards. In summer, the peaches, nectarines, plums... goodness! And the prices are half that in supermarkets.

At first glance, **Guisachan Village** (2355 Gordon Dr) may look like a humdrum strip mall but closer inspection reveals that it is a culinary mecca of fine food purveyors, including:

Codfathers Seafood Market (☎ 250-763-3474; ⊕ 9am-7pm) Fresh fish but picnickers love the array of smoked salmon and other fish to eat straightaway. A small café serves chowders, fish & chips etc.

L&D Meats & Deli (☎ 250-717-1997; ⊕ 9:30am-6pm Mon-Sat) Arrays of smoked meats and other deli items; vast choice of beautiful sandwiches.

Okanagan Grocery (☎ 250-862-2811; ⊕ 9:30am-5:30pm Tue-Sat) Artisan and organic bakery with breads from baguettes to croissants.

BUDGET
Bean Scene (☎ 250-763-1814; 274 Bernard Ave; coffee $2; ⊕ 6:30am-10pm) has a great bulletin board to check up on local happenings while you munch on a muffin. A quieter location, **Bean Scene North** (☎ 250-763-4022; 1289 Ellis St; ⊕ 6am-6pm) offers caffeinated respite in the Cultural District.

Mad Mango Café (☎ 250-762-8988; 551 Bernard Ave; meals from $7; ⊕ 8am-6pm Sun-Thu, to 9pm Fri & Sat) The creativity at this simple diner is in the food, not on the walls. Western breakfasts are served all day but the real stars are the many Asian dishes such as hot Thai soup, laksa and curried prawns with rice.

MIDRANGE & TOP END
Mamma Rosa (☎ 250-763-4114; 561 Lawrence Ave; mains $12-25; ⊕ 5-10pm Tue-Sun) OK, the red and white checked tablecloths may be plastic, but that just makes wiping up your slobber that much easier. And slobber you will over big bowls of excellent homemade pastas (about 100 varieties it seems) and more. Customize by adding meatballs, broccoli, anchovies etc. When the dessert arrives diners exclaim, 'Oh my word!'

La Bussola (☎ 250-763-3110; 1451 Ellis St; mains $15-30; ⊕ 5-10pm Mon-Sat) The Cultural District location is fitting. Since 1974 Franco and Lauretta Coccaro have worked to perfect their Italian supper house. The menu spans the lot, from pesto to red sauce, veal to seafood. Dine on the flower-bedecked sidewalk tables or in the stylish dining room.

Bouchons Bistro (☎ 250-763-6595; 1180 Sunset Dr; mains $20-35; ⊕ 5-10pm) This upscale café brings a bit of French flair to Kelowna. Gallic standards are faithfully rendered using local produce. Foie gras terrine, cassoulet, mussels and frites, fine cheeses and more make this a local favorite. Sit outside in summer.

Drinking
Kelowna's craft brewer, **Tree Brewing** (☎ 250-717-1091; 1083 Richter St; tours $7; ⊕ 3pm Fri), has an excellent range of beers, Hop Head IPA. Tours are friendly and fun.

You can always get food at Kelowna's pubs and bars.

Doc Willoughby's (☎ 250-868-8288; 353 Bernard Ave; ⊕ 11:30am-2am) Right downtown, this classic pub boasts a vaulted interior lined with wood and tables on the street. The beer selection is excellent, including brews from Tree Brewing and Penticton's Cannery Brewing.

Rose's Waterfront Pub (☎ 250-860-1141; Delta Grand Okanagan Hotel; 1352 Water St) Part of the upscale end of the waterfront, the vast lakeside terrace is the place for a sunset drink – from several hours before to several hours after.

Rotten Grape Wine & Tapas Bar (☎ 250-717-8466; 231 Bernard Ave; ⊕ 5pm-midnight Wed-Sun) Enjoy flights of local wines without the fru-fru in the heart of town. If you utter, 'Tannin, the hobgoblin of pinot.' at any point, be quiet and eat some of the tasty tapas (from $10).

Sturgeon Hall (☎ 250-860-3055; 1481 Water St; meals $7-15; ⊕ 11am-midnight Mon-Sat) Fanatical fans of hockey's Kelowna Rockets feast on excellent burgers and thin-crust pizza while quaffing brews at the bar or outside at sidewalk tables. In season every TV shows hockey.

Entertainment
CLUBS
Downtown Kelowna boasts several clubs. Several can be found in the 200 blocks of Lawrence and Leon Aves.

Flashbacks Nite Club (☎ 250-861-3039; 1268 Ellis St; cover varies; ✹ 8pm-late Wed-Sun) In a former cigar factory, this is the big mainstream venue for live music and name bands on tour.

PERFORMANCE VENUES
Free summer concerts, featuring everything from rock to classical music, take place in downtown's Kerry Park on Friday and Saturday nights and on Island Stage Wednesday nights. See www.parksalive.com for more info.

Rotary Centre for the Performing Arts (☎ 250-717-5304; www.rotarycentreforthearts.com; 421 Cawston Ave) This impressive facility anchors the Cultural District and has galleries, a theater, a café, workshops and more.

Kelowna Actors Studio (☎ 250-862-2867; www.kelownaactorsstudio.com; 1379 Ellis St; show tickets only from $38) Enjoy works as diverse as *The Producers* and *The Miracle Worker* at this dinner theater with serious ambition.

Kelowna Community Theatre (☎ 250-762-2471; 1375 Water St) is a venue for music and theater. The **Sunshine Theatre Company** (☎ 250-763-4025; www.sunshinetheatre.org) stages productions ranging from esoteric to dance to monologues at the Rotary Centre for the Performing Arts.

SPORTS
Kelowna Rockets (☎ 250-860-7825; www.kelownarockets.com; tickets from $18) is the much-beloved local WHL hockey team. It plays in the flashy 6000-seat **Prospera Place Arena** (☎ 250-979-0888; cnr Water St & Cawston Ave).

Getting There & Away
Kelowna airport (YLW; ☎ 250-765-5125; www.kelownaairport.com) is a busy place and has a surprisingly good wine shop. Discount carrier WestJet serves Vancouver, Victoria, Edmonton, Calgary and Toronto. Air Canada Jazz serves Vancouver and Calgary. Horizon Air has international service to Seattle. The airport is a long 20km north on Hwy 97 from Kelowna.

The **Greyhound Canada bus depot** (☎ 250-860-3835; 2366 Leckie Rd) is inconveniently east of the downtown area, off Hwy 97. Daily buses travel to other points in the Okanagan Valley such as Penticton ($21, 1½ hours, four daily), as well as Kamloops ($36, three hours, three daily), Vancouver ($74, six hours, six daily) and Calgary ($102, 10 hours, one daily). The station has coin lockers.

To get there, take city bus 9 or 10 from **Queensway station** (Queensway Ave btwn Pandosy & Ellis Sts). They run roughly every half-hour from 6:30am to 9pm. Better, use the depot phone to request a pick-up from your accommodations. A cab to the center costs a whopping $20.

Getting Around
TO/FROM THE AIRPORT
There are two buses connecting with the airport: **Kelowna Shuttle** (☎ 250-765-0182; www.kelownashuttle.com), costing $12 to $15 per person. Cabs cost about $30.

BUS
Kelowna Regional Transit System (☎ 250-860-8121; www.busonline.ca) runs local bus services. The one-way fare in the central zone is $2. A day pass for all three zones costs $5.50. All the downtown buses pass through **Queensway station** (Queensway Ave btwn Pandosy & Ellis Sts). Service is not especially convenient but some routes do boast double-decker buses just like those in London.

CAR & TAXI
Major car rental companies at Kelowna airport include Budget, Enterprise, Hertz and National.

Taxi companies include **Kelowna Cabs** (☎ 250-762-2222).

VERNON
pop 36,500

Elevations increase and winter temps decrease as you head north to Vernon. This precludes much grape-growing, although there are lots of orchards and truck farms. The compact city lies in a lovely valley encircled by three lakes: the Okanagan, Kalamalka and Swan.

Vernon itself is worth a stroll and there are some nearby farms worth visiting.

History
Once the hub of the Okanagan Valley, Vernon used to be a major crossroads town that connected the valley with the rest of the interior. Voyageurs first used its strategic location, followed by an onslaught of gold prospectors streaming up the valley to the Cariboo district. Later, cattle were brought in, and in 1891 the railway arrived. But it was in 1908, with the introduction of large-scale

---

BIG WHITE SKI RESORT

Known for perfect powder and plenty of it (750cm per year), **Big White Ski Resort** (☎ 250-765-8888, 800-663-2772; www.bigwhite.com; 1-day lift pass adult/child $75/35) is one of BC's best and most popular. The highest piste in the province, it features 12 sq km of runs, which are covered in the noted deep dry powder for excellent downhill and backcountry skiing, and big gullies that make for superb snowboarding. The stats: 777m drop, 16 lifts and 118 runs. There is also night skiing.

Big White's ski village has a great vibe, what with over a dozen restaurants, cafés and bars. You can ski almost up to the taps.

Contact **central reservations** (☎ 800-663-2772; www.bigwhite.com; r $100-900) for full accommodation details and pricing on the hundreds of condos and three hotels. With ski runs right outside the door, 42-room **Chateau Big White** (r from $175; 🖳 🛜) is a popular boutique hotel with a rooftop hot tub.

One of two hostels, **SameSun Ski Resort Hostel** (☎ 250-765-7050, 877-562-2783; www.samesun .com; Alpine Centre; dm/db from $29/80; 🖳 🛜) has direct ski access to the runs. Rooms have four to eight beds and there's a hot tub. There are daily shuttles to/from the Kelowna SameSun International Hostel (p264).

Big White is 55km east of Kelowna off Hwy 33. Ski buses run daily to/from Kelowna ($20), see the website for schedules. The resort operates a day-trip shuttle to its corporate cousin, Silver Star Ski Resort (p269).

---

irrigation, that the town took on an importance that was more than transitory. Soon the area was covered in orchards and farms.

Orientation & Information

Surrounded by rolling hills, downtown Vernon is a good respite along Hwy 97. Main St, also called 30th Ave, rarely clogs. At 25th Ave, Hwy 6, which leads southeast to Nakusp and Nelson, meets Hwy 97, which runs north-south, becoming 32nd St in Vernon and bisecting the city. On 32nd St, north of 30th Ave, you'll find a commercial strip with service stations, motels and fast-food outlets.

Bookland (☎ 250-545-1885; 3400 30th Ave) Topographical maps, travel guides and books on regional topics. Also magazines and newspapers.

Main post office (☎ 250-545-8239; 3101 32nd Ave, at 31st St)

Vernon Jubilee Hospital (☎ 250-545-2211; 2101 32nd St; 🕒 24hr)

Vernon Public Library (☎ 250-542-7610; 3001 32nd Ave; 🕒 10am-5:30pm Mon & Thu-Sat, 10am-4pm Tue & Wed) Free internet access; next to the Vernon Museum.

Visitor Centre North of town (☎ 250-542-1415; 6326 Hwy 97 N; 🕒 8:30am-6pm May-Oct) Near the southeastern shore of Swan Lake & 701 Hwy 97 S, about 5km north of town; South of town (☎ 250-545-3016, 800-665-0795; www.vernontourism.com; 701 Hwy 97 S; 🕒 8:30am-6pm May-Oct, 10am-4pm Nov-Apr) This is the main office, it's about 2km south of the center.

Sights

Vernon has over 30 **murals** (www.vernonmurals.ca) that have been painted by local artists with help from schoolkids and other volunteers. These are not your usual faded flag with skewed perspective murals either. Rather, these are building-sized works of art. Pick up a copy of the 'Heritage Murals' guide at the VCs (left).

You can do a complete tour on foot in under 90 minutes. A **trompe l'oeil scene** (3306 30th Ave) looks through the building wall to see orchard workers busily packing fruit. The **World Wars** (3202 32nd St) is a moving study of war and its effects. Note the text of the telegram carrying the news that families dread in wartime.

The **Vernon Museum** (☎ 250-542-3142; 3009 32nd Ave at 31st St; admission free; 🕒 10am-5pm Tue-Sat) has the usual collection of pioneer effluvium that would have been ideal for eBay, if it had existed in 1900.

The **Vernon Art Gallery** (☎ 250 545-3173; 3228 31st Ave; admission by donation; 🕒 10am-5pm Mon-Fri, 11am-4pm Sat) showcases the local art scene.

The **Allan Brooks Nature Centre** (☎ 250-260-4227; www.abnc.ca; adult/child $4/3; 🕒 10am-5pm Tue-Sun May-mid-Oct) is named for the famous local wildlife painter. It features interactive displays on the North Okanagan's diverse ecosystems. To find it, follow 34th St until it becomes Mission Rd. Follow that for about 2km, then turn left onto Allan

Brooks Rd. See the real thing on numerous nature walks in the area, including one past crowd-pleasing 'Marmot City.'

Davison Orchards (☎ 250-549-3266; 3111 Davison Rd; ☺ daylight May-Oct) is one of many orchards in the surrounding area, however Davidson is more attraction than farm. Kids love the tractor rides, homemade ice cream, fresh apple juice (for which it is justly famous), winsome barnyard animals and, yes, fudge.

Next to Davison Orchards, **Planet Bee** (☎ 250-542-8088; 5011 Bella Vista Rd; ☺ daylight May-Oct) is a working honey farm where you can learn all the sweet secrets of the nectar, see a working hive up close and taste a variety of honeys. Prices are reasonable, so you won't get stung.

Activities

Kalamalka Lake Park lies on the eastern side of its warm, shallow namesake lake (aka 'Kal' to locals), which is easily seen from Hwy 97 south of town. The 8.9-sq-km park offers great swimming at Jade and Kalamalka Beaches, as well as good fishing and picnic areas. A network of mountain biking and hiking trails takes you to places such as cougar-free **Cougar Canyon**, where the rock climbing is excellent. To get to the park from downtown Vernon, follow Hwy 6 east to the Polson Place Mall, then turn south on Kalamalka Lake Rd and proceed to Kal Beach.

Innerspace Dive & Kayak (☎ 250-549-2040; 3103 32nd St) rents all manner of gear. Kayaks good for the local lakes are $35 per day, snorkel sets are $15 and scuba gear for Ellison Provincial Park (opposite) is $55.

Sleeping

Vernon has some decent, if not brand-new, motels in the center. Many chains can be found among the strip malls north of town on Hwy 97. The VC (p267) has lists of B&Bs, many set among local farms. Ellison Provincial Park has camping (opposite).

Beaver Lake Mountain Resort (☎ 250-762-2225; www.beaverlakeresort.com; 6350 Beaver Lake Rd; campsites from $25, cabins $50-160; ☐) Set high in the hills east of Hwy 97 about midway between Vernon and Kelowna, this postcard-perfect lakeside resort has a range of rustic log and more luxurious cabins that sleep up to six people. Check out the bucolic scene on the internet with the live

BeaverCam, which must get some interesting Google hits.

Swan Lake RV Park (☎ 250-545-2300; www.swanlakecampground.com; 7255 Old Kamloops Rd; campsites from $25) On the west side of Swan Lake, 5km north of Vernon, this 34-pitch campground has shady grounds and rental canoes.

Tiki Village Motel (☎ 250-503-5566, 800-661-8454; www.tikivillagevernon.com; 2408 34th St; r $70-150; ☒ ☎ ☻) All this central motel needs are some namesake torches and you'll be right back in the 1960s. This living museum of the glory days of decorative concrete blocks has expansive plantings and 30 polychromatic rooms.

Schell Motel (☎ 250-545-1351, 888-772-4355; www.schellmotel.ca; 2810 35th St; r $75-135; ☒ ☎ ☻) Another vision in artful concrete blocks, this immaculate indie motel has a welcoming pool, barbeque and sauna. The 32 rooms have fridges and some have kitchens. Ideally central but out of range of the 32nd St roar.

Travelodge Vernon (☎ 250-545-2161, 800-255-3050; www.vernontravelodge.net; 3000 28th Ave; r $90-120; ☒ ☎ ☻) There's nothing special about this two-story 40-unit motel except that it has a lot of concrete. The central location is great and 32nd St is a sound-absorbing block away.

Eating & Drinking

The evening **Vernon Farmers Market** (☎ 250-546-6267; 2200 58th Ave; ☺ 4-8pm Fri) is the only reason to visit the Wal-Mart parking lot. There's also a **morning market** (cnr Hwy 97 & 43rd Ave; ☺ 8am-noon Mon &Thu).

More good picnic fare can be found at **Simply Delicious** (☎ 250-542-7500; 3419 31st Ave; ☺ 9am-5:30pm), with a good selection of organic prepared food. Across the parking lot, **Nature's Fare** (☎ 250-260-1117; 30th Ave; ☺ 9am-6pm Mon-Sat) has organic local produce plus prepared foods.

Bean to Brew (☎ 250-260-7787; 3202 31st Ave; meals from $5; ☺ 6am-10pm Mon-Fri, 8am-4pm Sat & Sun; ☎) The outdoor area here is in a heated yurt when it's cold. The amazing blueberry muffins are made with local berries. Soups and sandwiches are also good.

Talkin Donkey (☎ 250-545-2286; 3923 32nd St; meals $7; ☺ 7am-9pm, until 11pm Fri; ☎) When they talk about 'drinking responsibly' at this local institution, they mean ensuring that your coffee is fair trade. A good chunk of the proceeds at this funky with a spiritual edge place goes to charity. Tap your Birkenstock-clad toes to Friday night folk music or enjoy some of the soups, sandwiches and salads.

Sir Winston's Pub (☎ 250-549-3485; 2705 32nd St; mains $9-20; ☺ noon-late) A big, rollicking pub in the center of town. It has a good range of beer choices and a large patio. Burgers, steaks and fish & chips lead the parade of decidedly non-organic items.

Blue Heron Waterfront Pub (☎ 250-542-5550; 7673 Okanagan Landing Rd; mains $10-25; ☺ 11am-late Apr-Oct) Southwest of town. Enjoy sweeping views of Okanagan Lake from the big patio to keep things hopping all summer long. The meaty fare of excellent steaks and burgers is leavened by cheesy fare such as nachos. Good for boisterous groups.

Eclectic Med (☎ 250-558-4646; 2915 30th Ave; mains $12-25; ☺ 11:30am-2pm, 5-9pm Tue-Sun) The name sums up the menu which brings a Mediterranean accent to local standards like Alberta steaks, lake fish and lots of valley veggies. Plates are artfully presented and portions are unlikely to cause you to sink to the bottom of your motel pool. Service wins plaudits.

Getting There & Around

The **Greyhound Canada bus depot** (☎ 250-545-0527; 3102 30th St at 31st Ave) has service to Kelowna ($18, one hour, six daily), as well as Kamloops ($28, two hours, three daily) and Revelstoke ($36, 2½ hours, two daily).

Buses of the **Vernon Regional Transit System** (☎ 250-545-7221) leave downtown from the bus stop at 31st St and 30th Ave ($2). For Kalamalka Lake, catch bus 1 or 6; for Okanagan Lake, bus 7. A day pass costs $5; service is infrequent.

For a cab, call **Vernon Taxi** (☎ 250-545-3337).

AROUND VERNON

Beautiful **Ellison Provincial Park** on Okanagan Lake is only 16km southwest from Vernon. The 71 **campsites** (☎ 800-689-9025, information only 250-545-1560; www.discovercamping.ca; campsites $24; ☺ Apr-Oct) have showers and fill up in summer so reserve.

The park has hiking and biking trails and the only freshwater marine park in western Canada. Scuba divers can plunge into the warm water to explore a sunken wreck. Rent scuba gear and kayaks from Innerspace Dive & Kayak in Vernon (p268). Ellison is also known for its world-class rock

---

SILVER STAR

A classic BC ski resort of the kind you find outside of Whistler, **Silver Star** (☎ 250-542-0224, 800-663-4431, snow report 250-542-1745; www.skisilverstar.com; 1-day lift ticket adult/child $71/35) is relaxed, low-key, quiet at night and has lots of powder (over 700cm a year).

The resort area has a faux Gold Rush feel with brightly colored old west facades. There are a few pubs, a couple of restaurants and enough shops to keep you busy for almost an hour. The real focus, as it should be, is on the snow. There are 115 ski and snowboard runs, roughly 10% of which are double black diamond. The vertical drop is 760m from a peak elevation of 1900m. Twelve lifts, including one six-pack are placed for full ski-on, ski-off nirvana.

The ski season usually lasts from late October to early April. At the end of June - the official start of the summer season – the chairlifts begin operating again, and ski runs become excellent hiking and mountain biking trails. Stunning views let you see all the way west to the Coast Mountains.

Contact Silver Star for a range of accommodations options within the resort. Most let you ski right out your front door. **SameSun Budget Lodge** (☎ 250-545-8933, 877-562-2783; www.samesun .com; 9898 Pinnacles Rd; dm/d $30/80; ☐ ☺) is an upscale hostel of the usual SameSun quality. The common area is huge and the kitchen cozy. Reserve well in advance in winter. **Silver Creek Lodge** (☎ 250-549-5191, 800-610-0805; www.silverstarclubresort.com; r $170-300) has 69 fairly luxurious condostyle units in sizes from studio to two-bedroom. Enjoy the wonderful views from the two rooftop hot tubs.

To get to Silver Star, take 48th Ave off Hwy 97. The resort is 20km northeast of Vernon. **Vernon Airporter** (☎ 250-542-7574; www.vernonairporter.ca) operates shuttles between the resort and Vernon (one-way $27) and Kelowna Airport (round-trip $75) in the winter. The resort operates a day-trip shuttle to its corporate cousin, Big White Ski Resort (p267).

climbing. To get to Ellison from downtown, go west on 25th Ave, which soon becomes Okanagan Landing Rd. Follow that to the park.

East of Vernon on Hwy 6, farms and forests line the road to **Lumby** (population 1800) and **Cherryville** (population 1000), about 20km and 48km from Vernon, respectively. The many lakes draw lots of anglers.

From Cherryville, you can drive northeast 62km on rugged Sugar Lake Rd to the remote wonderland of **Monashee Provincial Park**. Old-growth cedars, spruce and hemlocks abound and you may spot rare mountain caribou among the myriad species. There's backcountry camping ($5) around pristine Spectrum and Big Peters Lakes, tucked away high in the mountains.

Hwy 6 heads east over a scenic road to Needles, where you can catch the ferry to the Kootenays and the road to Nakusp (p280).

VERNON TO SICAMOUS

Going north from Vernon, it is 78km on Hwy 97A to Sicamous and the junction with the Trans-Canada Hwy (Hwy1). This is a beautiful drive.

The **O'Keefe Historic Ranch** (☎ 250-542-7868; www.okeeferanch.ca; adult/child $12/10; ☼ 9am-5pm May, Jun, Sep & Oct, 9am-8pm Jul & Aug) is just what the name implies. Home to the O'Keefe family from 1867 to 1977, it still has an original log cabin, a general store and St Ann's, probably the oldest Roman Catholic church in the province. Before orchards – and later grapes – covered the valley, ranching as portrayed here was the way of life for most folk here. It is 12km north of Vernon on Hwy 97, just 4km after it splits from Hwy 97A.

Rolling farmlands give way to **Armstrong** (population 4500), 23km north of Vernon.

It's a historical village that has a couple of things going for it: a) it hasn't been overly restored, and b) it has train tracks going right down the middle of the main drag, giving the center an odd bifurcated charm. Good historical plaques dot the teetering buildings. Stop for lunch at the much-lauded **Brown Derby Café** (☎ 250-546-8221; 2510 Pleasant Valley Blvd; meals from $3; ☼ 7am-4pm Mon-Sat). Personality from the gregarious owners seasons the splendid breakfasts, specials and pies. The building dates from 1892.

Out by the highway, **Village Cheese Co** (☎ 250-546-8651; 3475 Smith Dr; ☼ 9am-5pm) manages to be, well, not cheesy thanks to its excellent products – which you can see being made (the five-year cheddar is superb). Try to catch the excellent **Farmers Market** (☎ 250-546-1986; ☼ 8am-12:30pm Sat May-Oct). It's the valley's oldest market, running since 1973, and is held downtown at the IPE Grounds.

Thirteen kilometers further north, **Enderby** (population 3100) is on the banks of the Shuswap River. Rock climbers scale the vertical rocks at Enderby Cliffs, north of town. The Enderby **Visitor Centre** (☎ 250-838-6727, 877-213-6509; www.enderby.com/chamber; 706 Railway St) has climbing information. The downtown is tree-lined and compact.

North of Enderby, Hwy 97A follows the simply gorgeous **Shuswap River Valley**. The fast-flowing waters curve through the wide, flat valley, which is dotted with red barns and horses, all backed by tree-covered hillsides. It's magical in winter after a fresh snow.

In Sicamous, be sure to pause at **D Dutchmen Dairy** (☎ 250-838-4304; www.dutchmendairy.ca; 1321 Maeir Rd; ☼ 9am-6pm), an old-school place where you can visit the Holsteins in the barn while curled up cats look on. Then you can sample the products, including artisan cheeses, buttermilk in glass bottles or one of several flavors of ice cream.

The Kootenays

Viewed from space, the Kootenays region of BC looks like a storm-tossed ocean: a never-ending series of huge mountains standing in for waves, with year-round snow-clad peaks providing the whitecaps. At ground level, you can spend weeks weaving in and out of the four major ranges: the Selkirks and Monashees in the west and the Rockies and Purcells in the east.

And if a voyage into space is an explorer's dream, so too is a trip to the Kootenays. There is one discovery after another along sinuous roads hanging on the sides of white-water canyons. Dreams of discovery formed silver and gold-mining towns like Fernie and Revelstoke 100 years ago and today you can revel in their well-preserved past. Go to the near ghost town of New Denver or wake up the dead in frenetic, funky and utterly captivating Nelson.

Discoveries can take many forms. In winter you'll not only find hundreds of meters of the region's renowned powder at serious resorts such as the one on Revelstoke Mountain, but you can also link them up on a series of good roads called the Powder Hwy. Summer will keep you busy for as many hours as there's daylight, with bike trails down the side of granite peaks such as those around Rossland, and rapids on rivers like the roaring Kicking Horse at Golden.

The Kootenays take their name from the Ktunaxa, a First Nations people David Thompson discovered on his explorations. As you make your own discoveries, you'll soon find that your own word for this region will definitely be fun.

HIGHLIGHTS

- Losing yourself in the merry vibe of **Nelson** (p283)
- Riding the trails in North America's mountain-biking capital **Rossland** (p289)
- Floating across one of the impossibly blue lakes served by **car ferries** (p281)
- Hunting glaciers in the remote regions of **Bugaboo Provincial Park** (p298)
- Finding a tiny wildflower that proclaims, 'I'm here,' in brilliant color in **Glacier National Park** (p278)

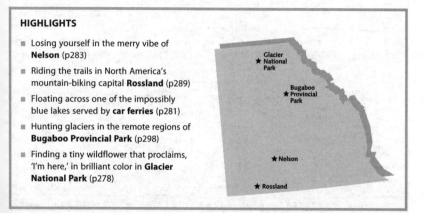

★ Glacier National Park

★ Bugaboo Provincial Park

★ Nelson

★ Rossland

WEST KOOTENAYS

Water and mountains define the West Kootenays. Between 230km-long Arrow Lake in the west and 145km-long Kootenay Lake in the east are quiet towns and trees – lots and lots of trees. New Denver and Kaslo are lost in an era a few decades back; the hardy independent folks living here wouldn't have it any other way.

If you're passing through on the Trans-Canada Hwy (Hwy 1) in the north or Hwy 3 in the south, take time for some exploring. Wilderness areas such as Valhalla Provincial Park provide natural isolation. Or enjoy the good life in Revelstoke and Nelson. The latter especially hums to a beat all its own.

Cross the lakes on the free ferries connecting highways throughout the region (p281) and count the shades of blue in the receding peaks of the Selkirk and Purcell Mountains.

History

Stern-wheelers on the long lakes in the late 1800s and early 1900s connected the area to the US. Later, trains added to the transportation network by carrying goods to and from the stern-wheeler ports. Busy ports included pretty Nakusp on Upper Arrow Lake and Kaslo on Kootenay Lake, where today you can visit the world's oldest surviving stern-wheeler. The Slocan Valley

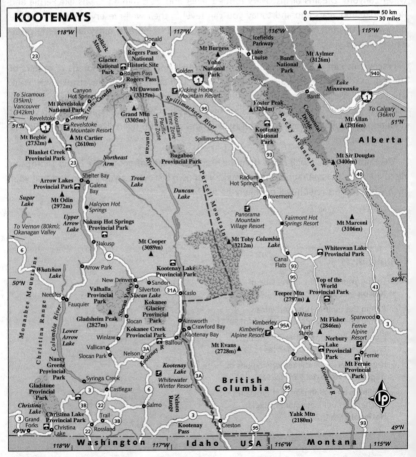

KOOTENAYS

boomed with silver mines during the late 1800s, and during WWII more than 20,000 Japanese Canadians were forced into internment camps throughout the valley.

The area around Castlegar and Grand Forks is rich in Russian Doukhobor history (see p290). Throughout the region, land and forest exploitation is being replaced by enjoyment. Ski resorts are proliferating across the remote peaks.

REVELSTOKE

pop 8000

Nestled between the Monashee and Selkirk mountain ranges, Revelstoke sits at the confluence of the rushing Illecillewaet River and the wide, slow-moving Columbia River. It perches on the western edge of Mt Revelstoke National Park, which is about halfway between the Okanagan Valley and the Rocky Mountains. All the hills and tumbling waters mean you can ski, snowboard, hike, bike or simply gaze at snowy peaks and alpine meadows depending on the season. This, coupled with a historic downtown that is perfect for an end-of-day stroll, make Revelstoke a pause that might become permanent.

History

Originally known to First Nations people as 'Big Eddy,' for the respite it offered canoe travelers, Revelstoke was later named for Edward Charles Baring (aka Lord Revelstoke), the British financier who came through with a much-needed cash advance that saved the Canadian Pacific Railway (CPR) from liquidation. The coming of the railway in the 1880s, along with the opening of the Trans-Canada Hwy in 1962, contributed to Revelstoke becoming a viable transportation hub.

Orientation

Revelstoke is south of the Trans-Canada Hwy. Victoria Rd parallels the very busy railway tracks that run along the northeast end of town. The main streets include 1st St and Mackenzie Ave. The center is just a few blocks square. Chain stores begin at the stoplight on the Trans-Canada.

Information

BOOKSTORES

Grizzly Book & Serendipity Shop (☎ 250-837-6185; 208 Mackenzie Ave) Offers magazines, a wide selection of New Age stuff and regional books.

INTERNET

The **SameSun Hostel** (p276) has public internet computers as does the summer location of the VC (below).

LAUNDRY

Family Laundry (☎ 250-837-3938; 409 1st St W; loads from $5; ⊙ 8am-8pm Mon-Sat, 8am-5pm Sun; ⊚) Enjoy vintage copies of *Gourmet* while you spin your load.

LIBRARY

Revelstoke Library (☎ 250-837-5095; 605 Campbell Ave; ⊙ noon-8pm Tue, 10am-5pm Wed-Sat) Has internet access.

MEDICAL SERVICES

Queen Victoria Hospital (☎ 250-837-2131; 6622 Newlands Rd; ⊙ doctor on call 24hr)

POST

Post office (☎ 250-837-3228; 313 3rd St W)

TOURIST INFORMATION

Parks Canada Regional Office (☎ 250-837-7500; revglacier.reception@pc.gc.ca; 301 3rd St W; ⊙ 8am-4:30pm Mon-Fri) Offers in-depth info about Mt Revelstoke National Park and Glacier National Park.

Visitor Centre (VC; ☎ 250-837-5345, 800-487-1493; www.seerevelstoke.com; 206 Campbell Ave; ⊙ 8:30am-4:30pm Mon-Fri; internet access 10 mins $1). From May to September, a second, larger VC at 110 Mackenzie Ave is open from 8:30am to 8pm; it has parking and internet access (10 mins $1).

Sights

Grizzly Plaza, between Mackenzie and Orton Aves, is a pedestrian square and the centre of downtown, where free live music performances – some achingly sincere if not good – take place in the evening throughout July and August and again on weekend nights in ski season. Life-sized bronze grizzly bears flank the plaza. Throughout downtown, look for historical plaques on the many restored buildings.

Don't miss the great **Revelstoke Railway Museum** (☎ 250-837-6060; www.railwaymuseum .com; adult/child $8/4; ⊙ 9am-8pm summer, 11am-4pm Fri-Tue winter), which houses restored steam locomotives, including one of the largest steam engines ever used on CPR lines. Photographs and artifacts document the construction of the CPR, pay tribute to its hardy workers and relate the railway's original financial woes. The museum bookstore

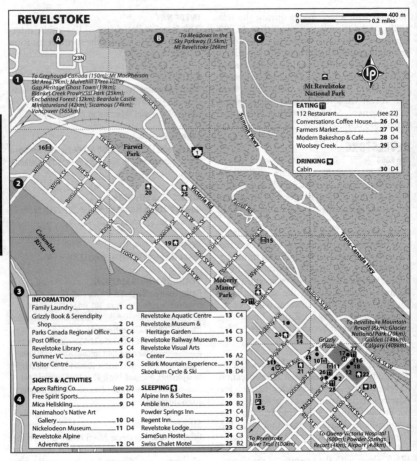

REVELSTOKE

0 ____ 400 m
0 ____ 0.2 miles

To Meadows in the
Sky Parkway (1.5km);
Mt Revelstoke (26km)

To Greyhound Canada (150m); Mt MacPherson
Ski Area (9km); Mulvehill Three Valley
Gap Heritage Ghost Town (19km);
Blanket Creek Provincial Park (25km);
Enchanted Forest (32km); Beardale Castle
Miniatureland (42km); Sicamous (74km);
Vancouver (565km)

Mt Revelstoke
National Park

Farwel
Park

Columbia
River

Moberly
Manor
Park

Grizzly
Plaza

To Revelstoke Mountain
Resort (6km); Glacier
National Park (70km);
Golden (148km);
Calgary (408km)

To Revelstoke
River Trail (100km)

To Queen Victoria Hospital
(600m); Powder Springs
Resort (4km); Airport (4.8km)

carries a huge selection of books about the building of the CPR, which was instrumental in linking Canada (p279). The grounds are picnic-perfect and you can watch the ceaseless passage of modern trains – which often cut off access to the museum.

The **Revelstoke Museum & Heritage Garden** (☎ 250-837-3067; 315 1st St W; adult/child $4/2; ✆ 9am-5pm Mon-Sat, 1-4pm Sun May-Sep, 1-4pm Mon-Fri Oct-Apr) holds a permanent collection of furniture and historical odds and ends that date back to the town's establishment in the 1880s. The prospector's chair tops most modern versions for comfort. Gardens out back bloom throughout summer.

Thrill to *The Titfield Thunderbolt* and other silent classics at the **Nickelodeon**

Museum(☎ 250-837-5250; www.revelstokenickelodeon .com; 111 1st St W; adult/child $10/5; ✆ 11am-6pm), which recalls thrills from a time pre-pre-pre-internet.

Nanimahoo's Native Art Gallery (☎ 250-837-0831; 113 1st St W; ✆ 11am-7pm) has a stunning collection of native art from more than 40 artists. The carvings are extraordinary. The **Revelstoke Visual Arts Centre** (☎ 250-814-0261; 320 Wilson St) has frequent exhibits by local artists.

Activities

Sandwiched in between the vast but relatively lesser-known Selkirk and Monashee mountain ranges, Revelstoke draws serious snow buffs looking for powder aplenty.

When the snow melts, white-water rafting is the thing.

Hiking opportunities abound in the region. Start close to the paved **Revelstoke River Trail**, which runs along the rivers at the south end of town.

Revelstoke is the gateway to the surrounding Alpine wilderness. Operators lead explorations for skiing, hiking and mountaineering by season. Two good ones are: **Revelstoke Alpine Adventures** (☎ 877-837-7141; www.revelstokealpine.ca; Mackenzie Ave) Ice- and rock-climbing, trekking.

Selkirk Mountain Experience (☎ 250-837-2381; www.selkirkexperience.com; Mackenzie Ave) Runs trips from a remote mountain lodge.

WINTER SPORTS

Hardy Scandinavians were Revelstoke's early settlers and they brought their habits from home, building North America's first ski jump in 1915 (p277). In the century since, the region's reputation as a ski center has continued to grow.

Just 6km southeast of town, the **Revelstoke Mountain Resort** (☎ 888-837-2188; www.revelstoke mountainresort.com; 1-day lift tickets adult/child $75/25) has ambitions to become the biggest ski resort this side of the Alps. But given that it only opened its seemingly endless virgin slopes in 2008, it has a long way to go. In the meantime while construction continues, you can in one run ski both 700m of bowl and 700m of trees. The vertical drop – accessed by a new gondola – is 1713m (over a mile), greater than Whistler's. There are

12 sq km of runs (the goal is 40) and 90% of the 40 runs are intermediate or advanced. Beginners need not apply (at least until the count reaches critical mass and the bunnies make demands).

Although the resort is making bowls accessible that were once helicopter- or cat-only, there are myriad more that are still remote. **Mica Heliskiing** (☎ 877-837-6191; www.micaheli.com; 207 Mackenzie Ave) offers three- to seven-day packages that include stays at a remote lodge. The cost is about $1200 per day. The resort offers both heli-skiing and has a cat operation.

For **cross-country skiing** (www.revelstokenordic.org), head to the Mt MacPherson Ski Area, 7km south of town on Hwy 23. You'll pay a mere $6 to use the 22km of groomed trails.

Snowmobiling is popular (almost every home seems to have one out front and most seem to be for rent). The **Snowmobile Revelstoke Society** (☎ 250-837-3325; www.sled revelstoke.com) has a vast range of information. **Great Canadian Snowmobile Tours** (☎ 250-837-9594; www.snowmobilerevelstoke.com) offers intro lessons (from $150) and a huge range of tours (from $180).

Free Spirit Sports (☎ 250-837-9453; 203 1st St W) rents a wide variety of winter gear including essential avalanche equipment.

WATER SPORTS

Apex Rafting Co (☎ 250-837-6376, 888-232-6666; www.apexrafting.com; 112 1st St E; adult/child $85/70) runs two-hour trips on the Illecillewaet

---

AVALANCHE WARNING

As you marvel at all the snowy peaks, take a second to realize that you are in the scary heart of avalanche country, where heavy slides of snow have enough power and weight to crush an entire city, although their destruction can be more personal. Avalanches kill more people in BC each year than any other natural phenomenon. In 2009, the toll was well into the double digits, including eight snowmobilers caught near Fernie.

Avalanches can occur at any time and even on terrain that seems relatively flat. Roughly 50% of people caught in them don't survive. It's vital that people venturing out onto the snow make inquiries about conditions first. Even resorts, which take many precautions, are not immune to avalanche deaths and it goes without saying: if an area is closed don't go there. Whether you're backcountry ski-touring or simply hiking in the alpine region, you'll want to rent a homing beacon; most outdoor shops can supply one.

In Revelstoke, the Canadian Avalanche Centre is operated by the **Canadian Avalanche Association** (CAA; ☎ 250-837-2435, 24hr info 800-667-1105; www.avalanche.ca). It analyzes avalanche trends, weather patterns and avalanche accidents and is a good source for conditions for the area covered by this book.

River in spring and summer. The trips are perfect for first-time rafters, kids or anyone wanting to just kick back and enjoy the scenery.

Navigate the rivers with a kayak from **Natural Escapes Kayaking** (☎ 250-837-2679; www .naturalescapes.ca). Rentals start at $35 for two hours and you can arrange tours of the region's waterways.

Very close to town, **Revelstoke Aquatic Centre** (☎ 250-837-9351; 600 Campbell Ave; ⊙ 9am-8pm) has a 25m pool, slides and more watery fun. Passes are included with most motel stays in the area.

MOUNTAIN BIKING

Mountain biking is huge here, as it is across the region. Pick up a copy of the *Biking Trail Map* from the visitor center or **Skookum Cycle & Ski** (☎ 250-814-0090; www.skookumcycle.com; 118 Mackenzie Ave), where you can rent bikes (from $20 for a half day).

Sleeping

There are lots of chain motels vying for attention out on the Trans-Canada Hwy, but you're much better off staying in town, where you can enjoy the vibe. See the VC for B&B lists.

BUDGET

Blanket Creek Provincial Park (☎ 800-689-9025; www.discovercamping.ca; campsite $15) This park, 25km south of Revelstoke along Hwy 23, includes 63 campsites, with flush toilets and running water. There's a playground, and a waterfall nearby.

SameSun Hostel (☎ 250-837-4050, 877-562-2783; www.samesun.com; 400 2nd St W; dm/d from $24/60; 🖳 🛜) In a labyrinthine heritage building, this 80-bed, 15-room hostel attracts an international crowd year-round. Consider the intricacies of foreign exchange in the outdoor hot tub.

MIDRANGE

Powder Springs Inn (☎ 250-837-5151, 800-991-4455; www.catpowder.com; 200 3rd St W; r $80-100; 🖸 🖳) The bummiest of the hostelries popular with ski bums. The location couldn't be better, otherwise it's strictly for those ready to pass out after a long day playing hard – or a long night in the raucous bar.

Alpine Inn & Suites (☎ 250-837-2116, 800-876-8206; www.alpineinnrevelstoke.com; 1001 W 2nd St;

r $70-140; 🖸 🖳 🛜) In a central spot, you can join the serious skiers who value the 38 quiet, clean and good-value rooms here. All have fridges and there's a small indoor hot tub.

Revelstoke Lodge (☎ 250-837-2181, 888-559-1979; www.revelstokelodge.com; 601 1st St W; r $70-150; 🖸 🖳 🛜 🖾) This 42-room pink-hued motel overcomes its inherent flaws, such as an all-encompassing parking area and stark cinder-block construction, thanks to its location. Check out a room or two to find one with recent paint and watch out for dark ones. Views of the CPR will excite train-spotters.

ourpick Swiss Chalet Motel (☎ 250-837-4650, 888-272-4538; www.swisschaletmotel.com; 1101 Victoria Rd; r $75-150; 🖸 🖳 🛜) Walk to town from this cozy 22-room motel while trains rumble past. Standards are high at this family-run place, which serves up enormo-muffins for breakfast.

Amble Inn (☎ 250-837-4665; 1221 1st St W; r $125-150) One of several heritage B&Bs in town, this 1897 inn is a credit to the carpenter's art. Ornate gingerbread is elaborately carved and painted myriad colors. Rooms are period posh with kitchen facilities and full breakfasts.

Regent Inn (☎ 250-837-2107, 888-245-5523; www .regentinn.com; 112 1st St E; r $120-180; 🖸 🖳 🛜) The nicest place in town is not posh but is comfy. The 50 modern rooms bear no traces of the hotel's 1914 roots (and exterior). The restaurant and lounge are both good and popular (opposite). Many soak the night away in the outdoor hot tub.

Eating

The **farmers market** (⊙ 8am-1pm Sat) sprawls across Grizzly Sq.

Modern Bakeshop & Café (☎ 250-837-6886; 212 Mackenzie Ave; meals from $5; ⊙ 7am-5pm Mon-Sat; 🛜) Try a *croque-monsieur* (grilled ham and cheese sandwich) or an elaborate pastry for a taste of Europe at this cute art moderne café. Many items are made with organic ingredients.

Conversations Coffee House (☎ 250-837-4772; 205 Mackenzie Ave; meals from $5; ⊙ 8am-8pm; 🛜) Local pictures line the bare brick walls at this loungey coffee place which has couches and tables for chilling. Bakery items, salads and sandwiches are available all day long.

ourpick Woolsey Creek (☎ 250-837-5500; 604 2nd St W; meals $10-20; ⊙ 8am-10pm) The food at this lively and fun place is the artistic result of two women, Sylvie and Sophie, and their passion for inventive fare. There are global influences across the menu (you won't go wrong with the prosciutto-stuffed chicken) and a fine wine list. Excellent starters encourage sharing and lingering on the large patio.

112 Restaurant (☎ 250-837-2107; Regent Inn, 112 1st St E; mains $24-35; ☯ noon-9pm) Dark and romantic, 112 is heavy on the woods and is good for an intimate night out. Steaks and seafood are artfully prepared and the starter list is long. Vegetarians, though, may have the inside edge with the excellent lasagne Florentine.

Drinking & Entertainment

The bar at Woolsey Creek (opposite) is popular on weekends and gets an arty crowd. The lounge at the Powder Springs Inn (opposite) is where you go to live out every wacky ski resort cliché. The bar at the Regent Inn (opposite) is probably the best all-around choice, it offers up great burgers, lots of good beers on tap and has pool tables and other diversions. Look for excellent local microbrews from Mt Begbie Brewing at all the above.

The Cabin (☎ 250-837-2144; 200 E 1st St; ☯) defies easy description: bowling alley, bar, outdoor gear store and art gallery. Maybe we should just call it 'fun'.

Getting There & Around

Greyhound Canada (☎ 250-837-5874; 1899 Fraser Dr) is west of town, just off the Trans-Canada Hwy. It has storage lockers. Buses go east to Calgary ($65, six hours, four daily) via Banff, west to Vancouver ($98, nine to 10 hours, four daily) via Kamloops or Kelowna.

A shuttle runs throughout the day to and from the ski resort in season.

MOUNT REVELSTOKE NATIONAL PARK

Known for their jagged peaks, the compact Selkirks are an espresso shot of rugged terrain and steep valleys. Just northeast of Revelstoke in the Clachnacudainn Range, the compact (260 sq km) **Mt Revelstoke National Park** (www.pc.gc.ca/revelstoke) is a stunner year-round. It comes alive with waves of wildflowers in summer while the winter vistas of blindingly white, jagged peaks against the azure sky is unforgettable.

From the 2223m summit of Mt Revelstoke, the views of the mountains and the Columbia River valley are excellent. To get to the summit, take the 26km **Meadows in the Sky Parkway**, 1.5km east of Revelstoke off the Trans-Canada Hwy. Open when enough snow melts (usually not until July, although officially it is mid-June to September), the paved road winds through lush cedar forests and alpine meadows and ends near Balsam Lake, within 2km of the peak. From here walk to the top or take the shuttle, which runs from 10am to 4pm daily. Along the way, watch for the site of Canada's **first ski jump**, where Nels Nelsen and Isabel Coursier coasted to world records beginning in 1915.

Umbrella-sized leaves are just some of the highlights of the **Skunk Cabbage Trail**, 28km east of Revelstoke on Hwy 1. Meanwhile, a 1.2km boardwalk along the Illecillewaet River gives an up-close view of the eponymous skunk cabbage, the marshes and myriad birds. Another 4km east, the **Giant Cedars Boardwalk** winds a 500m course around a grove of enormous old-growth cedars.

There are several good hiking trails from the summit. You can camp only in designated backcountry campgrounds, and you

THE KOOTENAYS

OH FUDGE!

West of Revelstoke on the Trans-Canada Hwy to Sicamous, kids shriek and parents try to distract them as one after another hackneyed roadside attraction comes into view. Prime examples include:

- **Three Valley Gap Heritage Ghost Town** (☎ 250-837-2109; www.3valley.com), 19km west of Revelstoke; ghost town, motel and more on a lake.

- **Enchanted Forest** (☎ 250-837-9477; www.enchantedforestbc.com), 32km west of Revelstoke; Jack (of Beanstalk fame) ponders BC's tallest tree house while fairies frolic.

- **Beardale Castle Miniatureland** (☎ 250-836-2268), 40km west of Revelstoke; tiny castles attract tiny fairies, tiny cars and tiny tourists.

must have a $10 Wilderness Pass camping permit (in addition to your park pass), which, along with lots of useful information, is available from **Parks Canada** in Revelstoke (p273) or from the **Rogers Pass Centre** inside Glacier National Park (opposite). Admission to both Mt Revelstoke and Glacier National Parks (the two are administered jointly) is

> ### WINTER ROAD CONDITIONS
>
> For up-to-date road conditions on the Trans-Canada Hwy and across the province, consult **DriveBC** (☎ 800-550-4997; www.drivebc.ca). This is essential in winter when storms can close roads for extended periods.

adult/child $8/4 per day. Developed campgrounds are few.

There's good cross-country skiing and snow-shoeing in the very long winters, but avalanches and bad weather require you to have the right gear and be prepared for anything (p275).

GLACIER NATIONAL PARK

Repeat the first word in the name **Glacier National Park** (www.pc.gc.ca/glacier) 430 times and you have the number of icy expanses located in this 1350-sq-km park.

Fans of rain and snow will revel in the almost constant precipitation. Annual snowfall can be as much as 23m. Because of the sheer mountain slopes, this is one

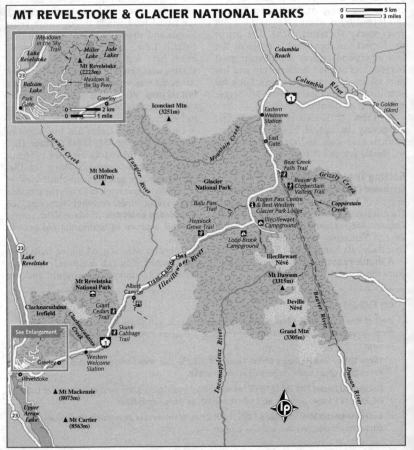

MT REVELSTOKE & GLACIER NATIONAL PARKS

TYING THE KNOT

British Columbia had an almost separate existence from the rest of Canada until 1885, when the Canadian Pacific Railway (CPR) completed its line over the previously impenetrable Rockies. These tracks for the first time linked the disparate territories of Canada and were part of the agreement that had brought BC into the confederation in 1871.

Running the rails through the Rockies was an enormous challenge that was accomplished by the work of thousands of immigrant laborers who endured harsh conditions to complete the dangerous task. Hundreds were killed by disease and accidents. Among the challenges they faced were the avalanches of Rogers Pass, which swept away people and trains like toys. Eventually long tunnels and snow sheds were laboriously constructed to protect the rails and the line was binding Canada together was completed on November 7, 1885.

East of the town of Field in Yoho National Park (p303), the gradients were so steep (4.5%), however, that any braking problem caused trains to lose control and plunge off the tracks, with all aboard dashed on the rocks below. To end this peril, two huge spiraling tunnels were laboriously blasted out of the granite mountains, which reduced grades to a more manageable 2.2%. Centennial celebrations for the tunnels were ongoing throughout 2009.

Along with the trains, the CPR built grand hotels in Calgary, Banff, Lake Louise, Vancouver and elsewhere to encourage travelers to ride the line and explore the region. People jumped at the chance to experience such rugged wilderness and still sip tea in luxury. Over a hundred years of passenger trains ended with a short-sighted government cutback that deprived Banff and the rest of the iconic route of a passenger service. Today the route is still busy with CPR freights and the occasional *Rocky Mountaineer* cruise train (p436). West of Calgary, the Trans-Canada Hwy runs parallel to much of the route.

There are four excellent places to learn about the history of this rail line in BC: a **lookout** from the Trans-Canada Hwy 8km east of Field (p303) offers a good view of the lower of the two spiral tunnels, with explanatory displays on how they work; the museum area inside the **Rogers Pass Centre** (below) in Glacier National Park shows the hazards of avalanches and features a model of the entire route over the Rockies; the **Revelstoke Railway Museum** (p273) documents the construction history of the entire CPR; and Cranbrook's **Canadian Museum of Rail Travel** (p295) preserves the beautiful trains that once ran on the line.

---

of the world's most active avalanche areas. For this reason, skiing, caving and mountaineering are closely regulated; you must register with park wardens before venturing into the backcountry.

Around Rogers Pass, you'll notice the many snow sheds protecting the highway. With the narrow road twisting up to 1330m, this is a dangerous area, sometimes called Death Strip; an unexpected avalanche can wipe a car right off the road. Still, the area is carefully controlled, and sometimes snows are brought tumbling down with artillery shells before they fall by themselves (on sunny afternoons in winter you may hear the big guns firing). Call for a daily **avalanche report** (☎ 250-837-6867) in season.

In summer the road is clear of snow, though you can encounter showers even on the sunniest of days. Whether you travel by car, bus, trail or bicycle (more power to you), Rogers will likely rank as one of the most beautiful mountain passes you'll ever have the pleasure of traversing. Be sure to pause at the **Hemlock Grove Trail**, 54km east of Revelstoke, where a 400m boardwalk winds through an ancient hemlock rainforest.

At the east side of the park is the dividing line between Pacific Standard and Mountain Standard time zones, which means that if it's noon in the park, it's 1pm just outside the east gate. Admission to this and Mt Revelstoke National Park (the two are administered jointly) is adult/child $8/4 per day.

Definitely plan to spend some time at the informative **Rogers Pass Centre** (☎ 250-814-5233; ⏰ 8am-8pm mid-June-Aug, 7am-5pm other months). Located 72km east of Revelstoke, the center shows films on the park and organizes guided walks in summer. Also check out the dramatic CPR dioramas documenting the railway's efforts to conquer the pass (in most cases it is: snow 1–0 railway). The center is also home to an excellent **bookstore** run by the Friends of Mt Revelstoke & Glacier (☎ 250-837-2010; www.friendsrevglacier.com). It's the place for books and maps on the region.

Across from the center, the 50-room **Glacier Park Lodge** (☎ 250-837-2126; www.glacierparklodge.ca; r $60-150; ✷ 🛜 🐾) is a good base for park explorations; it has a coffee shop.

Not far from here are the park's two campgrounds: **Illecillewaet Campground** and **Loop Brook Campground** (both $22 per campsite; ⦿ Jul-Sep). Both have running water and flush toilets. Backcountry campers must stick to designated backcountry sites and must have a $10 Wilderness Pass camping permit, which is available from the Parks Canada regional office in Revelstoke (p273) or the Rogers Pass Centre.

The Trans-Canada Hwy continues 40 km east to Golden (p299) and the East Kootenays.

NAKUSP

pop 1800

There are two good reasons to pass through Nakusp: you're on your way between Nelson and Vernon in the Okanagan Valley or you're traveling between Revelstoke and Nelson. Otherwise, while the nearby hot springs are diverting this is not the most compelling part of the Kootenays.

Nakusp, a First Nations word meaning 'sheltered bay,' was a major steamship port during the Slocan mining boom in the 1890s. Steamships carried ore up to the CPR tracks in Revelstoke.

The lakes were changed forever by the dams built as part of the Columbia River energy and flood control projects in the 1950s and 1960s. The level of Upper Lake was raised and several small towns were obliterated in the process. One of them, Beaton, was home to a remarkable pioneer woman named Mattie Gunterman who documented life there in the early 1900s with a camera. Her amazing pictures are now displayed online (www.vpl.ca/gunterman) by the Vancouver Public Library.

The dam-building is why even today you see little of the shoreline development you might expect and why Nakusp, which had to be relocated to higher ground, feels like a planned community.

Hwy 23 between Nakusp and Revelstoke is rather desolate. For details on the

Hwy 23 **Upper Arrow Lake ferry**, see opposite. While riding the ferry, check out the panels explaining the difficult and decades-long efforts to restore the ecological balance of the lake since the dams were built.

Southwest of Nakusp, Hwy 6 splits, heading southwest to Fauquier past Arrow Park, the official dividing line between Upper and Lower Arrow Lakes, and to the **Needles ferry**, which runs from Fauquier to Needles (opposite). Once on the other side, you'll climb over the 1189m-high Monashee Pass en route to Vernon (p266) in the Okanagan Valley. You'll pass a few small provincial parks along this route.

Nakusp VC (☎ 250-265-4234, 800-909-8819; www.nakusphotsprings.com; 92 W 6th Ave; ⦿ 9am-5pm Jun-Sep) has good hiking information for the area. Next door, the **Nakusp Museum** (adult/child $4/2; ⦿ 9am-5pm Jun-Sep) shows what the area looked like before the floods.

The area's hot springs attract a diverse crowd of families, hikers, bikers and others who want to soak up the hot water vibe. **Nakusp Hot Springs** (☎ 250-265-4528; www.nakusphotsprings.com; adult/child $9/free; ⦿ 9:30am-9:30pm), 12km northeast of Nakusp off Hwy 23, feel a bit artificial after a revamp that saw installation of a water filtration system. However, you'll forget this as the waters soak away your cares amidst an amphitheater of trees. Instead of driving you might want to make the beautiful 8km hike on the Kuskanax Interpretive Trail from Nakusp; the VC has a detailed brochure with the route. There are cramped sites for camping ($25), and simple chalets (from $70).

Anyone wishing to soak for free should ask around about two nearby natural hot springs: **St Leon's**, a favorite with locals for its seclusion and kidney-shaped pools, and **Halfway**, 24km north on Hwy 23. Getting to both undeveloped springs requires driving on logging roads, and a little hiking. Ask at the VC for specific directions, as these spots are, after all, secluded.

The best place to stay in the area is easily the **OUR PICK Hot Springs Guesthouse** (☎ 250-265-3069; www.enjoynakusp.com; 1950 Hwy 23 N; 🛜). This fun and friendly place has a superb location on the lake across from Hot Springs Rd. Enjoy the quiet in a hammock or borrow a kayak or bike. The owners excel as ambassadors for the area. Guests have a choice of a suite or a cabin, each with multiple

---

KOOTENAY FERRIES

The long Kootenay and Upper and Lower Arrow Lakes necessitate some ferry travel. All ferries (www.th.gov.bc.ca/marine/ferry_schedules.htm) are free. On busy summer weekends you may have to wait in a long line for a sailing or two before you get passage.

Upper Arrow Lake Ferry (☎ 250-837-8418) runs year-round between Galena Bay (49km south of Revelstoke) and Shelter Bay (49km north of Nakusp) on Hwy 23. The trip takes 25 minutes and runs from 6am to 11pm every hour on the hour from Shelter Bay and every hour on the half-hour between 6:30am and 11:30pm from Galena Bay.

Needles Ferry (☎ 250-837-8418) crosses Lower Arrow Lake between Fauquier (57km south of Nakusp) and Needles (135km east of Vernon) on Hwy 6; the trip takes five minutes. The ferry runs every day, leaving from Fauquier every 30 minutes on the hour and the half-hour from 5am to 10pm. From Needles it runs on the quarter and three-quarter hour between 5:15am and 9:45pm. After hours the ferry travels on demand only.

Kootenay Lake Ferry (☎ 250-229-4215) sails between Balfour on the west arm of Kootenay Lake (34km northeast of Nelson) and Kootenay Bay. Its 45-minute crossing makes it the world's longest free car ferry. In summer the ferry leaves Balfour every 50 minutes between 6:30am and 9:40pm, and from Kootenay Lake from 7:10am to 10:20pm. In winter the sailings are less frequent.

---

rooms and full kitchens (both $120). It is 2km north of the VC.

NEW DENVER

pop 560

Just a few moving vans away from being a ghost town, New Denver has an ideal position on Slocan Lake. Unlike Nakusp, it avoided the indignity of having to flee up a hill when a dam was put in, so it still feels rooted to its past. Prowl the quiet tree-lined streets and you might feel out of place not wearing a straw boater hat, corset or some other vintage wear.

A major boomtown in the heyday of the Silvery Slocan Mines and originally named Eldorado, New Denver grew quickly with seemingly endless potential, enough (boosters hoped) to rival the also-booming town of Colorado. As the boom subsided, this optimism – and the town – shrank.

Greatness, however, is subjective; today New Denver is a quiet (literally – locals are proud that there is no cell phone reception) and progressive community framed by tall mountain peaks on the shores of beautiful Slocan Lake.

Sights

The **Silvery Slocan Museum** (☎ 250-358-2201; 202 6th Ave; 🕑 9am-5pm Jun-Sep) is also home to the helpful **VC** (☎ 250-358-2719; www.slocanlake .com). Housed in the 1897 Bank of Montreal, it features well-done displays from the booming mining days and a tiny vault.

Look outside for the ongoing restoration of *The Lancet*, a home-built boat used by a Dr JE Brouse to control the spread of disease while spreading gossip around the lake in the early 1900s.

During WWII, more than 20,000 Japanese Canadians in Canada were rounded up and shipped to remote places in the BC interior for reasons of 'security.' The **Nikkei Internment Memorial Centre** (☎ 250-358-7288; www.newdenver.ca/nikkei; 306 Josephine St, New Denver; adult/child $6/4; 🕑 9:30am-5pm May-Sep) is on the site of one of 10 former internment camps in the Slocan Valley. One of the old huts has been furnished to show the stark conditions of the internees. There is a beautiful remembrance garden.

Nearby **Silverton** (population 220) also boomed but went bust; this pretty spot is even more of a ghost town than New Denver. If it's late summer and there's something in the air, it may be the annual **Hills Garlic Festival** (www.hillsgarlicfest.ca) when organic farmers and artisans come together for a weekend of fine food, crafts, music and plenty of garlic-laced treats.

Sleeping & Eating

New Denver Municipal Campground (☎ 250-358-2316; campsites $18-22) Enjoy lakeside camping with plenty of amenities at this 44-pitch site near the marina at the bottom of 3rd Ave.

Villa Dome Quixote (☎ 250-358-7242; www .domequixote.com; 602 6th Ave; r $60-80; 🖵) Tilt at windmills at this Buckminster Fuller fantasy of domed buildings. Corners are few in the 15 rooms, which have a certain minimalist flair (some share bathrooms). Revel in all things round as you bubble away in the hot tub.

Valhalla Inn (☎ 250-358-2228; www.valhallainn .biz; 509 Slocan Ave; r $65-120) The Valhalla has a lively pub with tables outside, a restaurant, 28 good-sized rooms and a bare-bones simplicity that will have you itching to get out in the natural beauty.

Silverton Resort (☎ 250-358-7157; www.silver tonresort.com; 15 Lake Ave, Silverton; cabins $150-300) Watch your step in the morning from some of the seven cabins at this waterside lodge or you'll fall in the lake – it's that close. Enjoy shady, woodsy charm and full kitchens plus TVs with a vintage concept called 'knobs'.

Appletree (☎ 250-358-2691; 210 6th Ave; meals $6; ⏱ 7am-4pm Mon-Sat) Enjoy a full plate of gossip with your tasty breakfast or lunch. Locals lounge around inside and out back under a big tree amiably decrying the state of the world.

Getting There & Away

New Denver is 47km southeast of Nakusp, along a gas station-free stretch of Hwy 6.

VALHALLA PROVINCIAL PARK

At almost 500 sq km, **Valhalla Provincial Park** (www.env.gov.bc.ca/bcparks) is paradoxically one of BC's most-accessible remote parks. On the west side of Slocan Lake from New Denver, it has no road access, yet it is a short boat ride away. Those who make the journey find an untrammeled wilderness that is excellent for hikers, canoeists and others looking for an escape.

The park encompasses most of the Valhalla Range of the Selkirk Mountains. The name comes from the Norse mythological palace for slain warriors. Ochre rock paintings along the shoreline are believed to represent the dreams and visions of ancient Arrow Lakes First Nations, who treasured the natural sanctuary.

Trails lace the park venturing to isolated lakes like Cahill and Beatrice and up to high-elevation glaciers. The **hiking** opportunities are many but they are only for those fully ready for a wilderness adventure. A popular **canoe trip** follows the Slocan Lake shoreline for two to five days. There are

---

HWY 6 TO NELSON

Leaving New Denver to the south, Hwy 6 runs alongside pretty Slocan Lake for about 30km. You'll see some dramatic rock faces, cool vistas of snow-clad peaks rising from the lake and little else with this option, which is 97km in total between New Denver and Nelson. If you're not doing a loop, the route via Kaslo is the more interesting option.

---

hikes from the nine lakeside **campgrounds** ($5, with fire rings, picnic tables and pit toilets) into the interior, where there are a few more basic campsites.

In New Denver, **Valla Venture** (☎ 250-358-7775) offers water-taxi services (from $35) to various spots, including the Nemo Creek trailhead, a good point of departure for day hikes.

Valhalla was protected as parkland in 1983, mostly due to the intense efforts of the **Valhalla Wilderness Society** (☎ 250-358-2333; www.vws.org; 307 6th St; ⏱ varies), an advocacy group that formed in the 1970s to save the Valhalla Range from logging. Since then the group has also successfully campaigned to protect the Khutzeymateen Grizzly Sanctuary near Prince Rupert, and the nearby White Grizzly Wilderness. A current focus is the commercialization of BC's parks (p57). When open, the society's office is a great place to learn more about current issues and to get excellent park topographic maps and trail information.

NEW DENVER TO KASLO

Even ghost towns shouldn't be this derelict. **Sandon** (☎ 250-358-7920; ⏱ 10am-6pm May-Oct), off Hwy 31A, 12km east of New Denver, is an old town that suffers from neglect of its obvious tourist potential. Modern-day junk litters the grounds of a town that once was home to 5000. The **museum** is the best feature, with lots of fascinating information on the prospectors of the 1890s.

Near Sandon you can get one of the best views of the Slocan Valley from the **Idaho Peak Lookout**, a 2244m-high viewpoint. A rough logging road leads up to a parking area, trailhead for an easy 1.5km (one-way) hike to sweeping vistas.

The **K&S Railway Historic Trail**, which also starts in Sandon, follows the old narrow-gauge railway tracks for 4.5km, passing interpretive signs, old mine shafts and remnants of the railway. You'll also get good views of the surrounding rugged terrain.

The entire 47km route along Hwy 31A traverses some gorgeous mountain scenery, replete with spurting springs and babbling brooks.

KASLO
pop 1100

Tree-lined streets, restored Victorian buildings and access to outdoor fun make Kaslo an excellent stop for travelers. Downtown's Front St is both busy and picturesque, with a good view of Kootenay Lake and a nice mix of shops, galleries, eateries and attractions.

Unlike surrounding towns in the Slocan Valley, it was timber, not silver, that lured the first European settlers to Kaslo. Later Kaslo became a thriving fruit-growing community noted especially for its cherries, some of which were said to be the size of plums, which in turn were said to be the size of melons etc.

The **VC** (☎ 250-353-2525; 324 Front St; ☻ 9am-5pm mid-May–mid-Oct) has good information on hiking and mountain biking trails in the area, as well as the diverse range of accommodations.

Sights & Activities
Right outside the VC, the 1898 **SS Moyie** (adult/child $7/3; www.klhs.bc.ca; ☻ 9am-5pm mid-May–mid-Oct) has been restored after much community agitation to prevent it suffering the fate of other riverboats. For 59 years the boat provided a vital link south to Nelson. Now a national historic site, the SS *Moyie* is moored permanently on the downtown lakeside and has a good museum that covers its active years.

The **Kootenay Star Museum** (☎ 250-353-2115; 402 Front St; admission by donation; ☻ 9am-5:30pm) is like a garage sale of old artifacts from the mines. It has a tiny café with home-baked items. The beautifully restored **Langham Cultural Centre** (☎ 250-353-2662; 477 A Ave; ☻ 1-4pm Thu-Sun) features displays by local artists in two galleries and live music performances in the 75-seat theater.

Kaslo Kayaking (☎ 250-353-9649; 438A Front St; rental per day from $50) rents kayaks, offers tours and gives lessons on paddle-perfect Kootenay Lake. They also rent bikes.

Sleeping & Eating
The Kaslo VC has a book bulging with B&B and rental accommodations. Front St is lined with good delis, bakeries, cafés and pubs.

Kaslo Municipal Campground (☎ 250-353-2662; www.kaslo.ca; Vimy Park; campsite $15-20; ☻ May-Sep) The 25 bare-bones pitches are close to Front St and the lake.

Kootenay Lake Guest House (☎ 250-353-2551; www.kaslohostel.com; 232 B Ave; dm/d $25/50; 🖳 🛜) This attractive European-style hostel has a big common kitchen, deck, sauna and organic vegetable garden. You can rent kayaks, canoes and bikes.

Kaslo Motel (☎ 250-353-7603; 330 D Ave; r from $60; 🐾) The 17 rooms at this central place are in a mix of cottages and a two-story block. Not all units have air-con but some have kitchens.

KASLO TO NELSON
The 70km drive to Nelson hugs the lake for most of the way. It's all very scenic. **Ainsworth Hot Springs** is a cute little old town with a spa resort. At Balfour, Hwy 31 ends at the Kootenay Lake Ferry (see boxed text, p281), but the road continues as Hwy 3A 34km to Nelson.

NELSON
pop 9900

Alluring, intriguing, amusing, confounding, Nelson is the star of the Kootenays. A beautiful hillside town that revels in its own spirit, Nelson combines excellent dining, solid green credentials, heritage charm and its own quirky sense of self in a package that demands a few days to fully explore.

'Keep Nelson Weird' is just one bumper sticker you'll spot around Nelson, where self-expression is an art, whether it's a guy riding a bike without handles down the street at midnight while making animal noises, or the range of works on display in its community galleries. The vibrant cultural mix is

---

DAY TRIP FROM NELSON

Doing a loop from Nelson north through Kaslo, west to New Denver and then south on Hwy 6 and back to Nelson is about as good a daytrip as you'll find in the Kootenays. The 217km route is a breeze for drivers and an impressive jaunt for cyclists.

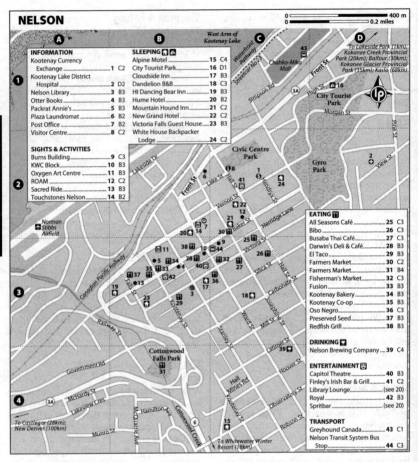

NELSON

0 — 400 m
0 — 0.2 miles

INFORMATION
Kootenay Currency
Exchange...........................1 C2
Kootenay Lake District
Hospital...........................2 D2
Nelson Library......................3 B3
Otter Books.........................4 B3
Packrat Annie's.....................5 B3
Plaza Laundromat...................6 B2
Post Office.........................7 B2
Visitor Centre......................8 C2

SIGHTS & ACTIVITIES
Burns Building......................9 C3
KWC Block..........................10 B3
Oxygen Art Centre.................11 B3
ROAM..............................12 C2
Sacred Ride........................13 B3
Touchstones Nelson................14 B2

SLEEPING
Alpine Motel.......................15 C4
City Tourist Park...................16 D1
Cloudside Inn......................17 B3
Dandelion B&B.....................18 C3
HI Dancing Bear Inn................19 B3
Hume Hotel........................20 B2
Mountain Hound Inn...............21 C2
New Grand Hotel...................22 C2
Victoria Falls Guest House..........23 B3
White House Backpacker
Lodge............................24 C2

EATING
All Seasons Café...................25 C3
Bibo..............................26 C3
Busaba Thai Café...................27 C3
Darwin's Deli & Café................28 B3
El Taco............................29 B3
Farmers Market....................30 C2
Farmers Market....................31 B4
Fisherman's Market................32 C3
Fusion............................33 B3
Kootenay Bakery...................34 B3
Kootenay Co-op....................35 B3
Oso Negro.........................36 C3
Preserved Seed....................37 B3
Redfish Grill......................38 B3

DRINKING
Nelson Brewing Company.........39 C4

ENTERTAINMENT
Capitol Theatre....................40 B3
Finley's Irish Bar & Grill............41 C2
Library Lounge....................(see 20)
Royal.............................42 B3
Spritbar...........................(see 20)

TRANSPORT
Greyhound Canada.................43 C1
Nelson Transit System Bus
Stop.............................44 C3

fueled by students at the renowned Kootenay School of the Arts, the Selkirk School of Music and a school of Chinese medicine.

Downtown is a compact hub of cafés, bars and shops, with nary a chain in sight. Down at the edge of the west arm of Kootenay Lake, paths, beaches and parks line the shore. Settle into a seat outside and enjoy the vibe. You never know what surprise will come your way next.

History

Nelson was born in the late 1800s, when two down-on-their-luck brothers from Washington sat bemoaning their bad fortune on top of Toad Mountain, just southwest of what is now Nelson. While the broth-

ers rested, some of their party found the copper-silver deposit that later became the Silver King Mine. A town began to build up around the ore-rich mine, and its mass production prompted two transcontinental railways to serve Nelson in order to carry the goods away to smelters. When this proved too costly, the mining company built its own smelter, which only lasted as long as the ore. The smelter buildings were destroyed in a massive fire in 1911, and like most mined-out towns, Nelson turned to its forests.

In 1977 Nelson was chosen for the government's project on heritage conservation. Today it boasts more than 350 carefully preserved and restored late-19th- to early-20th-century buildings.

Orientation

Nelson sits on the west arm of Kootenay Lake. Traveling from the north, Hwy 3A becomes a series of streets before heading west to Castlegar. Hwy 6 skirts the west side of downtown, joining Hwy 3A to Castlegar and going south to the small lumber town of Salmo before connecting with Hwy 3 which runs to Creston and the East Kootenays.

Baker St is the main drag and has many shops and restaurants. (And who couldn't love a town with a corner of Josephine and Baker? All it needs is a fruit stand.)

Information

For a good sense of the local scene, pick up a copy of the *Daily News*. Also worthy are the quarterly *Articulate* and *Route* 3. Events listings are posted at the Kootenay Co-Op (p287) at 295 Baker St. Hear local bands and local issues debated on community-run CJLY 93.5FM.

BOOKSTORES

Otter Books (☎ 250-352-7525; 398 Baker St) Excellent selection of local books, topographic maps and magazines.
Packrat Annie's (☎ 250-354-4722; 411 Kootenay St) Good array of used books and the delightful Vienna Café.

INTERNET ACCESS

Many cafés have internet access.
Nelson Library (☎ 250-352-6333; 602 Stanley St; ☽ 1-8pm Mon, Wed & Fri, 10am-6pm Tue & Thu, 11am-6pm Sat) Free internet access.

LAUNDRY

Plaza Laundromat (☎ 250-352-6077; 616 Front St; ☽ 8am-6pm)

MEDICAL SERVICES

Kootenay Lake District Hospital (☎ 250-352-3111; 3 View St; ☽ 24hr)

MONEY

Kootenay Currency Exchange (☎ 250-354-1441; 715 Vernon St; ☽ 9am-5pm Mon-Fri, 10am-3pm Sat) Typically for Nelson, this is also an art gallery.

POST

Post office (☎ 250-352-3538; 514 Vernon St)

TOURIST INFORMATION

Visitor Centre (☎ 250-352-3433, 877-663-5706; www .discovernelson.com; 225 Hall St; ☽ 8:30am-6pm May-Oct, 8:30am-5pm Mon-Fri Nov-Apr)

Sights

Almost a third of Nelson's buildings have been restored to their Victorian architectural splendor, spilling down its terraced hillsides. It's well worth a stop at the VC for the excellent companion brochures detailing self-guided tours of the area's architectural heritage by foot and car.

You can easily cover all 26 buildings on the walking tour in a couple of hours. Highlights include the 1899 **Burns Building** (560 Baker St), which has a carved cow's head over the door courtesy of its cattle-baron builder. You can't miss the turret on the **KWC Block** (498 Baker St), a 1901 landmark designed by the prolific Alexander Carrie.

Lakeside Park by the iconic Nelson Bridge boasts fusillades of flowers, shady trees and picnic tables. It backs a popular beach where swimmers debate whether to swim to the far shore. This area is a good destination for walkers from the center, who can follow the **Waterfront Pathway**, which runs all along the shore (it's western extremity past the airport has good and remote river vistas). You can walk one way to the park and ride **Streetcar No 23** (adult/child $3/2; ☽ 11am-5pm daily mid-Jun–Sep, 11am-5pm Sat & Sun May & Sep–mid-Oct) the other way. One of the town's originals, it follows a 2km track from Lakeside Park to the wharf at the foot of Hall St.

Nelson's baronial old city hall (1902) has been transformed into **Touchstones Nelson** (☎ 250-352-9813; www.touchstonesnelson.ca; 502 Vernon St; adult/child $10/4; ☽ 11am-7pm Wed-Sat, noon-4pm Sun), a museum of local history and art. Every month there are new exhibitions, many of which celebrate local artists. The history displays are engaging and interactive. Look for the First Nations canoes designed to look like sturgeon.

Creations as varied as film, prose, painting and dance can be seen at **Oxygen Art Centre** (☎ 250-352-6322; www.oxygenartcentre.org; 320 Vernon St; ☽ varies), a community-run gallery that showcases Nelson's deep pool of artistic talent.

Activities

Nelson is truly a four-season town of activities, whether on the lake or up in the beautiful surrounding mountains.

KAYAKING

The natural (meaning not dammed) waters of Kootenay Lake are a major habitat for kayaks. **ROAM** (☎ 250-354-2056; www.roam shop.com; 639 Baker St) sells gear, offers advice and works with the noted **Kootenay Kayak Co** (☎ 250-505-4549; www.kootenaykayak.com; rentals per day from $25, tours from $80). Kayaks can be picked up at Roam or Lakeside Park. The tours are highly recommended.

HIKING

The two-hour climb to Pulpit Rock affords fine views of Nelson and Kootenay Lake. Find the trailhead on your right at the west end of Johnstone Rd (on the north bank across the bridge). Excellent hikes abound at **Kokanee Creek Provincial Park** (☎ 250-825-4212; www.env.gov.bc.ca/bcparks), 20km northeast of town off Hwy 3A. Stop in at the park's visitor center for information on specific hikes, including the Canyon Trail, which winds through lush forest to views of waterfalls spilling off Kokanee Glacier. Eight trails begin right at the visitor center. **Kokanee Glacier Provincial Park** (☎ 250-825-3500 for trail conditions; www.env.gov.bc.ca/bcparks) covers 320 sq km and boasts dozens of lakes. Its 85km of hiking trails are some of the area's best. The fantastic 4km (two-hour) hike to Kokanee Lake on a well-marked trail can be continued to the treeless, boulder-strewn expanse around the glacier.

Summit Reflections (☎ 250-354-4884; www.summit reflections.com) offers a range of Alpine hikes and nature walks.

MOUNTAIN BIKING

Most of this area's mountain biking trails wind up from Kootenay Lake along steep and rather challenging hills, followed by wicked downhills. Trail names like 'Boneyard' and 'Fat Chance' are not misnomers, but there are some intermediate trails for those wishing to finish in one piece. **Sacred Ride** (☎ 250-354-3831; www.sacredride.ca; 213B Baker St; rental per day from $40) is also a good choice. It sells *Your Ticket to Ride*, an extensive trail map, for $10.

SKIING & SNOWBOARDING

Powder magazine said: 'If you put everything that really mattered into one little resort you would have Whitewater.' Known for its heavy powdery snowfall, which averages 1050cm per year, **Whitewater Winter Resort** (☎ 250-354-4944, 800-666-9420, snow report 250-352-7669; www.skiwhitewater.com; 1-day lift tickets adult/child $46/28) straddles the line between 'undiscovered gem' and 'legend.' Whitewater has only two double chairs and a rope tow, but they can take you to an elevation of 2040m (the drop is 396m), where you can enjoy great powdery snow on 46 runs. Several snowcat operators can take you to virgin territory from $400 for the day. It is revered for its easy access to the back-country. The resort is 18km south of Nelson off Hwy 6.

You can rent equipment at the resort or at most of the gear shops on Baker St.

Tours

Nestled on its hillside, Nelson is best viewed from the lake. And the views aren't just limited to the town either. Much of the surrounding region is still undeveloped, with iconic bands of blue mountains receding to the horizon.

Sail With Us (☎ 250-359-7772; www.sailwithus kootenaylake.com; Balfour) offers tours aboard a 10m sailboat. Lake tours for two start from $110 for two hours. It's located 30km east of Nelson in Balfour, near the Kootenay Lake Ferry.

Sleeping

By all means stay in the heart of Nelson so you can fully enjoy the city's vibe. The VC has a free phone for calling local accommodations. Ask for lists of B&Bs in heritage homes.

BUDGET

City Tourist Park (☎ 250-352-7618; 90 High St; sites from $20; ☼ May-Oct; ▣) Just a five-minute walk from Baker St, this small campground is right in an urban park and has 40 shady pitches.

Kokanee Creek Provincial Park (☎ 800-689-9025; www.discovercamping.ca; campsite $22; ☼ May-Sep) Situated 20km northeast of Nelson off Hwy 3A, this park contains 132 wooded pitches with toilets and showers. It has its own visitor center and offers daily interpretive programs. Redfish, set among old hemlocks, is the quieter of the two campgrounds here.

HI Dancing Bear Inn (☎ 250-352-7573, 877-352-7573; www.dancingbearinn.com; 171 Baker St; dm/r from $25/50; ▣ ☎) How many hostels have a concierge? This one does, offering advice and smoothing the stay of guests in the 14 shared and private rooms (all share bathrooms). Everything is immaculate.

our pick **White House Backpacker Lodge**
(☎ 250-352-0505; www.white-house.ca; 816 Vernon St; 198 Baker St; dm $25, r from $50; 🖳 🛜) Relax on the broad porch overlooking the lake at this comfy heritage house. Rooms are spotless and you'll get all the pancakes you can cook yourself for breakfast.

MIDRANGE
All of the following are in the centre, rates are surprisingly reasonable.

New Grand Hotel (☎ 250-352-7211, 888-722-2258; www.newgrandhotel.ca; 616 Vernon St; r $25-110; 🔀 🛜) Mustard stucco and wrought iron accents on the exterior give this 30-room hotel a vague Spanish/Old Hollywood feel. Stars will like the main rooms which have rich mission-style furniture and restored hardwood floors. Extras will enjoy the small economy rooms, some of which share bathrooms.

Mountain Hound Inn (☎ 250-352-6490, 866-452-6490; www.mountainhound.com; 621 Baker St; r $75-110; 🔀 🖳) The 19 rooms are small but have an industrial edge – to go with the cement block walls. It also offers high-speed internet and a continental breakfast. Rooms 121 and 122 have lake views.

Dandelion B&B (☎ 250-505-5466; www.bbcanada .com/thedandelion; 519 Carbonate St; r $85-100; 🛜 ; 📅 May-Sep) The Dandelion has two comfy rooms furnished in bright, contemporary hues. There's a patio and a view of the water from this restored old bungalow. Big breakfasts.

Alpine Motel (☎ 250-352-5501, 888-356-2233; www.alpine-motel.com; 1120 Hall Mines Rd; r $70-140; 🔀 🖳 🛜) The grounds at this Swiss-style motel are dotted with flowers and you can view the misty waters of the lake from the steaming waters of the hot tub. The 30 rooms are spacious; some are family size. It's near Observatory St, just up the hill south of the center.

Victoria Falls Guest House (☎ 250-352-2297; www.stanleyhousebb.com; cnr Victoria & Falls Sts; r $110-130; 🛜) The wide porch wraps right around this festive yellow renovated Victorian. The four rooms are more like suites with sitting areas and cooking facilities. Decor ranges from cozy antique to family-friendly bunkbeds.

Hume Hotel (☎ 250-352-5331, 877-568-0888; www .humehotel.com; 422 Vernon St; r $90-140; 🛜) This 1898 classic hotel is reclaiming its former grandeur – the red neon sign on the roof is a classic touch. The 43 rooms (beware of airless ones overlooking the kitchen on sultry nights) vary in quality; ask for the huge corner rooms with sweeping views of the hills and lake. Rates include a full hot breakfast; it has several appealing nightlife venues (p288).

Cloudside Inn (☎ 250-352-3226, 800-596-2337; www.cloudside.ca; 408 Victoria St; r $100-250; 🔀 🖳 🛜) Live like a silver baron at this vintage mansion run by two Brits who fled their jobs as suits in London. The six rooms are named after trees: Spruce will please antique lovers while Cedar will please view lovers. Luxuries abound; a fine patio overlooks the terraced gardens.

Eating
Nelson has a great range of eating options. Baker St and its precincts are lined with cool cafés, restaurants and pubs. Note that even in summer, Nelson betrays its small-town roots and starts putting away the sidewalk tables by 9pm.

FOOD PURVEYORS
Nelson has not one but two **farmers markets** where you can enjoy the local bounty. One is in the **centre** (cnr Josephine & Baker Sts; 📅 9:30am-3pm Wed Jul-Sep) and is a community event. The other in **Cottonwood Falls Park** (📅 8am-2pm Sat May-Oct) is both the largest in the region and also the best-sited: right next to a waterfall. There's live music, crafts and more.

Part community centre, part market, the **Kootenay Co-op** (☎ 250-354-4077; 295 Baker St; 📅 8am-7pm Mon-Sat) has local produce, foodstuffs and good prepared foods in its bakery.

Kootenay Bakery (☎ 250-352-2274; 377 Baker St; snacks from $2; 📅 7am-6:30pm) is a modern take on a old classic. Try the surprising root vegetable croissant or the apple fritter, which blows away the sad, corporate Timmy Ho's version.

BUDGET
Oso Negro (☎ 250-532-7761; 604 Ward St; coffee from $1.50; 📅 7am-5pm; 🖳) This local favorite corner café roasts its own coffee. Outside there are tables in a garden that burbles with water features set among statues.

El Taco (☎ 250-352-2060; 306 Victoria St; meals $5-8; 📅 11am-9pm Mon-Sat) All the colors of Mexico are crammed onto this tiny house. Eat at one of the art-accented tables outside or take food away. The burritos are hefty in size and flavor.

Darwin's Deli & Café (☎ 250-352-2120; 460 Baker St; meals from $6; ☺ 7:30am-10pm; 🖥 🛜) A classic Italian deli with good sandwiches, internet terminals and a few tables outside.

Preserved Seed (☎ 250-352-0325; 202 Vernon St; meals from $6; ☺ 5-11pm Mon, 8am-11pm Tue-Thu, till 4pm Fri) Classically Nelson: the food is vegan and organic, tables on decks outside have lake views, free poetry is on offer and hours respect the Sabbath. Oh, and they serve healthy teas.

MIDRANGE
Redfish Grill (☎ 250-352-3456; 491 Baker St; meals $5-20; ☺ 8am-11pm) Redfish serves excellent cuisine throughout the day. Breakfasts are large and traditional. At lunchtime there's a stylish mix of sandwiches and salads. At night the mood becomes whimsical and romantic. Tapas-style small plates and a range of global cuisine made with local produce include a killer Caesar salad redolent with garlic.

Fisherman's Market (☎ 250-505-5515; 577 Ward St; mains $8-20; ☺ 11am-8pm) With its roots as the region's best seafood shop, the dining area here is *the* place for fish and chips, wild caught salmon, crab and more. Specials depend on what's fresh. The furniture is a hoot: mismatched cast-offs that could have done duty in your high school.

Busaba Thai Café (☎ 250-352-2185; 524 Victoria St; mains $10-20; ☺ 11am-10pm) The iced Thai coffee here can turn around a hot day. The rich details of the interior have the lush elegance of a Bangkok gift shop where you'd actually buy something. The food is delicate, authentic and possibly best enjoyed on the patio under the stars.

Fusion (☎ 250-352-3011; 301 Baker St; mains $12-25; ☺ noon-2pm, 5-11pm Mon-Sat) This very popular tapas place has a menu with global influences. Specials change with the seasons. It has a broad deck outside and live acoustic guitar inside on some weeknights.

TOP END
All Seasons Café (☎ 250-352-0101; www.allseasons cafe.com; 620 Herridge Lane; mains $15-30; ☺ 5-10pm Mon-Sat) Sitting on the patio under the little lights twinkling in the huge maple above is a

Nelson highlight (in winter, candles provide the same romantic flair). One of BC's best restaurants, the eclectic menu changes with all the seasons. The wine list is iconic.

Bibo (☎ 250-352-2744; 518 Hall St; tapas $5-20; ☺ noon-11pm) Another star on Nelson's culinary list, Bibo is all exposed brick inside. Small plates celebrate local produce: go nuts and design your own cheese and charcuterie plate. In summer, the vast hillside terrace outside is simply seductive. (The wine list is memorable; service sublime.)

Drinking & Entertainment
Nelson has some good venues; many have live entertainment and also serve bar food such as burgers and nachos.

Most places in town serve the excellent organic beers from **Nelson Brewing Company** (☎ 250-352-3582; 512 Latimer St; ☺ tours 3:30pm Fri). The Paddywhack IPA is pure hoppy joy.

PUBS
Royal (☎ 250-352-1269; 330 Baker St; ☺ 11am-2am) A huge rollicking bar right on Baker St. There are tables out front and many more in the high-ceilinged space that sees many bands.

our pick **Library Lounge** (☎ 250-352-5331; Hume Hotel, 422 Vernon St; ☺ 11am-late) The corner bar in the vintage hotel is ornately decorated in traditional style. Easily the classiest venue in town, there is live jazz and acoustic guitar some nights. Ponder the passing parade from the sidewalk tables.

Finley's Irish Bar & Grill (☎ 250-352-5121; 705 Vernon St; ☺ noon-late; 🛜) This big, modern pub has a back deck with sweeping lake views. Inside, there's live music or DJs many nights, backed up by the beat of pool cues (or in the case of karaoke, hopefully drowned out).

CLUBS
Spritbar (☎ 250-352-5331; Hume Hotel, 422 Vernon St; ☺ 9pm-late Thu-Sat) The latest incarnation of the Hume's popular basement club is a minimalist black celebration of the 'art of mashup and turntablism'.

THEATER
Capitol Theatre (☎ 250-352-6363; www.capitoltheatre .bc.ca; 421 Victoria St) This restored 1927 theater has art films, performance art, ballet and drama.

Getting There & Around

The closest airport with commercial service to Nelson is in Castlegar (below). **Queen City Shuttle** (☎ 250-352-9829; www.kootenayshuttle.com; adult/child one way $22/11; 1hr) serves the Castlegar Airport.

Greyhound Canada (☎ 250-352-3939; Chahko-Mika Mall, 1128 Lakeside Dr) has services to Calgary ($110, 11 to 13 hours, two daily) via various south Kootenays cities and Vancouver ($125, 12 to 13 hours, two daily) via Kelowna ($63, 5½ hours, two daily).

The main stop for **Nelson Transit System Buses** (☎ 250-352-8228; www.busonline.ca) is on the corner of Ward and Baker Sts. Bus 2 serves Chahko-Mika Mall and Lakeside Park ($1.75). Bus 10 serves the North Shore and runs to the Kootenay Lake ferry in summer ($2.50).

Whitewater Winter Resort runs a **shuttle** (☎ 250-505-4921; return $15) to/from town during the ski season.

CASTLEGAR

pop 7800

You're bound to pass through Castlegar (or at most pause), a sprawling town that is a highway hub (Hwys 3 and 3A merge here). It sits at the confluence of the Kootenay and Columbia Rivers, which feed a huge pulp mill and Keenleyside Dam.

Head to the north end of Columbia Ave to see the strip of stores known as downtown Castlegar. In the southern part of town, you'll find the **VC** (☎ 250-365-6313; www .castlegar.com; 1995 6th Ave at 20th St; ☉ 9am-5pm Jun-Aug, 9am-5pm Mon-Fri Sep-May).

There are traces of the Eastern European cultures brought to the area by immigrants (including the Doukhobors, see p290).

DETOUR: KOOTENAY LAKE

If you're traveling south from Nelson, rather than travel through Salmo, you can follow Kootenay Lake the entire way. From Nelson head east on Hwy 3A to the Kootenay Lake ferry in Balfour (p281). The lake views will keep you on deck the entire journey. At Kootenay Bay (it's really just a ferry dock) Hwy 3A continues south 78km to Creston (p291). It's a quiet road, and except for a few villages, it'll just be you and the sweeping lake views.

Weezies Borscht Hut (☎ 250-304-2633; 2816 Columbia Ave, aka Hwy 22; meals $8; ☉ 10am-6pm) serves its namesake soup with all meals (it's a delicious tomato-cabbage version). Other treats worth the stop (at what really is a hut) include reubens, cabbage rolls and *pyrahi* (rolls filled with cheese and sauerkraut). In season, the strawberry-rhubarb pie is sublime and the ice cream the perfect bribe for anyone whining about cabbage.

Castlegar Airport (YCG; ☎ 250-365-5151) is on Hwy 3A southeast of town. It is the major airport for the region. Air Canada Jazz has daily flights to Vancouver and Calgary. Budget Rent A Car has offices in the airport terminal. Nelson is 41km northeast of Castlegar on Hwy 3A.

ROSSLAND

pop 3700

Perched high up in the Southern Monashee Mountains, Rossland's location 1023m up amidst the peak, is best appreciated if you're arriving from the west. All those vertical drops make it a top winter sports destination and an even bigger summer haven for mountain bikers. A history of mining has left the hills crisscrossed with old trails and abandoned rail lines, all perfect for riding.

The area was first encountered by Europeans in 1865, when builders of the historic Dewdney Trail passed by and simply marveled at the reddish mineral stains on nearby Red Mountain. Prospectors didn't come sniffing around for another 25 years. In 1890 Joe Moris decided to do more than admire the geology and tapped into the rich gold deposits that led to the town's birth. The town built up quickly. Sourdough Alley (today's Columbia Ave) became the province's wildest and roughest main thoroughfare, and by 1895, 7000 residents and hundreds of prostitutes could take their pick of 42 saloons. By 1929 most of the claims were mined out, and the boom went limp, having produced $165 million worth of gold.

Today the sturdy grid of streets lined with old wooden houses produces a new breed in search of gold: Olympic skiing medalists like Kerrin Lee-Gartner and Nancy Greene.

Information

Visitor Centre (☎ 250-362-7722, 888-448-7444; www .rossland.com; ☉ 9am-5pm May-Sep) Located in the Rossland Museum building, at the junction

THOSE DARN DOUKHOBORS

Castlegar's history is spiced up by the Doukhobors, members of a Russian Christian pacifist sect who followed their leader, Peter Verigin, west from Saskatchewan between 1908 and 1913. The Doukhobors, small groups of peaceful, communal-living people, rejected the teachings of the Russian Orthodox Church during the 18th century. They refused ritual worship, believing instead that god's spirit lived within each individual and that it was up to individuals, not an external god, to lead peaceful and harmonious lives. Needless to say, this sort of self-reliance was rejected by the church, which, in the timeless Russian manner, exiled the Doukhobors to cold, barren corners of Russia in the hope that the group would die out. Instead the Doukhobors thrived, and by 1899, 5000 members immigrated to Canada, first to Saskatchewan and then to Castlegar and nearby Grand Forks.

In the years since, the sect has largely dissolved into the community, although their legacy remains at two sights:

■ **Doukhobor Discovery Centre** (☎ 250-365-5327; www.doukhobor-museum.org; Hwy3A; adult/child $8/5; ⏰ 10am-5pm May-Sep) A couple of reconstructed buildings, weaving demonstrations and a small museum. It's across from the airport.

■ **Zuckerberg Island Heritage Park** (☎ 250-365-6440; admission by donation; ⏰ dawn-dusk) The island was the home of Alexander Feodorovitch Zuckerberg, a Russian teacher brought in to educate Doukhobor children. Today the park contains a suspension bridge, trails and restored onion-dome buildings.

of Hwy 22 and Hwy 3B. Ask about local walking tours. In winter the **VC** (☎ 250-362-5666; 2185 Columbia Ave; ⏰ 9am-4pm Mon-Fri) is in town.

Sights & Activities

The **Rossland Museum** (☎ 250-362-7722; adult/child $10/7; ⏰ 9am-5pm mid-May–mid-Sep, mine tours 9:30am-3:30pm) has displays on the rich local legacies of both skiing and mining. On the site of the former Black Bear Mine; 45-minute tours underground give you a good idea of what miners had to endure in blasting through the hard rock underfoot. There is also a section devoted to local skiing triumphs (which has limited winter hours). It's beside the VC.

MOUNTAIN BIKING

You can't go wrong cycling gut-clenching trails with names like Overdrive (a 1.5km drop), the Flume (tight trail flanked by slabs of rock) and the Dewdney Trail (75km of easy riding past lakes). Free-riding is all the rage, as the ridgelines are easily accessed andthere are lots of rocky paths for plunging downhill. The **Seven Summits Trail**, a 30.4km single track along the crest of the RosslandRange, has been officially designated as 'epic'.The VC has a **website** (www.bikerossland.ca) with maps, trail info, shuttle schedules, rentals and more. The **Kootenay**

Columbia Trails Society (www.rosslandtrails.ca) has tons of info, including downloadable maps; or pick up a copy of *Trails of the Rossland Range* ($8).

As you'd expect, local bike shops are fonts of knowledge. **Revolution Cycles** (☎ 250-362-5688; www.revolutioncycles.ca; 2044 Columbia Ave; rental per day from $40) has a wide range of rentals, maps, advice and much more.

Adrenaline Adventures (☎ 250-362-5005; www.adrenalinebc.com; Prestige Hotel, 1919 Columbia Ave) runs cycling shuttles, including one to a different ride each night of the summer ($12).

SKIING & SNOWBOARDING

Good in summer for riding, **Red Mountain Ski Resort** (☎ 250-362-7384, 800-663-0105, snow report 250-362-5500; www.redresort.com; 1-day lift pass adult/child $60/30) really shines in winter. Red, as it's known, includes the 1590m-high Red Mountain and 2040m-high Granite Mountain, for a total of nearly 5 sq km of powdery terrain. There are six lifts and a drop of 890m. Geared mostly toward intermediate and advanced skiers and snowboarders, the area is known for its 87 steep, tree-filled technical trails. It's only 5km north of downtown on Hwy 3B.

You can rent gear at the resort, and its website has links to various transport options for reaching Red from other parts of BC and the US.

Across the highway from Red Mountain, **Black Jack Cross Country Area** (☎ 250-364-5445; www.skiblackjack.ca; day pass adult/child $10/6) is a ski club with 25km of groomed skating and classic trails that are open to all. Top Canadian Nordic skier George Grey is a member.

Sleeping & Eating

The ski resort has detailed listings of places to stay near the slopes. The rates listed here cover the peak season, which in Rossland means winter; unlike much of BC, summer here is low season. Columbia Ave has several pubs and cafés.

Mountain Shadow Hostel (☎ 250-362-7160, 877-562-2783; www.mshostel.com; 2125 Columbia Ave; dm/d from $20/60; 🖳) Right near the center of town, this hostel has 48 beds in tidy and colorful rooms.

Rossland Motel (☎ 250-362-7218; www.stayand playrossland.com; 721 Hwy 22; r $70-120; 🛜) The solid-green credentials here (lots of recycling etc) are carried right through to the stark avocado-painted walls in the 10 rooms. Otherwise this classic motel is ideally located between town and the resort.

Ram's Head Inn (☎ 250-363-9577, 877-267-4323; www.ramshead.bc.ca; r $110-170; 🖳 🛜) A large common room with vaulted ceilings and a hefty stone fireplace, an outdoor hot tub and a games room make this 17-room lodge an oasis among the deep powder. It's 3km west of Rossland on Red Mountain Rd, off Hwy 3B at the base of the ski resort. (There are more resort-style choices here.)

Flying Steamshovel (☎ 250-362-7323; 2003 2nd Ave; r $90-110; 🎮 🖳 🛜) Popular with ski bums year-round, this lively pub (🕙 11am-late) and restaurant has three rather idiosyncratic rooms with narrow windows and Jacuzzi baths.

AROUND ROSSLAND

Leaving Rossland for the west, Hwy 3B runs for 28km of stunning Alpine mountain vistas through the mountains and 1575m Strawberry Pass.

Joining Hwy 3, the scenery continues to reward to **Christina Lake**, a bucolic spot for a pause, especially if you're camping at **Gladstone Provincial Park**. The **Texas Creek Campground** (☎ 800-689-9025; www.discovercamping .ca; campsite $15; 🕙 Jun-Oct) is 10km east of the town of Christina Lake off Hwy 3. It can be tricky to find, so watch for the signs for East

Lake Dr and then follow it for 1km to the campground. The 63 sites are large, private and shaded by the verdant forest.

Further west you'll hit the pretty border town of **Grand Forks**, known for its borscht and relatively abundant sunshine. The town was a byproduct of the Phoenix Mine, once the biggest copper-producing smelter in BC. Some of the Doukhobors (opposite) who settled in Castlegar later came here, and their influence still lends character and hearty food to the town. Another 140km on Hwy 3 brings you to Osoyoos (p245) and the Okanagan Valley.

Going east from Rossland on Hwy 3B you descend a steep grade and pass through one of the most industrialized parts of BC. Those smokestacks on the skyline belong to the industrial town of **Trail** (population 7900), where the main smelter has an illuminated sign giving the current price of zinc and lead. The good-sized town has traded a potentially scenic spot on the Columbia River for an economy based on mineral extraction.

CRESTON
pop 5100

Creston should probably be named Cornucopia given the amazing amount of produce that grows in the fertile fields locally. Fruit orchards thrive and Lapin cherries (large, juicy and dark red) are supplanting apples as the cash crop of choice.

Creston comes after the Crowsnest Hwy 3 climbs the 1774m Kootenay Pass east of Trail. The US is close by and Creston is only 11km from the border. It's a gateway to the Kootenays from Washington and Idaho. Hwy 3A heads north of here for a scenic 80km to the Kootenay Lake Ferry (p281), which connects to Nelson. This journey alone is worth the trip.

The **VC** (☎ 250-428-4342; www.crestonbc.com /chamber; 1607 Canyon St; 🕙 9am-5pm summer, 8:30am-4:30pm Mon-Fri winter) is near the center and has info on ag tours. Although most of the local produce is shipped out, you can still squeeze a few melons at the profusion of seasonal **fruit stands** and orchard markets east of town on Hwy 3. The choices are many, from those specializing in fudge to others with a full range of organic goods.

Bird-lovers flock to **Creston Valley Wildlife Management Area** (☎ 250-402-6900; www.creston wildlife.ca; admission free; 🕙 dawn-dusk), 11km west of Creston along Hwy 3. Some 70 sq km of marshy wetlands sit on protected provincial land. More than 100,000 migrating birds use the area to nest and breed each year. Look for black terns, white-fronted geese and blue herons as you walk along a 1km boardwalk to a watchtower, or on any of the more than 30km of dyke trails. An interpretive center is open for varying hours from May to mid-October.

For artisan baked goods and luscious sandwiches, try the **Creston Valley Bakery** (☎ 250-428-2661; 113 10 Ave; snacks from $3; ☯ 7am-5:30pm Mon-Sat), which is right in the otherwise forgettable center. It's hard to deny the appeal of the winsome weenie logo that proclaims 'Nice to meat you!' at **Famous Fritz** (☎ 250-402-9050; 1238 Northwest Blvd/Hwy 3; snacks from $3; ☯ 9am-5pm Tue-Sat), which has smoked meats among many deli items. It's west of the center.

EAST KOOTENAYS

Water, whether it is white as part of a class 3 rapid or white as powder on a black diamond ski run, defines the East Kootenays. The Purcell Mountains in the west and the Rocky Mountains in the east are the bookends to a region known for it's whitewater rafting (eg Golden, p299) and skiing (eg Fernie, below).

In winter the Powder Hwy links a string of ski resorts while in summer you can hit trails running, biking or simply hiking. A major feature is the Columbia River, which winds around BC, Washington and Oregon for 1953km before emptying into the Pacific Ocean.

FERNIE
pop 5200
Ringed by jagged peaks of stone that could have been placed there by the set designer of an mountain fantasy show, Fernie is the real deal. So real in fact that it is one of the best-preserved old towns in BC. The entire town has a vibrancy that radiates off the yellow brick buildings.

The town's history was tied to mining (coal was discovered in 1886), but when the mines closed many years ago the town went to sleep. Which is just as well, as nobody was awake to tear things down in the name

of progress, a fate that befell many another BC town.

You can still find a few old miners about town, happy to share harrowing tales of life underground. But these days you're more likely to find folks ready to share harrowing tales of their exploits on the slopes of the Fernie Alpine Resort. Outside of winter, Fernie seems to be half full of people lounging around while keeping one eye cocked for the first sign of snow.

Happily, constant winter storms travel over the Rockies and dump vast amounts of snow on the area, making it a powdery paradise for skiers and snowboarders. In summer the run-off means great rafting on local rivers, while the hills buzz with mountain bikers.

Orientation & Information
Downtown Fernie lies southeast of Hwy 3 (7th St), which manages to be not as ugly as many modern-day strips. Galleries, cheap variety stores, cafés, bakeries and outdoor shops can all be found along 2nd Ave (aka Victoria Ave). The historic center is bounded by 3rd and 7th Sts and 4th and 1st Aves.

Fernie District Hospital (☎ 250-423-4453; 1501 5th Ave; ☯ 24hr)

Fernie Heritage Library (☎ 250-423-4458; 492 3rd Ave; ☯ 11am-8pm Tue-Fri, noon-5pm Sat, also Sun Nov-Mar) In the 1907 Post Office & Customs House. Free internet access.

Polar Peek Books (☎ 250-423-3736; 592 2nd Ave) An eclectic mix of books with a good section of local interest. The bulletin board is a handy window into the community (but you might think most locals teach yoga).

Visitor Centre (☎ 250-423-6868; www.ferniechamber .com; 102 Commerce Rd; ☯ 9am-6pm summer, 9am-5pm

Mon-Fri winter) East of town off Hwy 3, just past the Elk River crossing. Good displays about the area.

Sights

Fernie experienced a devastating fire in 1908, which resulted in a brick-and-stone building code. Thus, today you'll see many fine **early-20th-century buildings**, many of which were built out of local yellow brick, giving the town an appearance unique to the East Kootenays. Between the shops and cafés, you can spend a few hours wandering this time capsule from decades ago.

Get a copy of *Heritage Walking Tour*, a superb booklet produced by the **Fernie & District Historical Society** (☎ 250-423-7016; 362 2nd Ave; admission by donation; ☒ 9:30am-5pm). This small museum has big displays on the area's skiing history. Check out the hand-built skis from the 1920s. Note that it hopes to leave its modest strip mall home for the grand surrounds of a heritage bank building at 491 2nd Ave by sometime in 2010.

Located in the old CPR train station, the **Arts Station** (☎ 250-423-4842; www.theartsstation .com; 601 1st Ave) has a small theatre for plays and films (think documentaries about Hugo Chavez), galleries and studios for some of the many local artists. Opening hours depend upon what's on.

Activities

Although much of the focus in winter is on the ski resort, there are hundreds of kilometers of cross-country trails in and around Fernie. Ask at the ski shops or the VC. The region is prime avalanche country, so be extra sure to take precautions (p275).

FERNIE ALPINE RESORT

A five-minute drive from downtown Fernie, this fast-growing resort, which has plenty of competition along the Kootenays' Powder Hwy, gets dumps amounting to 10m of snow per year on average. The **Fernie Alpine Resort** (FAR; ☎ 250-423-4655, 877-333-2339, snow conditions 250-423-3555; www.skifernie.com; 1-day pass adult/child $75/25) boasts five large bowls and 114 runs, including one 3km long. Thirty percent of the runs are rated expert. Condos and developments are proliferating like ski bums at a kegger. To get to the resort from town, follow Hwy 3 west and turn right onto Ski Hill Rd.

Cat-skiing is a popular way to get out into the vast expanse of country beyond FAR.

Fernie Wilderness Adventures (☎ 877-423-6704; www.fernieadventures.com; 1281 7th Ave) has many options starting from $350 per day.

You can rent equipment for about $30 per day at the resort or at the activity stores listed in this section. Also recommended is **Guides Hut** (☎ 250-423-3650; 671 2nd Ave), which has extensive winter sales and rentals. If you are planning any backcountry skiing, this is the place to get the scoop on conditions, rent avalanche kits, buy topographic maps and find out about organized tours.

MOUNTAIN BIKING

Mountain biking is almost as big as skiing. From easy jaunts in **Mt Fernie Provincial Park** (www.env.gov.bc.ca/bcparks), which is a mere 3km from town, to legendary rides up and down the hills in and around the ski resort (which runs lifts in summer), Fernie has lots for riders. Many come just to tackle the epic Al Matador, which drops over 900m before finishing in the terrific Three Kings trail. Get a copy of the widely available (and free) *Fernie Mountain Bike Map*.

Two bike stores have lots of advice and rent bikes from $35 a day: **Fernie Sports** (☎ 250-423-3611; 1191 7th Ave) and **Ski & Bike Base** (☎ 250-423-6464; 432 2nd Ave). Get a copy of *Fernie Trail Guide* at the shops or the VC and check out the **Crank Fernie** (www.crankfernie.com) website.

WHITE-WATER RAFTING

The Elk River is a classic white-water river, with three Class four rapids and 11 more class threes. It passes through beautiful country and you can often see large wildlife such as bears. Two Fernie outfits, **Canyon Raft Company** (☎ 250-423-7226, 888-423-7226; www .canyonraft.com) and **Mountain High River Adventures** (☎ 250-423-5008, 877-423-4555; www .raftfernie.com), offer day trips for about $110 and half-day floats for $60. At times you may be able to get a trip to the wilder Bull River.

HIKING

Great hiking trails radiate in all directions from Fernie. The excellent and challenging **Three Sisters hike** winds through forests and wildflower-covered meadows, along limestone cliffs and scree slopes. The 2744m summit offers incredible 360-degree views of the Elk Valley, Fisher Peak and surrounding lakes. From the VC, take Dickens Rd to

THE KOOTENAYS

FERNIE'S AMAZING COTTONWOODS

The world's oldest cottonwoods are only 12km west of Fernie. Look for Morrisey Rd and turn south off Hwy 3. Cross a bridge and look for a trailhead just on the far side. After only a 20-minute walk around the loop, you'll be in the midst of 400-year-old trees that are 10m in diameter. Amazingly, they were only discovered in 2003.

Hartley Lake Rd and follow it to the lake. Turn left onto the dirt track and hike 3km to the trailhead. Allow at least four hours each way. Another hike affording spectacular views, the **Hosmer Mountain Trail**, is also off Hartley Lake Rd (there is a parking area and a well-marked trailhead). This moderate hike takes about 2½ hours one way.

Explore the beautiful hills and flat canyon land around Fernie with **Fernie Nature Tours** (☎ 250-423-4306; www.fernienature.com; walks from $30). There's wildlife and wildflower viewing in summer and snow-shoeing in winter (including the intriguing star-gazing fondue dinner).

FISHING
Stretches of the Elk River offer superb fly-fishing. **Fernie Wilderness Adventures** (☎ 877-423-6704; www.fernieadventures.com) offers everything from fully guided outings (from $550) to the angling experience of a lifetime for those who like to sit on a frozen lake and stare into a dark hole (aka ice-fishing, $175).

Sleeping

Fernie's high season is the winter. **Fernie Central Reservations** (☎ 800-622-5007; www.fernie centralreservations.com) can book you a room in town or at the ski resort, although search a few internet booking sites first to look for deals.

Mt Fernie Provincial Park (☎ 800-689-9025; www.discovercamping.ca; campsite $15) Only 3km from town, leafy Mt Fernie Provincial Park features 40 sites, flush toilets, waterfalls, a self-guided interpretive trail and access to mountain-bike trails.

HI Raging Elk Hostel (☎ 250-423-6811; www .ragingelk.com; 892 6th Ave; dm/d from $25/50; 🖳) Broad decks allow plenty of inspirational mountain-gazing at this big red barn of a hostel that has good advice for those hoping

to mix time on the slopes and/or trails with seasonal work.

Powder Mountain Lodge (☎ 250-423-4492; www .powdermountainlodge.com; 892 7th Ave; dm/d from $30/80; 🟦 🖳 🟦) It looks a lot nicer inside the pool courtyard than outside the lodge at this popular budget place. Common areas include game rooms and billiards. Rooms come in several flavors; all have access to a large mountain-view deck.

Snow Valley Motel & RV Park (☎ 250-423-4421, 877-696-7669; www.snowvalleymotel.com; 1041 7th Ave; campsites $20-35, r $80-130; 🟦 🖳 🟦) The 21 flower-fronted rooms here are large and include newish cherrywood furniture fridges and microwaves (some have full kitchens). Outside there's a shady campground with 10 pitches and a barbeque. It's close to the center.

Red Tree Lodge (☎ 250-423-4622, 800-977-2977; www.redtreelodge.com; 1101 7th Ave; r $80-140; 🟦 🟦 🟦) Unprepossessing but ideally located, this modest two-story motel has recently refurbished rooms, which means no bedspreads with an explosion-at-the-crayon-factory color scheme. Instead there's a hot tub, a full shared kitchen, some balconies and lots of mountain views.

Park Place Lodge (☎ 250-423-6871, 888-381-7275; www.parkplacelodge.com; 742 Hwy 3; r $90-200; 🟦 🖳 🟦) There's a small pool inside under the atrium; most of the 64 comfortable rooms have balconies, fridges, microwaves and high-speed internet (but the cheapest look out onto the interior atrium – yuk). It's close to the center.

Eating & Drinking

Fernie has a good assortment of joints in and around the old center. On summer Sunday mornings, the **Mountain Market** is held in Rotary Park at 7th St and Hwy 3. It features a good mix of artists, bakers, farmers, musicians and more. **Cincott Farms Organic Market** (☎ 250-423-5564; 851 7th Ave; 🕙 8am-8pm) is like a daily farmers market. Look for the good ales of Fernie Brewing Co at most local pubs.

Mug Shots Bistro (☎ 250-423-8018; 591 3rd Ave; coffee $2; 🕙 7am-6pm; 🖳 🟦) Always hopping, there are coffees, baked goods, sandwiches and internet terminals. You can lounge on sofas or toil at tables.

Blue Toque Diner (☎ 250-423-4637; 601 1st Ave; meals $8; 🕙 8:30am-3:30pm) Located in the old train station, you can sip great coffee on the platform while CPR trains rumble past. Next to the Arts Station (p293) the menu is equally creative, featuring lots of seasonal and organic specials (trendy quinoa gets its due). Morning pancakes and omelettes are a hit, as are the lunch sandwiches.

Yamagoya Sushi (☎ 250-423-0090; 741 7th Ave; mains $8-20; ☺ 5-10pm) The views from the wrap-around porch may actually distract you from the beauty on your plate. Popular with the seasonal-worker crowd, who tear into the fusion rolls and tempura.

Brickhouse (☎ 250-423-0009; 401 2nd Ave; meals $8-25; ☺ 5pm-2am Mon-Sat) This upscale old pub serves steaks, burgers and other re-generative fare. The long wooden bar complements the bare brick walls. Some nights there's live jazz. Downstairs, there's a groovy lounge with pool tables and occasional dancing.

Royal Hotel (☎ 250-423-7750; 501 1st St; ☺ noon-late) The idiosyncratic corner bar in this 1909 hotel has live music many nights and an always affable crowd.

Getting There & Around

The Shuttle (☎ 250-423-4023, fernierentawreck@ hotmail.com) makes at least one run daily to/ from Calgary airport (adult/child $110/90; 4½ hours) and Cranbrook Airport (adult/ child $80/60, 90 minutes).

Greyhound Canada (☎ 250-423-6811; HI Raging Elk Hostel, 892 6th Ave) runs buses west to Kelowna ($108, 11½ hours, two daily) via Cranbrook and Nelson ($65, six hours, two daily) and east to Calgary ($65, 5½ to seven hours, two daily).

FERNIE TO CALGARY

If you are heading to Calgary Airport after Fernie, it's an easy 340km on Hwys 3 and 2. Plan on about four hours, however you might want to give yourself more time so you can stop and check out one of Western Canada's treasures: **Head-Smashed-In Buffalo Jump** (☎ 403-553-2731; www.cd.gov .ab.ca/hsibj). For nearly 6000 years First Nations people stampeded buffalo off the cliff here. The Unesco-recognized setting is more evocative than you'd imagine and the visitor center is a gem. It is close to Fort Macleod on Hwy 3.

Smokey Mountain Ski Shuttle (☎ 250-423-8605; fare $3) has a regular shuttle service between Fernie and the ski resort in winter. Most hotels run shuttles daily.

CRANBROOK
pop 19,800

Many a family holiday has foundered in the traffic-clogged streets of Cranbrook. 'The Strip,' a 2km slice of Hwy 3 called Cranbrook St as it runs through town, is dominated by fast-food chains, auto-parts stores, malls and midrange motels.

The downtown is diminutive and your best bet is to check out the city's one great museum and then literally head for the hills that ring the valley in snow-capped splendor. You can almost hear Fernie calling…

The magnificent **Canadian Museum of Rail Travel** (☎ 250-489-3918; www.trainsdeluxe.com; adult/ child $16/8; ☺ 10am-6pm summer, 10am-5pm Tue-Sat winter) is reason enough to stop in Cranbrook. The museum and its dozens of railcars stretch along Hwys 3 and 95 from the center at Baker St. It features much of the classic, luxurious 1929 edition of the *Trans-Canada Limited*, a legendary train operated by Canadian Pacific Railway from Montreal to Vancouver. The cars, along with those from other Canadian lines, are undergoing painstaking restoration.

Getting There & Away

Let the boosters loose and look what happens: Cranbrook's small airport gets a new name, **Canadian Rockies International Airport** (YXC; ☎ 250-426-7913; www.flycanadianrockies.com), and it becomes the lynchpin in the entire Powder Hwy strategy. Instead of weary skiers schlepping in from Calgary, Kelowna or even Vancouver, they fly right into Cranbrook, the hub of Kootenays skiing. To this end, Air Canada Jazz has daily flights to Vancouver and Calgary, Pacific Coastal Airlines also serves Vancouver and Delta puts the international in the airport name with three flights a week on 50-seat planes to/ from its hub at Salt Lake City in the US.

The **Greyhound Canada station** (☎ 250-489-3331; 1229 Cranbrook St N) is in the midst of the strip.

Around Cranbrook

Some 14km north of town, **Fort Steele Heritage Town** (☎ 250-426-7342; www.fortsteele.bc.ca; adult/child $14/3.50 summer, less other times; ☺ 9:30am-

THE MISSING PARK

Look at a map of the southeast corner of BC and you'll see an enormous hole where you might expect to find a park. South of the US border Glacier National Park protects a huge swath of land in Montana. This area extends well into Alberta as part of Waterton Lakes National Park. But on the BC side, there is the, by comparison, postage-stamp-sized Akima-Kishinena Provincial Park. Much of the **Flathead River Valley** that feeds into Glacier National Park is unprotected; these 500 sq km could easily become a major environmental battle zone over the next decade.

Already energy companies such as BP have been sniffing around. A proposal to sink 1500 natural gas wells in the valley was put on pause by the BC government after an outcry on both sides of the border. Proposals for vast coal mining operations east of Fernie are ongoing.

In the meantime, the very isolation that has protected the Flathead valley may be its undoing. Few people realize that this region is home to the greatest variety of large mammals on the continent (although poaching is said to be common in undeveloped and unmonitored Akima-Kishinena). Those that have seen its breath-taking beauty emerge committed to it getting the highest level of protection as a national park. *National Geographic* called the cross-border Flathead region the 'crown of the continent;' those working to protect this jewel include the **Sierra Club** (www.sierraclub.bc.ca) and **Wildsight** (www.wildsight.ca).

6:30pm Jul & Aug, 9:30am-5pm May-Jun & Sep, 10am-4pm Oct-Apr) takes historical preservation to histrionic extremes. Once an 1880s boomtown, then a ghost town, today it has more than 60 restored buildings, many populated by characters in historical garb during the summer. Unlike many tourist traps, it is well done and always a fave with kids.

KIMBERLEY
pop 6700

At the base of the Purcell Mountains, Kimberley is a former mining town that has worked hard to recreate itself as a sort of faux Bavarian village in the Alps. The center – called the Platzl (aka Spokane St) – has been remodeled with half-timbers and given a huge cuckoo clock, home to the town's mascot, Happy Hans. Every hour on the hour, people will stand in slack-jawed anticipation waiting for Hans to pop out of his oddly squat home and yodel. Between yodels, you may notice that all of the town's fire hydrants have been made to look like little people wearing lederhosen.

Although your instinct may be to snicker there's something oddly charming about all this nonsense. And over time, several shops and restaurants have appeared that make the Platzl a worthy stop – at least until Hans pops out. (Note: at peak times, there's singing and dancing, with a lot of oom-pah.)

Meanwhile, up the hill, where any Heidis are purely poseurs, yet another Powder Hwy resort is developing.

History

The discovery of rich minerals here in 1891 prompted the birth of the North Star Mine. The following year, on the other side of Mark Creek, another claim staked out what would grow to become the largest lead and zinc mine in the world, the Sullivan Mine. Mark Creek Crossing was renamed Kimberley in 1896, after the successful South African diamond mine. In 1909 Cominco took over operations, drawing more than 162 million tons of ore out of the Sullivan. The mine's closure in the 1970s and 1980s led to the focus on ersatz Bavarian tourism.

Information

The **VC** (☎ 250-427-3666; www.kimberleychamber.ca; 270 Kimberley Ave; ☺ 10am-6pm daily Jun-Aug, Mon-Sat Sep-May) sits in the large parking area behind the Platzl.

Sights & Activities

Take a ride on the tiny train at **Kimberley's Underground Mining Railway** (☎ 250-427-7365; www.kumr.ca; Gerry Sorensen Way; adult/child $15/7; ☺ 11am-3:30pm mid-May–mid-Sep) which putters 15km through the steep-walled Mark Creek Valley toward some sweeping mountain vistas. The trip ends at the base of the chairlift for the Kimberley Alpine Resort, from where you can ride to the top for more great views. The station is about 200m west of the Platzl.

The highlight of the **Kimberley Heritage Museum** (☎ 250-427-7510; 115 Spokane St; admission free; ⊙ 9am-4:30pm Mon-Sat summer, 1-4pm Mon-Fri winter) is the hapless Brutus, the stuffed remains of a grizzly bear bagged by a local 12-year-old. It's beside the library at the east end of the Platzl.

The 12-acre **Cominco Gardens**, beside the hospital above Kimberley, are full of roses, tulips and gnomes. If you're walking from town, take the stairway and trail at the west end of Howard St. It takes about 15 minutes.

KIMBERLEY ALPINE RESORT

Condos are more common than moguls at the **Kimberley Alpine Resort** (☎ 250-427-4881, 877-754-5462; www.skikimberley.com; 1-day lift pass adult/child $60/15), as speculators bet that lots of people will want to own a piece of the mountain – at least one they can time share. The resort boasts 7 sq km of skiable terrain, 80 runs and mild weather. There are five lifts and 45% of the runs are intermediate. The highlight is the 8200m Main Run, which has a 609m drop and is fully lit for night skiing. Note, however, that until the condo complement reaches full strength, life in the resort is fairly quiet. Nightlife and stores are minimal.

Sleeping & Eating

Most of Kimberley's accommodations are condos at the ski resort, which runs a central **reservations service** (☎ 877-754-5462; www.ski kimberley.com). Expect to pay $100 to $200 a night depending on season. Various no-name motels lurk around the outskirts of town.

The Edge (☎ 250-427-7744; www.theedgepuband hostel.com; 275 Spokane St; dm/d from $20/50; ⊠ ⊚) Right in the middle of the Platzl, this barhostel promotes its cheap drink prices and cheap beds. There's just no telling what that can lead too... But it's very clean and has an energy at night that's missing up the hill.

Mozart House (☎ 250-427-7671; 130 Spokane St; r $50; ⊙ 11am-9pm) Wake up to the smell of sauerkraut in one of eight simple rooms above this German restaurant (mains $10-20). You might even skip sheep and simply count wursts, schnitzels and cabbage rolls before sleep.

Chateau Kimberley (☎ 250-427-1500, 866-488-8886; www.chateau-kimberley.com; 78 Howard St; r $80-140; ⊠) There's a certain European minimalist charm in the 20 rooms at this modest boutique hotel immediately west of the Platzl. Bathrooms have deep tubs – perfect for soaking away post skiing kinks – and every room has high-speed internet.

Getting There & Away

Greyhound Canada (☎ 250-427-3722; 1625 Warren Ave), inconveniently 3km east of Kimberley, has pricey buses to Cranbrook ($13, 30 minutes, two daily).

KIMBERLEY TO RADIUM HOT SPRINGS

Hwy 95A heads northeast out of Kimberley for 30km and connects up with Hwy 93/95. Just south of the junction on Hwy 95, **Wasa Lake Provincial Park** (☎ 250-422-3003; campsite $19, reservations ☎ 800-689-9025; www.discovercamping .ca), is good for walking and home to the warmest lake in the Kootenays. The popular campground contains 104 pitches, 55 of which can be reserved, and offers good lake access, interpretive programs and flush toilets. The park protects an increasingly rare chunk of BC's grassland, most of which has been turned into golf courses or farmland. A 2.7km interpretive trail highlights the natural beauty, while an 8km loop circles the lake.

North from Wasa, Hwy 93/95 continues along the scenic Kootenay River. Almost 5km south of Canal Flats look for Whiteswan Forestry Rd, a gravel road that travels east 25km to **Whiteswan Lake**

DETOUR: TOP OF THE WORLD

If Whiteswan Lake isn't far enough off the beaten path, you can follow Whiteswan Forestry Rd for another 25 gravelly kilometers to remote **Top of the World Provincial Park**. When the road ends, it's an easy 6km hike or mountain-bike ride to Fish Lake, so named for its thick population of trout. You can camp at one of the backcountry sites ($15) at Fish Lake or stay in the large rustic cabin often used by anglers ($15 per person). Much of the park lives up to its name: the average elevation exceeds 2200m. All the BC wildlife heavyweights are found here: moose, bears, elk etc. In precolonial times, First Nations people came from as far away as Montana and Alberta to obtain chert, a grey, translucent, obsidian-like rock that was used in tools and weapons.

Provincial Park (☎ 250-422-3003; www.env.gov .bc.ca/bcparks), a remote 20-sq-km park that is home to both Whiteswan and Alces Lakes. This is the place to escape the touristy valley and enjoy fully loaded nature. The park's highlight, **Lussier Hot Springs**, is near the west entrance, some 17km from the turn off Hwy 93/95. Unlike many of the region's hot springs which look like they'd be at home in a Hampton Inn, the waters here flow through natural rock and sand pools. A well-marked trailhead leads you down to the springs, which can get oversubscribed in summer.

The park's five campgrounds have 114 rustic pitches ($15) with pit toilets. Trails lead to several more alpine meadows good for backcountry camping.

Fairmont Hot Springs Resort

Once you know that the waters have been filtered to remove any trace of mineral odor, you know you're not going to be taking a dip with Mother Nature. Condos surround the vast pool, which could be the centerpiece of a bland planned community…very like this one.

Windermere Valley

This narrow valley between the Purcell and Rocky Mountains was a key part of the Columbia Wetlands, a vital ecological area and wildlife habitat that stretches 180km along the Columbia River basin here. Most of the wetlands are intact except for those obliterated by golf courses and condos in **Windermere** and **Invermere**.

Panorama Mountain Village Resort

While some people whistle while they work, Kootenay ski resort execs must mutter 'Whistler' while they work. Yet another resort hoping to rival the big name to the west, **Panorama Mountain Village** (☎ 250-342-6941, 800-663-2929; www.panoramaresort.com; 1-day lift pass adult/child $72/30) boasts a 1220m drop, nine lifts and more than 120 trails, the longest of which is 5.5km. A gondola shuttles people between the upper and lower villages of the now-ubiquitous condos. Add in a golf course, summer lift service for mountain bikers and you have the possible future of outdoor activities in much of BC. The resort is at the end of an 18km drive up a winding road from Invermere. Many skiers find the isolation and somnolent nightlife nothing to whistle at.

RADIUM HOT SPRINGS
pop 900

There you sit, stuck out in the middle of this small mountain town, your car surrounded by Rocky Mountain bighorn sheep. You can't help but feel the palpable pull of the critters' namesake Rockies and the four Rocky Mountains national parks (Kootenay, Banff, Jasper and Yoho) just up the road.

Radium Hot Springs is named for the famed hot springs, which are just inside the southwest corner of **Kootenay National Park** (p306). Their name came after a government test conducted in 1914 showed minute levels of radioactivity in the springs, something that could only add to your healthy glow after a soothing soak.

The **Kootenay National Park & Radium Hot Springs VC** (☎ 250-347-9331, 888-347-9331; www .radiumhotsprings.com; 7556 Main St E/Hwy 93/95; ☯ 9am-7pm May-Sep, 9am-5pm Oct-Apr) has regional info and is staffed with Parks Canada rangers.

Sleeping & Eating

Radium Hot Springs contains more than 30 motels, most of which are close to the

---

BIG BUGABOO

Vast eroded pillars of granite mark the chiseled peaks of the Purcell Mountains, the range west of the Rockies. Hundreds of millions of years older, the ancient edifices of the Purcells are still being shaped by the largest icefields in BC. **Bugaboo Provincial Park** (www.env.gov.bc.ca) – the name is purported to have come from a term local lead miners used for a deadend mineral vein – is a place for serious outdoors adventure. Hikes that don't require mountaineering skills are the exception to the norm. Its highlight is the **Conrad Kain Hut** (☎ 403-678-3200; www.alpineclubofcanada .ca; per person $25; ☯ Jun-Sep), a legendary mountain cabin reached after a strenuous 5km hike from a small parking area. From here the Purcells are yours to explore.

The one road which reaches the park is gravel and runs for 45km west from Brisco, 27km north of Radium Hot Springs on Hwy 95.

highways. Book ahead for peak summer season. The best camping is in the park.

Misty River Lodge B&B (☎ 250-347-9912; www .mistyriverlodge.bc.ca; 5036 Hwy 93; r $60-100) Right outside the park gate, this five-room B&B has tri-lingual owners who cheerfully share their love for the parks with their guests. Rooms vary in size, but all have basic cooking facilities. Breakfast ($7) is continental.

Radium Gateway Motel (☎ 250-347-9655, 800-838-4238; Hwy 93; r $60-120; 🅿 🛜) Given how clean the 15 rooms are here, you may be tempted to eat the candy-cane-colored bedspreads. But best not. About 2km from the springs, the European family who run this flower-fronted motel have gone about 38 steps beyond their competition in adopting green practices.

Getting There & Away

Greyhound Canada (☎ 250-347-9726; Radium Esso, 7507 Main St W) has a service along Hwy 95 to Golden ($20, 1¼ hours, one daily) and Cranbrook ($23, 2½ hours, two daily). There's also a service through Kootenay National Park to Banff ($24, two hours, one daily).

GOLDEN

pop 4500

Golden is well situated for the national parks – there are six nearby. It's also an excellent place for white-water rafting on the Kicking Horse River, which converges with the Columbia here. Don't just breeze past the strip of franchised muck on Hwy 1 or you'll miss the tidy little town center right across the tracks. Although the main reason for being here are the mountains or the river valleys, take a moment to appreciate the stunning Kicking Horse Pedestrian Bridge, a covered bridge in the grand tradition that's right downtown. Opened in 2001, the bridge spans the turbulent – and picturesque – waters of the Kicking Horse River.

Orientation & Information

Expect delays for years to come on the Trans-Canada Hwy (Hwy 1) east of Golden as the road is reconstructed from scratch. The center of town lies 2km south of the highway.

Unfortunately, the glitzy **Visitor Centre** (☎ 250-344-7711; 🕐 9am-6pm), 1km east on Hwy 1 from the Hwy 95 turn-off into

Golden, primarily seems to promote the ski resort. For wide-ranging local info, visit the **Golden Chamber of Commerce** (☎ 250-344-7125, 800-622-4653; www.goldenchamber.bc.ca; 500 10th Ave North; 🕐 9am-5pm daily Jul & Aug, 10am-4pm Mon-Fri Sep-Jun).

Sights & Activities

WHITE-WATER RAFTING

Golden is the center for **white-water rafting** trips on the turbulent and chilly Kicking Horse River. Powerful Class III and IV rapids and breathtaking scenery along the sheer walls of the Kicking Horse Valley make this rafting experience one of North America's best. The fainter of heart can take a mellow but equally scenic float trip on the upper river. Many operators run the river in the busy summer season, sometimes creating jams.

Full-day trips on the river average about $120; half-day trips are about $75. Local operators include **Glacier Raft Company** (☎ 250-344-6521; www.glacierraft.com) and **Alpine Rafting** (☎ 250-344-6778, 888-599-5299; www.alpine rafting.com).

Creekboating, which involves kayak-like craft with extra flotation, is big with those who want to mount a frontal assault on the rapids.

KICKING HORSE MOUNTAIN RESORT

Sprawling across Whitetooth Mountain, **Kicking Horse Mountain Resort** (☎ 250-439-5400, 866-754-5425; www.kickinghorseresort.com; 1-day lift pass adult/child from $45/21) has a gondola and three lifts. A challenging 60% of its 106 runs are rated advanced or expert. The resort boasts a 1260m drop and a relatively snow-heavy, wind-free position between the Rockies and the Purcells. It is one of the wave of resorts built in the last few years which is now a core part of the Powder Hwy. Investors hope that the condo-count soon reaches critical mass. Like many of the newer resorts, Kicking Horse has minimal nightlife. And while it gets pluses for having good powder long after others, its main gondola can clog up on busy days, causing delays.

Kicking Horse Resort is 14km from Golden on Kicking Horse Trail.

MOUNTAIN BIKING

For easy riding in town, you can bike along the trails following the Kicking Horse River or head across the Columbia River to the West Bench, where you can tool around on 40km worth of trails. Summer lifts at Kicking Horse Mountain Resort access some of Canada's longest descents.

Summit Cycle & Ski (☎ 250-344-6600; 1007 11th Ave S; bike rental per day from $40) has knowledgeable staff. The **Golden Cycling Club** (www.golden cyclingclub.com) has maps and other info.

NORTHERN LIGHTS WOLF CENTRE

The **Northern Lights Wolf Centre** (☎ 250-344-6798; www.northernlightswildlife.com; adult/child $10/6; ☺ 9am-9pm Jul & Aug, 10am-6pm Sep-May) is a refuge in the wild for wolves born into captivity. Visitors can expect to meet a resident wolf or two and learn about their complex and humanly family structure. The goal of the center is to educate people about wolves, which are still being hunted to extinction to protect cattle and even other endangered species. The center is just west of Golden, 5km off the Trans-Canada Hwy. Look for signs or call.

Sleeping & Eating

There are scores of chain motels along Hwy 1. Check with the Chamber of Commerce for B&Bs.

Sander Lake Campground (☎ 250-344-6517; www.rockies.net/~bsander; campsites from $15) This campground, 12km southwest of Golden off Hwy 95, has a location amid trees and hills that would excite John Audubon. There are 27 pitches and three log cabins ($75).

Packers Place (☎ 250-344-5941; packerinn@cable rocket.com; 429 9th Ave; r $50-60; ☐) A bustling bar and restaurant where the food often shows color and flair. Tables overlooking the river and there's live music many nights. Packers has simple pub rooms.

Mary's Motel (☎ 250-344-7111, 866-234-6279; www .marysmotel.com; 603 8th Ave N; r $80-120; ☒ ☲ ☎) In town right on the river, Mary's has 81 rooms spread across several buildings; get one with a patio. Water features include a hot tub, pools inside and out and the roar of the river.

Kicking Horse River Chalets (☎ 403-720-0811, 866-371-6552; www.kickinghoseriverchalets.com; 2924 Kicking Horse Rd; cabins from $250) 'What a find!' is a common response among guests to this riverside retreat. The 18 log chalets have two levels and sleep up to six. There are soaker tubs, full kitchens and all the nature you can breathe in.

Kicking Horse Grill (☎ 250-344-2330; 1105 9th St S; mains $20-30; ☺ 5-9pm) Dishes at this creative log cabin change depending on the season, although excellent steaks are always on the menu. Try for a table outside under the huge tree.

Getting There & Away

Greyhound Canada (☎ 800-661-8747; www.grey hound.ca; Husky Travel Centre, 1050 Trans-Canada Hwy) serves Revelstoke ($30, two hours, four daily), Banff ($28, two hours, four daily) and Radium Hot Springs ($20, 1½ hours, one daily).

The Rockies

History doesn't record what various first-time visitors must have said when they first took stock of the Canadian Rockies. Does 'Wow!' cut it? Probably not, but we can assume that there were many exclamations of astonishment when the sheer beauty and majesty of these mountains struck each new visitor in turn.

Unesco has made its own exclamation and recognized the entire region as the Canadian Rocky Mountain Parks World Heritage Area. One of the largest protected sites in the world, it brings together Banff and Jasper National Parks in Alberta with Kootenay and Yoho National Parks in BC. Two BC provincial parks, Mt Robson and Mt Assiniboine, fill in the gaps.

It's a place that demands superlatives to match the beauty. Sawtooth-edged granite peaks march across the landscape. Permanent snow caps and vast snaking glaciers glow with inner luminescence year round. Cradled amongst the crags are alpine lakes that quite frankly don't look real with their gemstone shades of emerald and sapphire.

Water pours off the sheer cliffs in ribbons of waterfalls and thunders through canyons in torrents of white water. Much more pastoral are the carpets of wildflowers that grab their tiny moments in the sun during the short summer. Amidst the geological splendor, you can glimpse bears, elk, mountain goats, eagles and many more hardy species.

Travelers can revel in luxury in Banff, enjoy the small-town vibe of Jasper, camp next to a turquoise lake, chop wood at a remote hostel or savor the beauty around them at a remote lodge. Activities – from skiing to hiking to kayaking – will almost, but not quite, leave you too breathless to go 'Wow!'

THE ROCKIES

HIGHLIGHTS

- Finding the hidden beauty of the Rockies in **Yoho National Park** (p303)

- Leaving the drivers of the Icefields Parkway behind for the ethereal beauty of **Peyto Lake** (p323)

- Day-hiking the accessible wilderness surrounding **Jasper** (p324)

- Living the good life around the clock in **Banff** (p308)

- Soaking your cares away at **Radium** (p307), **Miette** (p331) or **Banff Upper Hot Springs** (p312)

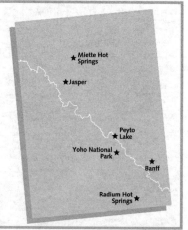

INFORMATION

On entering the national parks, you'll be given the excellent *Mountain Guide*. As well as outlining policies for the parks, the guide is full of information including what to do if you encounter a cougar (don't run, don't act like prey, find a rock and nail the sucker). There's lots more information available at the various park visitor centers (VCs). Booklets outlining the myriad hikes and other activities, as well as backcountry guides, can add greatly to your trip.

Parks Canada has links to all of the country's national parks from its website (www.parkscanada.ca). For more information, contact the VCs at the parks, which

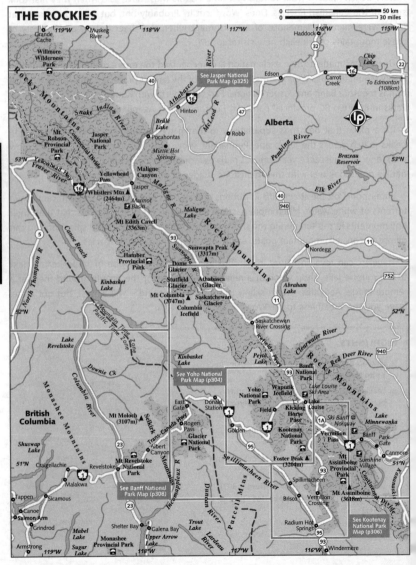

are often run with provincial and local tourism VCs as well as non-profit groups that support the parks.

Banff National Park (☎ 403-762-1550; www.parkscanada.ca/banff)

Jasper National Park (☎ 780-852-6176; www.parkscanada.ca/jasper)

Kootenay National Park (☎ 250-347-9331, 888-347-9331; www.parkscanada.ca/kootenay)

Yoho National Park (☎ 250-343-6783; www.parkscanada.ca/yoho)

Fees

You have to buy a park pass upon entry into any national park. The cost of **day passes** (adult/child/group of up to 7 people $10/5/20) quickly adds up, especially if you're spending a few days in the parks. It may make more sense to buy an **annual pass** (adult/child/group $66/34/137). Not only will this save you money but it will give you unlimited admission to Canada's national parks and historic sites.

Other fees, such as for camping, are outlined in the appropriate sections throughout this chapter. Many, as noted, can be reserved in advance.

Books

The bible for the region is the encyclopedic *Handbook of the Canadian Rockies* by Ben Gadd. You'll find a well-thumbed copy behind the counter at virtually every VC.

No Ordinary Woman: the Story of Mary Schaffer by Janice Sanford Beck is a highly readable biography of a woman who was an important early explorer of the Rockies. Schaffer's own book, *Old Indian Trails of the Canadian Rockies*, was first published in 1911 and has now been released with some of her own drawings and illustrations.

For passing the hours by the campfire, *Mountain Madness: An Historical Miscellany* by Edward Cavell and Jon Whyte is filled with entertaining yarns about oddball life in the Rockies. For more sober accounts, consider *The Canadian Rockies* by Roger Patillo, which details the tough-as-granite early explorers.

For a detailed look at Banff, Jasper and Glacier National Parks, look to Lonely Planet's *Banff, Jasper & Glacier National Parks*.

Admit it, you want to see lots of animals while you're in the parks. For background, consider *Wild Animals of the Canadian*

> **WINTER ROAD CONDITIONS**
>
> For up-to-date road conditions on the Trans-Canada Hwy and other roads in the national parks and BC consult the following:
>
> ■ **DriveBC** (☎ 800-550-4997; www.drivebc .ca) This is essential in winter when storms can close roads for extended periods.
>
> ■ **Rocky Mountains National Parks Road Report** (☎ 403-762-1450)

Rockies, by Kevin Van Tighem or the reliable *Canadian Rockies Guide to Wildlife Watching* by Michael Kerr and Grace Buzik.

For books on hiking, see p314.

YOHO NATIONAL PARK

Carrying boulders along like so many grains of sand, the Kicking Horse River tears through Yoho National Park like a rioting mob. It's a land of riotous drama, from the raw energy of the rivers to pounding waterfalls, from the sheer rock peaks to the colorful intensity of wildflower-strewn meadows.

Although the smallest (1310 sq km) of the four national parks in the Rockies, Yoho rewards anyone who turns off the Trans-Canada Hwy. Here you'll feel lost in the grandeur of the wilderness. Make the effort to see Lake O'Hara and some of the sights further afield and you'll understand why the Cree named this place Yoho, or 'awe.'

FIELD

The planets have somehow aligned for Field (maybe pushed there by the Kicking Horse River). This small village off the Trans-Canada Hwy has an alluring unfussy charm, around 40 or so B&Bs and two of the most creative bistro owners you'll find in these parts.

Sitting astride the river, many of Field's buildings date from the early days of the railways, when it was the Canadian Pacific Railway (CPR) headquarters for exploration and, later, for strategic planning when engineers were trying to solve the problem of moving trains over the Kicking Horse Pass. Check out the **'Dollhouse'** (2nd St E), a

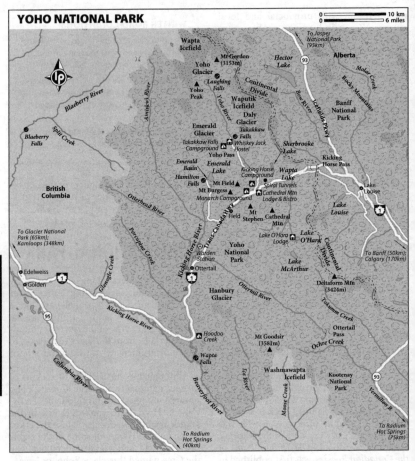

YOHO NATIONAL PARK

cute little 1927 house that was once a Royal Canadian Mounted Police (RCMP) jail and later – fittingly enough – a liquor store.

Field is home to the **Yoho National Park Information Centre** (☎ 250-343-6783; 9am-4pm Sep-Apr, 9am-5pm May & Jun, 9am-7pm Jul & Aug). Pick up the free *Backcountry Guide*; its map and trail descriptions give an excellent overview for exploring the park. Parks Canada rangers can advise on itineraries and conditions. Alberta Tourism staffs a desk here in summer for those heading east towards Banff. The non-profit group Friends of Yoho National Park has a useful website (www.friendsofyoho.ca).

Ask at the info center for a list of Field's numerous B&Bs or check the town's

website (www.field.ca). **Fireweed Hostel** (☎ 250-343-6999, 877-343-6999; www.fireweedhostel .com; 313 Stephen Ave; dm/r from $30/80;   ) has four spotless rooms with bunks and double beds.

ourpick **Truffle Pigs Bistro and Kicking Horse Lodge** (☎ 250-343-6303; www.trufflepigs.com; 100 Centre St; r $100-200;   ) has come far from its humble beginnings as a café in something of a shack. So successful was its inventive, high-concept bistro fare that it took over the hotel across the street in 2008. The 14 rooms now sport the same cheeky style as the bistro. Meanwhile the food is as good as ever (mains $8 to $25; confirm hours in advance) and is usually organic and locally sourced. Jen Coffman and Sean

Cunningham haven't lost pace even as the table count has multiplied.

Greyhound Canada buses stop at the info center on their trips west to Golden ($19, one hour, three daily) and beyond, and east to Banff ($24, 1½ hours, three daily).

LAKE O'HARA

A mountain lake right out of central casting, Lake O'Hara's impossibly blue waters, shining glaciers and tree-studded granite backdrop make it seem like a special effect. But real it is and, fortunately, draconian crowd control measures keep the hordes from turning this remote gem into Lake Louise.

First the good news: anyone can make the 11km hike up to the lake at any time (bikes not allowed, though). But most prefer the **shuttle bus** (adult/child $15/7.50; ☼ mid-Jun–early Oct) from the Lake O'Hara parking lot, 15km east of Field on the Trans-Canada Hwy. To alleviate human pressure on the trails and wildlife, there's a quota system for both the bus and the lake's popular backcountry **campgrounds** (backcountry permit per adult $10).

You can make **reservations** (☎ 250-343-6433) for the bus and camping up to three months in advance, and these are usually snapped up the same day. However, if you don't have advance reservations, six day-use seats on the bus and three to five campsites are set aside for 'standby' users. To snare these, try calling the day before and right as the phone lines open at 8am. Stay on hold until you hear one way or another. More details can be found at the Parks Canada website (www.pc.gc.ca /yoho) by following the links to Lake O'Hara. There are significant restrictions on what you can bring to the campsites (no guitars, dude) so check the website.

A basic day trip is definitely worthwhile, but if you stay overnight in the backcountry you'll be able to access many more trails, some quite difficult, all quite spectacular. Take the Alpine Circuit Trail (12km) for a bit of everything. The area around Lake O'Hara usually remains snow covered or very muddy until mid-July.

For posh accommodation at Lake O'Hara, see p306.

ELSEWHERE IN THE PARK

East of Field on the Trans-Canada Hwy is the **Takakkaw Falls road** (☼ late Jun–early Oct). At 254m, Takakkaw Falls is one of the highest water-

falls in Canada. Takakkaw is a Cree word for 'magnificent,' and they certainly are. From here **Iceline**, a 20km-hiking loop, passes many glaciers and spectacular scenery.

The beautiful green **Emerald Lake**, 10km north off the Trans-Canada Hwy, features a flat circular 5.2km walking trail with other trails radiating from it. The lake gets its incredible color from light reflecting off the fine glacial rock particles, deposited into the lake over time by grinding glaciers. In late summer the water is just warm enough for a dip. Look for the turnoff west of Field.

You can find solitude if you continue on from the lake to the **Emerald Basin**, a natural amphitheater of hanging glaciers punctuated by old avalanches. The hike is a 9.2km round trip; there is one steep climb (200m) near the start.

Sherbrooke Lake is another way to beat any crowds. Here a brilliantly colored glacial lake is surrounded by steep slopes and dramatic rock falls. The 6.2km round trip follows a moderately easy trail with a height gain of 165m. Look for the trailhead on the north side of the Trans-Canada Hwy from Wapta Lake.

The Unesco-recognized **Burgess Shale World Heritage site** protects stunning Cambrian-age fossil beds on Mt Stephen and Mt Field. These 515-million-year-old fossils, discovered by Charles Walcott in 1909, preserve the remains of marine creatures that were some of the earliest forms of life on earth. You can only get to the fossil beds by guided hikes, which are led by naturalists from the **Burgess Shale Geoscience Foundation** (www.burgess-shale.bc.ca). The 10-hour, 20km hike to Burgess Shale in **Walcott Quarry** (adult/child $100/25; ☼ Jun–Sep) explores how fossils for water-borne creatures came to be high in the mountains. See for yourself the rapid and dramatic changes occurring in the Rockies on the eight-hour **Climate Change Walk** (per person $50; ☼ Jun–Sep). You need to be in good shape for either, and you must make **reservations** (☎ 800-343-3006; info@burgess -shale.bc.ca) well ahead of time.

The famous **spiral tunnels** – the engineering feat that enabled CPR trains to navigate the challenging Kicking Horse Pass (p279) – lie 8km east of Field along the Trans-Canada Hwy. The viewpoint is a popular stop and you can see trains twisting in on themselves as they wind through the spirals.

THE ROCKIES

Near the south gate of the park, you can reach pretty **Wapta Falls** via a 2.4km trail. The easy walk takes about 45 minutes each way.

SLEEPING

Yoho National Park has five campgrounds (non-reservable); none are open October to April. Charming Field contains numerous B&Bs and a lodge (p304).

Monarch Campground (campsites $18) Right at the turnoff to Yoho Valley Rd, this quiet campground offers 46 basic sites. No fires are allowed here.

Takakkaw Falls Campground (campsites $18) Located 13km along the gravel Yoho Valley Rd, this place has 35 walk-in (200m) campsites for tents only. The absence of cars around the campsites makes this the most appealing of the Yoho trio.

Kicking Horse Campground (campsites $24) The only campground with showers, the 88 sites are popular with sweaty types. Interpretive programs run on summer nights. To get there, drive 3.2km east of Field on the Trans-Canada Hwy, then proceed 1km along the Yoho Valley Rd.

HI Whiskey Jack Hostel (☎ 403-670-7580, 866-762-4122; www.hihostels.ca; dm from $27; ☾ Jul-Sep) This isolated hostel offers 27 dorm-style beds in a chalet-style building. It is 15km off the Trans-Canada Hwy on Yoho Valley Rd, just before the Takakkaw Falls Campground and close to the falls themselves.

Lake O'Hara Lodge (☎ 250-343-6418; www.lake ohara.com; r per person per night from $270, 2-night minimum) An environmental legend, this lodge dates back to 1926 and offers the only place to stay at breathtaking Lake O'Hara beyond wilderness campsites. All wastewater is treated for recycling, and green cred is the street cred here. Eight rooms share bathrooms in the main lodge; 11 cabins are hidden in the trees. Rates include all meals and activities; transport from the parking area is on the lodge's biodiesel bus.

KOOTENAY NATIONAL PARK

Glaciers, deep canyons and ancient trees are some of the highlights in Kootenay National Park. A long park that snakes along Hwy 93, Kootenay came about because BC

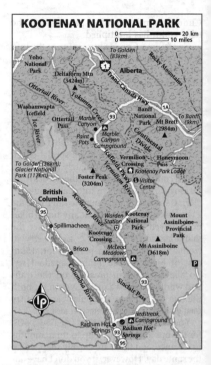

ran out of money in the 1920s when it was building the highway through the Rockies to Banff. The federal government stepped in with a solution: in return for money, the province would give the feds land comprising roughly 8km on either side of the road. The results were win-win.

Today there are popular campgrounds and trails leading off 94km-long Hwy 93. The main attraction is Radium Hot Springs, near the southern entrance. Otherwise it's pure wilderness, 13% of which is recovering from fires in 2003.

INFORMATION

Kootenay National Park & Radium Hot Springs VC (☎ 250-347-9331, 888-347-9331; www.radiumhot springs.com; 7556 Main St E/Hwy 93/95; ☾ 9am-7pm May-Sep, 9am-5pm Oct-Apr) Across the BC border the VC has regional information and is staffed with Parks Canada rangers.

Kootenay Park Lodge Visitor Centre (☾ 9am-6pm Jul & Aug, 10am-5pm mid-May–Jun & Sep) Located at Vermilion Crossing, 63km north from Radium Hot Springs; it has Parks Canada information.

SIGHTS

The park boundary between Banff and Kootenay National Parks marks the **Continental Divide**, which runs through Yellowhead, Kicking Horse, Vermilion and Crowitnest Passes. At the Divide, rivers flow either west to the Pacific or east to the Atlantic. The short interpretive **Fireweed Trail** loops through the surrounding forest at the north end of Hwy 93. Panels explain how nature is recovering from a 1968 fire here.

Some 7km further on, **Marble Canyon** has a pounding creek flowing through a nascent forest. Another 3km south on the main road is the short, easy trail through forest to ochre pools known as the **Paint Pots**. For years, the Kootenay people and then European settlers collected this orange- and red-colored earth. They'd shape it into patties, dry it, grind it, then mix it with fish or animal oil to make paint. Today you can walk past the muddy red pools and read panels describing both the mining history of this rusty earth and its past importance to First Nations people.

Learn how the park's appearance has changed over time at the **Kootenay Valley Viewpoint**, 16km east of Radium, where panels tracing the park's geological past vie with the view for your attention. Of course, with this view you may have a hard time looking down. Just 3km south, Olive Lake makes a perfect picnic or rest stop. A lakeside interpretive trail describes some of the visitors who've come before you.

Radium Hot Springs (☎ 250-347-9485; adult/child $7/6; ☼ 9am-11pm mid-May–early Oct, noon-9pm other times), 3km north of the town of Radium Hot Springs, are always popular. Even though they are the largest hot-spring pools in Canada and they are quite modern, they can get very busy in summer. Come early or late for a more intimate experience. The facilities include showers and lockers. The water comes from the ground at 44°C, enters the first pool at 39°C and hits the final one at 29°C.

SLEEPING

Radium Hot Springs (above) has scores of motels at all price ranges. Get info on the park's backcountry campsites at the VCs or online.

Marble Canyon Campground (campsites $22; ☼ Jul & Aug) Inside the park, 88km north

from Radium Hot Springs and about 8km from the park's east gate, this campground offers flush toilets but no showers with its 61 sites.

McLeod Meadows Campground (campsites $22; ☼ Jun-Aug) With similar facilities to Marble Canyon, this place features 98 pretty, wooded sites along the Kootenay River. Some are secluded, others are on the water.

Redstreak Campground (reservations ☎ 877-737-3783; www.pccamping.ca; campsites from $28; early May–early Oct) Near the park's west gate, Redstreak contains 242 sites (154 sites and 88 partial- and full-hookup sites for RVs). It's a busy place with many services, including flush toilets, showers, an interpretive trail and nightly interpretive programs.

Kootenay Park Lodge (☎ 403-762-9196; www .kootenayparklodge.com; r $90-190; ☼ mid-May–Sep) The 10 cabins here date from the 1930s and could be covered with frosting and decorated with gumdrops. The beds are snug and you can plop down on your porch and absorb nature. Fireplaces and homestyle cooking complete the scene.

AROUND KOOTENAY NATIONAL PARK
Mount Assiniboine Provincial Park

Often called the Matterhorn of Canada, the craggy summits of Mt Assiniboine (3618m) look down onto this remote 39-sq-km provincial park that's nestled between Kootenay and Banff National Parks. It's a magnet for experienced rock climbers and mountaineers. The park also attracts backcountry hikers and those who just want to sniff the alpine wildflowers.

This park takes its curious name from the Assiniboine (ass-*in*-a-boyne) First Nations, who are also referred to as 'Stoney' for the way they cook some foods – by putting hot stones in pots of water to heat them up. The park's main focus is **Lake Magog**, which is reachable only by hiking in summer or skiing in winter.

At the lake, **Mount Assiniboine Lodge** (☎ 403-678-2883; www.canadianrockies.net/assiniboine; r per person per night from $260) is the main point of contact for the park. It has accommodations for 30 guests each night in a combination of rooms and cabins. Originally built by the CPR in 1928, the main lodge is comfortable and well known for its tasty meals (included in room rates). Simple but renovated lakeside **Naiset cabins** ($15 per person)

THE ROCKIES

may also be reserved through the lodge. A **campground** (campsite $5) here is one of several rustic camping areas in the park.

The main trail to the lodge begins at Sunshine Village Ski Resort (p315) in Banff National Park; allow a good eight hours to make this 27km trek to Lake Magog. You can also arrange through the lodge for helicopter transport of you ($150 one way) or just your equipment ($2 per pound) if you're doing like most and going overland.

BANFF NATIONAL PARK

It's easy to be contrary and dismiss Banff National Park as being too crowded. Yes it is Canada's most popular national park but, as you'd suspect, there's layers of reasons for this. Banff town is big enough that anyone from shopper to skier will find ample diversion. And there's a long list of activity operators who can get you out in the beautiful wilderness. And, ultimately, that's what the park is all about: beautiful

wilderness. It's unlikely you'll stop discovering new stunning vistas no matter how long you stay. Twenty five peaks here top 3000m.

Established in 1885, Banff National Park is named for two CPR financiers who hailed from Banffshire in Scotland, and was Canada's first national park. The park covers an area of 6641 sq km and is home to almost every large mammal found in Canada.

BANFF
pop 7400

Banff gets five million visitors a year; many are day-trippers looking for fudge. Many others, however, are simply enjoying what is a cultured and ultimately very fun village in a gorgeous setting. The secret to enjoying Banff is not to fight it. Revel in the revelry made possible by the crowds. Enjoy the good museums, sniff the mountain air and remember that quicker than most people would think you can be alone in nature amidst soul-cleansing beauty.

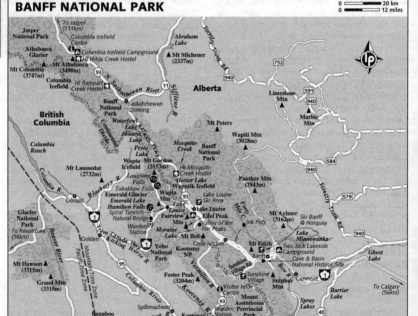

BANFF NATIONAL PARK

History

Created because of the CPR company's dream to build a health spa town in the middle of the park, Banff was destined to draw tourists from its beginnings in the 1880s. The growth happened quickly. Wealthy, well-traveled Victorian adventurers flowed into the park on the CPR trains, ready to relax in the rejuvenating hot springs or hire one of the many outfitters to take them up the mountains. In 1912 the decision to allow cars in Banff opened up the area to auto travelers. Soon, people other than the affluent wanted to check out the scene, and the town began pushing its boundaries. The south side of the river, with the Fairmont Banff Springs Hotel, catered to the wealthy crowd. The north side of the river, however, resembled more of a prairie town, with small lots zoned in a grid system. This class-distinctive boundary is still evident today.

Banff continues to face conflicts over its growth. Many people complain that the town site is too crowded and argue that it should build more hotels and streets to accommodate all the shopping-bag-laden tourists. Others decry this idea as only adding to the sprawl that has already claimed so much of the valley. Meanwhile, small buildings in the center are giving way to flashy enclosed low-rise malls filled with the likes of Gap, Burger King and Starbucks.

Orientation

Banff Ave, the main street, runs north–south through the whole length of town, then heads northeast to meet the Trans-Canada Hwy.

South of town past the Bow River Bridge, Mountain Ave leads south to Sulphur Mountain, while Spray Ave leads east to the Fairmont Banff Springs Hotel, the town's most famous landmark. To the west, Cave Ave goes to the Cave and Basin National Historic Site, which contains the first hot springs found in the area.

Information

BOOKSTORES

Indigo Spirits (☎ 403-760-2920; 317 Cascade Ave) Small chain bookstore where you can browse best-sellers amidst air laden with the scents of the nearby mall food court.

EMERGENCY

Emergencies (☎ 911) Use both in town and in the backcountry.

INTERNET ACCESS

Many cafés and motels have wi-fi.
CyberWeb (☎ 403-762-9226; 215 Banff Ave; per hr $6; 9am-9pm) In the Sundance Mall; has laptop connections and printers.
Underground Station (☎ 403-760-8776; 211 Banff Ave; per hr $6; 9am-10pm) In the Park Ave Mall.

LAUNDRY

Cascade Coin Laundry (☎ 403-762-3444; 317 Banff Ave; per load from $5; 8am-8pm) Situated on the lower level of Cascade Plaza.

LIBRARY

Banff Public Library (☎ 403-762-2661; 101 Bear St; 10am-8pm Mon-Fri, 11am-6pm Sat, 11am-5pm Sun) Internet access; reserve in advance. Good place for perusing old books on Banff.

MEDICAL SERVICES

Mineral Springs Hospital (☎ 403-762-2222; 301 Lynx St; 24hr) Treats 15,000 emergency patients each year.

MONEY

Currency Exchange (☎ 403-762-4478; 317 Banff Ave; 10am-7pm) In the Cascade Plaza.

POST

Post office (☎ 403-762-2586; 204 Buffalo St)

TOURIST INFORMATION

Parks Canada (☎ 403-762-1550; www.parkscanada.ca /banff) and **Banff/Lake Louise Tourism** (☎ 403-762-8421; www.banfflakelouise.com) both maintain counters inside the historic 1939 **Visitor Centre** (224 Banff Ave; 8am-8pm summer, 9am-5pm winter). Before commencing any hiking in the area check in here; Parks Canada publishes a detailed map, and the staff will tell you about current trail conditions and hazards. Anybody who plans on hiking overnight in the backcountry must sign in and purchase a wilderness permit. Free naturalist programs and guided hikes take place regularly, and every night in summer there is a lecture on some aspect of the area. There is even a handy drop box to pay your parking tickets.

To stay up to date with local events, tune into the Friends of Banff Park's (www .friendsofbanff.com) Park Radio (101.1FM),

THE ROCKIES

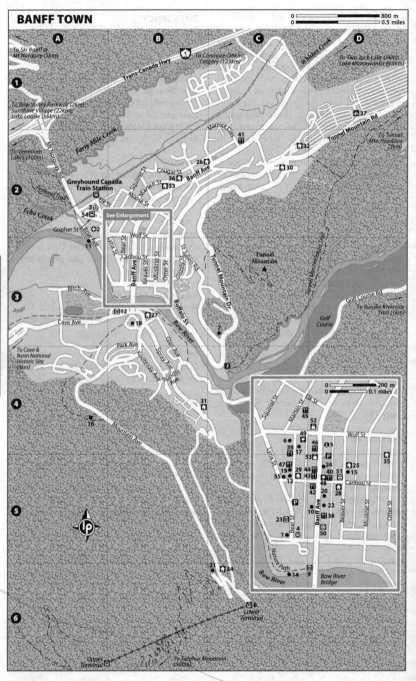

which features park news, condition reports and other interesting features. The group also runs a good bookstore located in the information center.

Dangers & Annoyances
The police are strict in Banff, and it's a bad idea to drive after a night at the bar; not only are you putting yourself and others at risk, but police often spot-check cars for drunk drivers and drugs. The fines are heavy. You'll have to work to avoid a parking ticket; they're given out in such great quantity that there's a place to pay them in the VC.

As for all those photogenic elk you may see wandering the streets, remember that they're wild animals and will charge at you if they feel threatened. Every year there are people who are attacked.

Sights
The stretch of Banff Ave between Wolf and Buffalo Sts is just one long glitzy strip mall. Pause for air at the **World Heritage Park**, with displays about Banff and Unesco. Toward the south end of Banff Ave you'll find

Central Park, where you can stroll alongside the mellow Bow River. Follow the signed **nature path** north along the river. Still further south across the Bow River Bridge is the **Park Administration Building**, a good place for a view and a photo of the town. Behind the building, the **Cascade Gardens** burst with flowers. A stream, ponds and a few benches dot the gardens. In summer the Siksika Nation erects a **tepee** with displays of traditional culture and dance exhibitions. Inside the building is the idiosyncratic Canada Place (p316).

BANFF PARK MUSEUM
Be sure to join Babe Ruth as one of the visitors who've signed the guest book at the **park museum** (☎ 403-762-1558; www.pc.gc.ca; 93 Banff Ave; adult/child $4/2; ⏰ 10am-6pm summer, 1-5pm winter) – he did so in 1922. Near the Bow River Bridge at the southern end of town, this lodge-style wood building was built by the CPR in 1903. Check out the surprising inner atrium and the oddball blonde beaver. Learn more on the summer tours (at 3pm).

Before trails first led curious wildlife watchers into the bush, the museum housed

THE ROCKIES

a zoo and aviary, so Victorian visitors to Banff could be guaranteed a glimpse of the park's wildlife. The museum, a national historic site, contains a collection of animals, birds and plants found in the park, plus a tree carved with graffiti dating back to 1841. A visit here is just like stepping back 100 years.

WHYTE MUSEUM OF THE CANADIAN ROCKIES

The **Whyte Museum complex** (☎ 403-762-2291; www.whyte.org; 111 Bear St; adult/child $6/3.50; ✆ 10am-5pm) features an art gallery and a vast collection of photographs telling the history of early explorers, artists and the CPR. Many of the exhibits rotate, but be sure to check out the Heritage Gallery with its story of the unlikely romance of Peter and Catharine Whyte, the museum's founders. On the property are four log cabins and two Banff heritage homes, one dating from 1907 and the other from 1931. The museum conducts tours of the complex and walking tours of the town year round (p316).

BUFFALO NATIONS MUSEUM

This **museum** (☎ 403-762-2388; 1 Birch Ave; adult/child $8/2.50; ✆ 11am-6pm summer, 1-5pm winter) is in the fort-like wooden building to the right as you head south over the bridge. Popular with kids, it mainly explores the history of the First Nations of the Northern Plains and the Rockies, but also covers indigenous groups from all over Alberta. Through life-sized displays, models and re-creations, it depicts traditions such as buffalo hunts. The museum was started by Norman Luxton in 1952, who had traded with many First Nations people from his souvenir shop.

HISTORIC BEAVER ST

Although development is relentless, you can still find areas of Banff unchanged from its early days as a tourist destination. Pick up the excellent *Banff Historical Walking Tour* at the VC. Several **historic buildings** on Beaver St recall the quaintness and charm that were once the local norm. They include:

- **206** The 1906 wood-frame home of George Luxton who founded the Buffalo Nations Museum.
- **208** Another Luxton holding, this was once an 1887 post office built from logs.
- **212** Yet another Luxton building, this eight-room log cabin has been a boarding house for thousands.

CAVE & BASIN NATIONAL HISTORIC SITE

Canada's national parks sprung from these springs in 1885, when the discovery of hot sulfur springs in a cave here led to the area being protected from development in 1885. Like coffee chain outlets today, the idea of preservation spread rapidly and soon Banff National Park and Canada's national park system were created. The **complex** (☎ 403-762-1557; www.pc.gc.ca; adult/child $4/2; ✆ 9am-6pm May-Sep; 11am-4pm Mon-Fri, 9:30am-5pm Sat & Sun Oct-Apr), southwest of town at the end of Cave Ave, has been restored to its 1914 appearance, complete with beautiful murals. Visitors can look at (and smell) the cave and sulfurous waters, but there's no bathing allowed. The **Middle Springs** a little further down the hill are closed to protect the delicate balance of waters.

You can stroll around the attractive grounds, where you'll see both natural and artificially made pools, for no charge. It's a good place for picnics, as there are tables, a fine view and a snack bar. Several pleasant **short walks** begin here: the 400m Discovery Trail, the 2.7km Marsh Loop and the 7.4km (round-trip) Sundance Trail.

UPPER HOT SPRINGS

You'll find a soothing hot pool and steam room at the **Upper Hot Springs spa** (☎ 403-762-1515; adult/child $8/7; ✆ 9am-11pm May-Sep, 10am-10pm Oct-Apr), 3km south of town on Mountain Ave. Besides parboiling in the pool (where water temperatures average 40°C), you can also indulge in a massage or aromatherapy treatment. You can rent bathing suits ($2), stylish sulfur-colored towels ($2) and lockers ($1). Note the heated floors in the changing rooms. Roam Rte (Banff's public bus system) 3 stops here.

FAIRMONT BANFF SPRINGS HOTEL

Since it was completed in the 1920s, the **Fairmont Banff Springs Hotel** (☎ 403-762-2211; 405 Spray Ave; public areas free), an 800-room baronial palace 2km south of downtown, has posed for thousands of postcards and millions of snapshots. The spectacular design includes towers, turrets and cornices, giving the impression that the hotel is full of fairy tales. Many people come just to wander the gardens and absorb the views (none are better than looking down the valley, the view perfectly framed by granite bluffs). See p318 for details on lingering overnight. Roam Rte 4 stops here.

BANFF GONDOLA

An excellent first stop in Banff to get the lay of the land. In less than 10 minutes, the **Banff Gondola** (☎ 403-762-2523; www.banffgondola .com; adult/child $29/14; ☺ approximately 10am-dusk) whisks you 1560m up to the 2281m summit for spectacular views over the surrounding mountains, Bow River and Banff town. The upper terminal has a café that's nothing special but who cares, given the killer views. Spiky peaks are arrayed in all directions and, if you don't mind a little chill, are especially breath-taking (literally) in winter when it's all an icy fantasy.

Alternatively, you can hike up the steep east side of the mountain in about two hours one way. You will be amply rewarded with great views. The trail starts from the Upper Hot Springs parking lot. Or ride up and hike down.

The lower terminal is just over 3km south of Banff on Mountain Ave; it's adjacent to the Upper Hot Springs pool. A cab ride costs about $16. Roam Rte 3 stops here.

LAKE MINNEWANKA

The largest reservoir in the national park, Lake Minnewanka is 11km east of Banff town. Forests and mountains surround this scenic recreational area.

Lake Minnewanka Boat Tours (☎ 403-762-3473; www.minnewankaboattours.com; adult/child $44/19; ☺ 9am-5pm, mid-May–mid-Oct) offers pricey yet popular 90-minute cruises on the lake to **Devil's Gap**. Unfortunately the boats are enclosed in order to protect the delicate sensibilities of the masses. To get to the lake from town, take Banff Ave east over the Trans-Canada Hwy to Minnewanka Rd and turn right.

OTHER MUSEUMS & GALLERIES

Banff has a thriving arts community thanks to the twin influences of money and lots of local inspiration (especially if you're a landscape painter).

Banff Centre (☎ 403-762-6301; www.banffcentre .ca; 107 Tunnel Mountain Dr), off St Julien Rd east of downtown, includes one of Canada's best-known art schools, complete with facilities for dance, theater, music and the visual arts. Exhibits, concerts and various other events take place regularly. During the Banff Summer Arts Festival, which lasts all season, students and internationally recognized artists present pieces in workshops and performances. The **Walter Phillips Gallery** (admission free; ☺ noon-5pm Wed-Sun, noon-9pm Thu) shows changing displays of contemporary art.

A large private gallery that sells work by Canadian artists and those from the Rockies in particular, **Canada House Gallery** (☎ 403-762-3757; cnr Caribou & Bear Sts; ☺ 9am-7pm) is an excellent place to see recent trends and works.

Scattered throughout the Cascade Plaza, **Canadian Ski Museum West** (☎ 403-762-8484; 317 Banff Ave; admission free; ☺ 7am-11pm) has exhibits chronicling Banff's skiing history through bronze statues of skiers, and panels describing the evolution of the sport and its growth in Banff.

Activities

Legendary skiing in winter, legendary scenery in summer: Banff is unparalleled for outdoor activities. Note that most of the much-touted white-water rafting trips happen in and around Golden, BC (p299). Avoid the commute and get wet once you're there.

OPERATORS

Banff has scores of small and focused activity operators, many listed below. There are also omnibus outfits that offer a myriad of activities year round.

Banff Adventures Unlimited (☎ 403-762-4554, 800-644-8888; www.banffadventures.com; 211 Bear St) Dog-sledding to fly-fishing.

Discover Banff Tours (☎ 403-760-5007, 877-565-9372; www.banfftours.com; Sundance Mall, 215 Banff Ave) Snowshoe tours to cave explorations.

Interpretive Guides Association (www .interpretiveguides.org) Umbrella accreditation group representing activity outfits and individual guides; can recommend guides no matter what you desire, from all-season virgin backcountry explorations to special-interest nature hikes.

HIKING

You'll find many good short hikes and day walks around the Banff area that will get you out into the beauty that's all around you. Parks Canada publishes an excellent brochure, *Day Hikes in Banff National Park*, outlining hikes accessible from the town.

You can take a pleasant, quiet stroll by **Bow River**, just three blocks west of Banff Ave beside Bow Ave. The trail runs from the corner of Wolf St along the river under the Bow River Bridge and ends shortly after on Buffalo St. If you cross the bridge, you can continue southwest through the woods to nearby **Bow Falls**.

For a short (2.3km one way) climb (260m) to break in your legs and survey the area, walk up stubby **Tunnel Mountain**, east of downtown. A trail leads up from St Julien Rd; you can drive here, but it's not a long walk from downtown to the start of the path. From the east end of Buffalo St, a 5.1km interpretive trail between Bow River and Tunnel Mountain heads north and east toward the **Tunnel Mountain Hoodoos**. The term 'hoodoo' refers to the distinctive vertical pillar shapes carved into the rock face by rainfall and glacial erosion.

Just west of downtown, off Mt Norquay Rd, is the 2km **Fenland Trail** loop, which goes through marsh and forest and connects the town with First Vermilion Lake.

Some excellent hiking trails meander off the Bow Valley Parkway (Hwy 1A), northwest of Banff. The Parkway branches off from, but finally rejoins, the Trans-Canada Hwy en route to Lake Louise. Waterfalls are the lure of a trail that follows the sparkling waters of **Johnston Creek**, which has creatively carved its way through the soft limestone of Johnston Canyon. The trail is paved as far as the **Lower Falls** (2.2km). The next 3.2km stretch to the **Upper Falls** is more challenging but worth it for the views. A further – and mostly untraveled – 6.2km brings you to the **Ink Pots**, five small springs of blue and green water surrounded by snowy peaks.

CANOEING

You can go canoeing on **Lake Minnewanka** and nearby **Two Jack Lake**, northeast of Banff. The **Vermilion Lakes**, three shallow lakes connected by narrow waterways, attract lots of wildlife and make excellent spots for canoeing. To get to the lakes, head northwest out of town along Lynx St and follow signs toward Hwy 1. Just before the highway, turn left onto Vermilion Lakes Dr, and you'll soon come to small parking areas for the lakes (a picnic out on the docks is iconic).

In town your best bet is the Bow River. **Blue Canoe Rentals** (☎ 403-762-5465; rentals per hr from $34; ☯ 10am-6pm mid-May–Jun & mid-Sep–mid-Oct, 9am-9pm Jul & Aug) hires out canoes at the corner of Bow Ave and Wolf St near the river. From here you can paddle to the Vermilion Lakes in about 30 minutes.

CYCLING & MOUNTAIN BIKING

You can cycle on the highways and on most of the trails in and around town. Excursions of all varieties are possible, whether you're looking to ride for a few hours, a day or several days with overnight stops at campgrounds, hostels or lodges. Two good, short cycling routes close to Banff run along **Vermilion Lakes Drive** and **Tunnel Mountain Drive**. Families enjoy the **Spray River Loop** (14.9km).

For something more challenging, go 1km past the Banff Springs Golf Course to the 14km **Rundle Riverside Trail**, which plunges into the backcountry with a lot of rough riding along the way.

Parks Canada publishes a brochure, *Mountain Biking and Cycling Guide Banff*

BACKCOUNTRY BANFF

Most of Banff National Park – and to an even greater extent the other nearby parks – is a remote land of raw natural beauty which will reduce you to about the status of a bug. Hikes into this land, where snow and June go together, require skills but offer huge rewards. Parks Canada maintains a network of rustic campsites and shelters that provide just enough comfort to let you rise above pioneer trailblazer status (which sounds good until you're sitting on a rock in freezing rain in the dark and you need to go to the can). Shelters have wood stoves, picnic tables, hard bunks and pit toilets; campsites have sleeping pads and outhouses.

Park Canada's *Backcountry Visitors' Guide* is an invaluable primer, with a simple map showing trails and coordinates. Recommended hiking guides include the discerning *Don't Waste Your Time in the Rockies* by Kathy and Craig Copeland, with good maps and trail descriptions, and the old standard *Classic Hikes in the Canadian Rockies* by Graeme Poole. *Canadian Rockies Trail Guide* by Patton and Robinson can take you far off the beaten path.

See Parks Canada information desks at visitor centers to check trail conditions and get recommendations for both Banff and the other national parks.

National Park, which describes trails and regulations.

Ski Stop (☎ 403-760-1650; www.theskistop.com; 203A Bear St; 1-day bike rentals $30-50; ☺ 9am-9pm summer, 7:30am-9pm winter) runs self-guided trips in the backcountry that include van shuttle, bike, gear and map as well as bike shuttles and guided rides around town.

Bactrax (☎ 403-762-8177; www.snowtips-bactrax .com; 225 Bear St; rentals per day $35-50; ☺ 8am-8pm) organizes two-hour rides from $40.

HORSEBACK RIDING

Hop on a horse and you can see the beautiful Banff area as it must have looked to outsiders in the 1880s. You can smell like them too. In Banff the most popular routes lie south of Bow River. **Holidays on Horseback** (☎ 403-762-4551; www.horseback.com), which operates out of the **Trail Rider Store** (132 Banff Ave; ☺ 9am-9pm), offers a variety of horseback riding trips around the region. Among the choices: an hour-long ride along Spray River ($40) and a three-hour Bow Valley Loop ($100). Much longer multi-day camping adventures in the backcountry start at $250 per night.

ROCK CLIMBING

The sheer number of the Banff area's rocky crags and granite peaks will excite even the most experienced climbers. This is not terrain for unguided novice climbers; even experienced climbers should talk to locals, do research and check weather conditions before venturing out.

Mountain Magic (☎ 403-762-2591; www.mountain magic.com; 224 Bear St; ☺ 9am-9pm) has an indoor climbing wall and staff are ready to share local expertise. **Banff Adventures Unlimited** (p313) offers lessons for all skill levels, beginning at $260 for a half-day.

SKIING & SNOWBOARDING

Three famous resorts with spectacular scenery surround Banff. Together they offer 248 trails, among other stats, so hot they'll melt your wax.

Ski Banff@Norquay (☎ 403-522-3555, 800-258-7669; www.banffnorquay.com; 1-day lift pass adult/child $55/17), just 6km from downtown Banff on Mt Norquay Rd, is the area's original resort. It's small – 0.77 sq km of skiable area, five lifts, 28 trails and a drop of 503m – but it does offer Friday-night skiing.

Sunshine Village (☎ 403-762-6500, 877-542-2633; www.skibanff.com; 1-day lift pass adult/child $76/26), 22km southwest of Banff, has a drop of 1070m and 13.6 sq km of skiable runs. In a region known for abundant powder, Sunshine gets the most: 30m on average. It's favored by serious skiers and is not overrun with beginners.

About 60km northwest of Banff, **Lake Louise Ski Area** (☎ 403-522-3555, 800-258-7669; www .skilouise.com; 1-day lift pass adult/child $76/25) ranks among Canada's largest ski areas, boasting a 1000m drop, 139 runs and 28.5 sq km of terrain spread over four mountain faces. Many skiers stop, mesmerized by the 360-degree views of peaks from the top, but few pause to count the seemingly unlimited numbers before the runs lure them down.

The three resorts have joint marketing (☎ 800-661-1431; www.skibig3.com) and operate the **Banff Ski Hub** (119 Banff Ave; ☺ 8am-9pm winter). You can buy passes good for all three (adult/child $240/115 for a three-day pass).

Numerous stores in Banff and the various ski resorts rent equipment. Ski Stop and Bactrax (left) are well regarded.

SPAS

Weary from a long day on the slopes, trails or at the shops? A spa is just the thing to relax and invigorate you.

Among the many choices:

Pleiades Massage and Spa (☎ 403-760-2500; www.hotspring.ca; Upper Hot Springs; 1-hr massage $85; ☺ 11am-9pm) Enjoy the historic springs and then choose from many massages and treatments including aromatherapy.

Red Earth Spa (☎ 403-762-9292; www.redearthspa .com; Banff Caribou Lodge; 521 Banff Ave; treatments from $100; ☺ 9am-8pm) Upscale spa with lavish baths, all manner of treatments and private spaces where couples can revive.

Banff for Children

Almost everything in Banff can be a treat for kids – well, their eyes might glaze over in the gold shops, but then adults' eyes do as well. Above all else, the Banff Gondola (p313) scores high on the fun meter. Also in the running is the Banff Park Museum (p311) with its many stuffed critters. Then there are the Upper Hot Springs (p312).

The VC can help with various short hikes aimed at kids, and in winter the area's three

THE ROCKIES

ski resorts each have children's programs – from special ski schools to play groups that let the adults swoosh off into the powder.

As a treat for good behavior, stop by **Welch's Chocolate Shop** (☎ 403-762-3737; 126 Banff Ave; ☺ 9am-10pm), where the little darlings can behave like kids in a candy store.

Quirky Banff

You will want to wave a maple leaf – or perhaps burn a copy of the iconic Molsen 'I am Canadian' beer ad – after you visit the delightfully chest-thumping **Canada Place** (☎ 403-760-1338; Park Administration Bldg, 1 Cave Ave; admission free; ☺ 10am-6pm May-Sep). Exhibits and interactive displays include the Canuckle-head trivia game. You can shoot virtual Bow River rapids in a birch-bark canoe but, sadly, there are no samples of Canadian cuisine like a Tim Hortons' doughnut.

Tours

WALKING

The **Whyte Museum** (p312) offers numerous guided walks and tours from $7 per person (Sundays year round, daily in summer). Itineraries include Heritage Homes and Historic Banff. The tours have excellent and enthusiastic guides and are highly recommended.

All of the main activity operators in Banff (p313) offer walks and hikes lasting from one hour to one day or even one week and more.

BUS

Brewster (☎ 403-762-6767, 877-791-5500; www.brewster.ca) has been a major player in developing tourism in Banff almost since the start. You may well find yourself stuck behind one of its ubiquitous buses throughout the Rockies and beyond. Among its myriad tours is a three-hour **Discover Banff tour** (adult/child $53/27) or a one-way trip to Jasper ($150/75) that stops at the icefields. The tours depart from the **Brewster Bus Station** (☎ 403-762-1092; 100 Gopher St) and various hotels.

Discover Banff Tours (p313) offers roughly the same lineup as Brewster and at similar prices, but uses much smaller buses. It also has tours aimed at spotting wildlife.

Festivals & Events

Banff/Lake Louise Winter Festival (☎ 403-762-0270; www.banfflakelouise.com) Annual town-wide party held in late January and early February since 1919 with much mirth and merriment.

Banff Mountain Film & Book Festival (☎ 403-762-6301; www.banffcentre.ca) International stories and movies about mountain adventure are honored in early November.

Sleeping

Accommodations are varied; from the storied heights – literally – at the Fairmont Banff Springs Hotel, to the humble pleasures of a hostel, there is something for every taste and budget.

Be sure to book ahead in summer. The staff at the VC are good, but they may not be able to pull a room out of the forest on a sunny weekend evening. There is a useful board listing accommodation outside the VC. It even has free phones so you can call around day or night.

Banff Ave is lined with places to stay from one end to the other. Most places are walkable from the center. Saunas and hot tubs are common, and it's not rare to find kitchen facilities.

B&Bs and vacation rentals are on the rise and Banff/Lake Louise Tourism shows dozens on its website (www.banfflakelouise.com).

There are hundreds more motel rooms in fast food – and chain store – laden Canmore, 26km east of Banff on the Trans-Canada Hwy. It's the place held up as the worst-case scenario by people arguing to rein in Banff's growth.

The rates listed here are for the peak summer season. Travelers in spring and fall will find bargains (but no crowds) everywhere. There are modest spikes in rates during the ski season coinciding with holidays.

BUDGET

Banff National Park contains 13 campgrounds, most of which lie right around the town or along the Bow Valley Parkway. Most are only open between May or June and September. They are all busy in July and August, and availability is on a first-come, first-served basis, so check in by noon or you may be turned away. Campgrounds with showers always fill up first.

Two Jack Main Campground (campsites $22; ☺ mid-May–Aug) Located 12km northeast of Banff on Lake Minnewanka Rd, it features 380 sites and flush toilets but no showers.

Two Jack Lakeside Campground (campsites $28; ☺ mid-May–Aug) About 1km south of Two Jack Main Campground and living up to the watery promise of its name, there are 74 sites and showers.

Tunnel Mountain Village Campground (☎ reservations 877-737-3783; www.pccamping.ca; campsites from $28) On Tunnel Mountain Rd, this campground actually includes three separate campgrounds: two primarily cater to RVs needing electrical hookups and one, Village 1, accommodates only tents, with a whopping 618 tenting sites. Close to town, it has flush toilets and showers. The sites vary widely in quality. Some are secluded, some have views of sheer-faced peaks and some are sheer nonsense. Village II remains open all year. Roam Rte 4 stops here.

HI Banff Alpine Centre (☎ 403-670-7580, 866-762-4122; www.hihostels.ca; 801 Coyote Dr; dm/d/cabins from $26/82/140; 🖵 🛜) This large facility, off Tunnel Mountain Rd, consistently scores among the top HI hostels worldwide. There's a café, patios and decks, fireplaces and numerous activities. It's a healthy 15-minute walk to town from this bucolic location; Roam Rte 4 stops nearby.

Banff Y Mountain Lodge (☎ 403-762-3560; www.ymountainlodge.com; 102 Spray Ave; dm/d from $32/70; 🖵) This unadorned dorm has a good central location. It accommodates men and women in its 100+ dorm beds and 44 privaterooms. Facilities include a café, a common cooking area and access to the gym ($5).

SameSun Banff (☎ 403-762-5521, 877-562-2783; www.samesun.com; 449 Banff Ave; dm/d from $35/100; 🖵 🛜) This old motel waited until an advanced age to become a swinger. It's pretty much always hopping at this very popular hostel. Misgivings are raised by those who say the popularity means the 130 beds never cool off. But if you're up for high energy, organized pub crawls and other highjinks, this is the place.

MIDRANGE

In spring and fall you can get rates well under $150 at the following listings. But in summer, things are more expensive. Check websites for deals.

Rocky Mountain B&B (☎ 403-762-4811; www.rockymtnbb.com; 223 Otter St; r from $65-130; 🛜) This 1918 boarding house was popular with CPR workers in the 1930s and remains a modest guest house today. The 10 rooms are basic, some share bathrooms and the TV is in the common area. It's a good deal though, especially as rates include breakfast.

Blue Mountain Lodge (☎ 403-762-5134; www.bluemtnlodge.com; 327 Caribou St; r $80-180; 🛜) Another fine midrange lodge right in the center, this one has 10 rooms and cabins. All are freshly decorated and many have themes: you'll have to decide on your fantasy of choice (nightstick? strip search?) in the Mountie room. We like the rough and ready charms of the Cowboy Bunkhouse.

Brewster's Mountain Lodge (☎ 403-762-2900, 888-213-1030; www.brewstermountainlodge.com; 208 Caribou St; r $90-180; 🖵 🛜) In Banff's ground zero, this 75-room hotel has heated underground parking (in case you get booted out of your room) and manages a mountain-lodge motif overlaid on the modern structure. Third-floor rooms have vaulted ceilings and forgo a balcony.

our pick **Banff Beaver Cabins** (Two Twenty Beaver Cabins; ☎ 403-762-5077; www.banffbandbcabins.com; 220 Beaver St; cabins from $125-200; 🛜) Pick your critter as each of the five cabins at this historic property smack dab in the center is named after an animal. You may be sleeping Beaver, but you may be sleeping in a gopher. Or an elk. Units vary in size but all have cooking facilities plus fresh buns in the am and fresh cookies in the pm.

Irwin's Mountain Inn (☎ 403-762-4566, 800-661-1721; www.irwinsmountaininn.com; 429 Banff Ave; r $130-200; 🖵 🛜 🍴) Banff Ave is lined with motels but this one stands out for its good value. The 65 spotless rooms win awards and the winsome staff win plaudits. Basic rooms are motel standard, but nudge up the budget and you can have a vast Jacuzzi right off the bed.

Banff Caribou Lodge (☎ 403-762-5887, 800-563-8764; www.bestofbanff.com; 521 Banff Ave; r $140-200; 🖵) One of the best large chalet-style motels on Banff Ave, the Caribou horns in with 195 large, comfortable rooms on four floors. Make new friends in the 35-person hot tub and have your cares rubbed away at the Red Earth Spa (p315).

TOP END

Most of the really luxury lodgings are in the hills overlooking the valley.

Buffalo Mountain Lodge (☎ 403-762-2400, 800-879-1991; www.crmr.com; 700 Tunnel Mountain Rd; r $170-320; 🖵 🛜) A slight jaunt from town by foot, the classic Banff scenery only gets better as you reach this little outcrop of inns. The 108 lush units here are large and lodgey:

expect working fireplaces, patios, a huge common hot tub and the feel that you've come to a camp for grown-ups.

Rimrock Resort Hotel (☎ 403-762-3356, 800-661-1587; www.rimrockresort.com; Mountain Ave; r from $250; ❄ ▣ ▨ ▨) Close to the Upper Hot Springs and the cable car, this luxurious resort has 346 rooms spread over nine stories. Rooms with balconies and valley views are best, but all have extra large baths and a formal, moneyed resort feel. There's a spa, indoor pool, ice rink and a host of noted restaurants.

Fairmont Banff Springs Hotel (☎ 403-762-2211, 800-441-1414; www.fairmont.com; 405 Spray Ave; r from $300; ❄ ▣ ▨) Few of the 770 rooms here are alike and that's central to this legendary property, which no one ever calls the Fairmont. (That's Banff Springs Hotel to you, *sir*.) The baronial walls reek of history; lose yourself in the stolid charms of one of the many common areas. Rooms with valley views are prized – despite their modern luxuries, don't take a room in one of the newer annexes, there's just no point. Spring or fall are the best times to stay, when the stretch-pants day-trippers are long gone and the ski bums absent.

Eating

There's all manner of cafés and restaurants in Banff offering a range of cuisines and catering to all budgets. Beware of tourist joints luring in the unwary, knowing they'll never return. For good tips on where to try, ask your bartender.

You can pick up some prepared deli foods and other picnic fixings at **Safeway** (☎ 403-723-3929; 318 Marten St; ❨ 24hr), just off Banff Ave.

BUDGET

Evelyn's Coffee Bar (☎ 403-762-0352; 201 Banff Ave, Town Centre Mall; snacks $3; ❨ 7am-11pm) Tightly packed with gossipers, Evelyn's dishes the dish – in this case baked goods, soups and excellent coffees. One of three.

Wild Flour (☎ 403-760-5074; 211 Bear St; meals from $5; ❨ 8am-8pm; ❨) From the coffee to the artisan bread, everything is organic at this bright bakery, which entices with a huge range of goods, soups and fine coffees and tea. Get a table outside.

Eddie (☎ 403-762-2230; 137 Banff Ave; meals from $6; ❨ 11am-3am) Best place in town for a late-

night burger (or food of any kind). Pitchers of beer, sports on TV and 2am food specials keep the ravenous hordes coming to this slightly stylish dive.

our pick Bruno's Café & Grill (☎ 403-762-8115; 304 Caribou St; meals $6-12; ❨ 8am-1am; ❨) Order your burger about 20 different ways, but know that they are all good. Thick and juicy, we like the grilled onions, swiss and mushroom option. Or order breakfast all day. Friendly staff pour excellent cocktails.

MIDRANGE

Nourish (☎ 403-760-3933; 2nd fl, Sundance Mall, 215 Banff Ave; meals $8-16; ❨ 9am-9pm) Take your pick of meals at this healthy place that's as unadorned as your colon after the high-fiber special. Choose from wheat-free, gluten-free, vegan, raw or plain old organic.

Balkan (☎ 403-762-3454; 120 Banff Ave; mains $10-20; ❨ 11am-10pm) Unless you've skied into a tree, you're unlikely to think you're in Mykonos at this low-concept Greek joint. But that's exactly the idea: housed in a former dance hall, the food is fun, the staff frolicsome and on some nights you get to throw plates, others you ogle the belly dancer.

Bison (☎ 403-762-5550; 211 Bear St; mains $15-30; ❨ 8am-10pm) Simple foods prepared beautifully is the hallmark of this excellent upstairs dining room. Relax on the terrace and watch the play of colors on the peaks during the long summer nights. Woodfired pizzas are tops, as are boldly flavored seafood and meat mains. Buttermilk waffles are the bomb at breakfast.

Grizzly House (☎ 403-762-4055; 207 Banff Ave; mains $15-30; ❨ 11:30am-late) Where your parents could have had their third date, whatever your age, Grizzly is a timeless lodge for fondue (about 12 kinds). In fact you'll dip yourself silly on three fondue courses with many meals. The other schtick is exotic meat, like rattlesnake, which is more often seen by the side of the road than on your plate.

Suginoya (☎ 403-762-4773; 225 Banff Ave; meals $20-30; ❨ 5-10pm) Sushi and sashimi as fresh as new fallen powder are the main attractions here. Everything is artfully prepared by chefs who've had years of training. Hot pots, sukiyaki, tempura and sake are options for those wishing things were hot.

TOP END

Bumper's Beef House (☎ 403-762-2622; 603 Banff Ave; mains $25-35; ☺ 5-10pm) Northeast of the center, Bumper's is a local institution. Prime ribs take center stage here and are simply superb. Everything else, the decor, the humdrum salad bar, the indifferent veggies, are barely in the chorus. (Note that the salad bar 'bacon' bits are garish red and artificial, while the bacon bits on the baked potatoes, served next to the prime rib, are real.)

Eden (☎ 403-762-1840; Rimrock Resort Hotel, Mountain Rd; mains from $40; ☺ 6-10pm) In a town where the dress code is usually 'what fits,' this luxurious cathedral of finer dining has a more formal one. The menu is French-accented and ever-changing with the seasons. Enjoy the full range of the kitchen's art with a 10-course tasting menu. Avoid strain choosing from the 17,000 bottles in the cellar: let the staff recommend. Apple-based desserts, when available, are sinful yet won't get you thrown out of Eden.

Drinking

Nightlife in Banff easily goes past midnight in the peak seasons. Most bars also serve food.

Rose & Crown (☎ 403-762-2121; 202 Banff Ave) Up on the sun-drenched rooftop deck, all of Banff's glory is arrayed around you, one peak after another. Inside there's pool tables, live music, frenetic dancing and one guy off in the corner enjoying his fish and chips.

St James Gate (☎ 403-762-9355; 205 Wolf St) An ersatz upscale English pub replete with dark wood and snugs, this place packs 'em in for the 24 beers on tap, stiff drinks and tasty fish and chips. The place to come if you like your color with a u or your Bond with a Q.

Tommy's (☎ 403-760-6610; lower level, 120 Banff Ave) Provide boozy commentary on the passing parade of footwear from the below-ground terrace at this humble old bar right in the center. The place to go for the scoop on seasonal jobs.

Entertainment

Banff has an entertainment calendar that, for its size, is the equal of Calgary's (note we didn't say Vancouver). You can find current entertainment listings in the 'Summit Up' section of the weekly *Banff Crag & Canyon* newspaper. Also check the schedule at the Banff Centre (p313), which has a full schedule of music and artistic performances.

Aurora Nightclub (☎ 403-760-3343; lower level, 110 Banff Ave, Clock Tower Village Mall; cover $5-10) is all Eurotrash flash and the wilder of the two main nightclubs.

Those ready to ski off a cliff if they hear one more lite rock hit of the 80s, will find respite – and deafness – at the **Devil's Gap** (☎ 250-762-8800; 306 Caribou St), a grungy metal bar upstairs past a lot of graffiti.

Shopping

St Moritz it's not. Banff is more suited to Gap than Fendi and you'll find a mixture of moderate chain, regional and local shops in the many modest malls along the three main blocks of Banff Ave.

Getting There & Away

Banff is 140km west of Calgary and 90km east of Field. If you're going or coming from the former, note that the Trans-Canada Hwy seems to be permanently clogged along its archaic Calgary stretch. If you're going to the airport, you could find yourself stuck in traffic admiring a seedy strip of porn peddlers and loan shops while your flight takes off. Give yourself at least three hours to get inside the terminal from Banff.

It's really a crime that VIA Rail no longer serves Banff, as the CPR tracks from Calgary to Vancouver go right through town. There is an ongoing effort to rectify this, but the petroleum-based economy of Alberta is unfriendly to mass transit.

BUS

Each year various operators run vans between Banff and Jasper over the Icefields Parkway. The following use large buses.

Brewster (☎ 403-762-6767; www.brewster.ca; 100 Gopher St) Operates express buses to/from Lake Louise (adult/child $22/11, one hour, four daily), Jasper ($70/40 four hours, one daily) and Calgary ($55/28, two hours, two daily).

Greyhound Canada (☎ 403-762-1092; 327 Railway Ave) Buses operate from Banff's forlorn train station. Services east to Calgary ($32, two hours, five daily) and west to Vancouver ($145, 13 to 15 hours, four daily) via Golden, Revelstoke, Kelowna and more.

Getting Around

TO/FROM THE AIRPORT

Brewster's service to Calgary (above) also serves the airport (adult/child $55/28).

THE ROCKIES

Banff Airporter (☎ 403-762-3330, 888-449-2901; www.banffairporter.com; adult/child $53/27) has frequent service to/from Calgary airport (two hours). Book in advance.

BUS
Roam (☎ 403-762-1215; www.banff.ca; adult/child $2/1; ☺ 6:30am-11pm), Banff's excellent public transit bus system, runs hybrid buses on two routes. Rte 3 Follows Banff Ave to the Bow River and then heads to the Gondola via Mountain Ave. Rte 4 Starts at Tunnel Mountain Campground, follows Tunnel Mountain Rd to the center and Banff Ave before crossing the river and following Spray Ave to the Fairmont Banff Springs Hotel. Buses run every 40 minutes.

CAR
All of the major rental-car companies have branches in Banff.
Avis (☎ 403-762-3222; Cascade Plaza, 317 Banff Ave)
Budget (☎ 403-762-4565; cnr Caribou & Bear Sts)
Hertz (☎ 403-762-2027; Fairmont Banff Springs Hotel, 127 Spray Ave)
National (☎ 403-762-2688; 102 Caribou St)

TAXI
Banff Taxi (☎ 403-762-4444)
Legion Taxi (☎ 403-762-3353)

LAKE LOUISE
The first person to spy Lake Louise must have had some sort of word or exclamation for the vista that presented itself: a huge glacier (now called Victoria after you-know-who) perched atop a mountain that backs a lake whose iridescent turquoise color changes with every movement of the sun. And all this framed by peaks that put the rocky in Rockies. Tarnation!

These days the buses come. And come. People walk about 50m, take a snapshot, say some modern-day equivalent of 'tarnation!' and go. All this makes the immediate area of Lake Louise something akin to the arteries of a bacon-cheeseburger addict: clogged. Yet amid the jam and the commercialism of iconic Fairmont Chateau Lake Louise on the north shore, there are escapes. You can enjoy the lake and the truly stunning surrounds and not get trampled. In fact, a short walk will have you far from the crowds and you'll be able to look back at them and say 'tarnation!' Or, visit

away from July or August, when you can drive right up and exclaim anything you want to barely anyone at all.

Orientation
The lake, known as the jewel of the Rockies, lies about 57km northwest of Banff, at the conjunction of Hwys 1 and 93. Before you get to the lake, you'll reach the uninspiring village of Lake Louise, which is essentially nothing more than the Samson Mall shopping center and a gas station. Though small, the strip of shops can provide you with everything from postal services to groceries and liquor, from restaurant meals to hiking boots (in case you left yours at home). The town is essentially a tourist attraction; few permanent residents actually live here except for those who staff the hotels.

The lake, named for Queen Victoria's daughter Louise (neither of whom ever came to the lake), is 5km uphill from the village. If you're walking, it takes about 45 minutes on the footpath.

Information
Parks Canada and Banff/Lake Louise Tourism offer information at the **VC** (☎ 403-522-3833; ☺ 9am-8pm Jul & Aug, 9am-4pm Sep-Jun) beside the Samson Mall in Lake Louise. Stop for advice on the many hikes away from the crowds and pick up the essential *Day Hikes in Banff National Park*; the center also features a good exhibition on the geological and natural history of the Rocky Mountains.

Woodruff & Blum (☎ 403-522-3842; Samson Mall; ☺ 9am-8pm) carries guides and maps to the Canadian Rockies; it's better than bookstore choices in Banff or Jasper.

Sights
First you'll want to go and see Lake Louise. The vast parking lot is a five-minute drive from Hwy 1. There are no trails circling the lake itself; in summer avoid going between 11am and 4pm, when the crowds peak. Easy walks are 1.1km one way along the southeast side of the lake to **Fairview Lookout** or 2km one way along the north lakeshore. This latter walk can be extended 3.3km to the self-explanatory **Plain of Six Glaciers** and then combined with the **Lake Agnes** trail for a mostly looping 14.6km hike that will give you some of the best five hours of your trip.

Overlooking the spectacle, the iconic Lake Louise Chalet opened in 1890 to alleviate some of the pressure on the Banff Springs Hotel. Renamed **Chateau Lake Louise** in 1925 (and Fairmont Chateau Lake Louise after the upscale chain absorbed it), the hotel features almost 500 rooms on eight floors, as well as restaurants and lounges. Though blander and less fabled than its Banff counterpart, it enjoys a grand lakeside setting. You can join the other millions of tourists who wander through the hotel every summer on their own. At certain times, **tours** (☎ 403-522-3511) are offered; check for details.

If you're thinking of a dip, consider this: at 1731m above sea level, Lake Louise peaks at a chilly 4°C.

Mt Whitehorn and the Lake Louise ski area lie east of the village, 4.5km along Lake Louise Dr. In summer the **Lake Louise Gondola** (☎ 403-522-3555; www.lakelouisegondola .com; adult/child $25/12.50; ◷ 9am-5pm mid-May–Sep) takes you to the top, where you can hike the trails and enjoy views of Lake Louise and Victoria Glacier. The ticket price includes an array of excellent programs, including guided walks and hikes, and there is an interpretive center. The outings into the alpine meadows are highly recommended and are a restful change from commercialism. You can upsize your ticket for a buffet meal at the top (breakfast/lunch $2.50/6), which is a good deal.

Though lesser known than Lake Louise, **Moraine Lake** always astounds. In fact the jade-green color entrances even the jaded. If you get your hands on an old $20 bill from 1969 to 1979, take a look at the picture on the back and you'll recognize the view of the lake. Look for a lodge (p322) and numerous trails. The lake sits in the gorgeous Valley of the Ten Peaks, 15km (mostly uphill) from the village. To get there, take Lake Louise Dr toward the chateau, turn left onto rugged Moraine Lake Rd and follow it to the end. If you're camping, you can also take the free shuttle from the campgrounds. A vendor often rents rowboats, so you can enjoy a 360-degree vista.

Activities

Lake Louise boasts 75km of **hiking** trails, many of which lead to beautiful alpine meadows that fill up with colorful wildflowers in July and August. It is common to see small, cute mammals such as pikas (plump, furry animals also called conies) and larger, more timid marmots along these trails. You often hear ice rumbling on the slopes too. Or it may be a bear: there are many. Trails may be snowbound and have avalanche warnings well into July.

Note that large numbers of trails are now often limited to groups of four or more; this includes all those in Paradise, Consolation and Larch Valleys. The idea behind group access is to bunch visitors together so that bears have peaceful interludes and aren't tempted to make a snack of individual hikers. The affected area is one of three main grizzly bear breeding areas in Banff National Park. Consult with the Parks Canada hiking experts at the VC for current conditions.

Many of the hiking trails become cross-country ski trails in winter. For downhill types, Lake Louise boasts the largest **skiing** area in Canada. The resort operates in conjunction with Ski Banff at Mt Norquay and Sunshine Village. See p315 for details on all three areas.

Rock climbing on the Back of the Lake, a backwater crag, is popular, partly because it's easy to access. There are lots of different routes with interesting names like 'Wicked Gravity' and 'Chocolate Bunnies from Hell.' Other places to climb, of varying degrees of difficulty and offering much more serenity, include Fairview Mountain, Mt Bell and Eiffel Peak. Everyone, even very experienced climbers, should first check full avalanche and trail conditions with one of the Parks Canada information centers.

Wilson Mountain Sports (☎ 403-522-3636; www .lakelouisewilsons.com; Samson Mall; ◷ 9am-8pm) rents out a full range of winter sports gear (ski packages from $33) as well as fairer weather gear such as mountain bikes (per day from $40), camping equipment and climbing gear.

Activity operators in Banff (p313) have many options for local fun.

Sleeping

Compared to Banff, Lake Louise has relatively few places to stay. However, the choices here are of high quality.

Lake Louise Campgrounds (☎ 403-522-3980; reservations 877-737-3783; www.pccamping.ca) Parks

Canada operates two campgrounds, both on the Trans-Canada Hwy. The tenting campground (campsite $28), off Moraine Lake Rd, contains 206 summer-only (May to September) sites, while the campground at the south end of Fairview Rd off Lake Louise Dr offers 189 year-round sites (from $33, RV-only when the tent campground is open). Both have flush toilets and showers.

HI Lake Louise Alpine Centre (☎ 403-522-2200, 866-762-4122; www.hihostels.ca; dm/d from $35/100; 🖳 🛜) On Village Rd north of Samson Mall, this huge lodge has all the appeal of a mountain chalet without requiring a mountain-sized budget. The 164 beds are split between two- to eight-bed rooms, many with private bathroom and some with lofts you'll love or loath. The hostel is co-owned by the Alpine Club of Canada, so hikers are catered for. See right for details on the café.

Deer Lodge (☎ 403-410-7417, 800-661-1595; www .crmr.com; 1109 Lake Louise Dr; r $110-220) About 28 fir trees to the left of Lake Louise, this old lodge feels just right (and so will you after a soak in the huge vista-viewing hot tub). Rooms are on the small side (think 'cozy') and there is no TV (think 'blissful') but at night you can sit outside and go 'ahhh.'

Fairmont Chateau Lake Louise (☎ 403-522-3511, 800-441-1414; www.fairmont.com; 111 Lake Louise Dr; r from $300; 🌀 🖳 🛜 🌀) Like its sister in Banff, the Chateau Lake Louise can get overrun by day-trippers in the summer. However it is not of the same grand baronial design and instead is a light tan that actually doesn't do much for the local beauty. The 486 rooms vary greatly in size and price. Obviously if you're going to go to the trouble of staying here you don't want to be on the wrong side of the hall – get a room with a view.

Moraine Lake Lodge (☎ 403-522-3733, 877-522-2777; www.morainelake.com; r $275-475) Saw logs in your log bed at this plush mountain boutique lodge overlooking the incomparable beauty of Moraine Lake. Rooms are in the main lodge, unassuming modern blocks and individual cabins. Splurge for the latter. Work up a sweat in one of the free canoes, then have cocktails on the dock, watching the play of light on the mountains.

Eating

Samson Mall has a small grocery and a couple of uninspired café-bakeries. The Fairmont Chateau Lake Louise offers some pricey places, including venues for afternoon high tea.

Bill Peyto's Café (☎ 403-522-2200; HI Lake Louise Alpine Centre, Village Rd; meals $7-20; 🕑 7am-9pm) This legendary café in the hostel has a vast range to choose from at affordable prices, including a lot of healthy and veggie options. Breakfast specials (under $6) are a bargain. Enjoy a microbrew out on the large terrace.

Lake Louise Station (☎ 403-522-2386; meals $8-30; 🕑 11am-9pm) Dine amidst cast-off baggage or in one of two restored dining cars at this 1909 station 1km from Samson Mall on Sentinel Rd. Food rises above the theme restaurant standard, with excellent steaks, roasts and seafood seasoned with organic herbs from the garden.

Getting There & Around

See p319 for transport details to/from Banff, Jasper and Calgary.

The **bus terminal** (☎ 403-522-3870) is at Samson Mall; Greyhound Canada and Brewster buses stop here.

ICEFIELDS PARKWAY

Let's see – there are 230km of Unesco-designated world heritage scenery that spans two famous parks, *and* it's traversed by a good truck-free road, *and* roadside critters such as mountain goats abound *and* there are lots of glaciers… Where do I sign up? Actually, all you need to do is hit the Icefields Parkway, an insignificant ribbon of pavement that winds through the beautiful spine of the Rockies.

Opened in 1940, this 230km road (Hwy 93) links Lake Louise with Jasper, following a lake-lined valley between two chains of the Eastern Main Ranges, which make up the Continental Divide. From here watershed rivers flow either eastward toward the Atlantic Ocean or westward toward the Pacific. These mountains are among the highest and craggiest in Canada.

The highway is in good condition, but it's slow going nonetheless. Animals including goats, bighorn sheep and elk often linger beside the road or even on it. If you're on the bus, you'll see the best scenery if you sit on the left-hand side going from Lake Louise to Jasper.

You can drive the route in a couple of hours, but stopping at the many viewpoints, picnic spots and sights, or hiking on one of the trails, will absorb a full day or longer. You can camp along the way or stay at one of the several rustic hostels. Cyclists on the Icefields Parkway often outnumber cars. Because of the terrain, it's easier to bike heading north.

Parks Canada publishes a worthwhile brochure, *The Icefields Parkway*, which includes a simple map and describes the sights along the way. It notes the seven major icefields – upland glaciers – and 25 smaller ones you'll pass along the way.

As is so often the case, the best time to see iconic **Peyto Lake** is early morning, when the sun adds a rosy contrast to the turquoise glacial waters. It's 40km north of the junction with the Trans-Canada Hwy near Lake Louise.

Some 17km further north, around eponymously named **Waterfowl Lake**, moose are plentiful (as are ducks!). After a long horseshoe curve around a small spring littered with intriguing rocks, the **Bridal Veil Falls** overlook is almost at the road's halfway point, 113km north of the start. Other key points of interest include **Sunwapta Falls**, which surge through a canyon (176km north) and **Athabasca Falls** (200km north), which have a powerful 23m drop.

Athabasca Glacier

The Athabasca Glacier, a fat tongue of the vast Columbia Icefield, can be glimpsed from the road. And we say glimpsed, because it's in serious retreat. Each year global warming is melting this enormous pile of ice – note the huge lakes forming at its base. Meanwhile commercialism here heats up.

The **Icefield Centre** (Map p325; ☎ 780-852-6288; ⏱ 9am-5pm mid-Apr–May & Sep–mid-Oct, 9am-6pm Jun-Aug) is a sprawling facility across from the glacier that is run by Brewster, the Kremlin of the Canadian Rockies. Much of the place is designed to get you to buy a glacier tour (don't hide in the toilets to escape the ads...), however there is a useful **Parks Canada information desk**, which does its best to toe an ideologically neutral line when it comes to global warming. Ask to see the annotated photo showing the glacier's rapid shrinkage year by year: it's startling.

Climate change is given a light hand throughout the displays, possibly to save guilt on the part of all the drivers of SUVs

that clog the parking lot. Worth seeking out however, is a time-lapse video showing how ice can slowly but surely literally move mountains.

In addition to the obligatory gift shop, the center has several restaurants.

You can take the walk to the toe of the glacier from the VC (1km and lengthening), or you can save yourself from slogging across a moonscape of gravel by driving part of the distance.

For an experience right on the ice, **Athabasca Glacier Icewalks** (☎ 800-565-7547; www.icewalks.com; Icefield Centre; ⏱ Jun-Sep) offers a three- to four-hour **Ice Cubed trip** (adult/child $60/30; ⏱ tours 10:30am Jun-Sep) up the glacier and a five- to six-hour **Icewalk Deluxe trip** (adult/child $70/35; ⏱ tours 10:30am Thu & Sun Jun-Sep) to various destinations in the snowfields. Bring warm clothes. Gear is provided.

Should you fall for the hype of Brewster's **ice tours** (☎ 403-762-6735, 877-423-7433; www.columbiaicefield.com; adult/child $50/25; ⏱ 9am-5pm Apr-Sep, 10am-4pm Oct), you'll be joined by up to 5000 people on busy days. The 90-minute trip in a special bus takes you out on the ice and to vast areas of the glacier that can't be seen from the road.

The Icefield Centre is 123km north of the parkway's start and 103km south of Jasper. Note: for truly amazing glaciers that are both remote and accessible (and make what you see along the Icefields Parkway look like frost in a freezer), see p382 for details on the ones around Stewart, BC.

Sleeping

Parks Canada campgrounds are strategically placed along the parkway, all with pit toilets and no showers. There is also a good batch of rustic HI hostels, mostly in scenic locations close to the highway. Though these small spots lack showers, there's

---

DETOUR: PARKWAY 93A

Starting at Athabasca Falls, Parkway 93A is the old highway that was replaced by the modern Icefields Parkway (Hwy 93). It's a meandering road that gives you a much more intimate feel for the park than the main road, and there are several picnic spots. After about 20km, it rejoins Hwy 93, 10km south of Jasper.

THE ROCKIES

usually a bracing stream nearby. Be sure to reserve through **HI hostels** (☎ 403-670-7580, 866-762-4122; www.hihostels.ca; ☒ Apr-Oct, call other times to confirm).

Columbia Icefield Campground (Map opposite; campsites $16; ☒ mid-May–mid-Oct) Close to the Icefield Centre, this campground has 33 tent-only sites, with picnic tables. Firewood is supplied.

Wilcox Creek Campground (Map opposite; campsites $16; ☒ Jun-early Sep) Near Columbia Icefield Campground and with similar amenities, this place has 46 sites. Remember, you're in glacier territory and it gets freezer-cold at night.

HI Mosquito Creek Hostel (Map p308; dm/r from $20/58) An excellent choice of the HI places, this hostel on the Icefields Parkway about 27km north of Lake Louise, has a fireplace, wood-burning sauna and 32 beds in four cabins and private rooms.

HI Rampart Creek Hostel (Map p308; dm/r from $20/58) Ice and rock climbers (the Weeping Wall is nearby) should head 11km north of the Saskatchewan River Crossing (88km north of Lake Louise) to this place with its sauna and 24 beds.

Closer to Jasper along the Icefields Parkway are two places managed by the **HI Jasper International Hostel** (Map opposite; ☎ 780-852-3215, 877-852-0781; www.hihostels.ca; ☒ Apr-Oct, call other times to confirm):

HI Beauty Creek Wilderness Hostel (dm from $20) Located 17km north of the Columbia Icefields, this 22-bed hostel was closed indefinitely in 2009, however it is a sweet spot so check for updates.

HI Athabasca Falls Hostel (Map opposite; dm from $20; ☒ Apr-Oct, call other times to confirm) 198km north of Lake Louise and 32km south of Jasper; has 40 beds.

Icefields Chalet (Map opposite; ☎ 780-852-6550, 877-423-7433; www.brewster.ca; r $110-245; ☒ May-Sep) The Icefield Centre contains this humdrum Brewster-run, bus-tour-filled place where some rooms lack glacier views.

JASPER NATIONAL PARK

Larger (10,878 sq km) yet calmer than Banff National Park, Jasper National Park does not have quite the same jaw-dropping scenery (think jaw-loosening) but in every respect it is the more manageable of the parks. Smaller crowds mean your chance of spotting bears, mountain lions, elk, beavers, mountain goats and other iconic critters is good.

Jasper has easily reached, must-see sights such as Maligne Lake and Canyon. But the backcountry is suitably wild and you can lose traces of civilization in minutes. The town of Jasper is compact yet big enough to amuse and entertain year round. Fires in 2003 charred many areas visible from the Yellowhead Hwy (Hwy 16) east of Jasper. Watching nature's vigorous recovery is an unexpected bonus.

JASPER

pop 4400

There are no malls but you'll still be able to lose a day or more wandering the relaxed streets of Jasper, a town that has been a symbiotic part of the national park since 1908. There's good nightlife, motels and plenty of services. From most parts of town, you can see a ring of snowy peaks, and trails will take you right into the wilderness from the center in 15 minutes.

Jasper, 369km southwest of Edmonton and 376km east of Prince George (p350), is a regional transportation hub. VIA Rail (p331) trains run east to Edmonton and west to both Vancouver and Prince Rupert (p367), while the famous Icefields Parkway travels 230km south to the Trans-Canada Hwy and Lake Louise.

Note that not everyone walking the streets of Jasper is human. Elk hang out downtown during the autumn rutting and spring calving seasons; you'll hear their haunting cry. They're prone to charging, so stay at least 30m away. (As if you'd want to get any closer to a rutting elk?)

History

Archaeological evidence shows that First Nations people lived here as early as 12,000 years ago. It is believed that the First Nations came here seasonally, arriving with the snowmelt to gather food, then leaving again once everything iced over. Many groups used the area, including Shuswap, Sekani and Beaver from the west, Iroquois and Stoney from the east, and Cree from throughout the area.

In the early 1800s David Thompson and the North West Company established a fur-trading route into the Kootenays over

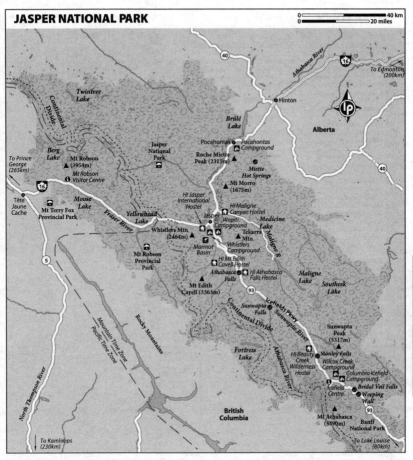

JASPER NATIONAL PARK

Athabasca Pass. Voyageurs soon intermarried with Iroquois and Cree, creating a Métis 'mixed-blood' group whose descendants shaped Jasper's history. Though the fur trade slowly died out, the steady flow of scientists and explorers did not. People were curious about the great glaciers, and soon adventurers and mountaineers were exploring the majestic peaks. In 1930 the National Parks Act was passed, fully protecting Jasper as a national park.

Orientation

The main street, Connaught Dr, has everything, including the train and bus station, banks, restaurants and souvenir shops. Patricia St, parallel to Connaught Dr, is also

parallel in terms of the services it offers. Street numbers throughout town, when posted at all, are difficult to follow.

Off the main street, small wooden houses line the streets, many with flower gardens befitting this alpine setting.

Information

The weekly community newspaper, *The Booster,* enthusiastically lives up to its name.

BOOKSTORES

In a glaring omission, Jasper lacks a good bookstore. Your best bets are small collections at gift shops. Try **Jasper Camera & Gift** (☎ 780-852-3165; 412 Connaught Dr).

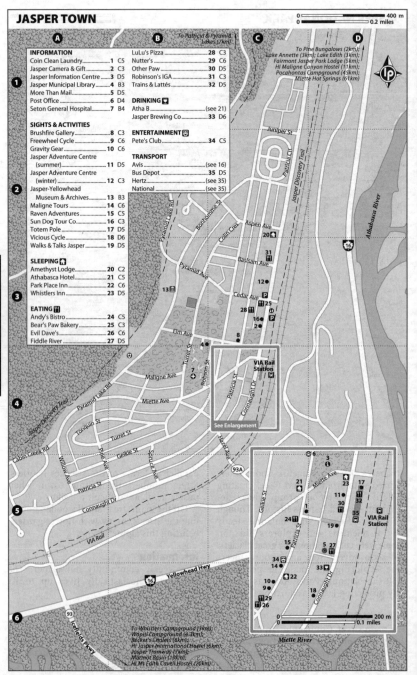

JASPER TOWN

0 — 400 m
0 — 0.2 miles

INFORMATION
Coin Clean Laundry	1 C5
Jasper Camera & Gift	2 C3
Jasper Information Centre	3 D5
Jasper Municipal Library	4 B3
More Than Mail	5 D5
Post Office	6 D4
Seton General Hospital	7 B4

SIGHTS & ACTIVITIES
Brushfire Gallery	8 C3
Freewheel Cycle	9 C6
Gravity Gear	10 C6
Jasper Adventure Centre (summer)	11 D5
Jasper Adventure Centre (winter)	12 C3
Jasper-Yellowhead Museum & Archives	13 B3
Maligne Tours	14 C6
Raven Adventures	15 C5
Sun Dog Tour Co	16 C3
Totem Pole	17 D5
Vicious Cycle	18 D6
Walks & Talks Jasper	19 D5

SLEEPING
Amethyst Lodge	20 C2
Athabasca Hotel	21 C5
Park Place Inn	22 C6
Whistlers Inn	23 D5

EATING
Andy's Bistro	24 C5
Bear's Paw Bakery	25 C3
Evil Dave's	26 C6
Fiddle River	27 D5
LuLu's Pizza	28 C3
Nutter's	29 C6
Other Paw	30 D5
Robinson's IGA	31 C3
Trains & Lattés	32 D5

DRINKING
Atha B	(see 21)
Jasper Brewing Co	33 D6

ENTERTAINMENT
Pete's Club	34 C5

TRANSPORT
Avis	(see 16)
Bus Depot	35 D5
Hertz	(see 35)
National	(see 35)

To Patricia & Pyramid Lakes (7km)

To Pine Bungalows (2km); Lake Annette (3km); Lake Edith (3km); Fairmont Jasper Park Lodge (5km); HI Maligne Canyon Hostel (11km); Pocahontas Campground (45km); Miette Hot Springs (61km)

Juniper St

Patricia Cir

Jasper Discovery Trail

Athabasca River

Pyramid Lake Rd

Bonhomme St

Colin Cres

Aspen Ave

Bastian Ave

Cedar Ave

Elm Ave

Pyramid Ave

Maligne Ave

Miette Ave

Turret St

Robson St

Pyramid Lake Rd

Jasper Discovery Trail

Cabin Creek Rd

Willow Ave

Torquin St

Pine Ave

Gelkie St

Spruce Ave

Turret St

Patricia St

Connaught Dr

VIA Rail

Yellowhead Hwy

(93A)

(16)

(93)

Icefields Pkwy

VIA Rail Station

See Enlargement

To Whistlers Campground (3km); Wapiti Campground (4.3km); Becker's Chalets (6km); HI Jasper International Hostel (6km); Jasper Tramway (7km); Marmot Basin (19km); HI Mt Edith Cavell Hostel (20km)

Enlargement
Miette Ave
Gelkie St
Patricia St
Connaught Dr
VIA Rail Station
Miette River

0 — 200 m
0 — 0.1 miles

INTERNET ACCESS

Some cafés have internet and wi-fi.
More Than Mail (☎ 780-852-3151, 888-440-3151;
620 Connaught Sq Mall; per 10 mins $1; ⊙ 9am-9pm
summer, 9am-6pm winter; ⊚) Also stores luggage (per
day $2.50) and offers business services.

LAUNDRY

Coin Clean Laundry (☎ 780-852-3852; 607 Patricia St;
per load $5; ⊙ 8am-9pm; ▣) Bright and airy, washes
sleeping bags, has showers, coffee bar and fast internet
access (per hr $8).

LIBRARY

Jasper Municipal Library (☎ 780-852-3652; 500
Robson St; ⊙ 11am-9pm Mon-Thu, 11am-5pm Fri & Sat)
Small, but cheery.

MEDICAL SERVICES

Seton General Hospital (☎ 780-852-3344; 518
Robson St; ⊙ 24hr)

POST

Post office (☎ 780-852-3041; 502 Patricia St) The 1939
building is worth checking out.

TOURIST INFORMATION

Right in the heart of town, the **Jasper Information Centre** (500 Connaught Dr; ⊙ 8:30am-7pm Jun-
Sep, 9am-5pm Oct-May) is easily one of Canada's
most attractive tourist offices, and that was
before renovations in 2009. Built in 1913
as the park office and superintendent's
residence, the stone building is surrounded
by flowers and plants. The large lawn is a
popular meeting and chilling spot. It has
three information desks: **Jasper Tourism &
Commerce** (☎ 780-852-3858; www.jaspercanadian
rockies.com), **Parks Canada** (☎ 780-852-6176; www
.parkscanada.ca) and the **Friends of Jasper National
Park** (☎ 780-852-4767; www.friendsofjasper.com),
which has a store for guides and maps. See
p328 for details on the group's excellent
guided walks.

Sights

Symbolic of the rail link from Jasper to
Prince Rupert (p367), a 21m **totem pole**
carved by a Haida artist from the Queen
Charlotte Islands in 1920 stands tall outside
the station.

The small but engaging **Jasper-Yellowhead
Museum & Archives** (☎ 780-852-3013; 400 Pyramid
Lake Rd; adult/child $4/3; ⊙ 10am-5pm daily May-Oct,
Thu-Sun only Nov-Apr) uses personal stories to

bring local history to life. Good ones cover
the development of tourism 100 years ago,
when swells swanned around the Rockies
literally on the backs of laborers earning
$3.50 per day.

Brushfire Gallery (☎ 780-852-3554; cnr Elm Ave &
Patricia St; ⊙ 10am-10pm May-Sep, 10am-5pm Sat & Sun
Oct-Apr) is run by the Jasper Artists Guild and
has rotating showings of works by the many
local artists.

Jasper Tramway (☎ 780-852-3093; www.jasper
tramway.com; adult/child $28/14; ⊙ 10am-9pm Jun-
Aug, 10am-5pm Apr & May, Sep-early Oct) glides up
Whistlers Mountain – named for the whistling marmots that live at the top – in seven
minutes. Board the tramway gondolas at the
terminal, about 7km south of town along
Whistlers Mountain Rd off the Icefields
Parkway. The upper terminal sits at a chilly
2277m, where there's the usual restaurant,
some good hiking trails and panoramic views
75km south to the Columbia Icefield and
100km west to Mt Robson in BC. The summit is a 45-minute walk over the tree line.

Lakes Annette and **Edith**, a 3km walk northeast of town along Lodge Rd (off the Yellowhead Hwy), sit at an altitude of about
1000m and can be warm enough for a refreshing swim. In the wooded parks around
the lakes, you'll find beaches, hiking and
biking on paved trails, picnic areas and boat
rentals.

The small and serene **Patricia** and **Pyramid
Lakes** are in the hills behind town, about
7km northwest along Pyramid Lake Rd.
Here you'll find picnic sites, hiking and
horseback riding trails, fishing and beaches,
canoe rentals, kayaks and windsurfers. In
winter you can go cross-country skiing or
ice skating.

Activities

See p328 for Jasper activity operators that
organize a variety of adventures in winter
and summer. **Kayaking Jasper** (www.kayakjasper.
ca), a group of local enthusiasts, has much
information.

HIKING

The 8.2km **Jasper Discovery Trail** circles the
town and takes about two hours on foot.
Follow the bear logo. Branches take you on
easy walks to all the lakes listed above.

Fewer hikers tramp through Jasper than
Banff, but more wildlife scampers through

the woods, which means that you stand a good chance of spotting some. In addition to the hikes around the lakes close to Jasper, many other paths meander through the terrain. Get Parks Canada's *Day Hikers' Guide to Jasper National Park*. It lists hikes lasting from a couple of hours to all day. If the weather has been wet, you may want to avoid the lower horse trails, which can become mud baths. Topographic maps are available for all routes; buy them at the Jasper Information Centre (p327).

If you're hiking overnight, pick up copies of Parks Canada's *Backcountry Visitors' Guide* and the *Summer Trails Jasper National Park*, which offers overnight trail descriptions along with a map. If you're camping in the backcountry, you have to obtain a backcountry permit from Parks Canada.

Just one of a myriad of choices, the **Mina Lakes – Riley Lake Loop**, covers three pristine lakes in the hills behind town. Start at the trailhead near the beginning of Pyramid Lake Rd; after a mere 2km you reach lower Mina Lake. A climb of 160m and you're at upper Mina Lake. Both are spring and glacier fed. Bear east and weave through the hills and forest to teardrop-shaped Riley Lake. From here it is an easy walk back to Jasper for a loop walk of 9km.

For books on hiking in Jasper and the other national parks see boxed text p314.

CYCLING & MOUNTAIN BIKING

As in Banff National Park, you can cycle on the highways and on most of the trails in the Jasper National Park. For more information, pick up the *Trail Bicycling Guide Jasper National Park* at the Jasper Information Centre. **Freewheel Cycle** (☎ 780-852-3898; www.freewheeljasper.com; 618 Patricia St; bike rentals per day from $32; 🕙 8am-8pm) has rentals and advice. Also good is **Vicious Cycle** (☎ 780-852-1111; www.viciouscyclecanada.com; 630 Connaught Dr).

ROCK CLIMBING

Experienced climbers head to the popular Mt Morro, Messner Ridge, Mt Athabasca, Mt Andromeda and Mt Edith Cavell. In winter you can ice climb on the frozen waterfalls. Stop by **Gravity Gear** (☎ 780-852-3155, 888-852-3155; www.gravitygearjasper.com; 618 Patricia St; 🕙 9am-8pm), where you can get good advice and leads on guides, and rent equipment.

WHITE-WATER RAFTING

Calm to turbulent rafting can be found on the class III **Sunwapta River** and the class II **Athabasca River** near Athabasca Falls. Rafting (or any boat usage) is prohibited on the **Maligne River** to protect the habitat for threatened Harlequin ducks.

Numerous companies offer trips of varying lengths, including the tour companies in Jasper (below). **Raven Adventures** runs trips on the Athabasca and Sunwapta Rivers (adult/child from $60/30).

SKIING & SNOWBOARDING

Jasper National Park's sole ski area is uncrowded **Marmot Basin** (☎ 780-852-3816, 800-473-8135; www.skimarmot.com; 1-day lift pass adult/child $67/24), which is easily the most mellow of the Rocky Mountain ski resorts. It features 84 trails for both beginners and experts, plenty of scenic cross-country trails, nine lifts and a chalet. The drop is 915m. Marmot Basin is 19km southwest of town off Hwy 93A. Shuttles run to/from town all day. Gear shops in town rent a huge range of gear.

Near Maligne Lake, the **Moose Lake Loop** (8km) and the trail in the **Bald Hills** (11km) are easy introductions to the 200km of cross-country skiing in the park. The skiing season usually runs from December to April. Numerous companies also offer snowshoe treks and other icy excitement like dog-sledding.

Tours

Historic walking tours of Jasper are offered by **Friends of Jasper National Park** (☎ 780-852-4767; Jasper Information Centre; tours by donation; 🕙 7:30pm Jun-Sep).

Walks & Talks Jasper (☎ 780-852-4994, 888-242-3343; www.walksntalks.com; 626 Connaught Dr) leads small groups of people on personalized excursions that include two-hour wildlife tours (adult/child $55/25) at 6:45am from June to October, and six-hour hikes (from $65/40) that vary the route for what's best that day. Winter trips include snow-shoeing and cross-country skiing.

Sun Dog Touring Co (☎ 780-852-9663; 888-786-3641; www.sundogtours.com; 414 Connaught Dr; tours adult/child from $60/35) offers the usual wildlife tours and interesting options such as guided train rides on VIA Rail and various winter adventures.

THE ROCKIES

Jasper Adventure Centre (☎ 780-852-5595; 800-565-7547; www.jasperadventurecentre.com; 604 Connaught Dr, in the Chaba Theatre in summer; 306 Connaught Dr winter) offers numerous walks and activities. **Birding & Beaver walks** (per person $55; ⊙ Apr-Nov) offer the promise of iconic critters.

Raven Adventures (☎ 780-852-4292; www.raven adventure.com; 610 Patricia St) leads nature walks lasting two to four hours (from $50/25 per adult/child). Winter options include dog-sledding and ice-walking.

Sleeping

There are good motels close to the center allowing you to enjoy the town's vibe, which, while low-key, is open and cheery. Hostels and campgrounds are not far away. There's an outcrop of low-key higher-end places to the north.

There are more than 100 tourist homes – private homes that offer rooms to travelers – in Jasper. Many have separate entrances, full facilities, amenities such as fireplaces, high-speed internet and more. They can be both comfortable and good value. B&Bs are rare because serving food requires several bureaucratic hoop jumps. Some places may sneak you a muffin with a cup of tea. Don't report them.

The **Jasper Home Accommodation Association** (www.stayinjasper.com) has a thick booklet of member accommodations, which you can get from the info center, view online or download. On average rates range from $60 to $125 and drop considerably in the off-season. Book online, by phone to the individual owners or at the info center.

BUDGET

Jasper National Park contains 10 campgrounds operated by **Parks Canada** (reservations ☎ 877-737-3783; www.pccamping.ca; campsite from $28). They are generally open from May to September, although a few stay open until the first snowfall (which may not be much later).

Wapiti Campground (campsites $18-33) The only year-round campground, the 362 sites (93 in winter) have flush toilets and showers. A pretty and easy 4.3km walk takes you into town.

Pocahontas Campground (campsites $22) At the turnoff to the Miette Hot Springs, Pocahontas has 140 sites and flush toilets, but no showers.

Whistlers Campground (campsites $28-39) The closest campground to town, 3.5km south on Whistlers Rd (off the Icefields Parkway), is a behemoth. The whopping 781 sites can get crowded in July and August. Services include electricity, showers and flush toilets. In summer, films and nature programs are presented nightly.

HI Jasper International Hostel (☎ 780-852-3215, 866-762-4122; www.hihostels.ca; dm/r from $24/60; 📠 ⊚) On Whistlers Rd toward the Jasper Tramway, 6.3km south of Jasper, this 84-bed hostel runs a shuttle bus into town. It is a fun scene, which is good as most of the beds are in two vast dorms.

Also south of Jasper are two HI hostels that can be booked through the Jasper hostel:

HI Mt Edith Cavell Hostel (dm from $20; ⊙ mid-Jun–mid-Oct) On Mt Edith Cavell Rd 13km from the junction with Hwy 93A, this 32-bed place sits below the Angel Glacier. It offers excellent access to hiking trails, including the gorgeous Tonquin Valley. The rustic accommodations include outhouses and creek water only.

HI Maligne Canyon Hostel (dm from $20; ⊙ closed Wed Oct-Apr) Barebones but close to good hiking, this place 11.5km east of town on Maligne Canyon Rd has 24 beds in two cabins.

MIDRANGE

ourpick **Athabasca Hotel** (☎ 780-852-3386, 877-542-8422; www.athabascahotel.com; 510 Patricia St; r $70-175; ⊚) Built in 1929, the historic, charming and idiosyncratic Athabasca Hotel has been much remodeled through the years, although the stuffed animal heads on the wall still look as they did the day they got plugged. Random antiques are found in the rooms, which may have an elaborate armoire but not a desk etc. Bargain rooms share bathrooms.

Whistlers Inn (☎ 780-852-3361, 800-282-9919; www.whistlersinn.com; 105 Miette Ave; r $100-250; 📠) The 63 rooms at this older hotel are fairly basic albeit modern. The real attraction is the rooftop hot tubs with their near 360-degree views. Unlike some other local inns, the stuffed critters on display have bodies to go with their heads.

Amethyst Lodge (☎ 780-852-3394, 888-852-7737; www.mpljasper.com; 200 Connaught Dr; r from $120-220; ⊠ 📠 ⊚) You want to be on the inside looking out of this architecturally challenged inn. But it's what's inside that counts: the 97 rooms are large, some with good views and/or balconies. Service is smooth. Watch for specials online, even in summer.

THE ROCKIES

Pine Bungalows (☎ 780-852-3491; www.pine bungalows.com; 2 Cottonwood Creek Rd; cabins $125-200; ☺ May-Oct) Wake up with an elk. Okay, it's not like waking up with Marilyn Monroe (Joe DiMaggio did when the pair stayed here in 1953), but the odds are good that one of the beasts will be ruminating outside your cabin door in the morning. A 20-minute walk from town, the 72 cabins could be made with gingerbread. Most have full kitchens; some have fireplaces and some are right on the river.

Becker's Chalets (☎ 780-852-3779; www.beckers chalets.com; Icefields Parkway; r $135-200; ☺ May-Oct) Located on a beautiful bend of the Athabasca River 6km south of town, spiffy Becker's has almost 200 units, some of them clumped together in blocks and others in cute little log cabin–style buildings down by the water. Styles vary greatly. The restaurant wins plaudits.

TOP END

Park Place Inn (☎ 780-852-9770, 866-852-9770; www .parkplaceinn.com; 623 Patricia St; r $130-250; ☒ ▣) It looks a bit modern and bland from the outside but, inside, the 14 rooms are decorated in different styles from the 1930s. Some have claw-foot tubs and some have beautiful wood floors.

Fairmont Jasper Park Lodge (☎ 780-852-3301, 800-441-1414; www.fairmont.com; r $300-750; ☒ ▣ ☎ ☒) A world apart from Jasper – and not just because of the intervening Lac Beauvert and the Athabasca Rivers – this famous lodge has a massive stone and log cabin-style main building, and nine restaurants and bars. The resort features enough amenities to placate even a frisky elk, including horseback riding and a world-class golf course. The 446 rooms are scattered amongst low-rise buildings.

Eating

The best supermarket is **Robinson's IGA** (☎ 780-852-3195; 218 Connaught Dr; ☺ 8am-6pm).

Nutter's (☎ 780-852-5844; 622 Patricia St; ☺ 9am-7pm) The name doesn't refer to the people who flock here for all manner of organic, vegan and macrobiotic foods.

Trains & Lattés (☎ 780-852-7444; Jasper Train Station; snacks from $3; ☺ 8am-6pm; ☎) Enjoy fresh sandwiches, soups, smoothies, coffees and more at this train station gem, which also sells train-related mags and books, plus

model trains. Trackside tables in the sun are a treat.

Bear's Paw Bakery (☎ 780-852-3233; 4 Cedar Ave; snacks from $3; ☺ 6am-6pm Tue-Sun) Luscious baked goods and sandwiches entice at this perennial fave. A second location, **Other Paw** (☎ 780-852-2253; 610 Connaught Dr; snacks from $3; ☺ 7am-10pm; ☎) has a larger menu.

LuLu's Pizza (☎ 780-852-3373; 407 Patricia St; meals $6-20; ☺ 9am-late) Breakfast served most of the day, thick burgers, pizza and fries, lots of fries. It's no wonder you'll find mountain hounds of all kinds here year round. Or they're home on the couch getting delivery until 2am.

Evil Dave's (☎ 780-852-3323; 622 Patricia St; mains $20-35; ☺ 5-10pm) It's the dark side of adjectives at this small and hip bistro where the dishes have names like Wacked Wings, Nefarious Chicken and Diabolical Tenderloin. Fortunately descriptions are much more positive when it comes to patrons: happy.

Fiddle River (☎ 780-852-3032; 620 Connaught Dr; mains $20-35; ☺ 5-10pm) There's fine dining on the 2nd floor of this long-running fine restaurant. Fresh seafood is the main event (think line-caught wild salmon, seasonal crab etc) but the steaks and pasta are also excellent. Good Okanagan wine list.

Andy's Bistro (☎ 780-852-4559; 606 Patricia St; meals $20-40; ☺ 5-10pm) Boasting an excellent wine list, Andy's has an ambitious and seasonal menu that fuses the fusion of Vancouver with Continental standards like veal. Seafood such as scallops enjoy creative preparations. The small dining room has tables topped with white tablecloths and fresh flowers. The Swiss chef will make you a sublime fondue for two.

Drinking & Entertainment

Except for the cries of rutting elk, Jasper gets quiet early. But a few venues let you buck the trend as listed here. Most of the pubs in this section do burgers etc.

our pick Jasper Brewing Co (☎ 780-852-4111; 624 Connaught Dr; ☺ 11am-11pm) Skeptics who don't believe that this is an excellent microbrewery should try the beer sampler. Among the highlights: smooth, creamy blueberry vanilla ale; hoppy Rockhopper; and the Liftline Cream, which apes an Irish McCaffrey's.

Atha B (☎ 403-852-3386; Athabasca Hotel, 510 Patricia St; ☺ 5pm-late) In the Athabasca Hotel, this raucous institution regularly features live rock and country plus dancing.

Pete's Club (☎ 780-852-6262; 614 Patricia St; ♥ 9pm-late) The place to boogie down with your ski instructor or arrange a liaison with the guide who showed you a beaver. Locals and visitors dance to rock, rasta, hip-hop and whatever else the DJs come up with. Watch for toga nights. Toga!

Getting There & Away

BUS

Each year various operators run vans between Jasper, Lake Louise and Banff over the Icefields Parkway.

Brewster (☎ 403-762-6767; www.brewster.ca; 607 Connaught Dr) Operates express buses to/from Banff (adult/child $70/40, four hours, one daily) via Lake Louise with connections to Calgary.

Greyhound Canada (☎ 780-852-3926; 607 Connaught Dr) In the bus depot in the VIA Rail station. Services to Edmonton ($72, five hours, four daily), Prince George ($75, five hours, two daily) and Vancouver ($140, 12 hours, two daily) via Kamloops. Luggage-storage service.

Sundog (☎ 780-852-4056, 888-786-3641; www .sundogtours.com; 414 Connaught Dr) Has service to Edmonton and its airport (adult/child $100/62, five hours, one daily); summer service to Banff via Lake Louise.

TRAIN

VIA Rail (☎ 780-852-4102; www.viarail.ca; 607 Connaught Dr) has a minihub in Jasper. The legendary *Canadian* stops at Jasper three times a week en route between Vancouver and Toronto. In addition, the *Skeena* runs three times a week to Prince George, where the train continues to Prince Rupert after an overnight stay.

Getting Around

CAR

Two rental-car firms share space in the train station, at 607 Connaught Dr: **Hertz** (☎ 780-852-9640) and **National** (☎ 780-852-1117). There is also **Avis** (☎ 780-852-3970; 414 Connaught Dr).

TAXI

Jasper Taxi (☎ 780-852-3600)

AROUND JASPER

A limestone gorge about 50m deep, with waterfalls and oddball rock formations, **Maligne Canyon** is a must-stop about 12km east of Jasper on the way to Maligne (ma-*leen*) Lake on – you guessed it – Maligne Lake Rd. Continue 16km further up the road to **Medicine Lake**, the level of which rises and falls due to underground caverns; sometimes the lake simply vanishes.

The largest glacier-fed lake in the Rockies and the second-largest in the world, **Maligne Lake** lies 48km southeast of Jasper at the end of Maligne Lake Rd. The lake's beauty is hyped by private operators as one of the most scenic of mountain lakes, but this will be difficult to understand if you only stay near the parking lots and chalet. Like Lake Louise, a little effort yields big rewards. Strolling the **east side lake trail** takes under an hour and leaves 90% of the crowds behind.

Maligne Tours (☎ ticket office 780-852-3370; www .malignelake.com; Jasper Tour Center, 616 Patricia St) has a lock on local activities. You can rent a canoe ($30 per hour) – recommended – at the historic Curly Philips Boathouse. **Spirit Island Boat Cruises** (adult/child $55/27; ♥ Jun-Aug) are essential for the clichéd shot of the lake, island and soaring peaks beyond. For something different, stop off on your drive to and from the lake – there are a number of uncrowded trails alongside the rushing **Maligne River**.

If you don't have a car to get to the lake, Maligne Tours runs a **shuttle service** (one way $20; ♥ mid-May–Oct) from Jasper.

To rest your weary bones, stop at **Miette Hot Springs** (☎ 780-866-3939; adult/child $7/6; ♥ 10am-9pm May–mid-Oct), 61km northeast of Jasper off the Yellowhead Hwy (Hwy 16) near the park boundary. Miette has the warmest mineral waters in the Canadian Rockies. Left alone, the springs produce a scalding 53.9°C, but the water is cooled to a more reasonable 39°C. The modern spa includes three pools (hot, warm and freezing) and sits amidst peaks and trees.

MOUNT ROBSON PROVINCIAL PARK

A BC provincial park has full bragging rights when it comes to claiming the tallest peak in the Canadian Rockies: 3954m Mt Robson rises triumphantly within its own namesake park to the west of Jasper National Park. This huge edifice has been wowing people since the first immigrants arrived over the ice bridge from Siberia.

TOP PLACES TO SEE WILDLIFE

Like most people, you're probably looking out for big game in the Canadian Rockies – black and grizzly bears, moose, bighorn sheep and elk – but keep your eyes and ears open and your senses in tune to the murmurings of nature. There's wildlife moving all around you, whether you can see it or not. Small animals such as pikas, martens, marmots and squirrels skitter by, while almost 300 species of birds nest, hunt, mate, sing and squawk in the parks. It's hard to say where you'll definitely spot critters, so your best bet is to stay watchful. Sometimes the best thing to do is just stand still for a while and see what pops up. However, if you want to narrow the odds, try one or more of our top places to watch wildlife:

■ Bow Valley Parkway in Banff National Park (p314)

■ Maligne Rd in Jasper National Park (p324)

■ Berg Lake Trail in Mt Robson Provincial Park (below)

■ Lake Annette in Jasper National Park (p327)

■ Hwy 93A in Jasper National Park (p328)

The Yellowhead Hwy (Hwy 16) follows some of the best scenery in the park and it parallels the mainline of the Canadian National Railroad, the second trans-continental line built after the CPR (p279). Driving east on the road from Prince George (p350) affords the most dramatic vistas along what is one of BC's most scenic drives. Things really intensify at Valemount and the junction with Hwy 5. The next 20km east on Hwy 16 yields one over-powering, windshield-filling view of the peaks after another.

Mt Robson has provided climbers with a *raison d'être* since at least 1907, but this treacherous ice-shrouded peak wasn't successfully tackled until 1913. Mountaineers from all over the world come every summer to try to repeat this feat, considered one of the world's most challenging climbs.

At the base of the mountain, 18km east of the Hwy 5 junction, the **Mount Robson Visitor Centre** (☎ 250-566-4325; ☯ 8am-5pm Jun & Sep, 8am-7pm Jul & Aug) offers context on the park and runs interpretive programs during summer. One of the highlights of the park is the 22km hike to ice-blue **Berg Lake**, a three-day hike that follows the base of Mt Robson and passes through the Valley of a Thousand Falls (that's water, not hikers). Along the way, you'll pass numerous glaciers, including the Berg Glacier, which clings to Robson's northwest face. Periodically, bits of glacier fall into the lake, filling it with icebergs. You need to register and pay at the park VC; it is a good idea to

reserve space at the seven **backcountry campsites** (☎ reservations 800-689-9025; www.discover camping.ca; backcountry fee $5) before venturing onto the Berg Lake Trail.

The Fraser River begins its long and sometimes tumultuous journey through BC at its headwaters in the southwest corner of the park. (The Fraser spills into the Pacific near Vancouver after traveling some 1280km.) In August and September you can see salmon spawning in the river at Rearguard Falls. You also stand a good chance of seeing a moose.

Adjoining the park's western end is the tiny **Mount Terry Fox Provincial Park**, named after the runner who lost a leg to cancer then attempted to run what he called the 'Marathon of Hope' across Canada, aiming to raise $1 from every Canadian for cancer research. Fox averaged a remarkable 37km a day until a recurrence of cancer forced him to end his run after 144 days and 5376km.

Accommodations include three park-run campgrounds and two private spots. Close to the VC, both **Robson Meadows Campground** and **Robson River Campground** (☎ 800-689-9025; www.discovercamping.ca; campsite $19; ☯ mid-May–Sep) offer showers, flush toilets and firewood. **Lucerne Campground** (campsite $14; ☯ mid-May–Sep) is 10km west of the Alberta border on the southern shore of Yellowhead Lake.

Mount Robson Lodge (☎ 250-566-4821, 888-566-4821; www.mountrobsonlodge.com; r $80-150; ☯ mid-May–mid-Oct) has 18 log cabins and rooms with fine views of the mountain and the Fraser River. It's off Hwy 16, 5km west of the VC.

Cariboo-Chilcotin & Coast

Although diverse, there is a unifying theme across this large central region of BC: emptiness. Towns are small and distances are great. The elemental stark beauty of the province is everywhere.

The Cariboo is furthest inland. It was first opened up to outsiders in the mid-1800s when the Cariboo Wagon Rd was completed in 1858. Homesteaders and gold-seekers followed its bumpy course, stopping at tiny settlements with geographically obvious names such as 100 Mile House, 108 Mile House and so on. There's no record to show if there was a You've Gone Too Far House. The goal was Barkerville, a gold rush town you can visit today in all its restored glory.

The Chilcotin is anchored by Williams Lake, a cowboy town if ever there was one. Large ranches sprawl across the rolling land of lakes and forests. Dude Ranches can be found along its one main road, Hwy 20, which shoots due west to the coast.

And what a coast it is. From the highway's perilous plunge down to the unspoiled, lush beauty of the Bella Coola Valley, this region is an unheralded gem. It's the one place along BC's long coast where you have relatively easy access to the Great Bear Rainforest, the earth's largest surviving temperate coastal rainforest. The adventure possibilities are as great as the magnificence of the huge spruces and rivers alive with prowling bears.

An ideal way to tour this untrammeled expanse is on a circle tour combining the BC Ferries Discovery Coast Passage linking Bella Coola and Port Hardy on Vancouver Island (p30).

HIGHLIGHTS

- Losing count of eagles, bears and more in the **Bella Coola Valley** (p343)
- Showing a cow who's boss at a **Chilcotin Dude Ranch** (p342)
- Not dying but still going to canoe heaven at **Bowron Lake** (p338)
- Paddling the azure lakes of underappreciated **Wells Gray Provincial Park** (p340)
- Finding your inner homesteader at **Cottonwood House** (p337)

★ Cottonwood House
★ Bowron Lake
★ Bella Coola Valley
★ Wells Gray Provincial Park

CARIBOO-CHILCOTIN & COAST

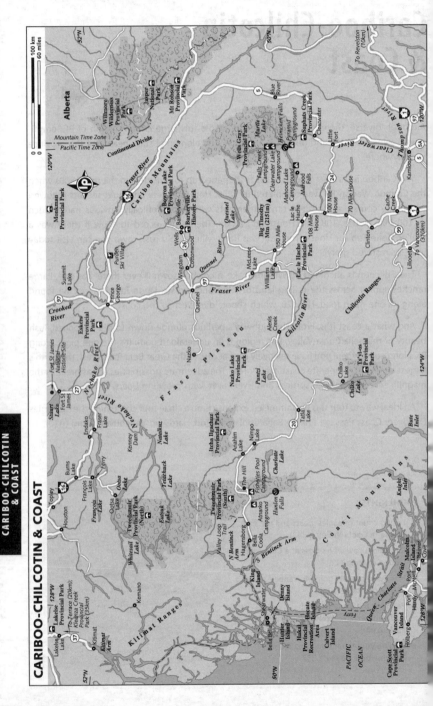

CARIBOO

Cowboy Country might as well be the name for the Cariboo region of BC. Working on the land is the way of life across this vast region, which stretches from the namesake Cariboo Mountains in the east to the Fraser Valley in the west. Ranchlands mix with forests. Hard winters give way to the long days of summer, when the grasses turn golden.

Small towns like Williams Lake provide focus for the hardy residents and offer sustenance to travelers ready to enjoy uncompromising outdoors experiences at Wells Gray Provincial Park and Bowron Lake. Cariboo was the site of a gold rush in 1862, and when word spread that gold had been found, thousands of gold-diggers came rushing in from California and the east. For more, see p337.

GOLD RUSH TRAIL/CARIBOO HIGHWAY

With boundless open ranges and rolling grassy hills, the southern interior makes excellent territory for cattle raising. Working ranches spill across the wide-open Cariboo-Chilcotin landscape.

Following the Gold Rush Trail (Hwy 97) north of Lillooet, you'll find **Clinton**, which in the 1860s had the evocative name Junction as numerous trails to the gold fields branched out from here. Its downtown streets feature western decor and some roaming dudes in cowboy boots.

100 Mile House is the retail and service hub of the south Cariboo and the place to come if you like comparing motels. Several guest ranches are located in these parts, see p342.

Williams Lake
pop 11,700

Williams Lake is a major crossroads: you can follow Hwy 20 west 456km to the coastal town of Bella Coola (p343); or you can follow the Cariboo Hwy (Hwy 97) north to McLeese Lake, a small lakeside resort with log cabins, then on to Quesnel and Prince George (240km). To the south are Kamloops and Vancouver.

Williams Lake is where trees usurp cattle as the resource of choice. Lumber yards, piles of logs and other evidence of the town's five mills surround the downtown area. About 65% of the population works in forestry. As such, the town is a workmanlike hub known mostly for a huge cowboy party that is BC's answer to the Calgary Stampede.

INFORMATION
Discovery Centre (☎ 250-392-5025; http://williams lakechamber.com; 1660 Broadway S off Hwy 97; ☼ 9am-5pm summer, 9am-4pm rest of yr; ☏) is one of BC's best VCs. Built by two local log-home builders, it's a soaring monument (memorial?) to trees. It has fascinating displays about the region and is an essential stop before heading west on Hwy 20 to the coast (p341). There's an excellent café.

SIGHTS
In 1919 the Pacific Great Eastern Railway (later BC Rail and now the Canadian National Railway) pushed its way into Williams Lake. People partied so much they decided to reenact the whole shebang again the following year. So began the **Williams Lake Stampede** (☎ 250-392-6585, 800-717-6336; williamslakestampede .com), an annual four-day hoedown that shakes the Stampede Grounds in late June and/or early July. The town's population more than doubles with cowpokes and poseur cowpokes. Cowboys compete in feats of derring-do, such as roping, barrel racing and bull riding, while companion events include the popular Stampede Queen Coronation and loggers' sports. Hotels fill and the event grows by the year. Tickets to festival events cost $15 to $60.

The small but interesting **Museum of the Cariboo Chilcotin** (☎ 250-392-7404; 113 4th Ave N; adult/child $3/free; ☼ 10am-4pm Mon-Sat Jun-Aug, 11am-4pm Tue-Sat Sep-May) features photos of Stampede Queens going back to 1933. My how hairstyles have changed! And back then racial attitudes required two queens: white and First Nations. Star bronc busters highlight the **BC Cowboy Hall of Fame**.

The old train station has been reborn as the **Station House Gallery** (☎ 250-392-6113; 1 Mackenzie Ave N; ☼ 10am-5pm Mon-Sat) with rotating exhibits by regional artists and lots of gifts.

WHITE-WATER RAFTING
Ride torrents of water for hours and never see anyone besides your raftmates, that's the experience offered by **Chilko Rafting Co**

BRIDGES OVER MANY WATERS

Cross 20 old bridges in a mere 12km on the **Williams Lake River Valley Trail**, which follows the lake's outlet through the rugged countryside to the fast-flowing waters of the mighty Fraser River. Listen for songbirds and the gnawing of a beaver. There are interpretive signs, benches and outhouses along the way. The gravel trail is good for hiking and biking.

(☎ 250-267-5258; 1118 Lakeview Crescent; trips from $125; ☑ Jul-Sep). Deep in the Cariboo region west of Williams Lake, the Chilcotin River pounds over rough lava beds and is a series of Class III and IV rapids. Trips last most of the day and include transport.

SLEEPING & EATING

Being a crossroads, Williams Lake has many chain motels. Outside of Stampede season (short as it is), you'll be able to find a room at a good price. Best picks are the string of well-maintained older motels overlooking the lake just south of the junction on Hwy 93.

Wildwood RV Park (☎ 250-989-4711; letscamp@ wlbc.net; 4195 Wildwood Rd; campsites $18-24) Located 14km north of Williams Lake, off Hwy 97, some of the 36 pitches are shaded and good for tents.

Drummond Lodge Motel (☎ 250-392-5334, 800-667-4555; www.drummondlodge.com; 1405 Hwy 97 S; r $75-120; ☒ ▢) This 23-unit place near the Discovery Centre has great views of the lake as well as beautiful gardens in the spacious grounds – get a room with a balcony. There's also high-speed internet access.

Valleyview Motel (☎ 250-392-4655; http://valley viewmoteljamboreemotel.bcmotels.com; 1523 Hwy 97 S; r $55-70; ☒) This very simple but clean roadside 18-room motel is cheaper for two people than many hostels, and you get to shut out the world and have your own bathroom. Oh, and the lake views are killer.

Gecko Tree (☎ 250-398-8983; 1024 Broadway S; meals $6-10; ☑ 8am-7pm Mon-Sat) Right at the junction, choose from (often organic) soups, baked goods, sandwiches and more. The coffees are the best in town.

GETTING THERE & AROUND

Buses run north to Prince George ($47, 3¼ hours, three daily) and south to Vancouver ($97, nine hours, three daily) from the **Greyhound Canada bus depot** (☎ 250-398-7733; 215 Donald Rd), just off Hwy 97.

Quesnel
pop 10,300

Quesnel's picturesque perch at the confluence of the Fraser and Quesnel Rivers and the impressive display of cultivated flowers along the riverfront trails are mere gloss on what is a huge logging town. The first major town after Williams Lake 124km south, it has a compact downtown with a couple of nice cafés and the aforementioned river walks to stretch your legs.

The **Visitor Centre** (☎ 250-992-8716; www .northcariboo.com; 703 Carson Ave; ☑ 8am-6pm Jun-Sep, 9am-4pm Tue-Sat Oct-May; ☞) is a winner. From Quesnel, Hwy 26 leads east to the area's main attractions, Barkerville Historic Park (p338) and Bowron Lake Provincial Park (p338).

SIGHTS & ACTIVITIES

The petite **Quesnel Museum** (703 Carson Ave; adult/ child $3/1.50; ☑ 8am-6pm Jun-Sep, 9am-4pm Tue-Sat Oct-May), in the same building as the VC, features a quirky array of antiques from the gold-rush days and a fascinating cache of historical photos of early residents, who look tough as nails.

An **observation tower** at the north end of town off Hwy 97 overlooks Two-Mile Flat, a large industrial area devoted to wood products. It's a vast, buzzing, humming and steaming place with action in all directions and all around the clock as beetle-killed trees (p59) are processed at a frantic rate. The VC may be able to arrange plant tours.

Skip driving Hwy 20 to the coast from Williams Lake and walk there from Quesnel. The 420km **Alexander Mackenzie Heritage Trail** follows ancient Nuxalk-Carrier First Nations 'grease' trails (used for trading oolichan, or fish oil) from the Fraser River west to Bella Coola, on the Pacific Ocean. In 1793 Alexander Mackenzie made the first recorded crossing of continental North America in his search to find a supply route to the Pacific Ocean. His carved graffiti can still be seen on a rock near Bella Coola (p346). The trail winds its way through forest and mountains and makes for a tough 16-day-plus walk. At least one food drop

CARIBOO-CHILCOTIN & COAST

is required. You can do some of the more accessible segments for just a few days – eg the section through the southern end of Tweedsmuir Provincial Park. You can also take day hikes from Quesnel. The **Alexander Mackenzie Voyageur Route Association** (www.amvr .org) sells *In the Steps of Alexander Mackenzie* ($20), a complete guide to the trail.

SLEEPING & EATING
Quesnel has it over Williams Lake when it comes to overnighting. Most motels and restaurants are arrayed around the compact center, meaning you can walk about with ease. The **farmers market** (☎ 250-747-8543; cnr Carson & Kinchent Sts; ☿ 8:30am-1pm Sat Mar-Oct) is a good one.

Talisman Inn (☎ 250-992-7247, 800-663-8090; www .talismaninn.bc.ca; 753 Front St; r $60-110; ☒ ▣ ⌨) Just north of downtown on Hwy 97, the Talisman is a gracious older 86-room motel kept in spotless order by the caring staff. Choose from king- or queen-size beds, then flop back and channel surf the big TVs.

Granville's Coffee (☎ 250-992-3667; 383 Reid St; meals $5-10; ☿ 7am-10pm Mon-Sat, 8am-5pm Sun) The sign out front, 'Sorry we're open,' sets the mood at this bakery/café with homemade baked goods, chili, huge sandwiches, ice cream and more. Don't pass without a muffin.

GETTING THERE & AWAY
Greyhound Canada (☎ 250-992-2231; 365 Kinchant St) buses run south to Kamloops ($62, six hours, one daily) and Vancouver ($115, 10½ hours, three daily), and north to Prince George ($26, two hours, three daily). Quesnel's small airport (YQZ) is just north of town at the junction of Hwys 97 and 26. Air Canada Jazz flies to/from Vancouver.

QUESNEL TO BARKERVILLE
Relive the pioneer days on this very worthwhile 82km jaunt off Hwy 97, which passes through country little changed since prospectors came with hope and left empty-handed. At the end you'll find Barkerville, a living ghost town replete with reenactors wandering about.

Between 1858 and 1861, when the Cariboo Wagon Rd (now Hwy 97) edged north from Kamloops to Quesnel, ramshackle towns hastily sprang up along the road built by gold prospectors, who had descended on

the region from around the world. In 1862 one member of this new international population hit the jackpot, making $1000 in the first two days of his claim. Despite his luck, Cornishman Billy Barker probably had no clue that more than 100,000 claim-jumping miners would run after his footsteps, crossing rivers, creeks and lakes to storm the Cariboo Wagon Rd in search of gold. Soon Barkerville became, for a brief time, the largest city west of Chicago and north of San Francisco. In its heyday, some 10,000 people jostled about the muddy town, hoping to hit jackpots of their own.

Cottonwood House Historic Site
The perfect appetizer for Barkerville, **Cottonwood House Historic Site** (☎ summer 250-992-2071, winter 250-983-6911; www.cottonwoodhouse .ca; adult/child $4.50/free; ☿ 10am-5pm mid-May–Aug) is a classic roadhouse from the 1860s, a time when stops like this lined the routes of the north, each about a day's ride apart. Now restored and run in conjunction with local schools, the complex evokes an older time as the wind rustles the birch and aspen trees. Apart from the roadhouse itself, there are trails that lead to other restored buildings, including a general store and barns. There are some interesting demonstration gardens and a café that sells homemade ice cream.

There's a **campground** and **rooms** (pitches $13, cabins for up to 6 people $35, r $40) where you can relax and fully absorb the quiet charms of the site. Rooms share a toilet and shower building.

Cottonwood House is 26km east of Quesnel on Hwy 26.

Wells
About 8km before you reach Barkerville, Wells is an historic gold rush town but the characters you see wandering around actually live here. The Wells **Visitor Information Centre** (☎ 250-994-2323, 877-451-9355; www.wellsbc .com; 4120 Pooley St; ☿ 9am-6pm May-Sep) runs an information center just off the highway in a small old general store. The town exists in two closely related parts: the older area up on the hill and the string of shops along the highway.

Wells Hotel (☎ 250-994-3427, 800-860-2299; www .wellshotel.com; 2341 Pooley St, Wells; r $75-130) The hub of Wells, it's been popular since 1933.

Recent renovations have restored the beautiful wooden floors and given each of the 13 rooms a private bathroom. Enjoy the good restaurant, pub and patio, then splash out in the rooftop hot tub.

Bear's Paw Café (☎ 250-994-2346; meals $5-8; 🕙 11am-9pm May-Sep) The sign out front is almost as big as the building, which should be reason enough not to miss this café right on Hwy 26 in Wells. The best food for miles is right here. Look for excellent grilled meats with Mediterranean-accented sides. The owners also run the funky Frog on the Bog gift shop/bakery across the street.

Barkerville Historic Park

What would Billy say if he saw his town today? Now called **Barkerville Historic Park** (☎ 888-994-3332 ext 29; www.barkerville.ca; adult/child $14/4; 🕙 8am-8pm mid-May–Sep), more than 125 buildings have been restored to their former glory, including a hotel, various stores and a saloon. In summer, people dressed in period garb roam through town, and if you can tune out the crowds it actually manages to create a historical mood. (In the Theatre Royal, dancing shows are staged in a family-friendly manner that would have caused mayhem among rough-and-tumble miners.)

Free historic walking tours relate the history of the gold rush, the experience of the Chinese workers who built the Cariboo Hwy, and the finer details of the art of panning for gold. Many businesses can be found along the streets, including one serving homemade root beer and another recreating baked goods from way back when (but without the wiggly things in the flour). The entire experience is less hokey than it sounds.

Outside of summer, the town site is open but most of the attractions are closed, which may actually make for a more evocative visit. Breezes rustle the trees and as you walk the quiet streets you might just be able to take yourself back in time.

SLEEPING & EATING

BC Parks (☎ 866-994-3297; www.barkervillecampgrounds.ca) runs three campgrounds with a total of 168 pitches around tiny Barkerville. Closest to the town site and mostly used by campers with tents (not RVs) is Government Hill Campground (campsites $17).

The 23 sites come with pit toilets but no showers.

Kelly House (☎ 250-994-3328, 866-994-0004; www.kellyhouse.ca; r $90-105) The three-room Kelly House is the sort of place you'd expect the 'dude' to live in old Westerns. The rooms have lots of flouncy fabrics and antiques (two share a bath). The owners can arrange activities from horse-riding to gold-panning.

St George Hotel (☎ 250-994-0008, 888-246-7690; www.stgeorgehotel.bc.ca; r $110-140) Inside historic Barkerville, the St George dates from the 1890s. The seven rooms look like scenes out of a Western, all are filled with antiques – it must be almost eerie after the last day-trippers have left. A stay here includes breakfast.

BOWRON LAKE PROVINCIAL PARK

This circular chain of lakes is the ultimate string of pearls for people who love to canoe. The 116km circular **canoe route** passes through 10 lakes: Bowron, Kibbee, Indianpoint, Isaac, McLeary, Lanezi, Sandy, Babcock, Skoi and Swan, and over sections of the Isaac, Cariboo and Bowron Rivers. In between are eight portages over well-defined trails that can accommodate wheeled canoe carriers, with the longest 2km. The trip takes six to 10 days. You'll find backcountry campgrounds along the way; to make sure there are sites for everyone, the park service only allows a limited number of canoes to start the circuit each day. You must bring your own food (or catch it).

The Mowdish Range runs right through the middle of the loop, while the Cariboo Range surrounds the perimeter of this amazing park, affording spectacular views no matter in which direction you look. And you might see moose, black and grizzly bears, caribou and mountain goats. In late summer you stand a very good chance of spotting bears on the upper Bowron River, where they feed on spawning sockeye salmon.

Weather will let you paddle this circuit anytime from mid-May to October. People generally choose to do the circuit in July and August, but September is also an excellent choice, since that's when the leaves change color. Mosquitoes, which thrive in the wet, relatively windless environment, are most ravenous in spring.

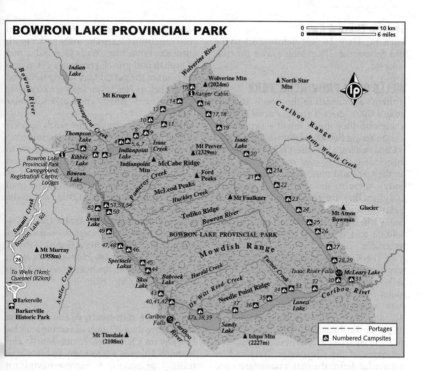

BOWRON LAKE PROVINCIAL PARK

Legend:
– – – – Portages
🔺 Numbered Campsites

Before planning your trip, visit **BC Parks** (www.env.gov.bc.ca/bcparks) and download the essential Bowron Lake Canoe Circuit Pre-Trip Information document. You will then need to make reservations with **BC Parks** (☎ 800-435-5622, outside North America 250-387-1642) to reserve your circuit. This can be done around January 2. The fee is $60 per person plus an $18 reservation fee. Once you get to the park, go to the **Registration Centre** (✆ 8am-6pm mid-May–Sep) at the time given when you make your reservation. Once there you'll be given an orientation.

If the full circuit doesn't sound like your thing, you can leave the multiday paddle to the hard-core types and just do day trips on Bowron Lake, which require no advance registration or fee.

Activities

Whitegold Adventures (☎ 250-994-2345, 866-994-2345; www.whitegold.ca; Hwy 26, Wells), based in Wells, offers four- to eight-day guided paddles around Bowron Lake. The full eight-day circuit, including guides and food, costs $1700 per person.

Bowron Lake Lodge (below) offers 10-day canoe rentals from $160. Becker's Lodge (below) offers similar services.

Sleeping

There are no independent licensed restaurants in the Bowron Lake area. You have to drive the 28km to Wells.

Bowron Lake Provincial Park Campground (campsites $15) Near the Registration Centre, this campground has 25 shady, nonreservable pitches and pit toilets.

Bowron Lake Lodge (☎ 250-992-2733, 800-519-3399; www.bowronlakelodge.com; r $65-90; ✆ May-Sep) With a postcard location right on the lake, this lodge is always popular. Decor of the motel rooms and cabins is, well, timeless. You can also camp at one of 50 pitches (some on the lake) for $24.

Becker's Lodge (☎ 250-992-8864, 800-808-4761; www.beckerslodge.ca; r $80-220) Just up the road, the attractive Becker's features nice log chalets and cabins. The 25 pitches cost $20 to $30, including firewood and use of facilities. The licensed restaurant may or may not be open from 2010 on.

Getting There & Away
Turn off Hwy 26 just before Barkerville and follow the 28km-long gravel Bowron Lake Rd.

WELLS GRAY PROVINCIAL PARK
If there's a waterfall in the woods and no-body's there, does it make a noise? That's a question they might ask at – supposedly – thundering **Helmcken Falls**, which at 141m is Canada's fourth-highest falls. And do the mist laden clouds over the falls rain dew on the tree- and moss-covered gorge if no-body's there to get wet? Good questions and ones that are germane given the utter isolation you'll find in Wells Gray Provincial Park, a wonderland of lakes, peaks, wildlife and dozens of purportedly noisy waterfalls.

In the Cariboo Mountains about half-way between Kamloops and Jasper, off the Yellowhead South Hwy (Hwy 5), the enormous 5410 sq km Wells Gray Provincial Park is a seldom-visited gem in the vast BC interior. It is the fourth-largest park in BC, after Tatshenshini-Alsek, Tweedsmuir and the Spatsizi Wilderness Plateau. The drainages of the Clearwater River and its tributaries define the park's boundaries and give visitors five major lakes, two large river systems and plenty of features to explore.

Though First Nations people have long lived in the area, it was a group of Over-landers (gold seekers who came from the east side of the Rockies, many starving), who named the river for its crystal-clear waters in 1862. The area remained vast wilderness until various settlers started moving in. Fur trapper John Ray was the first white man to settle in the area and one of the last to leave. Remnants of his homestead, the **Ray Farm**, are now a park attraction, reachable by a 1km hike.

When giant waterfalls were discovered in 1913, people began making appeals to the government to protect the area as parkland. It finally happened in 1939, and the park just happened to take its name from the government official responsible, Arthur Wellesley Gray.

Orientation & Information
Most people enter the park via the town of Clearwater on Hwy 5, 123km north of Kamloops and 216km south of the point where Hwy 5 splits off Hwy 16. A 36km paved road runs from Clearwater to the park's south entrance. From here, Wells Gray Rd, a mix of asphalt and gravel, penetrates 29km into the heart of the park. Many hiking trails and sights such as Helmcken Falls are accessible off this road, which ends at Clearwater Lake.

Alternatively, you can also reach the west side of the park from 100 Mile House on Hwy 97 via an 86km gravel road that leads to Mahood Falls and the west end of Mahood Lake. From Blue River, 107km north of Clearwater on Hwy 5, a 24km gravel road and 2.5km track lead to Murtle Lake in the southeast part of the park.

The **Visitor Information Centre** (☎ 250-674-2646; www.clearwaterbcchamber.com, www.wellsgray country.ca; 425 E Yellowhead Hwy at Clearwater Valley Rd, Clearwater; ☒ 9am-5pm daily Jul & Aug, Mon-Fri Apr-Jun & Sep-Dec) should be the mandatory first stop of your Wells Gray visit.

Activities
You can **hike**, **cross-country ski** and **ride a horse** along more than 20 trails of varying lengths. **Canoeing** on Clearwater, Azure, Murtle and Mahood Lakes is a good way to blaze new trails – or wakes. A narrow navigation channel from the north end of **Clearwater Lake** connects to the west end of **Azure Lake**; the two lakes form an upside-down 'L'.

You can only reach the 69 sq km **Murtle Lake** from the Blue River park entrance. It is renowned for being the largest lake without power boats in North America. The golden sand beach is simply a bonus. You can reach **Mahood Lake**, on the southwest side of Wells Gray, from 100 Mile House (see Orientation & Information, above).

Rustic backcountry campgrounds dot the area around all four lakes. To rent canoes, contact **Clearwater Lake Tours** (☎ 250-674-2121; www.clearwaterlaketours.com; per day from $50), which also leads a variety of canoe tours in the park.

The **Clearwater River** makes for some excellent, adrenaline-pumping white-water rafting. **Interior Whitewater Expeditions** (☎ 250-674-3727, 800-661-7238; www.interiorwhitewater.bc.ca; Clearwater; adult/child from $100/80) runs the river with a variety of trips.

Saying you can go backcountry hiking here is really an oxymoron as the entire place is backcountry, but among the dozens of hikes is a 15km one-way trek up to **Horse-shoe Falls** on the Murtle River. Side trips lead to panoramas atop Pyramid Mountain and azure Pyramid Lakes.

Sleeping & Eating

There are no commercial operations in the park, but just outside of the south gate you'll find a couple of excellent accommodations options along Clearwater Valley Rd. Clearwater is spread out but it is a convenient place for provisions. There are several motels on or – better – off Hwy 5. The town's main strip mall has the oddly named **Safety Mart Foods** (☎ 250-674-2632; Clearwater; ✆ 8am-8pm), an excellent supermarket with a good bakery and great deli.

There are three vehicle-accessible **campgrounds** (☎ 250-674-2194; pitches $15) in the park, all with pit toilets but no showers. One of the prettiest, the 50-pitch **Pyramid Campground** (✆ May-Oct), is just 5km north of the park's south entrance and close to Helmcken Falls.

Dutch Lake Resort (☎ 250-674-3351, 888-884-4424; www.dutchlake.com; 361 Ridge Dr, Clearwater; r $100-220) Nine cabins of varying sizes line part of the lakeshore of the diminutive namesake lake near the entrance to Clearwater. There are also a few motel units and 65 tent pitches (from $25). Rent a canoe and practice for greater fun in the park.

Helmcken Falls Lodge (☎ 250-674-3657; www .helmckenfalls.com; 4373 Clearwater Valley Rd; r $150-200; ✆ May–mid-Oct, late Dec-Mar) A rustic delight – guests stay in 21 modern rooms in four buildings, with delicious meals served in the red barn-like main lodge, which was built in 1948. The lodge rents canoes and offers horseback-riding trips. Cross-country skiers find warm refuge here in winter. Pitches are $15 to $25.

Wells Gray Guest Ranch (☎ 250-674-2792, 866-467-4346; www.wellsgrayranch.com; campsites $20, r $85-150) This ranch has 12 rooms in cabins and the main lodge building; everything seems to be made of logs. Live out the Wild West motif with a horseback ride; nature hikes and canoe trips are also offered. It's 27km north of Clearwater.

YELLOWHEAD SOUTH HWY

Confusingly dubbed the 'Yellowhead South Hwy,' Hwy 5 breaks with the main Yellowhead Hwy just west of Mt Robson Provincial Park (p331). The 349km stretch between this junction south to Kamloops (p239) doesn't have any *killer* scenery but it does have a lot of *nice* scenery. The gently rolling hills are occasionally punctuated by higher peaks and the road parallels the Thompson River – and the Canadian National Railway – for most of its length. Conditions are excellent and while not busy it is well used, especially by trucks linking Edmonton with the Lower Mainland.

The obvious highlight is Clearwater (opposite), gateway to Wells Gray Provincial Park, otherwise you'll find services and reasons to stop are few and far between.

CHILCOTIN

The Cariboo may seem thinly populated, but wait until you reach the Chilcotin. Vast cattle ranches and scattered Tsilhqot'in First Nations villages are about it civilization-wise for this vast high plateau of brown grasses, forests and lakes. Highway 20 barely makes a mark as it cuts across the middle to Bella Coola and the coast. For extensive information on the region, visit the Discovery Centre (p335) in Williams Lake.

HIGHWAY 20

Fabled and feared, this legendary road is really a pussycat. It's now paved for most of its 456km length and, with the exception of the Hill (p342), is a modern and pleasant road that you should easily traverse in five to six hours.

Just west of Williams Lake, Hwy 20 crosses over the Fraser River, which marks the boundary between the Cariboo and

---

DETOUR: TS'YL-OS PROVINCIAL PARK

You can get to the north end of 2332-sq-km **Ts'yl-os Provincial Park** (*sigh*-loss) by turning south off Hwy 20 at the town of Tatla Lake (219km west) and following the gravel road 63km to the rustic campground on the north tip of Chilko Lake, the largest high-altitude natural lake on the continent. Wildlife thrives here, and Chilko Lake is chock-full of fish.

GIDDYUP PILGRIM!

The Cariboo-Chilcotin has many cattle ranches that accept guests who revel in the chance to spend time playing cowboy in the kind of tree-studded pasturelands that bring a tear to the eye of John Wayne fans and cause suburbanites to go and buy SUVs.

The guest ranches span the spectrum of experiences. Some are little more than luxury resorts, with golf courses, spas and maybe a bean or two mixed in with the *pico de gallo* at the gourmet dinner. But others really are working ranches and guests do get a chance to experience the daily lives of ranchers – even if they are spared the constant concern about commodities prices, government bureaucrats, mad cow disease and the like.

Most charge about $150 to $250 per person per night (kids less) and that includes all meals and activities. Horseback riding is core to the ranch experience and at some you can go right along on a cattle drive (where the cowboys often say it's easier to herd the cattle – or even cats – than the dudes). Guided hikes are also favorites.

The **BC Guest Ranchers Association** (☎ 877-278-2922; www.bcgra.com) has detailed listings of ranches across the province. In the Cariboo-Chilcotin, popular ranches include:

■ **Big Creek Lodge** (☎ 250-394-4831; www.bigcreeklodgebc.com) In the deepest Chilcotin and in the shadow of the coast range, this hand-built lodge offers surprising comfort amidst a working ranch.

■ **Chezacut Wilderness & Ranch Adventures** (☎ 250-394-4410; www.chezacutwildernessadventures. com) One of the most environmentally conscious ranches in BC, cattle are raised organically; guests enjoy food that is both local and organic.

■ **Crystal Waters Guest Ranch** (☎ 604-465-9829; www.crystalwatersranch.com) Has log cabins at its lakeside location off Hwy 24 east of 100 Mile House.

■ **Wolf Valley Guest Ranch** (☎ 250-395-6694; www.wolfvalleyranch.com) You can work the trail kinks out in a sauna or gather round a campfire. Near 100 Mile House.

---

the Chilcotin. Enjoy the wide open landscape dotted by lakes for much of the route before you reach the coast mountains, where the landscape makes a dramatic shift to craggy bluffs and rushing rivers before dropping down into the wet, lush central coast (opposite).

Bella Coola is only accessible by car on Hwy 20 or by ferry (see p345) and there is no public transport on this route so you will need your own vehicle. Successful hitching is unlikely and cycling would only be for the most determined and fit. Gas is limited, as are cafés, so you should bring a full tank of gas and a picnic from Williams Lake. There is no cell phone service in the region so come prepared should your vehicle quit. All along the road you'll see evidence of beetle infestation (p401). The website for the West Chilcotin Tourism Association (www.visit thewestchilcotin.com) is an excellent resource.

From Hwy 20 you can take numerous side roads – most of which are gravel – to some of the province's most remote car-accessible provincial parks.

Great canoeing possibilities draw adventurers to seek out **Nazko Lake Provincial Park**, which is reached by 32km of graveled Alexis Lakes Rd, off Hwy 20 117km west of Williams Lake. Some 54km further on, **Puntzi Lake** (171km west) is good for picnics and echoes to the calls of trumpeter swans in the fall.

Nimpo Lake (295km west) is often abuzz with floatplanes serving fishing resorts on remote lakes. West of here, Hwy 20 wanders through mountains, passing by small towns with limited services, such as **Anahim Lake** (313km west). From here there's paved road as far as the Hill (356km west).

THE HILL

Prior to 1953 the only way out of Bella Coola was by boat or packhorse through the Chilcotin. Then a group of locals decided that enough was enough and they took matters into their own hands. Ignoring government engineers who said it was impossible, they carved their way up the side of the mountain, creating what is sometimes called the 'Freedom Rd.' It was perilous then and it seems perilous now. Over the 30km gravel stretch from Heckman's Pass (elevation 1524m) to the base of the hill (nearly sea level) there are 10% to 18% grades and constant sharp switchbacks. But that's just the dramatic stuff. The reality is that the road is wide, and sight lines are good. Put your vehicle in low gear, take your time and you'll actually enjoy the view. To get an idea of what lies ahead, stop at the viewpoint right before the grade begins.

THE COAST

It is only fitting that the dry plains of the Chilcotin suddenly give way to the temperate rainforest of the Coast region in dramatic fashion. And the Hill is all the drama most people could hope for. Reaching the bottom, you're in the wet and wonderful world of the Great Bear Rainforest (p346). Huge stands of trees line the steep peaks, punctuated by sheer rock faces. Here and there is the trace of a glacier and everything is cleaved by wild river valleys surging with white water.

Across this part of BC's coast, waters empty out into deep ocean fjords that curl majestically through coastal peaks and islands. It's all stunning but also very inaccessible. The area in and around Bella Coola is one of the few places easily reached in this enormous wild area between Prince Rupert (p367) in the north and Powell River (p157) on the Sunshine Coast.

Once you're at the bottom of the Hill (386km west of Williams Lake), you are in Bella Coola Valley that stretches 53km to Bella Coola and the North Bentinck Arm, the fjord which runs 40km inland from the Pacific. Your activities here have no limits. Hike into the hills and valleys starting from roads or at points only accessible by boat along the seemingly impenetrable shore.

And no matter what you do, you can enjoy the unique vibe of the valley, a delightful eccentricity common to end-of-the-road places everywhere. Artists, wanderers and dreamers abound.

TWEEDSMUIR PROVINCIAL PARK (SOUTH)

You are in this gigantic, roughly arrowhead-shaped park when you drive the Hill. At 9810 sq km, **Tweedsmuir** (☎ 250-398-4414; www.env.gov.bc.ca/bcparks) is the second-largest provincial park in BC (after Tatshenshini-Alsek in the northwest corner of BC); the southern part is 5060 sq km. The Dean River, roughly halfway up the park, divides Tweedsmuir into northern and southern portions. Hwy 20 is the only road through this wilderness park; it skirts the southern tip.

Tweedsmuir Provincial Park's features include the **Rainbow Range**, north of Hwy 20. The colorful dome of eroded rock and lava mountains appears, at certain lights, orange, red, yellow and purple. Most of the hiking in the park requires serious preplanning. The BC Parks website has good information and links to outfitters that support backcountry travel in the park. Many people access areas via floatplanes chartered in Nimpo on Hwy 20.

The most popular trek is to **Hunlen Falls**, which plummet 260m into the Atnarko River at the north end of **Turner Lake**. Access starts at Tote Rd, an 11km 4WD-only road that starts at the base of the Hill. From the road's end, it's a 16.4km hike up the side of a hill (78 switchbacks) in an area where grizzly bears are common. The reward is the stunning falls and the start of the Turner Lake chain. The latter is a canoeist's fantasyland; access is via floatplane.

Down in the Bella Coola Valley there's the just slightly wild **Valley Loop Trail** that includes the trailhead of the Alexander Mackenzie Heritage Trail (p336). It runs up one side of Burnt Bridge Creek, across a small suspension bridge and down the other side for a total of 5km of raw nature and valley vistas. The start is 402km west of Williams Lake.

The most developed and pleasant camping in the park is at **Atnarko Campground** (pitches $15; ⊗ Jun-Aug) on Hwy 20 at the start of Tote Rd. The 28 sites here are set in old-growth forest.

Tweedsmuir Provincial Park (North) is mostly reached by roads off the Yellowhead Hwy (see p361).

BELLA COOLA VALLEY

It may be the only valley in the Coast region that's easy to get to, but it's a stunner. Alexander Mackenzie would probably have agreed. He traveled through this area on his way to becoming the first white person to make it to the northwest coast, and indeed literally left his mark written in grease and vermilion on a rock near Bella Coola on July 22, 1793 (see p346 and p34). Long before that, Bella Coola and Chilcotin peoples thrived along the rivers, which were veritable supermarkets of salmon.

Although bears (and bald eagles and salmon and…) outnumber humans, about half of the population today is made up of First Nations people, descendants of the Nuxalk-Carriers. The Nuxalk (*new*-hawk) are well known for their carvings, paintings and trademark use of cobalt blue, which you'll see in artwork throughout the valley.

The two main towns, Bella Coola on the water and Hagensborg 15km east, run together, with most places of interest in or between the two. Some call Hwy 20 the Mackenzie Hwy.

Information

For information on the region, contact **Bella Coola Valley Tourism** (☎ 250-799-5202, 866-799-5202; www.bellacoola.ca; Co-op Store, cnr Mackenzie St & Burke Ave, Bella Coola; ☯ 9am-5:30pm Jun-early Sep, earlier for ferry arrivals). This well-run place can help you navigate the mysteries and delights of the valley. Most places aimed at visitors are open May to September, although some are year-round. Both the VC and your accommodations can point you to guides and gear for skiing, mountain biking, fishing, rafting and much more.

Services like car repair, ATMs, laundry and the like are easily found. **Kopas Store** (☎ 250-799-5553; Mackenzie St, Bella Coola) has gifts, art, outdoor gear and local books that include some by the store's owners and *Bella Coola, Life in the Heart of the Coastal Mountains*, co-authored by Hans Granander and Michael Wigle.

Another worthy tome is *Grizzlies & White Guys*, a great read by Clayton Mack, hunter, logger, tracker, guide and Nuxalk nation elder. His insight into the turbulent minds of bears and tourists is fascinating.

Sights & Activities

As you drive west on Hwy 20 from the Hill, you'll see the odd house here and there but little else in terms of development until you reach **Hagensborg** (population 530; 432km west), settled in 1895 by a hardy group of Norwegians whose hand-hewn homes were built with crude saws and axes. Attracted to the area because it resembled their homeland, the Norwegians stayed and entrenched themselves in Northern BC. Today the Scandinavian influence is still evident, and many residents still get cravings for lutefisk. Small, tidy farms line the road.

The valley is renowned for bears. our pick **Kynoch West Coast Adventures** (☎ 250-982-2298; www.kynochadventures.com; 1900 Hwy 20, Hagensborg) specializes in critter-spotting float trips down local rivers (from $95, three to five hours). It offers many other tours as well.

There's a good, short hike just west of Hagensborg at **Walker Island Park** on the edge of the wide and rocky Bella Coola River floodplain. Upon leaving the parking area you are immediately in the middle of a grove of cedars that are 500 years old. To fully appreciate some of the sylvan vistas, saddle up for a horse ride with **Rolling Pigeon Ranch** (☎ 250-982-0010; trail rides per hr from $45). Or peddle your way through the beauty with a bike from **Rick's Re:Cycling** (☎ 250-982-2722; Bella Coola; rental per day from $30).

The local rivers are alive with salmon and you can buy succulent smoked variations at **Bella Coola Valley Seafoods** (☎ 250-982-2716; ☯ 8am-6pm), where the motto is, 'Just say no to farmed salmon.' It's 5.7km off Hwy 20 on Salloompt River Rd.

Further east, at the small but exquisite **Petroglyph Gallery** (☎ 250-799-5673; www.petroglyph gallery.ca; Four Mile Reserve), you can marvel at the

---

DETOUR: ODEGAARD FALLS & PURGATORY POINT LOOKOUT

About 6km east of Hagensborg, Hwy 20 crosses the Nusatsum River Bridge. On the west side turn onto the forest service road and go 24km through rugged coast range forest until you reach an obvious clearing. Here there's a lookout over the river, and 1km further you'll find the trailhead for a 2km trail down to the river and on to crashing **Odegaard Falls**. Until this point the road, when dry, is just passable for cars. With a 4WD, continue over a very crude abandoned loggers road another 8km to the **Purgatory Point Lookout**. It's the end of the road, but the view down into the vast valley extending to the Pacific is really a backcountry hiker's dream.

work of Nuxalk artists like Alvin Mack and Silyas Saunders.

The village of **Bella Coola** (population 880; 437km west) sits at the mouth of the Bella Coola River where it spills into the deep North Bentinck Arm. Like the rest of the valley, it is surrounded by the sharp, spectacular Coast Mountains. The **Bella Coola Museum** (☎ 250-799-5657), on Hwy 20 just west of Mackenzie St, provides lots of valley context (phone to check for opening hours) and a good historical walking tour brochure.

About 2km west of town, **Government Dock** and the ferry terminal are an interesting stroll and good for gazing over the estuary; just beyond is a brief walk to **Clayton Falls**.

Sleeping & Eating

There are dozens of B&Bs and small lodges in the valley. Many offer evening meals; otherwise, there are a couple of cafés and motels in Bella Coola. There are grocery stores. In season, **Moore's Organic Market** (☎ 250-799-5975; 888 S Grand Rd; ☻ varies) has a luscious range of organic and local foods. The berries, yum!

Bailey Bridge Campsite & Cabins (☎ 250-982-2342; www.baileybridge.ca; Salloompt River Rd; pitches from $15, cabins from $55) Near the namesake bridge, nicely shaded pitches and cabins dot the river bank. A small store has gear and supplies.

ourpick **Bella Coola's Eagle Lodge** (☎ 250-799-5587, 866-799-5587; www.eaglelodgebc.com; 1103 Hwy 20, Bella Coola; r $70-200; ▯ ☎) Like a vacation retreat, Eagle Lodge is on a grassy spread and has nine rooms of varying sizes. There's a huge games room, a large hot tub and on request guests can enjoy great dinners. Ask Rosemary to give you her intriguing history talk.

Coast Mountain Lodge (☎ 250-982-2298; www.coastmountainlodge.com; 1900 Hwy 20, Hagensborg; r from $95; ▯ ☎) The 14 rooms are huge, and many have kitchen facilities. There's a cute little coffee bar with an internet terminal. The owners also run Kynoch West Coast Adventures (opposite); guests can rent minivans (per day $55).

Sinclair House (☎ 250-982-2435, 888-867-6668; www.bbcanada.com/2746.html; 3360 Hwy 20, Hagensborg; r $90-95; ▯) Rose gardens surround this shingled country house and there seems to be a mountain peaking behind every flowering shrub in summer. Full breakfasts and

a hot tub are included. Guests can arrange for elegant catered meals or simple sack lunches.

Tallheo Cannery Inn B&B (☎ 250-982-2344; www.centralcoastbc.com; r from $100) One BC's most amazing places to stay is across the inlet from Bella Coola in an old cannery. On approach by boat you may have misgivings – large portions over the water are collapsing. But, fear not, the rooms in an old 1920s bunkhouse are on solid ground. The adventurous will find that the views (stunning!), explorations (it's an entire village) and mystery (abandoned detritus of an old cannery) make this a fascinating stay.

Getting There & Away

Combining a trip on BC Ferries with Hwy 20 for an unbeatable circle tour of the Bella Coola Valley (p30), the Chilcotin and Cariboo is a great itinerary. **BC Ferries** (☎ 888-223-3779; www.bcferries.com) runs the Discovery Coast ferry (adult/child $150/75, car from $305), which links Bella Coola and Port Hardy on Vancouver Island on a schedule that is at times confounding. The boat normally used, the *Queen of Chilliwack* is not exactly the queen of the fleet and seems more barge than boat. It lacks cabins, so daytime trips are best but there are night services. The boat sometimes stops in remote coastal communities, which means the voyage can last anywhere from 13 to 25 hours. This journey covers part of the Inside Passage – for more on this route see the boxed text, p431.

There is no transport along Hwy 20 to Williams Lake although you can get there by charter plane. **Pacific Coastal Airlines** (☎ 800-663-2872; www.pacificcoastal.com) has flights (1¼ hours) between Bella Coola (QBC) and Vancouver's South Terminal.

Bella Coola's Eagle Lodge (left) rents out two-seater Smart cars ($65 per day, perfectly functional for all mainstream valley driving), which are mere cubs in comparison to the bear that is the other vehicle, a 4WD Suburban ($85 per day). Guests get reduced rates.

THE COAST & ISLANDS

The best way to appreciate the wild BC coast is from the deck of a BC Ferry on the Discovery Coast run to/from Bella Coola (above). This is the heart of the Great Bear

THE GREAT BEAR RAINFOREST

It's one of the last places like it on earth. The Great Bear Rainforest is a wild and remote region of islands, fjords and towering peaks on the BC coast, stretching south from Alaska along the BC coast and Queen Charlotte Islands to roughly Campbell River on Vancouver Island (which isn't part of the forest). Covering 64,000 sq km (or 7% of what's already a very large province), this is the last major tract of coastal temperate rainforest left anywhere. It's remarkably rich in life, from wild salmon and whales to eagles, elk and huge stands of ancient old-growth timber. It's also under huge threat.

As you survey the wilds around Bella Coola, which is roughly at the center of the Great Bear, you might not perceive the threat, but it's there. Remote river valleys are lined with forests of old Sitka spruce, Pacific silver fir and various cedars that are often 100m tall and 1500 years old. Logging companies eye the rest hungrily. In the meantime conservationists have achieved some modest victories. A 2006 agreement gave permanent protection to 18,000 sq km but also left the remaining 45,000 sq km open to 'sustainable' logging.

But the devil is in the details and BC government has missed deadlines for funding the conservation. As you gaze in rapt awe at the Great Bear's wild and mostly impenetrable beauty from the deck of a ferry or on a backcountry hike, you can think about what you can do to help save the rest. See p58 for some of the environmental groups active in the Great Bear Rainforest. The website www.savethegreatbear.org is also a good source of info.

And the name? That's in honor of the 'spirit bears' or Kermode bears that live in the rainforest here. In First Nations legend the raven turned one of every 10 bears white to show the people the earth's purity during the ice age. The bears, which are not albino but rather a genetic variation of black bear with white fur, only number a few hundred and live exclusively in the Great Bear Rainforest.

Rainforest and a place where even orcas outnumber people. Small First Nations villages like **Bella Bella**, on the west coast of Campbell Island, are isolated and not visited by many, but for the intrepid who do their homework the opportunities for having an ocean cove or entire driftwood-covered beach to yourself are unlimited.

Closer to Bella Coola, you should be able to arrange for a boat excursion if you ask around. Destinations can include hidden rivers where you might see a **Kermode bear** (above), the **rock** signed by Alexander Mackenzie in 1793 (someone later replaced the paint with carving) or a small **beachside hot spring** on the South Bentinck Arm.

Northern BC

A lone totem pole stands as a sentinel in the endless dusk of summer, its features at once animated and phlegmatic. The tall, erect fins of a pod of orcas cut across the water, hinting at the perfect marine athletes swimming below the surface. A long and lonely road stretches to an enigmatic horizon, offering escape, adventure, mystery and promise.

These are just some of the images you'll encounter in Northern BC, the largest region of the province. In the words of local author Betsy Trumpener, 'There's still the feeling here of being on the frontier, on the brink of the undiscovered.'

Going east to west, one important icon is found in Dawson Creek: Mile 0 of the Alaska Hwy, the road to the Yukon whose very name conjures up the images of the north. Near the center, Prince George is the ultimate crossroads, a place adept at sending travelers to the next destination even as it offers delights to those who linger.

Heading west, the Yellowhead Hwy curves through the ever-more-dramatic scenery to the coast. Smithers is a mountain town with a folk music vibe. Branching north, the lonely Stewart-Cassiar Hwy gives the Alaska Hwy stiff competition for Yukon access and it's the road of choice for anyone ready to stand awe-struck in the massive presence of glaciers.

On the Pacific, Prince Rupert is a town whose ups and downs form a dramatic arc to myriad diversions, while serving as a jumping-off point for Inside Passage voyages to the Yukon. Finally, the Queen Charlotte Islands (Haida Gwaii) are a treasure of First Nations culture and raw natural beauty.

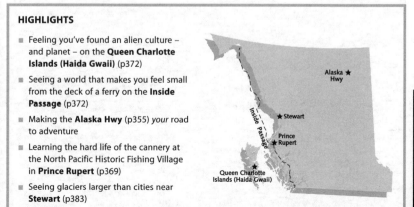

HIGHLIGHTS

- Feeling you've found an alien culture – and planet – on the **Queen Charlotte Islands (Haida Gwaii)** (p372)
- Seeing a world that makes you feel small from the deck of a ferry on the **Inside Passage** (p372)
- Making the **Alaska Hwy** (p355) *your* road to adventure
- Learning the hard life of the cannery at the North Pacific Historic Fishing Village in **Prince Rupert** (p369)
- Seeing glaciers larger than cities near **Stewart** (p383)

NORTHERN BC

NORTHERN BC

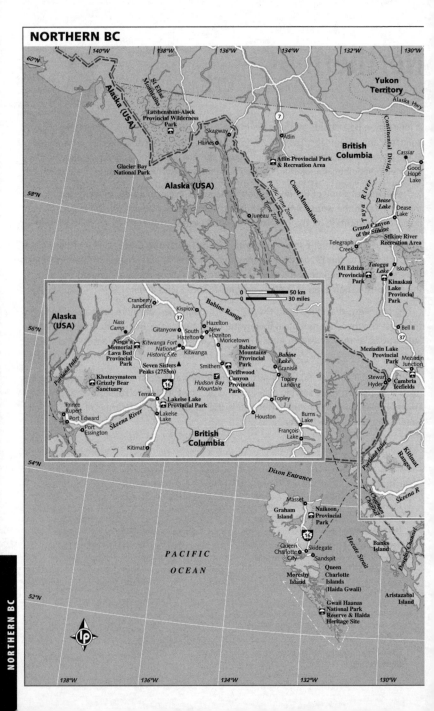

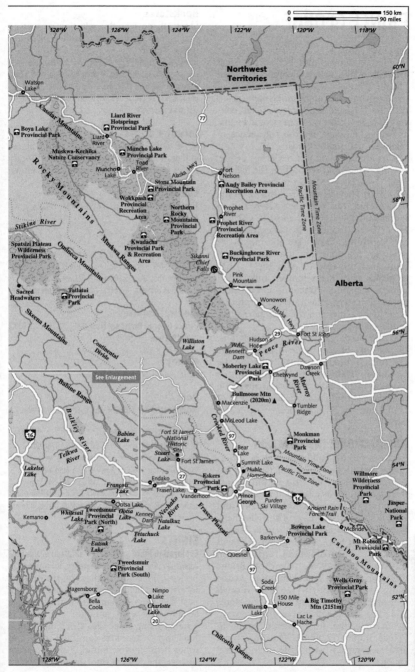

PRINCE GEORGE

pop 77,500

In First Nations times before outsiders arrived, today's Prince George was called Lheidli T'Enneh, which means 'people of the confluence,' an appropriate name given that the Nechako and Fraser Rivers converged here. Today the name would be just as fitting, although it's the confluence of highways that matters most.

Cars are sorted on Prince George's wide, ringing bypass and sent off on the Yellowhead Hwy (Hwy 16) west to the coast, the John Hart Hwy (Hwy 97) northeast to the Alaska Hwy, the Yellowhead Hwy east to Jasper and the Rockies, and the Cariboo Hwy (Hwy 97) south to its namesake region and Vancouver. Franchises and motels are ready for pit stops. But the city is worth more than a pause to reset the Garmin or glance at its many lumber mills. Good museums, natural attractions and nightlife reward lingerers. Penetrate the perplexing maze to the center and you find alternatives to the chain gang.

If the First Nations name is obvious, the origins of the name Prince George are not. A predecessor railroad to the Canadian National (CN) coined the moniker in the early 1900s and surviving records give conflicting accounts – it's not even known if 'Prince George' was a real person.

ORIENTATION & INFORMATION

Roads in this big confluence can be a confusing tangle. Hwy 97 from Quesnel becomes a commercial strip cutting across the edge of town as Central St before heading north to Dawson Creek (406km) and Mile 0 of the Alaska Hwy. The Yellowhead Hwy (Hwy 16) becomes Victoria St as it runs through town, coming to a dead end at 1st Ave. The Yellowhead turns east on 1st Ave and crosses the Yellowhead Bridge to Jasper (376km) and Edmonton. At the south end of town, Hwy 16 goes through a disheartening quadrant of big box stores and strip malls before it veers westward to become the long, scenic route to Prince Rupert (724km). The downtown area is compact, with little architectural character.

Bookstores

Stock up now as the selection as you go north does not get better until Whitehorse in the Yukon.

Books & Company (☎ 250-563-6637; www.booksand company.ca; 1685 3rd Ave; ☺ 8am-6pm Mon-Wed & Sat, 8am-9pm Thu, 8am-10pm Fri, 10am-5pm Sun; ☎) In an uncommonly beautiful building downtown with a huge selection; good café. The website is a hoot.

Internet Access

Wi-fi access is easy to find in public places and at motels. For a computer, try the library (below) or the Visitor Centre (VC; below).

Laundry

Just about every place to stay has a coin laundry.

Library

Prince George Library (Bob Harkins Branch; ☎ 250-563-9251; 887 Dominion St, Civic Centre Plaza; ☺ 10am-9pm Mon-Thu, 10am-5:30pm Fri & Sat year round, also 1-5pm Sun mid-Sep–Apr) One-hour free internet access.

Medical Services

Prince George Regional Hospital (☎ 250-565-2000; 2000 15th Ave; ☺ 24hr)

Money

Banks and ATMs abound.

Post

Main post office (☎ 250-561-2568; 1323 5th Ave)

Tourist Information

Visitor Centre Train Station (☎ 250-562-3700, 800-668-7646; www.tourismpg.com, www.initiativespg.com; VIA Rail Station, 1300 1st Ave; ☺ 8am-8pm May-Sep, 8:30am-5pm Oct-Apr); Branch (☎ 250-563-5493; Hwy 97 & Hwy 16; ☺ 8am-8pm May-Aug) The excellent train station VC can make bookings such as ferry tickets. Internet access per 30 minutes is $3.50.

SIGHTS

Exploration Place (☎ 250-562-1612; Fort George Park; adult/child $9/6; ☺ 10am-5pm Jun-Aug, 10am-5pm Wed-Sun Sep-May) has fine displays on the original locals, the Lheidli T'Enneh. Once you get past the gloss designed to attract people afraid of the word 'museum', the center is an engrossing stop. Check out the Nature Exchange, where kids can trade rocks and other items they've found. Kids also seem to love the SimEx ride simulator (where

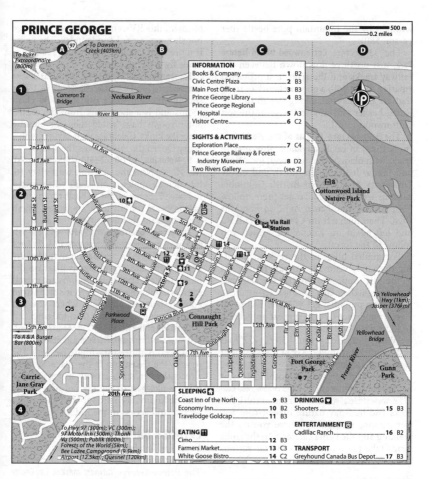

you get shaken up like a can of paint at the hardware store; no coney dogs first). It's southeast of the downtown area on the corner of 20th Ave and Queensway.

Prince George Railway & Forest Industry Museum (☎ 250-563-7351; 850 River Rd; adult/child $6/5; 🕙 10am-5pm) is beside Cottonwood Island Nature Park (p352) and does a surprisingly good job of making the local lumber industry and the trains that hauled away the wood interesting. There are lots of old locos for climbing on. Like everyone else, people here are mystified by the origins of 'Prince George.'

An excellent place to both view and buy works by members of the prolific local arts community is the **Two Rivers Gallery** (☎ 250-

614-7800; 725 Civic Centre Plaza; adult/child $5/2, admission free Thu; 🕙 10am-5pm Mon-Sat, to 9pm Thu, noon-5pm Sun). It has frequent special exhibitions and a striking design.

ACTIVITIES

There's something in the air in Prince George and it's probably from a pulp mill: six companies operate them (although the global economy hasn't been friendly here either). Learn about how trees are planted, cut down and turned into items as diverse as plywood and toilet paper on fascinating **guided forestry trips** with **Touchwood Tours** (☎ 250-964-1381; www.touchwoodtours.com). Several tours are offered, including one that explores the ongoing devastation wrought by the mountain pine beetle (per person $80).

The 33-hectare **Cottonwood Island Nature Park**, just north of downtown between the railway tracks and the river, is a protected riparian forest with a good network of trails that are perfect after a long day in the car. Birds, beaver and moose thrive in the wet cottonwood forest.

The 130-hectare **Forests of the World** features 15km of easily navigable interpretive trails, with plaques that tell about local flora and fauna. It lies at the north end of the University of Northern British Columbia campus west of town. To get there, follow 15th Ave west and turn right on Foothills Blvd. Then turn left on Cranbrook Hill Rd and left again on Kueng Rd, which you follow to the forest.

For guided hikes in the region, including the rarely visited temperate rainforests to the east (opposite), contact the **Caledonia Ramblers Hiking Club** (web.unbc.ca/~ramblers). For active pursuits, get yourself a copy of *Exploring Prince George*, a great guidebook to local trails and more.

Winter lasts a long time: −33°C (−27°F) is just another day in PG. Ask at the VC about **cross-country skiing**.

Hiking with a llama is nothing to spit at. **Strider Adventures** (☎ 250-963-9542, 800-665-7752; www.strideradventures.ca) runs multi-day treks and half-day nature hikes (from $30 per person, a bargain!) where you do the walking and the llama carries refreshments. Trips take place outside of PG on various preserved lands.

SLEEPING

There are a few decent places downtown, but those closest to the train station are a tad tattered. Hwy 97/Central St makes an arc around the center and this is where you'll find scads of motels.

An association of B&B owners operates the **Bed & Breakfast Hotline** (☎ 250-562-2222, 877-562-2626; www.princegeorgebnb.com), a free booking service that will help you arrange a B&B in your price range ($65 to $100). Members usually provide transportation from the train or bus stations. The VC (p350) also has B&B listings.

Bee Lazee Campground (☎ 250-963-7263, 866-679-6699; www.beelazee.ca; 15910 Hwy 97 S; campsite $20-25; ☼ May-Sep; ☒) A mere 10km south

of town, this RV-centric place features free hot showers, a pool and laundry. The name is more than fanciful: the owners sell honey made by local busy bees.

Economy Inn (☎ 250-563-7106, 888-566-6333; www .economyinn.ca; 1915 3rd Ave; r $55-90; ☒ ☐ ☞) This simple blue-and-white motel has 30 clean rooms and is a short walk from the center. Some rooms have 'jetted tubs' for blasting away the kinks. Celebrate your savings with a Dairy Queen dip cone across the street.

97 Motor Inn (☎ 250-562-6010; 2713 Spruce St; r $60-100; ☒ ☞) Near the junction with Hwy 16, this newish motel is on, wait, you guessed it: Hwy 97. Some of the 19 basic rooms have balconies and/or kitchens. The noted Thanh Vu restaurant (below) is right out front.

Travelodge Goldcap (☎ 250-563-0666, 800-663-8239; www.travelodgeprincegeorge.com; 1458 7th Ave; r $75-125; ☒ ☐ ☞) A real barker in the beauty department, the Travelodge is nicer on the inside (isn't everything?). Rooms are motel-standard but huge. Better yet, it's steps from good restaurants and bars, where you can get beer goggles for your own lodging.

Coast Inn of the North (☎ 250-563-0121, 800-663-114; www.coasthotels.com; 770 Brunswick St; r $125-200; ☒ ☐ ☞) A nine-story high-rise with 152 rooms, the Coast Inn is the place to crash a reception, er, smile sweetly as yet another bride walks past to the myriad of wedding parties. Rooms are a bit tight but have room service and access to the indoor pool.

EATING & DRINKING

Look for locally brewed Pacific Western Brewing beers (including organic amber ale). The Prince George **farmers market** (cnr George St & 3rd Ave; ☼ 8:30am-2pm Sat May-Sep) is a good place to sample the bounty of produce and foods made locally, such as the brick-oven breads from Red Rooster Bakery. Over the Nechako River, **Baker Extraordinaire** (☎ 250-614-2253; 556 N Nechako Rd; ☼ 10am-6pm Tue-Sat) lives up to its name with treats made from stoneground flour. Next door is an excellent deli and an organic produce vendor.

Books & Company (p350), the top-notch bookstore, is the place for coffees, baked goods and other snacks ($2 to $6).

Thanh Vu (☎ 250-564-2255; 1778 Hwy 97 S; mains $7-12; ☼ 11am-10pm) Out on the Hwy 97 strip you'll find real Vietnamese food, not just yet another garish emperor's chicken. Try the classic Halong pork or the salad rolls.

A&A Burger Bar (☎ 250-562-3456; 1393 West Central St; meals $7-12; ☽ 11am-10pm) Along Hwy 97, this local institution puts the surrounding chains to shame with fab gourmet burgers, poutine, milkshakes and more.

White Goose Bistro (☎ 250-561-1002; 1205 3rd Ave; mains $8-32; ☽ 11:30am-10pm) A touch of class downtown, chef Ryan Cyre cooks up surprising treats like lobster nachos in addition to more classic bistro fare at this white-tablecloth restaurant. Lunch sees salads, sandwiches and pastas.

Cimo (☎ 250-564-7975; 601 Victoria St; meals $10-25; ☽ noon-2pm Mon-Fri, 5-10pm Mon-Thu, until 11pm Fri & Sat) The pesto and other excellent Mediterranean dishes here never disappoint. Dine (or just enjoy a glass of BC wine) in the stylish interior or out on the patio. There's live jazz heard here many nights.

DRINKING & ENTERTAINMENT

Cadillac Ranch (☎ 250-563-7720; 1380 2nd Ave; cover varies; ☽ 8pm-3am Mon-Sat) For dancing, look for the parking lot of pick-ups at the bustling Cadillac Ranch, where the band or DJ plays mostly country music (classic rock does slip in) and you can two-step to your heart's content. The club gets many touring acts.

Publik (☎ 250-614-9111; Treasure Cove Hotel, 2005 Hwy 97 S; ☽ 11am-1am) Well-separated from the casino here, this pub brings a bit of fresh Vancouver style to PG. There's a great cocktail and wine list, good burgers and a lively vibe.

Shooters (☎ 250-563-4849; 611 Brunswick St; ☽ 4pm-2am) A mall of bars, this big downtown place has a room for upscale chillin', a room for hockey-fight watchin' and a big one with a fireplace for cheery drinkin'.

GETTING THERE & AWAY
Air
Prince George Airport (YXS; ☎ 250-963-2400; www.pgairport.ca) is on Airport Rd off Hwy 97. Air Canada Jazz and WestJet both serve Vancouver.

Bus
At **Greyhound** (☎ 250-564-5454; 1566 12th Ave) it's a confluence of buses. Greyhound runs west to Prince Rupert ($128, 11 hours, two daily), north to Dawson Creek ($78, six hours, two daily), east to Jasper ($72, five hours, two daily) and south to Vancouver ($138, 12 hours, three daily).

Train
VIA Rail's (1300 1st Ave) scenic *Skeena* heads west three times a week to Prince Rupert (12½ hours) and east three times a week to Jasper (7½ hours). Through passengers must overnight in Prince George.

GETTING AROUND
Prince George Transit (☎ 250-563-0011; www.busonline.ca) operates local buses (adult/child $2/1.50). Lines converge at 7th Ave and Dominion St.

Budget, Hertz and National have counters at the airport. For a cab, try **Prince George Taxi** (☎ 250-564-4444).

EAST OF PRINCE GEORGE
The Yellowhead Hwy (Hwy 16) runs 386km east to Jasper from Prince George. The first 270km to the junction with the Yellowhead South Hwy (aka Hwy 5, p341) pass through rolling oceans of green scenery paralleling the Fraser River before things get dramatic at Mount Robson Provincial Park (p331).

Just 60km east from Prince George, **Purden Ski Village** (☎ 250-565-7777; www.purden.com; lift pass adult/child $47/26) is a low-key hill with 25 runs, a 335m drop, two lifts and a rental shop.

Continuing east, you can find some of the rarest trees on earth along the **Ancient Rain Forest Trail**. About 1km of trails lead to some real behemoths of this temperate inland rainforest: old-growth red cedars and hemlocks that reach heights of 60m and more. Missed by loggers, the forest here teems with animal and plant life, much of it perfectly suited to the moist and misty conditions. Moss forms mats in the canopy that are another layer of life in the sky.

The trail is 113km east of Prince George (6.6km west of the Slim Creek rest area). Look for the sign that says simply 'Ancient Forest 1km Ahead.' Two websites have more info on this mystical area (http://wetbelt.unbc.ca/af-trail.htm and http://ancientcedar.ca).

Some 210km east of Prince George, **McBride** is a good quick stop for gas, food and refreshments – maybe not in that order.

PRINCE GEORGE TO DAWSON CREEK
As you travel north from Prince George, the mountains and forests give way to gentle rolling hills and farmland as Hwy 97 (at

NORTHERN BC

times called the John Hart Hwy) follows a portion of the meandering 1923km-long Peace River. If you're driving this route, you're probably linking it with the Alaska Hwy. Although there are a few diversions, there's no need to dawdle.

Beginning in the mid-1700s, the Cree and Beaver First Nations lived along the river and called it the 'river of beavers' for its huge populations of these thick-furred rodents. The two tribes periodically warred over the boundaries of the river, finally coming to an agreement about 200 years ago, renaming the river the 'Peace.' The east-flowing Peace River carves the only sizable opening through the Rockies to Alberta, making the climate in this region more similar to the prairie climate in Alberta. The climate also affects the political and social slant of the northeast communities; people read Alberta newspapers, know more about Alberta politics, get their city fix in Grand Prairie instead of, say, Prince George and even set their watches by Alberta time (opposite).

Two sights 40km north of Prince George also make good, short, day trips. **Huble Homestead** (☎ 250-564-7033; www.hublehomestead .ca; adult/child $5/3; ⏱ 10am-5pm daily mid-May–Aug, Sat & Sun Sep–mid-Oct) is the Little House on the Prairie come to life. Guides show how settlers at this 1905 farm lived off the land and made everything they needed, using tools such as the still-working forge in the blacksmith's shed. There's a good café.

The homestead is also the start of the area's second attraction, the **Giscome Portage** (www.env.gov.bc.ca/bcparks). Named for the Jamaican prospector John Giscome, the trail had already been in use by First Nations people for centuries when gold prospectors got it improved in the 1870s. A shortcut across the Continental Divide, the portage was a critical link in travel to the north. The trail is restored for 8.5km north to Summit Lake. The beautifully wooded trail is good for both hikers and bikers.

Low-key nature is found at Summit, Bear and MacLeod Lakes, which have provincial parks and camping along the 100km stretch after Huble Homestead. North of MacLeod Lake, Hwy 39 heads west for 29km to **Mackenzie** (population 5500), which sits on the southern shores of the 200km-long **Williston Lake**, the largest artificial reservoir in North America and the largest lake in BC. Environmentalists recoil with horror at Mackenzie's 'world's largest tree crusher,' a mammoth piece of machinery that sits, ironically, beside a wooded area along the town's main street. The big yellow monster was used to clear the floodplain under what is now Williston Lake.

The next stop off Hwy 97, **Chetwynd** (population 2700), 300km north of Prince George, is little more than a strip of services along the highway. This industrial town (motto: 'Success through effort') contains sawmills, a pulp mill and a gas plant; its unusual, but perhaps unsurprising, local hobby is chainsaw art. More than 50 carvings of varying sizes are spread around town, including the bears under the 'Welcome to Chetwynd' sign.

From Chetwynd you can head north through Hudson's Hope along Hwy 29 and avoid Dawson Creek and Fort St John on your way north (something you should consider, see opposite). Otherwise, it's 102km straight on to Dawson Creek.

DETOUR: TUMBLER RIDGE & BEYOND

You can penetrate deep into the seldom-visited heart of BC by taking Hwy 29 94km south from Chetwynd to **Tumbler Ridge** (population 2100). From here you can continue another 45km along the dirt Murray River Rd to **Kinuseo Falls**. Located inside **Monkman Provincial Park**, the spectacular falls are 60m higher than Niagara Falls. You can walk along a five-minute trail to the upper lookout or carry on 20 minutes further to the Murray River and look up at the falls. **Kinuseo Falls Campground** (campsite $15) offers 42 wooded sites close to the river and falls.

As for Tumbler Ridge, it was born in the early 1980s to service one of the province's enormous resource projects, Quintette Mine, the world's largest open-pit coal mine. But world energy prices cause the workforce to fluctuate like the rolling hills and the bad world economy has caused much hardship here. The next big hope is the mooted Northern Gateway Project (p366), which promises jobs building the huge pipeline through the region.

TIME FOR CHANGE

Many of BC's northwestern communities share the same time zone as Alberta – Mountain Standard Time (MST) – while much of the rest of the province is on Pacific Standard Time (PST). However, there's a twist: these communities – which include Chetwynd, Dawson Creek, Fort St John, Hudson's Hope and Tumbler Ridge – do not observe Daylight Saving Time. In winter these towns are one hour ahead of the rest of BC, but in summer they match time with the rest of BC as Pacific Daylight Saving Time is the same as Mountain Standard Time.

Whatever the time, daylight seems to last forever in summer, while winter is shrouded in darkness. In the more northerly reaches, in towns like Fort Nelson or Dease Lake, the summer sun might set at 1am and soon rise again at 5am. Come winter, the sun sets at 3pm, not rising again until 10am.

Highway 29 North

Driving along the spectacular Peace River is reason enough to take Hwy 29, which joins the Alaska Hwy 12km north of Fort St John (p356). As a bonus you'll save 47km of driving and avoid the congestion of Dawson Creek along Hwy 97.

Hudson's Hope (population 1200), 66km north of Chetwynd on Hwy 29, overlooks Peace River. The town's economy revolves around livestock ranching, grain and forage crops. Wildlife in the area is abundant (10 of North America's big game species are found here), but the biggest spectacle is the **WAC Bennett Dam** (☎ 250-783-5048; www.bchydro .com; admission free; ♡ 10am-6pm mid-May–Aug). One of the world's largest earth-filled structures, the hydroelectric dam is 24km west of Hudson's Hope. Tours take you 150m down inside the dam where you can learn about the wonders of electricity. What you don't learn about are the incredible hardships endured by the First Nations groups whose villages were inundated in the 1960s. Efforts at proper recompense only began in 2008.

Continuing east on Hwy 29 the road parallels the beautiful, broad Peace River Valley.

ALASKA HIGHWAY

Just the name of this legendary road conjures images of northern adventures. It's not quite boldly going where no man has gone before, but for most drivers it promises a break with the every day, the promise of the unexpected and a chance to see a moose.

This section covers the Alaska Hwy (Hwy 97) in BC. See p397 for the highway north of the Yukon border. Excepting some beautiful stretches near Muncho Lake, much of the road in BC passes through endless repetitions of rolling green wooded hills. For a discussion of travel options to the Yukon, see p388.

DAWSON CREEK

pop 11,400

Dawson Creek is primarily known for the road out of town. It's the starting point – Mile 0 – for the Alaska or Alcan (short for Alaska–Canada) Hwy. Beginning at Dawson Creek, the Alaska Hwy goes through Watson Lake and Whitehorse in the Yukon all the way to Fairbanks in Alaska, some 2237km (although progress in the form of road improvements keeps nibbling away at that total).

Once known only as the 'Beaver Plains,' the immediate area saw no outside settlement until the turn of the 20th century. In 1879, the town's namesake, Dr George Mercer Dawson, led a survey team through here in search of a route to bring the railway over the Alberta Rockies. Though the railway didn't happen until later, Dawson's studies aided settlement and prompted later exploration for oil and natural gas. Dawson studied Native communities and languages, which, along with his geological and botanical studies across Canada, earned him the portentous moniker 'Father of Canadian Anthropology.'

Although memories of the show are gathering dust in the video dustbin, there is virtually no local link to the TV show *Dawson's Creek* which ran from 1998 to 2003. It was set in a town near Boston.

The **Visitor Centre** (VC; ☎ 250-782-9595, 866-645-3022; www.tourismdawsoncreek.com; 900 Alaska Ave;

(🌣 8am-5.30pm May-Aug, 10am-5pm Tue-Sat Sep-Apr; 🛜) is in the Northern Alberta Railway Park along the highway, which becomes Alaska Ave as it runs through town. There's a large art gallery in an old grain elevator and a nice little museum. Kids will enjoy the dinosaur fossils on display and can ask for a guide to old bones on display throughout the region.

Few manage to pass the **Mile Zero Post** in the middle of the intersection of 102nd Ave and 10th St, one block south of the VC, without grabbing a cell phone photo. Locals have wisely capitalized on the interest with the new **Alaska Highway House** (☎ 250-782-4714; 10201 10th St; admission by donation; 🌣 9am-5pm daily May-Sep, Mon-Fri Oct-Apr), a museum in a vintage building overlooking the milepost. The stories of those who worked in impossible conditions building the road are told and there are some neat models, like one of the Kiskatinaw Bridge (right) under construction. (Pedants note: the true location for the Mile Zero Post should be at the train station with the VC; no one knows why it was moved.)

Sleeping & Eating

There are many places to stay – some belonging to chains that will seem ubiquitous as you journey north. Enjoy the regional bounty at the thriving **farmers market** (10200 8th St; 🌣 8am-noon Sat May-Oct) in the Co-op supermarket parking lot.

Mile 0 RV Park & Campground (☎ 250-782-2590; milopark@pris.ca; campsites $18-35; 🛜) This should actually be called the Kilometer 2.5 RV Park & Campground as that's where it is on the Alaska Hwy. It's a full-service place with hot showers and a laundry.

Inn on the Creek (☎ 250-782-8136, 888-782-8136; www.innonthecreek.bc.ca; 10600 8th St; r $90-120; ❌ 🖥 🛜) Don't let the name fool you – it's really the inn on the highway – but the 48 rooms are large, nicely remodeled and have fridges and large desks.

Granaries on Bear Mountain (☎ 250-782-6302; www.thegranaries.com; 2106 Ski Hill Rd; r $170-220; 🌣) Get away to luxury boutique accommodation in three restored old grain buildings or in rooms at a tiny inn at this sybaritic B&B 7km southwest of Dawson Creek. Set amidst beautiful forest, here you can enjoy whirlpools, large tubs, antiques and more. There's a strong commitment to green practices.

> ### DETOUR: AN ORIGINAL WOODEN BRIDGE
>
> Forget the bland modernity of the Alaska Hwy with an adventure that gives you a taste for the original road amidst some lovely surroundings. About 28km north of Dawson Creek, look for signs and a road to the east that is a 10km remnant of the original Alaska Hwy. The highlight of this pretty little drive is crossing the **Kiskatinaw Bridge**, a 163m curved wooden structure built by the US Army in 1942–43. (See details of its construction at Dawson Creek's Alaska Highway House, left). The north end of the road is 41km south of Fort St John.

Alaska Hotel (☎ 250-782-7625; 10209 10th St) If the walls could talk... Only the bar remains open for refreshments at this crusty old place right near the Mile Zero Post. But stories abound from the characters, many older than the road. Simple rooms upstairs (where the walls might talk) cost $55.

Getting There & Away

At the **Greyhound terminal** (☎ 250-782-3131; 1201 Alaska Ave) you'll find buses north to Whitehorse ($245, 20 hours, one daily) and the Yukon, and southwest to Prince George ($78, six hours, two daily).

DAWSON CREEK TO FORT NELSON

The wheat fields of Dawson Creek and NW Alberta are replaced by the low rolling terrain of the Rocky Mountains' foothills as you head north from Dawson Creek.

Fort St John, 75km north of Dawson Creek on Hwy 97, mainly functions as a service center for the oil and gas industries; in fact, its slogan is 'the energetic city'. There are few reasons to stop here, but should you need a break the **Fort St John – North Peace Museum** (☎ 250-787-0430; 9323 100th St; adult/child $6/3; 🌣 9am-5pm Mon-Sat) tells some good yarns about early residents, including how brain surgery was conducted by radio and the story of the first fort, which was built in 1794 (sadly, there's nothing left).

Hwy 29, the scenic shortcut (p355) to/from Prince George, meets the Alaska Hwy 12km north of Fort St John. There are many motels here.

DIY WATERFALL

Watch for a gravel road running west near Km 267. Drive 17km until you reach a small parking area and then follow a trail for 1.5km through spruce and poplar trees. You'll soon hear a roar and be rewarded with the 30m-tall **Sikanni Chief Falls**. It's a sylvan scene and rarely crowded. Watch for mountain goats and moose.

Continuing north, the population gets sparse along the Alaska Hwy – unless you're a moose or other critter like elk, deer or mountain goat. The terrain becomes rather monotonous, as each crest of a hill yields another crest of a hill straight ahead.

Most towns on the highway have only one or two service stations. **Wonowon** (One-o-One, get it?; 162km north) is at Mile 101 on the highway. During highway construction, soldiers were stationed here to search all cars at the Blueberry Checkpoint. If you didn't have enough provisions and spare parts to make it through the vast wilderness that lay ahead you were turned back. These days kids in the car might check to see if DVD supplies are sufficient for the journey

ahead. If not, it's back to the Wal-Mart in Fort St John.

Like so many tales along the Alaska Hwy, no one can seem to get straight why **Pink Mountain** (population 100, 226km north) is named Pink Mountain. The color of trees in fall, the sunlight reflecting off the mountain at sunrise, the hue from masses of fireweed blossoms in summer? Watch for **Moose Lick Creek**, so you can caption a photo with the name.

Before hitting Fort Nelson, you'll pass by a few provincial parks. First, at 278km north, is the 34-site **Buckinghorse River Provincial Park** (campsite $15), where you might see moose grazing alongside the river. It has pit toilets and fresh water.

Prophet River Provincial Recreation Area (350km north) has access to another original section of the Alaska Hwy.

FORT NELSON
pop 5100

It's a little bit of Alberta in Fort Nelson, at least when it comes to energy wealth. This once-sleepy outpost of filling stations and roadside cafés is entering its second decade as a boomtown, thanks to extensive deposits of oil and gas in the plains to the northeast.

SLOGGING THROUGH THE BOG

Northeastern BC was once just a massive tract of wilderness, with a geography of squishy muskeg ground and vast prairies so different from the rest of the province that no one really knew what to do with it. With harsh winters and short, hot summers, the massive area attracted few residents. While the rest of the province was settled and growing, the Peace region was home to scattered First Nations villages, voracious mosquitoes and little else.

During WWII, the US worried about its vast, unpopulated and unprotected Alaska coast. Other than wind and snow, there was little to prevent a Japanese attack on this remote territory. Moving troops or supplies here required perilous flights or slow voyages along the storm-tossed coast. What was needed was a road and, incredibly, one was built.

The engineering feat was remarkable by any measure. Under a wartime deadline, survey crews in 1942 stormed through the vast forests, followed by an army of 11,000 American troops (including many African-Americans, who were still banned from combat), 16,000 civilian workers (including large numbers of First Nations people for whom the work was their first employment) and 7000 pieces of equipment. From the air, it looked like a massive razor had shaved a thick strip off the forest's heavy green beard. More than 8000 culverts and 133 bridges crossed rivers. A mere nine months and six days after work started, the 2453km-long route from Dawson Creek to Fairbanks, Alaska, officially opened on November 20, 1942. The cost? A then-astonishing and today still-remarkable US$135 million (that's US$1.8 billion in today's dollars).

After the war, the road drove development in the entire northern region of BC and, vastly improved over the decades, it's an ever-busier link between the USA and Canada. To learn more about its construction, visit the Alaska Highway House in Dawson Creek (opposite). For more on the Alaska Hwy and its role in opening up the Yukon, see p398.

The fate of GM, Ford and Chrysler would be secure if everybody bought new pickup trucks and SUVs at the pace of local energy workers. Fans of chains and franchises will find department stores and strip malls a-plenty along the Alaska Hwy, which turns west here. And all the new workers have driven up the average price of a new subdivision house to well over $400,000.

Leasing of mineral rights has brought the Canadian and BC governments hundreds of millions of dollars but has also led to significant environmental impact. Oil and gas exploration is dirty business and drilling test holes has scarred the landscape. New pipelines, like the vast one serving the gas fields in nearby Horn River shale fields, are under continuous construction.

Fort Nelson is 456km north of Dawson Creek, so the main reason to stop here is to spend the night. You can't tour the world's largest gas processing or wood products plants.

The **Visitor Centre** (☎ 250-774-2541; www.tourism northernrockies.ca; 5430 50th Ave N; ☾ 8am-8pm May-Aug) has information about the surrounding area, including the scenic points east.

The **Fort Nelson Heritage Museum** (☎ 250-774-3536; www.fortnelsonmuseum.ca; adult/child $5/3; ☾ 8:30am-7:30pm May–mid-Sep), at the west end of town, has a stuffed albino moose and displays about the Alaska Hwy.

Sleeping & Eating

Motels are often booked out by house-hunting new arrivals. Fortunately there are new motels arriving too. Most are southwest of the center along the highway.

Fort Nelson Hotel (☎ 250-774-6971, 800-663-5225; www.fortnelsonhotel.com; 5110 50th Ave N; r $60-150; ✄ ▭ ⬚ ⬚) It's not quite a trip to the tropics, but a steak dinner in the Tiki Room, which is near the indoor pool, will transport you away from any blizzards outside. The 136 rooms are large with decor that was trendy when Tikis were big (circa 1978). Rates are 'combatively priced.'

Blue Bell Inn (☎ 250-774-6961, 800-663-5267; www.bluebellinn.ca; r from $95; ✄ ▭) Stay here and get gas, eat here and get gas, or maybe just drill here and get gas. This all-purpose stop has a restaurant, 24-hour convenience store and gas station, coin laundry, 57 comfortable rooms, many with kitchenettes, and 42 campsites (from $25).

FORT NELSON TO WATSON LAKE

Zipping along west from Fort Nelson you can leave the politics of energy exploration behind and savor some of BC's least appreciated scenery. On the 513km drive to Watson Lake in the Yukon you might just see more wildlife than in any other part of western Canada. On one drive we saw bears, elk, moose, caribou and lots of those smaller mammals that are called snacks by predators. Lakes, peaks and vistas add pizzazz.

At Km 484, 28km past Fort Nelson, the Liard Hwy (Hwy 77) heads north to the Northwest Territories, Fort Simpson and the remote Nahanni National Park.

At Km 594, 138km west of Fort Nelson, the Alaska Hwy passes through the north end of beautiful **Stone Mountain Provincial Park**, in the eastern Muskwa Ranges of the Rockies; the 'stone mountain' in question is Mt St Paul (2127m). From the top you see successions of tree- and snow-covered peaks in all directions. The park's 28-site **campground** (campsite $15; ☾ May–mid-Sep) offers access to hiking trails and backcountry camping. Look for the dramatic hoodoos – eroded stone pillars – at **Wokkpash Creek** and drink in the beauty of **Summit Lake**. Throughout this area you're likely to see stone sheep (small, dark cousins of bighorn sheep) licking salt off the road.

At the tiny town of **Toad River**, a former hunting lodge, **Toad River Lodge** (☎ 250-232-5401; www.toadriverlodge.com; Km 648; r $70-90), is a classic roadside icon: its pub has a ceiling lined with over a thousand baseball caps from around the world. It also has six cabins, six basic motel rooms and a camping area (campsites from $20).

Muncho Lake Provincial Park

It's a cliché but we would definitely call the 12km-long Muncho Lake the jewel of the Alaska Hwy in BC. In fact, one look at the virescent waters and we'd throw cliché avoidance to the wind and call it the 'emerald.'

The namesake 86,079-hectare park surrounding the lake begins at Km 695. Muncho means 'big lake' in the Tagish language (and is not to be confused with a call for salty snacks from the DVD-watchers in the back seat).

The road wends its way beautifully along the shore; for the Alaska Hwy construction crews, cutting the rocky terrace was the most difficult part of the construction in the region. Today salt-licking stone sheep serve as peanut gallery to the show. The backdrop mountains are part of the Terminal Range, which marks the northernmost section of the Rocky Mountains and ends at Liard River (60km northwest).

Of Muncho Lake's two campgrounds, the 15-site **Strawberry Flats Campground** (Km 700; www.env.gov.bc.ca/bcparks; campsite $15) has an unbeatable view of the lake, which just lasts forever on summer nights.

There are a few lodges scattered along the highway through the park. **Northern Rockies Lodge** (☎ 250-776-3481, 800-663-5269; www.northern rockieslodge.com; Km 708; campsite from $35, r $115-200) is both the nicest and open all year. The 45 rooms are split between the main lodge and chalets. There are 35 RV campsites along the water. The restaurant is good and residents receive discounts for filling their gas tanks.

Liard River Hot Springs Provincial Park

For thousands of years, Natives – including Sikanni and Nahanni – trappers, explorers like Robert Campbell, and weary travelers have paused to refresh at this oasis of warmth. Within the park, there's a micro, micro climate of lush boreal marsh and tropical vegetation that's home to 14 varieties of orchids and 250 other species of plants.

A 500m boardwalk leads to the large **Alpha pool** (day use adult/child $5/3), where you can sit and soak for hours. If you get tired of that, walk around and check out some of the strikingly green ferns and colorful wildflowers that, like you, revel in the heat and humidity. In the summer months, stroll five minutes further up the boardwalk to the deeper, slightly cooler 3m-deep **Beta pool** (☽ May-Jul). Fewer people come here, so take the opportunity to jump in and swim over to the sides where it's shallower; be sure to let the warm mud ooze between your toes. One of the great things about both pools is that they're natural – no concrete creations looking like motel refugees here.

Beware: it's crowded in July and August. If you can't come in the spring or fall, try coming later at night, when the families have gone off to dreamland. The park gate is closed from 11pm to 6am; outside of these hours non-campers must leave their vehicles outside the gate and walk in.

The park's **campground** (☎ 800-689-9025; www.discovercamping.ca; campsite $15-19) has 53 sites open year round that are reservable May to mid-October. Guides run interpretive programs throughout the summer.

From here it is 220km to Watson Lake and the Yukon (p397). Look for **scenic overlooks** of the Liard and Dease Rivers all the way to the Yukon border.

YELLOWHEAD HIGHWAY

The Yellowhead Hwy builds slow. It starts in the flatlands of Winnipeg and the prairies and finally gains some excitement as it passes through Jasper National Park and the Rocky Mountains. Continuing west, the road (Hwy 16) passes soaring Mt Robson (p331) before settling back to a scenic run through empty wilderness to Prince George (p353).

But the best is saved for the 705km run west to the coast. The Yellowhead first meanders into the heart of the Lakes District and then through the alpine adventure haven of Smithers. Reaching the Hazeltons, First Nations culture is everywhere, in particular those icons of the north, totem poles.

The road veers southwest to Terrace, passing the junction for Hwy 37, the Stewart–Cassiar Hwy (p381), an increasingly popular route to the Yukon. The final 147km drive from Terrace to Prince Rupert is consistently rated one of the most scenic in Canada. The road hugs the wide Skeena River, where the mists part to reveal glacier-clad mountains on the far shore.

From surprising Prince Rupert, ferries sail in every direction: north to Alaska, south to Vancouver Island and west to the Queen Charlotte Islands.

VIA Rail's *Skeena* parallels the Yellowhead from Jasper to Prince Rupert; it is an often stunning ride. The website www.nbctourism.com has regional information.

VANDERHOOF
pop 4700

Vanderhoof is 97km west of Prince George. It's the first town of any size that you'll encounter and is mainly a service center.

NORTHERN BC

For once the Dutch, rather than First Nations or the English, provided the local name, which means 'of the farm.' Indeed, these prime lands of the Nechako River Valley sustain oodles of farms and cattle. Proud locals note that this is the geographical center of BC.

Evidence of the beetle infestations that are killing trees across BC are especially obvious along this stretch of Hwy 16. For more information see p59.

FORT ST JAMES NATIONAL HISTORIC SITE

Simon Fraser may have been searching for a navigable route to the Pacific Ocean when he founded this site, but you don't need to search at all for this highlight. Just detour 66km north off the Yellowhead Hwy.

Fraser used this outpost as a place to trade furs with the area's trappers, mostly Carrier people, who were a branch of the Dene First Nations. The Carriers got their name from the mourning ritual of widows, who carried the ashes of their deceased husbands in pouches on their backs until a memorial potlatch could be held. Early French-speaking traders referred to them as 'Porteurs' (porters), which was translated by English-speaking traders.

The post became a commercial center and headquarters of the district of New Caledonia. In 1821 the fort became a Hudson's Bay Company outpost and operated until the early 20th century. Though the relationship between the fur traders and Carriers was an amicable one, it altered some of the hunter-gatherer instincts of the Carrier people and introduced rampant materialism. Hudson's Bay was the Wal-Mart of its time.

Restored in 1971, the **Fort St James National Historic Site** (☎ 250-996-7191; adult/child $8/4; ☻ 9am-5pm late May-Sep) closely resembles its 1896 appearance. The site gives visitors a fascinating glimpse into recent yet pivotal history. Costumed guides in each of the six major buildings provide background on the structure's function and on the people who lived there. Among the nuggets of information you'll learn is that trading for one blanket required a dozen or more beaver skins. There is a good place to picnic and enjoy the views of the placid lake.

Hwy 27 runs to the fort from the Yellowhead. The turn is 7km past Vanderhoof. The town of Fort St James (www.fsjames.com) has services and a couple of simple cafés.

BURNS LAKE
pop 1900

Burns Lake, 229km west of Prince George, serves as the center of the Lakes District and northern gateway to the north part of Tweedsmuir Provincial Park. It also hosts the popular **Burns Lake Bluegrass Festival**, which takes place in mid-July. Out in the middle of the lake is **Deadman's Island**, all 1 sq km of it, which is part of the Burns Lake Provincial Park (which exists in name only as it always seems to be a year away from opening). The island gets its inauspicious name from an accident that killed two men working on the Grand Trunk Railway (today the CN).

The carved trout sign that welcomes you to Burns Lake is a testimony to the serious anglers who descend upon the area's many lakes in spring and summer to catch rainbow and cutthroat trout, char, kokanee, ling cod and salmon, among other fish. In winter, look for the black beaks of snow-white trumpeter swans, who spend the season foraging in fields around frozen marshes.

Like other towns along the Yellowhead, Burns Lake experienced its population boom during the construction of the Grand Trunk Railway. Today, it's a lumber town that has a pretty location and services to speed travelers on their way.

For the best fishing holes, boat rentals and trail information, see the Burns Lake **Visitor Centre** (☎ 250-692-3773; www.burnslakechamber.ca; 540 Hwy 16; ☻ 9am-5pm Jun-Aug, Mon-Fri Sep-May). It adjoins a small museum.

One of the best spots for canoeing, kayaking and fishing is 177km-long **Babine Lake**, 34km north of Burns Lake on the Babine Lake Rd. The stunning lake is well worth the detour. You can also access the lake from Topley on Hwy 16.

Sleeping & Eating

There are a few chain motels on the edges of town. The small and simple **Burns Lake Municipal Campground** is near the center in a pretty area by the lake in Len Radley Memorial Park. The sites are – get this – free.

It's just south of the Yellowhead Hwy on Hwy 35; turn at the carved trout sign.

Sunshine Inn (☎ 250-692-7696, 866-388-1100; www.sunshineinn.ca; 940 Hwy 16 W; r $70-150;) Just west of the center, this modern 48-room motel has spotless rooms in two two-story blocks. Flat-screen TVs overlook plushly fitted queen- and king-size beds.

New Leaf Café (☎ 250-692-3800; 425 Hwy 16; snacks $4; 9am-7pm Mon-Sat) In a health food store, New Leaf serves up fair-trade coffee, smoothies, panini, waffles, pizza and many other healthy treats.

TWEEDSMUIR PROVINCIAL PARK (NORTH)

Canoers and kayakers with a real sense of adventure find maritime backcountry adventures galore at **Eutsuk Lake**, the highlight of 446,000-hectare **Tweedsmuir Provincial Park (North)**, the province's second-largest provincial park.

On the north and northwest, the park is bordered by the Ootsa-Whitesail Lakes Reservoir, on the west and southwest by the Coast Mountains and on the east by the Interior Plateau. The park is divided by the Dean River and the only access possible to Tweedsmuir Provincial Park (South) is off Hwy 20 (see p343).

Unlike many parks named for British dignitaries, Tweedsmuir took its moniker from someone who actually saw the park. In fact, John Buchan, Baron Tweedsmuir of Elsfield, and also Canada's 15th governor general, traveled extensively through the park on horseback and by floatplane before it took his name.

Wildlife abounds in this vast area and includes woodland caribou, goats, moose, black and grizzly bears and wolves. Up in the air, look for willow ptarmigans, gray-crowned rosy finches and golden-crowned sparrows. In the Nechako Reservoir, look for fish-hunting ospreys amidst the fallen logs.

Eutsuk Lake forms a system of joining waterways with **Ootsa**, **Whitesail** and **Tetachuck Lakes**. Except for Eutsuk, most lakes were dramatically raised in 1952 with the building of the Kenney Dam and the creation of the Nechako Reservoir. The raised waters were deemed necessary to generate enough power to serve the giant Alcan aluminum smelter in Kitimat. Eutsuk retains a natural purity the other lakes lack.

Anyone venturing into wild Tweedsmuir should plan carefully and be ready to experience full wilderness camping and boating. You will need to be totally self-sufficient and be prepared for any conditions.

Getting There & Away

From Burns Lake, access the park by following Hwy 35 23km south to the François Lake Ferry (free, every 50 minutes, 5:30am to 10:30pm) across François Lake. After about another 40km, you reach the **Little Andrews Bay Marine Park** (access fee per boat $50), where there are eight simple campsites. From here you boat Whitesail Lake to Chikamin Bay, site of the staffed **park ranger station** (May-Oct) where you pay the access fee. A mandatory boat winch ($50 each way, mid-June to August) covers the 600m portage and you're on Eutsuk Lake.

Lakes District Air Services (☎ 250-692-3229; www.lakesdistrictair.com; Burns Lake) has charter floatplane services to remote lakes and cabins in the park.

SMITHERS

pop 6000

Those who whizz past Smithers – or maybe just stop for gas – are seriously missing out. This Alpine-style town plays hard year round and if locals – 'Smithereens' – aren't out on the local slopes, trails and waters, they're busy creating. Lots of musicians, writers and artists live here.

Besides good places to stay, Smithers has fine places for food in its eminently walkable center. Roughly midway between the two Princes, Smithers is in the heart of the pretty Bulkley Valley, surrounded by the stunning Hudson Bay, Bulkley River and Babine Mountains.

History

The First Nations people locally are the Wet'suwet'en, who are organized among five clans. Smithers was chosen as the divisional headquarters of the Grand Trunk Railway and was the first village to be incorporated in BC (1921).

It became a town in 1967 and today is a government and administrative center with a progressive bent, which works to balance the advantages of tourist money and development with the downsides of growth.

Information

The weekly *Interior News* is a good local newspaper that provides a real window into the community. All through the region look for *Northword*, a brilliant free monthly with news and coverage of all things creative.

Mountain Eagle Books & Bistro (☎ 250-847-5245; 3775 3rd St; ☽ 9am-6pm Mon-Sat; �) Has a good range of new and used books and is an excellent spot for community information, including the area's thriving folk music scene and CDs. The tiny café has veggie soup and lunches.

Visitor Centre (VC; ☎ 250-847-5072, 800-542-6673; www.tourismsmithers.com; 1411 Court St; ☽ 9am-6pm May-Sep, 9am-5pm Mon-Fri Oct-Apr) Across the parking lot from the Bulkley Valley Museum, this center covers the region. It offers internet access.

Wash the Works (☎ 250-847-4177; 4148 Hwy 16; load $6; ☽ 8am-9pm) The name says it all: you can get coin-operated cleaning for your clothes, your car and your body.

Sights

Smithers' **Main St** is an intriguing place for a stroll, with a full range of local shops and services. There are enjoyable walks along the **Bulkley River** just north of the center at **Riverside Park**.

In the 1925 former courthouse at the crossroads of Main St and Hwy 16, you'll find the **Bulkley Valley Museum** (☎ 250-847-5322; admission free; ☽ 10am-5pm), which features exhibits on Smithers' pioneer days. In the same building, the **Smithers Art Gallery** (☎ 250-847-3898; admission by donation; ☽ noon-4pm Mon-Sat) displays and sells works by local and regional artists.

Activities

Mountain biking is popular throughout the Bulkley Valley and you'll find some well-maintained trails for all levels of rider. There are numerous outdoor gear stores on Main St, including **McBike & Sport** (☎ 250-847-5009; www.mcbike.bc.ca; 1191 Main St; ☽ 9am-6pm Mon-Sat), which rents bikes for $30 per day, sells cycling maps for $5 and leads guided tours. It also rents drift boats for fishing (from $150 per day).

In winter, the store is the contact point for the **Bulkley Valley Nordic Centre** (www.bvnordic.ca), which has more than 45km of groomed trails through a spruce forest. Over 5km are lit for night skiing.

Valhalla Pure Outfitters (☎ 250-847-0200; www.valhallasmithers.com; 1122 Main St) has gear, advice and trip reports for climbing, skiing, hiking,

paddling and more. It organizes tours for hiking, backpacking and climbing. The VC (left) can recommend guides and instructors for a range of activities. See opposite for excellent nearby parks and sites.

For an injection of pure adrenaline, join a white-water rafting trip on the Babine River to Hazelton in the Bulkley River Canyon. Several local companies offer trips, usually from about $100 per person. Kayaking is big, and the river and many lakes offer a lot of opportunities for one-day, or longer, trips. **Aquabatics** (☎ 250-847-3678; www.aquabatics.com; 1960 Hudson Bay Rd) has kayak rentals from $25 per day. In summer it usually has a location east of town near the airport (7391 Hwy 16).

Hudson Bay Mountain (☎ 250-847-2058; www.hudsonbaymountain.com; 1-day lift pass adult/child $45/25) is the fast-expanding local ski hill. The vertical drop is 533m and it has one chair lift but plans for more. Some 75% of the runs are intermediate or advanced. Most local sporting stores rent gear and a shuttle runs on weekends.

Festivals & Events

Don't miss the legendary **Midsummer Music Festival** (☎ 250-847-1971; www.bvfms.org; adult/child from $40/30), which is held in late June. It features more than 75 bands, including 45 from the valley. Mountain Eagle Books & Bistro (left) is a center of information for the three-day event, which is organized by the Bulkley Valley Folk Music Society.

Sleeping

The VC (left) makes free accommodations reservations and has lists of B&Bs and holiday homes. There are several motels on or near Hwy 16.

Riverside Park Municipal Campsite (☎ 250-847-1600; 3843 19th Ave; campsite $11-22) The sites have a lovely location right on the river and there are lockers. You can drive or make the 10-minute walk up Queen St to the town center.

Tyee Lake Provincial Park (☎ 800-689-9025; www.discovercamping.ca; Hwy 16; campsite $22) This is 8km east of Smithers off Hwy 16, and has 59 popular wooded sites and a playground.

Smithers Guesthouse (☎ 250-847-4862; www.smithersguesthouse.com; 1766 Main St; dm from $24, r $40-70; ☐ ☐) In a residential area close to both the center and Riverside Park, the five rooms are cozy and feature bunk beds. There's a large common kitchen and a covered deck with views of the mountains.

Stork Nest Inn (☎ 250-847-3831; www.storknestinn .com; 1485 Main St; r $65-80; ☒ ▣) The 23 basic and modern rooms are off inside corridors and have fridges. Guests receive a large breakfast and have access to high-speed internet and a steam room. The center is a brief walk.

Fireweed Motor Inn (☎ 250-847-2208; www .fireweedmotel.com; 1515 Main St N; r $65-85; ☒ ▣ ☜) Close to the center and a supermarket, this two-story motel-style place has 20 comfortable rooms with wi-fi, fridges, microwaves and more.

Two Rivers Lodge (☎ 250-846-6000; www.tworivers lodge.ca; Hwy 16, Telkwa; r $80-120; ☜) The 11 units here are a combination of suites in large buildings and cottages by the river. Our pick: number 7, a log cabin with a porch a few meters from the water.

Eating & Drinking

You can find excellent provisions for a picnic or an adventure in Smithers. The **farmers market** (☎ 250-847-8832; cnr Main St & Hwy 16; ☺ 8am-noon mid-May–Sep) is good for organic items. **Paul's Bakery** (☎ 250-847-9742; 3840 Broadway Ave; ☺ 7am-6pm Mon-Sat) is famous for whole-grain goodness. **Sausage Factory** (☎ 250-847-2861; 1107 Main St; ☺ 9am-6pm Mon-Sat) is redolent with smoked meats and makes excellent sandwiches to go.

Java's (☎ 250-847-5505; 3735 Alfred St; meals $7-12; ☺ 7am-7pm Mon-Fri, 5-9pm Sat) Great coffee yes, as well as tapas and early dinners from a limited menu (a steak, seafood, a curry). This large café is also the center of the thriving local folk music scene. There are performances and open-mike nights on many evenings after the official closing.

Alpenhorn Pub & Bistro (☎ 250-847-5366; 1261 Main St; meals $8-20; ☺ 11am-late) The patio here is so nice you may not wish to leave, except the mountain views will lure you to explore. Great pub food and many drinks specials (try the Rickards Red) keep the venue popular and packed.

Getting There & Away

Four kilometers west of town off Hwy 16 is **Smithers Airport** (YYD; ☎ 250-847-3664; www .smithersairport.com). Air Canada Jazz and Hawkair serve Vancouver.

Greyhound (☎ 250-847-2204; 4011 Hwy 16) serves Prince George ($69, five hours, two daily) and Prince Rupert ($64, five hours, two daily) along Hwy 16.

VIA Rail's *Skeena* stops in Smithers; the station is at the south end of Main St. The tri-weekly service takes six hours to both Prince George and Prince Rupert.

AROUND SMITHERS

The small and historic town of **Telkwa** (population 1500), 8km west on Hwy 16, has restored buildings and serene river walks. The **Old Ranger Station Gallery** (☎ 250-846-5454; Hwy 16) has art, books and more by local creative types.

The 1810m **Kathlyn Glacier** carved a 1.6km-wide gulch into Hudson Bay Mountain and recedes more each year. Gushing waterfalls cascade off its back, providing spectacular views in summer and world-class ice climbing in winter. From the parking lot, a short, easy trail leads to a viewing platform at the base of the glacier's **Twin Falls**, which plunge for 90m. Or tackle the steep three-hour climb to the toe of the glacier. Those in a hurry can view the glacier from the highway, a little further west of town. To get there, drive 4km west of Smithers, then take Kathlyn Glacier Rd and follow the signs for 6.1km.

Babine Mountains Provincial Park is a 32,400-hectare park deep in the glorious backcountry wilderness of the Babine Range of the Skeena Mountains. Trails to glacier-fed lakes and sub-alpine meadows provide accessible hiking and mountain biking during summer, while during winter the trails are ideal for snow-shoeing and cross-country skiing. The well-maintained **Fletcher-Gardner Trail** is a 13km hike through gorgeous wilderness to Lower Reiseter Lake, and makes a great spot for some wilderness camping.

Look for healthy populations of moose, marmots and mountain goats. To reach the park, follow Hwy 16 for 3km east of Smithers, and then turn northeast onto Babine Lake Rd, then north onto McCabe Rd, which zigzags into Driftwood Rd. It's about 16km total. You can backcountry camp here.

Driftwood Canyon Provincial Park (☎ 250-638-8490) was created in 1976 to protect the rich fossil beds that were discovered along the

Driftwood Creek around 1900. Formations found in the shale indicate that plants, insects and animals lived in the area some 50 million years ago. Over time, the running creek eroded through the sedimentation, finally exposing the fossil beds.

Today, you can walk to a viewing platform on the east bank of the creek, where interpretive panels describe the area's geological significance. It's on Driftwood Rd, 5km before Babine Mountains Provincial Park.

MORICETOWN
pop 670
The fast-flowing Bulkley River narrows to just a few meters across as it surges between two sheer rock walls. Generations of First Nations Wet'suwet'en people have used the **Bulkley River Gorge** to spear and net salmon. The view of the water, the leaping silver fish and the skill displayed in catching them is mesmerizing. It is right beside Hwy 16, 20km west of Smithers, in the small town of Moricetown.

NEW HAZELTON & AROUND
If you haven't seen forests of totem poles yet, the towns of New Hazelton, Hazelton and South Hazelton (area population 6500) are the bases for your viewing. Several smaller villages nearby mean you can spend a day or more searching out these most-iconic of all First Nations symbols (below).

Named for the hazelnut bushes growing along the river terraces, the three main towns have large First Nations populations and sit within the walls of the rugged Rocher de Boule (Mountain of Rolling Rock), near the confluence of the Skeena and Bulkley Rivers.

The Skeena River (*skeena* means mist) has long been central to people's lives in the area. The Gitksan and Wet'suwet'en people, who have lived here for more than 7000 years, first navigated cedar canoes along the treacherous Skeena all the way out to the coast. Fur trappers arrived in the area around 1866.

The area became an active and boisterous commercial center in the early 1900s. Soon, the influx of people spread, scattering inland to find riches in the mines, to stake land claims and to build farms. When the Grand Trunk Railway construction crews rolled through in 1914, they brought more people, more rowdiness and some general confusion about the profusion of Hazeltons.

For the record: **Hazelton** (also called the Old Town) was the original settlement, established long before the train showed up. Once it did, Hazelton was slated to become a ghost town with the founding of the 'South' and 'New' Hazeltons. The new communities vied for the position of commercial center and remained in a bitter and senseless battle while the railway went bankrupt. Today, **New Hazelton** is the commercial center along Hwy 16; South Hazelton is essentially tacked onto it. The original Hazelton has found new life as a pioneer town with shops and the 'Ksan Historical Village.

New Hazelton's **Visitor Centre** (VC; ☎ 250-842-6071; www.newhazelton.ca; junction Hwys 16 & 62; ☸ 8am-7pm Jul & Aug, 9am-5pm mid-May, Jun & Sep)

TOTEMS OF THE YELLOWHEAD

You can easily spend a day searching out totem poles in and around the Hazeltons. Often they are found in small First Nations villages, which are interesting in their own right. To understand the complex story behind each pole, see p43. The New Hazelton VC has a handy map 'Tour of the Totems.' Sites include:

- **'Ksan Historical Village** (opposite)
- **Kispiox** (opposite)
- **Kitwanga** (opposite)
- **Gitanyow** (p382)

Further afield, **Prince Rupert** has totem poles at the excellent Museum of Northern British Columbia (p368) while there are totems aplenty on the **Queen Charlotte Islands**, including at the Haida Heritage Centre at Qay'llnagaay (p377). See p37 for more on the history of totems.

is an essential stop for sorting through the various local sights. In the summer there's a weekend **farmers market** in the VC parking lot, with excellent local berries.

There are motels, campgrounds and restaurants in each of the Hazeltons.

Hazelton

Amidst the rolling hills, the dramatic **Hagwilget Bridge** stands out – literally. It soars 100m over the Skeena River and is 2km into the 7km drive to Hazelton from the VC. You can stop and walk across for some vertigo-inspiring views. In Hazelton stroll the banks of the Skeena River and explore the historic buildings. Placards along the river detail local history.

Named using the Gitksan name for the Skeena, which flows right outside, **'Ksan Historical Village & Museum** (☎ 250-842-5544; www.ksan.org; admission $2; ⊙ 9:30am-4:30pm Mon-Fri Oct-Mar, 9am-5pm daily Apr-Sep) is a replicated First Nations village that offers an absorbing look at the local culture. **Guided tours** (adult/child $10/8.50; ⊙ every 30 min) are essential for a full understanding and are led by the Gitksan. Among the sights: the Frog House of the Distant Past, the Wolf House of Feasts and the Fireweed House of Masks and Robes. Note that in summer it can seem like the Lemmings House of Crowds. Eagle House sells aboriginal snacks.

Kispiox

The small First Nations village of **Kispiox** (population 800) has a stunning line of 16 totem poles. Many are recent, a result of the continuing resurgence of First Nations culture and art. Stop by the **Community Centre** (Lac Seel St), where you may be able to arrange a detailed tour. Kispiox is reached by a 13km paved road of the same name that begins near Hazelton. In summer, watch for farm stands along the road selling the best raspberries you've ever had.

KITWANGA

The junction with the **Stewart-Cassiar Highway** (p381; Hwy 37), an increasingly popular route north to the Yukon that also gives access to splendid Stewart and Hyder (p382) and totem-pole-filled Gitanyow (p382), is 44km west of New Hazelton. A dozen **vintage totem poles** stand to attention on a grassy verge by the Skeena River.

TERRACE

pop 12,800

This a logging, government, service and transportation center astride the Skeena River. Although Terrace (www.kermodei tourism.ca) itself is no looker, it's a hub for tourism to fascinating places right around the compass. In town, trail-filled **Ferry Island** is just off Hwy 16 immediately east of the center. **Heritage Park Museum** (☎ 250-635-4546; www.heritageparkmuseum.com; 4702 Kerby Ave; adult/ child $5/3; ⊙ 9:30am-5:30pm Mon-Fri mid-May–Aug, daily Jul & Aug) has eight old pioneer buildings built from logs. Who knew there were so many styles?

Skeena Valley Expeditions (☎ 866-918-7238; www .skeenavalleyexpeditions.com; trips from $150) is a high-end operator of white-water rafting trips in Northern BC. A six-hour trip from Terrace hits the class 3+ rapids of the Copper River. Many more remote trips are available.

AROUND TERRACE

The 146km **Skeena River drive** between Terrace and Prince Rupert is one of the most scenic in BC. Hwy 16 runs right alongside the ever-widening river. At times there is barely enough room for the road and the parallel CN train tracks between the river and the sheer rock walls of the hillside. Roadside pull-outs let you absorb the spectacle.

Nisga'a Lava Bed

Ready for a big blow? Volcano lovers will be fascinated by **Nisga'a Memorial Lava Bed Provincial Park** (☎ 250-798-2277, tour information 250-633-2991), one of the most extraordinary parks in BC. Jointly managed by the Nisga'a Nation and the government, this 18,000-hectare park (Nisga'a name: Anhluut'ukwsim Laxmihl Angwinga'asanskwhl) is in the beautiful Nass Basin, 91km north of Terrace along the Nisga'a Hwy.

About 250 years ago, a massive volcanic eruption spilled hot, heavy lava onto the Nass floodplain. Destroying entire villages, suffocating vegetation and killing more than 2000 Nisga'a ancestors, the lava covered an area 10km long and 3km wide. It even rerouted the Nass River to the north edge of the valley, where it still flows today.

The lava created various formations (depending on the speed at which it flowed), including lava tubes, chunks and ropelike Pahoehoe lava. The pale gray rocks look almost furry with the hardened ash; the effect is reminiscent of a lunar landscape. Most of the **trails** in the park are short and accessible from the highway. One of the best is about 4km south of the Visitor Centre and goes to **Vetter Falls**. The short trail traverses a lava bed before plunging into thick forest, where you'll find the namesake waterfall. It's both misty and mystical.

At the edge of the main lava bed the **Visitor Centre** (☎ 250-638-9589; ☿ 10am-6pm mid-Jun–Aug) is in a traditional Nisga'a longhouse. Here you can get information on the history of the Nisga'a and pick up the *Self-Guided Auto Tour* brochure ($1), which offers good descriptions of park highlights.

You can book **Nisga'a tours** (☎ 250-633-5150, 866-633-2696; www.ncgtourism.ca; adult/child $40/25; ☿ 10am Sat mid-Jun–Aug) of the lava fields, go on a hunt for mushrooms and herbs in the surrounding rainforests or see a First Nations fishwheel scooping up salmon.

There's a pretty 16-site **campground** (campsite $15) beside the visitor center.

Vetter Falls Lodge (☎ 250-633-2929, 877-917-1177; vetterfalls@telus.net; New Aiyansh; r $90-130) is close to the falls and has six rooms (some with wood stoves) in a lodge and cabins. Breakfast is included.

The Nisga'a village of **Nass Camp** is about 7km northwest of the visitor center. Near here is the junction with the logging road that connects to the Stewart-Cassiar Hwy at Cranberry Junction. See p383 for details.

Kitimat
pop 9000
Ideally situated on the Douglas Channel's Kitimat Arm, 58km south of Terrace (at the southernmost point of Hwy 37), Kitimat has great natural potential: towering mountains, a deep protected port and fresh- and salt-water fishing. But another of

---

IN THE PIPES

Running 1170km from northern Alberta to the industrial coastal town of Kitimat, the proposed **Enbridge Northern Gateway Pipeline** (www.northerngateway.ca) is a $4 billion project that would bring 500,000 barrels of oil daily to the BC's coast from the tar sands fields. A companion pipeline will take 'condensate', a by-product of natural gas, from Kitimat to Alberta where it will be blended with the crude oil to make it flow easier.

As you'd surmise, the project has stirred controversy from communities – especially First Nations ones – along its entire path. But what has really concerned environmental groups is the new port in Kitimat that will see tankers carrying both crude oil and distillate. The consequences of an *Exxon Valdez*-style spill are unthinkable. At present oil tankers have been banned from BC's Inside Passage for three decades. The pipeline will require a change to this as well as securing environmental approvals all along its route. Enbridge has a powerful argument in its favor: jobs. The lure of 4000 jobs constructing the two-way pipeline is undeniable in depressed industrial towns like Tumbler Ridge and Kitimat, and to the cash-strapped federal and provincial governments.

But there are also issues at the other end of the pipeline. Extracting oil from tar sands is an enormous undertaking with huge environmental cost. Forests have to be cut down, top soil stripped away, water heated and used to extract the tar from the sand, that same water sent to vast contamination ponds (just one covers 130 sq km), then refining and – if the pipeline from Kitimat arrives – mixing in petroleum products piped to Alberta so the tar by-product can be piped to BC and put aboard tankers that will sail the Inside Passage to refineries elsewhere. According to *National Geographic*, producing oil this way releases three times as much carbon dioxide into the atmosphere as an oil well.

In 2009, the global bust in oil prices put a pause in developing the tar sands, but Enbridge has been resolute in pushing the pipeline forward. Opponents – there are many – include the Living Oceans Society (www.livingoceans.org) and the Dogwood Initiative (www.dogwoodinitiative.org). The latter group got headlines when it produced stickers that made the duck on the $1 coin (the loonie) appear covered in oil. One argument against the project is that it is designed to put price pressure on the US, which is the primary market for the tar sands oil and which receives the oil through existing pipelines across Alberta. If the price from south of the border isn't sufficient, the oil can be sent to tankers in BC and shipped to buyers willing to pay more in Asia.

BC's 1950s Stalinist projects – an enormous aluminum smelter and dam – has blighted the beauty. Kitimat is now intent on luring a controversial new oil pipeline (see the boxed text opposite).

PRINCE RUPERT

pop 15,200

The biggest thing on the coast between Vancouver and Alaska, Prince Rupert isn't just a maritime transport hub but also a destination in itself that is good for a few days of enjoyment. It may rain 220 days a year, but even when it's raining, misty, foggy or cloudy, its rugged mountain beauty and fjord-like coastal perch atop solid granite rocks is profoundly lovely.

Besides plenty of places to get great seafood while enjoying views of the harbor and islands, it has two dynamite museums: one on First Nations culture and another located in an amazing preserved cannery and village. Opportunities to see wildlife, from bears to orcas, are almost as prolific as the critters themselves.

History

If the reasons for Prince George's name are unknown (p350), little more is known about why Prince Rupert came to be named for an obscure German prince who fought for the English monarchy in the 1600s.

Perhaps Charles Hays was a fan. He was the general manager of the Grand Trunk

PRINCE RUPERT

INFORMATION		
Eddie's News	1	C2
Java Dot Cup	2	C2
King Koin	3	C3
Post Office	4	C2
Prince Rupert Library	5	D2
Prince Rupert Regional Hospital	6	C3
Rainforest Books	7	C2
Visitor Centre	8	D1
SIGHTS & ACTIVITIES		
Carving Shed	9	D1
City Hall	10	C2
Firehall Museum	11	C2
Ice House Gallery	(see 16)	
Kwinitsa Station Railway Museum	12	C2
Museum of Northern British Columbia	13	C1
Oceanwild	14	D1
Prince Rupert Adventure Tours	15	D1
Prince Rupert Adventure Tours	16	D1
Prince Rupert City & Regional Archives	17	D1
Seashore Charters	(see 16)	
SLEEPING		
Andree's B&B	18	D2
Black Rooster Roadhouse	19	C3
Crest Hotel	20	C2
Eagle Bluff B&B	21	D1
Inn on the Harbour	22	C2
Ocean View Hotel	23	B3
Pacific Inn	24	C3
Pioneer Hostel	25	D2
Prince Rupert RV Campground	26	A4

EATING		
Baker Boy	27	C3
Cow Bay Café	28	D1
Cowpuccino's	29	D1
Dolly's Fish Market	30	D1
Opa Sushi	31	D1
Rain	32	C2
Safeway	33	C2
Smiles Seafood	34	D1
Waterfront Restaurant	(see 20)	

DRINKING		
Breakers Pub	35	D1
Charley's Lounge	(see 20)	

SHOPPING		
Rupert Square Mall	36	C2

TRANSPORT		
Greyhound Canada Bus Depot	37	C2
Hawkair	(see 38)	
Highliner Plaza Hotel	38	B2
National	(see 38)	

Cow Bay

Pacific Mariners Memorial Park

Prince Rupert Harbour

Pattulo Park

Roosevelt Park

Centennial Golf Course

To Yellowhead Hwy; Hertz (1.5km); Butze Rapids (6km); Mount Hays (6km); Diana Lake Provincial Park (16km); Prudhomme Lake Provincial Park (16km); North Pacific Historic Fishing Village (20km); Port Edward (22km); Terrace (146km)

To Ferry Terminal (2km); Train Station (2km); Viewing Area (3km)

NORTHERN BC

Railway who, in 1906, saw in the vast harbor setting the potential to build a town that would rival Vancouver. Serious financial problems plagued the railway when Hays, who was off touring, fatefully (and fatally) booked his passage home on the *Titanic*. To make matters worse, WWI came along, stripping the region of young men, and the railway eventually suffered the indignity of having its assets frozen by the courts. The town never developed into the vast metropolis Hays envisioned but instead became a fishing center for the Pacific Northwest.

The Grand Trunk Railway ultimately became part of the CN system which, 100 years later, is working to allow Hays' ambitions for the world's deepest natural ice-free port finally to be realized. Prince Rupert now has a modern container terminal that handles container ships from Asia. Coupled with the CN line along the Skeena (which continues via downtown Jasper, p324), days are lopped off the travel times of shipments of Chinese-made TVs, toasters and T-shirts to the heart of the US. That the new port opened just as the economy went into reverse is just another bit of bad luck Prince Rupert will have to overcome.

Orientation & Information

Rupert, as everyone calls it, is on Kaien Island and is connected to the mainland by a bridge on Hwy 16. Cow Bay, named for a dairy farm that used to be located here, has become a historic waterfront area full of shops, restaurants and the cruise ship port, Atlin Terminal. Cow Bay is just north of the compact and somewhat hilly downtown, which has that baffling Canadian system of naming intersecting streets and avenues with the same number.

BOOKSTORES
The shop in the Museum of Northern British Columbia (right) has a great range of books.

Eddie's News (☎ 250-624-4134; 611 2nd Ave W) Lots of magazines and a few books.

Rainforest Books (☎ 250-624-4195; 251 3rd Ave W) This place has a good selection of new releases and used books.

INTERNET ACCESS
Java Dot Cup (☎ 250-622-2822; 516 3rd Ave W; per hr $3; 🕑 7:30am-9pm; 🛜) Has numerous terminals plus a café in a heritage building.

LAUNDRY
King Koin (☎ 250-624-2667; 745 2nd Ave W; per load $4; 🕑 8am-10pm) Self-serve or drop clothes off for royal treatment.

LIBRARY
Prince Rupert Library (☎ 250-627-1345; 101 6th Ave W; 🕑 10am-9pm Mon-Thu, 10am-5pm Fri, 1-5pm Sat & Sun; 🛜) Thirty minutes free use of computers.

MEDICAL SERVICES
Prince Rupert Regional Hospital (☎ 250-624-2171; 1305 Summit Ave; 🕑 24hr) In Roosevelt Park.

POST
Post office (☎ 250-627-3085; Rupert Sq Mall)

TOURIST INFORMATION
Visitor Centre (☎ 250-624-5637, 800-667-1994; www.tourismprincerupert.com; Cow Bay Atlin Terminal; 🕑 9am-8pm Jul-Sep, 10am-3pm Oct-Apr) For regional info, see www.travelnorthwestbc.com.

Sights

Don't miss the fabulous **Museum of Northern British Columbia** (MNBC, ☎ 250-624-3207; www.museumofnorthernbc.com; 100 1st Ave W; adult/child $5/1; 🕑 9am-8pm Mon-Sat, 9am-5pm Sun Jun-Aug, 9am-5pm Mon-Sat Sep-May), which resides inside a post-and-beam building styled after a First Nations longhouse. Excellent exhibits and superb documentation show how local civilizations enjoyed sustainable cultures that lasted for thousands of years. Using technologies based on steam, the people were able to make items as diverse as soup ladles (from goat horns) to canoes (from huge spruce logs). The displays include a wealth of excellent Haida, Gitksan and Tsimshian art. Tours of the museum and walking tours of the town are well worth it.

You'll see **totem poles** all around town; two flank the stoic statue of Charlie Hays beside City Hall on 3rd Ave. Many totems are replicas of well-known traditional works. In summer, the MNBC offers guided **heritage** and **totem walking tours** around town ($5). Check for tour times. To witness First Nations artistry in action, stop by the **Carving Shed** (🕑 times vary, Jun-Aug), next door to the courthouse. Often you'll see local artists there working on jewelry or cedar carvings.

Housed in an old train station, the **Kwinitsa Station Railway Museum** (🕑 9am-5pm Jun-Aug) documents the drama surrounding the building of the railway to Rupert. Located down the hill on Bill Murray Dr, entry is included with the MNBC admission.

Rupert's center, and especially the prominent Rupert Square Mall, gets shabbier by the year, so the short stroll down to **Cow Bay** is a welcome change of scenery. The eponymous spotted decor is everywhere but somehow avoids being grating. There are shops, cafés and a good view of the waterfront where you can see both fishing boats and cruise ships unloading their catch.

The **Prince Rupert City & Regional Archives** (☎ 250-624-3326; 100 1st Ave E; ❧ 10am-3pm Mon-Fri) contains a huge collection of photographs, nautical charts and books.

Fire engine buffs – and confused rock fans – will seek out the rebuilt 1925 REO Speedwagon fire engine at the small **Firehall Museum** (☎ 250-627-4475; 200 1st Ave W; admission by donation; ❧ 10am-4pm summer), beside the real fire hall.

Rupert's vibrant creative community runs the light and airy **Ice House Gallery** (☎ 250-624-4546; Atlin Terminal; ❧ 10am-5pm Tue-Sun), where a huge range of works in many mediums are for sale.

For sweeping views of the harbor, channel and islands beyond, wander over to **Pacific Mariners Memorial Park**, a simple place with a low brick memorial to the scores of local people lost in Pacific waters. To see Rupert's maritime future, head towards the ferry harbor but then take the turn to the Port of Prince Rupert and go another 1km, following signs to the **viewing area** (❧ daytime). It's fascinating watching huge container ships disgorging their cargo in a mechanical ballet. And what's in all those little containers anyway…

The **North Pacific Historic Fishing Village** (☎ 250-628-3538, 250-624-3207; www.cannery.ca; 1889 Skeena Dr; adult/child $12/6; ❧ 10am-7pm May-Sep but phone to confirm), near the town of Port Edward (22km from Prince Rupert), explores the history of fishing and salmon-canning along the Skeena River. The sprawling complex was used from 1889 to 1968 and is a real world unto itself. Exhibits document the miserable conditions of the workers, along with the workings of the industry that helped build the region. Guides provide insight into working conditions; watch the restored canning line in action and think about what was required of the average worker to fill 14

trays of cans in four minutes. You can easily spend a half day or more wandering the old wooden buildings, which are built over the water. A good café often serves excellent homemade chowder and baked goods. Various oral history books with compelling stories are for sale. To really get a flavor for the cannery, spend the night. Simple B&B rooms ($40 to $50) share bathrooms and overlook the channel.

Activities

You can picnic, swim, fish, hike or take out a canoe at **Diana Lake Provincial Park** and **Prudhomme Lake Provincial Park**, about 16km east of town on Hwy 16.

Dozens of charter-boat operators run **fishing trips** out of Prince Rupert. Local specialties include rockfish, halibut, crabs and shrimps. The VC (opposite) has a comprehensive list of operators, or you can wander Cow Bay and chat with the skippers.

Skeena Kayaking (☎ 250-624-5246; www.skeena kayaking.ca; rentals per 24hr $90) offers both rentals and custom tours of the area, which has a seemingly infinite variety of places to put into the water.

Of the many **hiking** trails in and around town, one path goes up 732m **Mt Hays** from the Butze Rapids parking lot, east of town on Hwy 16. On a clear day, you can see local islands, the Queen Charlotte Islands and even Alaska.

Beginning at a parking lot on the Yellowhead Hwy, 3km south of town just past the industrial park, trails lead to Mt Oldfield, Tall Trees (you'll see some old cedars) and **Butze Rapids**. The rapids walk is a flat, 4km loop to Grassy Bay with interpretive signs; the others are more demanding. The VC offers details on these and others.

Tours

All that water, all that life. You can see minke and gray whales plus porpoises all year round around Prince Rupert. Orcas swim through in summer while humpbacks feed from July to November. Several local firms offer boat trips to watch. To see bears in their habitat, see p372.

Pike Island is a small island outside of the harbor where villages thrived as long as 2000 years ago, and remains of them can still be seen today. **Seashore Charters** (☎ 250-624-5645, 800-667-4393; www.seashorecharters.com; Atlin

Terminal; tours adult/child from $60/44) runs half-day trips to Laxspa'aws, as the island is known, that include a 40-minute boat ride each way and the services of a First Nations guide. Seashore Charters also offers various harbor, whale and wildlife tours.

Prince Rupert Adventure Tours (☎ 250-627-9166; www.adventuretours.net; 207 3rd Ave E; adult/child from $55/50) offers boat tours that circle Kaien Island May to October. It also runs tours to see whales and various other wildlife-related trips. It also has a desk at the Atlin Terminal.

Oceanwild (☎ 250-622-7659; www.oceanwild.ca; 23 Cow Bay Rd) lives up to its name with scuba diving trips, coastal hiking, remote bird viewing and more. Tours start at about $100 per person for four hours.

Festivals & Events

In mid-June, **Seafest** celebrates Rupert's seaside location with parties and parades on land and water. **Udderfest** (☎ 250-624-3626; www.harbourtheatre.princeruperttoday.com) in early August presents five days of captivating fringe theater performed by local groups and national performers.

Sleeping

Rupert has a range of accommodations, but when all three ferries have pulled in (a sort of nautical hat trick), competition gets fierce; book ahead. Rupert has more than a dozen B&Bs, of which the VC (p368) has lists.

Rooms with harbor views may enjoy the spectacle of one of Rupert's technicolor sunsets.

BUDGET

Prince Rupert RV Campground (☎ 250-624-5861; www.princerupertrv.com; 1750 Park Ave; campsite $21-30; 💻) Near the ferry terminal, it has 88 sites, hot showers, laundry and flush toilets.

Pioneer Hostel (☎ 250-624-2334, 888-794-9998; www.pioneerhostel.com; 167 3rd Ave E; dm/d from $22/56; 🛜) Bold colors enliven the compact and clean rooms, some with bunk beds. The hostel has a small kitchen and barbeque facilities out back; it provides bikes rentals and ferry/train pick-ups.

Black Rooster Roadhouse (☎ 250-627-5337; www.blackrooster.ca; 501 6th Ave W; dm/d from $25/55; 💻 🛜) A renovated house in an old neighborhood just up the hill from the center is the basis for this excellent hostel. Guests enjoy lounging on the patio or in the bright common room, or picking up refreshments from the nearby corner store. Call for shuttle pick-up.

Ocean View Hotel (☎ 250-624-6117; www.oceanviewhotel.ca; 950 W 1st Ave; r $35-75; 🛜) Lovingly maintained by its longtime family owners, the Ocean View dates back to 1910, although serial renovations through the years have erased much of the past. Only two of the 36 rooms have the views suggested by the name, but all are spotless, if a bit idiosyncratic. The cheapest are a bargain and share bathrooms. The pub serves seafood and is a popular spot for anglers to ponder the one that got away.

MIDRANGE

Eagle Bluff B&B (☎ 250-627-4955; www.citytel.net/eaglebluff; 201 Cow Bay Rd; r $50-90; 💻) Ideally located on Cow Bay, this basic place is in a heritage building that has a striking red-and-white paint job. Inside, however, the seven rooms have decor best described as homestyle; some share bathrooms. The deck views are sublime.

Andrée's B&B (☎ 250-624-3666; www.andreesbb.com; 315 4th Ave E; r $75-110; 🛜) In a historic residential neighborhood close to the center, this four-room B&B is in a grand house that's got old nautical stuff out front and great harbor views out back. The rooms (named for plants like honeysuckle) have character, with gleaming hardwood floors and period furniture.

Pacific Inn (☎ 250-627-1711, 888-663-1999; www.pacificinn.bc.ca; 909 3rd Ave W; r $75-140; 🛜) This flash-free place has 77 large and modern motel rooms. It is one of many midrange motels in the direction of the ferry terminal and the best in terms of still being a short walk to the center. The underground garage ensures you can load your car rain-free.

Inn on the Harbour (☎ 250-624-9107, 800-663-8155; www.innontheharbour.com; 720 1st Ave W; r $85-160; 🛜) Sunsets may dazzle you to the point that you don't notice the humdrum exterior of this modern, harbor-view motel. The 49 rooms have been revamped with a stylish combo of rich dark colors and beige. Non-view rooms catch glimpses of the grim Rupert Square Mall – don't look!

TOP END

Crest Hotel (☎ 250-624-6771, 800-663-8150; www.cresthotel.bc.ca; 222 1st Ave W; r $100-300; ❌ 💻 🛜)

Prince Rupert's premier hotel has harbor-view rooms that are worth every penny, right down to the built-in bay window seats. The smallish rooms overlooking the parking lot are a different matter; your money will buy more elsewhere. There's a new floor of suites that are downright opulent. Charley's Lounge (right) and the Waterfront Restaurant (right) are excellent.

Eating

All those fishing boats in the harbor mean you can enjoy fresh seafood (halibut and salmon star) all over town.

Stock up on food for the ferry or expeditions at the **Safeway** (☎ 250-624-5125; 200 2nd Ave W; ☽ 7am-10pm). **Baker Boy** (☎ 250-624-4031; 617 3rd Ave; ☽ 7am-5pm Mon-Sat) is a traditional bakery with unusual cookies like Bird's Nest (white coconut with a jam center).

Cowpuccino's (☎ 250-627-1395; 25 Cow Bay Rd; coffee $2; ☽ 7am-8pm) A funky coffeehouse and local meeting place with good M&M cookies.

Dolly's Fish Market (☎ 250-624-6090; 7 Cow Bay Rd; ☽ 10am-6pm) The café is burgeoning at this purveyor of locally caught seafood (anything smoked, yum!). Chowders and the crab sandwiches are winners, and the menu keeps expanding. The eating area may be small but the salt grinders show they're serious.

Opa Sushi (☎ 250-627-4560; 34 Cow Bay Rd; meals $8-18; ☽ noon-9pm Tue-Sat) Another fine venue for bounty from the docks. Enjoy top-notch sushi in a historic net loft with views of the harbor. For a treat, order the spectacular sashimi on a hand-carved cedar plank. There's a tree-covered terrace out back.

Smiles Seafood (☎ 250-624-3072; 113 Cow Bay Rd; meals $8-25; ☽ 11am-9pm) Flip over the placemat at this 1934 veteran for a look at the menu from 1945, when a sardine sandwich on toast cost 25¢. Prices have changed but little else, from the booths to the welcome. Excellent shrimp chowder.

Cow Bay Café (☎ 250-627-1212; 205 Cow Bay Rd; meals $10-20; ☽ 11:30am-9pm) Fun, clever and interesting, this bistro shines, rain or, er, shine. Cookbooks are strewn around the tables and herbs grow right outside the door. Lunch features soups and salads, dinner seafood with global influences. Set right on the water, get a table on the deck.

our pick **Rain** (☎ 250-627-8272; 737 2nd Ave; meals $10-30; ☽ 5pm-midnight Mon-Sat) A little bit of Vancouver has fallen on Rupert. A stylish combo of lounge and bistro, Rain has a long list of small plates for sharing plus regular meals. You'll be thunderstruck by the calamari dijonaise, a succulent creation that actually melts in your mouth.

Waterfront Restaurant (☎ 250-624-6771; Crest Hotel, 222 1st Ave; mains $15-30; ☽ 11am-10pm) This open kitchen turns out a long list of excellent fare that – no surprise – does a lot with seafood, but also has creative pastas and specials. Large salads are excellent and you can order from casual to fancy. Great wine list and views.

Drinking

Feel like hanging out in a dive? There are a few old seamen's joints along 2nd Ave W.

Breakers Pub (☎ 250-624-5990; 117 George Hills Way; meals $8; ☽ 11am-late; ☜) Right on the water at Cow Bay, take in the big views of the fishing boats while the skippers grouse at the bar. The food is fine (good fish sandwiches) and you can play darts or shoot pool.

our pick **Charley's Lounge** (☎ 250-624-6771; Crest Hotel, 222 1st Ave; meals $8-15; ☽ noon-late) Half the town is here on Friday nights for the heated patio and fantastic harbor views. Enjoy a creative pub menu and many choices of BC wines by the glass.

Getting There & Away

Rupert is an air, land and sea hub.

AIR

Prince Rupert Airport (YPR; ☎ 250-622-2222; www.ypr.ca) is on Digby Island, across the harbor from town. The entire process of getting between town and the airport is an adventure involving a bus and a ferry. Given the complexities, you must be ready to be picked up by the shuttle bus at an unmarked stop in front of the **Highliner Plaza Hotel** (815 1st Ave ☜) two hours before flight time. Be sure to confirm all the details with your airline or the airport.

Air Canada Jazz serves Vancouver; check-in is at the airport. **Hawkair** (☎ 866-429-5247; www.hawkair.ca; check-in Highliner Plaza Hotel, 815 1st Ave W) also serves Vancouver.

BUS

Greyhound Bus Depot (☎ 250-624-5090; 112 6th St) buses depart to Prince George ($128, 10½ hours, two daily).

BEAR HEAVEN

For bears, the **Khutzeymateen Grizzly Bear Sanctuary**, a 45,000-hectare park 40km northeast of Prince Rupert, is like being a kid locked in a candy store. Khutzeymateen is a Tsimshian word meaning 'confined space of salmon and bears' and that's just what it is. At least 50 grizzlies hang out here munching on salmon; viewing them is popular.

The remote sanctuary is jointly managed by BC Parks and the Tsimshian First Nations. It was permanently protected as parkland in 1992 and two years later the area was officially designated as a 'grizzly bear sanctuary.'

Because grizzlies are reclusive by nature and do better when left alone, the human presence in the park is heavily restricted, though you can join a boat tour or take a floatplane in for a peek. Both Seashore Charters and Prince Rupert Adventure Tours (see Tours, p369) offer these types of tours. You can usually see other wildlife, besides bears, sheltering and feeding in the thick rainforest and along the river estuary at the mouth.

The number of guides allowed to lead people right into the sanctuary is extremely limited. One, Dan Wakeman of Prince Rupert, has written *Fortress of the Grizzlies: The Khutzeymateen Grizzly Bear Sanctuary*, a book about the reserve. His company, **Sun Chaser Charters** (☎ 250-624-5472; www.sunchasercharters.ca), runs multi-day trips into the park from about $2000 per person for four days.

Greg Palmer runs day tours and overnight trips into the reserve with **Palmerville Adventures** (☎ 250-624-8243; www.palmerville.bc.ca). Three-hour trips via floatplane and Zodiac boat cost $450. Three-day trips, with two nights aboard a floating dock in the sanctuary, cost $1600.

FERRY

Ferries share the same general harbor area, although the Alaska Marine Highway terminal is behind large fences as it is considered a US border crossing. All the boats listed here have cafeterias and will let you pitch a tent on deck. For more on the Inside Passage journey see p431.

The Inside Passage run to Port Hardy (adult/child $150/75, car from $350, cabin from $80, 15 to 25 hours, three per week summer, two per week winter) with **BC Ferries** (☎ 250-386-3431; www.bcferries.com), is justifiably hailed for its amazing, wild scenery and wildlife viewing. The Queen Charlotte Islands service goes to Skidegate (adult/child $35/17.50, car from $125, cabin from $50, seven to nine hours, six per week summer, three per week winter).

Alaska Maritime Highway (☎ 250-627-1744, 800-642-0066; www.alaskaferry.com) is an excellent service going to Ketchikan, Wrangell, Petersburg, Juneau and, most importantly, the Yukon-connecting towns of Haines ($160, 33 hours, two to three per week) and Skagway ($171, 35 hours, two to three per week). Cabins cost from $160 and vehicles start at $370.

TRAIN

The western terminus VIA Rail station (at the BC Ferries Terminal south of down-town), operates the tri-weekly *Skeena* to/from Prince George (12½ hours) and, after an overnight stop, Jasper in the Rockies.

Getting Around

Prince Rupert Transit (☎ 250-624-3343; www.busonline.ca) has service in the central area (adult/child $1.25/1) and infrequent service to the ferry port and North Pacific Historic Fishing Village ($2.50). The main downtown bus stop is at the Rupert Sq Mall on 2nd Ave.

Major car rental companies include **Hertz** (☎ 250-624-3673; 970 Saskatoon Ave) and **National** (☎ 250-624-5318; Highliner Plaza Hotel, 815 1st Ave W).

A one-way trip to the ferries or train with **Skeena Taxi** (☎ 250-624-5318) is about $12.

QUEEN CHARLOTTE ISLANDS (HAIDA GWAII)

pop 6100

Not far off the coast of the BC mainland is a world like no other in Canada. The Queen Charlotte Islands (QCI), or Haida Gwaii, are a sparsely populated, wild, rainy and almost magical place which abounds with flora and fauna, including enormous thousand-year-old cedars that are markedly different

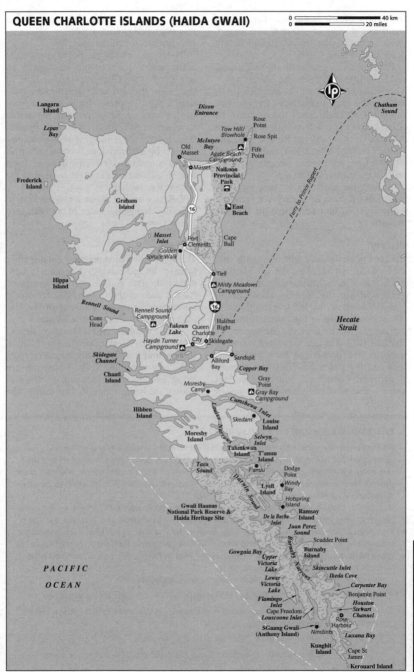

QUEEN CHARLOTTE ISLANDS (HAIDA GWAII)

0   40 km
0   20 miles

Langara Island
Lepas Bay
Frederick Island
Dixon Entrance
Chatham Sound
Rose Point
Tow Hill/ Blowhole
Rose Spit
McIntyre Bay
Old Masset
Agate Beach Campground
Fife Point
Masset
Naikoon Provincial Park
Graham Island
East Beach
16
Cape Ball
Masset Inlet
Port Clements
Golden Spruce Walk
Hippa Island
Tlell
Misty Meadows Campground
Ferry to Prince Rupert
Hecate Strait
Rennell Sound
Rennell Sound Campground
Cone Head
Yakoun Lake
Halibut Bight
Queen Charlotte City
Haydn Turner Campground
Skidegate
Skidegate Channel
Chaatl Island
Alliford Bay
Sandspit
Copper Bay
Gray Point
Gray Bay Campground
Moresby Camp
Cumshewa Inlet
Hibben Island
Skedans
Louise Island
Moresby Island
Selwyn Inlet
Talunkwan Island
T'anuu Island
Tasu Sound
T'anuu
Dodge Point
Windy Bay
Lyell Island
Hotspring Island
Gwaii Haanas National Park Reserve & Haida Heritage Site
De la Beche Inlet
Ramsay Island
Juan Perez Sound
Scudder Point
Gowgaia Bay
Upper Victoria Lake
Burnaby Island
Lower Victoria Lake
Skincuttle Inlet
Ikeda Cove
Carpenter Bay
Benjamin Point
Flamingo Inlet
Houston Stewart Channel
Cape Freedom
Louscoone Inlet
SGaang Gwaii (Anthony Island)
Rose Harbour
Ninstints
Luxana Bay
Kunghit Island
Cape St James
Kerouard Island
PACIFIC OCEAN
Darwin Sound
Burnaby Narrows
Lumber Narrows

NORTHERN BC

from those on the mainland. Hundreds of waterfalls, dozens of streams, and jagged, random peaks that top 1500m in height draw adventurers.

But it's the culture of its traditional residents that really sets the islands apart. The Haida people have old and rich traditions going back thousands of years. You can witness its resurgence today across the islands. You can touch its ancient mysteries at Gwaii Haanas National Park Reserve and Haida Heritage Site, a lost and preserved world where abandoned villages of totem poles stare silently out to sea.

Visiting the islands is not easy and they don't reward those in a hurry. but for those ready to invest time and attention, they are magical.

History

Believed to be the only part of Canada that escaped the last Ice Age, the islands have been inhabited continuously for 10,000 years and are the traditional homeland (Haida Gwaii) of the Haida nation, generally acknowledged as the prime culture in the country at the time the Europeans arrived in 1774. Though they were fearsome warriors who dominated BC's west coast, they had few defenses against the diseases – primarily smallpox, tuberculosis and greed – that were introduced by European explorers. In 1835, the Haida population was estimated at 6000 people; in 1915, that number had shrunk to only 588.

Today, the Haida are proud, politically active and defiant people who make up one-third of the Charlottes' population. In the 1980s, they led an internationally publicized fight to preserve the islands from further logging. More recently the Haida have successfully negotiated with institutions to have the remains of ancestors, once dug up by anthropologists, returned. And you're bound to see evidence of a campaign to stop affluent bear hunters coming to the islands for trophies.

Talk is ongoing about a referendum to officially change the name of the islands to Haida Gwaii.

Culture

The arts of the Haida people – notably their totem poles and carvings in argillite (a dark, glass-like slate found only in southeast Alaska and on these islands) – are world renowned. You'll see evidence of the Haida's artistry throughout the islands.

It's a rich culture that is resurgent, thanks to the original efforts of people like Bill Reid (below) and to artists today like carvers Reg Davidson and Billy Bellis. Potlatches are being held to select community leaders and efforts are being made to ensure that the

---

BILL REID, WATCHMAN OF A CULTURE

Bill Reid became engrossed in Haida culture in the 1950s. His maternal grandmother had grown up on the small island of Tanu in the southern QCI. Diseases caught from Westerners and other calamities left her village empty, with just a few totems to attest to the people who had once thrived there. Reid organized the removal of totem poles to Vancouver in an effort to preserve the artistic achievement of a vanished way of life.

Reid also took up carving, learning the skill from some surviving Haida masters. By the 1980s his works were internationally recognized and his carved cedar canoe, Loo Taas, was the star of Vancouver's Expo 86. But Reid was not only an artist, he was also on the front lines in the fight against logging on the Charlottes and was an activist promoting the rebirth of Haida culture. When he died in 1998, his ashes were taken on Loo Taas to T'anuu, now part of the Gwaii Haanas National Park Reserve and Haida Heritage Site.

You can see Reid's remarkable work in many places, including:

■ Haida Heritage Centre at Qay'llnagaay in Skidegate (p377) – Loo Taas, his iconic canoe.

■ University of British Columbia Museum of Anthropology in Vancouver (p101) – Raven and the First Men, an extraordinary carving.

■ The Bill Reid Gallery of Northwest Coast Art in Vancouver (p96).

■ Your wallet – the reverse of the Canadian $20 bill has depictions of two of Reid's works.

Haida language doesn't join 10 other aboriginal languages in Canada that have gone extinct in the last 100 years.

The obvious starting point to appreciate Haida culture is the remarkable Haida Heritage Centre at Qay'llnagaay (p377) in Skidegate. The Carving Shed in Skidegate (p377) is another great place, but you'll encounter the culture throughout the islands.

Look for copies of the free *Haida Laas*, a monthly publication of the Haida nation. It details the ever-more vigorous cultural lives of the people.

Environment

The wedge-shaped Queen Charlotte archipelago of some 154 islands lies 80km west of the BC coast and about 50km from the southern tip of Alaska. They are warmed by an ocean current that rolls in from Japan, giving the islands 127cm of rain annually.

Poor drainage near the north end of Graham Island results in the growth of sphagnum moss and gentian, surrounded by lodgepole pine and yellow cedar. Elsewhere, mighty stands of western hemlock, Sitka spruce and western red cedar still cover the landscape in places not decimated by 20th-century clear-cutting.

The islands also have their own unique species of pine marten, deer mouse, black bear and short-tailed weasel. Unfortunately, introduced species such as beavers, raccoons and rats have altered the natural balance. Sitka blacktail deer were introduced at least five times between 1880 and 1925 as an alternate food source. Lacking natural predators, the deer became so prolific that hunting is encouraged to control the population; even so they are easily spotted.

Home to 15% of all nesting seabirds in BC, the Queen Charlottes contain the only confirmed nesting site of horned puffins in Canada. A whopping 30% of the world's ancient murrelets nest here, as do most of the province's Peale's peregrine falcons.

From late April through late June, gray whales pass by on their 16,000km annual migration route between Mexico's Baja and Alaska. The islands also include the largest sea lion rookery in BC.

Although logging is in decline due to economics, it destroyed enormous swaths of old-growth forest. The largest surviving tracts are found in the southern third of the archipelago, within the boundaries of the national park. New environmental questions include a proposal to build an enormous wind farm in the comparatively shallow waters of the Hecate Straight off the north end of Graham Island.

Orientation

Mainland ferries dock at Skidegate on Graham Island, the main island for population (80%) and commerce. The principal town is Queen Charlotte City (QCC), 7km west of Skidegate. The main road on Graham Island is Hwy 16, which is fully paved. It links Skidegate in the south with Masset, 101km north.

Graham Island is linked to Moresby Island to the south by a small ferry from Skidegate. The airport is in Sandspit on Moresby Island, 12km east of the ferry landing at Alliford Bay. The only way to get to Gwaii Haanas National Park Reserve, which covers the south part of Moresby Island, is by boat or floatplane.

Information

It is important for visitors to the remote Queen Charlotte Islands to make arrangements for accommodations and tours in

---

TIMING YOUR VISIT

If you plan to visit the Gwaii Haanas National Park Reserve and Haida Heritage Site then you should understand that a visit takes several days (see p380). Those expecting to hop off the ferry and see everything in a few hours and then depart, won't. But don't be discouraged if you have neither time nor money to do a long boat or kayaking trip into the park; you can always arrange a one-day paddle or boat trip, and you can actually see a lot of interest on Graham Island by car or bike. Explore the forests, go beachcombing and chat with the locals, whose ideas and lifestyles are shaped by the salty fresh air and isolation.

Although most tourist activities are dormant out of season, you can visit the islands. It's cold, wet and deeply rewarding for those looking for a lonely, storm-tossed beach.

advance and understand that services are limited. Cell phone reception is patchy and should not be relied upon.

Pick up a copy of the weekly **Queen Charlotte Islands Observer** (www.qciobserver.com; $2), a lively newspaper that doesn't shy away from local debates and includes the views of columnists like the rapier-witted Jane Wilson. The paper publishes the annual *Guide to the Queen Charlotte Islands / Haida Gwaii* (www.queencharlotteislandsguide.com), an indispensable compendium of information and listings.

See p380 for information on visiting Gwaii Haanas National Park Reserve and Haida Heritage Site.

BOOKSTORES
Northwest Coast Books (☎ 250-559-4681; 3205 3rd Ave, QCC; ◷ 10am–4:30pm Tue-Sat) Great collection of QCI books and good recommendations; commentary by Buster, the profane parrot.

EMERGENCY
Ambulance (☎ 800-461-9911)
Police (☎ QCC 250-559-4421, Masset 250-626-3991)

INTERNET ACCESS
The QCC Visitor Centre (right) has internet terminals (per 15 minutes $2.50). Don't expect wi-fi.

LAUNDRY
Coin laundry (117 3rd Ave, City Centre Store complex, QCC; ◷ 8am-6pm) Also has locations in Port Clements and Masset.

MEDICAL SERVICES
In cases of major emergencies, patients are generally sent to Prince Rupert by air ambulance.
Northern Haida Gwaii Hospital (☎ 250-626-4700; 2520 Harrison Ave, Masset; ◷ 24hr) New in 2008, largest on the islands.
Queen Charlotte Islands General Hospital (☎ 250-559-4300; 3209 3rd Ave, QCC; ◷ 24hr)

MONEY
ATMs are found in QCC, Skidegate, Masset and Sandspit.

POST
QCC post office (☎ 250-559-8349; 117 3rd Ave) In the City Centre Store complex; service changes by Canada Post mean that delivery times to the mainland can be s-l-o-w.

TOURIST INFORMATION
Your first stop should be the excellent **Visitor Centre** (VC; ☎ 250-559-8316; www.qcinfo.ca; 3220 Wharf St, QCC; hours and days vary). It occupies a building on the water and has natural history displays, a good website and a small library. A second VC at the airport opens for arriving flights in summer. Both carry marine and topographical charts. For a fee the VC will arrange even the most complex details of a visit to the reserve.

In Masset, the **Visitor Centre** (☎ 250-626-3995; www.massetbc.com; 1450 Christie St; ◷ 10am-4pm Jun-Aug) is near the south entrance to town.

A good website for information is www.haidagwaiitourism.ca. Pick up a copy of *Art Route*, a guide to more than 40 studios and galleries.

QUEEN CHARLOTTE CITY
pop 1100

This small fishing village serves as the commercial center of the islands. The community of permanent residents takes the massive summer influx of tourists in its stride. It's useful as a base and for arranging details of your visit but shouldn't be your focus. Efforts continue to give a new unified name to the town's main road, which at present goes by Hwy 33, 3rd Ave and Cemetery Rd.

Sleeping
Haydn Turner Campground (campsites $15) Deeply shaded at the west end of town, there are pit toilets here. Three walk-in sites ($5) are on the beach. Follow 3rd Ave to the end.

our pick Premier Creek Lodging (☎ 250-559-8415, 888-322-3388; www.qcislands.net/premier, 3101 3rd Ave, QCC; dm $25, r $35-95) Dating from 1910, this friendly lodge has eight beds in a hostel building out back and 12 rooms in the main building, ranging from tiny but great-value singles to spacious rooms with views and porches. There's high-speed internet.

Hecate Inn (☎ 250-559-4543, 800-665-3350; www.qcislands.net/hecateinn; 321 3rd Ave, QCC; r $80-120; ▣) Surrounded by flowers, the 16 spotless rooms here have high-speed internet and kitchens.

Eating & Drinking
Growing food is a popular summer pastime on the Charlottes. Peruse the bounty at the **farmers market** (◷ 8am-noon Sat Jun-Sep). Choices

---

YAKOUN LAKE

Hike about 20 minutes through ancient stands of spruce and cedar to pristine **Yakoun Lake**, a large wilderness lake towards the west side of Graham Island. A small beach near the trail is shaded by gnarly Sitka alders. Dare to take a dip in the bracing waters or just enjoy the sweeping views.

The trailhead to the lake is just off the main dirt and gravel logging road between QCC and Port Clements. It runs for 70km; watch for signs for the lake.

---

include a lot of local foodstuffs. **Isabel Creek Store** (☎ 250-559-8623; 3301 3rd Ave; ☽ 9am-5pm Mon-Sat) is an organic market with fish fresh from the docks 100m away. There's also a basic grocery.

Ocean View Restaurant (☎ 250-559-8503; Sea Raven Motel, 3301 3rd Ave; ☽ 11am-9pm) Good fresh seafood is the specialty at this casual dining room, where some tables look out to the harbor.

Purple Onion Deli (☎ 250-559-4119; 3207 Wharf St; meals $5-8; ☽ 8am-5pm; 🖳) A bright deli with a cute decor accented by little garlic heads and onions. There's a long list of coffee drinks, bakery items and sandwiches. Enjoy 'em at tables outside. There's internet access (per 15 minutes $2.50).

Queen B's (☎ 250-559-4463; 3201 Wharf St; meals $7-15; ☽ 9am-5pm) In the lower level of an old Canadian Legion hall, this funky place excels at baked goods, which emerge from the oven all day long. There are tables with water views outside and lots of local art inside. In summer there are dinners on Friday and Saturday nights that feature local foods like salmon.

SKIDEGATE
pop 740

Skidegate (pronounced 'skid-a-git'), a Haida community on the shores of Rooney Bay, is leading the revival of Haida culture and art. Its museum is reason enough to visit the Charlottes.

The town has a small shopping strip with a good market and bakery. At the north end of town, look for a **carving shed** (☽ 9am-4pm) on the water's edge, where new works of art are in constant creation. **Jags Beanstalk** (☎ 250-559-8826; 100 Hwy 16; ☽ 8am-5pm) serves superb

coffee drinks (with artful foam!) with views and flowers.

Haida Heritage Centre at Qay'llnagaay

One of BC's top attractions, the recently dedicated **Haida Heritage Centre at Qay'llnagaay** (☎ 250-559-4643; www.haidaheritagecentre.com; adult/child $12/5; ☽ 10am-6pm Mon-Sat May-Sep, open Sun also Jul & Aug, 11am-5pm Tue-Sat Oct-Apr) is a magnificent monument to the islands and their culture. It's a living monument: workshops and carving sheds buzz with Haida artisans creating new canoes and totem poles (there are 11 already on site; for more information see p43). Interactive displays detail how humans have changed the islands over thousands of years (mostly by logging in the last 50). Learn about the 12 species of trees on the islands and listen to hydrophones underwater at East Limestone Island, just outside the museum – you may hear a whale. Among the fascinating things you'll learn is that bears usually eat their salmon under certain trees and these trees end up being especially vigorous – the perfect candidate for a totem pole. There are daily programs in summer.

TLELL
pop 400

The 40km road from Skidegate north to Tlell follows the dramatic, rocky coast right at the water's edge and is a QCI highlight. About 18km past Skidegate, look for a **spring** by the side of the road, where locals stop to fill jugs. After 4km there's a fine shady **rest stop** on a rocky shore with picnic tables. Look overhead for bald eagles giving you a beady eye.

Tlell is barely definable as a village – it's more a small collection of artsy places along the road. Look for the **Rising Tide Bakery** (☎ 250-557-4677; ☽ 8am-5pm Wed-Sun Jun-Aug), loved by locals and visitors alike for its sticky buns made with flour ground on site. It serves soups and sandwiches also.

Tlell is the southern gateway to **Naikoon Provincial Park** and home to the **park headquarters** (☎ 250-557-4390; ☽ 9am-4pm Jun-Aug). Here you can obtain information on the tides and check out the interpretive displays. The beautiful 72,640-hectare park, extending to the northeast tip of Graham Island, is comprised mostly of sand dunes and low sphagnum bogs surrounded by stunted and gnarled lodgepole pine and red and yellow cedar. The word 'naikoon' is a corruption of 'nai-kun', meaning 'long nose' – the name for the 5km-long Rose Spit that separates the stormy Hecate Strait and Dixon Entrance. The park is loosely divided into North (at Masset) and South (at Tlell). You'll find campgrounds and interesting hikes at either end.

From Tlell, take the worthwhile **Pesuta Trail** to the wreck of the *Pesuta,* a timber-hauling ship that ran aground in 1928. The trail begins at the Tlell River Picnic Area, just off Hwy 16 past the park headquarters, and follows the river to East Beach. You then follow the high-tide line out to the wreck. Allow about seven hours to make the 10km round-trip.

See opposite for details on the north end of the Naikoon Provincial Park.

Just off Hwy 16, **Crystal Cabin Gallery** (☎ 250-557-4383; 778 Richardson Rd; ☽ 9am-6pm) has works by local artists, some of it quite exquisite. There are a couple of other shops selling art nearby.

Sleeping

Naikoon Provincial Park (☎ 250-557-4390) contains two excellent campgrounds. **Misty Meadows Campground** (campsite $15; ☽ mid-May–Sep), just off Hwy 16 at the south end of the park, features 30 shaded sites, some of which have platforms so your tent doesn't get soaked. A short trail leads to the beach. See opposite for information on Agate Beach Campground.

Cacilia's B&B (☎ 250-557-4664; www.qcislands.net /ceebysea; r $40-80) Let the surf lull you to sleep at this beechwood-shingled beach house surrounded by dunes just off Hwy 16 as it turns inland. There are six sizable rooms and the chance to start a huge driftwood collection.

PORT CLEMENTS
pop 500

This logging and harbor town lies 21km north of Tlell on Hwy 16. For years it was famous for the **Golden Spruce**, a huge genetically unique spruce that had a low chlorophyll count and thus a golden color. In 1997, Grant Hadwin, an anti-logging logger and zealot, cut it down to protest 'the hypocrisy of logging.' The act didn't just kill the tree, it traumatized the community as

well. (Hadwin supposedly drowned while trying to return to the islands by kayak from Prince Rupert.) The entire affair is brilliantly chronicled in *The Golden Spruce* by John Vaillant.

Today, a 1m-tall tree sprouted from a golden spruce pinecone grows gamely behind a huge fence near the museum. Is that golden tinge due to its parent's gene or ill health?

There are two good walks near Port Clements. About 1km south on Juskatla Rd is **Sunset Park**, which has a 2km boardwalk into the marshes and a tall watchtower from where you can see oodles of birds, otters and other critters. The **Golden Spruce Walk**, 5km further south, may now only feature the stump of its namesake but this actually lets you focus more on the amazing and verdant coastal rainforest along the 3km trail. Just after the start, bear to the right and you'll see a huge cedar growing on the side of a yet larger spruce.

The **Port Clements Museum** (☎ 250-557-4285; admission $2; ☽ 9am-1pm Jun-Aug, 2-4pm Sat & Sun Sep-May) on Bayview Dr has artifacts from the era of clear-cutting. As the economy has killed logging on the islands (bringing much economic hardship), the collection has multiplied.

Golden Spruce Motel (☎ 250-557-4325, 877-801-4653; www.qcislands.net/golden; 2 Grouse St; r $55-85; ▢ ⊚) is a rambling place where the 12 rooms are more brown than golden. Owner Urs Thomas can organize all sorts of adventures on sea and land. (If that includes some of the island's legendary fishing, he'll barbeque your fish.) There's a laundry and a good breakfast café.

MASSET & OLD MASSET
pop 1700

These two adjoining towns divide right along cultural lines: Haida live in Old Masset, others live in Masset, the commercial center of the north end of the island. There are a few artists with studios here and the setting, on broad and flat Masset Inlet, gives it the feel of a village in the Maritimes.

You'll see marinas and harbors here and the seafaring heritage is preserved at the **Dixon Entrance Maritime Museum** (☎ 250-626-6066; 2182 Collison Ave, Masset; adult/child $2/free; ☽ 1-4pm Jun-Aug, 2-4pm Sat & Sun Sep-May). It also has a good gallery of local art.

Sleeping & Eating

A few shops, cafés and groceries are along Main St, Masset. By far the best supermarket on the islands is the **Co-op Marketplace** (☎ 250-626-3933; Main St; 8am-7pm), which has a deli, bakery and more.

Hidden Island RV & Resort (☎ 250-626-5286, 866-303-5286; www.hidden-island-resort.ca; 1440 Tow Hill Rd; campsites from $20) About 1km from Masset on Tow Hill Rd, this has 16 shady sites. It has a café (open noon to 8pm) with superb fish and chips sourced from halibut caught in nearby waters.

our pick **Copper Beech House** (☎ 250-626-5441; www.copperbeechhouse.com; 1590 Delkatla Rd, Masset; r from $100) Run by legendary chef and bon vivant David Phillips, this rambling old house backs onto the Masset harbor and features three unique rooms, all with private bathrooms. There's always something amazing cooking in the ever-expanding kitchen.

Haida Rose Café (☎ 250-626-3310; 415 Frog St; snacks $3-5; 8am-5pm;) This community hangout and gallery in Old Massett serves excellent coffee and is just a short stroll from totem polls and a carving shed.

Masset's small airport (p380), 1km east of town, is also the site of **HaidaBucks Lounge** (☎ 250-626-5548; meals $8-12; noon-late), which gained fame after Starbucks threatened legal action for trademark infringement (they desisted after lots of bad PR).

NORTH COAST

Tow Hill Rd runs 26km east of Masset along a constantly storm-tossed beach. Flotsam from as far as Japan washes ashore daily. A long stretch of the road runs under a canopy of moss-draped trees arching overhead like a living cathedral. The last 12km are packed sand, which is fine for cars except after a storm. Scattered all along here are funky little businesses run by the kinds of eccentric owners you find at the end of a remote road.

At about 9km, look for **Trout House** (☎ 250-626-9330; 9102 Tow Hill Rd; summer, varies), which seems half constructed from driftwood. Cozy up to the pot-bellied stove for a cup of coffee and enjoy organic and healthy fare.

Just past the 15km marker, look for two sets of beach cabins. By now you're off the grid, meaning that cooking is by propane and lighting is by lantern. It's hard to

imagine more restful surroundings far from contemporary life.

Rapid Richie's Rustic Rentals (☎ 250-626-5472; www.beachcabins.com; cabins $70-90) Has five cabins; the Zendo is right in the dunes.

North Beach Cabins (☎ 250-557-2415; www.northbeachcabins.com; cabins $75-90) Four cabins near the water with wrap-around decks.

Embodying the spirit of this road to the end of everything, **Moon Over Naikoon** (☎ 250-626-5064; 8am-5pm Jun-Aug), 17 km east of Masset, has a bakery and a kaleidoscopic collection of artworks and stuff found on the beach.

Bed down while tides driven from Asia hit the beach at Naikoon Provincial Park's **Agate Beach Campground** (☎ 250-557-4390; campsites $15; mid-May–mid-Sep), 23km east. The 43 sites sit right on the sand. On clear days you can see Alaska. Named for the pretty glass-like stones found along the beaches, Agate Beach can get windy and quite chilly after dark. Outside of the season, you can camp here for free but there are no pit toilets or firewood.

Near the end of the road lies **Tow Hill**, a columnar basalt outcrop an hour's hike from a parking lot. At the top, you'll enjoy incredible views of the north end of Naikoon Provincial Park as well as north to Alaska. Also worth checking out is the **Blowhole**, which spurts out ocean water on incoming tides.

For real adventure, hit the **Cape Fife Loop Trail**, a 21km loop that takes you over the Argonaut Plain to Fife Point and Rose Spit through the northern part of Naikoon Provincial Park.

At the very end of the road you can park on packed sand and see **Tow Hill Beach** stretching seemingly forever east into the mists. It's mystical, beautiful and a bit primordial. Pitch a tent at **Hiellen Campground** (☎ 250-626-5115; campsite $20), a Haida-run facility with sites just off the beach under moss-draped cedars.

SANDSPIT

pop 470

Sandspit is just that – a long sandy spit jutting out into Hecate Strait. The only community on Moresby Island, Sandspit is home to the airport, a grocery and simple inns aimed at people heading into the park or fishing. It's also the major gateway into the Gwaii Haanas reserve.

Moresby Island Guest House (☎ 250-637-5300; www.moresbyisland-bnb.com; 385 Beach Rd; r $35-75) has 10 rooms which share bathrooms in a large modern house right on the bay. You can rent a bike here.

In the airport terminal, **Java on the Spit** (☎ 250-637-2455; meals $6-8; ☺ 9am-4pm; 🛜) is *the* place for lunch (and not just because options are few). Wondrous baked goods, sandwiches and soups.

GWAII HAANAS NATIONAL PARK RESERVE & HAIDA HERITAGE SITE

Other-worldly and ethereal, this huge, wild park encompasses parts of Moresby and 137 smaller islands at the south end of the Queen Charlottes. The 640km-long stretch of rugged coastline is true wilderness at its best. If you take out a kayak, you can paddle for days without seeing another human being. (Although you might find a few at the hot springs.)

Archaeological finds have documented more than 500 ancient Haida sites, including villages and burial caves dotted throughout the islands. The most famous (and photographed) village is **Ninstints**, on SGaang Gwaii (Anthony Island), where rows of totem poles stare eerily out to sea. This ancient village was declared a Unesco World Heritage site in 1981. Other major sights include Skedans on Louise Island and Hotspring Island, where you can soak away the bone-chilling cold in natural springs. The ancient sites are protected by the Haida Gwaii Watchmen, who live on the islands during summer. Their name comes from human figures at the top of totem poles who looked over villages and warned of danger.

Information

Access to the park is by boat or floatplane only. A visit demands advance planning and usually requires several days. If you want to travel independently, you need to reserve ahead, as only a limited number of people can be in the park at any given time (see Reservations & Fees, right).

Anyone who has not visited the park during the previous three years must attend a free 90-minute orientation session that's instructive and entertaining. Sessions are held at the **Haida Heritage Centre at Qay'llnagaay** (☺ 9am Mon-Fri Jun-early Sep, also Sat Jul & Aug) in Skidegate (see p377). You may also be able to arrange a session at Sandspit's airport if you did not plan on taking the ferry to Graham Island. Ask when you reserve. Contact Parks Canada's **Gwaii Haanas office** (☎ 250-559-8818; www.pc.gc.ca/gwaiihaanas) in the heritage centre with questions. The website is a thorough resource; download the Trip Planner.

RESERVATIONS & FEES

For travel from May 1 through September 30 you must obtain one of a limited number of daily **reservations** (☎ 250-387-1642, 800-435-5622; per person $15) unless you have a guide who has arranged this. In addition there are user fees (per night adult/child $20/10). Each day from May 1 to September 30, six standby spaces are made available and demand for these can be fierce as a winter gale – call **Parks Canada** (☎ 250-559-8818; www.pc.gc.ca /gwaiihaanas) or check at the QCC **Visitor Centre** (p376) for details.

Activities

The easiest way to get into the park is with a tour company. The QCC **Visitor Centre** (p376) can provide names of operators or, for a fee, it can plan and organize even the most complex trips. Some will outfit independent travelers with gear and other essentials such as kayaks (average per day/ week $75/350).

Anvil Cove (☎ 250-559-8207; www.queencharlotte kayaking.com) QCC based; tours combine kayaks with nights on a namesake eight-passenger sailboat; six- to 10-day trips from $2300.

Moresby Explorers (☎ 250-637-2215, 800-806-7633; www.moresbyexplorers.com) Sandspit based; has one-day tours from $190 and much longer ones. Rents kayaks and gear.

Ocean Sound Kayaking (☎ 403-609-5576; www .oceansoundkayaking.com) Leads well-regarded eight- to 11-day kayaking tours from $2000 per person.

Queen Charlotte Adventures (☎ 250-559-8990, 800-668-4288; www.queencharlotteadventures.com) QCI based; offers one- to 10-day trips using power boats, kayaks or sailboats. A six-day trip that covers the park using kayaks and a camping mothership costs $2000. Does kayak rentals and transport.

GETTING THERE & AWAY
Air

The main airport for QCI is at **Sandspit** (YZP; ☎ 250-559-0052) on Moresby Island. Masset has a small airport (YMT) 1km east of town.

Air Canada Jazz (☎ 888-247-2262; www.aircanada .com) flies daily between Sandspit and Vancouver. **Pacific Coastal Airlines** (☎ 800-663- 2872; www.pacific-coastal.com) flies between Masset and Vancouver's South Terminal several times each week. **North Pacific Seaplanes** (☎ 800- 689-4234; www.northpacificseaplanes.com) offers a picturesque service between Prince Rupert and Masset, QCC and pretty much any place else a floatplane can land (one-way fares start from $260).

Note that reaching the airport from Graham Island is time consuming: if your flight is at 3:30pm, you need to line up at the car ferry at Skidegate Landing by 12:30pm (earlier in summer or you'll be left at the dock) in order to make the 1pm ferry in order to have time to check in for your flight.

Ferry
BC Ferries (☎ 250-386-3431; www.bcferries.com) has services between Prince Rupert and Skidegate Landing (adult/child $35/17.50, car from $125, cabin from $50, seven to nine hours, six per week summer, three per week winter).

GETTING AROUND
Once you leave Hwy 16, most of the roads are gravel or worse. Many are logging roads and, while activity is down, watch out for trucks.

BC Ferries operates a small and less-than-convenient **ferry** linking the two main islands at Skidegate Landing and Alliford Bay (adult/child $7/4, cars from $17, 20 minutes, almost hourly 7am to 10pm). The schedule pauses about the time flights arrive, meaning a major delay for many; worse, new restrictions limit passengers and cars to well under the boat's capacity, which causes some to wait one or more sailings in summer.

Eagle Transit (☎ 877-747-4461; www.qcislands.net /eagle) meets flights and ferries. The fare from the airport to QCC is $20/13 per adult/ child. It also runs a ferry connector for all Prince Rupert services. Fares range from $2 to QCC to $20 to Masset.

If you want to get around in a car, you are going to have to weigh the high cost of local car rental against the cost of bringing a vehicle on the ferry. **Budget** (☎ 250-637-5688; www .budget.com) has locations at both the airport and QCC. The slightly cheaper **Rustic Car**

Rentals (☎ 250-559-4641, 877-559-4641; citires@ qcislands.net; 605 Hwy 33, QCC) operates out of a gas station. Rates at both can run from $60 to $100 or more per day as mileage is not included.

STEWART-CASSIAR HIGHWAY

Dare we say it? This is the better way to the Yukon. Over its 727km length, the Stewart-Cassiar Hwy traverses some of the rawest and wildest country in BC. It's your gateway to enormous glaciers, vast, barely explored lands and, simply put, the sense of adventure that's brought you north in the first place.

Perhaps your biggest stumbling block will be the road's reputation. For years it was a crude connector known for its ability to shred tires and constitutions. But years of steady improvements have made it accessible for all vehicles. While it still isn't the breeze that the Alaska Hwy has become, it has opened up an exciting route to the north.

Even if you're not going to the Yukon, use the Stewart-Cassiar to get to jaw-dropping glaciers and the fun vibe of Stewart, BC and Hyder, Alaska (p382).

Orientation & Information
The Stewart-Cassiar Hwy (Hwy 37) starts and heads north from Hwy 16 at Kitwanga (p382), 468km west of Prince George and 241km east of Prince Rupert. Officially it takes the name Stewart-Cassiar Hwy at Meziadin Junction.

Less than 10% of the highway is still not paved, and even these gravel stretches are kept in good shape. In summer, cars will have no problem. But you should also prepare for contingencies – bad weather can make conditions tough – and keep your tank full: services are sparse. Many services and businesses are not open outside of summer and road conditions may be hopeless in winter.

The **Stewart-Cassiar Tourism Council** (☎ 866- 417-3737; www.stewartcassiar.com) is a good source of info. BC provides **road condition reports** (☎ 250-771-3000, 250-771-4511; www.drivebc.ca).

For a discussion of travel options to the Yukon, see (p388).

NORTHERN BC

HIGHWAY 37 QUICK REFERENCE

Here's a primer to conditions and services (confirm they're open outside June to September) with distances going north from the Hwy 16 junction:

- Hwy 16 Junction–Meziadin Junction: Road is paved and modern for entire length. Meziadin Junction (156km north) has junction for Hwy 37A to Stewart & Hyder (below) and gas, a café and groceries.

- Meziadin Junction–Bell II: Road is modern and paved for the entire length. Bell II (250km north) has gas, a café, camping and a lodge.

- Bell II–Tatogga Lake: Road is paved except for one 20km stretch. Tatogga Lake (390km north) has gas, a restaurant (summer) and lodging.

- Tatogga Lake–Iskut: Road is paved. Iskut (405km north) has gas and lodging.

- Iskut–Dease Lake: Road has one unpaved 20km section. Dease Lake (488km north) has gas, repairs, shops, cafés and lodging.

- Dease Lake–Good Hope Lake: Paved road has one short, unpaved portion along the lake. Good Hope Lake (626km north) has gas.

- Good Hope Lake–Junction Hwy 37 and Alaska Hwy: The road is paved but narrow and curvy. Numerous warnings for animals. The junction with the Alaska Hwy (p397; 727km north); gas, repairs and cafés here and in nearby Watson Lake.

KITWANGA

Kitwanga, along with nearby Gitanyow and Kispiox (p365), is the traditional home of the Gitksan First Nations people, who traded along this section of the Skeena River for centuries. The area includes spectacular **totem poles**, as well as the small **Kitwanga Fort National Historic Site**. A path with interpretive signs follows a route up Battle Hill, where Canada's only First Nations fort commanded the valley in pre-colonial days.

GITANYOW

Otherwise known as Kitwancool, this small First Nations town is home to more than a dozen stunning **totem poles** dating from over 100 years ago to the present (for more on the meaning of totem poles, see p43). Behind the array is a community center that is sometimes open and which has displays of local cultural items. The town is 21km north of Hwy 16 and well worth the detour, even if you are not going any further on Hwy 37.

MEZIADIN JUNCTION

About 155km north of Kitwanga, this is the junction with Hwy 37A to Stewart and Hyder. Nearby, **Meziadin Lake Provincial Park** (☎ 250-638-8490) has become a popular fishing spot and campground with pit toilets,

a boat launch and 60 sites ($15), some of which are on the lake.

STEWART & HYDER

If you've come this far, don't miss the chance to take the 67km side trip west to the twin border towns of Stewart, BC, and Hyder, Alaska, which sit on the coast at the head of the Portland Inlet. Glaciers like you'll see no place else, waterfalls, ravenous bears and hapless salmon are some of the unforgettable sights.

Stewart's **Visitor Centre** (☎ 250-636-9224, 888-366-5999; www.stewart-hyder.com; 222 5th Ave; ⌚ 9am-6pm Jun-Sep, limited hr winter) covers the region.

Sights

The ride in on Hwy 37A is a sight in itself: midway to Stewart you'll see more and more of **Bear Glacier** until you round a bend and there's a hill-sized icefield flowing into a lake next to the road and glowing an ethereal blue. You've now already seen more glacial ice than people see all day on the Icefields Parkway in the Rockies (p322).

The long Portland Inlet, a steep ocean fjord that extends from the coast 90km into the mountains, finally stops at Stewart, Canada's most northerly ice-free port. The fjord cuts a natural border between Canada and the USA, which is why Hyder,

---

DETOUR: CRANBERRY JUNCTION ROUTE

At the mythical 'Cranberry Junction' (it's little more than a signpost) 82km north of Hwy 16, a logging road runs 51km east to the Nisga'a Lava Bed (p365). This is a great shortcut between Prince Rupert and the Stewart-Cassiar Hwy and it gives you an easy way to see the lava beds. One caveat: the logging road is unpaved for its length. During the late spring, summer and early fall when it's dry, cars should not have a problem but watch out for logging trucks. Another attraction is that it is a scenic, quiet road. One October day we saw over a dozen bears.

3km away, is only connected to other parts of Alaska by water and air. For a good look at the isolated beauty of the area, watch *Insomnia*, a 2002 thriller with Robin Williams and Al Pacino.

Stewart (population 700) was once a bustling mining town where prospectors flocked after hearing about the discovery of gold. The boom, however, was short lived, and when the riches ran dry, so did the population. Today, Stewart's port shuffles logs to southerly ports. Its center, **5th Ave**, is lined with vintage buildings.

Hyder (population 60, give or take a couple of sled dogs) ekes out an existence as a 'ghost town', although here the spooks sell trinkets. Some 40,000 tourists come through every summer avoiding any border hassle from US customs officers – there aren't any (although going back to Stewart you'll pass through a Canadian customs post – keeping a gimlet eye out for liquor and guns smuggled into Hyder by boat). It has muddy streets and a long **pier** you can drive out on for great harbor views.

The towns collectively greet visitors to the area, and you'll barely know they're in separate countries. They say the postal code (V0T 1W0) sums it up: Very Old Town, One Way Out. You can use Canadian currency in both towns.

GLACIER HIGHWAY

The name is a bit of a misnomer – it's all rough gravel – but this road takes you through rich scenery and to what can best be described as a glacial orgasm.

Fish Creek (www.fs.fed.us), about 3km past Hyder, is a major run for pink and chum salmon. From mid-July through September, the salmon run and you can watch the drama from a long, wooden, elevated walkway. Spent fish lay their eggs and die in the shallows while bears stalk about feasting. Bald eagles and gulls dart in for their share.

It may smell like a fish store three days after the power quit, but it's riveting.

Continue on for 20km and slowly a vast icefield will come into view. Continue up the hill to a **viewpoint** (33km from Hyder) where the sheer immensity of **Salmon Glacier** spreads in all directions. Unlike other glaciers, here the striated ice of the continent's fifth largest glacier flows to the horizon through two series of peaks. Bring a picnic, settle back, sniff an alpine wildflower and just soak up the splendor.

Pick up the excellent *Salmon Glacier Self Guided Auto Tour* from the Stewart VC.

Sleeping

Stewart's 5th Ave has a number of off-beat cafés, shops and places with internet access.

Rainey Creek Campground (☎ 250-636-2537; 8th Ave; campsites $12-25) Showers, kitchens, tent pads and flush toilets ensure the 98-site municipal Rainey Creek Campground is a good choice.

ourpick Ripley Creek Inn (☎ 250-636-2344; www .ripleycreekinn.com; 306 5th Ave; r $50-120; 🖳 🛜) Spread across five historic buildings in Stewart's center, the 32 rooms are decorated with a stylish mix of new and old. Venues range from simple rooms in a former brothel to large rooms with private decks overlooking the estuary. Ask if you can see the toaster museum of early kitchen conveniences.

King Edward Hotel & Motel (☎ 250-636-2244, 800-663-3126; www.kingedwardhotel.com; 405 5th Ave; r $60-100; 🍴 🖳 🛜) Of the two buildings here, the two-story motel-style one has the nicest rooms. Some of the 65 rooms have kitchens. There's a popular coin laundry.

Eating & Drinking

For the tastiest local seafood, look around Hyder for the mobile **Seafood Express** (☎ 250-636-9011; meals from $7; 🕑 erratic), which serves up stupendous plate meals from a kitchen in a school bus. Dine at picnic tables outside.

Bitter Creek Café (☎ 250-636-2166; 311 5th Ave, Stewart; meals $10-30; ⏱ 5-10pm May-Sep) An artifact-filled pub run by the Ripley Creek Inn folks, the menu features excellent chowder, steaks, seafood and oven-fresh biscuits. Tables on the terrace shine in summer.

Glacier Inn (☎ 250-636-9248; Hyder) Looks like hell from the outside and only a tad better inside. Ignore the touristy 'get Hyderized' shot-swilling shtick and you can settle back for a good session in this old boozer.

NORTH OF MEZIADIN JUNCTION

At **Bell II**, an outpost 94km north of the Meziadin Junction, **Bell II Lodge** (☎ 604-639-8455, 800-530-2167; www.bell2lodge.com; campsite $20-31, r $125-180; 🖥) has 22 upscale chalets and 15 campsites. You can heli-ski from here in the winter.

North of here, the highway passes through a series of canyons with rushing white-water rivers. Some 120km east over roadless mountains is the Sacred Headwaters, a pristine sub-alpine basin that is under threat by energy companies (p59).

At the Tahltan town of **Iskut**, the gateway to Spatsizi Plateau Wilderness Park (below), you'll find a grocery store, gas station and places to stay.

Just south of Iskut, the **Red Goat Lodge** (☎ 250-234-3261, 888-734-4628; www.redgoatlodge.com; campsite $15-25, r from $90; 🛜), on the shores of Eddontenajon Lake, is a haven for travelers, with hotel rooms and upscale B&B rooms. There are campsites and you can rent kayaks and canoes; llamas wander about.

Parks

Kinaskan Lake Provincial Park is excellent for trout fishing, offers 50 lakeside campsites ($15) with pit toilets (but no showers) and free wood. Access is about 115km north of Bell II.

Spatsizi Plateau Wilderness Provincial Park is a vast and wild place that is mostly inaccessible. The park entrance is 136km east of Hwy 37 at Tatogga along primitive roads, which pretty much end when you get to the park. The park's trails are often little more than vague notions across the untouched landscape.

Stikine River Recreation Area, a narrow park west of Dease Lake (right), connects the Spatsizi Plateau Wilderness Park with the Mt Edziza Provincial Park and serves as the pull-out for canoe trips starting in Spatsizi. Past the bridge, the river thrusts through the spectacular **Grand Canyon of the Stikine**, an 80km stretch through a steep and sheer-walled canyon that is completely unnavigable by boat but beautifully scenic by car.

The 230,000-hectare **Mt Edziza Provincial Park** protects a volcanic landscape featuring lava flows, basalt plateaus and cinder cones surrounding an extinct shield volcano. Though it's inaccessible by car, you can hike, horseback ride or fly into the park by making arrangements in Telegraph Creek or Dease Lake.

The stunning little **Boya Lake Provincial Park**, about 100km north of Dease Lake, surrounds the shockingly turquoise Boya Lake. Dotted with small tree-covered islets, this warm lake looks like something out of the tropics. You can camp right on the shore. The campground includes pit toilets, a boat launch and 45 campsites ($15).

Dease Lake & North

Although the area was once an important supply point for construction of the Alaska Hwy to the north, Dease Lake is today a small stop on the highway, a halfway point between Hwy 16 and Whitehorse. There are stores and motels.

Northway Motor Inn (☎ 250-771-5341, 866-888-2588; www.northwaymotorinn.bcnetwork.com; r $85-100; 🛜) has 44 large rooms. The restaurant is a cut above the norm, with fresh service and friendly food – wait!

Relive the Lincoln Logs of your youth at **Arctic Divide Inn & Motel** (☎ 250-771-3119; www .arcticdivide.ca; r $85; 🛜). Logs and post-and-beam construction give this midrange motel a little flair.

West from Dease Lake is **Telegraph Creek**, a minute wilderness town 113km along rugged Telegraph Creek Rd. Part ghost-town, it's located in the heart of Stikine River country. **Stikine RiverSong** (☎ 250-235-3196; www.stikineriversong.com; 🖥) is a café, inn, general store and guiding service located in an 1898 heritage building.

Hwy 37 is paved the rest of the way north to the Yukon. The road becomes narrow and winding but there are some pristine lakes along the way and lots of wildlife. Watch for moose.

GLACIER BAY NATIONAL PARK (ALASKA)

South of BC's Tatshenshini-Alsek Provincial Wilderness Park, this spectacular US park fits into the amazing jigsaw puzzle of borders and beauty here. Sixteen tidewater glaciers spill out from the mountains to the sea, making these unusual icefields some of the most renowned in the world. The glaciers here are in retreat, revealing remains of plants and animals that fascinate naturalists. Most people prefer to kayak the small inlets and bays, particularly Muir, where cruise ships are not allowed. There are few trails except around the **park headquarters** (☎ 907-697-2627; www.nps .gov/glba) in Bartlett Cove. Lonely Planet's *Alaska* has extensive coverage of this wonderland.

ATLIN
pop 470

If you make the journey to Atlin, then stay. Bouncing over the at-times-rough 98km road to this time capsule of a frontier town will reward those who get with the laid-back, iconoclastic vibe – something you can't do in an afternoon.

Surrounded by the huge icefields and glaciers of the northern Coast Mountains, Atlin sits alongside the 145km-long land-locked fjord known as Atlin Lake. Isolated in the northwestern-most corner of BC, Atlin was born in 1898 on the back of the Klondike gold rush. In town, colorful houses face the lake, with boats or float-planes parked in front. Atlin served as the location for the 1983 Brian Dennehy film *Never Cry Wolf* about a government researcher who comes to love wolves.

At the southwest corner of the lake is the imposing **Llewellyn Glacier**, whose meltwater carries glacial sediment to the lake, making it a seemingly too-beautiful-not-to-be-fake turquoise.

The small **Atlin Museum** (☎ 250-651-7522; ⓨ mid-May–early Sep), housed in a 1902 schoolhouse, offers area information, historical displays and walking tours. Volunteers and staff are doing a fine job restoring the retired 1917 gas-powered lake cruiser *MV Tarahne* (tah-ron). Right down by the waterfront, the **Atlin Inn & Kirkwood Cottages** (☎ 250-651-7546; Lake

St; r from $70) has basic rooms in a vintage hotel and nearby log cabins. It's *the* local pub.

The partial-gravel Atlin Rd (Hwy 7 in the Yukon) runs south from the Alaska Hwy in the Yukon. The junction is at **Jake's Corner** and is 346km west of the junction of Hwy 37 with the Alaska Hwy and 62km southeast of Whitehorse. Notwithstanding glaciers and impenetrable peaks, you're only 150km from Juneau, Alaska.

TATSHENSHINI-ALSEK PROVINCIAL WILDERNESS PARK

Jointly managed by BC Parks and the Champagne and Aishihik First Nations, this park on the northwest tip of BC is part of the Unesco World Heritage site that includes Kluane National Park and Reserve in the Yukon (p400), and Glacier Bay and Wrangell-St Elias National Parks in Alaska. It is only accessible through the Yukon or Alaska, with Haines being a good starting point. At nearly a million hectares, it is the largest park in BC. Created in the early 1990s to protect the area from mining, the park superseded Tweedsmuir Provincial Park (981,000 hectares) as the largest park in the province. It's entirely wilderness although its two namesake rivers attract hardy and expert river-rafters and kayakers. The BC Parks website (www.env.gov .bc.ca) has a series of good downloadable maps covering the rivers in detail.

NORTHERN BC

Yukon Territory

Just the name Yukon stirs the soul. Derived from the First Nations word *Youcon*, which means 'big river,' this mountainous northern territory reaches past the Arctic Circle to the Arctic Ocean.

The namesake big river has been a vital link from the past to the present. Tens of thousands of gold seekers, drawn by the fantasy of riches, floated down the Yukon River in a motley collection of rafts and homemade boats in 1897. Many perished and those who survived to reach Dawson City mostly discovered failure and ruination.

These days legions of paddlers travel the Yukon River during a barely three-month-long season combining spring, summer and fall. For many it is the trip of a lifetime as the glacier-fed waters move them swiftly past pristine river banks teeming with wildlife.

In Dawson, whether arriving by road or river, visitors discover a town whose storied past is on display in an evocative mix of restored gold-rush buildings and structures rotting away, each weathered board telling a story. But what makes Dawson a real gem is that, the past aside, it's a vibrant, quirky town filled with creative characters who find their life's direction at the end of the road.

Far up the Yukon River, Whitehorse, the territory's capital, is another surprising place. At the crossroads of the Alaska Hwy and the Klondike Hwy, it has a rich cultural life and is the base for adventures throughout the territory. Many of these include time in Kluane National Park and Reserve, a vast wilderness of glaciers in the west.

HIGHLIGHTS

- Plotting your course in forbidding **Kluane National Park** (p400)
- Discovering **Fort Selkirk** (p407) on the Yukon River
- Catching the vibe in intoxicating **Dawson City** (p407)
- Paddling the glacier-fed **Yukon River** (p389) or its tributaries
- Taking in the arctic beauty of **Tombstone Territorial Park** (p416)

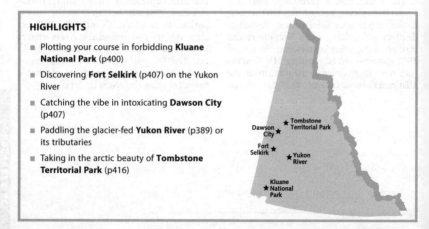

YUKON TERRITORY

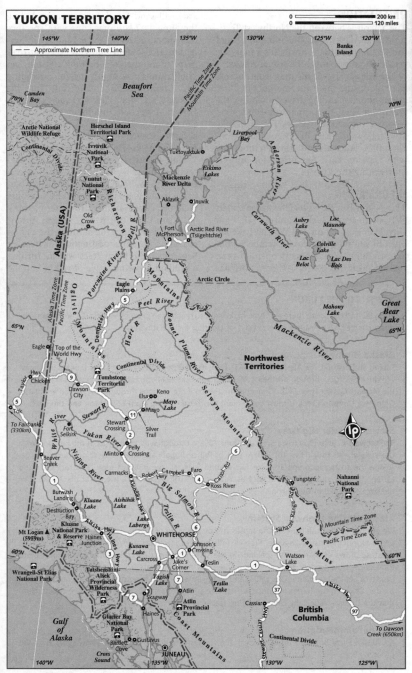

ORIENTATION

The Yukon is between the Northwest Territories and Alaska, with BC to the south and the Beaufort Sea to the north. It's a subarctic region about one-third the size of Alaska.

The Alaska Hwy is the main route across the Yukon, and there are a number of other scenic and demanding drives, including the Dempster Hwy, the only north–south road to cross the Arctic Circle. The Klondike Hwy follows the path of the gold rush from Klondike, Alaska, and links Whitehorse with Dawson City. See below for options on reaching the Yukon.

INFORMATION

The Yukon has six **visitor information centers** (VICs). Beaver Creek, Carcross, Dawson City, Haines Junction and Watson Lake are open in summer (May to September) from 8am to 8pm; Whitehorse is open all year. **Tourism Yukon** (☎ 800-661-0494; www.travelyukon

.com) will send free information, including the annual *Yukon* magazine with specifics on regional activities, events and accommodation. It also distributes an excellent road map. A number of other official tourism publications are highly useful, including *Art Adventures on Yukon Time*, *Into the Yukon Wilderness*, *Viewing Yukon's Natural History Attractions* and many more.

Two magazines to look for on your travels have excellent features on the Yukon: *Up Here* and *Yukon: North of Ordinary*.

Note the extremes in daylight hours and temperatures. Whitehorse may experience long, 19-hour sunny days in July but, come January, it's light for a mere six hours (actually, 'light' is the wrong term, think 'less dark') and the average temperature is −18.7°C. For all but the hardiest, the Yukon is truly a summer destination. In fact by September the birch trees will be turning a brilliant, glowing shade of yellow and the

NORTH TO THE YUKON

From BC and the south there are three main ways to reach the Yukon by vehicle. All are potentially good choices, so you have several ways of creating a circle itinerary.

Alaska Highway

Fabled and historic, the Alaska Hwy (p355), from its start point in Dawson Creek (364km northeast of Prince George), through northeast BC to Watson Lake (944km), is being somewhat eclipsed by the Stewart-Cassiar Hwy. Still, it's an epic drive even if the sections through Fort Nelson are bland. Going via Dawson Creek is most convenient for those coming from Edmonton and the east.

Stewart-Cassiar Highway

The Stewart-Cassiar Hwy (Hwy 37; p381) runs 700km through wild scenery from the junction with the Yellowhead Hwy (Hwy 16) 240km east of Prince Rupert and 468km west of Prince George. A side trip to the incomparable glaciers around Stewart (see p383) is easy. This route is good for people from most of BC, the Rockies, Alberta and the western US. It ends at the Alaska Hwy near Watson Lake in the Yukon.

Alaska Marine Highway System

We are big fans of the car-carrying ferries run by the state of Alaska (www.dot.state.ak.us/amhs; p431) along the Inside Passage. Free of frills, you simply relax and enjoy one of the world's greatest shows of marine life, soaking up the same scenery that cruise-ship passengers spend thousands more to see. You can take a three-day ride on boats from Bellingham, Washington (north of Seattle) to Haines (see p403) and Skagway (see p404) in southeast Alaska on the Yukon border. Or catch the ferries in Prince Rupert (see p372) for services to the same two towns. Note that the boats – especially cabins – fill up fast in summer, so reserve.

Our Recommendation

An Alaska Ferry between Prince Rupert and Haines one way and the Stewart-Cassiar Hwy the other.

ONLY IN THE YUKON

Certain details about the Yukon are different from BC. Important ones are:

Emergencies (☎ 867-667-5555, in Whitehorse 911)

Telephone area code (☎ 867; Alaska 907)

Road condition information (☎ 511; www.511yukon.ca)

Government campgrounds Also known as territory campgrounds, they cannot be reserved. The fee at all campgrounds is $12 per tent/RV per night.

---

winds of winter will be blowing seasonal residents and visitors south. Much of the territory's tourism industry is then closed until May or June.

ACTIVITIES

Yukon VICs can supply you with information and answer questions on hiking, canoeing, rafting, cycling, gold prospecting, skiing, fishing and various adventure trips. There are outfitters and tour companies to handle arrangements, but you don't need an organized trip and you don't need your own gold mine to enjoy the Yukon fully.

Whitehorse (p390) is the place to get guides and gear for adventures across the territory.

Hiking

If you've got the skills, hiking in the Yukon is unforgettable. The Chilkoot Trail (p405), which begins in Alaska, fully deserves its legendary reputation. Kluane National Park (p400) in the territory's southwest corner also has excellent hikes, from short and easy to long and demanding. Tombstone Territorial Park (p416) near Dawson also offers unlimited possibilities for challenging backcountry trekking.

Canoeing & Kayaking

Paddle heaven! Canoeists and kayakers have many choices, from easy float trips down the Yukon River and its tributaries to challenging white-water adventures.

Trips down the Yukon from Whitehorse can last from a few hours to the full 16-day campaign to Dawson. Many people start or end at Carmacks, the halfway point, making an eight-day trip. Boat rental and return

charges for an eight-day, one-way trip are about $210 to $350 and transport can be arranged. See Whitehorse (p390) and Dawson City (p407) for more details. *Paddling the Yukon River and its Tributaries* by Dan Maclean (www.publicationconsultants .com/paddle.htm) is an invaluable primer.

White-water Rafting

The Alsek and Tatshenshini Rivers are ranked among the best and wildest in North America. They're found in BC, south of Kluane, and are accessible from Haines Junction. Other major areas are the Lapie (near Ross River) and Takhini (north of Whitehorse) Rivers.

Fishing

For anglers, www.yukonfishing.com provides regulations and a list of what's where, as well as the best time and means to catch your prize salmon, trout or grayling.

Watching Wildlife

Yukon Tourism publishes a number of guides, such as the excellent *Yukon's Wildlife Viewing Guide*, that detail the critters you can expect to see in the territory, many right along the highways. Bear, caribou and moose are just some of the larger animals commonly seen.

For an unforgettable introduction into the world of Yukon hunting, take a look at the government publication *Hunting Regulations Summary*. Besides telling you how to bag a moose, it has a section on determining the sex of caribou that will stay with you long after other memories of your trip fade.

FESTIVALS & EVENTS

The Yukon has a number of events that are important throughout the territory. See p394 for events in Whitehorse and p413 for the many fun happenings in Dawson City.

February

Yukon Quest (www.yukonquest.com) This legendary 1600km dog-sled race goes from Whitehorse to Fairbanks, Alaska through darkness and −50°C temperatures. Record time: 10 days, 2 hours, 37 minutes.

June

Kluane Chilkat International Bike Relay (www .kcibr.org) Bikers ride 238km from Haines Junction to Haines, Alaska.

Yukon River Quest (www.yukonriverquest.com) The world's premier canoe and kayak race, which covers the classic 742km run of the Yukon River from Whitehorse to Dawson City. Record times include team canoe (39 hours, 32 minutes) and solo kayak (44 hours, 14 minutes).

August

Discovery Days (3rd Mon of the month) Many head to Dawson (p413) to celebrate the discovery of gold or just to discover fun. Most of the territory shuts down to celebrate this holiday.

September

Klondike Trail of '98 Road Relay (www.klondikeroad relay.com) Some 100 running teams of 10 each complete the overnight course from Skagway to Whitehorse.

WHITEHORSE

pop 23,700

Whitehorse doesn't immediately impress: it's got a bustle you don't associate with the Yukon and many of the buildings are more utilitarian than evocative (and those strip malls, ewww). But pause, and you begin absorbing its charms. Whitehorse is the heart of the territory and its museums and sights can be the bedrock of your trip. Add in more culture than you'll find in places bigger by a factor of 10 and enough nightlife to rival the midnight sun and you'll be hooked.

Whitehorse's airport is a vital outside link and the Yukon's two main roads – the Alaska Hwy and the Klondike Hwy – form an X with Whitehorse in the crosshairs. It's the place to get outfitted for adventures into the Yukon, to stock up on anything you need for your journey and to kick up your heels.

HISTORY

Whitehorse has always been a transportation hub, first as a terminus for the White Pass & Yukon Route Railway from Skagway. During WWII it was a major center for work on the Alaska Hwy and its airport played a vital role. In 1953 Whitehorse was made the capital of the territory, to the continuing regret of the much smaller and more isolated Dawson City.

ORIENTATION

Whitehorse sits just off the Alaska Hwy between Dawson Creek in BC (1430km to the east), where the highway starts, and Fairbanks, Alaska (970km west). The official city limits cover 421 sq km, making it one of the largest urban-designated areas in the whole of Canada. Despite this, the central core is quite small and you can walk everywhere. Downtown is designed on a grid system; the main traffic routes are 2nd and 4th Aves.

INFORMATION

Among local newspapers, the *Yukon News* is feisty while *What's Up Yukon* (www .whatsupyukon.com) is the source for entertainment listings.

Bookstores

Mac's Fireweed Books (☎ 867-668-2434; www .macsbooks.ca; 203 Main St; ⊗ 8am-midnight May-Sep, 8am-9pm Oct-Apr) Splendid selection of local titles plus a section on First Nations culture. Carries topographical maps, road maps, magazines and newspapers. It sells Yukon maps and books online at www.yukonbooks.com.

Well-Read Books (☎ 867-393-2987; cnr Jarvis St & 4th Ave; ⊗ 9am-6pm Mon-Sat, 10am-5pm Sun) Good range of used books.

Internet Access

The laundry and library have internet access. Many motels and cafés have wi-fi.

Laundry

Norgetown (☎ 867-667-6113; 4213 4th Ave; per load from $5; ⊗ 8am-9pm; 💻) Has a drop-off service and internet terminals.

Libraries

Whitehorse Library (☎ 867-667-5239; 2071 2nd Ave; ⊗ 10am-9pm Mon-Fri, 10am-6pm Sat, 1-9pm Sun; 💻) Free internet access for 15 minutes; good selection of Yukon books.

Medical Services

Whitehorse General Hospital (☎ 867-393-8700; 5 Hospital Rd; ⊗ 24hr)

Post

Post office (☎ 867-667-2485; Shoppers Drug Mart, 211 Main St; ⊗ 9am-6pm Mon-Fri, 11am-4pm Sat)

Tourist Information

Tourism Whitehorse (☎ 867-668-8629; www .visitwhitehorse.com; 3128 3rd Ave; ⊗ 9am-4pm Mon-Fri) Located next to the Yukon Historical & Museums Association in a 1905 house, information is strictly for the city; good website.

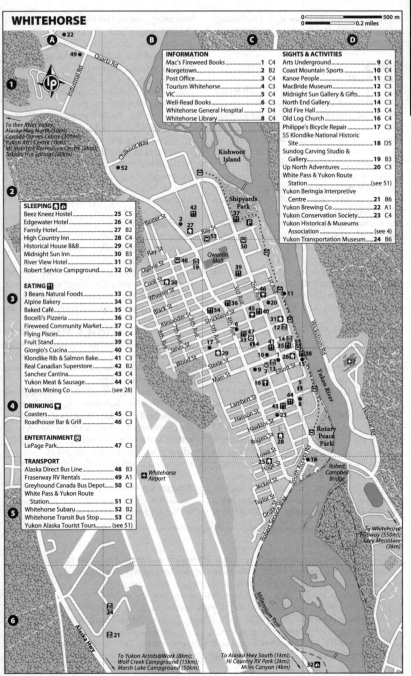

WHITEHORSE

0 — 500 m
0 — 0.2 miles

Quartz Rd

To Ibex River Valley;
Alaska Hwy North (50m);
Canada Games Centre (200m);
Yukon Arts Centre (1km);
Mt McIntyre Recreation Centre (5km);
Takhini Hot Springs (30km)

Chilkoot Way

Kishwoot Island

Shipyards Park

Baxter St
Ray St
Ogilvie St
Cook St
Wheeler St
Black St
Alexander St
Jarvis St
Wood St
Steele St
Main St
Lambert St
Hanson St
Hawkins St
Rogers St
Lowe St
Hoge St
Jeckell St
Taylor St

Qwanlin Mall

Strickland St

2nd Ave
3rd Ave
4th Ave
5th Ave
6th Ave

Wickstrom Rd

Yukon River

Hospital Rd

Whitehorse Airport

Robert Service Way

Drury St

Rotary Peace Park

Robert Campbell Bridge

Millennium Trail

To Whitehorse Fishway (550m); Grey Mountain (3km)

To Yukon Artists@Work (8km);
Wolf Creek Campground (15km);
Marsh Lake Campground (50km)

To Alaska Hwy South (1km);
Hi Country RV Park (2km);
Miles Canyon (4km)

Alaska Hwy

VIC (☎ 867-667-3084; 100 Hanson St; ☺ 8am-8pm May–mid-Sep, 9am-4:30pm Mon-Fri mid-Sep–May) Territory-wide information, enough to feed a campfire all night.

SIGHTS
Waterfront
Dawson ahoy! The **SS Klondike** (☎ 867-667-4511; South Access Rd & 2nd Ave; adult/child $6/2; ☺ 9am-6pm mid-May–mid-Sep) was one of the last and largest stern-wheelers used on the Yukon River. Built in 1937, it made its final run upriver to Dawson in 1955 and is now a museum and national historic site.

One look at the majestic Yukon River and you'll understand why the waterfront is being reborn. The beautiful **White Pass & Yukon Route Station** (Front St) has been restored and anchors the area. Next door, the **Old Fire Hall** (☎ 867-333-4255; Front St) has sales by local artists and live performances of music and comedy on a shifting schedule.

Rotary Peace Park is in the south. At the north end, **Shipyards Park** has a growing collection of historic structures gathered territory-wide and a skateboard track and toboggan hill. Linking it all is a cute little **waterfront trolley** (adult/child $2/free; ☺ 9am-9pm May-Sep).

Museums
Giving new meaning to 'spend a penny,' a moose-sized 'nugget' of copper stands outside the **MacBride Museum** (☎ 867-667-2709; cnr 1st Ave & Wood St; adult/child $7/3.50; ☺ 9am-6pm mid-May–Sep, noon-4pm Tue-Sat Oct–mid-May), which is much improved of late. Tales of the gold rush, First Nations, legendary characters and lots of stuffed critters are all here. At the entrance, check out the good camera shot of the old Whitehorse waterfront.

Up by the airport you can see a moose-sized beaver outside the engaging **Yukon Beringia Interpretive Centre** (☎ 867-667-8855; www.beringia.com; Km 1473 Alaska Hwy; adult/child $6/4; ☺ 10am-6pm) which focuses on Beringia, an area that, during the last Ice Age, encompassed the Yukon, Alaska and eastern Siberia yet was untouched by glaciers. Interactive displays re-create the time. From downtown, take the airport bus and then walk south for five minutes.

Nearby, the **Yukon Transportation Museum** (☎ 867-668-4792; 30 Electra Circle; adult/child $6/3; ☺ 10am-6pm May-Aug) covers the perils and adventures of getting around the Yukon by plane, train, truck and dog sled. See what happened when thousands of troops had to mud-wrestle the very earth to build the Alaska Hwy.

Art Galleries
There are more artists than bears in Whitehorse. The well-funded arts community has a lot on display.

Arts Underground (☎ 867-667-4080; www.artsunderground.com; Hougen Centre lower level, 305 Main St; ☺ 9am-5:30pm Mon-Sat), run by the Yukon Arts Society, is a good-sized gallery with rotating exhibits.

Exhibits at the **Yukon Arts Centre** (☎ 867-667-8484; www.yukonartscentre.org; Yukon College, 300 College Dr; ☺ noon-5pm Tue-Sun) are well curated and rotate every few months. This is also a performing arts venue.

The name says it all: **Yukon Artists@Work** (☎ 867-393-4848; www.yaaw.com; 3B Glacier Dr; ☺ noon-5pm daily Jun-Aug, Fri-Sun Sep-May) displays the creations of more than three dozen local artists, some of whom may be busy creating when you visit. It's in a warren of rooms in a warehouse 10km south of the airport.

Other galleries:
Midnight Sun Gallery & Gifts (☎ 867-668-4350; 205C Main St; ☺ 9am-8pm) Past the fudge is a good selection of Yukon arts, crafts and products.

KILL YOUR DINNER...

Worried that the increasing sophistication of Whitehorse was causing Yukoners to become too citified (read: Southern or south of the Yukon border) *Up Here* (www.uphere.ca), the magazine of Canada's north, offered the following suggestions to avoid going soft:

'Be Northern. Build a house out of town. Wear moosehide and sealskin. Park your car in your yard. Pee by the highway. Take your dog to work. Smoke 'em if you've got 'em. Say 'the Yukon' (What gutless bureaucrat dropped the 'the'?). Jaywalk. Commute on your quad. Look people in the eye. Don't shave – and ladies, that goes for you. Curse. Spit. Enter without knocking. Eat bannock, dry-meat and tea. Build campfires in your yard. Shop at the dump. Call the rest of world 'Outside.' Kill your cellphone. Kill your dinner. And stop acting like a goddamn southerner.'

North End Gallery (☎ 867-393-3590; 1116 1st Ave; ✆ 10am-6pm Mon-Sat) High-end Canadian art.

Sundog Carving Studio & Gallery (☎ 867-633-4186; 4194 4th Ave; ✆ 9am-4:30pm Mon-Fri) First Nations artists sell their own works at this cooperative store.

Whitehorse Fishway

our pick Whitehorse Fishway (☎ 867-633-5965; admission by donation; ✆ 9am-9pm Jun-Aug) has a 366m wooden fish ladder (the world's longest). Large viewing windows let you see chinook salmon swim past starting in late July (before that it's grayling; go online and watch www .yukonenergy.ca/community/multimedia /fishcam); 2008 was a terrible year for fish counts however, a feared result of climate change. Outside amid the thunderous roar of the river's spillway, there's usually a tent where you can learn about the ingenious traditional aboriginal fishing methods.

The fishway is past the hydroelectric plant just south of town; it's easily reached on foot.

Other Sights

Built by the town's first priest in 1900, the **old log church** (☎ 867-668-2555; 303 Elliott St; adult/child $3/free; ✆ 10am-6pm mid-May–Aug) is the only log-cabin-style cathedral in the world, and the oldest building in town. Displays inside include the tale of one Bishop Stringer who was trapped in the wilds and resorted to boiling and eating his boots to stay alive. Part of one – perhaps an uneaten midnight snack – survives.

Yukon Brewing Co (☎ 867-668-4183; www.yukon beer.com; 102 Copper Rd; ✆ 11am-6pm, tours 2pm Jun-Aug), the maker of enormously popular Yukon Gold, Arctic Red, Lead Dog Ale and Chilkoot Lager, is based in Whitehorse. All are good and easily found Yukon-wide.

About 10km off the Klondike Hwy (Hwy 2) north of town in a quiet wooded area are the **Takhini Hot Springs** (☎ 867-633-2706; Km 10 Takhini Hot Springs Rd; adult/child $10/6; ✆ 8am-10pm Jun-Aug). The pools are almost suburban but it's a good place to avoid frostbite even in summer.

ACTIVITIES

Whitehorse is the place to gear up for the entire province, although you can have some fun here first.

Coast Mountain Sports (☎ 867-667-4074; Hougen Centre lower level, 305 Main St; ✆ 9:30am-6pm Mon-Sat,

to 9pm Thu & Fri, noon-4pm Sun) has a large selection of outdoor clothing and gear. **There & Back Again** (☎ 867-633-5346; www.thereandback again.ca; 108 Elliott St, Ste 219) lets you pack light; it rents backpacking and backcountry gear.

Yukon Pride (☎ 867-668-2932; www.yukonpride.ca) specializes in gay and lesbian adventure travel in the Yukon.

Cycling

Whitehorse has scores of **bike trails** along the Yukon River and into the surrounding hills. All along the **Ibex River Valley** west of Whitehorse is good for biking. The VIC has maps, or pick up a copy of *Whitehorse Mountain Bike & Recreational Trails*.

For bike rentals, **Philippe's Bicycle Repair** (☎ 867-633-5600; 508 Wood St) has good ones from $25 per day (or $50 for the entire summer!). It's a local expert hang-out.

Walking & Hiking

You can walk a scenic 5km loop around Whitehorse's waters that includes a stop at the fishway. From the SS *Klondike* head south on the **Millennium Trail** until you reach the Robert Service Campground (p394) and the Rotary Centennial Footbridge over the river. The fishway (left) is just south. Head north along the water and cross the Robert Campbell Bridge back to the town center.

Even better is the **Yukon River Loop Trail**, a 16km variation that comprises the waterfront footpath but goes much further south to the stunning sheer rock river passage at **Miles Canyon**. You cross to the east side of the river over a dramatic suspension footbridge.

Around Whitehorse you can go hiking at the **Mt McIntyre Recreation Center**, up Two Mile Hill Rd, and at **Grey Mountain**, east of town. The hiking trails become cross-country ski trails in winter.

Swimming

Canada Games Centre (☎ 867-668-7665; 200 Hamilton Blvd; adult/child $7/3.50; ✆ 7am-10pm) was renamed for the major national winter games held in Whitehorse in early 2007. It is a fantasyland of pools, skating rinks and other indoor activities.

Canoeing & Kayaking

Whitehorse is the starting place for popular canoe and kayak trips to Carmacks or on to Dawson City. It's an average of eight days to the former and 16 days to the latter. Outfitters offer rentals that include transport back to Whitehorse. Canoe/kayak to Carmacks is about $210/300, and $350/500 to Dawson City. You can get a taste for the adventure on the popular 34km run north to Lake Laberge.

Kanoe People (☎ 867-668-4899; www.kanoepeople .com; cnr 1st Ave & Strickland St), at the river's edge, can arrange any type of trip including paddles down Teslin and Big Salmon Rivers. They sell gear, maps and guides, and rent bikes.

Up North Adventures (☎ 867-667-7035; www .upnorth.yk.ca; 103 Strickland St) offers rentals and transport on the major rivers, as well as paddling lessons, guided mountain-bike trips and winter sports.

Most paddlers use *The Yukon River: Marsh Lake to Dawson City* map available at www.yukonbooks.com.

TOURS

Learn about the secret American toilet still in plain sight and other Whitehorse facts on a downtown walking tour with the **Yukon Historical & Museums Association** (☎ 867-667-4704; 3126 3rd Ave; tour $4; 🕙 9am-3pm Mon-Sat Jun-Aug). Tours depart from its office in the 1904 Donneworth House.

Meet at the old log church (p393) for summer **cemetery tours** ($2); check schedules.

our pick **Yukon Conservation Society** (☎ 867-668-5678; www.yukonconservation.org; 302 Hawkins St; 🕙 Jul-Aug) runs 10 different free nature hikes, including fun children's programs and more serious six-hour hikes for adults.

FESTIVALS & EVENTS

Several Yukon events are based in Whitehorse.

Whitehorse's **International Storytelling Festival** (www.storytelling.yk.net), usually in October, features First Nations participants.

SLEEPING

Whitehorse can get almost full during the peak of summer, so you should certainly book ahead. The VIC has lists of B&Bs and holiday homes.

Steadfastly sticking to its policy of letting recreational vehicles (RVs), primarily from the US, park for free in its lot, Wal-Mart has been tough competition for local RV parks. Worse, there's been an increase in

RVs discharging waste along Yukon roads since people began parking their $250,000 rigs in the service-free Wal-Mart lot.

Budget

There are several RV campgrounds on the Alaska Hwy near the airport.

Yukon Government Campgrounds (☎ 867-667-5648; campsite $12) South of Whitehorse on the Alaska Hwy are two campgrounds: Wolf Creek (16km from town), set in a wooded area, and Marsh Lake (50km) with nearby beach access. Sites include firewood.

Hi Country RV Park (☎ 867-667-7445; www.hi countryrvyukon.com; 91374 Alaska Hwy; campsite $15-35; 🖳 🛜) At the top of Robert Service Way, this wooded campground offers hookups, showers, laundry and a playground.

our pick **Robert Service Campground** (☎ 867-668-3721; www.robertservicecampground.com; Robert Service Way; campsite $16; 🕙 mid-May–mid-Sep; 🖳 🛜) It's a pretty 15-minute walk from town on the Millennium Trail to the 70 sites at this tents-only campground on the river 1km south of town. Excellent coffee, baked goods and ice cream in the café.

Beez Kneez Hostel (☎ 867-456-2333; www.bz kneez.com; 408 Hoge St; dm/r $25/50; 🖳 🛜) Like the home you've left behind, this cheery hostel has a garden, deck, grill and free bikes. The two cabins ($50) are much in demand.

Midrange & Top End

Whitehorse has a lot of midrange motels that earn the sobriquet 'veteran.' Try to compare a few.

Family Hotel (☎ 867-668-5558; 314 Ray St; r $80-140; 🕷 🛜) The only quality about this clean, simple three-story place that's especially 'family' is the huge coin laundry. Won't Junior always remember washing his undies on the family's trip of a lifetime? Rooms are large, with plenty of room for board games – and undies folding – on the floor.

Edgewater Hotel (☎ 867-667-2572, 877-484-3334; www.edgewaterhotelwhitehorse.com; 101 Main St; r $80-200; 🕷 🖳 🛜) Much updated, the Edgewater has a dash of style. The 30 rooms are smallish (some lack air-con) but have flat-screen TVs. Better rooms have river views; some have kitchens. The basement bar is popular.

Historical House B&B (☎ 867-668-2526; www .yukongold.com; cnr 5th Ave & Wood St; r $85-110; 🕷 🖳)

A classic wooden home from 1907, there are three rooms here. Top-floor ones have individual bathrooms down the hall and angled ceilings. A larger unit has a huge kitchen; the common area has a wood stove. There's high-speed internet and a nice garden.

Midnight Sun Inn (☎ 867-667-2255, 800-284-4448; www.midnightsunbb.com; 6188 6th Ave; r $85-125; ✂ ▣) A modern B&B in a sort of overgrown, suburban-style house, the Midnight Sun Inn offers four themed rooms. However, the decor is restrained: a few dried reeds and dark prints pass for 'Egypt.' Brighter is the 'Northern.' The Sun is downtown, has high-speed internet and serves big breakfasts.

River View Hotel (Canada's Best Value Inn; ☎ 867-667-7801, 888-315-2378; www.riverviewhotel.ca; 102 Wood St; r $90-150; ▣ ☎) Recently renovated, the floors still sound hollow here, but many of the 53 rooms have the views implied by the name and all are very large. Close to everything, yet on a quiet street, it's a good choice.

High Country Inn (☎ 867-667-4471, 800-554-4471; www.highcountryinn.ca; 4051 4th Ave; r $90-220; ✂ ▣ ☎) Towering over Whitehorse (four stories!), the High Country is popular with business travelers and high-end groups. The 84 rooms are large – some have huge whirlpools right in the room, a bonus the hotel notes will make your stay 'memorable.' A deranged-looking 40-foot Mountie stands guard in the parking lot.

EATING

Whitehorse has several excellent places to eat, at all budgets. And in summer you can drink half the night and still pass out in the sun.

Budget

Baked Café (☎ 867-633-6291; 100 Main St; snacks $4; ✿ 7am-7pm; ☎) In summer, the outdoor tables at this stylish café attract swells in shades who you'd think would be reading *Daily Variety*. Smoothies, soups, daily lunch specials, baked goods and more.

Yukon Meat & Sausage (☎ 867-667-6077; 203 Hanson St; sandwiches $6; ✿ 9am-5:30pm Mon-Sat) The smell of smoked meat wafts out to the street and you walk right in. This great deli has a huge selection of prepared items and custom-made sandwiches. Great for picnics or eat in.

Alpine Bakery (☎ 867-668-6871; 411 Alexander St; snacks from $6; ✿ 8am-6pm Mon-Sat) Everything is organic at this serious bakery where there are daily wholegrain and lunch specials. Fresh juices are just the thing to cool down from yoga classes and other healthy activities. They have an ad that reads: 'Wanted: Interesting Salad Greens.'

Flying Pisces (meals $7-14; ✿ 11am-2pm, 4:30-9pm Tue-Sat) Look for this unassuming white trailer parked by the Old Fire Hall, or follow those in the know who revel in the fresh halibut fish and chips. Choose your batter (a first!): original, tempura, crispy cashew or Thai curry, and then find a picnic table.

Midrange & Top End

Don't be fooled by the midnight sun. People are done eating by 9pm in summer so they can, what? Get tans?

Yukon Mining Co (☎ 867-667-6457; High Country Inn, 4051 4th Ave; meals $7-20; ✿ 11am-late Apr-Oct) The sprawling covered deck here draws crowds of locals, tourists and guides ('and when you see the whites of his eyes…') through the season. Backed by a huge bar, diners choose from huge burgers, salads and fresh Yukon fish. The Arctic char is sublime.

Bocelli's Pizzeria (☎ 867-667-4838; cnr 4th Ave & Alexander St; meals $8-16; ✿ 4-9pm Tue-Sat) Every pizza here comes with homemade basil tomato sauce and a lash of garlic. Chef Mitch Cormier takes her pizza seriously – ask for more than four toppings and she'll tell you that the toppings turn into one taste, a crime given she makes her own sausage. They deliver.

ourpick Sanchez Cantina (☎ 867-668-5858; 211 Hanson St; meals $10-20; ✿ 11:30am-3pm, 5-9:30pm) You have to head south across two borders to find Mexican this authentic. Burritos are the thing; get them with the spicy mix of red and green sauces. It all comes from a tiny, home-style kitchen. Settle in for what may be a wait on the broad patio.

Klondike Rib & Salmon Bake (☎ 867-667-7554; 2116 2nd Ave; mains $12-25; ✿ 4-9pm) It looks touristy and it is, but the food is excellent at this sprawling casual place with two decks. Two of the main items are in the name. Fresh halibut also wins raves as does the wild-game stroganoff.

Giorgio's Cucina (☎ 867-668-4050; 206 Jarvis St; mains $12-30; ✿ 11:30am-2pm, 5-10pm) The best place in town for Italian has creative specials. The semi-open kitchen flames things up and the steaks are prime. Portions are mother-lode size – make certain your room has a fridge. The refined service does credit to the long wine list.

Groceries

The growing season may be short but the Yukon makes up for it in produce. Summer sees local foods aplenty in stores.

Fireweed Community Market (www.yukonfood .com; Shipyards Park; ☺ 3-8pm Thu mid-May–mid-Sep) This farmers market draws vendors from across the region. It's a real showcase.

Fruit Stand (☎ 867-393-3994; 208 Black St; ☺ 10am-7pm May-Sep) You can buy fresh fruit and veggies at this cross between a stand and a store, which sells lots of Yukon-grown produce (berries!) and prepared items such as fireweed honey. Yum.

3 Beans Natural Foods (☎ 867-668-4908; 308 Wood St; ☺ 10am-5:30pm Tue-Sat) This health food store has a good range of organic foods.

Real Canadian Superstore (☎ 867-456-6635; 2270 2nd Ave; ☺ 8am-9pm) A vast superstore with aisles of bulk-size foods. Stock up here.

DRINKING

Coasters (☎ 867-633-2788; 206 Jarvis St; ☺ 3pm-late) Hidden in the pedestrian 202 Motor Inn, this surprisingly huge bar has deejays and bands playing rockabilly, hip-hop or something trendy from Vancouver. Sunday is open mike.

Roadhouse Bar & Grill (☎ 867-668-7263; 2163 2nd Ave; ☺ 11am-late) The patio here is a fave and draws locals ready to air-kiss their neighbors between slugs of serious booze.

ENTERTAINMENT

You can always find a local band playing in Whitehorse. Watch for fliers that appear on poles and trash cans around town. There are also lots of thespians. Look for shows throughout the year, especially at the Yukon Arts Centre (p392).

All summer, there are free **lunchtime concerts** by Yukon musicians and artists at **LePage Park** (cnr Wood St & 3rd Ave; ☺ noon, Mon-Fri May-Sep).

GETTING THERE & AWAY
Air

Whitehorse Airport (YXY; ☎ 867-667-8440; www.gov .yk.ca/yxy) is five minutes west of downtown off the Alaska Hwy. It has a small café

inside and an iconic DC-3 weathervane (it works!) out front. It is served by the following airlines:

Air North (☎ 800-661-0407; www.flyairnorth.com) Whitehorse-based, serves Dawson City, Old Crow, Inuvik in the NWT, Fairbanks in Alaska, and Vancouver, Edmonton and Calgary.

Condor (☎ 800-364-1667, in Germany 01805 707 202; www.condor.com) Twice-weekly flights to/from Frankfurt May to October.

First Air (☎ 800-267-1247; www.firstair.ca) Flies to Yellowknife in the NWT via Fort Simpson.

Jazz (☎ 888-247-2262; www.flyjazz.ca) Serves Vancouver.

Bus & Train

Bus companies come and go; check the latest with the VIC.

Alaska Direct Bus Line (☎ 867-668-4833; www .alaskadirectbusline.com; 501 Ogilvie St) offers a summer service to Dawson ($150, eight hours, twice weekly); Tok, Alaska (US$135, 10 hours, three times weekly), running via the Alaska Hwy; and Haines Junction (US$75, two hours).

Alaska/Yukon Trails (☎ 800-770-7275; www .alaskashuttle.com) runs shuttles between Whitehorse and Dawson (US$150 6½ hours, three times weekly in summer); it also links Whitehorse with Fairbanks via Haines Junction and Tok (US$195, 12 hours, three times weekly in summer).

Greyhound Canada (☎ 867-667-2223, 800-661-8747; www.greyhound.ca; 2191 2nd Ave) reaches the end of the line in Whitehorse. Services south along the Alaska Hwy to Dawson Creek ($240, 20 hours, three times per week) connect with buses for the rest of BC and Canada.

White Pass & Yukon Route (☎ 867-633-5710; www.wpyr.com; Whitehorse ticket office, 1109 Front St) offers an enjoyable and scenic rail and bus connection to/from Skagway (adult/child from US$116/58, 4½ hours, two daily, mid-May to mid-September). The transfer point is Fraser, BC or Carcross.

Yukon Alaska Tourist Tours (☎ 867-668-5944; www.yukonalaskatouristtours.com; White Pass & Yukon Route Station; 1109 Front St) runs twice daily to Skagway (US$60, four hours, mid-May to mid-September).

GETTING AROUND
To/From the Airport

Yellow Cab (☎ 867-668-4811) charges about $18 from the center for the 10-minute ride.

Bus
Whitehorse Transit System (☎ 867-668-7433; ticket $2.50; every 30-70min; ☺ Mon-Sat) has a transfer point at the Qwanlin Mall. Route 2 serves the airport, the center and the Robert Service Campground.

Car & RV
Check your rate very carefully as it's common for a mileage charge to be added after the first 100km, which will not get you far in the Yukon. Also, check whether your insurance will cover damage from Yukon's rugged roads – there's a reason for all those windshield replacement ads.

Budget (☎ 867-667-6200; www.budget.com), **Hertz** (☎ 867-668-4224; www.hertz.com) and **National/ NorCan** (☎ 867-456-2277; www.national.com) are at the airport.

Whitehorse Subaru (☎ 867-393-6550; www .whitehorsesubaru.com; 17 Chilkoot Way) can usually beat the biggies on price.

Fraserway RV Rentals (☎ 867-668-3438; www .fraserwayrvrentals.com; 9039 Quartz Rd) rents all shapes and sizes of RV from $80 to $300 per day depending on size (it matters) and season. Mileage extra.

ALASKA HIGHWAY

'I'm gonna drive the Alaska Hwy!' has been the start of many an adventure. In fact, the very name means adventure. These days it is as much a well-traveled corridor between Alaska, the Yukon and the rest of North America as it is a route of dreams.

The 2237km-long road is generally in good condition (bar annual improvements and maintenance). It starts in Dawson Creek, BC (p355), enters the Yukon in the southeast and passes through Watson Lake, Whitehorse, Haines Junction and Beaver Creek en route to Fairbanks, Alaska. It is Hwy 97 in BC, Hwy 1 in the Yukon and Hwy 2 in Alaska.

If you like the outdoors, you'll like the Alaska Hwy: the scenery from BC to Whitehorse is verdant and at times striking. The real stunner is the run west from Whitehorse that passes the peaks of Kluane National Park.

BC TO WHITEHORSE
This section of the Alaska Hwy has a lot of rolling hills and reasonably sedate scenery. The road itself teases the Yukon before dropping back into BC. Then it crosses into the Yukon almost for good just southeast of Watson Lake (though, it does flirt with BC again west of Swift River).

Watson Lake
Originally named after Frank Watson, a British trapper, Watson Lake is the first town in the Yukon on the Alaska Hwy and is just over the border from BC. It's merely a useful rest stop except for the excellent **VIC** (☎ 867-536-7469; www.watsonlake.ca; ☺ 8am-8pm summer), which has an entertaining museum about the highway and piles of territory-wide info. The town offers campgrounds, roadside motels, full services and a Greyhound Canada stop.

The town is famous for its **Sign Post Forest** just outside the VIC. The first signpost, 'Danville, Illinois,' was nailed up in 1942. Others were added and now there are 63,000 signs, many liberated from municipalities worldwide.

The Robert Campbell Hwy (p399) runs northwest from here.

Twenty-six kilometers west of Watson Lake you come to the junction of the Stewart-Cassiar Hwy (Hwy 37), which heads south into BC (p381).

Just west of the junction, family-run **Nugget City** (☎ 867-536-2307, 888-536-2307; www .nuggetcity.com; campsite from $20, cabins from $80; ⬚) has accommodations and food that's three cuts above the Alaska Hwy norm (especially the berry pie).

Another 110km west, past the 1112km marker, look for the **Rancheria Falls Recreation Site**. A boardwalk leads to picturesque and powerful twin waterfalls. It's an ideal place to stop.

Teslin
Teslin, on the long, narrow lake of the same name, is 272km west of Watson Lake and long a home to the Tlingits (lin-*kits*). The Alaska Hwy brought both prosperity and rapid change to this aboriginal population. The engrossing **George Johnston Museum** (☎ 867-390-2550; www.gjmuseum.yk.net; Km 1294 Alaska Hwy; adult/child $6/3; ☺ 9am-5pm mid-May– early Sep) details the life and culture of this 20th-century Tlingit leader and self-taught photographer.

Just west of town, the **Teslin Tlingit Heritage Centre** (☎ 867-390-2526; ☺ 9am-5pm Jun-Sep) has

NORTH TO ALASKA

Nowadays the aura of the Alaska Hwy is more hype than fact. In every way it's a modern two-lane road, with smooth curves, broad sight lines and paving from one end to the other. But that has not always been the case. A famous 1943 photo shows a jeep seemingly being sucked down to China through a morass of mud while soldiers look on helplessly.

With the outbreak of WWII, Canada and the US decided that years of debate should end and that a proper road was needed to link Alaska and the Yukon to the rest of Canada and the US.

That a road, any road, could be carved out of the raw tundra and wilderness of the north in little over a year was a miracle. The 2450km gravel highway ran between Dawson Creek in BC and Fairbanks in Alaska. The route chosen followed a series of existing airfields – Fort St John, Fort Nelson, Watson Lake and Whitehorse – known as the Northwest Staging Route. It was an undertaking on par with building pyramids or going to the moon. For more on the construction, see p357.

Ceaseless Toil

In the six decades since WWII, various governments and contractors have never stopped widening, straightening and otherwise creating the modern road you drive today. In fact one of the biggest jobs today is simply trying to stay ahead of the endless subsidence that happens from the annual thawing and freezing of the land

Known variously as the Alaskan International Hwy, the Alaska Military Hwy and the Alcan (short for Alaska-Canada) Hwy, it's now called the Alaska Hwy. It has transformed both the Yukon and Alaska, opening up the north to year-round travel and forever changing the way of life of the First Nations along the route. Whitehorse went from a backwater airstrip to capital of the territory in 1953 because it was on the ever-more-vital road.

Measuring Apples & Oranges

The Alaska Hwy begins at 'Mile 0' in Dawson Creek in northeastern BC and goes to Fairbanks, Alaska, although the official end is at Delta Junction, about 155km southeast of Fairbanks. Mileposts long served as reference points but improvements shortening the road and the adoption of the metric system have made mileage references archaic along the 1965km in Canada. However, mileposts are still very much in evidence in Alaska, and communities on both sides of the border use the original mileposts for postal addresses and as reference points.

For more on the Alaska Hwy and its harrowing past, check out the VIC in Watson Lake (p397), the Yukon Transportation Museum in Whitehorse (p392) and the Alaska Highway House in Dawson Creek, BC. For a minutely detailed guide to every feature, including seemingly every roadside trash can, look for *Milepost* (www.milepost.com), a legendary annual publication sold throughout the north.

---

a pretty lakeside spot. The focus here is on Tlingit culture and artwork, especially the rich tradition of carved masks.

Johnson's Crossing

Some 53km north of Teslin is Johnson's Crossing, at the junction of the Alaska Hwy and Canol Rd (Hwy 6; box opposite).

Jake's Corner

The junction with the road to Atlin (p385) is at **Jake's Corner**, 47km west of Johnson's Crossing. The Tagish Rd here goes west 55km to Carcross (p406), which is a recommended detour off the Alaska Hwy.

WHITEHORSE TO ALASKA

The most rewarding portion of the Alaska Hwy, it gets you up close and personal with Unesco-recognized Kluane National Park and Reserve. Plan to take time for making impromptu stops to go 'gosh!'

First, however, from Whitehorse to Haines Junction the road has been massively improved and the wide cuts and broad turns have obliterated a lot of scenery.

Haines Junction

There are several good reasons to pause in Haines Junction but the best one is looming right in front of you: the soaring

DETOUR: ROBERT CAMPBELL HIGHWAY

From Watson Lake (p397), this 588km rough gravel road (Hwy 4) is an alternative route north to Dawson City; it meets the Klondike Hwy near Carmacks (p407). Named after Robert Campbell, a 19th-century explorer and trader with the Hudson's Bay Company, it's a scenic and lightly traveled route that parallels several major rivers. It has no services except in **Ross River** (pop 350), 373km from Watson Lake. At the junction with the Canol Rd (Hwy 6), the town is home to the Kaska First Nations and a supply center for the local mining industry. There's a campground and motels in town, and a government campground at **Lapie Canyon**.

A historic military boondoggle of epic proportions, the **Canol Rd** runs 230km south from Ross River to Johnson's Crossing (opposite) on the Alaska Hwy. During WWII, the US army built the Canol pipeline and parallel road at tremendous human and financial expense to transport oil from Norman Wells in the Northwest Territories to Whitehorse. However, it was only used for a brief period and then abandoned after countless hundreds of millions of dollars (in 1943 money no less) had been spent. North of Ross River, the Canol Rd runs for about 240km before ending near the Northwest Territories border; to go any further you have to hike the demanding **Canol Heritage Trail**.

Faro (www.faroyukon.ca), 10km off the Robert Campbell Hwy on the Pelly River, was created in 1968 to support the huge copper, lead and zinc mine in the Anvil Mountains. Downtown, the **Campbell Region Interpretive Centre** offers advice on viewing the abundant wildlife, particularly Fannin sheep, which live only in the Yukon.

silhouette of the Kluane National Park and its peaks, which wear a beanie of white even in summer. The town makes an excellent base for exploring the park or staging a serious mountaineering, backcountry or river adventure. German travelers will hear their language spoken throughout town.

The magnificent Haines Hwy heads south from here to Alaska (p402), passing the raft-ready white water of the Tatshenshini River.

Yukon Tourism (☎ 867-634-2345; www.hainesjunctionyukon.com; ☒ 10am-6pm May & Sep, 8am-8pm Jun-Aug) and **Parks Canada** (☎ 867-634-7250; www.parkscanada.gc.ca/kluane; Logan St; ☒ 10am-6pm mid-May–Aug, 10am-4pm Sep–mid-May) share the **VIC** in the Kluane National Park headquarters building. There's lots of info from the two agencies and a good model of the park terrain. In summer, rangers give regular nature talks.

All shops, lodging and services are clustered around the Alaska and Haines Hwys junction. And that thing that looks like an acid-trip cupcake? It's a **sculpture** meant to be a winsome tableau of local characters and critters. Repairs are constant as it proves an inviting target – and not just for art critics.

The post office, bank and ATM are inside **Madley's Bigway Foods** (☎ 867-634-2200; Hwy 3; ☒ 8am-9pm; ☐), which has dreadful fast food but stocks basic camping supplies and groceries.

ACTIVITIES

Although stunning, the ridges surrounding Haines Junction don't begin to hint at the beauty of Kluane National Park (p400). Escape your car for the 5.5km **nature walk** along Dezadeash River where Hwy 3 crosses it at the south end of town.

Paddlewheel Adventures (☎ 867-634-2683; www.paddlewheeladventures.com; 116 Kathleen St), opposite the VIC, arranges Tatshenshini rafting trips ($125 per person, includes lunch), scenic white-water trips and guided interpretive hikes ($55 to $125). It rents mountain bikes or canoes ($30 per day) and provides local transportation.

Owned by a longtime park warden and guide, **Kruda Ché Boat Tours** (☎ 867-634-2378; www.krudache.com) will arrange any number of custom tours by boat and on foot within Kluane National Park. Wildlife, history and aboriginal culture are among the themes.

An aerial tour around the icy heart of Kluane National Park is a splurge you should budget for. **Sifton Air** (☎ 867-634-2916; www.yukonairtours.com; Km 1632 Alaska Hwy) charges from $115 per person for a 40-minute tour of the largest icefields outside of the polar caps.

SLEEPING & EATING

Haines Junction has a cluster of motels and RV parks. Campers can enjoy a beach and shade at **Pine Lake**, a territorial

---

A TASTE OF CHAMPAGNE

About 75km west of Whitehorse look for the turn to **Champagne**, a former popular stop on the old Alaska Hwy (the charmless modern replacement opened in 2002). A trading post during the gold rush, it now boasts a huge collection of hubcaps mounted on a fence. The entire detour lasts about 14km before you rejoin the bland bit of the Alaska Hwy. Haines Junction is 60km west.

---

campground 6km east of town on the Alaska Hwy. Cerulean waters highlight **Kathleen Lake** (campsite $15), a Parks Canada campground 24km south of Haines Junction off the Haines Hwy.

The Cabin B&B (☎ 867-634-2600; www.thecabin yukon.com; cabin $90-120) South of town and close to Kathleen Lake are five basic cabins scattered in the woods. Cooking and heating is by propane and the toilets are outside, but the views from the rustic porches are bucolic.

Alcan Motor Inn (☎ 867-634-2371, 888-265-1018; www.alcanmotorinn.com; s/d $90/150; 🅿 🛜) The modern two-story Alcan has 23 large rooms with great views of the jagged Auriol Range. Some have full kitchens and there's a public coin laundry. It also has **Northern Lights** (⏰ 7am-9pm) – a cafe as opposed to a celestial attraction. It's good for breakfasts and burgers.

Raven Motel (☎ 867-634-2500; www.yukonweb .com/tourism/raven; 181 Alaska Hwy; r $130-150; meals $35-50; ⏰ May-Sep; 🅿 🛜) There are 12 comfortable motel-style rooms here and guests can partake of a vast German-style breakfast buffet. But the real star is the restaurant, which has the best food between Whitehorse and Alaska. Menus are complex and continental.

Village Bakery & Deli (☎ 867-634-2867; Logan St; meals $6-10; ⏰ 7am-9pm May-Aug; 🛜) Across from the VIC, this bakery turns out excellent goods all day while the deli counter has sandwiches you can enjoy on the huge deck. On Friday night there's a popular barbeque with live folk music.

Frosty Freeze (☎ 867-634-7070; Alaska Hwy; ⏰ 11am-10pm May-Sep) What looks like a humdrum fast-food joint is several orders of magnitude better. The shakes are made with real ice cream, the sundaes feature fresh

berries and the burgers (try the mushroom-Swiss number) are huge and juicy.

GETTING THERE & AWAY
Alaska Direct Bus Line (☎ 867-668-4833; www .alaskadirectbusline.com) offers a summer service on the Alaska Hwy to Tok, Alaska (US$90, seven hours, three times weekly) and Whitehorse (US$75, two hours).

Alaska/Yukon Trails (☎ 800-770-7275; www .alaskashuttle.com) links Whitehorse and Fairbanks (US$175, 10 hours, three times weekly in summer) via Haines Junction and Tok.

Kluane National Park & Reserve
Unesco-recognized as an 'empire of mountains and ice,' Kluane National Park looms south of the Alaska Hwy much of the way to the Alaskan border. This rugged and magnificent wilderness covers 22,015 sq km of the southwest corner of the territory. Kluane (kloo-wah-neee) gets its far-too-modest name from the Southern Tutchone word for 'lake with many fish.'

With BC's Tatshenshini-Alsek Provincial Wilderness Park (p385) to the southeast and Alaska's Wrangell-St Elias National Park to the southwest, this is one of the largest protected wilderness areas in the world.

INFORMATION
Parks Canada has two **VIC**s (www.pc.gc.ca/kluane). One is in Haines Junction (p398) and the other at **Tachal Dhal** (Sheep Mountain; Alaska Hwy; ⏰ 9am-3:30pm late May-early Sep), 130km west of Haines Junction. The latter has binoculars for spotting Dall sheep impossibly hopping about a sheer cliff face just west. Feel the weight of a set of sheep horns on display and catch an alluring glimpse of the Kluane interior up the Slims River valley. At either center, pick up a copy of *Recreation Guide*, which shows the scope of the park (and how little is easily accessible). The map shows hikes ranging from 10 minutes to 10 days.

Winters are long and harsh. Summers are short, making mid-June to mid-September the best time to visit. Note that winter conditions can occur anytime, especially in the backcountry. See Haines Junction (p398) for the park's campground.

SIGHTS
The park consists primarily of the **St Elias Mountains** and the world's largest non-polar

icefields. Two-thirds of the park is glacier interspersed with valleys, glacial lakes, alpine forest, meadows and tundra. The **Kluane Ranges** (averaging a height of 2500m) are seen along the western edge of the Alaska Hwy. A greenbelt wraps around the base where most of the animals and vegetation live. Turquoise **Kluane Lake** is the Yukon's largest. Hidden are the immense icefields and towering peaks, including **Mt Logan** (5959m), Canada's highest mountain, and **Mt St Elias** (5488m), the second highest. Climbing the former is the perilous goal of only a few a year who typically endure temperatures of −90°C near the summit.

Partial glimpses of the interior peaks can be found at the Kilometer 1622 **viewpoint** on the Alaska Hwy, but the best views are from the air. You can arrange tours and charters of planes or helicopters in Haines Junction (p398).

ACTIVITIES

There's excellent **hiking** in the forested lands at the base of the mountains, along either marked trails or less-defined routes. There are about a dozen in each category, some following old mining roads, others traditional aboriginal paths. Detailed trail guides and topographical maps are available at the VICs. Talk to the rangers before setting out: they will help select a hike and can provide updates on areas that may be closed due to bear activity. Overnight hikes require backcountry permits ($10 per person per night).

our pick **Guided hikes** (per person $5-20) that venture into the park and cover topics as diverse as traditional First Nations culture and bears are offered by the rangers in summer. Schedules vary so confirm in advance.

The Tachal Dhal VIC is the starting point for **Slims West**, a popular 60km round-trip trek to **Kaskawulsh Glacier** – one of the few that can be reached on foot. This is a difficult route that takes from three to five days to complete and includes sweeping views from Observation Mountain (2114m). An easy overnight trip is the 15km **Auriol loop**, which goes from spruce forest to subalpine barrens and includes a wilderness campground. The trailhead is 7km south of Haines Junction.

To learn more about spruce beetle blight (below), which has killed so much of the forest, and witness the forest's regeneration, stop at the **Spruce Beetle Walk**. Just 18km west of Haines Junction on the Alaska Hwy, Parks Canada has a 1.7km loop trail into the forest with good explanatory signs on the disaster.

BEETLES RIP?

Even as beetles wreak havoc on forests across BC and the Rockies (see p59), the forests of the Yukon may be recovering.

Certainly you can't miss the vast swaths of brown as you drive the Alaska Hwy past Kluane National Park: millions upon millions of dead trees killed by the spruce beetle starting in 1994. Normally the spruce beetles claim a tree here and there every year, part of nature's process that thins out weak and old trees so that new and healthy ones can thrive. But huge areas where all the trees were killed were previously unknown.

As 3500 sq km in the park and much more in the surrounding region were lost, the search for answers was furious. It was clear that the beetle population had exploded and they were burrowing in and killing every tree they encountered. The causes were many:

- Warmer summers were weakening the trees due to drought.

- Warmer winters were allowing far more beetles than usual to survive from one year to the next.

- Fire suppression meant that the forest was aging faster than normal, with fewer opportunities for young trees.

By 2006 however, several factors were now working against the beetles: they had decimated their environment, a very cold winter killed many and there was now a population explosion of beetle-eaters. New attacks on trees plummeted back towards historic levels. Meanwhile, nature has opened the door to other trees: birch and alder, which grow fast and are favored by a burgeoning population of moose and other critters.

Fishing is good and **wildlife-watching** plentiful. There's a large and diverse population of grizzly bear, as well as black bear, moose, caribou, goats and 150 varieties of birds, among them eagles and the rare peregrine falcon.

Many enjoy **skiing** or **snow-shoeing** during the short days of winter.

Destruction Bay
pop 60

This small village on the shore of Kluane Lake is 107km north of Haines Junction. Like Haines Junction and Beaver Creek, it started off as a camp and supply depot during the construction of the Alaska Hwy. It was given its present name after a storm tore through the area. There's boating and fishing on Kluane Lake and a gas station in the village.

Near the town, **Congdon Creek** (Km 1723 Alaska Hwy; campsite $12) is a beautiful location with views across a sparkling mountain lake with snowy peaks in the background. It's cliché city! The campsites are well spaced and there's a playground. Read the warnings and don't become a box of chocolates for a bear who's a fan of Forrest Gump.

Burwash Landing
pop 90

Burwash Landing, 19km north of Destruction Bay, pre-dates the road as a Kluane First Nations village. It saw a brief gold rush on nearby 4th of July Creek. During the construction of the Alaska Hwy it was an oasis for weary soldiers who came here for hearty portions of fine food. Times have changed, although you can still get gas.

The highlight here is the excellent **Kluane Museum** (☎ 867-841-5561; Km 1759 Alaska Hwy; adult/child $4/2; ☺ 9am-8pm mid-May–early Sep), which is inside a former church (it was too big). The museum features a huge stuffed moose, ancient mammoth teeth and displays on natural and First Nations history. Take a copy of the local walking tours and stretch your legs, looking at old cabins being subsumed into the permafrost.

Beaver Creek
pop 110

Wide-spot-in-the-road Beaver Creek is a beacon for sleepy travelers or those who want to get gas. Fans of dismal food will find much to cheer here. The Canadian border checkpoint is just north of town; the US border checkpoint is 27km further west. Both are open 24 hours.

The **VIC** (☎ 867-862-7321; Km 1202 Alaska Hwy; ☺ 8am-8pm May-Sep) has information on all of the Yukon. A bizarre **sculpture garden** – check out the rabid beaver – just north tempts the silly (or intoxicated) into unnatural acts.

Of the four motels in town, the **1202 Motor Inn** (☎ 867-862-7600, 800-661-0540; 1202 Alaska Hwy; r from $50) is the least offensive and does have a certain frontier charm. The 30 rooms are basic and functional. Get a newer one away from the idling trucks.

Alaska

You'll note that the incredible scenery of the Alaska Hwy dims a bit once you cross into its namesake state. The Alaska Hwy department seems to have a 'bulldoze it and leave' philosophy, so the route is much more torn up and despoiled here than in the pristine conditions in the Yukon.

From the US border, it's 63km (39 miles) to the **Tetlin National Wildlife Refuge** (http://tetlin .fws.gov) on the Alaska Hwy. About 117km (73 miles) past Tetlin, you'll reach the junction with the Taylor Hwy (Hwy 5), which connects with the Top of the World Hwy (p415) to Dawson City. Another 19km (12 miles) on the Alaska Hwy west of the junction is **Tok** (population 1400; www.tok alaskainfo.com), which has a slew of motels, some good restaurants and services.

HAINES HIGHWAY

Glaciers, looming snow-clad peaks, lush and wild river valleys, wind-swept alpine meadows and a bald-eagle-laced river delta are just some of the highlights crammed into the Haines Hwy. It links the important ferry port and fun town of Haines, Alaska, with Haines Junction and the Alaska Hwy in the Yukon. Paved and in good shape for its entire length, this is the favored route for Alaskans heading to ferries to Juneau or further south.

If you're only doing a short loop between Haines and Skagway via Whitehorse, this 259km road might be the highlight of your trip. In fact, no matter what length your Yukon adventure, the Haines Hwy (Hwy 3) might be the high point.

Heading south from Haines Junction, look west for a close-up of the St Elias Mountains, those glaciers glimpsed at the top stretch all the way to the Gulf of Alaska. About 80km south, look for the **Tatshenshini River viewpoint**. This white-water river flows through protected bear country and a valley that seems timeless.

About 10km further, look for **Million Dollar Falls**. For once the sight lives up to the billing as water thunders through a narrow chasm. Let the roar lull you to sleep at the nearby territorial **campground**.

The highway crosses into BC for a mere 70km but you'll hope for more as you traverse high and barren alpine wilderness where sudden snow squalls happen all year round. At the 1070m Chilkat Pass, an ancient aboriginal route into the Yukon, the road suddenly plunges down for a steep descent into Alaska. The US border is 72km north of Haines, along the wide **Chilkat River Delta**, home to scores of **bald eagles**. The handsome birds flock like pigeons each fall when they mass in the trees overlooking the river, drawn by the comparatively mild weather and steady supply of fish.

Pullouts line the Haines Hwy (Hwy 7 in Alaska), especially between mileposts 19 and 26. Take your time driving and find a place to park. Just a few feet from the road it's quiet, and when you see a small tree covered with 20 pensive – and sizable – bald eagles, you can enjoy your own raptor version of *The Birds*.

Each June more than 1200 riders and hundreds of volunteers take to the highway for the **Kluane Chilkat International Bike Relay** (www.kcibr.org), a huge event from Haines Junction to Haines. The winning teams boast a time of only six hours; others take longer, especially the teams that don costumes and party more than they pedal.

HAINES (ALASKA)

Haines is spared the cruise-ship hordes of Skagway just across the Lynn Canal (North America's longest and deepest fjord) and that's fine. It's a real community with a real downtown close to a working waterfront. As you gaze out over the beautiful mountain-backed waters – possibly with a relaxing beverage in hand – you're unlikely to be jealous of those aboard the conga line of cruise ships puffing (and we mean puffing

– the pollution clouds the air) their way to the next port.

Coming from the south on Alaska Marine Highway ferries (see p405), Haines is definitely the port of choice for accessing the Yukon.

Lonely Planet's *Alaska* has complete coverage of Haines; alternatively, download the Southeast Alaska chapter at www.lonely planet.com.

Information

Prices for Haines are in US$. Haines is on Alaska time, one hour earlier than Yukon time. **Haines Convention & Visitors Bureau** (☎ 907-766-2234, 800-458-3579; www.haines.ak.us; 122 2nd Ave; ☉ 8am-5pm Mon-Fri, 9am-5pm Sat & Sun) has rest rooms, free coffee and racks of free information.

Sights & Activities

Walk the center and waterfront then amble over to **Fort Seward**, an old army post dating back 100 years. Now a national historic site, the many mannered buildings have been given a range of new uses, from art galleries to funky stores to B&Bs.

Haines makes the most of its bald eagles and has a **festival** (http://baldeaglefest.org) in their honor every November. Numerous local guides will show you eagles in ways you can't see them from the Haines Hwy.

Sleeping & Eating

Portage Cove State Recreation Site (Beach Rd; campsite US$5; ☉ 15 May-Aug.) A 2-mile (3.2km) walk from downtown, this scenic campground overlooks the water and has nine sites that are for backpackers and cyclists only. Follow Front St south; it becomes Beach Rd near Fort Seward.

Fort Seward Lodge (☎ 907-766-2009, 877-617-3418; www.ftsewardlodge.com; 39 Mud Bay Rd; s/d $95/110, € shared bathroom $75; ☎) Fort Seward's former post exchange is a great choice with, well, great views. The rooms are a good size and comfortable, if simple. It's an easy walk to most of town and there's a free ferry shuttle.

Mountain Market & Spirits (☎ 907-766-3340; 3rd Ave at Haines Hwy; meals US$4-10; ☉ 7am-7pm Mon-Fri, 7am-6pm Sat & Sun) The hippest spot in Haines has excellent coffee and a range of organic baked goods, snacks and sandwiches. The grocery selection is simply fun.

Stock up for the ferry or get a picnic for the highway.

Fireweed (☎ 907-766-3838; Bldg 37, Blacksmith Rd; meals US$6-16; ✆ 11am-10pm) In Fort Seward, Fireweed mixes funk and style. The menu has organic and veggie items plus excellent burgers, pizzas, chowders and seafood. Swoon like we do over the Haines Brewing Spruce Tip Ale while out on the deck overlooking the Lynn Canal.

Getting There & Away

There's no public transportation from Haines into the Yukon.

Alaska Marine Highway System (☎ 800-642-0066; www.ferryalaska.com) is a superb service that links Haines and the Yukon to BC and the US. Boats serve Skagway (US$31, vehicles from US$41, two hours, five to seven weekly), Juneau, Petersburg, Wrangell, Ketchikan and, importantly, Prince Rupert in BC (US$160, cabins from US$160, vehicles from $370; 33 hours; two to three per week) as well as Bellingham, Washington, in the US (US$353, cabins from US$340, vehicles from US$800; 68 to 80 hours; one to two per week). For more information on this service, see p431. The ferry terminal is situated 6.5km south of town.

The **Haines-Skagway Fast Ferry** (☎ 907-766-2100, 888-766-2103; www.hainesskagwayfastferry.com) carries passengers only (adult/child US$31/16, 35 minutes, three or more per day June to September) and docks near the center.

KLONDIKE HIGHWAY

This 716km road is the spine of the Yukon. It traces much of the Gold Rush Trail that 40,000 hopeful yet increasingly desperate people took to Dawson City in 1898. It runs from the notorious port of Skagway in Alaska through the northwestern corner of BC to Whitehorse and Dawson City. It is paved and open year round. The initial stretch from Skagway to Carcross is a natural wonder of lakes and mountains.

SKAGWAY (ALASKA)

pop 850

Skagway. Derided by some, eulogized by others, this tiny gold rush town can be overrun with cruise-ship passengers or offer a moody window to the past, all in the same

day. Although it's in the US, it can only be reached by car using the Klondike Hwy from the Yukon through BC. It's the starting point for the legendary Chilkoot Trail and the White Pass & Yukon Route railroad.

In summer, Skagway is a zoo as mammoth cruise ships disgorge up to 8000 passengers each day. But by night they are safely back at the buffets and Skagway takes on a serene calm.

This is the last stop on the Alaska Marine Highway ferry run from Prince Rupert, BC (p367) and Bellingham, Washington, in the US, making it an important entry point for the Yukon, although you may prefer the more salubrious port of Haines (p403).

Lonely Planet's *Alaska* has complete coverage of Skagway; alternatively, download the Southeast Alaska chapter at www .lonelyplanet.com.

Orientation

From the ferry terminal, foot and vehicle traffic spills onto Broadway St and the center of town, which offers complete services and shops. From here the Klondike Hwy sets off for Whitehorse and beyond.

Skagway is on Alaska time, which is one hour earlier than the Yukon. Most places close outside of summer. Prices in this section are in US dollars.

Information

Chilkoot Trail Centre (☎ 907-983-9234, 800-661-0486; cnr Broadway St & 2nd Ave; ✆ 8am-6pm summer) Run by Parks Canada (www.pc.gc.ca/chilkoot) and the US National Park Service (www.nps.gov/klgo); provides advice, permits, maps and a list of transportation options to/from the Chilkoot Trail.

Klondike Gold Rush National Historical Park Visitor Centre (☎ 907-983-2921; www.nps.gov/klgo; cnr Broadway St & 2nd Ave; ✆ 8am-6pm May-Sep) Offers free walking tours daily and the Skagway Trail Map for area hikes.

Skagway News Depot & Books (☎ 907-983-3354; 264 Broadway St; ✆ 9am-6pm) Good selection of regional titles, guides and topographical maps.

Skagway Visitor Bureau (☎ 907-983-2854, 888-762-1898; www.skagway.com; 245 Broadway St; ✆ 8am-6pm) In an amazing building with a driftwood facade.

Sights

Skagway is filled with **historic buildings** restored to their gold rush appearance. Get a self-guiding map from the information centers and set off on your exploration.

our pick **White Pass & Yukon Route** (WP&YR; ☎ 907-983-2217, 800-343-7373; www.wpyr.com; cnr 2nd Ave & Spring St; adult/child US$103/52; ☻ mid-May–late Sep) is reason enough to visit Skagway. The visually stunning railroad twists up the tortuous route to the namesake White Pass, tracing the notorious and deadly White Pass trail used during the Klondike gold rush.

Sleeping

Reservations are essential in summer although, if time allows, there's no reason not to head into the Yukon to spend the night. There are many places to eat and drink on or just off Broadway St.

Pullen Creek RV Park (☎ 907-983-2768, 800-936-3731; 501 Congress St; sites from US$14) There are 46 sites here, right near the ferry dock and State St.

Skagway Home Hostel (☎ 907-983-2131; www .skagway.com; cnr 3rd Ave & Main St; dm US$15-20, r US$50; 🖳) Not a far walk from the ferry dock (or call for free pick-up), this family-run hostel couldn't be more welcoming, right down to the free produce from the garden.

Sergeant Preston's Lodge (☎ 907-983-2521; http://sgtprestons.eskagway.com; 370 6th Ave; r US$90-120; 🖳) The 37 rooms here are scattered among a few unassuming buildings right off Broadway. All are large and comfortable.

Getting There & Away

From Skagway to Whitehorse on the Klondike Hwy (Hwy 2) is 177km. The road is modern and paved, and customs at the border usually moves fairly quickly.

BOAT

The excellent **Alaska Marine Highway** (☎ 800-642-0066; www.ferryalaska.com) service goes to Haines (US$31, vehicles from US$41, two hours, five to seven weekly), Juneau, Petersburg, Wrangell, Ketchikan and, importantly, Prince Rupert in BC (US$171, cabins from US$160, vehicles from $370, 35 hours, two to three per week); it also goes to Bellingham, Washington, in the US (US$363, cabins from US$340, vehicles from US$900, 68 to 80 hours, one to two per week). For more on the Inside Passage journey, see p431.

The **Haines-Skagway Fast Ferry** (☎ 907-766-2100, 888-766-2103; www.hainesskagwayfastferry .com) carries passengers only (adult/child US$31/16, 35 minutes, three or more per

day June to September) and docks near the center.

BUS & TRAIN

See Whitehorse, p396, for transport options to the Yukon capital.

CHILKOOT TRAIL

Arduous at best and deadly at worst in 1898, the Chilkoot Trail was the route most prospectors took to get over the 1110m Chilkoot Pass from Skagway into the Yukon. Today, hikers reserve spots months in advance to travel the same route.

The well-marked 53km trail begins near **Dyea**, 14km northwest of Skagway, and heads northeast over the pass. It then follows the Taiya River to Lake Bennett in BC, and takes three to five days to hike. It's a hard route in good weather and often treacherous in bad. You must be in good physical condition and come fully equipped. Layers of warm clothes and rain gear are essential.

The trip begins in lush coastal forest and ascends into alpine tundra, where you will be above the treeline. In between sudden snow squalls (common all summer), you will see beautiful lakes and carpets of wildflowers. The trail then descends into hardy boreal forest. At trail's end in **Bennett**, there are artifacts aplenty from the gold rush, including the imposing hulk of St Andrew's Church.

Hardware, tools and supplies dumped by the prospectors still litter the trail. At several places there are wooden shacks where you can put up for the night, but these are usually full so a tent and sleeping bag are required. There are 10 designated campgrounds along the route, each with bear caches.

At the Canadian end you can either take the White Pass & Yukon Route train from Bennett back to Skagway or further up the line to Fraser in BC, where you can connect with a bus for Whitehorse.

The Chilkoot Trail is a primary feature of the **Klondike Gold Rush International Historic Park**, a series of sites managed by both Parks Canada and the US National Park Service that stretches from Seattle, Washington, to Dawson City. Each Chilkoot hiker must obtain one of the 50 permits ($54 plus $12 for a reservation) available each day

---

TOUGH, FOOLHARDY & FUTILE

Some 40,000 dreamers traveled from Skagway to Dawson City in 1897 and 1898 in search of gold. Most didn't strike it rich and, in fact, most left the Yukon poorer than when they arrived – a consequence of overly optimistic claims, bad luck and the highly efficient apparatus in place to fleece even those few who did strike it rich.

It started when ships docked in Seattle and San Francisco in the summer of 1897 crammed with gold from the Yukon. Word spread fast and soon thousands of mostly ill-prepared fortune seekers were headed north. Boats poured into Skagway that fall, turning it into the boomtown recalled today. That winter – could there have been a worse time for this? – thousands made their way up the Chilkoot Trail to the Canadian border, a sight John Muir said looked like 'an anthill stirred with a stick.' Only those with at least a thousand pounds of supplies were allowed into Canada; the country wanted to avoid starving miners dying all over the place. Meeting this hurdle required the average miner to trudge, in the snow, the equivalent of 1800 miles carrying their supplies one load at a time (few could afford animals or help to cover the 30 miles between Dyea and Bennett).

Once in Bennett, the prospective prospectors built boats out of whatever they could find. When the ice broke at the end of May, 1898, one of the motliest flotillas ever assembled set sail for Dawson on the Yukon. Few knew what to expect or had any experience with white-water rafting. Although the number is unknown, it's thought that far more drowned that summer on the Yukon's rivers than perished on the Chilkoot Trail. And reaching Dawson offered no respite: lawlessness, claim-jumpers, deprivation and myriad other hardships were constant. Adding an exclamation point to the futility, by the time news of the gold finds had set off the gold rush, the most valuable claims were already staked. The would-be millionaires arrived a year too late.

The Klondike Hwy generally follows the Gold Rush Trail (as Parks Canada calls it) past Whitehorse as far north as Minto. If you want to stay on the route of the prospectors to Dawson City, you'll need a canoe from one of the outfitters in Whitehorse and several days to navigate the Yukon River.

---

in summer; reserve in advance. Each day at 1pm eight permits are issued on a first-come, first-served basis for the next day. For further information contact the **Chilkoot Trail Centre** in Skagway (p405).

CARCROSS

pop 430

Long a forgotten gold rush town, beguiling little Carcross, 74km southeast of Whitehorse, is a worthy stop. It's the first settlement you reach in the Yukon from Skagway on the Klondike Hwy. The site was once a major seasonal hunting camp of the Tagish people, who called the area *Todezzane* (literally 'blowing all the time'). The present town name is an abbreviation of Caribou Crossing and refers to the local woodland caribou herds.

There are daily trains in summer from Skagway on the **White Pass & Yukon Route** (p405; round-trip adult/child $228/152), which cover a large section of the line most day trippers miss. Some old buildings, such as the 1903 Caribou Hotel, are being restored

and the site on the shores of Lake Bennett is picture-perfect (although Klondike prospectors who had to build boats here to cross the lake didn't think so).

The **VIC** (☎ 867-821-4431; ☼ 8am-8pm May-Sep) is in the old train station and has an excellent walking tour booklet of the town. The station also has good displays on local history and can steer you to local galleries with First Nations artisans.

Carcross Desert, the world's smallest, is the exposed sandy bed of a glacial lake. It's 2km north of town.

WHITEHORSE TO CARMACKS

North of Whitehorse, between the Takhini Hot Springs Rd and Carmacks, the land is dry and scrubby, although there are some farms with cattle and horses. After about 40km, however, look for serene **Lake Laberge**, which has a beach, followed by **Fox Lake**, 24km further north, and **Twin Lakes**, 23km south of Carmacks. Each has a government campground with shelters and pump water.

You can cover the 525km between Whitehorse and Dawson City in six hours, although there's plenty of reason to dawdle. As you whiz along, think back 100 years to when people traveled this route in winter by open sleigh, taking a week in sub-zero conditions. Bring a picnic, food choices along the road are uninspired – including the Brobdingnagian cinnamon rolls hawked everywhere.

CARMACKS

pop 400

Perched on the banks of the Yukon River, Carmacks is named for one of the discoverers of gold in 1896, George Washington Carmacks. A rogue seaman wandering the Yukon, it was almost by luck that Carmacks (with Robert Henderson, Tagish Charlie and Keish – aka Skookum Jim) made their claim on Bonanza Creek. Soon he was living the high life and it wasn't long before he abandoned his First Nations family and headed south to the US.

Given his record as husband and father, it's fitting that Carmacks is honored by this uninspired collection of gas stations and places to stay. The main reason to stop is the excellent **Tage Cho Hudan Interpretive Centre** (☎ 867-863-5830; admission by donation; ☼ 9am-4pm May-Sep) where volunteers explain aboriginal life past and present. Like elsewhere in the territory, residents here are keenly attuned to the land, which supplies them with game and fish throughout the year. A pretty 15-minute interpretive walk by the river provides a glimmer of insight into this life.

The junction for the Robert Campbell Hwy (see boxed text, p399) is also here.

About 25km north of Carmacks, the **Five Finger Recreation Site** has excellent views of the treacherous stretch of rapids that tested the wits of riverboat captains traveling between Whitehorse and Dawson. There's a steep 1.5km walk down to the rapids.

MINTO

Easily missed – unless you've got plans – Minto, 72km north of Carmacks and 250km south of Dawson, is where the Klondike Hwy leaves the route of the Gold Rush Trail and the Yukon River. This is a popular place to put in for a four- to five-day trip down the Yukon River to Dawson City.

Minto is also the place to pick up a boat to Fort Selkirk (below).

STEWART CROSSING

Another popular place to get your canoe wet, Stewart Crossing is on the Stewart River, which affords a narrow and somewhat more rugged experience before it joins the Yukon to the west for the trip to Dawson.

Otherwise unexceptional in the extreme, the village is the junction of the Klondike Hwy (Hwy 2) and the Silver Trail (Hwy 11).

North of Stewart Crossing the Klondike Hwy continues for 139 bland kilometers to the junction with the Dempster Hwy (p416). From here it's only 40km to Dawson City.

DAWSON CITY

pop 1700

In 1896 today's Dawson City was a sandy shoal at the confluence of the Yukon and Klondike Rivers. In 1897 it was the destination for tens of thousands of fortune hunters lured by the promise of gold. Within

---

THE LONELIEST FORT

For over 100 years **Fort Selkirk** was the most important stop on the Yukon River between Whitehorse and Dawson City. Founded as a trading post in 1849 by Robert Campbell, the post grew over the decades and was used by the army, trappers, First Nations people looking to trade and settlers looking for shelter. It was still going strong in the 1950s when it suffered a fate known to small towns in the wrong place everywhere: the new Klondike Hwy bypassed it. By a lot. River traffic ended and so did Fort Selkirk, its once busy streets and dozens of sturdy log buildings left to rot. But over the years it became a popular spot for anybody passing in a canoe or kayak, and in the 1980s the Yukon government began modest preservation.

Today Fort Selkirk is an isolated time capsule of the Yukon pre-car. If you aren't paddling by, you can enjoy a day-trip by river from Minto, 40km upstream, with **Big Bend Enterprises** (☎ 867-537-3551; www.bigriveryukon.ca; adult/child $125/63; ☼ late May-early Sep).

DAWSON CITY

0 _____ 400 m
0 _____ 0.2 miles

DRINKING 🍷
Bars at Westminster Hotel........**51** B3
Bombay Peggy's.......................(see 39)
Downtown Hotel......................(see 41)
Midnight Sun............................**52** B3

ENTERTAINMENT 🎭
Diamond Tooth Gertie's.............**53** B3

SHOPPING 🛍
Dawson Trading Post.................**54** B3
Dog House................................**55** B3
Wild & Wooly...........................**56** B4

TRANSPORT
Ferry.......................................**57** C1

INFORMATION
CIBC ATM................................**1** B3
Dawson City Community
  Library.................................**2** B4
Dawson Medical Clinic..............**3** B5
Maximilian's............................**4** B3
Post Office...............................**5** B3
TastyByte Internet Cafe.............**6** B3
VIC...**7** B3
Western Arctic Information
  Centre..................................**8** B3

SIGHTS & ACTIVITIES
3rd Ave Veterans......................**9** B4
Canadian Bank of Commerce......**10** B3
Cemetery.................................**11** D6
Cemetery.................................**12** D6
Cemetery.................................**13** D6
Cemetery.................................**14** C6
Cemetery.................................**15** D6
Circle Cycle.............................**16** C3
Commissioner's Residence.........**17** A5
Crocus Bluff............................**18** C6
Dänojà Zho Cultural Centre.......**19** B2
Dawson City Museum................**20** B5
Fortymile Gold
  Workshop/Studio...................**21** B3
Goldbottom Tours.....................**22** B3
Harrington's Store....................**23** B4
Historical Plaques.....................**24** B3
Jack London Interpretive
  Centre..................................**25** B5
Klondike Institute for Art &
  Culture.................................**26** B3
Klondike Spirit Tickets (Triple
  J Hotel)................................**27** C4
No Gold Gallery.......................**28** B3
Northern Commercial Co
  Warehouse............................**29** C3
ODD Gallery............................**30** B4
Old Post Office.........................**31** B3
Palace Grand Theatre................**32** B3
Princess Sophia Memorial..........**33** B3
Robert Service Cabin.................**34** B5
SS Keno..................................**35** B3
St Andrew's Presbyterian
  Church..................................**36** B5

SLEEPING 🛏
5th Ave B&B............................**37** B5
Aurora Inn...............................**38** B4
Bombay Peggy's........................**39** B4
Dawson City Bunkhouse.............**40** B4
Downtown Hotel.......................**41** B3
El Dorado Hotel........................**42** B4
Gold Rush Campground RV
  Park.....................................**43** C3
Klondike Kate's........................**44** B3
Yukon Hotel.............................**45** A4

EATING 🍴
Antoinette's Food Cache............**46** B4
Bonanza Market........................**47** B3
Drunken Goat Taverna..............**48** B3
Farmers Market........................**49** B3
Klondike Kate's........................(see 44)
La Table on 5th........................(see 38)
River West...............................**50** B3

DETOUR: SILVER TRAIL

Exactly what the name implies, this old mining road (Hwy 11) heads east from Stewart Crossing. The first 52km to **Mayo** (www.yukonweb.com/community/mayo) is paved and there are some turnouts for nature walks along the way. Mayo dates to 1903, when it was a busy river port for the surrounding silver industry. Today it has a couple of motels and a cute little downtown on the river with restored buildings and plaques detailing its history.

From here the road turns to gravel. The first of two nearly abandoned mining towns, Elsa, is 45km from Mayo (sadly no one thought to name any nearby places Ham or Rye) and is closed to the public. But **Keno** (www.kenocity.info), a further 16km, has a small **mining museum** that's usually open at peak times in summer. There are good hikes here to alpine meadows, snowy peaks and up **Keno Hill**, which has a signpost with distances to cities worldwide (eg Melbourne 8300 miles).

In summer, there's a Silver Trail **Information Centre** (9am-5pm Jun-Aug) in Stewart Crossing, just south of the bridge on the Klondike Hwy. The walking tour brochures for Keno and Mayo really cut the mustard.

---

two years the Klondike Gold Rush had peaked and the 99% who didn't make a fortune were slinking off home (see the boxed text, p406, for more on these characters). Dawson began to molder away. But something happened on the way to legendary ghost town status: it didn't die.

Today Dawson is one of North America's most authentically colorful towns. A hardy crew lives here year round, joined each summer by thousands who come for the beautiful locale and tangible links to the past. Many buildings remain from the gold rush era and Parks Canada is involved in restoring or preserving those considered historically significant; regulations ensure that new buildings are built in sympathy with the old. With unpaved streets and board sidewalks, the town still has a gritty feel.

Dawson also has the intangible pull of an end-of-the-road vibe that rewards those unwilling to march to anyone's drum – even their own. Long summer nights let you enjoy both raw nature and raw nightlife. But note, by September, 'flee sale' signs appear around town as seasonal residents (about half) head south. For those remaining, Dawson is a cold (average temperature in January is −27°C) and quiet place.

HISTORY

First Nations trapping villages always dotted the banks of the rivers here. Prospectors – and bar keeps, floozies, outfitters, con men etc – began congregating here in late 1896. They named their 'townsite' of tents pitched in the mud Dawson after the geologist George Dawson, who had mapped the area in 1887. The city grew to a population of 40,000 almost as fast as its boom faded. Once known as the 'Paris of the North,' by 1920 Dawson had become a small frontier town of a few hundred sustained by miners who persevered on and bureaucrats who'd made it the capital of the territory (a status it lost in 1953 when the seat moved to Whitehorse amid much local anguish).

Dawson is built on permafrost, which begins just a few centimeters down. Buildings have foundations of planks resting on gravel and many show the seasonal effects of heaving. Outside of town are the eerie piles of tailings, which look like the work of mammoth gophers. These huge mounds are actually from giant gold dredges that sucked up the swampy earth at one end and left it behind sans gold at the other. Today dozens of enterprises are still mining for gold in the region around Dawson City.

ORIENTATION

You can walk around town in a few hours. The Klondike Hwy leads into Front St (also called 1st Ave) along the Yukon River. Just north of town, a free ferry crosses the Yukon River to the Top of the World Hwy (p415) and onward to Alaska. Dawson is 527km from Whitehorse and 240km south of the Arctic Circle.

Like a ray of sunshine in January, street numbers are a rarity in Dawson. Unless noted otherwise, opening hours and times given below cover the period mid-May to mid-September. For the rest of year, most sights, attractions and many businesses are closed.

INFORMATION

The biweekly, volunteer-run *Klondike Sun* (www.klondikesun.com) covers news and events. Dawson's lively community radio station is at 106.9 FM. Note that Dawson can still get raucous on a weekend night; the bright Gore-tex jackets of tourists can be red flags to drunks.

CIBC ATM (2nd Ave)

Dawson City Community Library (☎ 867-993-5811; cnr 5th Ave & Queen St; ☯ noon-8pm Tue-Sat but can vary) Has internet access.

Dawson Medical Clinic (☎ 867-993-5744; Church St; ☯ 9am-noon & 1-5pm Mon-Fri) A private clinic and pharmacy; nurses are always on call at the adjoining government clinic (☎ 867-993-4444).

Maximilian's (☎ 867-993-6537; Front St; ☯ 8am-8pm) Excellent selection of regional books, magazines, out-of-town newspapers and topographical and river maps.

Post office (☎ 867-993-5342; 3rd Ave; ☯ 8:30am-5:30pm Mon-Fri, 11:30am-2:30pm Sat)

TastyByte Internet Cafe (☎ 867-993-6105; Front St; per hr $6; ☯ 9:30am-5:30pm; ☞) Good coffee and a view.

VIC (☎ 867-993-5566; cnr Front St & King St; ☯ 8am-8pm) Parks Canada information is split between here and the Palace Grand Theatre (King St).

Western Arctic Information Centre (☎ 867-993-6167; Front St; ☯ 9am-8pm) Maps, road condition reports and information on the NWT and Dempster Hwy.

SIGHTS

In summer, if the historic center of Dawson feels like a claim with paydirt, just wander off uphill a few blocks, where you'll find timeless old houses and streets.

Klondike National Historic Sites

Parks Canada (www.pc.gc.ca/dawson) does an excellent job of providing information and tours of Dawson's principal historic sights. In addition to the individual sight fees listed below, there is a good-value **pass** (adult/child $29/15) valid for all Parks Canada sites and tours. For tickets go to the Parks Canada window at the **Palace Grand Theatre** (King St; ☯ 9:30am-5:30pm), though you won't be able to get seats for the opening night show of July 18, 1899: 'Arizona Charley & Forty Shapely Ladies.'

ROBERT SERVICE CABIN

Called the 'Bard of the Yukon,' poet and writer Robert W Service lived in this typical gold rush **cabin** (cnr 8th Ave & Hanson St; admission free; ☯ 1-4:30pm) from 1909 to 1912. Don't miss the **dramatic readings** (admission $7; ☯ 1:30pm & 7pm). From here he was known to wander the hills at odd hours talking to himself before locking himself inside for weeks on end writing. In other words, he was a typical writer.

COMMISSIONER'S RESIDENCE

Built in 1901 to house the territorial commissioner, this proud **building** (Front St; admission $7; ☯ 10am-5pm, tour times vary) was designed to give potential civic investors confidence in the city. The building was the longtime home of Martha Black who, despite being deserted by her husband and pregnant on the way to the Yukon in 1898, pressed on to Dawson, bought a lumberyard and married George Black, who became a legendary Yukon politician. Oh, and she was elected to the Canadian Parliament at the age of 70 (*Martha Black* by Flo Whyard is a great book about this grande dame of the Yukon).

SS *KENO*

The voyage from Whitehorse to Dawson was not easy. The season was short and there were perilous areas of white water to navigate. The **SS** *Keno* (admission $7; ☯ 10am-6pm) was one of a fleet of paddle-wheelers that worked the rivers for over half a century. Now on dry land by the river, it houses many good displays about travel 100 years ago.

HARRINGTON'S STORE

This old store has been converted to a **historic gallery** (cnr 3rd Ave & Princess St; admission free; ☯ 9am-4:30pm) with photos from the peaks and valleys of Dawson's existence.

Other Historic Sites

Old buildings in every state of repair dot the dirt streets of Dawson – wander around and see what you find...

Old Post Office (cnr 3rd Ave & King St; ☯ 9am-3pm Tue-Sat) Built in 1901. You can still mail a card here ($5 to anywhere in the world) but the mail only goes out once a year as part of the annual Percy De Wolfe Mail Race (www.thepercy.com), which covers the old dog-sled mail route 336km to Eagle, Alaska.

3rd Ave Veterans (3rd Ave) Often-photographed, this 1901 troika have settled against each other like puppies huddling for warmth.

St Andrew's Presbyterian Church (cnr 4th Ave & Church St) Gently settling into the permafrost, this 1901 church was designed by Warren Porter, who also did the Canadian Bank of Commerce building.

Canadian Bank of Commerce (Front St) Robert Service worked as a teller here in 1908-09 before he found his real calling as a writer. Now derelict, this suitably imposing building is actually made of pressed metal made to look like carved stone. That it sits abandoned contributes to Dawson's unrestored charm.

Princess Sophia Memorial (Front St) On October 18, 1918, the SS Princess Sophia sank off the coast of Alaska killing all 353 aboard. Some 125 were Dawsonites heading south for the winter and the community was traumatized. Before the ship sank – storms prevented rescue or escape – many passengers wrote last letters to loved ones that were later found.

Historical Plaques (Front St) A series of engaging riverside plaques combine photos with highlights of Dawson's history.

Northern Commercial Co Warehouse (cnr King St & 5th Ave) One of Dawson's very first buildings (1897), this sturdy structure was erected away from the hodge-podge of filthy riverbank tents that marked early Dawson. It has stolidly withstood more than a century of weather extremes.

Jack London Interpretive Centre

In 1898 Jack London lived in the Yukon, the setting for his most popular animal stories including *Call of the Wild* and *White Fang*. At the writer's **cabin** (8th Ave at Firth St; admission by donation; 10am-1pm & 2-6pm) there are daily interpretive talks. A labor of love by historian and writer Dick North, Dawne Mitchell and others, this place is a treasure trove. Read the stories about 'Jack,' a local dog, which Jack, the noted author, used as a model for Buck in *Call of the Wild*. North's *Sailor on Snowshoes* is a wonderfully readable account of London's time in the Yukon.

Dawson City Museum

This **museum** (867-993-5291; 5th Ave; adult/child $9/7; 10am-6pm) houses a collection of 25,000 gold rush artifacts. Engaging exhibits walk you through the hard-scrabble lives of the miners. The museum is housed in the landmark 1901 Old Territorial Administration building. It was designed by noted architect Thomas W Fuller, who also designed the old post office and other buildings around town. Next door is a barn with old mining trains. Be sure to attend the daily re-enactment of a miners' meeting, the goldfield version of justice. Here a miscreant is accused of claim jumping and, after evidence is heard, the crowd decides what to do: hang him, lash him, banish him or set him free.

Dänojà Zho Cultural Centre

Inside a beautiful wooden building on the riverfront, this **cultural centre** (867-993-6768; www.trondek.com; Front St; adult/child $5/2.50; 10am-6pm) has displays and interpretive talks on the *Hän Hwäch'in* (River People), who were the first to inhabit the area. The collection includes traditional artifacts and a re-creation of a 19th-century fishing camp. Locally made crafts are for sale. Check the schedule of cultural tours and performances of authentic dances. The striking building was designed by noted Yukon architects KVA.

Midnight Dome

The slide-scarred face of this hill (it's not due to mining) overlooks the town to the north, but to reach the top you must travel south of town about 1km, turn left off the Klondike Hwy onto New Dome Rd, and continue for about 7km. At 880m above sea level, the Midnight Dome offers sweeping views of the Klondike Valley, Yukon River and Dawson City. There's also a steep **trail** that takes 90 minutes from Judge St in town; maps are available at the VIC.

Cemeteries & Crocus Bluff

A 15-minute walk up King St and Mary McCloud Rd behind town leads to 10 **cemeteries** that are literally filled with characters, among them Joe Vogler, who fought to have Alaska secede from the US. He was buried here in 1993, having vowed not to be buried in an Alaska that wasn't free. During the 2008 US presidential election, Sarah Palin stirred controversy when it was revealed that her husband Todd was a Vogler follower.

The Dawson City Museum (left) leads two-hour **cemetery tours** (tour $5; 7pm) here or pick up the excellent walking tour brochure from the VIC. If you're driving, ignore the 'local traffic only' signs coming up King St. On New Dome Rd, turn at Mary

MINING: THEN & NOW

The more you learn about the early gold miners in the Dawson area, the more you learn about their unrelenting sacrifice in pursuit of gold. And this isn't just the thousands who lost everything trying to get there during the gold rush, it's the miners who worked their claims during the long and brutal winters after 1897. Miners would build fires on the frozen ground to melt the ice below. Then they would dig down. They would repeat the process again and again until they were several meters down. At this point they would start tunneling along the seams of gold-laden dirt, scooping out gravel so it could be panned after the thaw. And they did this in the dark.

Today, miners with the same spirit work to ferret out the precious metal. Despite backhoes, pumps and other tools, it is still dirty, hard work. As one, David Millar, told us: 'The early miners were looking for gold nuggets the size of their toes; I'm looking for ones the size of sea salt.' Like most of the current Dawson-area miners – about 200 – he's mining placer (which means sand or gravel bank) areas that have already been worked once or twice but counts on modern methods to find gold others have missed. 'You work long days,' he says, 'you keep working until it just gets so cold, you have to do something else.'

Millar and his family also operate GoldBottom Tours (opposite).

McLeod Rd (ignoring the 'no exit' signs). There's also a short path out to pretty **Crocus Bluff**, which has excellent views of Dawson and the Klondike and Yukon Rivers.

Mine Sites

The scarred valleys around Dawson speak to the vast amounts of toil that went into the gold hunt. Most emblematic is Bonanza Creek, where gold was first found. Miners still work claims here that yield some gold.

Over 100 times more fun than being a miner, **Claim 33** (☎ 867-993-6626; Bonanza Creek Rd; ☯ 10am-5:30pm) is part museum, part roadside attraction and full-time performance venue for owner Jerry Bryde. Using bone-dry Norwegian humor, he gives gold-panning lessons that almost always yield a few flakes for visitors (the cost is pegged to the price of gold, eg if its $1000 per ounce, it costs $10 for a panning lesson). The site is about 9km up Bonanza Creek Rd from the Klondike Hwy.

About 4km further on, **Dredge No 4** (Bonanza Creek Rd; admission $7; ☯ 10am-4pm, tour times vary) is a massive dredging machine that tore up the Klondike Valley and left the tailings behind, which remain as a blight on the landscape. Parks Canada offers fascinating tours of this monster that worked something like a sinister gopher in a science fiction novel.

Just 1.5km further up the valley, the **Discovery Site** is roughly where gold was first found in 1897. It's a quiet site today with a little water rippling through the rubble. Another 2km brings you to **Claim No 6**, a site

where you can pan for your own gold for free (rent a pan for $3 at Claim 33).

Ship Graveyard

When the Klondike Hwy was completed, the paddle-wheel ferries were abandoned. Several were sailed just downstream from town and left to rot on the bank. Now overgrown, the remains are a fascinating destination for a short hike. Take the ferry across the river, then walk north through the Yukon River Campground for 10 minutes and then another 10 minutes north along the beach.

Moosehide

This tiny First Nations village is 3km downstream from Dawson. Moosehide thrived during the gold rush as a refuge for indigenous people fleeing the sleaze of Dawson. Today it is a short but challenging **hike** that takes about three hours. There are caveats: check with the VIC as the route is weather dependent, there may be bears, and you need a permit to visit (ask at the Dänojà Zho Cultural Centre, p411).

Galleries

Dawson has a thriving arts community – even the mayor is an artist. The well-funded **Klondike Institute for Art & Culture** (KIAC; ☎ 867-993-5005; www.kiac.org; cnr 3rd Ave & Queen St) has an impressive new studio building, galleries and educational programs.

KIAC's exhibition space, the **ODD Gallery** (☎ 867-993-5005; cnr 2nd Ave & Princess St; ☯ hrs vary), shows local works.

No Gold Gallery (☎ 867-993-5203; cnr Front St & Queen St) has works by a dozen local artists (and cartographic maps). **Fortymile Gold Workshop/Studio** (☎ 867-993-5690; 3rd Ave) has gold creations from 30 local artists. Watch as jewelry is made from local refined gold, which is silky and has a rich yellow color as opposed to the bling you see on *The Sopranos*.

ACTIVITIES

Besides the many walks and hikes described above, you can mountain bike throughout the area. The **Ridge Road Heritage Trail** winds through the goldfields south of town combining Bonanza Creek Rd with the equally historic Hunker Creek Rd. The VIC has a trail description. **Circle Cycle** (☎ 867-993-6270; cnr King St & 7th Ave; per day $25) rents mountain bikes.

Besides arriving by **canoe** or **kayak**, many people also exit Dawson via the Yukon River. A popular three- to four-day trip, good for novices, goes 168km downstream from Dawson to Eagle, Alaska.

Dawson Trading Post (p415) rents canoes and arranges longer trips. **Dawson City River Hostel** (right), across the river, also rents canoes, arranges transport and helps organize trips.

For a daytrip to the real wild side, consider Tombstone Territorial Park on the Dempster Hwy (p416).

TOURS

Parks Canada guides, often in period garb, lead excellent **walking tours** (tour $7; ☾ 9:30am, some days extra tours) of Dawson. Learn about individual buildings and Paradise Alley, demure today but home to more than 400 prostitutes in its time. You can also take a self-guided **audio tour** (rental $7; ☾ 9:30am-4:30pm).

GoldBottom Tours (☎ 867-993-5750; www.gold bottom.com; ticket office Front St) runs daily tours during the summer at the site, 15km up Hunker Creek Rd, which meets Hwy 2 just north of the airport. The 3½-hour tours cost $25 (children free); you can include transport to/from Dawson for $40. If you catch gold fever, you can stay in one of four cabins ($65) and pan as much as you like (and keep what you find).

Sail the Yukon on the **Klondike Spirit** (☎ 867-993-5323; tickets Triple J Hotel, cnr 5th Ave & Queen St; tours from $40), a modern re-created paddle-wheeler that offers day and dinner cruises.

FESTIVALS & EVENTS

Spring Breakup (late Apr) No, not the time when relationships end after a long winter cooped up in a cabin arguing about whose turn it is to chop wood, but rather the moment when the winter ice on the Yukon River breaks apart with a roar. The focus of much debate, guessing the moment of each year's breakup is the subject – you'll be shocked to learn – of much gambling. More ominously, it now happens on average a week earlier than it did 100 years ago.

Dawson City Music Festival (mid-Jul; ☎ 867-993-5384; www.dcmf.com) This festival features well-known Canadian musicians. It's very popular – tickets sell out two months in advance and the city fills up – so reservations are a good idea.

Discovery Days (3rd Mon in Aug) The premier annual event in Dawson City celebrates the you-know-what of 1896. There are parades and picnics. Events, including a very good art show, begin days before.

SLEEPING

Reservations are a good idea in July and August, although the VIC can help. Many places will pick you up at the airport; ask in advance. Unless otherwise stated, the following are open year round.

As you approach Dawson from the south, you'll pass several large RV-style commercial campgrounds.

Budget

Yukon River Campground (campsite $12) On the western side of the river, about 250m up the road to the right after you get off the ferry, this territorial campground has 98 shady sites.

Dawson City River Hostel (☎ 867-993-6823; www .yukonhostels.com; dm $18-22, r from $46; ☾ mid-May–Sep) This delightfully eccentric hostel is across the river from town and five minutes up the hill from the ferry landing. It has good views, cabins, platforms for tents and a communal bathhouse. Tent sites are $14. Owner Dieter Reinmuth is a noted Yukon author.

Gold Rush Campground RV Park (☎ 867-993-5247; 866-330-5006; www.goldrushcampground.com; cnr 5th Ave & York St; sites $20-40; ☾ mid-May–mid-Sep; ☞) Convenience trumps atmosphere at this 83-site gravel parking lot for RVs.

Midrange

Dawson City Bunkhouse (☎ 867-993-6164; www .dawsoncitybunkhouse.com; cnr 2nd Ave & Princess St; r $65-120) Built like buildings were during the gold rush, the bunkhouse has economy (small, shared bathroom) and larger rooms with private bathrooms and TVs. Noise carries. Half the units are monthly ($400).

5th Ave B&B (☎ 867-993-5941; www.5thavebandb .com; 702 5th Ave; r $80-135; ❄ 🖵 🛜) Eleven large and comfortable rooms are spread across two adjoining buildings. Breakfast is serve-yourself-as-much-as-you-want. A large patio has high-quality chairs for gazing at the light playing off the hills.

Bombay Peggy's (☎ 867-993-6969; www.bombay peggys.com; cnr 2nd Ave & Princess St; r $80-200; ❄ Mar-Dec; ❄ 🛜) A renovated brothel, Peggy's allure is its period furnishings and spunky attitude. Budget 'snug' rooms share bathrooms. The rooms are plush in a way that will make you want to wear a garter, while the bar is a classy oasis (opposite).

Downtown Hotel (☎ 867-993-5346, 800-661-0514; www.downtownhotel.ca; cnr Queen St & 2nd Ave; r $90-150; ❄ 🖵 🛜) A landmark hotel on a prominent corner, the Downtown has 34 rooms in the main heritage building and 25 more in a modern annex. Not all have air-con; ask to see a couple as some are small and/or frumpy. The bar (opposite) is literally a riot.

El Dorado Hotel (☎ 867-993-5451, 800-764-3536; www.eldoradohotel.ca; cnr 3rd Ave & Princess St; r $100-160; ❄ 🛜) The El Dorado has 46 contemporary rooms, including six recently built air-con suites. There are another six rooms in the old 1897 **Yukon Hotel** building on Front St, although the rooms are strictly motel-modern.

ourpick Klondike Kate's (☎ 867-993-6527; www .klondikekates.ca; cnr King St & 3rd Ave; cabins $120-140; ❄ Apr-Sep; 🖵) The 16 cabins here behind the ever-popular restaurant of the same name are rustic without the rusticisms. High-speed internet, microwaves and fridges ensure comfort. The porches are perfect for decompressing. Green practices are many: locally handmade organic soap, bamboo flooring and blinds, compostable consumables and more.

Aurora Inn (☎ 867-993-6860; www.aurorainn .ca; 5th Ave; r $120-160; 🖵 🛜) All 20 rooms in this European-style inn are large and comfortable. And if there's such a thing as Old World cleanliness, it's here: the admonishments to remove your invariably muddy shoes start at the entrance.

EATING

Picnickers, hikers and backcountry campers will find two good grocery stores in town. A **farmers market** (❄ 11am-5pm Sat mid-May–mid-Sep)

thrives by the iconic waterfront gazebo. The sweet-as-candy carrots are the product of very cold nights. Try some birch syrup.

Most hotels have so-so restaurants that cater to the crowds that troop through all summer. With exceptions noted below, most places close outside of summer.

River West (☎ 867-993-6339; cnr Front St & Queen St; meals $4-8; ❄ 7am-7pm Mar-Oct) Busy throughout the day, this excellent coffeehouse, bakery and cafe looks out on the Front St action. Grab an outside table and watch the passing parade of gossiping locals.

Bonanza Market (☎ 867-993-6567; 2nd Ave; sandwiches $6; ❄ 8am-6pm) A good market with interesting produce and some organic fresh foods. The deli makes excellent sandwiches.

ourpick Drunken Goat Taverna (☎ 867-993-5800; 2nd Ave; mains $7-25; ❄ noon-9pm, very late Fri & Sat) Follow your eyes to the flowers, your ears to the Aegean music and your nose to the excellent Greek food, served 12-months-a-year by Tony Dovas. Out back there's a simple take-out that opens from midnight to 3am on weekends selling 'snacks for drunks.'

Klondike Kate's (☎ 867-993-6527; cnr King St & 3rd Ave; mains $8-25; ❄ 8am-9pm Apr-Sep) Two ways to know spring has arrived: the river cracks up and Kate's reopens. Locals count the days for both. The long and inventive menu has fine sandwiches, pastas and fresh Yukon fish. Specials are often just that. This is *the* place for breakfast.

La Table on 5th (☎ 867-993-6860; Aurora Inn, 5th Ave; mains $15-40; ❄ 5-9pm) Cornish game hen fondue is one of the intriguing choices on the Swiss haute cuisine menu here. Or ponder a passel of schnitzels or a bevy of steaks. Make arrangements in advance and a local storyteller will join you at your table.

Antoinette's Food Cache (☎ 867-993-6822; 3rd Ave; mains $20-35; ❄ 5-9pm Tue-Sat) Look for the leaning Mountie out the front of this house where noted chef Antoinette Oliphant both lives and prepares a short but exquisite fusion menu each night. Inside or on the patio, it feels like a dinner party at a friend's.

DRINKING

The spirit of the prospectors lives on in several saloons in Dawson. On summer nights the action goes on until late (there's nothing like stumbling out of a bar to watch the sunset at 2am).

Bars at Westminster Hotel (3rd Ave; ☺ noon-late) These two bars carry the mostly affectionate monikers 'Snakepit,' 'Armpit' or simply 'Pit.' The places for serious drinkers, there's live music many nights.

our pick Bombay Peggy's (☎ 867-993-6969; cnr 2nd Ave & Princess St; ☺ 11am-11pm) There's always a hint of pleasures to come swirling around the tables of Dawson's most inviting bar. Enjoy good beer, wine and mixed drinks inside or out on the back patio. Drink specials add to the festive air, which attracts *everybody* in town.

Downtown Hotel (☎ 867-993-5346; cnr Queen St & 2nd Ave; ☺ 11am-late) This unremarkable bar comes to life at 9pm in summer for what can best be called the 'Sourtoe Schtick.' Tourists line up to drink a shot of booze ($10) that has a pickled human toe floating in it. It's a long-running gag that's delightfully chronicled in Dieter Reinmuth's *The Saga of the Sourtoe*. (That the toe – it *is* real – looks much like a bit of beef jerky should give pause to anyone who gets the Slim Jim munchies…)

Midnight Sun (☎ 867-993-5495; cnr Queen St & 3rd Ave; ☺ noon-late) The boozy venue for live music; it jumps with people shaking it to good local and regional bands.

ENTERTAINMENT

Diamond Tooth Gertie's (☎ 867-993-5575; cnr Queen St & 4th Ave; admission $6; ☺ 7pm-2am mid-May–mid-Sep) This popular re-creation of an 1898 saloon is complete with small-time gambling, a honky-tonk piano and iconic dancing girls. The casino helps promote the town and fund culture. Each night there are three floor shows, heavy on corn and kicking legs. The available food won't improve your mood if you're losing.

SHOPPING

Dawson Trading Post (☎ 867-993-5316; Front St; ☺ 9am-7pm) Sells interesting old mining gadgets, bear traps ($500) and old mammoth tusks so you can take up carving. It has a good bulletin board.

Dog House (☎ 867-993-5405; Front St; ☺ 10am-7pm) The local center for dog-sledding. Dress as a musher and get your picture taken.

Wild & Wooly (☎ 867-993-5170; cnr 3rd Ave & Queen St; ☺ 10am-7pm) This place has all sorts of lovely, locally made jewelry along with quite fashionable men's and women's clothes. Or,

if you simply forgot your tidy-whiteys, they have those too.

GETTING THERE & AWAY
Dawson City Airport (YDA) is 19km east of town off the Klondike Hwy. **Air North** (☎ 800-661-0407; www.flyairnorth.com) serves Whitehorse, Old Crow, Inuvik in the NWT and Fairbanks in Alaska.

There are no rental cars available in Dawson and bus services seem to be in a constant state of flux. Check with the VIC for details.

Alaska Direct Bus Line (☎ 867-668-4833; www.alaskadirectbusline.com) offers a summer service to Whitehorse ($150, eight hours, twice weekly).

Alaska/Yukon Trails (☎ 800-770-7275; www.alaskashuttle.com) runs shuttles between Whitehorse and Dawson (US$150, 6½ hours, three times weekly in summer). It also links Dawson to Fairbanks over the Top of the World Hwy via Chicken and Tok (US$170, 9½ hours, three times weekly in summer).

DAWSON TO ALASKA

At the northern end of Dawson City's Front St the free ferry crosses the Yukon River to the scenic **Top of the World Hwy** (Hwy 9). Open only in summer, the road is mostly paved in Canada for the beautiful 106km to the US border that runs along ridge tops.

You'll continue to feel on top of the world as you cross the border, the land is barren alpine meadows with jutting rocks and grazing caribou. The **border crossing** (☺ 9am-9pm Yukon time/8am-8pm Alaska time, 15 May-15 Sep) has strict hours; if you're late you'll have to wait until the next day.

On the US side the road becomes gravel, with stretches of dirt that are okay for cars in summer but possibly dodgy after rains. After 19km (12 miles) you reach the Taylor Hwy (Hwy 5). The old gold mining town of **Eagle** on the Yukon River is 104km (65 miles) north of this junction.

Some 47km (30 miles) south over dirt roads (expect to get dirt in parts of your vehicle and person you didn't think possible), you hit **Chicken** (www.townofchicken.com), a delightful place of free-thinkers happy to sell you a stupid T-shirt at one of the gas stations/cafes or share their caustic views on bureaucrats.

Another 124km (77 miles) south over decent roads and you reach the Alaska Hwy (p398) where a turn east takes you to the Yukon. Just a tick west, **Tok** (www.tokalaskainfo.com) has services and motels. Alaska time is one hour earlier than the Yukon.

DEMPSTER HIGHWAY

Maybe the E should be a U? D-U-M-P-S-T-E-R. That's the destination for your tires if they're not up to snuff for one of North America's last roads that still carries real bragging rights. At its northeast end is Inuvik, a First Nations town amid the vast tundra expanse of the Northwest Territories. After the mountains of the Yukon, flat Inuvik, which is right on the broad Mackenzie River, is a real gear shift. It's also your ticket to the Arctic Ocean. Now that's adventure!

The 736km Dempster Hwy (Hwy 5 in the Yukon, Hwy 8 in the Northwest Territories) makes the journey the reason for going. It winds through stark mountains and emerald valleys, across huge tracts of tundra and passes Tombstone Territorial Park (right). It starts 40km southeast of Dawson City off the Klondike Hwy and heads north over the Ogilvie and Richardson Mountains, crossing the Arctic Circle.

Almost all gravel, the Dempster is open most of the year but the best time to travel is between June and early September when the ferries over the Peel and Mackenzie Rivers operate. In the winter, ice forms a natural bridge over the rivers, which become ice roads. It's closed during the spring thaw and winter freeze-up; these vary by the year and can occur from mid-April to June and mid-October to December respectively.

The road is a test for drivers and cars. Travel with extra gas and tires, and expect to use them. For information, the **Western Arctic Information Centre** in Dawson City (p410) is an excellent resource. Check out road conditions in the Yukon (☎ 511; www.511yukon.ca) and the NWT (☎ 800-661-0750; www.dot.gov.nt.ca).

Accommodations and vehicle services along the route are scarce. There is a gas station at the southern start of the highway at **Klondike River Lodge** (☎ 867-993-6892). The lodge will rent gas cans that you can take north and return on the way back.

The next services are 369km north in Eagle Plains. The **Eagle Plains Hotel** (☎ 867-993-2453; www.eagleplainshotel.com; r $100-150) is open year round and offers 32 rooms. The next service station is 180km further at **Fort McPherson** in the Northwest Territories. From there it's 216km to Inuvik.

The Yukon government has three campgrounds – at **Tombstone Mountain** (below), **Engineer Creek** (194km) and **Rock River** (447km). There's also a Northwest Territories government campground at **Nitainlaii Territorial Park**, 9km south of Fort McPherson.

TOMBSTONE TERRITORIAL PARK

Shades of green and charcoal color the wide valleys here and steep ridges are dotted with small glaciers and alpine lakes. Summer feels tentative but makes its statement with a burst of purple wildflowers in July. Clouds sweep across the tundra bringing squalls punctuated by brilliant sun. Deeper inside, other-worldly mountains, eroded into forbidding shapes, bring to mind the color of the moon.

Tombstone Territorial Park (www.yukonparks.ca) lies along Dempster Hwy for about 50km. The park's only formal **campground** (campsite $12) has a small but excellent **Interpretive Centre** (☑ 9am-5pm late May–mid-Sep). It's 72km from the start of the highway and is set in along the headwaters of the Yukon River just before **Tombstone Mountain**, the point where the trees run out and the truly wild northern scenery begins.

There are good **day hikes** near the campground, as well as longer, more rigorous **treks** for experienced wilderness hikers. Permits are required for backcountry camping, especially at several lakes popular in summer. (The park's backcountry camping guide shows refreshing honesty in answer to this frequently asked question: 'Will you come looking for me if I don't return?' 'No.')

Tombstone is an easy day-trip from Dawson City (112km each way). With preparations, however, a multi-day park expedition will be like few others.

INUVIK (NWT)
pop 3300

Inuvik is the reward at the end of the Dempster Hwy. Although it's in the Northwest Territories, its main access is from the Yukon. It is also the staging point for trips to Vuntut and Ivvavik National Parks and Herschel Island Territorial Park in the far north of the Yukon.

Inuvik lies on the east channel of the Mackenzie River 97km south of the Arctic Coast. It was built in 1955 as an administrative post for the government. It's somewhat tattered and won't give you cause to linger long on your course to greater adventure. In a different time zone to the Yukon, Inuvik has 24 hours of sunlight for an average of 56 days from late June. In early December the sun sets and does not rise until January.

Lonely Planet's *Canada* has complete coverage of Inuvik and the NWT; alternatively, download the Northwest Territories & Nunavut chapter at www.lonelyplanet.com.

The **Western Arctic Visitors Centre** (☎ 867-777-4727, winter 867-777-7237; www.inuvik.ca; 284 Mackenzie Rd; ◷ 9am-7pm Jun–mid-Sep) has numerous displays about the area and its ecology.

Parks Canada (☎ 867-777-8800; www.parkscanada .ca; 187 Mackenzie Rd; ◷ 8:30am-5pm Jun-Aug, call other times) has information on Vuntut and Ivvavik National Parks.

Several local companies specialize in tours of varying duration to the Yukon parks. Other services include logistical work for independent travelers as well as gear rental.

Arctic Nature Tours (☎ 867-777-3300, fax 867-777-3400; www.arcticnaturetours.com; 65 Mackenzie Rd) has tours to places like Herschel Island ($480 per person).

Arctic Chalet (☎ 867-777-3535; www.arcticchalet.com; 25 Carn St; r from $110) has bright, cabin-style rooms in a sylvan setting. The genial owners rent canoes, kayaks and cars, run dog-sledding tours and are good sources of adventure info.

Most people drive the Dempster Hwy to Inuvik, but flying can save you two days' traveling time and about four tires. **Mike Zubko Airport** (YEV) has services with **Air North** (☎ 800-661-0407; www.flyairnorth.com) to Whitehorse and Dawson City, some via Old Crow.

ARCTIC PARKS

Nature, nature, nature and nothing else marks three remote parks in the far north of the Yukon. Casual visits are impossible but with money, fortitude or slight insanity (or bits of all three) you can see parts of the planet few will ever see.

The 280-person village of **Old Crow** (www .oldcrow.ca) is home to the Vuntut Gwich'in First Nations and is unreachable by vehicle. Residents subsist on caribou from the legendary 130,000-strong Porcupine herd, which migrates each year between the Arctic National Wildlife Refuge (ANWR) in Alaska and the Yukon. Not surprisingly, the locals are against the threat of oil drilling on the US side of the border in the ANWR. Life here is hard, as shown in the American PBS documentary *Arctic Son*.

On the Yukon side of this vast flat Arctic tundra, a large swath of land is now protected in two adjoining national parks, Vuntut and Ivvavik. Information on both can be obtained from the Parks Canada office in Inuvik (left), where you can get information on the very limited options for organizing visits to the parks (think chartered planes, long treks over land, water and ice and total self-sufficiency). There are no facilities of any kind in the parks.

VUNTUT NATIONAL PARK

Vuntut, a Gwich'in word meaning 'among the lakes,' is about 100km north of Old Crow, where there is a one-person **park office** (☎ 867-667-3910; www.pc.gc.ca/vuntut). The 4345-sq-km park was declared a national park in 1993. It lives up to its name with scores of lakes and ponds, home to 500,000 shore birds in late summer. Archaeological sites contain fossils of ancient animals such as mammoths, plus evidence of early humans.

IVVAVIK NATIONAL PARK

Ivvavik, meaning 'a place for giving birth to and raising the young,' is situated along the Beaufort Sea adjoining Alaska and covers 10,170 sq km. The **park** (www.pc.gc.ca/ivvavik) is one of the calving grounds for the Porcupine caribou herd; thousands are born over a three-week period beginning in late May. As forbidding as it is, there's evidence of human habitation here going back 8000 years.

The park holds one of the world's great white-water rivers, the **Firth River**, which can be navigated for 130km from Margaret Lake near the Alaskan border north to the Beaufort Sea. When the river meets Joe Creek, the valley narrows to a canyon and there are numerous areas of white water rated Class II and III+.

DISSOLVING LIKE A SUGAR CUBE

Visitors to **Herschel Island** (below) are in for a macabre sight: coffins rising from the ground. That's because warming temperatures are causing long-buried coffins to float up through the melting permafrost. At the same time the sharp decline in Arctic ice means that the shoreline is now exposed to pounding ocean waves; the island is literally dissolving. The water itself is no longer crystal clear; the thawing of the land and sea means that run-off into the Arctic Ocean is filling the water with silt and debris.

Of course, one island's demise can be others' gain. International shipping lines are making preliminary investigations into running tankers and freighters through newly ice-free waters between Asia and Europe (the fabled Northwest Passage is no longer a myth). Meanwhile the US, Canada and a newly aggressive Russia are sparring over ill-defined Arctic boundaries that now have new meaning and value.

HERSCHEL ISLAND (QIKIQTARUK) TERRITORIAL PARK

Its aboriginal name means 'it is island,' and indeed it is. Barely rising above the waters of Mackenzie Bay on the Beaufort Sea, **Herschel Island** (☎ 867-667-5648; www.yukonparks.ca) has a long tradition of human habitation. There have been several waves of people through the area, but the Thule, expert whale hunters, were thought to be the first to make a permanent settlement here, about 1000 years ago. In the late 1800s American whalers set up shop at **Pauline Cove**, a natural port deep enough for ocean vessels and protected from northerly winds and drifting pack ice. They hunted bowhead whales, which had the longest bones and were the most desirable for women's corsets. Fashion nearly drove them to extinction.

The whalers abandoned the port in 1907, leaving behind several wooden buildings that survive today, often appearing ghost-like out of the gloom. Evidence can also be found of missionaries, whose position as redeemers of souls was never embraced locally. Today Inuvialuit families use the island for traditional hunting.

There are no permanent residents, although in summer scientists camp out, monitoring the island's steady disintegration as it melts away (above). It has been named one of the world's most endangered cultural landmarks by the World Monuments Fund and is a contender to become a UNESCO World Heritage Site.

Visits to Hershel Island during the short summer (late June to late August) are possible via daytime tours from Inuvik (p417). The flight across the Mackenzie Delta to reach the island is spectacular; park rangers usually give tours. Backcountry camping during the short summer season is possible, although most of the 500 annual visitors only spend half a day. There are fire rings, wind shelters, pit toilets and limited water. Some tourists visit the island at the end of a kayak trip in the Ivvavik National Park.

Directory

CONTENTS

ACCOMMODATIONS

Most areas of BC have abundant accommodations options, available for a wide range of prices. Northern BC and the Yukon are the only exceptions; these far-flung regions have few budget accommodations outside of the cities, and their relatively few (and generally spartan) motel rooms are priced higher than comparable establishments elsewhere.

It's always good to reserve in advance. This is vital during the peak season and on busy weekends around holidays. Conversely, it's usually not necessary to reserve in a town like Dawson Creek in the north, which has a string of largely similar motels aimed at people traveling the Alaska Hwy.

British Columbia Approved Accommodation Guide, an annual directory published by **Tourism BC** (☎ 800-435-5622; www.hellobc.com), is a detailed guide with options in all classes of lodgings. It's free and is available at visitor information centers, from Tourism BC or online.

In this book, accommodations are listed in order of ascending price. This means that, where applicable, campgrounds and hostels will be listed first. The price range is as follows:

Budget under $70 per night
Midrange $70 to $170 per night
Top End over $170 per night

Accommodation Types
B&BS
With over 3000 B&Bs in BC and the Yukon, your choices are myriad. North American B&Bs are typically more upscale than the casual, family-style pensions found in Europe. Many (especially those catering to romantic escapists) require reservations and have strict policies on children, pets and so on. Prices span the gamut, although basic places are generally in the $50 to $100 range.

Local VCs usually have complete listings, along with photos and descriptions. In the Rockies, B&Bs are prevalent in towns and can provide good basic and private lodging. Other B&Bs may be in wilderness settings and offer a range of activities. B&Bs can also be a good source of local information on activities, particularly in an area like the Queen Charlotte Islands.

CAMPING
Camping is one of the most popular activities enjoyed by residents and visitors, and there are many places to camp, from primitive forest sites to deluxe campgrounds with resort-style amenities. Reservations are

---

BOOK ACCOMMODATIONS ONLINE

For more accommodations reviews and recommendations by Lonely Planet authors, check out www.lonelyplanet.com/hotels. You'll find the true, insider lowdown on the best places to stay. Reviews are thorough and independent. Best of all, you can book online.

a good idea during the summer – they're essential over long weekends.

Depending on the services (electricity, water, cable TV) your RV requires, private campgrounds cost about $20 to $35 a night for two people. Tent campsites usually charge between $15 and $25.

For details on camping in Parks Canada, BC Parks and Yukon territorial campgrounds, see p76.

There are over a thousand Ministry of Forests campgrounds but, in a bid to save money, the ministry has deemed that most are 'user managed', which means you stay there for free and take care of everything yourself.

The annual Tourism BC *Super Camping Guide* (www.camping.bc.ca) is a good source for private, RV-oriented campgrounds and it lists BC Parks sites. *Camping on Yukon Time* is a good annual government publication that lists the territory's campgrounds.

GUEST RANCHES

BC has dozens of guest ranches, the euphemism for dude ranches of *City Slickers* fame, where you can join a trail ride or sit by a mountain lake. Many are in the Cariboo-Chilcotin region (see p342).

HOSTELS

Hostels are common in tourist areas and most have beds for about $18 to $28 per person per night. These are usually in dorm-style rooms with four to six beds, although many hostels offer private rooms for $50 to $60. Expect shared bathrooms, kitchen facilities and common areas. Amenities might include laundry facilities, internet access, game rooms,

bike or other sporting gear rentals, and group outings to local pubs and attractions.

Some of the hostels listed in this book are affiliated with **Hostelling International** (HI; www .hihostels.ca). **SameSun** (www.samesun.com) also operates budget lodges and hostels. There are also many independent hostels in Vancouver.

MOTELS & HOTELS

Rates vary tremendously around the province. Plan to spend $100 for a basic double room with a private bathroom during high season in Vancouver and Victoria. In less popular areas, $80 is the norm.

The quality of hotels and motels varies greatly. Generally the typical motel room includes a private bathroom, one or two large beds, a tea and coffee maker, and a TV with dozens of channels. Luxury and boutique hotels/resorts are found in Vancouver, Vancouver Island and the Rockies. Ski resorts offer comfortable lodge and condo accommodation. Conversely, in remote areas such as Northern BC and the Yukon, you'll find that standards can be folksy at best.

Many motels (and an increasing number of suite-style hotels) offer kitchenettes. Quite a few midrange motels now include a small refrigerator and microwave in their standard-room price. Children can often stay free in the same room as their parents, but the age limit varies.

Discounts

To look for deals, check out an establishment's website first and then cross-reference it with one of the large internet booking services (though these services often do not list interesting, independent places). It is always worthwhile calling a place you are interested in staying to ask about any special deals: we saved 50% and got a whole host of – normally costly – extras for free at one well-known resort just by asking: 'Do you have any specials?'

Seasonal Rates
The prices given in this book are for the peak season, which is usually summer; in ski areas, like Whistler, peak season is winter. Other times you can expect discounts of up to 50% off the high-season rates.

Vancouver's accommodations rates ebb and flow depending on conventions, events and other factors. Often good deals are available for midrange accommodations on weekends, when the business travelers stay away. Rates listed do not include the various taxes (see p425).

ACTIVITIES
You name it, you can do it. See the British Columbia & the Yukon Outdoors chapter (p61) for details.

BUSINESS HOURS
Listings in this book don't include hours when they are in line with the following standard hours (Sunday hours are usually shorter):
Downtown stores 9am or 10am to 5pm or 6pm
Post Offices 8am-5pm Mon-Fri
Pubs 11am-1am; food until 10pm
Restaurants breakfast 6-11am, lunch 11:30am-2pm, dinner 5-9pm (8pm in rural areas)
Suburban stores 9am-9pm
Supermarkets 9am-9pm

CHILDREN
BC and the Yukon are excellent destinations for children. Parks and museums often have programs geared toward youngsters, all but the most extreme activities are suitable for children and, quite simply, kids are welcome everywhere. Vancouver for Children (p105) brims with ideas on where to take the little ones. See p53 for info on eating with kids.

Most public restrooms have diaper-changing facilities and the better motels and hotels can suggest child-minding facilities. Car seats are available from rental firms and

breast-feeding won't raise an eyebrow. At ski resorts, there are usually programs for kids. Rural and wilderness places may or may not welcome children: ask first.

CLIMATE
BC has a varied climate influenced by latitude, mountainous terrain and distance from the moderating effects of the Pacific Ocean. Along the coast it's mild, with warm, mostly dry summers (June through September) and cool, very wet winters (December through March). The interior of the province is much drier, particularly in the south along the Okanagan Valley, which gets less than 347mm of rain each year (compared with 6550mm at Henderson Lake on Vancouver Island's Barkley Sound); summers are generally hot and winters are cold. In the mountain regions summers are short, with warm

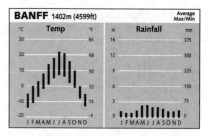

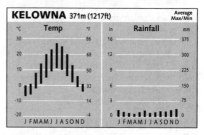

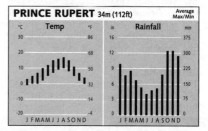

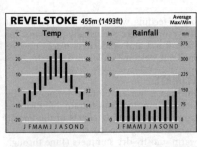

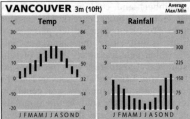

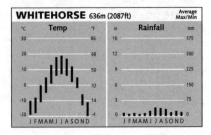

days and cool nights; winter snowfalls are heavy.

The Yukon has short, mild summers with midnight sun; these can be lovely, but the other eight to 10 months of the year are cold, with temperatures well below freezing during the dark winters.

See p23 for additional details.

DANGERS & ANNOYANCES

BC and the Yukon are generally safe places. Violent crime is unusual, but theft can occur. See p95 for things you should consider in urban Vancouver, which has had problems with violent gangs.

Outdoor Hazards

There are some precautions you should take to fully enjoy the great outdoors of BC, the Rockies and the Yukon. For health information, see p437.

BEARS

Bear attacks, though rare, are a very real threat. See p62 for tips on ways to protect yourself.

BLACK FLIES & MOSQUITOES

During spring and summer black flies and mosquitoes blight the interior and northern reaches of BC and the Yukon. The cumulative effect of scores of irritated, swollen bites can wreck your trip.

Building a fire will help, and camping in a tent with a zippered screen is a necessity. In clearings, along shorelines or anywhere there's a breeze you'll be safe, which is why Vancouver and the coast are relatively bug-free.

Wherever you go, bring liquid repellents. DEET, a common ingredient, is both effective and essential. Get a product with at least 15% DEET and read the precautions carefully.

FIRE

Campfires, when allowed, must be confined to fire rings at designated campgrounds or fire pans in the backcountry. Before turning in for the night or leaving an area, make sure fires (including cigarettes) are completely extinguished. Special care must be taken during the summer months, when fire danger is at its highest. Forest fires often force campfire bans (even far from the burning areas), so check conditions.

SWIMMER'S ITCH

A tiny parasite found in some of BC's lakes can generate this pesky rash. However, warnings are usually posted at places where it's a problem. To help prevent itching, apply baby oil before you enter the water then dry yourself off completely with a towel after getting out.

TICKS

Wood ticks hop onto warm-blooded hosts from tall grasses and low shrubs throughout the region. They're most troublesome March through June. Protect your legs by wearing gaiters or tucking your pants into socks. Give yourself, your children and pets a good going over after outdoor activities. If you find a tick burrowing into your skin it's most easily removed by grasping and pulling it, gently, straight up and out with a small pair of tweezers. Disinfect the bite site with rubbing alcohol. Save the tick in a small plastic or glass container if possible. That way, a doctor can inspect it if a fever develops or the area around the bite appears to be infected. See p437 for information on Lyme disease.

WATER
Tap water in the region is safe to drink, but in the backcountry you'll need to purify water you collect before drinking it. The simplest way of purifying water is to boil it – vigorous boiling for five minutes should be satisfactory, even at high altitude.

Simple filtering will not remove all dangerous organisms, so if you cannot boil water it should be treated chemically. Chlorine tablets (Puritabs, Steritabs or other brand names) will kill many pathogens, but not giardia or amoebic cysts. Iodine is very effective in purifying water and is available in tablet form (such as Potable Aqua), but be sure to follow the directions carefully.

DISCOUNT CARDS
Seniors (generally those over 65) and students (those with a valid International Student Identity Card) will qualify for discounts on admission to many of the museums, parks and other attractions listed in this book. The cost is usually somewhere between the children's and adult's.

FOOD
In Vancouver you'll find food in every price range. Elsewhere prices tend to be moderate so as to be affordable by locals. You'll always find pricey places in resort areas.

At eating places in this book, the following price ranges (not including drinks) apply:
Budget Under $12 per meal
Midrange $12 to $25 per meal
Top End Over $25 per meal

For a full discussion of when to eat, what to eat and how to eat it, see the Food & Drink chapter, p50.

GAY & LESBIAN TRAVELERS
In BC the attitude toward gays and lesbians is open in urban areas like Vancouver (see p108) and Victoria. While you won't find as open a gay and lesbian culture in other parts of BC, throughout the province and the Yukon attitudes are tolerant. That

said, the lack of prominent gay and lesbian communities outside urban centers tends to mean that most people keep their orientation to themselves.

In 2003, BC became the second province after Ontario to allow gay marriage. The BC Ministry of Health maintains a website with information for couples who would like to marry (www.vs.gov.bc.ca/marriage/howto.html).

HOLIDAYS
National public holidays are celebrated throughout Canada. Banks, schools and government offices (including post offices) are closed, and transportation, museums and other services operate on a Sunday schedule. Holidays falling on a weekend are usually observed the following Monday and long weekends are among the busiest on BC's roads and waterways. To avoid inconvenience, either plan your visit for a different time or make sure you secure accommodations in advance. The following is a list of the main public holidays:

January
New Year's Day (January 1)

March/April
Easter (Good Friday, Easter Monday)

May
Victoria Day (Monday preceding May 25)

July
Canada Day (July 1)

August
BC Day (first Monday of the month; BC only)
Discovery Day (third Monday of August; Yukon only)

September
Labour Day (first Monday of the month)

October
Thanksgiving (second Monday of the month)

November
Remembrance Day (November 11)

December
Christmas Day (December 25)
Boxing Day (December 26; many stores open, other businesses closed)

DIRECTORY

INSURANCE

Residents of BC are covered by the provincial healthcare system, but visitors to the province are not, so you need to check your insurance before you leave home. Many policies will cover you for travel in BC but many won't. The critical questions to ask your current insurer and those offering coverage are: 'Who pays if I get sick in BC and the Yukon?', 'Who pays if my trip is canceled or delayed (assuming you would have a liability)?' or 'Who pays if my belongings are stolen?'

You may need to take out travel insurance for health coverage. Not only does it cover you for medical expenses and luggage theft or loss, but also for cancellations or delays in your travel arrangements under certain circumstances, such as becoming seriously ill on the day before your scheduled departure.

TRAVEL INSURANCE

Worldwide travel insurance is available at www.lonelyplanet.com/travel_services. You can buy, extend and claim online anytime – even if you're already on the road.

INTERNATIONAL VISITORS
Entering Canada

Entering Canada is normally a straightforward affair, assuming you have the proper documents such as passports and visas. The **Canada Border Services Agency** (www.cbsa .gc.ca) runs the border crossings and entry points.

PASSPORTS & VISAS

All people need a passport to enter Canada, including US citizens.

Visitors from most of the US, Western Europe and many Commonwealth countries normally don't require a visa for a tourist stay of less than 180 days. But citizens of another 130 countries do. **Citizenship & Immigration Canada** (www.cic.gc.ca) has visa details on its website and it has links to Canadian embassies and consulates worldwide so you can check requirements locally.

US BORDER

Points of entry on the US–Canada border are open 24 hours except for some minor ones and those in the Yukon that have limited hours and/or close for the season. Entering Canada by land from the US usually goes smoothly at the dozens of border crossings from the continental US and Alaska. But there may be a wait on weekends and at other busy times, particularly at the I-5/ Hwy 99 crossing south of Vancouver, where you may have to wait several hours. Either avoid crossing at these times, or drive to one of the other Lower Mainland crossings such as Aldergrove or Huntingdon.

The website, www.borderlineups.com, has live cameras showing the situation at major crossings as well stats on wait times.

US citizens flying home should note that you must clear US Immigration and Customs at Vancouver and Calgary airports *before* you fly to the US. This means two things: a) get to those two airports at least an hour earlier than normal as the US lines can be long, and b) when your plane arrives in the US, you are treated as a domestic passenger, so you're on your way.

Customs

The duty-free allowance coming into Canada is 1.14L (40oz) of liquor, 1.5L (or two 750mL bottles) of wine or 24 cans or bottles of beer, as well as up to 200 cigarettes, 50 cigars or 200g of tobacco. You are allowed to bring in gifts up to a total value of $60. Gifts with a value higher than $60 are subject to duty and taxes on the over-limit value.

Fresh and prepared foods are the subject of myriad rules and regulations. Just buy what you need in Canada.

Register excessive or expensive sporting goods and cameras with customs, as this will save you time and trouble when leaving, especially if you plan on crossing the Canada–US border.

If you are bringing a dog or cat into the country you will need proof that it has had a rabies shot in the past 36 months.

Pleasure boats may enter Canada either on a trailer or in the water and can stay for up to one year. An entry permit is required and is obtainable from the customs office at, or closest to, the point of entry.

Pistols, fully automatic weapons, any firearms less than 66cm (26in) in length and self-defense sprays (like pepper or mace) are not permitted into the country.

Embassies & Consulates

Consulates in Vancouver include the following:

Australia (Map p88; ☎ 604-684-1177; Ste 2050, 1075 W Georgia St)

France (Map p88; ☎ 604-681-4345; Ste 1100, 1130 W Pender St)

Germany (Map p88; ☎ 604-684-8377; Ste 704, 999 Canada Place)

Ireland (Map p93; ☎ 604-683-9233; 100 West Pender St)

Netherlands (Map p88; ☎ 604-684-6448; 595 Burrard St)

New Zealand (Map p88; ☎ 604-684-7388; Ste 1200, 888 Dunsmuir St)

UK (Map p88; ☎ 604-683-4421; Ste 800, 1111 Melville St)

USA (Map p88; ☎ 604-685-4311; 1095 W Pender St)

Money

The Canadian dollar ($) is divided into 100 cents (¢). Coins come in 1¢ (penny), 5¢ (nickel), 10¢ (dime), 25¢ (quarter), $1 (loonie) and $2 (toonie) pieces. Notes come in $5, $10, $20, $50 and $100 denominations; $50 and $100 bills can prove difficult to cash. Canadian bills are all the same size but vary in their colors and images.

See p23 for information on costs and the inside front cover for exchange rates. Prices in this book are quoted in Canadian dollars except for entry points in the US, such as Haines, Alaska, where US dollars (US$) are used.

ATMS

ATMs are common throughout BC, the Rockies and the larger towns of the Yukon.

CHANGING MONEY

If you're not going to withdraw cash as needed from ATMs, exchange cash when you arrive in Canada. There are 24-hour currency exchange machines and counters in Vancouver International Airport. Currency exchange offices are common in Vancouver and Victoria, as well as other larger towns throughout the province. Note: fees mean that an ATM is a better deal.

CREDIT CARDS

Credit and debit cards are almost universally accepted and, in fact, you'll find it hard or impossible to rent a car, book a room or order tickets online or over the phone without one.

TAXES & REFUNDS

The federal Goods and Services Tax (GST) adds 5% to nearly every product, service or transaction. To this BC adds a 7% BC provincial sales tax (PST). Alberta and the Yukon have no extra sales taxes.

Accommodations (aka 'cash cows' to revenue authorities) draw an 8% provincial tax plus local taxes that average 2%. In Alberta there is a provincial hotel tax of 4% and possibly a local tax of 2%. The Yukon levies no added hotel taxes.

Almost all tax rebate schemes have been killed, but if you booked your trip as part of a package, you may be able to get 50% of the 5% federal GST refunded from your accommodations. Fill out the GST/HST Refund Application for Tour Packages form available from the **Canada Revenue Agency** (☎ 902-432-5608, 800-668-4748; www.cra -arc.gc.ca/E/pbg/gf/gst115). Start counting your pennies.

TIPPING

Tips are expected by restaurant and bar servers, as well as by taxi drivers and anyone else providing a personal service, such as a guide. Workers are paid a low base wage in the expectation they will earn tips. Never tip less than 10% of the total bill; leave 15% if the service was fine and up to 20% if it was excellent. Some restaurants impose a service charge on the bill (especially to people with accents – we're serious), in which case don't tip. And don't tip in fast food, take-out or buffet-style self-service restaurants.

Baggage carriers in airports or hotels receive $1 per bag. Don't forget to leave a couple of dollars for the housekeeping staff for each night you stay.

Post

Canada Post (www.canadapost.ca) is reliable and easy to use. Postal service counters have been installed in convenience stores, drug stores and supermarkets. Rates for postcards and letters to the US are 98¢, to the rest of the world $1.65.

INTERNET ACCESS

Wi-fi is commonplace in BC, the Rockies and the Yukon in places to stay, many cafés and other public places. Some places to stay have high-speed access requiring an Ethernet connection.

DIRECTORY

You'll find internet computers in libraries, some cafés and internet cafés in larger towns, as well as in accommodations. Paid access usually costs about $1 per 10 minutes. There are no unusual security concerns associated with using these public computers.

For useful and fun websites that can improve your trip, see p25.

In this book, the internet icon (🖳) is used for places with public internet computers. The wi-fi icon (🛜) is used for any place with wi-fi access. For accommodation it also means that at least some rooms have wi-fi.

LEGAL MATTERS

The Canadian federal government permits the use of marijuana for medicinal purposes, but official prescription cannabis is strictly regulated. It's illegal to consume alcohol anywhere other than a residence or licensed premises, which puts parks, beaches and other public spaces off limits.

You can incur stiff fines, jail time and penalties if caught driving under the influence of alcohol or any illegal substance. The blood-alcohol limit is 0.08%, which is reached after just two beers. Penalties include being thrown in jail overnight, followed by a court appearance, heavy fine and/or further incarceration.

Canada has strict regulations banning smoking in all public places. This can include patios and other outdoor spaces. Your best bet to light up: the middle of a big empty parking lot.

LEGAL AGE

- Driving: 16
- Voting: 18
- Drinking: 19

MAPS

Members of the Canadian Automobile Association (CAA), American Automobile Association (AAA) or affiliated clubs can get free road maps before leaving home or from offices throughout BC. Bookstores, gas stations and convenience stores usually sell a wide variety of maps ranging from regional overviews to detailed street atlases.

For extended hikes or multi-day backcountry treks, it's a good idea to carry a topographic map. The best are the series of 1:50,000 scale maps published by the government's **Centre for Topographic Information** (www.maps.nrcan.gc.ca). These are sold by approximately 900 map dealers around the country; check the website for vendors. You can also download and print maps from www.geobase.ca.

Gem Trek Publishing (www.gemtrek.com) offers some of the best Rocky Mountains maps in scales from 1:35,000 to 1:100,000.

SHOPPING

The best souvenirs and gifts are items made by local artisans. We list scores of galleries and shops throughout this book where you can buy works made in BC, the Rockies and the Yukon.

Although you need to make certain that you won't have customs problems with foodstuff when you get home, edible items like superb smoked salmon are widely sold. If in doubt, a bottle of Okanagan Valley wine always goes down well.

SOLO TRAVELERS

BC and the Yukon are good for solo travelers, male and female. The people are generally friendly – chatty even – and many activities and attractions lend themselves to meeting others. However, this is also an excellent place to enjoy perfect solitude if that's what you're looking for. There's no end to the natural places you can find solitude. The one caveat is going out into the backcountry, where traveling alone can be dangerous if a bear attacks, you have an accident or other calamity occurs.

TELEPHONE

If you are calling a number within the same area code, you need to dial all 10 digits. If you are dialling any other number in North America, you also need to dial 🕾 1, then the 10 digits.

For calling outside of North America dial 🕾 011 followed by the country code and the number. When calling North America from abroad the country code is 🕾 1.

Pay phones are common in cities and towns, however you'll need coins or a long-distance phone card to work them. Phone cards are available from myriad companies and are sold in myriad places (convenience stores, gas stations etc). Compare prices.

Cell (mobile) phones use the GSM and CDMA systems, depending on the carrier. If you have an unlocked GSM phone, you should be able to buy a SIM card for under $50, which will include a bit of talk time. Using your home-country cell phone service in Canada will be subject to rates much like those of hotel phones: extortionate. And note that much of the backcountry has no cell phone signal.

TIME

Most of BC and the Yukon operate on Pacific Time, which is eight hours behind Greenwich Mean Time. Both BC and the Yukon generally observe daylight saving time; clocks are turned forward one hour on the second Sunday in March and are turned back one hour on the first Sunday in November. For exceptions to this, see p292 and p355.

The Alberta part of the Rockies is on Mountain Time, which is one hour later than Pacific Time. Alaska is on Alaska Time (so there!), which is one hour earlier than Pacific Time.

TOURIST INFORMATION

With tourism being such a major part of the economy for both BC and the Yukon, it's no surprise that the tourism infrastructure is well funded and easy to use.

Tourism BC (☎ 800-435-5622; www.hellobc.com) has over a 100 VCs in towns and cities throughout the province. These excellent resources can assist you with planning, reservations, maps, activities information and much more. They are usually along major roads and are well marked with blue and white signs with a big yellow 'i.' Hours vary, but larger offices are typically open from at least 8am to 6pm daily during summer and from 9am to 5pm on weekdays throughout the rest of the year. These offices used to be called Visitor Information Centres and you'll still see references to VIC. (The name change makes it easier for them to offer products beyond mere information – like fudge.)

Yukon Tourism and Culture (☎ 800-661-0494, outside North America 867-667-5340; www.touryukon.com) maintains six VICs at major entry points to the territory. See p388 for more information.

Besides providing gobbets of excellent free literature to supplement your reading – and kindling – needs for the trip, the BC and Yukon tourist offices can be good places to buy specialist guidebooks and maps.

TRAVELERS WITH DISABILITIES

Guide dogs may legally be brought into restaurants, hotels and other businesses. Many public-service phone numbers and some payphones are adapted for the hearing impaired. Most public buildings are wheelchair accessible and many parks feature trails that are likewise accessible.

Getting around on public transport is possible but requires some planning. The best place to start is **Access to Travel** (www .accesstotravel.gc.ca), the federal government's website with information on accessible air, bus, rail and ferry transportation.

Other helpful resources include:

BC Coalition of People with Disabilities (☎ 604-875-0188, 604-875-8835; www.bccpd.bc.ca)

BC Paraplegic Association (☎ 604-324-3611; www.bcpara.org)

CNIB (Canadian National Institute for the Blind; ☎ 604-431-2121; www.cnib.ca)

Mobility International (www.miusa.org) Has links to hundreds of Canadian organizations in a searchable database.

Society for Accessible Travel & Hospitality (www.sath.org)

VOLUNTEERING

The omnibus www.volunteerbc.bc.ca is a good starting point for those who want to volunteer for programs (literacy, assisting the disabled, cleaning up the environment etc) while they're in BC.

WOMEN TRAVELERS

BC, the Rockies and the Yukon are generally safe places for women traveling alone, although the usual precautions apply. In Vancouver, the Main and Hastings Sts area is best avoided and it's probably not a good idea to go for a walk in Stanley Park on your own after dark. In more remote parts of the province, particularly in Northern BC, women traveling alone will find themselves in a distinct minority although there's no shortage of feisty locals ready to assist a sister in need, especially in the Yukon.

The more populated and frequently visited parts of BC are great for women travelers. Hostels usually have formal or informal group outings to pubs and local attractions, and many outfitters, ski areas and the like offer trips and classes geared towards women.

WORK

In almost all cases, non-Canadians need a valid work permit to get a job in Canada. Obtaining one may be difficult, as employment opportunities go to Canadians first. Some jobs are exempt from the permit requirement. For full details on temporary work, check with **Citizenship & Immigration Canada** (CIC; www.cic.gc.ca/english/work/index.asp).

People aged 18 to 30 may be able to get work permits as students or as part of a working holiday program. See the CIC website for details.

Those wanting short-term jobs, such as restaurant and bar work, should be able to find seasonal work in popular tourist spots. Ski resorts always need people; it's worth emailing them ahead of winter to find out how each one fills its many openings. Often there will be postings on the resort website. Many of these jobs ignore permit requirements if you're not Canadian but, if you get caught, you will be leaving Canada immediately.

Transportation

GETTING THERE & AWAY

British Columbia is easily reached from major international points as well as from the rest of North America. Getting to the Yukon usually requires a plane connection. However both BC and the Yukon are best enjoyed from the ground and sea. Road trips and ferry links are as much a part of the experience as the destination. Flights, tours and rail tickets can be booked online at www.lonelyplanet.com/travel_services.

AIR

Though many BC-bound travelers will fly into Vancouver, if your trip includes the Rockies or the Kootenays, Calgary may be a useful hub and could be part of an open-jaw itinerary, eg fly into one and out of the other.

See p424 for details on documents and immigration formalities.

Airports
Vancouver International Airport (YVR; ☎ 604-207-7077; www.yvr.ca) is 13km south of downtown Vancouver near the suburb of Richmond. It's Canada's second-busiest airport and likely to be your port of entry into BC if you fly. It has good connections throughout western Canada, and there are international services to the US, Europe and Asia.

The main airport has two terminals: international and domestic. It has some pretty features but also some annoying ones: poor signage and walkways that run temptingly right through the middle of duty-free shops. The smaller south airport terminal, located off Inglis Dr, handles small regional airlines and seaplanes. There is a shuttle bus between the two terminals.

For Rockies-bound travelers, **Calgary International Airport** (YYC; www.calgaryairport.com) has services from the USA and Europe. **Edmonton Airport** (YEG; www.edmontonairports.com), good for Jasper or a shortcut right to Dawson Creek and the start of the Alaska Hwy, has services from the USA.

Kelowna Airport (YLW; p266) has services to/from Seattle with Horizon Air, which makes the Okanagan Valley an easy connection for travel from the USA.

Whitehorse Airport (YXY; p396) in the Yukon has services to Alaska and summer flights to/from Germany.

Airlines
International airlines serving Vancouver include:
Air Canada & Air Canada Jazz (airline code AC; ☎ 888-247-2262; www.aircanada.ca) Services worldwide.
Air New Zealand (airline code NZ; ☎ 800-663-5494; www.airnewzealand.ca) Serves Auckland.
Alaska Airlines (airline code AS; ☎ 800-252-7522; www.alaskaair.com) Serves the US west coast and Alaska.
American Airlines (airline code AA; ☎ 800-433-7300; www.aa.com) Services across the US.
British Airways (airline code BA; ☎ 800-247-9297; www.britishairways.com) Serves London.
Cathay Pacific (airline code CX; ☎ 604-606-8888, 888-338-1668; www.cathaypacific.com) Serves Hong Kong.
China Airlines (airline code CI; ☎ 604-682-6777; www.china-airlines.com)
Continental Airlines (airline code CO; ☎ 800-231-0856; www.continental.com) Services across the US.
Delta (airline code DL; ☎ 800-221-1212; www.delta.com) Services across the US.
Horizon Air (airline code QX; ☎ 800-547-9308; www.horizonair.com) Serves the Pacific Northwest of the US.

Japan Airlines (airline code JL; ☎ 800-525-3663; www
.jal.co.jp/en/) Serves Tokyo.
KLM (airline code KL; ☎ 800-447-4747; www.klm.nl)
Serves Amsterdam.
Lufthansa (airline code LH; ☎ 800-563-5954; www
.lufthansa.com) Serves Frankfurt.
United Airlines (airline code UA; ☎ 800-241-6522;
www.united.com) Services across the US.

The following airlines fly to Vancouver
from other parts of Canada:
Air Canada & Air Canada Jazz (airline code AC;
☎ 888-247-2262; www.aircanada.ca) Services
worldwide.
WestJet (airline code WS; ☎ 800-538-5696;
www.westjet.com)

Airlines with services to Whitehorse (p390)
in the Yukon include:
Air Canada Jazz (airline code AC; ☎ 888-247-2262;
www.aircanada.ca) Serves Vancouver.
Air North (airline code 4N; ☎ 800-661-0407;
www.flyairnorth.com) Serves Vancouver, Calgary,
Edmonton and Fairbanks, Alaska.
Condor (☎ 800-364-1667; www.condor.com) Serves
Frankfurt.
First Air (☎ 800 267-1247; www.firstair.ca) Serves
the NWT.

Tickets

With so many international airlines serving it, Vancouver is a great destination for
competitive airfares. To get a good idea of
what's being charged, check out websites
like Expedia (www.expedia.com), Kayak
(www.kayak.com), Orbitz (www.orbitz.com)
and Travelocity (www.travelocity.com).
Individual airline websites often feature
unique special offers. Further connections
to various BC cities may add little to the
airfare. The regional chapters list important airports, so it's worth checking fares
to those as well, if you want to get close to
your final destination.

LAND

For details on border crossings into Canada
from the US, see p424.

From the USA
BUS

You can travel to many places in BC (and
Whitehorse in the Yukon) from the USA
via **Greyhound** (☎ 800-661-8747; www.greyhound
.com). Most routes require you to travel between Seattle and Vancouver, then transfer,
or go via Calgary.

CLIMATE CHANGE & TRAVEL

Climate change is a serious threat to the ecosystems that humans rely upon, and air travel
is the fastest-growing contributor to the problem. Lonely Planet regards travel, overall, as a
global benefit, but believes we all have a responsibility to limit our personal impact on global
warming.

Flying & climate change

Nearly every form of motorized travel generates CO_2 (the main cause of human-induced climate
change), but planes are by far and away the worst offenders, not just because of the sheer distances
they allow us to travel, but because they release greenhouse gases high into the atmosphere.
The statistics are frightening: two people taking a round trip flight between Europe and the
USA will contribute as much to climate change as an average household's gas and electricity
consumption over a whole year.

Carbon offset schemes

Climatecare.org and other websites use 'carbon calculators' that allow travelers to offset the level
of greenhouse gases they are responsible for by making financial contributions to sustainable
travel schemes that reduce global warming – including projects in India, Honduras, Kazakhstan
and Uganda.

Lonely Planet, together with Rough Guides and other concerned partners in the travel
industry, support the carbon offset scheme run by climatecare.org. Lonely Planet offsets all of
its staff and author travel.

For more information, check out our website: www.lonelyplanet.com.

For details of small bus lines linking the Yukon with Alaska, see p396.

CAR

The US highway system connects directly with Canadian roads at numerous points along the BC border. Gas is generally cheaper in the USA.

TRAIN

Amtrak (☎ 800-872-7245; www.amtrak.com) connects Vancouver to Bellingham and Seattle with one train and two buses daily, in a journey that takes four hours. See p125 for details. From Seattle, Amtrak trains go south to Portland, San Francisco and Los Angeles, and east to Minneapolis and Chicago.

From Canada

BUS

Greyhound Canada (☎ 800-661-8747; www.greyhound.ca) has routes into BC from Edmonton to Dawson Creek and the Alaska Hwy, as well as via Jasper. In the south buses run from Calgary through Banff and the Rockies, and south via Fernie.

TRAIN

VIA Rail (☎ 888-842-7245; www.viarail.ca) runs the *Canadian* between Vancouver and Toronto. Stops include Kamloops (p241), Jasper (p331), Edmonton, Saskatoon and Winnipeg. It's a beautiful trip, but it only runs three times a week.

SEA
Alaska Cruises

The BC and Alaska coast is one of the world's most popular – and profitable – cruise destinations. In total, close to 40 vessels from over a dozen cruise lines make hundreds of sailings between the US West Coast, Vancouver and Alaska every year from May to October. Some boats make the run from US ports such as Seattle and San Francisco, making it possible to tailor a package whereby you can sail one-way to/from BC, or even the Yukon via Skagway in Alaska, and travel overland or by air the other way. However a complex itinerary such as this requires the services of a travel agent. Some websites with useful info include:

Cruisejunkie.com Takes an unvarnished look at issues surrounding the cruise ship industry.

Cruisemates.com Has a useful and enthusiastic roundup of Inside Passage services.

Vacationstogo.com Has deeply discounted and last minute fares.

Of the various lines, **Holland America Line** (☎ 877-724-5425; www.hollandamerica.com) is the largest to ply the Inside Passage. It operates numerous trips and land-based tours throughout the Yukon that are sometimes open to non-cruise ship passengers.

Ferry

Alaska Marine Highway ferries (AMH; ☎ 800-642-0066; www.ferryalaska.com) sail from Bellingham, WA along the stunning Inside Passage to Haines (p403) and Skagway (p404) in Alaska, which are key entry ports to the Yukon. These trips take almost four days, running twice a week in summer and once a week in winter. It is one of the most spectacular voyages anywhere in the world – note the number of cruise ships that do it – and the advantage of the ferry is that you can bring your car to the Yukon with you.

The AMH ships are very comfortable, with decent cabins, good, freshly cooked food and usually a park ranger offering commentary on the many sights, including scads of

TRANSPORTATION

SAILING THE INSIDE PASSAGE

Taking an **Alaska Marine Highway ferry** (above) or **BC Ferries** ship (p432) along the stunning Inside Passage and the BC and Alaska coasts can be the highlight of any trip. Expect to see marine life ranging from whales to dolphins to orcas. Look for eagles overhead and bears on the shore. The rugged coastline is largely part of the Great Bear Rainforest (see boxed text, p346) and you will spend hours passing deserted islands and rocky coasts accented by waterfalls. On these runs the crews are friendly and captains will slow the ships when, say, a pod of dolphins swims past. On most of the vessels (but sadly not BC Ferries to Bella Coola), you can get a cabin and just spend a day or more relaxing, reading and gazing. Note: none of the ships is flashy, although the Alaska fleet has better food – lots of fresh seafood.

TRANSPORTATION

wildlife such as whales; lots of people pitch tents on the deck. Reservations for this route are a must. One of the ferries' other great advantages is just what they aren't: cruise ships. There's no planned fun, no endless buffets, no stupid games – just scenery and serenity. For more on these trips, see boxed text p431.

Another AMH option is to take the boat from Prince Rupert (p372) in BC to Haines or Skagway and then on to the Yukon. This route is nearly the equal in terms of scenery with the Bellingham run and it takes half as long. Both routes to Haines and Skagway stop at southeast Alaska towns such as Juneau and Ketchikan.

You can get to Victoria by ferry (p178) from Port Angeles, Washington.

GETTING AROUND

AIR
Air Canada is the country's main domestic airline and flies to Vancouver from other major Canadian cities. Its regional affiliate Air Canada Jazz flies to numerous smaller cities in BC. The other major airline is WestJet, which flies to Vancouver, Victoria, Prince George, Kelowna and other cities. See p396 for details of Yukon air links.

Airlines
Airlines providing regional services in BC and the Yukon include:

Air Canada & Air Canada Jazz (airline code AC; ☎ 888-247-2262; www.aircanada.ca)

Air North (airline code 4N; ☎ 800-661-0407; www.flyairnorth.com)

Central Mountain Air (airline code 9M; ☎ 250-877-5000, 888-865-8585; www.flycma.com)

Harbour Air (airline code H3; ☎ 604-274-1277, 800-665-0212; www.harbour-air.com)

Hawkair (airline code BH; ☎ 800-487-1216; www.hawkair.ca)

Pacific Coastal Airlines (airline code 8P; ☎ 604-273-8666; www.pacific-coastal.com)

West Coast Air (airline code 80; ☎ 604-606-6800, 800-347-2222; www.westcoastair.com)

WestJet (airline code WS; ☎ 800-538-5696; www.westjet.com)

BICYCLE
British Columbia Cycling Coalition (www.bccc.bc.ca) is the best source of information on bicycling in BC. Bike rentals are widely available,

and in the various regional chapters of this book you will find bicycle rental listings for many towns. If you bring your own bike you can take it on most forms of public transportation. Check with air, ferry, bus and train companies to see what their rates and requirements are.

Rental
Mountain bikes usually rent for about $35 per day and are available in most larger towns and cities. A credit card will cover the deposit.

Purchase
The same places that rent bikes also sell them at prices similar to those in other developed areas.

BOAT
The blue-and-white BC Ferries are a symbol of coastal British Columbia as well as a mode of transportation. You'll find extensive details about BC Ferries' services in the Vancouver & Around, the Vancouver Island and the Whistler & the Sunshine Coast chapters.

What follows is an overview of services, plus details on the long-distance Inside Passage and Discovery Coast Passage routes.

BC Ferries Corporation (☎ 888-223-3779; www.bcferries.com) operates a fleet of 36 ferries on BC's coastal waters. Formerly government-run, it has been part privatized amid much controversy. Fares have risen ('temporary' fuel surcharges never seem to go away even when the price of fuel drops), there are questions about the levels of service, and, most disastrously, in 2006 the *Queen of the North* sank, killing two, when the crew forgot to make a routine course change and the ship ran aground on a remote part of the BC coast.

However the company remains integral to traveling the coast and it hopes that new boats will restore its luster in time for the Olympics and beyond.

Tickets
You can reserve space in advance and buy tickets online or over the phone. You can also do so at the entrance to docks, although if it is a busy time, you may have to wait one or two sailings to get aboard.

Look for specials, such as winter sales. One popular package is SailPass, which gives you either four consecutive days of ferry travel for $165 or seven consecutive days for $195. The pass includes unlimited travel for a car and two people on the Southern Gulf Islands, Northern Gulf Islands and Brentwood Bay–Mill Bay routes, along with one round trip on each of the Mainland–Vancouver Island and Sunshine Coast crossings.

Another good package is CirclePac, a four route travel package that gives you up to 15% off regular, one-way fares on each of the following routes: Horseshoe Bay–Langdale, Earls Cove–Saltery Bay, Powell River–Comox, and Vancouver Island–Mainland (your choice of Nanaimo–Horseshoe Bay, Nanaimo–Tsawwassen or Swartz Bay–Tsawwassen).

Vancouver Area Service

The two busiest routes are from Tsawwassen (about an hour's drive south of downtown Vancouver) to Swartz Bay (a half hour drive north of Victoria), and from Horseshoe Bay (a half hour drive north of downtown Vancouver) to Departure Bay near Nanaimo on Vancouver Island. The ferries on these routes are huge, holding hundreds of cars and passengers.

From Tsawwassen, ferries also go to Duke Point near Nanaimo, and to the Southern Gulf Islands (Salt Spring, Galiano, Mayne, Saturna and the Pender Islands). From Horseshoe Bay, ferries also go to Bowen Island and the Sunshine Coast.

Other BC Ferries routes cover Gabriola Island, Thetis Island, Kuper Island, Texada Island and the Northern Gulf Islands (namely Denman, Hornby, Quadra, Cortes, Malcolm and Cormorant).

It's always much cheaper to travel on BC Ferries without a motorized vehicle. You can take bicycles, canoes or kayaks onboard.

Vehicle **reservations** (☎ 888-223-3779; www .bcferries.com) are recommended for weekends on the Tsawwassen-Swartz Bay, Horseshoe Bay–Departure Bay and Tsawwassen–Duke Point routes.

Inside Passage

The Inside Passage route between Port Hardy and Prince Rupert is among the most scenic boat trips in the world. In summer the service is scheduled for 15-hour daylight runs between Port Hardy and Prince Rupert, in different directions on alternate days. Sailings in October through May typically include stops in tiny First Nations villages and can take up to two days.

This spectacular route is usually served by the new *Northern Expedition*, which was launched in 2009. It's a plush vessel with amenities on a par with cruise ships. Veterans of the route worry that the very lack of ostentation that made these trips so special will be lost, and that revenue-producing lounges have replaced open deck space that made for such fine viewing of nature.

You must reserve space on Inside Passage sailings. See p372 for more details on schedules and fares, as well as p431 for more on the route and voyages.

Discovery Coast Passage

This journey covers the dramatic route between Port Hardy and Bella Coola on the central BC coast. It's shorter than the Inside Passage route, but equally scenic. Ships run only from mid-June to mid-September. Reservations are necessary.

There are no cabins on the *Queen of Chilliwack*, which usually plies the Discovery Coast Passage, but there are reclining lounge seats and floor space where you can stretch out. Some passengers set up tents on deck and sleep outside. For more details, see p345.

Queen Charlotte Islands

For details on the Queen Charlotte Islands services from Prince Rupert, see p372. The much loved veteran of the route, *Queen of Prince Rupert*, was retired in 2009 and replaced by the *Northern Adventure*, a ship that previously sailed in Europe.

BUS

Greyhound Canada (800-661-8747; www.greyhound .ca) covers most of BC and has services into the Yukon along the Alaska Hwy to Whitehorse. You can find various discounts by booking online. The fares listed throughout this book are full price. But there are many discounts. With planning you could reduce the $76 full fare from Vancouver to Kelowna with the following discounts:

- **Advance Purchase:** up to 60% off for buying a non-refundable ticket in advance.
- **Companion Fare:** A traveler with a full-fare ticket can buy a second ticket for $30.

- **eSavers:** 20% discount for booking online.
- **HI Discount:** 25% discount for members of Hostelling International.
- **Student Fares:** 25-50% off with ID.

If you purchase a ticket online, you will receive it as an email attachment that you must print out. There are no ways to do this at Greyhound Canada stations. Alternatively, you can pick up the ticket at ticket counters at major stations.

Pacific Coach Lines (☎ 800-661-1725; www.pacific coach.com) has services between Whistler, Vancouver and Victoria.

Note that places off the main highways have no public bus services of any kind.

Backpackers Bus

Moose Travel Network (☎ 888-244-6673, outside North America 604-297-0228; www.moosenetwork.com; ⊙ Jun-Sep, less often May & Oct), runs small buses catering to single backpackers on a series of routes that take in Vancouver, Jasper, Banff, Victoria and Kelowna. For one fare ($250 to $960) you can get on and off anywhere along the route you've paid for. The buses stop at major (and minor) scenic highlights that they pass and there are group activities. Each day's run ends with drop-offs at hostels.

CAR & MOTORCYCLE

British Columbia, the Rockies and the Yukon cover a huge area. Driving is the best way to travel in the region. You can go where and when you want, use secondary highways and roads, and get off the beaten track. You can use car ferries to cover some segments and create interesting circular routes.

Automobile Association

With 24 offices throughout the province, the **British Columbia Automobile Association** (BCAA; ☎ 877-325-8888; www.bcaa.com; membership per year $81) provides its members, and the members of other auto clubs (such as the

---

ROAD REPORTS

BC (☎ 800-550-4997; www.drivebc.ca)
Rocky Mountains (☎ 403-762-1450)
Yukon (☎ 511; www.511yukon.ca)

AAA in the USA), with travel information, maps, travel insurance and hotel reservations. It also provides a service in the Yukon. Many people join for the **emergency roadside assistance** (☎ 604-293-2222, Lower Mainland 800-222-4357).

Bring Your Own Vehicle

Cars licensed to drive in North America may be driven in Canada.

Distances

A few sample distances and average travel times (without stopping):

Banff–Fernie 360km, 4 hours
Dawson Creek–Whitehorse 1420km, 16 hours
Kelowna–Banff 480km, 6 hours
Prince George–Dawson Creek 405km, 4¾ hours
Prince George–Prince Rupert 705km, 8½ hours
Prince Rupert–Whitehorse (via Stewart-Cassiar Hwy) 1375km, 19 hours
Vancouver–Kelowna 390km, 4 hours
Vancouver–Prince George 790km, 9 hours
Whitehorse–Dawson City 530km, 7 hours

Driver's License

Generally your driver's license from home is good in Canada.

Fuel & Spare Parts

At the time of writing, gasoline (petrol, usually just called gas in Canada) costs about $1 per liter in BC, this is about a third more than the cost of gas in US border areas. Prices are higher in remote areas and the Yukon.

In the north, along major roads such as the Alaska Hwy, service stations are spaced at regular intervals. That said, don't expect to find a gas station on some side roads. A good rule is to fill up your tank when it's half empty. Don't be like the guy we rescued on a remote Yukon road who had set off with a van full of kids and a nearly empty tank (and no map)!

Auto parts and mechanics who've seen it all are also to be found at regular intervals on major roads in the north, but it's still a good idea to carry at least one full-service spare tire – especially if you'll be driving on gravel highways.

Insurance

Cars from North America usually have insurance coverage in Canada. If in doubt ask your agent. Wherever you're from, if you are renting, check to see if your auto policy or credit card covers you while driving the rental. If so, you can avoid buying the extortionate insurance offered by rental companies. No matter what kind of insurance coverage you have, it may be void if you stray off major roads in the north.

Rental

Major car-rental firms have offices at airports in BC and Whitehorse, as well as some city centers. In smaller towns there may be independent firms; these are listed throughout the book. Clarify your insurance coverage for things like gravel damage if you're going to be driving off major paved roads.

Shop around for deals but watch out for offers that don't include unlimited kilometers of driving. And never buy the rental-car company's gas if offered when you pick up your car – it's a bad deal. Buy your own and return it full. If you are considering a one-way rental, look out for high fees.

RENTAL-CAR FIRMS

Alamo (☎ 800-462-5266; www.alamo.com)
Avis (☎ 800-272-5871; www.avis.com)
Budget (☎ 800-268-8900; www.budget.com)
Hertz (☎ 800-263-0600; www.hertz.com)
National (☎ 800-227-7368; www.nationalcar.com)

RECREATIONAL VEHICLES

Recreational vehicles (RVs) are hugely popular in BC and the Yukon, and rentals must be booked well in advance of the summer season. In high season, RVs cost $100 to $200 or more a day, including a mere 100km per day. One-way rentals are possible, but you'll pay a surcharge. Also budget plenty for fuel, because RVs typically get miserable gas mileage.

Large rental companies have offices in Vancouver, Calgary, Whitehorse and large BC towns.

CanaDream (☎ 800-461-7368; www.canadream.travel)
Fraserway RV Rentals (☎ 867-668-3438; www.fraserwayrvrentals.com)
West Coast Mountain Campers (☎ 604-279-0550; www.wcmcampers.com)

Road Hazards

It's best to avoid driving in areas with heavy snow, but if you do, be sure your vehicle has snow tires or tire chains as well as an emergency kit of blankets etc. If you get stuck, don't stay in the car with the engine going: every year people die of carbon monoxide poisoning. A single candle burning in the car will keep it reasonably warm.

Make sure the vehicle you're driving is in good condition and take along some tools, flares, water and food. Rural areas usually do not have cell phone service.

Be careful on logging roads as logging trucks always have the right of way and often pay little heed to other vehicles. It's best not to drive on logging roads at all during weekday working hours.

Gravel roads of all kinds – such as those in the Yukon – can take a toll on windshields and tires. Keep a good distance from the vehicle in front of you, and when you see an oncoming vehicle (or a vehicle overtaking you), slow down and keep well to the right. Carry a spare tire.

Wild animals are another potential hazard. Most run-ins with deer, moose and other critters occur at night when wildlife is active and visibility is poor. Many areas have roadside signs alerting drivers to possible animal crossings. Keep scanning both sides of the road and be prepared to stop or swerve. A vehicle's headlights often mesmerize an animal, leaving it frozen in the middle of the road.

Road Rules

North Americans drive on the right side of the road. Speed limits, which are posted in kilometers, are generally 50km/h in built-up areas and 90km/h on highways. A right turn is permitted at a red light after you have come to a complete stop, as is a left turn from a one-way street onto another one-way street; U-turns are not allowed. Traffic in both directions must stop when stationary school buses have their red lights flashing – this means that children are getting off and on. In cities with pedestrian crosswalks, cars must stop to allow pedestrians to cross.

Seat belt use is compulsory in Canada. Children under the age of five must be in a restraining seat. Motorcyclists must use lights and wear helmets. The blood-alcohol limit when driving is 0.08% (about two drinks) and is strictly enforced with heavy fines, bans and jail terms.

TRANSPORTATION

HITCHHIKING

Hitchhiking is not common in BC and the Yukon. It's never entirely safe in any country in the world, and is not recommended. Travelers who decide to hitchhike (or pick up hitchhikers) should understand that they are taking a risk. If you do choose to hitchhike, do it only in pairs. Hitching on the Trans-Canada Hwy is illegal until 40km past the Vancouver city limits.

LOCAL TRANSPORTATION

British Columbia has excellent, widespread local public transportation in the area around Vancouver and Victoria. Outside of these areas service can be sparse, erratic or infrequent. Look in the regional chapters for details on each town's offerings, or see the province-wide website (www.transitbc .com), which features links to the local bus systems. Most places have taxi companies.

In the Yukon, public transit in Whitehorse will suffice for getting around town but, as in much of BC, you'll have a hard time getting around without a car.

TRAIN

Railroad service is limited in BC. The national carrier, **VIA Rail** (☎ 888-842-7245; www .viarail.ca), has only one route from Vancouver. The *Canadian* departs a paltry three times a week and makes a few stops in BC, including outside of Kamloops, before reaching Jasper. The 18½-hour trip takes in some beautiful scenery. Fares range from $185 for a coach seat to about $2000 for two people in a sleeping car, which includes gourmet meals, access to a dome car etc.

VIA Rail also runs the *Skeena* between Prince Rupert and Jasper thrice weekly. It's a daytime-only trip with an overnight stay in Prince George, and stops in Terrace, New Hazelton, Smithers, Houston and Burns Lake. Passengers on the *Skeena* have a choice of service class and fare, and you find your own lodgings in Prince George. Prince Rupert to Jasper costs $110 or more and a deluxe service is available in summer.

Like airlines, VIA Rail offers various discounts for advance purchase and round trips. Fares can change daily depending on demand, so it's worth checking regularly.

On Vancouver Island, VIA Rail runs the *Esquimalt & Nanaimo Railiner,* also known as the *Malahat,* a short, scenic trip from Victoria to Courtenay up the coast of Vancouver Island, with one train daily in each direction (p178) despite often being threatened with permanent closure.

Rocky Mountaineer Vacations (☎ 877-460-3200; www.rockymountaineer.com) runs 'cruise-train' trips between Vancouver and Whistler (p151) as well as trains on the historic Canada Pacific Railway (CPR) line to Banff and the Canadian National (CN) line to Jasper. A route from Whistler to Jasper follows the starkly beautiful course of the mighty Fraser River. The latter two journeys in particular are sold as part of 'trip of a lifetime' packages and aren't really aimed at independent travelers.

Health Dr David Goldberg

There's a high level of hygiene found in this region, so most common infectious diseases will not be a significant concern for travelers. Also, good medical care is widely available.

BEFORE YOU GO

INSURANCE

The Canadian healthcare system is one of the best in the world. Excellent care is widely available. Benefits are generous for Canadian citizens, but foreigners aren't covered. Make sure you have travel-health insurance if your regular policy doesn't apply when you're abroad. Find out in advance if your insurance plan will make payments directly to providers or reimburse you later for overseas health expenditures.

ONLINE RESOURCES

There is a wealth of travel-health advice on the internet. The World Health Organization publishes a superb book, called *International Travel and Health,* which is revised annually and is available free online at www.who.int/ith. Another website of general interest is **MD Travel Health** (www.mdtravel health.com), which provides complete travel-health recommendations for every country, is updated daily and is available for free.

It's usually a good idea to consult your government's travel-health website, if one is available, before departure:
Australia (www.smartraveller.gov.au)
United Kingdom (www.nhs.uk/livewell/travelhealth /pages/travelhealthhome.aspx)
United States (www.cdc.gov/travel)

IN CANADA

AVAILABILITY & COST OF HEALTHCARE

For immediate medical assistance anywhere in BC, call ☎ 911; in the Yukon, call ☎ 867-667-5555. In general, if you have a medical emergency, the best bet is to find the nearest hospital and go to its emergency room.

If you have a choice, a university hospital can be preferable to a community hospital, although you can often find superb medical care in small local hospitals and the waiting time is usually shorter. If the problem isn't urgent, you can call a nearby hospital and ask for a referral to a local physician, which is usually less expensive than a trip to the emergency room.

Pharmacies are abundantly supplied, however you may find that some medications which are available over-the-counter in your home country require a prescription in Canada.

INFECTIOUS DISEASES

There are several infectious diseases that are unknown or at least uncommon outside North America. Most are acquired by mosquito bites, tick bites or environmental exposure.

West Nile Virus

Infections were unknown in Canada until recently, but West Nile virus has now been observed in many provinces, including Saskatchewan, Alberta, Ontario, Québec and Manitoba. The virus is transmitted by Culex mosquitoes, which are active in late summer and early fall, and generally bite after dusk. Most infections are mild or asymptomatic, but the virus may infect the central nervous system, leading to fever, headache, confusion, lethargy, coma and sometimes death. There is no treatment for West Nile virus.

At the time of writing there was no evidence of the virus in British Columbia or the Yukon. For the latest update on the areas affected by West Nile, go to the Health Canada website at www.hc-sc.gc.ca/english /index-eng.php. See also Mosquito Bites (p439).

Lyme Disease

This has been reported from the southern parts of the country. The infection is transmitted by deer ticks, which are only 1mm to

2mm long. Most cases occur in late spring and summer. The first symptom is usually an expanding red rash that is often pale in the center, known as a bull's eye rash. However, in many cases, no rash is observed. Flu-like symptoms are common, including fever, headache, joint pains, body aches and malaise. When the infection is treated promptly with an appropriate antibiotic, usually doxycycline or amoxicillin, the cure rate is high. For prevention tips, see Tick Bites (p439)

Giardiasis

This parasitic infection of the small intestine occurs throughout North America and the world. Known colloquially in BC as 'beaver fever,' Giardiasis has symptoms that may include nausea, bloating, cramps, and diarrhea, and may last for weeks. Avoid drinking directly from lakes, ponds, streams and rivers, which may be contaminated by animal or human feces.

Rabies

Rabies is a viral infection of the brain and spinal cord that is almost always fatal. In Canada most cases of human rabies relate to exposure to bats. Rabies may also be contracted from raccoon, skunk, fox, and unvaccinated cats and dogs. All animal bites and scratches must be promptly and thoroughly cleansed with large amounts of soap and water, and local health authorities contacted to determine if there is a risk of rabies. If there is any possibility, however small, that you have been exposed to rabies, you should seek preventative treatment, which

consists of rabies-immune globulin and rabies vaccine, and is quite safe. In particular, any contact with a bat should be discussed with health authorities, as bats have small teeth and may not leave obvious bite marks.

HIV/AIDS

This infectious disease occurs throughout Canada.

ENVIRONMENTAL HAZARDS
Cold Exposure

Cold exposure may be a significant problem, especially in the northern parts of the country. To prevent hypothermia, keep all body surfaces covered, including the head and neck. Synthetic materials such as Gore-Tex and Thinsulate provide excellent insulation. Since the body loses heat faster when wet, stay dry at all times. Change inner garments promptly when they become moist. Keep active, but get enough rest. Consume plenty of food and water. Be especially sure not to have any alcohol. Caffeine and tobacco should also be avoided.

Watch out for the 'Umbles': stumbles, mumbles, fumbles and grumbles, important signs of impending hypothermia. If someone appears to be developing hypothermia, you should insulate them from the ground, protect them from the wind, remove wet clothing or cover with a vapor barrier such as a plastic bag, and transport immediately to a warm environment and a medical facility. Warm fluids (not coffee or tea) may be given if the person is alert enough to swallow.

RECOMMENDED VACCINATIONS

No special vaccines are required or recommended for travel to Canada. All travelers should be up-to-date on routine immunizations, listed below.

Vaccine	Recommended for	Dosage	Side effects
tetanus-diphtheria	all travelers who haven't had booster within 10 yrs	one dose lasts 10 years	soreness at injection site
measles	travelers born after 1956 who've had only one measles vaccination	one dose	fever; rash; joint pains; allergic reactions
chickenpox	travelers who've never had chickenpox	two doses one month apart	fever; mild case of chickenpox
influenza	all travelers during flu season (Nov-Mar)	one dose	soreness at the injection site; fever

MEDICAL CHECKLIST

- Acetaminophen/paracetamol (Tylenol) or aspirin
- Anti-inflammatory drugs (eg ibuprofen)
- Antihistamines (for hay fever and allergic reactions)
- Antibacterial ointment (eg Neosporin) for cuts and abrasions
- Steroid cream or cortisone (for poison ivy and other allergic rashes)
- Bandages, gauze, gauze rolls
- Adhesive or paper tape
- Scissors, safety pins, tweezers
- Thermometer
- Pocket knife
- DEET-containing (at least 25%) insect repellent for the skin
- Permethrin-containing insect spray for clothing, tents and bed nets.

Bring medications in their original containers, clearly labeled. A signed, dated letter from your physician describing all medical conditions and medications, including generic names is also a good idea. If carrying syringes or needles be sure to have a physician's letter documenting their medical necessity.

Mosquito Bites

When traveling in areas where West Nile or other mosquito-borne illnesses have been reported, keep yourself covered (wear long sleeves, long pants, hats and shoes rather than sandals). Apply a good insect repellent, preferably one containing DEET, to exposed skin and clothing. Avoid contact with eyes, mouth, cuts, wounds or irritated skin. Products containing lower concentrations of DEET are as effective, but for shorter periods of time. In general, adults and children over 12 should use preparations containing 25% to 35% DEET, which lasts about six hours. Children aged between two and 12 years should use preparations containing no more than 10% DEET, applied sparingly, which will last about three hours. Neurologic toxicity has been reported from DEET, especially in children, but appears to be extremely uncommon and generally related to overuse. DEET-containing compounds should not be used on children under the age of two. Insect repellents containing certain botanical products, including oil of eucalyptus and soybean oil, are effective but last only 1½ to two hours. Products based on citronella are not effective.

For additional protection, you can apply permethrin to clothing, shoes, tents and bed nets. Permethrin treatments are safe and remain effective for at least two weeks, even when items have been laundered. Permethrin should not be applied directly to skin.

Tick Bites

To protect yourself from tick bites, follow the same precautions as for mosquitoes, except that boots are preferable to shoes, with pants tucked in. Be sure to perform a thorough tick check at the end of each day, with the aid of a friend or mirror. Ticks should be removed with tweezers, grasping them firmly by the head. Insect repellents based on botanical products unfortunately cannot be recommended to prevent tick bites.

Mammal Bites

Most animal injuries are directly related to a person's attempt to touch or feed the animal. Any bite or scratch by a mammal, including bats, should be promptly and thoroughly cleansed with large amounts of soap and water, followed by application of an antiseptic such as iodine or alcohol. The local health authorities should be contacted immediately for possible post-exposure rabies treatment.

HEALTH

Glossary

aurora borealis – charged particles from the sun that are trapped in the earth's magnetic field and appear as colored, waving beams; also called the northern lights

beaver fever – giardiasis; disease affecting the digestive tract caused by bacteria found in many freshwater streams and lakes; can be avoided by boiling drinking water
boreal – refers to the Canadian north and its character

Canadian Shield – a plateau of rock formed 2.5 billion years ago that covers much of the northern region of Canada; also known as the Precambrian or Laurentian Shield
clear-cut – an area where loggers have cut every tree, large and small, leaving nothing but stumps
coulees – gulches, usually dry
CN – Canadian National Railroad; one of two main railroads in Canada
CPR – Canadian Pacific Railway; the other main railroad in Canada

down-island – on Vancouver Island, anywhere south of where you are

First Nations – denotes Canada's aboriginal peoples; often used instead of Native Indians or Native people

gasoline – petrol, known as gasoline, fuel, or simply gas; mostly sold unleaded in Canada
GST – the 7% goods and services tax levied on most purchases throughout Canada

hoodoo – distinctive vertical pillar shape carved into a rock face by rainfall and glacial erosion

icefield – a large, level expanse of floating ice
Inside Passage – sea route from the Alaskan Panhandle to Washington state that runs between mainland BC and the chain of islands off the coast

Kermode bear – sometimes called spirit bears, have white fur and live in the Great Bear Rainforest

loon – aquatic bird
loonie – slang term for Canada's one-dollar coin, which depicts a loon on one side
Lower Mainland – common term for the southwestern part of BC, including metropolitan Vancouver

Métis – Canadians of mixed French and First Nations ancestry

Mounties – Royal Canadian Mounted Police (*RCMP*)
muskeg – undrained boggy land found in northern BC

névé– compacted snow that forms the surface of the upper part of a glacier
no-see-um – various tiny biting insects that are difficult to see and can annoy travelers in the woods or along beaches; can be kept out of tents with no-see-um netting, a very fine mesh screen
NWT – Northwest Territories, the part of Canada to the east of the Yukon.

Ogopogo – monster similar to the Loch Ness monster, thought to reside in Okanagan Lake; has never been photographed
oolichan – aka eulachon and candlefish; small, oil-rich fish important to *First Nations* people

portage – process of transporting boats and supplies overland between navigable waterways
petroglyphs – ancient paintings or carvings on rock
potlatch – competitive ceremonial activity among some BC *First Nations* people (usually coastal), involving the giving of lavish gifts to emphasize the wealth and status of a chief or clan; now often just refers to a wild party or revel
PST – Provincial Sales Tax; currently 7% in BC; when coupled with the *GST*, it can bring the tax on many purchases to 14%

quay – pronounced 'key'; a city's waterfront docks area, as in North Vancouver's Lonsdale Quay or Port Alberni's Harbour Quay

RCMP – Royal Canadian Mounted Police; the main law-enforcement agency throughout Canada

sourdough – a person who has completed one year's residency in northern Canada
spelunking – exploration and study of caves

taiga – coniferous forests extending across much of subarctic North America and Eurasia
toonie – slang name for a Canadian two-dollar coin
trailer – caravan or mobile home

up-island – on Vancouver Island, anywhere north of where you are

VC –Visitor Centre; Official tourism offices in BC
VIC –Visitor Information Centre; former name of VCs in BC

The Authors

RYAN VER BERKMOES
Coordinating Author

Ryan's been bouncing around BC and the Yukon for more than two decades. Memorable jaunts have included going to the end of the road in the Queen Charlotte Islands, to the end of all the roads in the Yukon and to the end of the line on the Kettle Valley Rail Trail. It's fitting that Ryan's now covering Canada for LP given his background with moose. At his first newspaper job he was tasked with placing random moose jokes in the classifieds to pique reader interest (eg What's a moose's favorite condiment? Moose-turd). For better jokes than that, surf over to www.ryanverberkmoes.com.

JOHN LEE

Born in the southeastern English city of St Albans, John attended BC's University of Victoria to study utopian political theory, which was much more interesting but not quite as lucrative as an MBA. He launched his full-time travel-writing career in 1999 after a Road to Damascus-style trip on the Trans-Siberian Railway and has since contributed to hundreds of publications, some of them still in business. Many of his travel stories – including quite a few about beer – can be found online at www.johnleewriter.com.

CONTRIBUTING AUTHOR

Dr David Goldberg MD completed his training in internal medicine and infectious diseases at Columbia-Presbyterian Medical Center in New York City, where he has also served as voluntary faculty. At present, he is an infectious diseases specialist in Scarsdale NY and the editor-in-chief of the website www.MDTravelHealth.com

---

LONELY PLANET AUTHORS

Why is our travel information the best in the world? It's simple: our authors are passionate, dedicated travellers. They don't take freebies in exchange for positive coverage so you can be sure the advice you're given is impartial. They travel widely to all the popular spots, and off the beaten track. They don't research using just the internet or phone. They discover new places not included in any other guidebook. They personally visit thousands of hotels, restaurants, palaces, trails, galleries, temples and more. They speak with dozens of locals every day to make sure you get the kind of insider knowledge only a local could tell you. They take pride in getting all the details right, and in telling it how it is. Think you can do it? Find out how at **lonelyplanet.com**.

THE AUTHORS

Behind the Scenes

THIS BOOK

This 4th edition was researched and written by Ryan Ver Berkmoes and John Lee, who both also wrote the 3rd edition. The 2nd edition was written by Ryan and Graham Neale. The 1st edition was written by Debra Miller and Julie Fanselow. This guidebook was commissioned in Lonely Planet's Oakland office, edited and laid out by Cambridge Publishing Management, UK, and produced by the following:

Commissioning Editors Jennye Garibaldi, Suki Gear, Emily K Wolman

Coordinating Editor Catherine Burch

Coordinating Cartographer Corey Hutchison

Coordinating Layout Designer Paul Queripel

Managing Editors Melanie Dankel, Bruce Evans

Managing Cartographer David Connolly

Managing Layout Designer Sally Darmody

Assisting Editors Tom Lee, Scarlett O'Hara, Michala Green

Assisting Cartographers Andy Rojas, Xavier di Toro, Tom Webster

Assisting Layout Designers Nicholas Colicchia, Julie Crane

Cover image research provided by lonelyplanetimages.com

Indexer Marie Lorimer

Project Manager Ruth Cosgrove

Thanks to Lucy Birchley, Jessica Boland, Ellen Burrows, Rebecca Dandens, Heather Dickson, Mark Germanchis,

Michelle Glynn, Martin Heng, Lauren Hunt, Laura Jane, Chris Lee Ack, Raphael Richards, Fabrice Rocher

THANKS
RYAN VER BERKMOES

The number of folks to thank outnumber Kermode bears but here's a few: Jim Kemshead never fails to deliver both beer and info in the Yukon as does Dan Davidson and dancer extraordinaire Rachel Wiegers (well at least info). In BC, Prince Rupert's Bruce Wishart is good for both info and drinks of all kinds as is Prince George's Michalle Clark (even when it's −38°C). Deanna Steven showed me the uphill side of Rossland while John Schreiner was a gentleman as always. The New Pornographers supplied music, Betsy Trumpener did her best to plug sex in the snow and John Lee is simply the best. And Erin? She needs to not miss a trip.

JOHN LEE

Thanks are due to the unfailingly friendly staff at regional visitor centers large and small as well as to the locals encountered en route, especially those in the tiniest communities who were generally more than happy to stop and chat. A tip of the hat is also due to Ryan for his slick ability to be the ideal co-conspirator on this project. Finally, thanks to all my Vancouver buddies for keeping me relatively

---

THE LONELY PLANET STORY

Fresh from an epic journey across Europe, Asia and Australia in 1972, Tony and Maureen Wheeler sat at their kitchen table stapling together notes. The first Lonely Planet guidebook, *Across Asia on the Cheap*, was born.

Travelers snapped up the guides. Inspired by their success, the Wheelers began publishing books to Southeast Asia, India and beyond. Demand was prodigious, and the Wheelers expanded the business rapidly to keep up. Over the years, Lonely Planet extended its coverage to every country and into the virtual world via lonelyplanet.com and the Thorn Tree message board.

As Lonely Planet became a globally loved brand, Tony and Maureen received several offers for the company. But it wasn't until 2007 that they found a partner whom they trusted to remain true to the company's principles of traveling widely, treading lightly and giving sustainably. In October of that year, BBC Worldwide acquired a 75% share in the company, pledging to uphold Lonely Planet's commitment to independent travel, trustworthy advice and editorial independence.

Today, Lonely Planet has offices in Melbourne, London and Oakland, with over 500 staff members and 300 authors. Tony and Maureen are still actively involved with Lonely Planet. They're traveling more often than ever, and they're devoting their spare time to charitable projects. And the company is still driven by the philosophy of *Across Asia on the Cheap*: 'All you've got to do is decide to go and the hardest part is over. So go!'

sane during the late nights, early mornings and eye-drooping afternoons of write-up when my fingers were permanently stapled to this keyboard.

OUR READERS
Many thanks to the travelers who used the last edition and wrote to us with helpful hints, useful advice and interesting anecdotes:

Tom Andrews, Jo Barrett, Jochem Bijnsdorp, Chirs Bilton, Mario Bless, Francine Brondex, Tony Carter, James Cox, Sue Crimp, Alison Davis, Gail Fawley, Gregg Fawley, Christina Freymann, Stephanie Goldsmith, Paul Griffiths, Bert Groenenberg, Bonnie Hardy, David Harmer, Carly Harris, Judith Harrison, Camilla Heath, Robert Holder, Claire James, Tracy Jeffery, Nicola Kaiser, Craig Kelley, Robin Kop, Aaron Lasota, John Marino, Maren Martens, Brandon Ngai, Elizabeth Niznik, Annie Oudijk, Debbie Querner, Martin Reuss, Caroline Roussy, Colin Smith, Rob Stewart, Alex Stirkul, Yvonne Symons, Manuela Tobler, Gijsbert Van Den Brandhof, Pat Warrington, Mark Weatherby, Ciska Winter.

ACKNOWLEDGMENTS
Many thanks to the following for the use of their content:

Globe on title page ©Mountain High Maps 1993 Digital Wisdom, Inc.

SEND US YOUR FEEDBACK

We love to hear from travelers – your comments keep us on our toes and help make our books better. Our well-traveled team reads every word on what you loved or loathed about this book. Although we cannot reply individually to postal submissions, we always guarantee that your feedback goes straight to the appropriate authors, in time for the next edition. Each person who sends us information is thanked in the next edition – and the most useful submissions are rewarded with a free book.

To send us your updates – and find out about Lonely Planet events, newsletters and travel news – visit our award-winning website: **lonelyplanet.com/contact**.

Note: we may edit, reproduce and incorporate your comments in Lonely Planet products such as guidebooks, websites and digital products, so let us know if you don't want your comments reproduced or your name acknowledged. For a copy of our privacy policy visit lonelyplanet.com/privacy.

Index

INDEX

000 Map pages
000 Photograph pages

000 Map pages
000 Photograph pages

INDEX

GreenDex

The following listings for British Columbia and the Yukon have been selected by Lonely Planet authors because they demonstrate an active sustainable-tourism policy. Some are involved in conservation or environmental education while others are owned and operated by locals committed to responsible tourism. Sustainable practices garnered mentions for farmers markets and restaurants.

Accommodation listings are limited to those that show a much greater commitment to the environment than just asking you to help them save money by reusing your towels.

We want to keep developing our sustainable-tourism content. If you think we've omitted someone who should be listed here, or if you disagree with our choices, email us via www.lonelyplanet.com /contact. For more information about sustainable tourism and Lonely Planet, see www.lonelyplanet .com/responsibletravel.

MAP LEGEND

ROUTES

Tollway	Mall/Steps
Freeway	Tunnel
Primary	Pedestrian Overpass
Secondary	Walking Tour
Tertiary	Walking Tour Detour
Lane	Walking Trail
Under Construction	Walking Path
Unsealed Road	Track
One-Way Street	

TRANSPORT

Ferry	Rail (Underground)
Metro	Tram
Bus Route	Cable Car, Funicular
Rail	

HYDROGRAPHY

River, Creek	Glacier
Intermittent River	Canal
Swamp	Water
Mangrove	Lake (Dry)
Reef	Lake (Salt)

BOUNDARIES

International	Marine Park
State, Provincial	Cliff

AREA FEATURES

Airport	Land
Area of Interest	Mall
Beach, Desert	Market
Building	Park
Campus	Reservation
Cemetery, Christian	Rocks
Cemetery, Other	Sports
Forest	Urban

POPULATION

CAPITAL (NATIONAL)	CAPITAL (STATE)
Large City	Medium City
Small City	Town, Village

SYMBOLS

Sights/Activities
- Beach
- Buddhist
- Christian
- Golf
- Hindu
- Monument
- Museum, Gallery
- Point of Interest
- Pool
- Ruin
- Sikh
- Skiing
- Trail Head
- Winery, Vineyard
- Zoo, Bird Sanctuary

Eating
- Eating

Drinking
- Drinking
- Café

Entertainment
- Entertainment

Shopping
- Shopping

Sleeping
- Sleeping
- Camping

Transport
- Airport, Airfield
- Border Crossing
- Bus Station
- Cycling, Bicycle Path
- Parking Area
- Petrol Station
- Taxi Rank

Information
- Bank, ATM
- Embassy/Consulate
- Hospital, Medical
- Information
- Internet Facilities
- Police Station
- Post Office, GPO
- Telephone
- Toilets

Geographic
- Lighthouse
- Lookout
- Mountain, Volcano
- National Park
- Pass, Canyon
- Picnic Area
- River Flow
- Shelter, Hut
- Spot Height
- Waterfall

LONELY PLANET OFFICES

Australia
Head Office
Locked Bag 1, Footscray, Victoria 3011
☎ 03 8379 8000, fax 03 8379 8111
talk2us@lonelyplanet.com.au

USA
150 Linden St, Oakland, CA 94607
☎ 510 250 6400, toll free 800 275 8555
fax 510 893 8572
info@lonelyplanet.com

UK
2nd fl, 186 City Rd,
London EC1V 2NT
☎ 020 7106 2100, fax 020 7106 2101
go@lonelyplanet.co.uk

Published by Lonely Planet Publications Pty Ltd
ABN 36 005 607 983

© Lonely Planet Publications Pty Ltd 2009

© photographers as indicated 2009

Cover photograph: Revelstoke, British Columbia, Canada, Jakob Helbig Hansen/Photolibrary Many of the images in this guide are available for licensing from Lonely Planet Images: www.lonelyplanet images.com.

Printed by SNP Printers Limited
Printed in Singapore

Lonely Planet and the Lonely Planet logo are trademarks of Lonely Planet and are registered in the US Patent and Trademark Office and in other countries.

Lonely Planet does not allow its name or logo to be appropriated by commercial establishments, such as retailers, restaurants or hotels. Please let us know of any misuses: www.lonelyplanet.com/ip.

Although the authors and Lonely Planet have taken all reasonable care in preparing this book, we make no warranty about the accuracy or completeness of its content and, to the maximum extent permitted, disclaim all liability arising from its use.